The selection of behavior

The selection of behavior

The operant behaviorism of B. F. Skinner: Comments and consequences

Edited by

A. CHARLES CATANIA
and
STEVAN HARNAD

CAMBRIDGE UNIVERSITY PRESS

Cambridge
New York   Port Chester   Melbourne   Sydney

CAMBRIDGE UNIVERSITY PRESS
Cambridge, New York, Melbourne, Madrid, Cape Town,
Singapore, São Paulo, Delhi, Mexico City

Cambridge University Press
The Edinburgh Building, Cambridge CB2 8RU, UK

Published in the United States of America by Cambridge University Press, New York

www.cambridge.org
Information on this title: www.cambridge.org/9780521348614

First published 1988
Reprinted 1989
First paperback edition 2011

A catalogue record for this publication is available from the British Library

Library of Congress Cataloguing in Publication Data
The selection of behavior:
the operant behaviorism of B. F. Skinner: comments and consequences/
edited by A. Charles Catania and Stevan Harnad.
p. cm.
Consists of articles by B. F. Skinner, commentaries on the articles,
and Skinner's responses to the commentaries.
"Bibliography of works by B. F. Skinner": p.
Bibliography: p.
Includes index.
ISBN 0 521 34388 7 ISBN 0 521 34861 7 (pbk.)
1. Behaviorism (Psychology) 2. Skinner, B. F. (Burrhus Frederic), 1904–
I. Catania, A. Charles. II. Harnad, Stevan R.
III. Skinner, B. F. (Burrhus Frederic), 1904–
[DNLM: 1. Skinner, B. F. (Burrhus Frederic), 1904–
2. Behaviorism. BF199 S464]
BF199.S45 1988
150.19´434–dc 19
DNLM/DLC
for Library of Congress 87-33750

ISBN 978-0-521-34388-6 Hardback
ISBN 978-0-521-34861-4 Paperback

Contents (overview)

Contents (detailed)

Summing up

Preface

The core of this volume consists of several classic articles by B. F. Skinner, commentaries on those articles by scholars in a variety of disciplines, and Skinner's responses to those commentaries. That core is preceded by a brief introduction to Skinner and his work; it is followed by a summing up – an exchange between Skinner and the editors on some of the major issues raised in the articles, commentaries, and responses.

Each "target" article is followed by commentaries arranged in alphabetical order by first author. Skinner's response follows immediately after each commentary, and is distinguished by his initials, BFS, and a change in type size. The affiliations listed for each commentator are those current at the time the commentary was submitted.

The volume also includes a bibliography of Skinner's published work, a reference section keyed to the articles and commentaries in which a given reference appears, and name and subject indexes.

This project began in a casual way. In 1980, Stevan Harnad, Editor of *Behavioral and Brain Sciences* (henceforth *BBS*), had asked me to serve as Associate Editor for the experimental analysis of behavior. At the time when Skinner's research laboratory was still active I had been a graduate student in the Department of Psychology at Harvard, my current research involved work with both human and nonhuman organisms, and I was past editor of the *Journal of the Experimental Analysis of Behavior*. But after the first couple of years of my *BBS* term I had been singularly unsuccessful in generating new material.

My task was to invite or encourage authors to submit works that would eventually become "*BBS* treatments": After review for suitability, the papers would be sent out for commentary to scholars in the relevant disciplines and the author would then reply. The issues of *BBS* usually consisted of several treatments, supplemented occasionally by "continuing commentary" on earlier material. By the spring of 1982, I had reviewed some *BBS* papers that had been submitted independently of any initiative of mine, but not one of the authors I had suggested had yet come through with a manuscript.

In a telephone discussion with Harnad about this situation, I was trying to come up with a contribution and happened to ask whether he had ever considered doing a treatment of a classic published article rather than one written especially for *BBS*. When he asked what sort of article I had in mind, I named Skinner's "Operational analysis of psychological terms." Harnad liked the idea, though he wondered whether Skinner's history of not responding to his critics, and in particular to Chomsky's review of his book *Verbal behavior*, made it unlikely that Skinner would participate in such a project (Skinner once wrote "I have escaped from the punishers. . . . I do not often read my critics"). But Harnad encouraged me to give it a try.

At the May 1982 meeting of the Association for Behavior Analysis, I met Skinner in a corridor and asked whether he would consider doing the replies to the commentaries if the "Operational analysis" paper were given a *BBS* treatment. He replied that the idea sounded fine, and he and I went our separate ways for the remainder of that meeting. It had not occurred to me at the time that he might have said no, but every colleague to whom I have told this story has been surprised by his answer.

After I returned from the meeting, I reported my conversation with Skinner to Harnad. I am still impressed by the short latency of his response, in which he suggested that if Skinner were willing to do one treatment we should see whether he would be willing to do several, so that a special issue of *BBS* could be devoted to his papers. The subtitle, "The canonical papers of B. F. Skinner," for which Harnad is responsible, may even go back to that particular telephone conversation.

In June I called Skinner to propose the special issue. By July 1982, the project had begun, and I wrote to confirm the plans for an issue of *BBS* devoted to a selection of his papers. We quickly agreed on "The operational analysis of psychological terms" ("Terms"), "An operant analysis of problem solving" ("Problem solving") and, tentatively, "The phylogeny and ontogeny of behavior" ("Phylogeny"). The next step was to settle on the remaining selections and their formats. By letter, we reviewed the criteria for inclusion of each article: Each should be a self-contained unit; each should deal with issues that did not overlap with those in the other papers; the papers as a group should have a coherent structure; the papers should not omit any major areas critical to the contemporary analysis of behavior; and, of course, the whole package had to fit within the available page limits.

Soon Skinner took up the contents with his "powwow," a group that met at Harvard on an occasional basis to discuss behavioral issues; of that group, Margaret Vaughan was particularly involved in the consideration of the *BBS* contents and in some of the relevant correspondence. "Selection by consequences" ("Consequences") was added to the existing list, and next "Behaviorism at fifty" ("Behaviorism-50") was chosen in preference to "Why I am not a cognitive psychologist." Some consideration was given to including one or more excerpts from the book, *Verbal behavior*, but it was difficult to find sections that would stand alone, and by May 1983 it was decided that "Terms" and "Problem solving" would have to be the vehicles for the discussion of verbal behavior. By the end of June 1983 the list of articles to be treated had been made final with Skinner's approval of edited versions of "The flight from the laboratory" (1961) and "Are theories of learning necessary?" (1950), which I had abridged and combined into a single paper called "Methods and theories in the experimental analysis of behavior" ("Methods").

Well before this time, work had begun on other aspects of the project. Permissions to reprint the articles were requested, editing of the articles for uniformity of reference format and other details began, and abstracts were prepared. Skinner had declined to write the abstracts, so I produced them on a word processor by entering and then rearranging and deleting key sentences from each article. Skinner approved each abstract with only minor modifications; his satisfaction with them must be attributed at least in part to the fact that they were essentially made up of his own sentences.

Another major task was to compile a list of potential commentators to whom each article would be sent. Harnad's lists were combined with my suggestions and those of Skinner's "powwow." A major part of the job was paring the combined lists down to manageable size. Some decisions were easy. For example, Chomsky was included in most of the mailings. But some of our choices were inevitably arbitrary. For our first mailing, which was fittingly "Terms," chronologically Skinner's earliest article of those that would be included in the *BBS* treatments, we had by December 1982 reduced an initial list of about 200 names to a mailing of about 60. The response was light, probably because of the preholiday timing of the mailing, and "Terms" was sent to about another 30 scholars in early March 1983.

Thereafter each article was sent to about 100 potential commentators, with only a small overlap of names across lists, for a total of more than 600 mailings over the course of the project. "Consequences" was mailed in late March 1983 and "Problem solving" in late May, and the remaining three, "Phylogeny," "Behaviorism-50" and "Methods," were mailed during the fall of 1983. Commentators were given about five weeks to provide their commentaries, except that some additional leeway was given to overseas scholars.

The statistics were as follows: "Terms" received 21 commentaries out of 101 mailings, "Consequences" 24 out of 107, "Problem solving" 18 out of 95, "Phylogeny" 26 out of 106, "Behaviorism-50" 36 out of 113, and "Methods" 17 out of 108. The total was 142 commentaries out of 630 mailings, or about 23%. (*BBS*'s submission ratio varies from about 20 to 60%.)

Some time after the closing date for the commentaries on "Terms," Harnad provided a tongue-in-cheek analysis in which he characterized the responses as coming from one of five groups: party-line eulogists; reconstructed kindred spirits; defectors who had left the behavior analytic fold; unapologetic cognitive scientists; and the never-were-behaviorists. A group of commentaries that did not readily fit into any of these categories he described as philosophical and methodological papers in which the relevant arguments were not made.

Almost all of the commentaries received were included in the treatments. Over the six sets, fewer than a dozen commentaries were declined; the grounds included excessive length, irrelevance, and lateness. In a very few cases, a commentary was returned to an author for revision, and occasionally it was possible to accommodate a latecomer. Each set of treatments required record-keeping and review, and was sent out to Skinner within a month or two of the closing date for each treatment. He received commentaries on "Terms" and on "Consequences" in June 1983 and on "Problem solving" in August; those on the remaining three target articles were sent to him within a one-week period in mid-December.

Skinner mailed his replies to the commentaries on "Terms" in October and had completed his replies to all six sets of commentaries by January 1984. But the chores associated with the issue dragged on for some time more. Section headings needed titles, references needed checking, and so on. In a cover letter of 12 March 1984, Skinner wrote: "I feel like Job with no comforter, but it is all over."

That was not yet to be, however. In our review of the six treatments, Harnad and I felt that the material did not have proper closure, and so we prevailed upon Skinner to write replies to some of our questions about various general issues raised and developed in the course of the commentaries. That work ended in July 1984, after which the issue was in the hands of Cambridge University Press and appeared as *BBS* Volume 7, Number 4 (December 1984).

In response to the *BBS* issue, some continuing commentaries were submitted, but only one has been incorporated into this volume with Skinner's reply (Hershberger on "Methods"). As of this writing the rest is not yet history. Already the pieces in the special issue have begun to be cited (e.g., as documented in the *Social Sciences Citation Index* for 1986). No doubt the discussions initiated by these treatments will continue, with new participants joining those represented in these pages. May this historic interaction between B. F. Skinner and a cross-disciplinary spectrum of commentators serve not only to correct misunderstandings and misrepresentations but also to widen constructive dialogue about the work of one of the most significant contributors to twentieth-century behavioral science.

Columbia, Maryland A. CHARLES CATANIA

Contributors

JONATHAN E. ADLER [5]
Department of Philosophy
Brooklyn College, City University of New York

STUART A. ALTMANN [6]
Department of Biology
University of Chicago

GERARD P. BAERENDS [6]
Department of Zoology
University of Groningen, The Netherlands

DAVID P. BARASH [6]
Departments of Psychology and Zoology
University of Washington

JEROME H. BARKOW [6]
Department of Sociology and Social Anthropology
Dalhousie University
Halifax, Nova Scotia, Canada

GEORGE W. BARLOW [1]
Department of Zoology and Museum of Vertebrate Biology
University of California, Berkeley

MARC BELTH [5]
School of Education
Queens College, City University of New York

JONATHAN BENNETT [3]
Department of Philosophy
Syracuse University

D. CAROLINE BLANCHARD [6]
John A. Burns School of Medicine and Department of Psychology
University of Hawaii at Manoa

ROBERT J. BLANCHARD [6]
John A. Burns School of Medicine and Department of Psychology
University of Hawaii at Manoa

ROBERT C. BOLLES [1]
Department of Psychology
University of Washington
Seattle, Washington

KENNETH E. BOULDING [1]
Department of Economics
Swarthmore College

RICHARD P. BRINKER [3]
Educational Testing Service
Princeton, New Jersey

JERRAM BROWN [6]
Department of Biological Sciences
State University of New York at Albany

GORDON M. BURGHARDT [6]
Department of Psychology
University of Tennessee

C. B. G. CAMPBELL [1]
Division of Neuropsychiatry
Walter Reed Army Institute of Research
Washington, D. C.

JAIME G. CARBONELL [5]
Department of Computer Science
Carnegie-Mellon University

A. CHARLES CATANIA [0, 7]
Department of Psychology
University of Maryland Baltimore County

L. JONATHAN COHEN [4]
The Queen's College
Oxford University, England

ANDREW M. COLMAN [6]
Department of Psychology
University of Leicester, England

BO DAHLBOM [1]
Department for the Theory and Philosophy of Science
Umeå University, Sweden

DENISE DANIELS [6]
Institute for Behavioral Genetics
University of Colorado

ARTHUR C. DANTO [3]
Department of Philosophy
Columbia University

LAWRENCE H. DAVIS [5]
Department of Philosophy
University of Missouri–St. Louis

RICHARD DAWKINS [1]
Department of Zoology
University of Oxford, England

JUAN D. DELIUS [6]
Experimentelle Tierpsychologie
Psychologisches Institut
Ruhr-Universität
Federal Republic of Germany

DANIEL C. DENNETT [3]
Department of Philosophy
Tufts University

SAMUEL M. DIETZ [2]
Educational Foundations Department
Georgia State University

P. C. DODWELL [4]
Department of Psychology
Queen's University, Canada

JOHN W. DONAHOE [1]
Neuroscience and Behavior Program
Department of Psychology
University of Massachusetts, Amherst

IRENÄUS EIBL-EIBESFELDT [6]
Forschungstelle für Humanethologie
Max-Planck-Institut für Verhaltensphysiologie
Seeweisen, Federal Republic of Germany

H. J. EYSENCK [6]
Department of Psychology
Institute of Psychiatry
University of London, England

B. A. FARRELL [5]
Corpus Christi College
University of Oxford, England

JEROME A. FELDMAN [4]
Department of Computer Science
University of Rochester

KEVIN J. FLANNELLY [6]
Department of Psychology
University of Hawaii at Manoa

JOHN J. FUREDY [5]
Department of Psychology
University of Toronto, Canada

GORDON G. GALLUP, JR. [5]
Department of Psychology
State University of New York, Albany

THOMAS J. GAMBLE [1]
Department of Psychology
Yale University

K. R. GARRETT [3]
Department of Philosophy
Brandeis University

MICHAEL T. GHISELIN [1, 6]
Department of Invertebrates
California Academy of Sciences

ALISON GOPNIK [5]
Department of Psychology and Linguistics
University of Toronto, Canada

ROBERT M. GORDON [5]
Department of Philosophy
University of Missouri–St. Louis

GILBERT GOTTLIEB [6]
Department of Psychology
University of North Carolina at Greensboro

GEORGE GRAHAM [3]
Department of Philosophy
University of Alabama at Birmingham

STEPHEN GROSSBERG [4]
Center for Adaptive Systems
Department of Mathematics
Boston University

KEITH GUNDERSON [5]
Department of Psychology and Minnesota Center for Philosophy of Science
University of Minnesota at Minneapolis/St. Paul

JACK P. HAILMAN [6]
Department of Zoology
University of Wisconsin–Madison

C. R. HALLPIKE [1]
Department of Anthropology
McMaster University, Canada

STEVAN HARNAD [7]
Editor, Behavioral and Brain Sciences
Princeton, New Jersey

ROM HARRÉ [4]
Sub-Faculty of Philosophy
Oxford University, England

MARVIN HARRIS [1]
Department of Anthropology
University of Florida

PETER HARZEM [3]
Department of Psychology
Auburn University

JOHN HEIL [5]
Department of Philosophy
Virginia Commonwealth University

WAYNE HERSHBERGER [2]
Department of Psychology
Northern Illinois University

PHILIP N. HINELINE [3]
Department of Psychology
Temple University

LAURENCE HITTERDALE [5]
Santa Ana, California

MAX HOCUTT [3]
Department of Philosophy
University of Alabama

JERRY A. HOGAN [6]
Department of Psychology
University of Toronto, Canada

ROBIN M. HOGARTH [4]
Graduate School of Business
University of Chicago

WERNER K. HONIG [1]
Department of Psychology
Dalhousie University, Canada

ALASDAIR HOUSTON [6]
Edward Grey Institute of Field Ornithology
Department of Zoology
University of Oxford, England

GRAHAM HOYLE [6]
Institute of Neuroscience
University of Oregon

EARL HUNT [4]
Department of Psychology
University of Washington

FRANCIS W. IRWIN [5]
Department of Psychology
University of Pennsylvania

JULIAN JAYNES [3]
Department of Psychology
Princeton University

CARL N. JOHNSON [5]
Program in Child Development and Child Care
University of Pittsburgh

PERE JULIÀ [4]
Department d'Ensenyament Universitari Generalitat de Catalunyà
Barcelona, Spain

ALEJANDRO KACELNIK [6]
Edward Grey Institute of Field Ornithology
Department of Zoology
University of Oxford, England

STEPHEN KAPLAN [6]
Departments of Psychology and Computer and Communications Services
University of Michigan

MICHAEL J. KATZ [1]
Department of Developmental Genetics and Anatomy
Case Western Reserve University

GEIR KAUFMANN [4]
Department of Cognitive Psychology
University of Bergen, Norway

RICHARD C. KEEFE [3]
Department of Psychology
Arizona State University

DOUGLAS T. KENRICK [3]
Department of Psychology
Arizona State University

MANFRED KOCHEN [4]
Mental Health Research Institute
University of Michigan

MICHAEL LEBOWITZ [5]
Department of Computer Science
Columbia University

C. FERGUS LOWE [3]
Department of Psychology
University College of North Wales, Wales

R. DUNCAN LUCE [2]
Department of Psychology and Social Relations
Harvard University

WILLIAM G. LYCAN [5]
Department of Philosophy
University of North Carolina at Chapel Hill

WILLIAM LYONS [5]
Department of Moral Philosophy
University of Glasgow, Scotland

BRIAN MACKENZIE [2]
Department of Psychology
University of Tasmania, Australia

M. JACKSON MARR [5]
Department of Psychology
Georgia Institute of Technology

F. H. C. MARRIOTT [2]
Department of Biomathematics
University of Oxford, England

JOHN C. MARSHALL [5]
Neuropsychology Unit, Neuroscience Group
The Radcliffe Infirmary
Oxford, England

J. MAYNARD SMITH [1]
School of Biological Sciences
University of Sussex, England

PAUL E. MEEHL [3]
Department of Psychiatry
University of Minnesota at Minneapolis/St. Paul

RICHARD MILLWARD [2]
Walter S. Hunter Laboratory of Psychology
Brown University

J. MOORE [3]
Department of Psychology
University of Wisconsin–Milwaukee

ROBERT C. MOORE [5]
Artificial Intelligence Center, SRI International
Menlo Park, California and
Center for the Study of Language and Information
Stanford University

J. M. E. MORAVCSIK [2]
Department of Philosophy
Stanford University

CHRIS MORTENSEN [5]
Department of Philosophy
University of Adelaide, Australia

R. J. NELSON [2]
Department of Philosophy
Case Western Reserve University

JOHN M. NICHOLAS [2]
Department of Philosophy and History of Medicine and Science
University of Western Ontario, Canada

F. J. ODLING-SMEE [1]
Departments of Applied Biology and Psychology
Brunel University, England

DONALD PERLIS [5]
Computer Science Department
University of Maryland at College Park

ANTHONY J. PERZIGIAN [6]
Departments of Anthropology and Anatomy
University of Cincinnati

ULLIN T. PLACE [3]
Department of Philosophy
University of Leeds, England

ROBERT PLOMIN [6]
Institute for Behavioral Genetics
University of Colorado

H. C. PLOTKIN [1, 6]
Department of Psychology
University College London, England

ROBERT R. PROVINE [1]
Department of Psychology
University of Maryland Baltimore County

KJELL RAAHEIM [4]
Department of Cognitive Psychology
University of Bergen, Norway

HOWARD RACHLIN [3]
Department of Psychology
State University of New York, Stony Brook

ANATOL RAPOPORT [4, 6]
Institute for Advanced Studies
Vienna, Austria

JAN G. REIN [4]
Department of Social Sciences
University of Tromsoe, Norway

GEORGES REY [5]
Department of Philosophy
University of Colorado

MARC N. RICHELLE [2]
Laboratoire de Psychologie Expérimentale
University of Liège, Belgium

JON D. RINGEN [3]
Philosophy Department
Indiana University at South Bend

DIANE M. RILEY [5]
Addiction Research Foundation
Toronto, Ontario, Canada

SETH ROBERTS [2]
Department of Psychology
University of California, Berkeley

LYNN C. ROBERTSON [3]
Veterans Administration Medical Center
Martinez, California

Daniel N. Robinson [5]
Department of Psychology
Georgetown University

Alexander Rosenberg [1]
Department of Philosophy
Syracuse University

David M. Rosenthal [5]
Program in Philosophy
Graduate Center, City University of New York

William W. Rozeboom [2]
Department of Psychology
University of Alberta, Canada

Duane M. Rumbaugh [1]
Department of Psychology
Georgia State University and
Yerkes Primate Institute
Emory University

S. N. Salthe [6]
Department of Biology
Brooklyn College, City University of New York

Kenneth M. Sayre [2]
Department of Philosophy
University of Notre Dame

Joseph M. Scandura [4]
Interdisciplinary Studies in Structural Learning and Instructional Science
University of Pennsylvania

Morton L. Schagrin [2]
Faculty for Arts, Education and Humanities
State University of New York, Fredonia

Roger Schnaitter [5]
Department of Psychology
Illinois Wesleyan University

Jonathan Schull [1]
Department of Psychology
Haverford College

Miriam W. Schustack [5]
Department of Psychology and Social Relations
Harvard University

Charles P. Shimp [2]
Department of Psychology
University of Utah

Michael A. Simon [5]
Department of Philosophy
State University of New York at Stony Brook

B. F. Skinner [1–7]
Department of Psychology and Social Relations
Harvard University

Paul R. Solomon [1]
Department of Psychology
Williams College

Ernest Sosa [2]
Department of Philosophy
Brown University

Edward P. Stabler, Jr. [4]
Centre for Cognitive Science
University of Western Ontario
London, Ontario, Canada

J. E. R. Staddon [5, 6]
Department of Psychology
Duke University

Douglas Stalker [3]
Department of Philosophy
University of North Carolina at Chapel Hill

Stephen C. Stearns [1]
Biological Laboratories
Reed College
Portland, Oregon

Robert J. Sternberg [4]
Department of Psychology
Yale University

Stephen P. Stich [5]
Center for Advanced Study in the Behavioral Sciences
Stanford, California

H. S. Terrace [3]
Department of Psychology
Columbia University

William S. Terry [5]
Department of Psychology
University of North Carolina at Charlotte

Roger K. Thomas [5]
Department of Psychology
University of Georgia

William Timberlake [1]
Department of Psychology
Indiana University, Bloomington

Frederick M. Toates [5]
Biology Department
The Open University
Milton Keynes, England

James T. Townsend [2]
Department of Psychological Sciences
Purdue University

WILLIAM VAUGHAN, JR. [1]
Department of Psychology and Social Relations
Harvard University

WILLIAM S. VERPLANCK [4]
Department of Psychology
University of Tennessee at Knoxville

DOUGLAS WAHLSTEN [6]
Department of Psychology
University of Waterloo, Canada

GERHARD D. WASSERMANN [6]
Reader in the Theory and Philosophy of Biology
University of Newcastle upon Tyne, England

HENRY M. WELLMAN [5]
Department of Psychology
University of Michigan

N. E. WETHERICK [4]
Department of Psychology
University of Aberdeen, Scotland

LEROY WOLINS [2]
Department of Psychology
Iowa State University

MICHAEL L. WOODRUFF [5]
Department of Anatomy
Quillen–Dishner College of Medicine
East Tennessee State University

COLIN WRIGHT [3]
Department of Philosophy
University of Exeter, England

EVERETT J. WYERS [5]
Department of Psychology
State University of New York at Stony Brook

WANDA WYRWICKA [1]
Brain Research Institute and Department of Anatomy
University of California School of Medicine, Los Angeles

THOMAS R. ZENTALL [5]
Department of Psychology
University of Kentucky

PAUL ZIFF [3]
Department of Philosophy
University of North Carolina at Chapel Hill

G. E. ZURIFF [3]
Department of Psychology
Wheaton College
Norton, Massachusetts

Introduction

The operant behaviorism of B. F. Skinner

A. Charles Catania

Of all contemporary psychologists, B. F. Skinner is perhaps the most honored and the most maligned, the most widely recognized and the most misrepresented, the most cited and the most misunderstood. Some still say that he is a stimulus–response psychologist (he is not); some still say that stimulus–response chains play a central role in his treatment of verbal behavior (they do not); some still say that he disavows evolutionary determinants of behavior (he does not). These and other misconceptions are common and sometimes even appear in psychology texts (e.g., Todd & Morris 1983). How did they come about, and why do they continue? The present treatments may help to clarifly some of the misunderstandings.

The articles sampled here represent a range of Skinner's work (in the treatments, each article is referred to by its abbreviated title). The first but most recent, "Selection by Consequences" ("Consequences," Skinner 1981), relates operant theory to other disciplines, and in particular to biology and anthropology. The second, "Methods and Theories in the Experimental Analysis of Behavior" ("Methods"), outlines some of the basic concepts of operant theory in the context of a discussion of methodological and theoretical issues; it is an amalgamation of revised versions of "The Flight from the Laboratory" (Skinner 1961) and "Are Theories of Learning Necessary?" (Skinner 1950) and a portion of the preface to *Contingencies of Reinforcement* (Skinner 1969). "The Operational Analysis of Psychological Terms" ("Terms," Skinner 1945) is the earliest work treated; its special concern is with the language of private events, and many features of Skinner's analysis of verbal behavior are implicit in it. "An Operant Analysis of Problem Solving" ("Problem Solving," Skinner 1966a) continues the interpretation of verbal behavior in distinguishing between rule-governed and contingency-shaped behavior. "Behaviorism at Fifty" ("Behaviorism-50," Skinner 1963) addresses the status of behaviorism as a philosophy of science, and points out some of the difficulties that must be overcome by any science of behavior. "The Phylogeny and Ontogeny of Behavior" ("Phylogeny," Skinner 1966c), the last of the works sampled, considers how evolutionary variables combine with those operating within an organism's lifetime to determine its behavior.

Biography [*see also* "Appendix: Biographical Sketch..."]

Burrhus Frederic Skinner was born on March 20, 1904, in Susquehanna, Pennsylvania. After majoring in English at Hamilton College, he tried a career at writing but gave it up after finding he had nothing to say. Having a long-standing interest in human and animal behavior and some familiarity with the writings of Watson, Pavlov, and Bertrand Russell, he then entered the graduate program in psychology at Harvard University (Skinner 1976). There he began a series of experiments that led to more than two dozen journal articles and culminated in *The Behavior of Organisms* (1938). In the manner of *The Integrative Action of the Nervous System* (Sherrington 1906) and *Behavior of the Lower Organisms* (Jennings 1906), the work presented a variety of novel research findings and provided a context for them. The extensive data illustrated many properties of reinforcement and extinction, discrimination and differentiation; the concept of the three-term contingency was to become the cornerstone for much else that would follow.

In 1936, after three years as a Junior Fellow in the Harvard Society of Fellows, Skinner moved to the University of Minnesota. His basic research continued, but during World War II he also worked on animal applications of behavior principles, including the training of pigeons to guide missiles (Skinner 1960; 1979). Although the project never got beyond demonstrations, a major fringe benefit was the discovery of shaping, the technique for creating novel forms of behavior through the differential reinforcement of successive approximations to a response.

Another product of those days was the Aircrib, which Skinner built for his wife and his second daughter (Skinner 1945). It was a windowed space with temperature and humidity control that improved on the safety and comfort of the ordinary crib while making the care of the child less burdensome. It was not used for conditioning the infant (contrary to rumor, neither of Skinner's daughters developed emotional instability, psychiatric problems, or suicidal tendencies). Soon after came the utopian novel, *Walden Two* (1948). Some who later criticized the specifics of that planned society failed to observe that its experimental character was its most important feature: Any practice that did not work was to be modified until a more effective version was found.

In 1945, Skinner assumed the chairmanship of the Department of Psychology at Indiana University. Then, after delivering the 1947 William James Lectures at Harvard University on the topic of verbal behavior, he returned permanently to the Harvard Department of Psychology (Skinner 1983). There he completed his book *Verbal Behavior* (1957) and, in collaboration with Charles B. Ferster, developed the subject matter of schedules of reinforcement (Ferster & Skinner 1957). Much else has been omitted here (e.g., *Science and Human Behavior* [1953] and teaching machines); the articles and books Skinner has since written are numerous. All but one of the articles treated ("Terms") are drawn from those later pieces; they constitute a sample of his most seminal works. Many others are cited in the course of the treatments.

Operant behaviorism

Operant behaviorism (or radical behaviorism) is the variety of behaviorism particularly identified with Skinner's work, It provides the systematic context for the research in psychology sometimes referred to as the experimental analysis of behavior. Behavior itself is its fundamental subject matter; behavior is not an indirect means of studying something else, such as cognition or mind or brain.

A primary task of an experimental analysis is to identify classes of behavior on the basis of their origins. Some classes of responses, *respondents*, originate with the stimuli that elicit them (as illustrated by the stimulus–response relations called reflexes). Others, called *operants*, are engendered by their effects on the environment; because they do not require eliciting stimuli, they are said to be *emitted* rather than elicited. Admitting the possibility that behavior could occur without eliciting stimuli was a critical first step in operant theory. Earlier treatments had assumed that for every response there must be a corresponding eliciting stimulus. The rejection of this assumption did not imply that emitted responses were uncaused; rather, the point was that there are other causes of behavior besides eliciting stimuli. Adding operants to respondents as behavior classes did not exhaust the possibilities, but it was critical to recognize that the past consequences of responding are significant determinants of behavior.

The consequences of a response may either raise or lower subsequent responding. Consequences that do so are respectively called *reinforcers* and *punishers* (punishment has sometimes been confused with negative reinforcement, but positive and negative reinforcement both involve increases in responding; they differ in whether the consequence of responding is the addition to or removal of something from the environment, as in the difference between appetitive procedures and those involving escape or avoidance). The particular relations that can be established between responses and their consequences are called *contingencies* of reinforcement or punishment.

But the consequences of responding are also typically correlated with other features of the environment (some consequences of stepping on the brake pedal or the gas pedal, for example, depend on whether the traffic light is red or green). When a stimulus sets the occasion on which responding will have a particular consequence, the stimulus is said to be *discriminative*. If responses then come to depend on, or come under the control of, this stimulus, the response class is called a *discriminated operant*. Both respondents and discriminated operants involve an antecedent stimulus, but the distinction between them is crucial and depends on whether consequences of responding play a role. A response that depends only on the presentation of a stimulus, as in a reflex relation, is a member of a respondent class. One that depends on the relations among the three terms – *stimulus*, *response*, *consequence* – is a member of a discriminated operant class. Thus, discriminated operants are said to be defined by a *three-term contingency*. The three-term contingency is often neglected by those who think of behavior change only in terms of the instrumental and classical procedures of earlier conditioning theories.

Much of the research that helped to establish this vocabulary was conducted in the experimental chamber that for a while was known as the Skinner box (that term was more often used by those outside than by those within the experimental analysis of behavior). Simple stimuli (lights, sounds), simple responses (lever presses, key pecks), and simple reinforcers (food, water) were arranged for studying the behavior of rats or pigeons. Many responses automatically have particular consequences (to see something below eye level, for example, we look down rather than up). But natural environments do not ordinarily include levers on which presses produce food pellets only when lights are on. Operant chambers were designed to create arbitrary *contingencies*; they were arbitrary, but only in this sense. As for responses such as the pigeon's key peck:

> Such responses are not wholly arbitrary. They are chosen because they can be easily executed, and because they can be repeated quickly and over long periods of time without fatigue. In such a bird as the pigeon, pecking has a certain genetic unity; it is a characteristic bit of behavior which appears with a well-defined topography. (Ferster & Skinner 1957, p. 7)

Given this recognition of genetic determinants in the specification of operant classes, it is ironic that some species-specific characteristics of lever presses and key pecks later became the basis for criticisms of operant theory. Perhaps these responses were not arbitrary enough. But given that the concern was to study the effects of the consequences of responding, it would hardly have been appropriate to have sought out response classes so highly determined in other species-specific ways that they would have been insensitive to their consequences.

There are "natural lines of fracture along which behavior and environment actually break" (Skinner 1935a, p. 40). "We divide behavior into hard and fast classes and are then surprised to find that the organism disregards the boundaries we have set" (Skinner 1953, p. 94). Operant theory is not compromised by demonstrations that some response classes are more easily established than others, or that some discriminations can be more easily established with some reinforcers than with others. Consequences are important, but they do not operate to the exclusion of other sources of behavior, including phylogenic ones. Phenomena such as autoshaping (producing a pigeon's pecks on a key by repeatedly lighting the key and then operating the feeder) were discovered in the course of operant research, and present no more of a problem to operant accounts than do the respondent conditioning phenomena studied by Pavlov.

The discovery that behavior could be maintained easily even when only an occasional response was reinforced led to the investigation of schedules of reinforcement. Schedules arrange reinforcers on the basis of the number of responses, the time at which responses occur, the rate of responding, or various combinations of these and other variables. In more complicated cases, different schedules operate either successively or simultaneously in the presence of different stimuli or for different responses. Reinforcement schedules have proven useful in such areas as psychopharmacology and behavioral toxicology. The performances generated by complex schedules are also sometimes analogous to performances that in humans are discussed in terms of preference, self-control, and so on (e.g., see "Methods").

In its extension to verbal behavior, a primary task of an operant analysis is again that of identifying the various sources of behavior. Its concern is with the functions of language rather than with its structure. In the *tact* relation, for example, an object or event is a discriminative stimulus that sets the occasion for a particular utterance, as when one says "apple" upon seeing an apple (tacting is not equivalent to naming or referring to; the relation called reference involves another class of behavior, called *autoclitic*). Through the tact relation, verbal behavior makes contact with events in the world. Other relations include (but are not limited to) the *intraverbal*, in which verbal behavior serves as a discriminative stimulus for other verbal behavior (as in learning addition or multiplication tables), the *textual*, in which written text provides the discriminative stimuli (as in reading aloud), and the *mand*, in which the verbal response specifies a consequence (as in making a request or asking a question). Any utterance, however, is likely to involve these and other relations in combination; verbal behavior is a product of multiple causation. Novel utterances may be dealt with by showing how their various components (words, phrases, grammatical forms) have each been occasioned by particular aspects of a current situation; novelty, in other words, comes about through novel combinations of existing verbal classes.

More important, these elementary relations are only the raw materials from which verbal behavior is constructed. A sentence cannot exist solely as a combination of these elementary units. Speakers report on the conditions under which they are behaving verbally (as when someone says, "I am happy to report that..."), they cancel the effects of their own verbal behavior (as when they include "not" in a sentence), they indicate its strength (as when they speak of being sure or uncertain), and so on. In each of these cases, some parts of the speaker's verbal behavior are under the discriminative control of the various other verbal relations. These processes, called *autoclitic*, are the basis for larger verbal units (e.g., sentences) and for the complexities of self-editing, logical verbal behavior, and so on. The nestings and orderings and coordinations of these processes are intricate, but they can nevertheless be accommodated by the discriminative stimuli and the responses and the consequences of the three-term contingency. This sort of analysis is illustrated in "Terms"; although that article predated Skinner's development of the vocabulary of *Verbal Behavior*, these relations are implicit in it, and more is involved in it than simply the tacting of private events.

These and other aspects of operant behaviorism are discussed in the treatment that follow. For the commentators, the articles are the stimuli, their commentaries are the responses, and Skinner's replies are the consequences. For Skinner, the commentaries are the stimuli and his replies are the responses; some of the consequences will be evident only in the effects of the treatments on their readers. Other potential responses and consequences produced by these treatments are even more remote and also remain to be seen. To the extent that they may correct some misreadings of operant theory, they are steps in the right direction. Given that we have already taken more than a single step, our journey has begun. This is as it should be. There is much to explore and our journey will not be short.

Canonical papers of B. F. Skinner

1 Selection by consequences

Abstract: Human behavior is the joint product of (i) contingencies of survival responsible for natural selection and (ii) contingencies of reinforcement responsible for the repertoires of individuals, including (iii) the special contingencies maintained by an evolved social environment. Selection by consequences is a causal mode found only in living things, or in machines made by living things. It was first recognized in natural selection. Reproduction, a first consequence, led to the evolution of cells, organs, and organisms reproducing themselves under increasingly diverse conditions. The behavior functioned well, however, only under conditions similar to those under which it was selected.

Reproduction under a wider range of consequences became possible with the evolution of processes through which organisms acquired behavior appropriate to novel environments. One of these, operant conditioning, is a second kind of selection by consequences. New responses could be strengthened by events which followed them. When the selecting consequences are the same, operant conditioning and natural selection work together redundantly. But because a species which quickly acquires behavior appropriate to an environment has less need for an innate repertoire, operant conditioning could replace as well as supplement the natural selection of behavior.

Social behavior is within easy range of natural selection, because other members are one of the most stable features of the environment of a species. The human species presumably became more social when its vocal musculature came under operant control. Verbal behavior greatly increased the importance of a third kind of selection by consequences, the evolution of social environments or cultures. The effect on the group, and not the reinforcing consequences for individual members, is responsible for the evolution of culture.

The history of human behavior, if we may take it to begin with the origin of life on earth, is possibly exceeded in scope only by the history of the universe. Like astronomer and cosmologist, the historian proceeds only by reconstructing what may have happened rather than by reviewing recorded facts. The story presumably began, not with a big bang, but with that extraordinary moment when a molecule came into existence which had the power to reproduce itself. It was then that selection by consequences made its appearance as a causal mode. Reproduction was itself a first consequence, and it led, through natural selection, to the evolution of cells, organs, and organisms which reproduced themselves under increasingly diverse conditions.

What we call behavior evolved as a set of functions furthering the interchange between organism and environment. In a fairly stable world it could be as much a part of the genetic endowment of a species as digestion, respiration, or any other biological function. The involvement with the environment, however, imposed limitations. The behavior functioned well only under conditions fairly similar to those under which it was selected. Reproduction under a much wider range of conditions became possible with the evolution of two processes through which individual organisms acquired behavior appropriate to novel environments. Through respondent (Pavlovian) conditioning, responses prepared in advance by natural selection could come under the control of new stimuli. Through operant conditioning, new responses could be strengthened ("reinforced") by events which immediately followed them.

A second kind of selection

Operant conditioning is a second kind of selection by consequences. It must have evolved in parallel with two other products of the same contingencies of natural selection – a susceptibility to reinforcement by certain kinds of consequences and a supply of behavior less specifically committed to eliciting or releasing stimuli. (Most operants are selected from behavior which has little or no relation to such stimuli.)

When the selecting consequences are the same, operant conditioning and natural selection work together redundantly. For example, the behavior of a duckling in following its mother is apparently the product not only of natural selection (ducklings tend to move in the direction of large moving objects) but also of an evolved susceptibility to reinforcement by proximity to such an object, as Peterson (1960) has shown. The common consequence is that the duckling stays near its mother. (Imprinting is a different process, close to respondent conditioning.)

Since a species which quickly acquires behavior appropriate to a given environment has less need for an innate repertoire, operant conditioning could not only supplement the natural selection of behavior, it could replace it. There were advantages favoring such a change. When members of a species eat a certain food simply because eating it has had survival value, the food does not need to be, and presumably is not, a reinforcer. Similarly, when sexual behavior is simply a product of natural selection, sexual contact does not need to be, and presumably is not, a reinforcer. But when, through the evolution of special susceptibilities, food and sexual contact become reinforcing, new forms of behavior can be set up. New ways of gathering, processing, and ultimately cultivating foods and new ways of behaving sexually or of behaving in ways which lead only eventually to sexual reinforcement can be shaped and maintained. The behavior so conditioned is not necessarily adaptive; foods are eaten which are not healthful, and sexual behavior strengthened which is not related to procreation.

Much of the behavior studied by ethologists – courtship, mating, care of the young, intraspecific aggression, defense of territory, and so on – is social. It is within easy range of natural selection because other members of a species are one of the most stable features of the environment of a species. Innate social repertoires are supplemented by imitation. By running when others run, for example, an animal responds to releasing stimuli to which it has not itself been exposed. A different kind of imitation, with a much wider range, results from the fact that contingencies of reinforcement which induce one organism to behave in a given way will often affect another organism when it behaves in the same way. An imitative repertoire which brings the imitator under the control of new contingencies is therefore acquired.

The human species presumably became much more social when its vocal musculature came under operant control. Cries of alarm, mating calls, aggressive threats, and other kinds of vocal behavior can be modified through operant conditioning, but apparently only with respect to the occasions upon which they occur or their rate of occurrence. (The imitative vocal behavior of certain birds may be an exception, but if it has selective consequences comparable with those of cries of alarm or mating calls, they are obscure. The vocal behavior of the parrot is shaped, at best, by a trivial consequence, involving the resemblance between sounds produced and sounds heard.)

The ability of the human species to acquire new forms through selection by consequences presumably resulted from the evolution of a special innervation of the vocal musculature, together with a supply of vocal behavior not strongly under the control of stimuli or releasers – the babbling of children from which verbal operants are selected. No new susceptibility to reinforcement was needed because the consequences of verbal behavior are distinguished only by the fact that they are mediated by other people (Skinner, 1957).

The development of environmental control over the vocal musculature greatly extended the help one person receives from others. By behaving verbally people cooperate more successfully in common ventures. By taking advice, heeding warnings, following instructions, and observing rules, they profit from what others have already learned. Ethical practices are strengthened by codifying them in laws, and special techniques of ethical and intellectual self-management are devised and taught. Self-knowledge or awareness emerges when one person asks another such a question as "What are you going to do?" or "Why did you do that?" The invention of the alphabet spread these advantages over great distances and periods of time. They have long been said to give the human species its unique position, although it is possible that what is unique is simply the extension of operant control to the vocal musculature.

A third kind of selection

Verbal behavior greatly increased the importance of a third kind of selection by consequences, the evolution of social environments or cultures. The process presumably begins at the level of the individual. A better way of making a tool, growing food, or teaching a child is reinforced by its consequence – the tool, the food, or a useful helper, respectively. A culture evolves when practices originating in this way contribute to the success of the practicing group in solving its problems. It is the effect on the group, not the reinforcing consequences for individual members, which is responsible for the evolution of the culture.

In summary, then, human behavior is the joint product of (i) the contingencies of survival responsible for the natural selection of the species and (ii) the contingencies of reinforcement responsible for the repertoires acquired by its members, including (iii) the special contingencies maintained by an evolved social environment. (Ultimately, of course, it is all a matter of natural selection, since operant conditioning is an evolved process, of which cultural practices are special applications.)

Similarities and differences

Each of the three levels of variation and selection has its own discipline – the first, biology; the second, psychology; and the third, anthropology. Only the second, operant conditioning, occurs at a speed at which it can be observed from moment to moment. Biologists and anthropologists study the processes through which variations arise and are selected, but they merely reconstruct the evolution of a species or culture. Operant conditioning is selection in progress. It resembles a hundred million years of natural selection or a thousand years of the evolution of a culture compressed into a very short period of time.

The immediacy of operant conditioning has certain practical advantages. For example, when a currently adaptive feature is presumably too complex to have occurred in its present form as a single variation, it is usually explained as the product of a sequence of simpler variations, each with its own survival value. It is standard practice in evolutionary theory to look for such sequences, and anthropologists and historians have reconstructed the stages through which moral and ethical codes, art, music, literature, science, technology, and so on, have presumably evolved. A complex operant, however, can actually be "shaped through successive approximation" by arranging a graded series of contingencies of reinforcement. (Patterns of innate behavior too complex to have arisen as single variations may have been shaped by geologic changes due to plate tectonics: Skinner 1975a.)

A current question at level i has parallels at levels ii and iii. If natural selection is a valid principle, why do many species remain unchanged for thousands or even millions of years? Presumably the answer is either that no variations have occurred or that those which occurred were not selected by the prevailing contingencies. Similar questions may be asked at levels ii and iii. Why do people continue to do things in the same way for many years, and why do groups of people continue to observe old practices for centuries? The answers are presumably the same: Either new variations (new forms of behavior or new practices) have not appeared or those which have appeared have not been selected by the prevailing contingencies (of reinforcement or of the survival of the group). At all three levels a sudden, possibly extensive, change is explained as due to new variations selected by prevailing contingencies or to new contingencies. Competition with other species, persons, or cultures may or may not be involved. Structural constraints may also play a part at all three levels.

Another issue is the definition or identity of a species, person, or culture. Traits in a species and practices in a culture are transmitted from generation to generation, but reinforced behavior is "transmitted" only in the sense of remaining part of the repertoire of the individual. Where species and cultures are defined by restrictions imposed upon transmission – by genes and chromosomes and, say, geographical isolation, respectively – a problem of definition (or identity) arises at level ii only when different contingencies of reinforcement create different repertoires, as selves or persons.

Traditional explanatory schemes

As a causal mode, selection by consequences was discovered very late in the history of science – indeed, less than a century and a half ago – and it is still not fully recognized or understood, especially at levels ii and iii. The facts for which it is responsible have been forced into the causal pattern of classical mechanics, and many of the explanatory schemes elaborated in the process must now be discarded. Some of them have great prestige and are strongly defended at all three levels. Here are four examples.

A prior act of creation. (i) Natural selection replaces a very special creator and is still challenged because it does so. (ii) Operant conditioning provides a similarly controversial account of the ("voluntary") behavior traditionally attributed to a creative mind. (iii) The evolution of a social environment replaces the supposed origin of a culture as a social contract or of social practices as commandments.

Purpose or intention. Only past consequences figure in selection. (i) A particular species does not have eyes in order that its members may see better; it has them because certain members, undergoing variation, were able to see better and hence were more likely to transmit the variation. (ii) The consequences of operant behavior are not what the behavior is now for; they are merely similar to the consequences which have shaped and maintained it. (iii) People do not observe particular practices in order that the group will be more likely to survive; they observe them because groups which induced their members to do so survived and transmitted them.

Certain essences. (i) A molecule which could reproduce itself and evolve into cell, organ, and organism was alive as soon as it came into existence without the help of a vital principle called life. (ii) Operant behavior is shaped and brought under the control of the environment without the intervention of a principle of mind. (To suppose that thought appeared as a variation, like a morphological trait in genetic theory, is to invoke an unnecessarily large *saltum*.) (iii) Social environments generate self-knowledge ("consciousness") and self-management ("reason") without help from a group mind or zeitgeist.

To say this is not to reduce life, mind, and zeitgeist to physics; it is simply to recognize the expendability of essences. The facts are as they have always been. To say that selection by consequences is a causal mode found only in living things is only to say that selection (or the "replication with error" which made it possible) defines "living." (A computer can be programmed to model natural selection, operant conditioning, or the evolution of a culture but only when constructed and programmed by a living thing.) The physical basis of natural selection is now fairly clear; the corresponding basis of operant conditioning, and hence of the evolution of cultures, has yet to be discovered.

Certain definitions of good and value. (i) What is good for the species is whatever promotes the survival of its members until offspring have been born and, possibly, cared for. Good features are said to have survival value. Among them are susceptibilities to reinforcement by many of the things we say taste good, feel good, and so on. (ii) The behavior of a person is good if it is effective under prevailing contingencies of reinforcement. We value such behavior and, indeed, reinforce it by saying "Good!" Behavior toward others is good if it is good for the others in these senses. (iii) What is good for a culture is whatever promotes its ultimate survival, such as holding a group together or transmitting its practices. These are not, of course, traditional definitions; they do not recognize a world of value distinct from a world of fact and, for other reasons to be noted shortly, they are challenged.

Alternatives to selection

An example of the attempt to assimilate selection by consequences to the causality of classical mechanics is the term "selection pressure," which appears to convert selection into something that forces a change. A more serious example is the metaphor of storage. Contingencies of selection necessarily lie in the past; they are not acting when their effect is observed. To provide a current cause it has therefore been assumed that they are stored (usually as "information") and later retrieved. Thus, (i) genes and chromosomes are said to "contain the information" needed by the fertilized egg in order to grow into a mature organism. But a cell does not consult a store of information in order to learn how to change; it changes because of features which are the product of a history of variation and selection, a product which is not well represented by the metaphor of storage. (ii) People are said to store information about contingencies of reinforcement and retrieve it for use on later occasions. But they do not consult copies of earlier contingencies to discover how to behave; they behave in given ways because they have been changed by those contingencies. The contingencies can perhaps be inferred from the changes they have worked, but they are no longer in existence. (iii) A possibly legitimate use of "storage" in the evolution of cultures may be responsible for these mistakes. Parts of the social environment maintained and transmitted by a group are quite literally stored in documents, artifacts, and other products of that behavior.

Other causal forces serving in lieu of selection have been sought in the structure of a species, person, or culture. Organization is an example. (i) Until recently, most biologists argued that organization distinguished living from nonliving things. (ii) According to Gestalt psychologists and others, both perceptions and acts occur in certain inevitable ways because of their organization. (iii) Many anthropologists and linguists appeal to the organization of cultural and linguistic practices. It is true that all species, persons, and cultures are highly organized, but no principle of organization explains their being so. Both the organization and the effects attributed to it can be traced to the respective contingencies of selection.

Another example is growth. Developmentalism is structuralism with time or age added as an independent variable. (i) There was evidence before Darwin that species had "developed." (ii) Cognitive psychologists have argued that concepts develop in the child in certain fixed orders, and Freud said the same for the psychosexual functions. (iii) Some anthropologists have contended that cultures must evolve through a prescribed series of stages, and Marx said as much in his insistence upon historical determinism. But at all three levels the changes can be explained by the "development" of contingencies of selection. New contingencies of natural selection come within range as a species evolves; new contingencies of reinforcement begin to operate as behavior becomes more complex; and new contingencies of survival are dealt with by increasingly effective cultures.

Selection neglected

The causal force attributed to structure as a surrogate of selection causes trouble when a feature at one level is said to explain a similar feature at another, the historical priority of natural selection usually giving it a special place. Sociobiology offers many examples. Behavior described as the defense of territory may be due to (i) contingencies of survival in the evolution of a species, possibly involving food supplies or breeding practices; (ii) contingencies of reinforcement for the individual, possibly involving a share of the reinforcers available in the territory; or (iii) contingencies maintained by the cultural practices of a group, promoting behavior which contributes to the survival of the group. Similarly, altruistic behavior (i) may evolve through, say, kin selection; (ii) may be shaped and maintained by contingencies of reinforcement arranged by those for whom the behavior works an advantage; or (iii) may be generated by cultures which, for example, induce individuals to suffer or die as heroes or martyrs. The contingencies of selection at the three levels are quite different, and the structural similarity does not attest to a common generative principle.

When a causal force is assigned to structure, selection tends to be neglected. Many issues which arise in morals and ethics can be resolved by specifying the level of selection. What is good for the individual or culture may have bad consequences for the species, as when sexual reinforcement leads to overpopulation or the reinforcing amenities of civilization to the exhaustion of resources; what is good for the species or culture may be bad for the individual, as when practices designed to control procreation or preserve resources restrict individual freedom; and so on. There is nothing inconsistent or contradictory about these uses of "good" or "bad," or about other value judgments, so long as the level of selection is specified.

An initiating agent

The role of selection by consequences has been particularly resisted because there is no place for the initiating agent suggested by classical mechanics. We try to identify such an agent when we say (i) that a species adapts to an environment, rather than that the environment selects the adaptive traits; (ii) that an individual adjusts to a situation, rather than that the situation shapes and maintains adjusted behavior; and (iii) that a group of people solve a problem raised by certain circumstances, rather than that the circumstances select the cultural practices which yield a solution.

The question of an initiating agent is raised in its most acute form by our own place in this history. Darwin and Spencer thought that selection would necessarily lead to perfection, but species, people, and cultures all perish when they cannot cope with rapid change, and our species now appears to be threatened. Must we wait for selection to solve the problems of overpopulation, exhaustion of resources, pollution of the environment, and a nuclear holocaust, or can we take explicit steps to make our future more secure? In the latter case, must we not in some sense transcend selection?

We could be said to intervene in the process of selection when as geneticists we change the characteristics of a species or create new species, or when as governors, employers, or teachers we change the behavior of persons, or when we design new cultural practices; but in none of these ways do we escape from selection by consequences. In the first place, we can work only through variation and selection. At level i we can change genes and chromosomes or contingencies of survival, as in selective breeding. At level ii we can introduce new forms of behavior – for example, by showing or telling people what to do with respect to relevant contingencies – or construct and maintain new selective contingencies. At level iii we can introduce new cultural practices or, rarely, arrange special contingencies of survival – for example, to preserve a traditional practice. But having done these things, we must wait for selection to occur. (There is a special reason why these limitations are significant. It is often said that the human species is now able to control its own genetics, its own behavior, its own destiny, but it does not do so in the sense in which the term control is used in classical mechanics. It does not for the very reason that living things are not machines: selection by consequences makes the difference.) In the second place, we must consider the possibility that our behavior in intervening is itself a product of selection. We tend to regard ourselves as initiating agents only because we know or remember so little about our genetic and environmental histories.

Although we can now predict many of the contingencies of selection to which the human species will probably be exposed at all three levels and can specify behavior that will satisfy many of them, we have failed to establish cultural practices under which much of that behavior is selected and maintained. It is possible that our effort to preserve the role of the individual as an originator is at fault, and that a wider recognition of the role of selection by consequences will make an important difference.

The present scene is not encouraging. Psychology is the discipline of choice at level ii, but few psychologists pay much attention to selection. The existentialists among them are explicitly concerned with the here and now, rather than the past and future. Structuralists and developmentalists tend to neglect selective contingencies in their search for causal principles such as organization or growth. The conviction that contingencies are stored as information is only one of the reasons why the appeal to cognitive functions is not helpful. The three personae of psychoanalytic theory are in many respects close to our three levels of selection; but the id does not adequately represent the enormous contribution of the natural history of the species; the superego, even with the help of the ego ideal, does not adequately represent the contribution of the social environment to language, self-knowledge, and intellectual and ethical self-management; and the ego is a poor likeness of the personal repertoire acquired under the practical contingencies of daily life. The field known as the experimental analysis of behavior has extensively explored selection by consequences, but its conception of human behavior is resisted, and many of its practical applications rejected, precisely because it has no place for a person as an initiating agent. The behavioral sciences at level iii show similar shortcomings. Anthropology is heavily structural, and political scientists and economists usually treat the individual as a free initiating agent. Philosophy and letters offer no promising leads.

A proper recognition of the selective action of the environment means a change in our conception of the origin of behavior which is possibly as extensive as that of the origin of species. So long as we cling to the view that a person is an initiating doer, actor, or causer of behavior, we shall probably continue to neglect the conditions which must be changed if we are to solve our problems (Skinner 1971).

POSTSCRIPT

It is curious that the notion of selection by consequences should have appeared so late in the history of human thought. Selection is found only in living things, and that is no doubt relevant, but people have been interested in living things as long as in nonliving. A possible explanation is that the effect of selection is somewhat delayed. We see the product but not the process; hence, we are likely to attribute the product to a current product of the selective contingencies rather than to the contingencies themselves.

A creative act is a kind of surrogate of selection; purpose is another. Biologists have dealt with their supposed place in the origin of species. Psychologists show less agreement about their place in the origin of behavior. Cognitive psychologists, for example, tend to call operant behavior "goal-directed," but goal-directedness is only a current surrogate of a history of reinforcing consequences. The intentionalism of modern philosophy also serves as a surrogate of a personal history.

The reason why selection by consequences has been so long neglected may be the reason it is still so widely misunderstood.

COMMENTARIES AND RESPONSES

Skinner on selection: A case study of intellectual isolation

George W. Barlow

Department of Zoology and Museum of Vertebrate Zoology, University of California, Berkeley

Ask yourself the following question: Would "Consequences" have been published in *Science* in 1981 if the author had been anonymous? The answer would be a resounding no, and it would not be difficult to confirm this assertion experimentally now, some years later. Surely the editors of *Science* must have had good reasons for publishing his article. We can only guess the reasons, but I doubt we would be far wrong.

First and foremost, B. F. Skinner is a major figure in modern psychology. Almost anything he has to say in the realm of behavior is of widespread interest whether one's opinion is that it is right or wrong, and with or without adequate documentation. He has made enormous contributions to the field and demonstrated the awesome control the experimenter can have over the behavior of an animal under specified conditions.

That very control seems to have shaped Skinner's perception of the biological world. It has also produced a vision of human behavior that can be disquieting. In "Consequences" Skinner asserts that a person is not "an initiating doer, actor, or causer of behavior." He states further that it is possible to "construct and maintain new selective contingencies" by reinforcing the "good" behavior of such a person. Taken at face value that sounds harmless enough, except for two things: Someone else decides what is good behavior, and we have no clear prescription for how that decision might be reached or who makes it. The definition of good behavior appears simply to evolve by trial and error at three levels, and perhaps it has. That is the major thesis of "Consequences."

The first level is that of Darwinian natural selection. That kind of selection is treated superficially and conventionally. (I return to his views on natural selection below.) The second kind of selection is that of operant conditioning, and the third is that of cultural evolution, the course of both being molded by their consequences. His treatment of the last two levels does not find universal acceptance.

I take exception to Skinner's portrayal of selection at the level of operant conditioning. For one, I prefer to call this level that of phenotypic modification or intraindividual adaptation; the terminology is not important. What is important is that individual adaptability is a much richer set of phenomena than is even remotely embraced by operant conditioning.

Ectothermic animals, for instance, acclimate to the temperature at which they are found; the thermal preferendum of an individual depends on its thermal acclimation, which varies with the season and microhabitat (Hutchison & Maness 1979). Sexual maturity, with its attendant changes in behavior, can occur at radically different ages in platyfish depending on dominance relationships that are independent of the respondent's behavior (Borowsky 1978). The maternal digger wasp learns how much to provision her nest site in one trial, without the benefit of overt reinforcement, and the appropriate response is delayed several hours (Baerends 1941). Early experience appears to have pervasive effects on behaviors that are first manifest only in adulthood. One such phenomenon is sexual imprinting; attempts to fit it into a conditioning paradigm present difficulties and suggest a procrustean resolution.

The manner in which Skinner contrasts natural selection and conditioning as two distinct kinds of selection also has a major fault. Genetic and experiential factors are conveyed as being fundamentally separate. This separation is inherent in the way Skinner relegates biologists' interests to unlearned behavior and evolutionary phylogenies. The rigidity is also apparent in his insistence that "most operants are selected from behavior which has little or no relation to" eliciting or releasing stimuli. An epigenetic approach provides a more realistic view.

Evidence is growing rapidly that there are evolved predispositions for animals to learn to respond in particular ways to particular kinds of stimulation. The example most appropriate to Skinner's essay, and also the most debatable, is that of language. People learn a given language, and conditioning doubtless plays a role. But humans may also be predisposed to speak, and the structure of language may have properties that transcend the process of operant conditioning (Lenneberg & Lenneberg 1975). This possibility is ignored in Skinner's essay.

The range of interaction between experience and species-specific constraints on learning is nowhere better and more convincingly documented than in the elegant comparative studies on the acquisition of song among birds (Green & Marler 1979). Likewise, sexual imprinting is proving increasingly to involve both constraints and plasticity; recognizing one's species is an ability that requires little experience. Rather, imprinting's function seems to be the learning of closeness of relationship (P. Bateson 1980). Finally, I disagree with Skinner's easy and almost casual equating of genetic with fixed behavior.

I do agree with Skinner on the other hand, that cultures have evolved because of the consequences of their practices. Many will differ with us on this.

A major weakness of "Consequences" is that it has been written in a vacuum. Skinner's remarks on natural selection show a lack of understanding as well as total isolation from the noisy arguments that have been heard throughout the land for the last 20 years about group versus individual selection. It is almost embarrassing to read in a 1981 paper that "what is good for the individual or culture may have bad consequences for the species" – or, when writing about the origins of behavior and clearly not about humans, "The behavior so conditioned is not necessarily adaptive; foods are eaten which are not healthful, and sexual behavior strengthened which is not related to procreation." Lest I be misunderstood, let me point out that I am not saying that group selection is inconceivable (see D. S. Wilson 1975; 1980) but that this loose application of the species-benefit argument reveals a fundamental failure to understand modern theorizing about natural selection.

This confusion is apparent in the conclusion of "Consequences." Skinner argues with regard to altruism that selection operates at three different levels, paralleling his opening remarks. The three kinds of selection are (*i*) biological (here kin selection), (ii) psychological (through reinforcement of individual behavior), and (iii) cultural (as in inducing heroism). He claims that "the contingencies of selection at the three levels are quite different, and the structural similarity does not attest to a common generative principle."

What we have here is a failure to distinguish between proximate and ultimate mechanisms (E. O. Wilson 1975). The hero is taught to behave that way, which is the proximate mechanism. In the small societies in which heroism must have evolved, the hero's kin enjoyed improved reproductive fitness superior to that of individuals who were not so easy to train. This is kin selection, the ultimate causation. A common generative principle is reasonable.

I was equally taken aback by the absence of references to highly relevant literature closer to home for Skinner. In a classic paper Pringle (1951) explored the parallels between learning and natural selection. Campbell (1975) has written on almost the same theme as Skinner and is often cited. Pringle's and Campbell's treatments are more sophisticated than the essay before us. Skinner has also overlooked the literature on constraints on learning and the ethologists' resolution of the nature–nurture issue.

Why, indeed, should *Science* have published this essay? Perhaps the editors felt that we should know Skinner's mind well, including the box within which it operates, precisely because his writings have been so influential, extending into the sociopolitical arena. Skinner should respond to this type of criticism and not just by asserting that he is not understood. He should acknowledge these other fields by learning more about them than is found in the secondary literature. It may yet be possible to bring this great thinker out of the walls he has erected around his intellect.

BFS: I am sorry that in the four or five thousand words that were available to me when I wrote "Consequences" I have not covered the field of natural selection to Barlow's satisfaction. I am also sorry that he appears not to be aware of the extent of current research on operant conditioning. I am happy that he agrees with me on the evolution of culture, but he seems to miss its relevance to the question of who is to decide what is good behavior.

So far as the point of "Consequences" is concerned, it does not matter in the least whether any of the behavior Barlow mentions is the product of natural selection, operant conditioning, the evolution of cultural practices, or any combination thereof. The same issues arise: the need to abandon the concept of a creator, purpose, essences like life, mind, and zeitgeist as contemporary surrogates of histories of selection, and values. I repeat: All these issues demand attention regardless of whether the consequences are found in natural selection, operant conditioning, or the evolution of cultures. Although there is lively controversy at all three levels, the basic notion of selection by consequences survives and raises the questions I addressed.

On the status of causal modes

Robert C. Bolles

Department of Psychology, University of Washington

The modern Western world grew up being thoroughly familiar with two traditional causal modes. We knew about the mental mode, the world of ideas and feelings and the associations among ideas and feelings. We knew how to explain behavior in terms of ideation and volition. We also knew about the mechanical mode, the world of machines and billiard balls, projectiles and things in orbit. We knew how to explain behavior in terms of neural impulses and muscle contractions. These modes were familiar; they did not enjoy a great deal of practical success, but they were familiar.

Not so familiar were some other explanatory modes that had been around since antiquity. There was Aristotle's fourfold approach, which showed up from time to time, and which is still fashionable among Jesuit scholars. And there was the empirical approach of Hume. Hume observed, rightly, that we really do not know how the mind works, or even what is really happening on the billiard table. All that we can actually know is that our observations are orderly and, with experience, predictable. If we have observed this following that many times before, then we can count on this following that again. Psychologists have never been very comfortable with Aristotle's approach, nor, for a long time, did they take very kindly to Hume's empirical approach. In the heady days of early behaviorism, the mechanistic bias precluded any alternative to a mechanical mode of causation. All other modes were dismissed, so that behavior could be explained only in terms of neural impulses and muscle contractions.

It is greatly to his credit, I think, that Skinner has always stood opposed to this mechanistic bias. In one of his earliest publications Skinner (1931) considered the question of how one knows that one is looking at a reflex. How can we tell that this regularly elicited reaction really is a reflex? Do we know this because of our underlying knowledge of the neural mediation involved: the afferent, the synapse, and the efferent? No, not at all. We know we have a reflex for simple, empirical, Hume-like reasons: The stimulus regularly elicits the reaction. Back in those days, back at the beginning of Skinner's career, such an empirical orientation was not very popular, but he stuck with it, defended it ably, and continued to promote it. And gradually the empirical causal mode began to catch on.

But meanwhile subtle changes could be seen in Skinner's behavior. He pointed out that just as an elicited response is perfectly well explained by citing the antecedent eliciting stimulus, so an emitted response can be perfectly well explained by citing the consequent reinforcing stimulus (Skinner 1937). Only a mechanist would insist upon the emitted response having an elicitor. Deny the mechanists their fundamental assumption, and you have behavior explained by its consequences. Adhere to a purely empirical mode of causation, and you have operants being explained by their reinforcers. If you have a stream of operants, and a stream of reinforcers, these streams turn out to be so well correlated that you do not even have to have a "theory" to explain the correlation (Skinner 1950). If the stream of reinforcers really controls the behavior, then you have the behavior under control and you do not have to be bothered by the question of how it is mediated, because you have your own kind of causal mode.

It may be noted that there is nothing teleological about control by consequences, because by the time you actually get behavior under control there will be a history of reinforcement for it, and if one were interested in questions of mediation then that history could be assumed to be acting proactively. But the question of whether the past acts proactively or the future acts retroactively hardly ever arises when one is committed to Skinner's kind of causal mode.

For some years now (e.g., Campbell 1956) parallels have been noted between the selection of responses by reinforcement and the selection of species by evolutionary processes. In "Consequences" Skinner has elaborated some of these parallels. Thus, he proposes that causation by consequences is the proper explanatory mode for both evolutionary scholarship and the experimental analysis of behavior. And he extends the argument to include a third area, social organization and evolution. Perhaps it was thought that the emphasis upon a common causal mode for these three areas would help to legitimize one or another of them, or the causal mode itself. However, this emphasis overlooks a fundamental point. One can understand that a theorist would want to push an idea as far as it can go, particularly when it is a good idea. But we also have to understand that parallels may be no more than parallels.

The problem is this. Although it is quite true that evolutionary theorists like to think of consequences (the survival and prosperity of a species) selecting genotypes, very little of the explaining they do takes this form. Evolutionary theory is constantly on the search for mediating mechanisms, for the antecedent conditions that present challenges to animals' survival, and for the complicated interactions between animal and environment. In short, the great bulk of evolutionary scholarship involves itself with proximate causation and mediating mechanisms. And the great overriding principle of ultimate causation, the causation by consequences, although very widely believed in, is rarely cited as explaining anything. In Skinner's analysis of behavior the situation is very much the opposite. He tends to rely on reinforcement as an explanatory principle, and to dismiss mediating mechanisms (for example, when there is a discriminative stimulus that might be thought of as eliciting the operant, it is not allowed to do anything, it merely "sets the occasion"). So the selection by consequences idea has to carry the whole explanatory burden.

The problem is that different explanatory modes should not compete with each other, they should complement each other. Aristotle was basically right, I think, in that we should use a variety of explanatory modes rather than trying to rely on just one. Perhaps if one is only interested in controlling behavior, then Skinner's causal mode suffices. But a lot of psychologists want to do more than control behavior. The truth is that the mind is full of ideas and feelings and associations; the head is full of neurons and synapses. And a lot of psychologists want to know how these things work, and in their searches they will, no doubt, be using the familiar, traditional explanatory modes.

BFS: Bolles gives 1956 as the date of the first observation of similarities between operant conditioning and natural selection, but in 1953 in *Science and Human Behavior* (p. 430) I wrote: "We have seen that in certain respects operant reinforcement resembles the natural selection of evolutionary theory. Just as genetic characteristics which arise as mutations are selected or discarded by their consequences, so novel forms of behavior are selected or discarded through reinforcement." And I went on to say that "[t]here is still a third kind of selection which applies to cultural practices. . .[a] practice modifies the behavior of members of the group. The resulting behavior may affect the success of the group in competition with other groups or with the nonsocial environment."

In his last paragraph, Bolles brings up an interesting point. As an explanatory mode, selection is responsible only for novelty, for origins. That is the way in which it differs from the causal mode of physics. Once a given structure has been selected by natural selection and once a bit of behavior has been shaped by operant reinforcement, selection as a causal mode has done its work and a mechanical model may suffice. A survey of the current state of the organism – the responses in its repertoire, the relevant reinforcing consequences, the controlling stimuli – need not involve selection at all. Nor will the neurological account of how these variables are interrelated. Only if these structures are still changing will selection need to be considered as a causal mode. So far as they are the products of selection, a "mechanical" causality suffices.

B. F. Skinner: A dissident view

Kenneth E. Boulding

Department of Economics, Swarthmore College

I write out of an imperfect and probably biased knowledge of Skinner's work, my reading not extending much beyond his popular works and the present article, "Consequences." It is only by the clear statement of current images and subsequent testing by critique or experience, however, that knowledge becomes more perfect. The following is my current image, subject to future revision.

1. I still have to be persuaded that experimental psychology, especially with animals, has contributed much even to the understanding of animals, still less to the understanding of the immense complexity of the human organism. The experimental method is useful only in a very limited area of scientific inquiry, where systems are simple and repeatable, as in chemistry. It is on the whole an inappropriate methodology in developing improved cognitive images of complex, unstable systems with changing parameters and cumulative structures, where rare events are significant. Humans are a supreme example of systems of this kind.

2. The whole black-box, input–output, behavioral approach strikes me as having very limited value in understanding behavior, even of animals. In the case of humans we have a key to opening the black box of our minds in our capacity for reflection and communication. It seems the height of absurdity to dismiss this as "operant control" of "vocal musculature."

3. Skinner's basic theoretical concepts, such as reinforcement, rest ultimately on a largely unexamined selection of mental images out of a potentially very large and unexamined repertoire. It simply assumes that there is a valuation structure within the organism which, for instance, can distinguish, and at least rank, pleasures and pains, and this assumption presumably is derived from human introspection and then applied to rats and pigeons. Valuations, however, although they are in part genetically created, are also, even in animals, learned, and in humans the learning process is very large. The evaluative structure, for instance, by which we learn to speak and write "correct" English is wholly learned – we have a genetically produced potential for the learning of language, but there is no gene for English or Chinese.

4. The evolutionary theory, as expounded in "Consequences," is a middling first approximation, but quite inadequate even for the complexities of biological, much less for social, evolution. It neglects the complexity of ecological selection, and even more the complexity especially of societal mutation, which is often highly teleological

and much influenced by the capacity of humans for images of the future. Together with the sociobiologists, Skinner neglects the process of transmission of learned structures from one generation to the next by a learning process, which I have called "noogenetics," and which is of some importance even in animals, and of overwhelming importance in humans. Skinner does recognize, however, that selective processes that lead to the spread of a particular mutation (and this goes for the noogenetic as well as the biogenetic) through the field of a species may be adverse to the survival of the species itself. The reverse may also be true – that obstacles to the spread of certain mutations through the species may help the survival of the species itself.

5. With Skinner's protest against crude applications of classical mechanics I have a lot of sympathy; the very success of Newtonian and Laplacian mechanics has had a most unfortunate effect on those sciences that study complex systems with ustable parameters, where whatever "laws" there are change all the time. He constantly seems to be slipping back, however, into the quasi-mechanical determinism the theory of operant conditioning represents, which is inappropriate to biological and especially to human and societal systems. Skinner, and many other psychologists, have trapped themselves in a methodology inappropriate to the system they are studying, so much so that it is hard not to feel that we can learn more about human structure and process from the poets than from the psychologists. It could be, of course, that when and if we ever find out the actual processes in the nervous system by which images are coded and changed, this could lead to a radical change in the understanding and practice of human learning. This, however, requires observational and descriptive science, guided by fine instrumentation, rather than experimental science. Here again the principle that nothing fails like imitated success seems to apply; the success of experimental science in its appropriate fields, which are quite limited, has led to its extension into fields in which it is not appropriate. The psychologists, and Skinner in particular, seem to have been caught in this trap.

BFS: Boulding has offered an image to be corrected "so that knowledge becomes more perfect." A few corrections:

1. There are many fields which now lie beyond prediction and control. Evolution is one, plate tectonics another, and astronomy beyond the solar system a third. Do we remain silent about them? No, we interpret observations in those fields by using what we have learned from research in which we *can* predict and control. Most educated people accept such interpretations in lieu of the explanations which have come down to us from folk culture and religion. Human behavior is such a field, and I am confident that an experimental analysis has contributed much more to understanding it than Boulding says.
2. The experimental analysis of behavior is not a "black box, input–output...approach." (See "Terms" and "Problem Solving.") Input–output suggests a stimulus–response formulation to which operant conditioning and an emphasis on selection by consequences were correctives.
3. Reinforcers are not defined in terms of pleasure and pain. They are defined in terms of their effects in strengthening behavior. How we come to talk about them and call them pleasant and painful is mentioned in "Terms."
4. I had no space to expound evolution fully. But I *did* explain the trans-

mission of learned structures from one generation to the next in the discussion of imitation and related topics.

5. Operant conditioning is not quasi-mechanical. It is, as I point out in my paper, the clearest evidence we have of the process of selection by consequences. As I say in my reply to Bolles, selection is concerned with origins; once a system has come into existence it can be studied in other ways. I would not look for much help, however, from processes in the nervous system by which images are coded.

Behaviorism and natural selection

C. B. G. Campbell

Division of Neuropsychiatry, Walter Reed Army Institute of Research, Washington, D. C.

Much of the content of "Consequences" has appeared previously in other publications of Professor Skinner. I have taken this opportunity to read some of them also. It is interesting to see so much emphasis on evolution and natural selection in the work of a distinguished experimental psychologist. As he himself points out, few psychologists afford selection much attention. Surely one of his many contributions has been the stressing of selection and the role of behavior in it. Nevertheless, there are some elements in the paper with which I disagree.

Although Skinner inserts the disclaimer that his three levels of contingencies are ultimately all a matter of natural selection, throughout the bulk of his discussion here and elsewhere he treats them quite separately. Further, he emphasizes their distinctness by his statement that each of the three levels of variation and selection has its own scientific discipline: biology, psychology, and anthropology. He suggests that operant conditioning, the second level or kind of selection by consequences, could supplement natural selection or replace it. It is my contention that subsuming these three entities – natural selection, operant conditioning, and social environment or culture – under the umbrella of "selection by consequences" is misleading.

The modern definition of natural selection stresses reproductive success. The genotypes of a species possess a large pool of variation. This produces phenotypic variation in the populations of the species, some of which is morphological and some behavioral. Natural selection is a statistical concept. The better genotype has a better chance of surviving long enough to reproduce itself and add some of its genes to the next generation. It should be remembered that natural selection favors or discriminates against phenotypes, not genotypes. When genotypic differences are not expressed in the phenotype they are not accessible to selection. This process is said to be selective because some genes increase in frequency while others decrease.

Operant conditioning or contingencies of reinforcement may be said to select for increased or decreased frequency of some form of behavior in the repertoire of individuals. Such behaviors might become shaped in such a way as to be appropriate for novel environments and lead to differential reproduction. For this to occur these behaviors or their possessors would have to be acted upon by natural selection. Operant conditioning is here acting much like mutation or gene recombination, producing new variation on which natural selection may act. It does not have a power equivalent to that of natural selection insofar as evolution is concerned. The evolution of social environments or cultures is perhaps analogous to biological evolution. Certainly it has had an impact on human evolution. In my view, classifying natural selection, operant conditioning, and the evolution of culture as three "kinds" of selection by consequences is akin to classifying a child's ball, the planet earth, and an orange as spheroids.

In "Consequences" Skinner again deplores the use of the term "selection pressure" because he considers it to be an example of an attempt to assimilate selection by consequences to the causality of classical mechanics. It appears to convert selection into something that forces a change. In his book *About Behaviorism* (1974) he raises the same complaint and adds that the notion that the "pressure" is exerted primarily by other species is erroneous. The definition of selection pressure with which I am familiar is: the degree of systematic bias or enhanced probability in favor of increase, from one generation to the next, of the frequency of a given genetic factor or type of genetic system (Jepsen, Simpson, & Mayr 1949). I do not see how this concept could be considered to be an attempt to assimilate selection to the causality of classical mechanics. Perhaps the term "pressure" is too reminiscent of physics, but the actual definition gives no such impression. Skinner does not reveal the origin of the idea that selection pressure is exerted primarily by other species. I do not believe that such an idea is common among biologists.

Skinner clearly believes that the concept of selection by consequences is an explanatory scheme or causal mode with more explanatory power and verifiability than some of the more traditional schemes. As he indicates, natural selection occupies a very special place. Although Darwin was able to persuade many that evolution had indeed occurred, he had more difficulty convincing them that natural selection was and is the creative force of evolution. Certainly it can be said that among biologists its validity is reasonably well established now. The punctuationalists are, however, currently contending with the gradualists concerning the temporal relationships of its actions (Eldredge & Gould 1972). The evidence for social and cultural change brought about by changing environments is all about us. These changes result less from alterations in the physical environment than from human activity. I am not convinced that a strict analogy with natural selection is possible in all instances. My value system tells me that many of these changes are deleterious. Operant conditioning is certainly a very powerful tool for understanding and in many cases controlling behavior. Where it is appropriately applied it is vastly more useful than the invention of forces, essences, and deities.

BFS: Unlike Campbell I believe it is correct to classify "a child's ball, the planet earth, and an orange as spheroids" and conceivably useful to do so in raising the question of why things so diverse are nevertheless roughly spherical. I think it is useful to point out that the four issues I raise – origination, purpose, essences, and values – are due to the nature of selection as such and not to any particular variations or selected consequences common to the three levels.

Campbell seems to feel that all selection must be due to genetic change. Thus, in discussing operant behavior he says that "behaviors might become shaped in such a way as to be appropriate for novel environments *and lead to differential reproduction*. For this to occur these behaviors or their possessors would have to be acted upon by natural selection" (my italics). But the italicized phrase had nothing to do with operant conditioning. The *process* has presumably evolved because it led to differential reproduction, but it operates through consequences of its own.

I have no objection to the definition of selection pressure that Campbell cites. My objection is not that it is "an attempt to assimilate selection to the causality of classical mechanics" but merely that, as Campbell says, "the term 'pressure' is too reminiscent of physics." By saying that selection pressure is not necessarily exerted by other species, I meant merely to defend evolution against Social Darwinism. Such an idea may not be common among biologists, but it has been vigorously discussed.

I believe that operant conditioning supplements natural selection, but I did not suggest that it could replace it completely. A far greater fraction of the behavior of a species like *Homo sapiens* is due to operant conditioning than is, say, that of an insect. The human species has shown a much greater capacity to adjust to novel environments by turning to operant conditioning as the principal source of its behavior.

Skinner, selection, and self-control

Bo Dahlbom

Department of the Theory and Philosophy of Science, Umeå University, Sweden

Recognizing that Skinner wants us to accept the metaphor of "natural selection" as the exclusive metaphor for theorizing in psychology, we can simply retort that we find this metaphor not helpful enough, that we find his arguments and facts supporting the role he wants to give this metaphor not convincing enough. Outstanding examples of this line of criticism are Chomsky (1959) and Dennett (1978b).

The problem with this criticism is that however convincing it is to most of us, Skinner himself does not seem to give it much weight. His view seems to be that whatever critics profess to show along this line, it is still the case that his choice of metaphor is superior and exclusive. But if Skinner's reason for his choice of metaphor is not its proven value, what could his reasons possibly be? Well, one might think that Skinner does not really think of "selection by consequences" as a metaphor at all. There are indications of this in "Consequences." Current theorizing in cognitive science is characterized as operating with "the metaphor of storage," but selection by consequences is said to be "first *recognized* in natural selection" (my italics) and "*discovered* very late in the history of science" (my italics). But there should be no doubt that the idea of natural selection is a metaphorical extension of a notion used to characterize the human practice of animal and plant breeding ("artificial selection"). In some of Darwin's forerunners (see the discussion of Wells and Matthew in Mayr 1982) this was explicitly indicated. Darwin himself was immensely happy with this analogy, and it colored his language to the extent of describing nature as a selecting agent on a par with a human being. He viewed "artificial selection" as an experimental verification of his theory, but more important, I think, is the vestige of "goal directedness" assigned the process of evolution by this metaphor.

The obvious problem we will have in understanding Darwin's theory is to a large extent attributable to difficulties in sorting out what should be taken literally and what should be seen as only metaphorical in this notion of "selection." What does it mean to say that "nature selects"? In what sense is the process of evolution a matter of "selection"? In view of this it is unreasonable to treat "selection by consequences" as anything but a metaphor. This is not to degrade it: Theorizing thrives on good metaphors. But it leaves us with a substantial problem of analysis: What does "selection by consequences" mean? And is this metaphor good enough? To say that "selection by consequences" was recognized or discovered may seem harmless enough, but it can convey a seriously misleading impression.

Now, I don't think that Skinner really wants to convey this impression, and this is indicated by claims like the following, when he is comparing the "prescientific" view of persons with his own (Skinner 1971, p. 101): "Neither view can be proved, but it is in the nature of scientific inquiry that the evidence should shift in favor of the second."

Thus another reason for Skinner's confidence might be found in "the nature of scientific inquiry." Skinner derives his views on psychology and anthropology from the field of biology. And he seems to be taking the development within biology as an indication of what direction "scientific inquiry" will take. Just as biology, with the aid of "natural selection," has done away with a "prior act of creation," "purpose or intention," "certain essences," and "certain definitions of good and value," according to Skinner, so will psychology and anthropology as they mature. This brings us to a second line of criticism of Skinner's position.

This line is more interesting if one really wants to disturb Skinner, something the first line obviously hasn't been able to do. Let us then tentatively accept Skinner's claim that "selection by consequences" is the supreme and exclusive metaphor for theorizing in psychology. Is Skinner's understanding of this metaphor, his understanding of Darwin's theory of natural selection, accurate? Specifically, does the acceptance of this metaphor, the extension of Darwin's theory into psychology, commit one to a view of persons as not "initiating agents" ("causal forces")? There are at least five aspects of Darwin's theory that point to negative answers to these questions. (Dennett 1978c, which arrives at a similar conclusion using different arguments, is an admirable example of this line of criticism.)

1. Darwin's theory of evolution has two major components: a principle of variation and a principle of selection. Skinner is influenced by the synthetic theory of evolution and its simplistic view of the first of these principles. But once the processes of variation are taken seriously, and recent trends in evolutionary theory indicate that they again will be, the organism itself becomes an important object of study. This means, among other things, an interest in embryology and morphology (epigenetics). A consequence of this interest is a questioning of the hegemony of adaptationism in favor of "structural" considerations (Gould & Lewontin 1979; Grene 1959).

2. Obviously, natural selection works only if organisms are mortal. Only if organisms are threatened by destruction and failure to procreate will there be any "consequences" to consider. This was the very important truth that Darwin learned from Malthus. His theory of evolution rested squarely on the premise of there being a struggle for survival. But this necessitates an interest in the characteristics of organisms determining their conditions of survival.

3. Natural selection favors organisms with adaptive traits. Traits, however, are not adaptive as such, but only relative to other traits of the organism. What good will the long neck do the giraffe if its teeth are not strong enough to chew the leaves, or its stomach not strong enough to digest them? Selection by consequences is not a process determined by the environment alone; it is the combination of organism and environment that does the selecting.

4. Organisms with their behavioral repertoires are selected by their environment. But there is an opposite process of selection by which organisms select their environment. This is perhaps a more important process of adaptation in cultural species. Thus, organisms adapt by changing and by changing their environment. Indeed, the latter process is central to Skinner's program of education and social reform. Just as we can learn about a well-adapted organism by studying its environment, so we can learn about its environment by studying the organism.

5. Romantic Europeans in the early 19th century dreamed of the liberation of nations, the usurpation of the power of despots, of self-rule and democracy. Darwin's theory of evolution usurped a "very special creator," to use Skinner's phrase. But Skinner doesn't see that this liberation of nature involves a transfer from outside control to self-control. The very essence of Darwin's "Copernican revolution" is, I think, the idea of nature as a self-regulating, self-controlling system. But if control can be transferred from a creator to the system of nature, it can be delegated from nature to its subsystems.

A first step toward the liberation of nature is made possible by viewing nature as a machine, which once started will run by itself. This mechanistic view was central to 18th-century deism. The idea is that a rigid universe needs no controller. But a flexible, evolving nature must be controlled to be protected from destruction. Nature controls its own flexibility by constraining it – "Natura non facit saltum" – and its consequences – through immediate, constant, and relentless selection – according to Darwin.

In an evolving nature there is flexibility, variation, in the reproduction of organisms. Darwin's theory explains how such a flexible reproductive system can survive through self-control. But for the system to survive its organisms must survive long enough to reproduce. This, again, can be ensured by the organisms being rigid, like machines. But if an organism is flexible it must be protected. Darwin was struck by the enormous waste in nature, by the fierceness of the "struggle for existence." Nature is very different from the benign environment of the Skinner box. It must therefore be possible for a flexible organism to avoid self-destructive behavior by self-control, rather than by environmental control, since the latter, in a harsh environment, is equal to destruction. Responses must be killed off without killing the organism. If the organism can foresee the consequences of its behavior, it can avoid self-destructive behavior. Selection must be delegated from the environment to the organism itself. Rather than taking a step over a cliff and dying, a human being can let the step die instead. In this way, nature can admit flexibility in its subsystems by delegating control. Organisms, too, must be liberated.

As this liberation of subsystems proceeds, systems will appear with goals that, temporarily at least, may conflict with the goals of the total system. From the Darwinian perspective it is clear that the behavioral capacity of a human being is part of a functional system in which the goals themselves are flexible, and only indirectly related to survival and procreation. But even to the extent that the goals of human beings can be related to goals in systems of which human beings are subsystems, it is still interesting to pursue the functional analysis at the level of human beings. Even if, as Dawkins (1976) has put it, human beings are only "survival machines" for genes (which seems clearly spurious), this does not make a functional characterization at the level of human beings uninteresting or mistaken. (To believe so is to commit a very simple reductionist mistake. See below.)

Together these five points encourage an interest in the study of the internal structure and functioning of organisms, and a view of human beings as self-controlling. There are, I think, three ways for Skinner to avoid this conclusion.

1. He can claim that his theory of selection by consequences stands by itself without the support of Darwin's theory. But then he can hardly defend the exclusive supremacy of his choice of metaphor. If it is in the "nature of scientific inquiry" in biology that human beings are self-controlling, his case will be lost.

2. He can rely on reductionism and argue that since organisms and their behavioral repertoires can be studied in the process of evolution, we should study this process rather than the organisms. There are hints in this direction in "Consequences": "It is true that all species, persons, and cultures are highly organized, but no principle of organization explains their being so. Both the organization and the effects attributed to it can be traced to the respective contingencies of selection." But so what? The

theory of evolution is a theory of change, and it helps us understand the origin of the characters of organisms, but this does not mean that our study of these characters is best pursued in terms of their origin. Nor does Skinner really want to be committed to such an extreme version of reductionism. Observing that human behavior is ultimately "all a matter of natural selection" he still wants to pursue psychology and anthropology as separate disciplines rather than reduce everything to biology. And his argument for this move reveals his understanding of the business of science ("operant conditioning, occurs at a speed at which it can be observed from moment to moment"), namely, to produce results. But the same argument can be directed against Skinner's impossible dream of gaining complete control, both theoretically and practically, of the environment.

3. Finally, Skinner can accept that human beings are self-controlling systems, but claim that this does not make them "initiating agents." He has left the notion of "initiating agent" so vague as to make this move possible. But such a move seriously limits the force of his position, making it no longer incompatible with the current paradigm of cognitive psychology.

The Darwinian solution to the problems facing our species amounts to increasing the knowledge we as human beings have of our place in nature so that we can increase the level of self-control of our interaction with nature. To increase our self-control means to increase our liberty. The Skinnerian solution is radically different. Skinner's program for education and social reform delegates no control to human beings, except to the cadre of educational officers working on how to control us (and themselves) by controlling our environment. My point is only that this program, with its views of human beings, is in no way supported by the Darwinian theory of natural selection.

BFS: I did not choose "the metaphor of natural 'selection'" to describe operant conditioning. I had done research on the selection of behavior by consequences for many years before the similarity to natural selection suggested itself. Selection is not a metaphor, model, or concept; it is a fact. Arrange a particular kind of consequence, and behavior changes. Introduce new consequences, and new behavior will appear and survive or disappear. Individuals gain the "flexibility" that Dahlbom regards as essential precisely from the fact that their behavior is modified by consequences in their lifetime rather than through natural selection. Thus, I can claim that my "theory of selection by consequences" stands by itself without the support of Darwin's theory, and there is no "exclusive supremacy of [my] choice of metaphor" to defend.

Dahlbom may be surprised to learn that my *Science and Human Behavior* (1953) is said to be the first text in psychology to have a chapter on self-control. We do control ourselves, but not as initiating agents. We control ourselves as we control the behavior of others (by changing our environment), but we do so because we have been exposed to contingencies arranged by the social environment we call our culture.

Organisms avoid self-destructive behavior without foreseeing the consequences, but, as I explain in "Problem Solving," people no doubt do so more effectively when they have analyzed the contingencies and, in that sense, have foreseen the consequences.

I agree that any dream of gaining complete control of the environment is "impossible," but from what we learn when the environment is reasonably well controlled, we can at least interpret what is happening under more chaotic conditions.

Replicators, consequences, and displacement activities

Richard Dawkins

Department of Zoology, University of Oxford, England

I find Skinner's article "Consequences" admirable. Selection by consequences is a good phrase, which puts a correct emphasis on the radical difference between active selection by a choosing agent on the one hand, and the blind – I almost said inconsequential! – mechanical purposelessness of the Darwinian and quasi-Darwinian processes that Skinner lists, on the other. Konrad Lorenz (1966a) reached similar conclusions about the relationship between natural selection and reinforcement learning. But I believe it is important to be even clearer than Skinner and Lorenz were about *exactly what* the entities being selected are, and exactly how they are to be distinguished from their consequences. The entities that are selected, at whatever level, must be "replicators," entities capable of forming lineages of duplicates of themselves in some medium. At Skinner's level i, the ordinary Darwinian level, the replicators are genes, and the consequences by which they are selected are their phenotypic effects, that is, mostly their effects on the embryonic development of the bodies in which they sit. A gene affecting running speed in an antelope, for instance, survives or fails to survive in the form of copies down the generations, by virtue of those consequences on running speed. Genes whose consequence is a slow gait tend to end up in predators' stomachs rather than in the next generation of antelopes. Individual organisms are *not* replicators: They are highly integrated bundles of consequences (Dawkins 1982).

A case can be made for generalizing the idea of consequences to "extended phenotypes," to consequences of a gene upon the world outside, for instance consequences of a beaver gene upon dam size and hence lake size. Such consequences could be important for the survival of the gene itself. Be that as it may, the important point is that the distinction between "that which is selected" (the gene) and "the consequences by which it is selected" (phenotypic effects) is stark and clear, and is made particularly so by the central dogma: There are causal arrows leading from genes to phenotypes but *not* the other way around (the other way around would constitute the well-known Lamarckian heresy). I would like to know whether the equivalent of the central dogma holds at Skinner's other levels.

At Skinner's level ii the replicators are habits in the animal's repertoire, originally spontaneously produced (the equivalent of mutation). The consequences are reinforcement, positive or negative. The habits can be seen as replicators because their frequency of emergence from the animal's motor system increases, or decreases, as a result of their reinforcement consequences. Note that, in their role as replicators, if habits are analogous to anything in the Darwinian scheme, it is to genes, not to individual organisms. But they are clearly not very close analogues of genes, and this makes the whole application of the Darwinian analogy at this level difficult.

Something like level ii selection by consequences can go on in imagination – simulation in the brain. The animal sets up a simulation in its head of the various actions that it might pursue and, importantly, their probable consequences. The simulated consequences feed back and influence the choice of action. The process can easily be described in subjective shorthand – "If I do *P*, I can see that the consequence would be *X*, so I had better do *Q* instead" – but there is nothing mystical or necessarily conscious about it: It goes on in electronic computers all the time, and the computer programs that do it are not necessarily very complex, although the more interesting ones are. This process should probably not be lumped under level ii, but given its own level ii-½.

I have a misgiving about Skinner's level iii, the cultural level. This is not because, as we shall probably be repetitiously told by other commentators, he is "reductionist" (whatever in the world that may mean), but because he is insufficiently clear about exactly what the entities are that are being selected, and what the consequences are by which they are selected. Is it the cultural practices themselves that replicate, that survive or fail to survive in the milieu of a single society in virtue of their consequences (Cloak 1975)? An example of this might be a hit tune that survives in the milieu of American society in virtue of its catchiness. Here the tune (or, more strictly, the representation of the tune in people's brains) is the replicator; it replicates itself when its engram is duplicated into a new brain, when a new person learns the song after hearing the pleasing acoustic consequences of the engram. Society is the medium within which the duplication, and hence survival, of the tune, takes place, but the survival, or otherwise, of the whole society is not, on this view, at issue.

Alternatively is it, as Skinner seems to suggest for level iii, whole societies that are the entities that survive or fail to survive, bag and baggage with all their cultural practices? I object to this suggestion on various grounds: It is factually implausible, and it probably suffers from analogues of many of the notorious theoretical difficulties of "group selection" (Williams 1966): An awful lot of societies would have to go extinct for even a modest amount of evolutionary change to occur. But all I want to do here is to point out that, logically, the application of the model of selection by consequences to the cultural domain has no necessary connection with group survival or extinction in a metapopulation of groups, as Skinner implies. Similarly, if – which I doubt – group survival or extinction were an important kind of "consequence," it might operate at the level of genetic replicators no less than at the level of cultural ones.

I would not dare to criticize Skinner on his own territory of reinforcement learning, but may I close by briefly offering what I hope is a constructive suggestion? It concerns that ethological chestnut, the "displacement activity." Why does an animal, when "frustrated," "thwarted," or "in conflict," perform an irrelevant act, scratch its head, say, or preen its wing? McFarland (1966) reviews the theories, including his own ingenious theory of attention switching, which seems to me to lead to the following functional hypothesis: Displacement activities may be to Skinner's level ii what mutations are to level i.

If a selective process is to result in improvement it must have variation upon which to work: genetic mutation in the case of ordinary Darwinian selection. The variation offered is random with respect to improvement. The Darwinian theory predicts that, since mutation is a recurrent phenomenon, the mutations we see should mostly be deleterious – the good ones having been already selected into the gene pool long ago – and the prediction is fulfilled. But it is still true that although particular mutations are nearly all deleterious, the phenomenon of mutation itself is vitally necessary for continued evolution. It has therefore frequently been suggested that mutation rates themselves might be adaptive, boosted in evolution in the interests of providing raw material for further evolution. This would have to work by selection favouring "mutator genes," genes whose consequence is to raise the general mutation rate of the animal. Mutator genes exist, but for various reasons the theory is probably wrong (Williams 1966): The optimal mutation rate favoured by selection on mutator genes is probably zero – an optimum fortunately never reached. But the boosted optimal mutation rate theory is wrong only at level i; maybe an analogue of it is valid at Skinner's level ii.

Consider a pigeon in one of Professor Skinner's boxes, under an extinction regime. It has been a statistical law of its world that if you press the red key you get food, and now the law is being violated: No food is forthcoming. What does the pigeon do about it? It preens its feathers, and if an ethologist happens to be looking he will label the movement a displacement activity because it is obviously irrelevant to the task in hand: Any fool can see that you cannot get food by preening. But wait. Any fool might have said that you can't get food by pecking at bits of red plexiglass, and yet the experimenter set up a world in which that was precisely how you did get food. In the world of nature, the big Skinner Box out there, a bird cannot predict what will be good: If it could, it wouldn't need to *learn* what to do, it would just get on and do it. The whole point of level ii selection by consequences is that it can solve problems that level i selection has not solved.

If the animal is frustrated or thwarted, say, because it can see food under the glass, it is clear that whatever solution to the problem it is attempting, say pecking at the glass, is not working. There may in fact be a good solution to the problem – hook the beak under the glass and tweak it off the food – but the pigeon cannot be expected to know this, since neither it nor any of its ancestors has met the problem before. Reinforcement learning is designed to discover the solution to such problems by its special application of the general method of selection by consequences, but it cannot go to work unless there is "mutation" – random production of spontaneous behaviour. No doubt such "mutations" may be produced at any time. But there is obviously something to be said for boosting the "mutation rate" at *particular* times, times when there is a problem at hand and it is not being solved: times, in other words, of thwarting and frustration. So the pigeon boosts its rate of spontaneous behaviour production during times of frustration, the very times when displacement activities are said to occur. If the resulting behaviour should happen to be the correct solution to the problem, the watching ethologist says "clever bird," and the thought of displacement activity does not cross his mind. It is only when the bird does not immediately hit the solution, when it preens itself instead, say, that the ethologist says "Aha, displacement activity." But as far as the bird is concerned, both may be manifestations of the same thing: turning up the spontaneous random "mutation" generator in response to thwarting. Just as most mutations are failures, so too, by definition, are displacement activities. It is only the failures that qualify to be called displacement activities. But that there should sometimes be failure is of the essence of selection by consequences.

BFS: I thank Dawkins for his refreshingly helpful commentary and confine my remarks to questions he asks about levels ii and iii.

I do not know whether an "animal sets up a simulation in its head of the various actions that it might pursue and, importantly, their probable consequences," but people do something much like that when they examine prevailing contingencies and construct rules to be followed to respond to them effectively (see "Problem Solving"). Dawkins's suggestion that displacement activities at level ii may have the effect of mutations at level i throws light on creativity – another chestnut in evolutionary theory closely related to this paper. Creative artists know how to create mutations from which they then select those that are beautiful in the sense of reinforcing to them, greatly increasing the chances that their work will be original. My only trouble with Dawkins's suggestion is that displacement activities tend to be stereotyped, but – who knows? – mutations may be, too.

There is clearly a question about what exactly is being selected and what are the selecting consequences. Within a given group, the answer seems to be practices – better ways of hunting, gathering, growing, making tools, and so on. The practices are transmitted from generation to generation when those who acquire them under the contingencies arranged by one generation become the transmitters for the next. There is no competition between cultures, no Social Darwinism, in such a formulation. But cultures as a whole have also come into existence and perished. As I point out in my replies to Harris and Maynard Smith, the evolution of cultural practices is like the evolution of heart, stomach, eye, ear, fin, leg, wing, and so on. The evolution of cultures is like the evolution of species, each of which may have a particular kind of heart, stomach,. . .and so on. It is clear that cultural *practices* do not evolve because of successful competition between cultures, except where the practices have to do with conflicts between cultures – for example, the invention of more powerful weapons. A culture which strengthens itself by developing new methods of agriculture, new social systems, and so on is more likely to compete successfully with another culture, but the practices themselves evolve because of contributions to the group that would also prevail if there were no competition with other groups.

Skinner: The Darwin of ontogeny?

John W. Donahoe

Neuroscience and Behavior Program, Department of Psychology, University of Massachusetts, Amherst

Skinner proposes that the contemporary environment has a selecting effect on individual development (i.e., ontogeny) in a manner that is functionally equivalent to that of the ancestral environment on species development (i.e., phylogeny). The principle of reinforcement is intended to describe the environmental control of ontogeny, the principle of natural selection that of phylogeny. The arguments invoked to support Skinner's and Darwin's common claims appear to be fundamentally similar. Additional evidence of similarity are Darwin's frequent remarks on the special difficulties in understanding natural selection encountered by those trained in mathematics and physical science. In pointing to limitations in "the causality of classical mechanics," Skinner has isolated the locus of the problem.

Skinner and Darwin are also alike in provoking fundamentally identical counterarguments from their critics. Leaving aside those criticisms that could only have arisen from failure to read the original writings – and this is a substantial portion of the lot – both Darwin and Skinner have been charged with asserting just about every absurdity that they did not specifically deny. As a historian of biology has observed, selectionist theory "is so easy almost anyone can misunderstand it" (Hull 1972, p. 389).

The differences among scientists regarding natural selection have been "to a large extent determined by ideological factors" and have centered upon "the fundamental scale of values" (Ellegård 1958, pp. 8, 197). So too with the reinforcement principle. Chief among Darwin's and Skinner's shared differences with nonselectionists are the attitudes toward essentialism and teleology. Skinner notes these ideological factors here, and they had been previously identified in accounts of natural selection (Mayr 1976b). The critics concur that the dispute involves basic philosophical issues, as when the approach to language by transformational generative grammarians is self-described as a "triumph of rationalism over empiricism" (Katz & Bever 1976, p. 10).

The arena in which these values most openly conflict is, as Skinner notes, the treatment of complex human behavior – especially memory and language. (It should be noted that even Wallace, the cooriginator of the theory of evolution through natural selection, demurred in its application to the human species.) That philosophical differences are at stake is illustrated by comparing the treatment of reinforcement by a modern linguist (Chomsky 1959) with that of natural selection by a 19th-century linguist (Müller 1872). Present-day generative grammarians posit universal linguistic rules of such an abstract character that their origins are claimed to be beyond the impoverished input afforded by the contemporary environment. Reinforcement is therefore said to be incapable, in principle, of engendering language. In its stead, an appeal is made to a genetically based universal grammar resulting from natural selection (Chomsky 1980a, pp. 263, 321; 1980b, pp. 3, 9). Nineteenth-century linguists also characterized the defining features of language as universal and abstract. Moreover, the same philosophers – Plato and Kant – are favorably cited by both generations of linguists (Chomsky 1966; Weimer 1973). Although their characterizations of language were highly similar, 19th-century linguists reached a very different conclusion: They concluded that language was, in principle, beyond the reach of natural selection! What is common to both eras is a resistance to selectionist thinking for as long as the evidence permits.

Although most apparent in the treatment of complex human behavior, nonselectionist thinking also continues to leave its mark on the interpretation of simpler learning processes in animals, albeit more subtly. Consider an influential current account of conditioning with the Pavlovian procedure in which the conditioned response (e.g., salivation) is said to be acquired when there is a discrepancy between the asymptotic association value supportable by the unconditioned stimulus, or reinforcer (e.g., meat powder in the mouth), and the initial association value of all contiguous environmental stimuli, notably the conditioned stimulus (e.g., a tone; Rescorla & Wagner 1972). This description of the conditioning process has an implicit teleological flavor: A *future* event, the asymptotic association value, is required as a reference point from which the discrepancy is measured. Even if the learner were endowed by natural selection with "foreknowledge" of the asymptotic association value of all potential unconditioned stimuli – a large order in itself – how such information would be available for all potential learned reinforcers remains a puzzle.

Although I believe that a precise parallelism exists between natural selection and reinforcement as selectionist accounts of organic change, Skinner's article "Consequences" contains two potential impediments to the acceptance of reinforcement as the transcendent principle of ontogeny. First, although culture is a crucial influence on human behavior and reinforcement contributes centrally to an understanding of that influence, the mode of action proposed by Skinner is problematic. The appeal to a new "kind" of selection involving an "effect on the group, not the reinforcing consequences for individual members" seems unnecessary. The proposal is reminiscent of the generally unhelpful concept of group selection (Wynne-Edwards 1963) and might better be replaced by a treatment analogous to kin selection (Hamilton 1964) or reciprocal altruism (Trivers 1971) in sociobiology (E. O. Wilson 1975). Second, although the distinction between respondent and operant conditioning probably served an important function historically, it would no longer seem best to describe them as different "kinds" of selection, or different "processes" of behavioral change. After all, the selecting environment responsible for conditionability included neither Pavlov's conditioning frame nor Thorndike's puzzle box. Respondent and operant conditioning might best be regarded as simply different *procedures* for studying behavioral change, procedures that are potentially understandable in terms of a common reinforcement principle (see Donahoe, Crowley, Millard & Stickney 1983). Skinner was prudent to have focused initially on the implications of reinforcement rather than the microbehavioral and physiological mechanisms that subserved the process. (Darwin's ill-fated theory of pangenesis will be remembered as his attempt to identify the mechanism of natural selection.) Nevertheless, it is also well to recall that the scientific acceptance of natural selection as the primary principle of phylogeny did not occur until over 75 years later with the modern synthesis of evolution and population genetics (Mayr 1982).

The assessment of reinforcement as the fundamental principle of ontogeny will probably follow the steep and thorny path taken earlier by natural selection. To quote Darwin (1888, pp. 148–49) in a letter to Huxley, "It will be a long battle, after we are dead and gone." Let us hope that the matter is resolved before our species is "dead and gone" from the potentially harsh verdict of natural selection.

BFS: Donahue wonders whether cultural evolution, or the evolution of cultural practices, is a different *kind* of selection. I think it is, although I see in it no new behavioral process. I think operant conditioning explains the discovery of new practices and their transmission to other (especially younger) members of a group. But one may still identify variations (new practices), reproduction (the transmission to others), and selection through consequences, whether for the individual or the group (and that last phrase distinguishes between the evolution of cultural practices and the evolution of cultures). For example, the use of a new food or a new way of planting or storing it will be transmitted to other members of a group because of its reinforcing consequences for individuals, who are thereby more likely to escape hunger. The group may then complete more successfully with another group (say, for available land). In neither case is a special genetic trait at work, as in kin selection. The evolved process of operant conditioning is a sufficient explanation.

I do not agree that respondent and operant conditioning are best regarded as "simply different *procedures* for studying behavioral change." As Ferster and I pointed out in *Schedules of Reinforcement* (Ferster & Skinner 1957), a term like "conditioning" or "extinction" is traditionally used to refer or two very different things: (1) the role of the experimenter or the environment in bringing about a change, and (2) the resulting change in the organism. Donahue seems to add a third, "*procedures* for studying behavioral change." We are concerned here with behavioral processes as they must have existed before anyone promoted them or studied them. Whether there is a neurological principle common to respondent and operant conditioning is a question that will presumably be answered by neurologists; the two types of conditioning are still clearly distinguished by the contingencies under which they occur.

The wider context of selection by consequences

Thomas J. Gamble

Department of Psychology, Yale University

Many of us in the social and behavioral sciences welcome and applaud Professor Skinner's continual attempts to clarify the nature of causation in "purposive" systems. However, a reader unfamiliar with current extensions of Darwinian models to nongenetic aspects of adaptation (i.e., learning or social evolution) may get the impression that this work is being done primarily by the field known as "the experimental analysis of behavior." This is not the case.

In psychology the analogy between trial and error learning and the selection of unforesightful variations has long been recognized and developed. Campbell (1956; 1974b) traces the trend back to Baldwin (1900), Thurstone (1924), Tolman (1926), Ashby (1952), and many others. Work in this area continues unabated in traditions other than that designated by Skinner. An especially relevant introduction to such work is available in the exchanges between Ghiselin (1981) and his commentators in the journal *Behavioral and Brain Sciences*. Important psychological work on selection by consequences by Campbell (1956), Pulliam and Dunford (1980), Ghiselin (1973; 1981), Simon (1966), and many others should also be consulted by those interested in the model.

In sociology and anthropology the situation is much the same. Aspects of these fields are characterized by vital and growing communities of scientists working with extensions of the Darwinian model. Mathematical formalisms attempting to model the nongenetic diffusion of cultural traits have been developed and tested by Boyd and Richerson (1980) and Cavalli-Sforza and Feldman (1973; 1981). Other important work in this area includes that of Waddington (1968) and Plotkin and Odling-Smee (1981). Hence the behavioral sciences at Skinner's levels ii and iii may not be as limited in this regard as he suggests.

Skinner's article may also give the impression that modern selection theory generates a relatively unproblematic research program. This is not the case. Although many of us find it the most promising among current alternatives it is inundated with conceptual and empirical puzzles. Some examples include whether one-trial learning is not a more appropriate analogue to the Darwinian model than is the model of gradual approximation. Another has to do with how to conceptualize units of variation. Are they specific movements? classes of functionally or conceptually similar behaviors? mental representations of the opportunity space? There are also questions about the mode of retention of selected variations, and concerning conflicts between individual selection and group cooperation. Another of these important issues is whether all selection takes place in regard to direct contact with contingencies or through vicarious selection systems such as thought trials. These are all important challenges to the research program of which the interested reader should be aware.

BFS: I certainly do not claim that experimental behavior analysts were the first to suggest a parallel between Darwinian selection and "trial and error learning," but I contend that the experimental analysis of behavior is by far the most detailed examination of the contingencies of selection responsible for the behavior of the individual. I also believe that selection at level iii does not require a process different from natural selection or operant conditioning. I certainly did not mean to suggest that very much has been done in those fields by operant conditioners. Indeed, I regret that more has not been done.

I do not see the relevance of Gamble's comments on one-trial learning. As I showed more than 50 years ago (Skinner 1932c), an operant like pressing a lever is easily conditioned by one reinforcement. I do not suppose Gamble means that a complex bit of phylogenic behavior (say, building a nest) once occurred in that form as a variation and was selected by its consequences. It must have been the end result of a long process of shaping. I have reviewed a few established geological processes which could have supplied conditions for a gradual approach to complex phylogenic behavior (Skinner 1975).

The emancipation of thought and culture from their original material substrates

Michael T. Ghiselin

Department of Invertebrates, California Academy of Sciences

We should be grateful to Skinner for his attempts to purge psychology of unnecessary metaphysical encumbrances. Getting rid of a vital principle of life and its analogues is conducive to clear thinking and to the effectual solution of legitimate scientific problems. Yet, especially in the light of developments in evolutionary biology over the past few years, I wonder if some of his efforts have perhaps led to oversimplification.

For one thing, those of us who have been working on adaptation over the last two decades have learned not to ask what is good for the species or anything else. It was long forgotten that what organisms do happens because of differential reproduction among other organisms in ancestral populations. Right thinking means asking, not what is good, but what has happened. Otherwise we are apt to misconstrue the underlying mechanisms, with unfortunate consequences. This should apply to natural selection, learning, and cultural transmutation.

Skinner's analysis of cultural evolution is a case in point. He treats culture as if it were identical with verbal behavior, implicitly embodying it in the organisms who behave verbally. This implies that the culture *is* those organisms, and that anything exterior to them constitutes part of the culture's social environment. The organisms themselves, and groups composed of such organisms, would be the replicanda which, by analogy with ordinary biological evolution, are selected and evolve. This gives us a model of cultural evolution that links the survival of the culture to the survival of its biological substratum. Evidently Skinner wants to treat culture as a class of verbal behaviors, inseparable from a class of verbally behaving organisms. Unfortunately "culture" is a mass noun, and it is not clear what the individuals are. As I see it, culture is a class of cultural individuals, such as words, sentences, and languages. Its connection to organisms is accidental, not necessary. (See Ghiselin 1980; 1981; 1982.)

Just as the gene (in two senses) is the replicandum and also the lineage of replicated genes, and just as the species is the nexus of successive generations of parents and offspring, so the culture is the totality of replicated individuals and all of their descendants, which itself forms a larger individual, lineage, and whole. In other words, culture is made up of everything that is produced through behavioral replication and its indirect consequences. It evolves through selection of those products, not necessarily of their producers. These products include artifacts. For example, someone writes a book. It is copied, revised, duplicated, cited, perhaps translated, imitated, and even plagiarized. It might spawn a lineage of similar works – a genre even. At any rate, the book is not dependent upon any particular piece of matter in which it happens to be embodied. Equating culture with verbal behavior is like failing to distinguish between literature and publishing. The medium definitely is not the message. An element of a book (a copy) is no more a receptacle for culture than its author is. The cultural whole is incarnate in both. By the same token it is erroneous to claim that the artifacts are the "environment" of the culture. Like the organisms that make up a species, they are integral parts of it. The author may die without biological issue: Yet his literary child may endure for ages. In this sense, at least, culture may be said to have a life of its own.

On the other hand cultural entities, like organisms, do form parts of environments in both biological and cultural evolution. A myth can function as a selective influence just as much as a predator can. We fear both, and act upon it. When we consider how the nervous system operates, it is not clear how we should extrapolate to it from other entities subject to selection. That some kind of parallelism exists, as Skinner maintains, seems eminently reasonable. We might nonetheless ask just how far the genes possess hegemony over the intellect. The automaton theory of behavior would have it that the soma is a mere puppet to the germ – or to some antecedent condition of the soma. Yet if culture can be autonomous – and a selective agent in its own right – why not thoughts? Is the mind nothing more than the slave of the gonads? We cannot evade this issue merely by complaining about the metaphorical language. However we choose to express it, we have a substantive issue about how behavior relates to that which behaves. Skinner may have gone too far beyond freedom and dignity.

BFS: I do not treat culture "as if it were identical with verbal behavior." I said that verbal behavior (which I had just discussed) greatly increased the importance of a third kind of selection by consequences. Other ways in which new forms of behavior are transmitted to new members of a group include imitation and modeling. I would define a culture as "a mass noun" as a social environment. Children are born into a culture simply in the sense that their behavior will be shaped and maintained by contingencies of reinforcement in which other people play a part. If a group of people is confined to one locality, its physical features may also be included as part of a culture. A child's behavior is the result of both.

Features of a social environment (separate cultural practices as variations) come into existence for many reasons which need not be related to their effects upon members of a group. They are transmitted to new members when the members learn either by imitation without modeling or by explicit modeling, or through advice, warnings, maxims, rules, laws, and other verbal devices, and when those who have thus been changed become in turn those who compose the social environments of others.

Ghiselin reports that those who have been working on adaptation have "learned not to ask what is good for the species or anything else." In the experimental analysis of behavior, a specific example concerns what is reinforcing. I might paraphrase Ghiselin by saying "Right thinking means asking, not what is reinforcing, but what has happened." We *discover* what is reinforcing to an organism; we do not predict it. Things do not reinforce because they are good or feel good. I believe the same point can be made for natural selection and the evolution of cultures. I discussed the issue briefly in "Consequences" under the heading "Certain Definitions of Good and Value."

I am not sure that Ghiselin is characterizing my position as "the automaton theory of behavior," but automaton suggests the classical mechanical causal mode, which I am suggesting is not applicable. I cannot say "how far the genes possess hegemony over the intellect," but in "Consequences" I said, "Ultimately, of course, it is all a matter of natural selection, since operant conditioning is an evolved process, of which cultural practices are special applications." I do not believe that there is something called "intellect" or "thought" which belongs in a different world.

Fitting culture into a Skinner box

C. R. Hallpike

Department of Anthropology, McMaster University, Canada

As an anthropologist, I would like to address those aspects of "Consequences" that seek to apply the notion of "selection by consequences" to social and cultural evolution.

The first and perhaps most fundamental objection is that, whatever "consequences" may mean, *something* has first to come into existence before it can be "selected" by them. The sources of novelty are just as important as the success or failure of novelty, but Skinner has nothing to say about the sources of social innovation except that they are variations that are reinforcing to the individuals who introduce them. This attitude to innovation is not, of course, surprising in someone who believes that creativity is nothing more than random variation of existing procedures, and who is trying to show that a simple model – "variation proposes; environment disposes" – will apply equally to biological evolution, individual learning, and social evolution. The model, however, is totally inadequate in the face of social reality. For example, the supersession of stone tools by metal tools is a clear instance of "selection by consequences," but the reasons for preferring metal to stone tools are perfectly obvious: Metal tools do not break, can be easily resharpened, and are far more versatile in shape than stone. The real problem is *not* to explain why metal was preferred to stone but to understand how and why metal technology originated in the first place, and it is therefore sheer mystification to treat innovation as "random variation."

Unlike biological mutations, which do not occur as responses to the environment, and are not under the control of the organisms in which they occur, social and cultural innovations are conscious responses to certain aspects of the organisms' social environment. In the case of social evolution, therefore, we cannot operate on the basis of that neat separation between variation and selection that is favored in neo-Darwinian biological theory. Although social innovations are initially produced by individuals, individuals do not innovate in a vacuum, or in some entirely private and idiosyncratic world of their own, but as members of a particular society at a particular period in history.

Again, although organic mutations do not change the physical environment of the organism, social innovations very definitely do change their social "environment" – printing, the steam engine, and universal suffrage being obvious examples. Here, too, the desired analogy between social and biological evolution breaks down because in the case of social evolution there is a dialectical interaction between innovation and society, by which innovation is a function of society, and in turn changes society.

For this reason to talk of "selection by consequences" fails to grasp that "consequences" not only "select" but can provide *new* opportunities and new problems as the basis for further change, and are therefore themselves an integral part of the process of change, not simply the *conclusion* to change, as Skinner presents them.

With these considerations in mind the apparent emptiness of what Skinner has to say about change and stability becomes especially clear:

> Why do people continue to do things in the same way for many years, and why do groups of people continue to observe old practices for centuries? The answers are presumably the same: Either new variations (new forms of behavior or new practices) have not appeared or those which have appeared have not been selected by the prevailing contingencies (of reinforcement or of the survival of the group)....change is explained as due to new variations selected by prevailing contingencies or to new contingencies.

In short, either people go on doing what they have always done, or they do not, and innovations may occur in existing circumstances or in new ones!

Another fundamental defect in Skinner's account of social evolution derives from his failure to come to terms with the notion of structure or organization. On the one hand he seems to resort to individualism, as when he says that the evolution of social environments or culture "presumably begins at the level of the individual. A better way of making a tool, growing food, or teaching a child is reinforced by its consequences – the tool, food, or a useful helper, respectively." He also denies to structure or organization any causal efficacy, and says that "organization and the effects attributed to it can be traced to the respective contingencies of selection." It should also be noted that although he frequently refers to contingencies of selection, and to circumstances that "select the cultural practices which yield a solution" to a problem, and to a situation that "shapes and maintains adjusted behavior," and says that after introducing "new cultural practices...we must wait for selection to occur," in all these cases the circumstances and situations which are presented so impersonally actually consist, causally speaking, of the behavior and dispositions of *people*.

But, on the other hand, he wishes to treat cultures or societies as real entities that are comparable to biological organisms, some of which are more effective than others and which will therefore be subject to natural selection. Thus he says "it is the effect on the group, not the reinforcing consequences for individual members, which is responsible for the evolution of...culture." One can appreciate that even Skinner might shrink from "explaining" slavery by claiming that owning slaves is reinforcing for the masters, and that submitting to slavery is reinforcing for the slaves. But having dispensed with the notion of structure as a distinct factor in social evolution he seems to be left with nothing better than the old structural–functionalist, holistic notion of societies as real entities with goals and needs of their own distinct from those of their members. So cultures can, for example, "induce individuals to suffer or die as heroes or martyrs."

The solution to this dilemma is to recognise that although of course structure or organization cannot by itself *do* anything, and that only real, individual people have any *causal* powers in space and time, the individual members of a society are not causally *autonomous*. That is, what they do and why they do it are also expressions of the institutions, categories, rules, beliefs, and values of the particular society into which the individuals composing it have been socialized, which they did not create as individuals, and which will outlast them. Now, while these institutions and cultural forms cannot do anything, they certainly possess structural properties, as objective as those of the natural world, and it can easily be shown that some institutions will not fit with others, or can be elaborated in certain directions and not in others. In the same way, belief and value systems have an internal logic of their own, and certain innovations will not work because they are inconsistent with the basic principles of these systems. Social evolution is, among other things, a process of exploration of the objective properties of social and cultural structures. By ignoring the objective properties of structure, Skinner deprives himself of any means of bridging the gap between the characteristics of individual behavior and those of society.

The statement by Skinner in his abstract that "social behavior is within easy range of natural selection, because other members are one of the most stable features of the environment of a species" is therefore profoundly incorrect, because it totally ignores the dialectical interaction between individual behavior and sociocultural structure.

Skinner maintains that "selection by consequences" is superior to other theories because it refutes "the supposed origins of a culture as a social contract or of social practices as commandments" and also disposes of theories of "group minds" and "zeitgeists." Must one point out that relatively few of us in the social sciences believe that societies were created by wild men emerging from the forests and shaking hands, or by the fiat of culture heroes, and that theories of group minds and zeitgeists have long gone the way of the Absolute as serious subjects for debate in social evolution? Not only is it unnecessary to use Skinner's theory to refute these ideas, but it is far from obvious that "selection by consequences" could refute them anyway.

The search for parsimonious and general theories is all very well, but such theories must also be adequate to the facts, and the facts of biological evolution, individual psychology, and social evolution are so vast and diverse that there seems no good reason to believe that *any* general law could encompass them all. As the law of "selection by consequences" illustrates, the result of such an endeavor is likely to be a combination of the trivial and the profoundly misleading.

BFS: Hallpike lists his objections in very strong terms. I have "nothing to say about" *A*; my model *B* "is totally inadequate"; *C* is "sheer mystification." I fail to grasp that *D*...; there is "apparent emptiness" in *E*; *F* is a "fundamental defect"; an important point *G* is ignored. *H* is "profoundly incorrect, because it totally ignores...." Yet I do not see any great difference between us except in Hallpike's understanding of what I have written.

"*Something* has first to come into existence before it can be 'selected.'" Of course. It is an old problem in operant behavior: A response must occur before it can be reinforced. Cultural practices no doubt have many kinds of origins. Some may be accidental, some may be designed ("conscious?"). Design may take selective consequences into account (see "Problem Solving") but even so may be random with respect to the evolution of the practice. Both accidental and designed practices are effective first in reinforcing people. They become practices only when they are transmitted as parts of a social environment. I do not know how metal tools were discovered, but the advantages Hallpike singles out all have to do with contingencies reinforcing the behavior of an individual. I can easily compose a scenario in which the smelting and use of metals came into existence through entirely accidental contingencies, and I do not think the account would be mystification.

I do not see that the analogy between social and biological evolution breaks down because of "dialectical interaction between innovation and society." Certainly changes due to natural selection alter the contingencies for further selection.

A current problem in evolutionary theory has to do with the fact that some species do not change during very long periods of time. I thought it worthwhile to mention the parallel in human cultures, but Hallpike's summary ("In short, either people go on doing what they have always done, or they do not, and innovations may occur in existing circumstances or in new ones!") is "emptier" than what I said. If cultures do not change, it is either because new variations have not appeared or because those which have appeared have not been selected for by the prevailing contingencies.

I can understand why Hallpike may regard my neglect of structure or organization as a fundamental defect, since he is apparently a structural anthropologist for whom those are fighting words. But I should want to underline his admission that "of course structure or organization cannot by itself *do* anything." Hallpike's solution – that although only real, individual people have any real causal powers in space and time, the individual members of a society are not causally autonomous – is my own. They are not causally autonomous because their behavior is controlled by a social environment. (Naturally "even" I would "shrink from 'explaining' slavery by claiming that owning slaves is reinforcing for the masters, and that submitting to slavery is reinforcing for the slaves." The word "slavery" suggests different contingencies.)

Of course I do not say that societies are "real entities with goals and needs of their own distinct from those of their members" except in the sense that a social environment is distinct from the individuals whom it affects.

Hallpike misunderstands my point that social behavior is within easy reach of natural selection because other members are among the most stable features of the environment of the species. There is a reason why so much of the behavior studied by ethologists emphasizes courtship, mating, nest building, and the care of young. In addition to their obvious relevance to individual survival, these classes of behavior could evolve because mates and offspring are necessarily constant parts of the environment – unlike, for example, a particular food supply or nesting material, where phylogenic behavior has a lesser chance to evolve. To call that point profoundly incorrect because it totally ignores the dialectical interaction between individual behavior and sociocultural structure is putting it rather strongly.

I am glad that Hallpike does not believe that societies were created by wild men emerging from the forest and shaking hands. I did not say that selection by consequences is superior to *all* other theories, but I do wish that it were true that "theories of group minds and zeitgeists [had] long gone the way of the Absolute as serious subjects for debate in social evolution."

Group and individual effects in selection

Marvin Harris

Department of Anthropology, University of Florida

Anthropologists would benefit from arguments on behalf of selection by consequences as a metaprinciple for explaining cultural as well as biological evolution and the acquisition of individual response repertoires. Contemporary anthropology (with the exception of archaeology) is not only "heavily structural" as Skinner states, but heavily ideographic, emic, voluntarist, mentalist, and even mystical or obscurantist (Harris 1979). Since I wish to be none of these, the critical remarks that follow should not be viewed apart from my fundamental agreement with Skinner's positivism and materialism and my own intellectual grounding in reinforcement principles as taught by William Schoenfeld and Fred Keller (Keller & Schoenfeld 1950) many years ago.

"Consequences" is flawed by the slipshod manner in which Skinner characterizes the contingencies responsible for cultural selection (iii) and the nature of behavioral selection (ii) as it applies to the human case. The author states: "It is the effect on the group, not the reinforcing consequences for individual members, which is responsible for the evolution of culture." This is both an epistemological lapse (unoperationalized entity) and counterfactual. Effects on the group are aggregate effects on the individuals in the group (Harris 1964). This is not to deny the occurrence of group selection in cultural evolution, but to identify it exclusively with extinctions of regional or local repertories caused by war, famine, and other catastrophes. Group selection is only one of two forms of selection by consequences that characterize cultural evolutionary processes. The other, selection of behavioral innovations in individual repertories, is far more common. In fact, group selection is merely the limiting case of individual selection in which the consequences are catastrophic for all group members. Sociocultural systems usually change long before catastrophic consequences lead to group extinction. One has merely to cast an eye at the rapid pace of changes in technology and domestic life to get the point. Automobiles and electric lights were not selected for as a consequence of their contribution to group survival (cf. "contingencies...promoting behavior which contributes to the survival of the group") but because they constituted reinforcements for specific individuals whose behavior was thereby shaped.

When we say that behavior has been selected for as a result of its favorable consequences for a group, we can only mean that it has had favorable consequences for some or all members of the group sufficient to outweigh its adverse effects on some or all of the members. The cumulative shaping of individual behavior is precisely what cultural evolution is all about. Of course, these behaviors are interrelated and in conjunction with various environmental and social feedback processes possess systemic properties that are the logico-empirical basis for the concepts of society, culture, and sociocultural systems. For an anthropological behaviorist, events on the sociocultural level are necessarily abstractions (but concrete and real) derived from the observation of behavioral changes in individuals, and the evolution of sociocultural systems is necessarily the evolution of such behavior.

Thus human behavioral repertories consist overwhelmingly of operantly conditioned responses that are at the same time culturally conditioned responses, that is, responses shaped in conformity with culturally determined reinforcement schedules and contingencies. Therefore Skinner's claim that "the contingencies of selection at the three levels are quite different" is incorrect in the human case as regards levels ii and iii. In the human case the contingencies of selection are not random but occur in conformity with programs encoded primarily in the brains (or other neural pathways as distinguished from the genes) of enculturated individuals (and not, as Skinner proposes, merely in "documents, artifacts, and other products of. . . behavior").

Behaviorist principles can tell us how these individuals shape each other's behavior, but they cannot tell us what behavior they will shape. Skinner's criterion for separating levels ii and iii in the human case obscures this problem and deters fruitful collaboration between materialist, behaviorist, nomothetic anthropologists and like-minded psychologists.

Practitioners of the science of culture need to know more from psychologists than the general laws of operant behavior. In order to predict or retrodict favored or unfavored innovations in cultural repertories and hence to understand the divergent and convergent (not merely unilinear) trajectories of sociocultural evolution, we need to be able to measure cost–benefit consequences as "currencies" relevant to the biologically determined discriminative stimuli and biologically determined reinforcers that underlie operant conditioning in the human case (i.e., innate biopsychological drives, needs, instincts, etc.). Without such knowledge we cannot specify the consequences of behavioral innovations and hence cannot operationalize the principle of selection by consequences.

BFS: As Harris points out, I defined "a third type of selection by consequences" as "the evolution of social environments or cultures." The examples I gave, however, – better ways of "making a tool, growing food, or teaching a child" – are far from the "extinctions of regional or local repertories caused by war, famine, and other catastrophes," which sounds more like Social Darwinism. I said quite explicitly that, as Harris insists, the first effect occurs "at the level of the individual," but there is another effect which can be stated only at the level of the group in spite of the fact that it is always an individual who behaves. If the evolution of a culture could be said to correspond to the evolution of a species, then the evolution of cultural practices corresponds to the evolution of eyes and ears and hearts and legs and wings.

It is not hard to define a cultural practice, but what is a culture? It is more than a group in the sense of the inhabitants of a given place. To speak of their common values is simply to appeal to common selective contingencies, as I note in "Consequences." I have taken a culture to be a social environment, the contingencies of reinforcement maintained by a group which, in addition to the physical environment, are responsible for the repertoires of new members of the group. Harris puts it this way: "Human behavioral repertories consist overwhelmingly of operantly conditioned responses that are at the same time culturally conditioned responses, that is, responses shaped in conformity with culturally determined reinforcement schedules and contingencies." But a culture is *transmitted* (and the mode of transmission is at the heart of selection) when individuals who have been changed by the contingencies maintained by a group become part of a maintaining group. That process requires operant conditioning, but it is a different contingency of selection.

I did *not* say that contingencies of selection occur *merely* in "documents, artifacts, and other products of... behavior." I was speaking of the metaphor of the storage of contingencies of selection in genes and the nervous system, and I said that the social environment could be regarded as an exception because "*parts* of [it were physically] stored in documents, artifacts, and other products of that behavior" (italics added).

When Harris writes: "Behaviorist principles can tell us how these individuals shape each other's behavior, but they cannot tell us what behavior they will shape," I would put it this way: Individuals shape each other's behavior by arranging contingencies of reinforcement, and what contingencies they arrange and hence what behavior they shape are determined by the evolving social environment, or culture, responsible for their behavior.

On the stabilization of behavioral selection

Werner K. Honig

Department of Psychology, Dalhousie University, Canada

The processes of change described by Skinner in "Consequences" are clearly "retrospective"; neither successful nor unsuccessful changes are selected in an anticipatory fashion. Genetic alterations are not decided in advance by environmental pressures; the strengthening or weakening of behavior is not carried out in anticipation of its outcomes; social structures are not established with the intent of effecting social change. Where there is an apparent anticipation of successful change, this is owing to biases (of the form of responding, for example) or to "rules" that have themselves been selected in retrospective fashion. In fact, much of Skinner's argument was anticipated in a provocative article by Campbell (1960), concerning variation and selective retention in cognitive and creative behavior.

While we recognize the retrospective action of the consequences of genetic or behavioral or social variation, we must also note that these changes each incorporate mechanisms for stability that oppose further change. In the case of evolution, this is perhaps a trivial point; a morphological change is permanent until modified by a further, presumably random, successful mutation. The change is "stored" genetically. Social change is "codified" and transmitted as law or tradition (Tevye's sons in *Fiddler on the Roof*), and the retrospective origins of the change are readily forgotten by those who are controlled by social institutions. But how is behavioral change "fixed" and used by individual organisms? Skinner is, as ever, silent on this question. The functional definition of reinforcement as a retrospective process cannot at the same time explain the action of reinforcement in fixing behavior.

Skinner suggests that the reinforceability of behavior is itself a consequence of evolution, because adaptiveness of behavior enhances survival value. It is equally reasonable to suppose that animals evolved mechanisms for rendering the selected behavior resistant to change. The physiological forms of such mechanisms still need to be identified, but students of animal learning seem generally to agree that "associations" are formed either between the behavior and its consequences (instrumental conditioning) or between an initial signal and a primary or unconditioned stimulus that elicits a response (classical conditioning). The nature of association as a psychological concept has been the object of intense study in recent years. Much current evidence suggests anticipatory mechanisms both in instrumental learning and in classical conditioning. For example Breland and Breland (1961) showed in their study of the "misbehavior" of organisms that the instrumental response would "drift" toward the consummatory response required by the reinforcer that follows the response. Likewise, in autoshaping (a classical conditioning procedure) the responses elicited by the conditioned stimulus take a form that is appropriate for consumption of the reinforcer (Jenkins & Moore 1973). In fact, classical conditioning is generally viewed as the development of an anticipatory process. Skinner has never claimed that the change of behavior that is part of classical conditioning results from selection by reinforcement following the conditioned response.

Many other findings suggest the importance of anticipatory mechanisms in learning. The "blocking" of conditioning when a second CS is redundantly added to an established CS (Kamin 1969) is usually explained by the fact that the UCS can be anticipated from the latter; only when the outcome of the trial is "surprising" does the second CS gain control of the conditioned response. Likewise, the "value" of a reinforcer can be enhanced or reduced "off baseline," and this will subsequently be reflected in the performance of the acquired response that precedes the reinforcer (see Adams & Dickinson 1981).

Similar findings support anticipatory processes in the production of established behavior; in particular, animals seem to anticipate temporal durations and delays (see Honig 1981, for a review). In "short-term" memory procedures, performance based upon an initial stimulus in a trial is markedly enhanced when different outcomes can be expected following different initial stimuli (Peterson, Wheeler & Trapold 1980). Evolution may well have selected a capacity in animals for developing anticipations that guide appropriate behavior and enhance the likelihood of survival. The maintenance of behavior through anticipatory and associative mechanisms may well be parallel to the genetic template, and to the maintenance of social custom through rules, codes, and other directives.

BFS: I have not read Campbell's 1960 paper, and it may well have anticipated the argument of "Selection by Consequences." But I had already made my point in *Science and Human Behavior*, published in 1953. As I said in my reply to Bolles, I wrote on page 430.

> We have seen that in certain respects operant reinforcement resembles the natural selection of evolutionary theory. Just as genetic characteristics arise as mutations and are selected or discarded by their consequences, so novel forms of behavior are selected or discarded through reinforcement. There is still a third kind of selection which applies to cultural practices.

A rather elaborate analysis of survival value and its relation to other kinds of value then follows.

The Breland and Breland (1961) report is now more than 20 years old and, in spite of the attention it aroused, it has not, so far as I know, been analyzed in controlled scientific research. Most of the instances reported were not examples of a "'drift' toward the consummatory response required by the reinforcer that follows the response" but a sudden intrusion of phylogenic behavior. I myself did experiments on what Jenkins and Moore (1973) called autoshaping as early as 1946 and referred to it in my notes as the classical conditioning of a stimulus eliciting an exploratory response (Skinner 1983b; 1983d, p. 134). If Honig is using the word "anticipatory" in its dictionary sense, it is a problem to explain rather than an explanatory principle. How can an anticipated event affect behavior?

Cause and effect in evolution

Michael J. Katz

Department of Developmental Genetics and Anatomy, Case Western Reserve University

Professor Skinner argues that the analogy between evolutionary processes in biology and learning processes in behavior is a good one, and, along the way, he bares a number of epistemological assumptions common to biology and to psychology. Central to his discussion is a particular sequence of causes and effects, the unfolding of which produces "selection by consequences" – an *overall* effect with a somewhat peculiar flavor. Perhaps a more extended analysis of this idea can be even more revealing.

"Selection by consequences" – generally called natural selection – is the broad-scale effect generated by a particular underlying sequence of events. What exactly is this sequence? Usually, natural selection is thought of in terms of populations, but for simplicity let me begin with the existence of a single animal, *A*. Next, we introduce a test – does animal *A* match some necessary requirement of its environment? If the match between animal and environment is appropriate, then the animal survives. If the match is not appropriate, the animal dies. Thus, the basic sequence of events is: existence of *A*, test of matching, existence (or nonexistence) of *A*.

Natural selection is most often envisioned as a continual process. This means that natural selection consists of an extended iteration of the basic sequence of events, namely: . . . , existence of *A*, test of matching, existence (or nonexistence) of *A*, test of matching, existence (or nonexistence) of *A*, test of matching, ... Furthermore, in the biological world there is one additional step added to each iteration of the basic sequence: Animal *A* may change. Therefore, the full sequence is really: . . . , existence of *A*, change to A_1, test of matching, existence (or nonexistence) of A_1, change to A_2, test of matching, existence (or nonexistence) of A_2, change to A_3, test of matching, ...

Where is the cause and effect in this sequence? At any one time, the direct cause of the existence (or nonexistence) of *A* is a preceding test of matching. Conversely, the direct effect of a test of matching is the existence (or nonexistence) of *A*. This appears to be entirely consistent with the classical notion of cause and effect – in other words, a sequence of events can be defined such that the preceding event can be considered to be the direct cause of the next event, which, in its turn, can be considered to be the direct effect of the preceding event.

In addition, the statement "change to A_2" contains another implicit cause and effect relation. Although I have not specified it in this abstraction, the common presumption is that changes in *A* are effects directly brought about by mechanisms (causes), such as mutations, that are entirely consistent with the well-understood laws of the physical world.

On the other hand, as Skinner points out, the idea of natural selection includes something a bit peculiar, something that appears different from the traditional notions of cause and effect as they are usually applied in the physical world. If this new something is not the cause and effect relations themselves, then what might it be? Perhaps it is the highly ordered nature of the *overall* effect that is produced. Specifically, the new idea in natural selection appears to be that although they lack rationality, forethought, or purposive organization, the standard cause and effect relations operating in the natural world nonetheless do not lead to homogeneous or random phenomena. Instead, natural selection results in certain particular, complex, and well-organized phenomena. Here, in fact, is the apparent paradox: How can undirected causes produce apparently directed effects?

There are a variety of ways in which direction is built into the process of natural selection in the biological realm. Let me just mention two of the most fundamental directional forces. First, there are the nature and the specificity of the operative matching test. The particular matching criterion that determines survival can strongly shape the form of the surviving population. Even homogeneously or normally distributed populations can be drastically restructured by certain matching constraints (Katz & Grenander 1982), especially when the sequence of existence, testing, existence, testing,...is very long. For example, when bacteria are forced to match very peculiar environments, natural selection can readily produce homogeneous bacterial populations with very peculiar biochemistries.

Second, there is the intrinsic nature of the precursors themselves, which can strongly direct the step "change to A_1." Intrinsic constraints mean that A can change into only a certain select set of A_1's. Although certain matching tests can produce unusual bacterial populations, these populations are only amplifications of the limited potentials of the bacterial genome. For example, it appears that bacteria do not have the intrinsic potential to develop mitochondria; therefore, it is unlikely that natural selection can readily produce bacteria with mitochondria. Moreover, although almost any part of the genome of an organism can, in theory, change, many of the potential mutations cannot actually be incorporated into a viable organism. And of those mutations still compatible with a viable organism, some will be otherwise detrimental and others will be effectively invisible.

In most biological situations, natural selection operates on a complex precursor. Complex precursors have, by definition, a great many possible features to change. However, the highly interactive nature of most complex biological entities further constrains the actual changes that can be successfully instituted (Katz 1983). Although not preplanned, all of these intrinsic constraints end up channeling and thereby giving direction to the overall effects that are produced in long causal sequences of natural selection.

Sometimes the intrinsic constraints are readily apparent in the systems that are undergoing natural selection. Frequently, however, the intricacy and the complexity of biological systems make it difficult to distinguish immediately the inherent directional effects. This is especially a problem in those cases, such as most multicellular organisms, in which the systems are composed of a great many different interacting elements, all balanced in a dynamic equilibrium. Here it is necessary to perturb the system in a controlled manner to reveal many of the influences that direct the causal sequences of natural selection.

These controlled perturbations are actually "evolutionary experiments," because the causal sequences of natural selection – composed of the repeated iteration "existence of A, change to A_1, test of matching" – are synonymous with "evolution." As Skinner has emphasized, essentially the same evolutionary process found in the realm of natural selection among organisms can also be seen in the realm of behavior and in the realm of culture. Such evolution is not peculiar in its cause and effect relations. Rather, it is peculiar in its apparent directedness. Evolution is truly directed, in the sense that it flows along in only certain channels. Professor Skinner reminds us that although the complex order that is thereby created is wonderful, it does not countermand any natural laws.

BFS: Katz gives a useful statement of natural selection, emphasizing that it is "brought about by mechanisms...entirely consistent with the well-understood laws of the physical world" yet containing something new. What is new is appropriately enough called "novelty." The key word in Darwin's title was "origin." Selection is creative, in spite of the fact that, as Katz points out, "although the complex order that is thereby created is wonderful, it does not countermand any natural laws."

A one-sided view of evolution

J. Maynard Smith

School of Biological Sciences, University of Sussex, England

Skinner draws an analogy between evolution by natural selection and both learning and social change. This raises two questions. How adequate is his picture of evolution? How good are the analogies?

On the first point, I agree that life is best defined by the possession of those properties – multiplication, heredity, variation – that make evolution by natural selection possible, and indeed inevitable. The other properties of living things, and in particular their apparent adaptedness, follow necessarily from these three. I agree that there is no need for a "vital principle called life." Yet I think Skinner's view of evolution is one-sided. This comes out when he rejects "a species adapts to an environment," in favour of "the environment selects the adaptive traits."

The environment can only select traits that arise in the first place, and hence the course of evolution depends on the repertoire of variation. For example, palms grow intermingled with broad-leaved trees in the same forest, subject to the same environment, but their forms are characteristically different. This is because their mode of growth is different: Palms have never evolved the device of "secondary thickening," whereby the trunk thickens by the addition of annual rings of growth. So far as we know, there is little limitation on the kinds of changes that can occur by mutation in the sequence of DNA in the genome. But changes in DNA have their effects (which are naturally selected) by influencing a complex developmental process. Consequently, only certain variations are possible to a given kind of organism. For example, no vertebrate has ever evolved six legs, handy as an extra pair would sometimes be.

For these reasons, I prefer to think of species as adapting to their environments. I am also puzzled by Skinner's objection to the "storage" of genetic information. As it happens, I dislike the claim that "genes...'contain the information' needed by the fertilized egg in order to grow into a mature organism," but my reasons are different from Skinner's. I object because the phrase suggests that we understand the process of development and its genetic control, when in fact we do not. However, the statement "genes contain the information needed to make all the proteins of the mature organism" has a precise and quantifiable meaning, and is correct (except, perhaps, for antibody proteins). Of course, insofar as there is information in the genome, it is there only because of past natural selection, but it is still there.

Thus I think Skinner's picture of evolution is correct but one-sided, because it ignores the structure and development of the organism, and the resulting constraints on the repertoire of variation, and it ignores the mechanisms whereby genetic information is stored and transmitted. I suspect that this one-sidedness reflects an analogous one-sidedness in his concept of learning and behaviour. Thus in his theory of learning, there are no constraints on the kinds of actions an animal may try out, so that the end result depends only on the pattern of reinforcement, just as in his picture of evolution there are no constraints on variation. Similarly, in Skinner's theory of behaviour, there seems to be nothing in the animal's head, just as there is no storage of information in his picture of the genome.

Thus his analogy between natural selection and operant conditioning is a good one, but it is an analogy between a one-sided theory of evolution and a one-sided theory of learning. I can understand the wish of psychologists to study behaviour while ignoring neurophysiology. Analogously, Weismann's (1889) concept of the separation of germ line and soma made it possible to study genetics and evolution without understanding development, and considerable progress has resulted. But it does not, or at least should not, lead biologists to think that development does not happen, or that the structure of organisms does not place constraints on future evolution. In the same way, it may sometimes be fruitful for psychologists to treat the brain as a black box, but that is no excuse for claiming that the box is empty.

Skinner's second analogy is between biological evolution and culture: "It is the effect on the group, not the reinforcing consequences for individual members, which is responsible for the evolution of...culture." For this to be true, we must suppose the following. There are a number of different human groups, each with a different culture. The culture of a given group changes from time to time, in ways unrelated to the overall trend of cultural evolution (just as mutation causes changes unrelated to the trend of evolution). The cultural changes that do occur alter the chances of extinction, survival, and splitting of the group. The overall trend of cultural change is determined by this differential survival. Groups will therefore tend to have cultures that ensure their survival.

I have spelt out this argument more explicitly than Skinner has done, because I want to be sure I understand him. I'm not sure he would go as far as I have gone, but unless the assumptions of the last paragraph are correct, then the analogy between evolution and cultural change is a misleading one. In prehistoric times, when there may have existed a number of culturally isolated groups, the process outlined may have played some role in directing cultural change. As a causal explanation of, for example, the change from the feudal England of the Middle Ages to the England of today, it will not do, if only because the requisite group structure has not existed. For example, during my lifetime there have been dramatic changes in attitudes towards birth control and abortion. For these to have been brought about by a mechanism of the kind Skinner proposes, society would have to consist of a series of groups, some practising birth control and others not, the former being more successful in dividing to form new groups: This is manifestly not the case.

To sum up, Skinner's analogy between natural selection and operant conditioning is a close one, but it is made possible only by the one-sided nature of his pictures of evolution and learning. His analogy between cultural and biological evolution seems to me to be of little value.

BFS: Maynard Smith is right in saying that I am not interested in the structure and (physiological) development of the organism, but I believe it has a structure and that that structure develops. I simply think that structure is appropriately studied by those who possess the proper instruments and methods. I have objected only to theories of structure and development which put researchers on the wrong track. I would cite "information" as an example. I do not believe the genes "tell" the fertilized egg how to grow. Perhaps that metaphor will cause no harm, but it has caused a great deal of harm in the field of human behavior. People are changed by contingencies of reinforcement, they do not store information about them.

Maynard Smith seems to feel that the evolution of cultures must be very close to Social Darwinism. There must be many cultures, and they must compete, and some must survive and some perish. But, as I have said in reply to Dawkins and Harris, I am concerned with the evolution of cultural *practices* – with features that would correspond to heart, stomach, eye, ear, leg, fin, wing, and so on – features characteristic of many different species as cultural practices are characteristic of many different cultures. A man may invent a quicker way of making a fire because of the consequences for him. If that is imitated and transmitted, it becomes a consequence for the group and survives as such. It is the practice which survives, not the group. The practice may well contribute to the survival of the group in competition with other groups or in "competition" with the natural environment.

Linear and circular causal sequences

H. C. Plotkin and F. J. Odling-Smee

Department of Psychology, University College London (HCP) and Departments of Applied Biology and Psychology, Brunel University, England (FJOS)

Skinner seems wrong on almost every point that he makes in "Consequences," with one important exception. That is that selection is the basis by which living systems gain knowledge of themselves and their world. Selection operates at the genetic, developmental, individual learning, and cultural levels (see Plotkin & Odling-Smee 1981). How then could he be wrong about everything else? It is, we think, because he makes a fundamental error in asserting that selection by consequences is a "causal mode" (whatever that is) which is somehow different from other causes – indeed he contrasts it with "the causal pattern of classical mechanics." It is hard to know what Skinner means by this because he is not explicit, but the implication seems to be that causation in biology and the social sciences is somehow different from that in the physical sciences. He is, of course, in very good company. Mayr's assertions (1961; 1982) that ultimate causes (changes in the genetic program brought about by natural selection) and proximate causes (the expression of the genetic program in phenotypic form) are different, constitute a similar claim. But it seems to us that causation cannot be arbitrarily divided in this way. The causation of the physicist cannot be different from that of the biologist. What is different is that causal sequences in physical systems are typically linear, whereas causal sequences in living systems are invariably circular. The circularity, however, is not static. Living systems are a set of processes moving in time and tied together by a nexus of causal sequences. Each process is a causal influence on some other process, and in a system with a limited number of such processes, each eventually feeds back on itself. Such circular causal sequences might more accurately be labelled as spiral.

The failure to note *this* difference leads to a failure to see the reasons and consequences of such spiral causal sequences. The error then ripples through the whole conceptual structure that Skinner attempts to build in "Consequences."

There are at least two reasons for this pervasive circularity of causal sequence. One is that phenotypes are not mere passive vehicles for genes and victims of natural selection. Phenotypes are operators (Waddington 1969) in that they alter their environments in many different ways and hence change the selection forces that act upon them. This is how the differential propagation of genes occurs. It is pointless to ask which is prior, the nature of the environment or the activity of the organism. They are inextricably bound together in what Lewontin (1982) calls the "interpenetration of organism and environment" (p. 159). It is simply incorrect to offer a dichotomy of either "a species adapts to an environment" or "the environment selects the adaptive traits." The error is compounded by asserting that the latter is correct. Neither is correct – nor are any of the other alternative interpretations that Skinner offers for a range of biological and psychological issues. What happens is that a species, in adapting (it is never adapt*ed*) to an environment changes that environment, which then requires further processes of becoming adapted, which in turn imposes more environmental change, and so on. Exactly the same applies to the individual learner. Thus learners *are* doers, and sometimes what they do occurs largely in their heads. In doing they change themselves and their worlds. Piaget's dialectic of assimilation and accommodation captures this endless interplay more nearly than any other formulation. Skinner's static view doesn't begin to approach the complexity of living things.

The other source of circular (spiral) causal sequence is the hierarchical organization of living systems. Genes partly determine phenotypic features, and phenotypic fitness determines the differential propagation of genes. Several different hierarchies are available in the literature. A serious problem for theoretical biology is that the obvious phenomenological, structural hierarchy (macromolecules, organelles, cells, tissues, organs, organisms, ecosystems), which everyone recognizes, may not match the hierarchy of dynamic processes that embodies the functioning of living systems. A similar point has been made by Dawkins (1978), Hull (1980), and ourselves (Plotkin & Odling-Smee 1979), and it is not trivial because the obvious hierarchy may get in the way of our seeing the functionally important one. An example of a nonobvious hierarchy is the one we have put forward. Genetic processes, variable development, individual learning, and socioculture at no level map out in any simple way onto an organism. Each level partitions individuals or aggregates them. This conceptual difficulty aside, if one attempts to analyse such hierarchies in any depth, circular causal sequences immediately become apparent in the form of "upward" and "downward" causation (Campbell 1974a). An example of two-way causation in such a hierarchy occurs when genes are important and inevitable determiners of how and what is learned, but what is learned is often an important determiner of what genes are fed back (downward) into the gene pool.

The interconnectedness of living systems may be complex, but interconnected they are. It is the characteristic and essence of living things. The levels never become decoupled. Skinner is in error when he writes that "operant conditioning could not only supplement the natural selection of behavior, it could replace it." The logical requirement of hierarchical organization, however, is that learning as a more subordinate process in the hierarchy can never be decoupled from the less subordinate processes in the hierarchy. Learning of any and every sort must be primed by more fundamental processes, be they genetic or developmental. Skinner's is the erroneous thinking that underpins general process learning theory with its now invalidated notion of stimulus, response, and reinforcer equivalence. This same erroneous idea of a single and unencumbered learning process is what underlies Skinner's continuing and astonishing assertion that language and its social correlates are "simply the extension of operant control to the vocal musculature." Oh Chomsky, where are you now! Writing, we hope, a commentary for these treatments.

There is an unsettling similarity between Skinner's levels 1, 2, and 3 and our levels 1, 3, and 4. It is unsettling because Skinner does not arrive at his levels by analysis, and as a result they appear to have very little in them and the structure as a whole has no conceptual force. By his own assertions, his levels contain no stored information (actual or metaphorical) and no organization. How, then, are they to be explained and what do they explain? According to Skinner "at all three levels the changes can be explained by the 'development' of contingencies of selection." Can they?

Our challenge to Skinner is to abandon easy assertion and take up some kind of analysis of his levels in terms of their interrelationships and their processes. If he can do so without having to have recourse to concepts of information, storage, and organization then all the more interesting. The point, though, is to show us, not just tell us.

BFS: Plotkin & Odling-Smee nicely define their position by appealing to Piaget and, with rather more passion, to Chomsky. The question is not whether learning is doing, whether learners are doers, but whether they are initiators. Selection is a causal mode only in the sense of causing novelty – whether in the *origin* of species, the *shaping* of new operants, or the *invention* of cultural practices.

What can I reply to commentators who say that "the point. . .is to show us, not just tell us?" True, I am not a biologist or an anthropologist, but as a psychologist I have certainly published more than most of my contemporaries, and there is a very extensive literature in the experimental analysis of behavior which will *show* Plotkin & Odling-Smee what I am talking about, if they care to look. ("Methods" is one place to start.)

Contingency-governed science

Robert R. Provine

Department of Psychology, University of Maryland Baltimore County

Skinner has provided an insightful and useful analysis of contingency-governed phenomena in the biological and behavioral sciences. "Consequences" is more than a clever attempt to build bridges between operant psychology and indifferent or often hostile disciplines in the biological sciences such as ethology. It reveals a common, unifying theme that runs through most of the biological and behavioral sciences, the notion that selection by consequences, in some form, is a feature of all living things. The organism is viewed as a theory of its environment. Skinner does an admirable job of developing his argument. I would like to comment on a complementary issue, the role played by contingencies in shaping an operant science of behavior. The focus on contingencies encourages self-correction by investigators, a characteristic that may be the most powerful recommendation for the operant approach. This property of contemporary operant psychology may be a surprise to those who confuse the behavior-analytic approach with the radical environmentalism of a half-century ago.

If an operant psychologist finds that contingencies under his control fail to influence the behavior of an organism, he may conclude either that the behavior is refractory to contingencies or that the wrong contingencies were tried. In either case, the investigator is forced to reexamine and adjust his method and approach. Recent challenges to the operant position usually fail to consider this property of self-correction, and that operant psychology is not a form of environmentalism. Three such challenges are the discovery of "biological constraints on learning," "feature detectors" in sensory systems, and "pattern-generating circuits" in motor systems.

All would structure and therefore restrict the ways organisms learn, perceive, or move. I presume that Skinner would say that all three evolved in response to the contingencies of natural selection. The discovery of behavior that seems refractory to contingency management or is amenable only to highly specific contingencies is hardly a defeat for the operant approach. The constraints on learning and perceptual or motor processes simply define the context and limit the degrees of freedom in which operant learning may occur.

In conclusion, the operant analysis of behavior provides rapid feedback and encourages one to "go with what works." This basically atheoretical approach is itself sensitive to contingencies and seems quite adaptive.

BFS: "Consequences" is, in a way, an answer to the three challenges Provine mentions. One might as well speak of biological constraints on medicine as on learning. We study the effects of drugs, surgery, and other therapeutic practices on the organisms which present themselves for treatment as we study the learning processes in the organisms in which we are interested. In neither case is anyone claiming a universal science of medicine or learning. That a given species is predisposed by its genetic history to see particular stimuli in preference to others or to behave in particular ways in preference to others is a fact of the same sort. A different kind of selection has been at work.

Fitness, reinforcement, underlying mechanisms

Alexander Rosenberg

Department of Philosophy, Syracuse University

Skinner is right: Natural selection and operant conditioning are two versions of the same phenomenon. This fact explains not only their form, content, and relations to findings in biology and psychology, but also the complete parallel in their respective intellectual histories. In particular, their relation to these findings both explains and enables us to refute persistent though mistaken charges made against the two theories. It also points to the direction in which both of these theories must be extended. Skinner's account of the identity of selection and reinforcement, however, blocks the explanation, the defense, and the elaboration that the two theories require.

The most venerable charge against the theory of natural selection is that it is unfalsifiable: Its claims about differences in fitness can only be substantiated in the differential reproduction it cites fitness to explain. The way to refute this charge is to specify the mechanisms that characterize differences in fitness independent of their effects in differential reproduction. The practical difficulty of specifying these mechanisms on which fitness supervenes arises because they involve an overwhelmingly large number of disjunctions of physical factors that differ from case to case, so that no general characterization of fitness combining precision, manageability, and truth can actually be constructed. However, once it is seen that in principle this independent specification of fitness can be accomplished, the charge of vacuity is easily undercut. More important, by exposing the underlying factors that make for fitness differences from case to case, the explanatory and predictive power of applications of the theory of natural selection is increased (see Rosenberg 1983).

By reflecting on the relation between fitness differences and their underlying mechanisms among organisms in environments, we may put to rest the venerable charge's latest versions, like Gould and Lewontin's (1979) complaint that the adaptationist program is but a sterile Panglossianism ("everything is for the best"). It is therefore ironic that, as Dennett (1983) has shown, Gould and Lewontin's unavailing arguments against adaptationism are identical to Skinner's arguments against mentalism. It is even more deeply ironic that extending operant theory and defending it against accusations that it mirrors the alleged Panglossianism of evolutionary theory requires that operant theory be developed in a direction Skinner has categorically abjured: the direction, if not of mentalism, then of "centralism," taking seriously the psychological states that intervene between initial reinforcement of emitted behavior and its subsequent recurrence.

Skinner's critics have long chided the law of effect with vacuity, on the grounds that the only general characterizations of reinforcers available make the law an empty tautology. The criticism has warrant in texts that define a reinforcer as "any stimulus which if presented (or withdrawn) contingent on an operant, increases (decreases) the probability of the occurrence of the operant." (Compare criticisms of evolutionary theory spawned by definitions of fitness or adaptation as whatever increases subsequent reproduction.) Of course, the actual laboratory practice of operant psychologists in uncovering particular contingencies of reinforcement leads them to identify particular reinforcers independently of the change in the frequency or character of particular operants. Thus they have produced quantitative instantiations of the law of effect for small numbers of organisms in specific experimental settings. But to unify and theoretically substantiate these findings under a general theory we need to find a feature common to all reinforcers, aside from their operant consequences. Without one we cannot identify and measure reinforcers independently – and therefore we cannot use the general version of the law to explain and predict anything. Independent identification of reinforcers is needed to link the law to something not already identified as a reinforcer or an operant, and such linkage is required for the provision and improvement of explanatory and predictive content. Despite a great deal of contemporary research, no feature common and peculiar to reinforcers has so far been found. This is because what makes a contingency reinforcing must ultimately be some common effect of reinforcers inside the body of the organism. This common effect, or disjunction of effects, will be the intermediate links, the immediate causes of subsequent emission of operant behavior. (Compare evolutionary theory's need for a common denominator of fitness independent of the reproductive effects fitness is intended to explain.)

Now, looking for the causes of behavior inside the body is not by itself under Skinnerian anathema. As Skinner (1963a) has written, "The skin is not that important a boundary." But looking for causal mechanisms is excluded. Finding the proximate causes of behavior inside the body is not only demanded by the defense and the development of operant theory, but is an exemplification of the "causal pattern of classical mechanics" which Skinner rejects. It is also in his view the first step toward "mentalism."

The signal accomplishment of the theory of natural selection was not to supersede classical mechanics, but to show how the physical sciences can be expected to subsume biological phenomena. It relies on this relation between selection on heritable variation on the one hand and the forces and factors of physics and chemistry that fitness consists in on the other, to defend itself against charges of vacuity. It dispenses with creativity by appeal to prior noncreative phenomena; it accords to living systems the same essence it accords to physical ones. If, as Skinner rightly claims, operant theory has all the strengths of natural selection, it must have these properties as well. Just as evolutionists have progressively found the required causal intermediaries between selection and evolution, so operant psychologists must find causal intermediaries between reinforcers and operants. Only such intermediaries can satisfy the physical requirement of no action at a (temporal) distance, and provide the linkage to nonbehavioral factors that entrench and substantiate the law of effect. Operant psychology must find a mechanism parallel to the physical factors on which fitness supervenes. This is the course of development that Skinner wants to exclude, however. He rejects the "attempt to assimilate selection by consequences to the causality of classical mechanics." "People," he writes in "Consequences," "behave in given ways because they have been changed by. . .[reinforcing] contingencies. The contingencies can perhaps be inferred from the changes they have worked, but they are no longer in existence." But the direct inference back from changes in behavior to prior contingencies of reinforcement is too easy to have much content; in this respect it is like facile inferences from current adaptation to prior selection, inferences that the opponents of adaptationism have seized upon. In both cases, causal intermediaries are required.

What will these intermediaries look like? Some of Skinner's arguments against mentalism are good ones, and suggest convincingly that we should not look to "folk psychology" for these intermediaries. On the other hand, if the only other source for manageable classes of identifiable intermediaries (the common effects diverse reinforcers share, which enable us to explain and predict the behavioral consequences of reinforcement) are to be found in neuroscience, then the entrenchment and further development of the law of effect will have to be postponed, pending the establishment of a neuroscience with the desired manageable classes. The discovery of biochemical mechanisms of synaptic transmitter modulation by classical conditioning (reported in Kandel & Schwartz 1982) may justify some optimism in this regard, but what it shows is that the elaboration of a psychological theory of selection by consequences must, like its evolutionary big brother, proceed in the direction of a molecular biological, that is physical, theory.

Of course, there may be intermediaries of the required sorts at higher levels of organization than those treated in molecular neuroscience. This is the hypothesis of the cognitive psychologist, among others. There is, moreover, some reason to suppose that if such intermediaries exist, their behavior is shaped by selection for consequences as well (see Dennett 1978a). If so, Skinner will have been vindicated in spite of himself, for the fundamental units of an operant psychology will be the kind of ghostly intermediaries he has so long condemned. But given the parallels between operant psychology and evolutionary biology, this should come as no surprise, for just as the units of selection and evolution are in dispute among biologists (see Ghiselin 1981), we should expect that in the parallel science of psychology, the units of selection may not, as Skinner blithely supposes, be "selves or persons." In either case, the future direction of development for a psychology of selection by consequences must be away from behavior and its environmental conditions, in the very direction Skinner has so sternly enjoined.

BFS: I see nothing tautological about the definition Rosenberg gives of a reinforcer as "any stimulus which if presented (or withdrawn) contingent on an operant, increases (decreases) the probability of the occurrence of the operant." It is no more tautological than the definition of an allergen. One may guess fairly accurately that certain standard things will be reinforcers, but beyond that one must find out what is reinforcing to a particular person. The unconditioned reinforcers gain their power from phylogeny. Susceptibilities to reinforcement have had advantageous consequences and have evolved as traits.

I agree that no feature common and peculiar to reinforcers has so far been found, and I shall be surprised if one is ever found. I also agree that reinforcers have a common effect inside the body. But that is not the centrism to which I object. We commonly say that reinforcers feel good, taste good, look good, and so on, but as I suggest in this paper "good" appears at all three levels as more or less synonymous with selective advantage.

I would certainly reject any "attempt to assimilate selection by consequences to the causality of classical mechanics." Selection is responsible for novelty, but as something new comes into existence the structures involved obey the laws of classical mechanics. I have not "categorically abjured" movement in the direction of studying the "states that intervene between initial reinforcement of emitted behavior and its subsequent recurrence." I have simply left that to those who have the proper instruments and practices. Introspective mentalists simply put the neurologist on the wrong track, and so I believe do cognitive psychologists. It is the function of a science of behavior at the present time to give neurologists their assignments, as it was the function of genetics prior to the discovery of DNA to give modern geneticists their assignment with respect to the gene. I look forward to a comparable development in behavior, though I do not expect to live to see it.

Perspectives by consequences

Duane M. Rumbaugh

Department of Psychology, Georgia State University and Yerkes Regional Primate Research Center, Emory University

Skinner argues persuasively that behavior is selected by consequences and that contingencies of reinforcement shape operant responses. Consistent with this principle is the conclusion that perspectives on behavior held by scientists are themselves formulated or shaped by contingencies of reinforcement, by consequences. Skinner himself recognizes this congruence and has on several occasions denied that he is to receive any personal credit for his contributions to science: Those contributions have been beyond his personal control in that they have been shaped and articulated by the same set of principles that he attempts to define as sufficient for the entire behavioral domain.

It is concluded that the formulation of the laws of behavior by scientists will be dictated by those same laws; however, only if validity is reinforcing will their articulation eventually be errorless and complete. By the same reasoning, those laws and principles will also serve to shape acceptance, or rejection, by the scientific community and by the public at large of the laws and principles as articulated. It is to be hoped that the responses of acceptance by scientists will become increasingly enthusiastic as the articulation of the principles or laws becomes increasingly sufficient. But will this be the case? If so, will it also be the case that societies at large will respond with increased acceptance as scientists more closely approximate the translating of natural law into the language of humans?

Skinner argues in "Consequences" that society is selected for and shaped by "whatever promotes its ultimate survival." Each society has had its own set of characteristics shaped by contingencies spanning millions of years, and no radically new characteristic can accrue to a society as though it were a biologic mutation. Consequently, it is improbable that we can anticipate or define for an array of diverse societies all of the conditions that will prove requisite to acceptance of the principles of behavior as articulated by even the ablest scientist; however, and this is consonant with Skinner's view, their acceptance should be enhanced to the degree they are viewed as complementary to ultimate survival.

Skinner notes near the end of "Consequences" that the efforts of those who have made experimental analyses of behavior have been rejected. The reason, he states, is that this approach has "no place for a person as an initiating agent." To hold that individuals' behavior is attributable solely to the contingencies of reinforcement of those individuals' lives as the contingencies have shaped and changed their beings to the present is, from the individuals' perspective, to deny responsibility and control over their lives. On the contrary, societies have generally fostered perspectives that do attribute control to the individual, or, rather, societies generally have been selected for espousing such perspectives, probably because they have strengthened their bases for holding individuals responsible for their behaviors in the framework of what is presumed to be "good and bad" for the well being and the survival of those societies.

On the other hand, the possibility should not be ruled out that the trend of human evolution has included selection for those individuals whose views were readily shaped by environmental contingencies to the conclusions (i) that as individuals they live in a cause and effect determined world and (ii) that their behavior can be self-controlled and used causally to achieve reinforcing effects (i.e., goals).

Clearly, persons persist in perceiving their actions as efforts to transcend their environmental pressures and crises so as to become controllers of these forces and thus avoid being controlled by them. Even Skinner asks whether we can "take explicit steps to make our future more secure?"; and he then asks if to do thus "must we not in some sense transcend selection?" Skinner clearly hopes that success will be obtained through certain steps, which would include "showing or telling people what to do with respect to relevant contingencies – or [how to] construct and maintain new selective contingencies."

Sadly, there is little empirical evidence to warrant optimism for success through the initiation of such steps. Such methods have been relatively ineffective to date in building a world in which peace, safety, security, health, and happiness are ensured. Quite the contrary has prevailed, and the picture grows less bright each year.

In short, though many are ready to join Skinner in such steps, the fact is that we do not know how to incorporate behavioral science into the operations of society so that it will be a powerful contingency of its present and future. Surely the appeal of a cognitive psychology, lamented by Skinner, is in part based on its assumption that some control of behavior is retained by intraorganismic operations, though those operations are not held to be apart from the prescriptions of natural laws.

One hopes that scientists will unite quite involuntarily in support of a perspective of behavior to the degree that it is valid. Only if we are educating scientists improperly should it be otherwise. Even so, the question remains, Why should a society want to incorporate a perspective of behavior that places the control of behavior, not in the individual, but solely in the contingencies of reinforcement as they have brought change in the individual to the present point in time? To be zealous about doing so would seem tantamount to justifying efforts to preserve life, as we know it, only to the end that the contingencies of the environment will continue to have something on which to operate and to shape – a somewhat less than compelling raison d'être.

Paradoxically, a valid perspective of behavior, whether at hand or to be obtained in the future, might inherently be unpalatable to society and be viewed as antithetical to its welfare and survival. It might prove to be the case that for a valid perspective of behavior to be incorporated into the fabric of world societies it will have to be coupled with a social philosophy, not yet in hand, that will provide or define a "purpose" for existence for the individual.

Whatever our individual perspectives regarding behavior and the future, we have been very fortunate to have the brilliant contributions of B. F. Skinner. His contributions to psychology will serve in perpetuity as part of those contingencies that will continue to bring it to new states across time. It has been a personal privilege to be challenged by his life and perspective through the 30 years of my own career.

BFS: I found two points in Rumbaugh's commentary particularly interesting. Not much attention has been paid in this treatment to the possibility of intervening in selection by design. The evolution of domestic animals has been altered for centuries, and genetic engineering now appears as a much more effective discipline. We have designed individuals through the special contingencies arranged in education, therapy, and other fields, and we have proposed and tested new cultural practices. We have even altered selective contingencies to permit cultures to survive that would otherwise become extinct.

But, as Rumbaugh points out, even with these interventions the prospect of effective action with respect to the frightening problems faced by the world today is not promising. Would there be more survival value in the traditional view of man as originator and creator? Are we worsening our chances by taking a view which so many people find hard to accept – namely, that our behavior is determined by our genetic and personal histories? Two points are relevant:

1. Man the initiator, the master of his fate, has been the established view for several thousand years. Perhaps he can be given credit for the human achievement, but he is also responsible for our problems.
2. The alternative view seems to me to be promising because it points to something that is more easily changed. Rather than save the world by changing how people feel and think about it, it may be possible to create an environment in which they will acquire more effective behavior, work more productively, treat each other better, and take the future more effectively into account.

Selectionism, mentalisms, and behaviorism

Jonathan Schull

Department of Psychology, Haverford College

"So long as we cling to the view that a person is an initiating doer, actor, or causer of behavior, we shall probably continue to neglect the conditions which must be changed if we are to solve our problems." No wonder Skinner finds the "present scene" discouraging. *Species do* adapt to an environment *and* the environment selects adaptive traits; individuals patently *do* adjust to situations *and* situations maintain and shape adjusted behavior; groups of people *do* solve problems, *even* as circumstances do select cultural practices that (sometimes) yield solutions. The problem with Skinner is that he has always insisted that recognition of the importance of selection would require abandoning any appreciation of purposes or persons as causal agents. The problem with the present scene is that it has taken him at his word and chosen dignity, purpose, and the acknowledgment of cognition over behaviorism and selectionism.

The cultural practice we should all consider abandoning is the premise that selectionism necessarily implies behaviorism. That Skinner would resist such a move is not surprising, given his history of reinforcement. His position was shaped at a time when cogent arguments against a scientifically sterile and metaphysically dubious mentalism were amply rewarded, and with good reason. But today, disciplined analyses of cognitive functions in psychology, biology, and cognitive science are among the most fertile approaches, and they are implicitly or explicitly founded upon the rejection of the vitalistic mentalism that so incensed behaviorists. Perhaps the time has come to try to understand the cultural context that selected for behaviorism, to understand why selection by consequences remains an underappreciated causal mode, and to understand how the cultural (and probably innate) tendency to impute purposes to biological phenomena can persist in a world that is (undeniably and crucially) produced through selection by consequences occurring at many levels.

In the context of a Cartesian dualism which said that phenomena were caused *either* by mindless, mechanical, material, and scientifically explicable processes *or* by nonphysical, scientifically inexplicable mentalities, William Paley's (1836) pre-Darwinian review of the otherwise inexplicable fitness of organisms to their environments was justifiably taken to provide strong evidence for the existence of an intelligent, purposive, divine "designer" of the biological world. Paley argued for Descartes' god. The theory of "natural selection replaces a very special creator" precisely because it explained adaptedness in terms of purely material processes. The mind of god was therefore expunged from biology. Skinner's and Thorndike's (1911) own advancement of the physically realizable principle of reinforcement was similarly taken to be incompatible with the idea that mental processes underlie voluntary behavior. But if we abandon the idea that physical realizability precludes mentality then we are free to get on with the business of using selectionist principles to explain behavior *and* cognition in initiating agents, without blinding ourselves to the facts of life and mind.

This is not to say that any of us initiating agents are unmoved movers, only that we, and our feelings of causal efficacy, are worth attending to. An example which Skinner ought to accept might help us make this point. The initiating conditions of the *evolution* of new behavior patterns are woefully neglected in biology because biologists tend to shy away from phenomena in which the achievements of individuals could instigate evolutionary change. Such phenomena are suggestive of purposivism, Lamarckism, and other bugaboos, and have therefore been eschewed. However, one of the few recent discussions of a probably important phenomenon of this sort comes from none other than Skinner himself. In a note on the phylogeny and ontogeny of behavior Skinner [see "Phylogeny," this volume] supposes that an ancestor of the modern dog had no instinctive tendency to turn around as it lay down, but learned the behavior as an operant reinforced by the production of a more comfortable bed. Once instigated, however, the behavior might have had adaptive consequences (permitting quicker movement in emergencies, etc.) which could select for genes that promote the behavior. If so, "Dogs in which the response was most readily conditioned must have been most likely to survive and breed," and the behavior may have "eventually become so readily available as an operant that it eventually appeared without reinforcement" (Skinner 1966c). Evolutionarily speaking, that first creative individual was an initiating agent even though its behavior (like all events) had causal and selective antecedents. The example suggests

1. that species with some developmental plasticity may be able to "experiment" with potentially adaptive traits for many generations before they become "committed" to the relatively "expensive," slow, and hard-to-reverse process of genetic institutionalization of the trait;
2. that recognition of initiating agents need not entail neglect of selection by consequences; and
3. that interactions between the kinds of selection Skinner mentions bear further discussion (Baldwin 1896; G. Bateson 1963).

In a similar manner, intelligent agents (like ourselves, for example) "experiment" "mentally" with potentially productive courses of action (rehearsing various scenarios, envisioning their probable consequences, and selecting the one that has produced the most desirable imagined consequence) before committing themselves to the relatively expensive, slow, and hard-to-reverse process of behaving. If the imagined consequence is in fact experienced, their "foresight" is rewarded – which is just to suggest (with James 1890, Dennett 1978, and others)

1. that thought processes themselves involve selection by consequences; and are selected by mental and environmental consequences;
2. that the parallel between selection in individuals, in species, and in cultures goes deeper than Skinner permits himself to imagine; and
3. that imputing a causal role to thought, purpose, and goals does not force one to abandon the ideal of physiological realizability (or physical determinism, for that matter).

The investigation and exploitation of the neural and environmental processes underlying such phenomena would proceed more rapidly if Skinner's habitual linkage of selectionism with behaviorism and antimentalisms were rethought. Selectionism does not preclude mentalism, and I believe Skinner has made it clear that mentalism requires selectionism.

On the other hand, it should be noted that if a materialistic cognitivism is permissible in contemporary psychology, it may not be excludable from evolutionary biology. The parallels between evolution, learning, and thinking in species and in individuals serve to make another point. If species are hierarchically organized selection-by-consequence systems (as Skinner has insightfully argued), and if selection-by-consequence mechanisms provide the modern explanation for intelligence and purpose (as Skinner affirms), and if such mechanisms need not be seen as denying the existence of the phenomena they explain (as many modern mechanistic mentalists maintain), then on what grounds do we dismiss the possibility that evolving species are not in some sense individuals (Ghiselin 1981) of limited but genuine intelligence and purpose? The very question is enough to drive one back to behaviorism.

BFS: Is there a word or two missing near the end of Schull's first paragraph? I am puzzled by his statement that "the problem with the present scene is that it has taken [me] at [my] word and chosen dignity, purpose, and the acknowledgment of cognition over behaviorism and selection." "My word" is to the effect that doing so raises problems, and I have certainly not counseled doing so.

Cognitive science is most "fertile" in breeding promises of great achievement, such as the "disciplined analyses of cognitive functions" Schull mentions. The achievements have yet to be realized. Most of what is called cognitive science is work that was carried on in more or less the same way before that magical term was added.

I am all for *feelings* of causal adequacy as I am for feelings of freedom and dignity. I want people to be adequate, unhampered, successful, and aware of the fact that they are so, and I have suggested ways in which that may be brought about – by changing their environment.

To shift the origination of a genetic trait to something that happened in an individual is perhaps to make the individual an initiating agent for the genetic trait, but we have still to explain the origin of the behavior of the individual. We have only moved a little further along in the search for the initiating agent. As for "experimenting mentally," rehearsing, imagining, foreseeing, I am in no better position to say what is happening than anyone else, including cognitive scientists. An answer will probably come from neurology, but only in the distant future. Meanwhile, we can approach these activities without committing ourselves to any position as to their nature by looking, for example, at how we teach children to experiment mentally, to rehearse, and so on, and at how we know that they are doing so.

Bridges from behaviorism to biopsychology

Paul R. Solomon

Department of Psychology, Williams College

It would be difficult to overstate the magnitude of Skinner's contribution to psychology and related disciplines. Many of the approaches to the study of behavior that we take for granted can be traced to his initiative. Yet Skinner has not been without his critics. On the one hand there are those who express moral or philosophical outrage at some of his ideas about the control of behavior. At a more concrete level, there are those who have criticized specific aspects of Skinner's views. Some of the most severe criticisms have come from biopsychologists and neuroscientists. Skinner has often been criticized for his treatment of the biological aspects of behavior. This is especially true concerning his treatment of language and the predispositions for learning, and his general views on the brain. And although some of the tensions between radical behaviorism, biopsychology, and neuroscience will not be easily resolved, in "Consequences," Skinner appears to be building some bridges.

One of the most stinging criticisms of Skinner's work concerns his view on language. The major thrust of this criticism is that Skinner has ignored the biological aspects of language. A second point of contention between Skinner and his critics concerns the apparent incompatibility between Skinner's views on the acquisition of operantly conditioned responses and the work showing that certain associations are more easily learned than others (e.g., Garcia, McGowan & Green 1972). Here Skinner has been criticized for ignoring biological predispositions which either facilitate or hinder learning. A third criticism leveled by biopsychologists and neuroscientists concerns Skinner's treatment of the brain. To some, Skinner's assertion that it is not useful to study and model the nervous system through inference from behavior ignores many of the insights obtained about brain–behavior relationships using just this strategy.

Skinner has not ignored his critics. In "Consequences" he both revitalizes earlier arguments and marshals new ones to answer these criticisms. Yet the tone of this article seems more compromising than that of earlier treatments. In discussing language, Skinner seems to have modified his earlier views somewhat. In considering the importance of language he notes that "vocal behavior can be modified through operant conditioning, but apparently only with respect to the occasions upon which [the various kinds of vocal behavior] occur or their rate of occurrence." With this statement, it appears that Skinner has made room for the biological aspects of language, while at the same time providing an important role for operant conditioning.

In "Consequences" Skinner also attempts to accommodate the compelling data concerning biological predispositions for learning. For example, he notes that a duck may follow a large moving object (in this case its mother) both because it has been selected to do so and because of "an evolved susceptibility to reinforcement by proximity to such an object." This is a far cry from Skinner's earlier statement.

> Pigeon, rat, monkey, which is which? It doesn't matter. Of course, these species have behavioral repertoires which are as different as their anatomies. But once you have allowed for differences in the ways in which they make contact with the environment, and in the ways in which they act upon the environment, what remains of their behavior shows astonishingly similar properties. (Skinner 1959a)

In addressing language and biological predispositions for learning Skinner appears to have accommodated the concerns of many biopsychologists. But what about Skinner's treatment of the brain? Many have accused Skinner of treating the brain as a black box and simply ignoring it. This, of course, is not true. Rather, Skinner has asserted that the brain should be studied in much the same way that all other events are studied – by examining observables. Skinner therefore soundly rejects the notion of the "conceptual nervous system." He argues that a conceptual nervous system cannot be used to explain the behavior from which it is inferred (Skinner 1974, p. 213). Many behavioral neuroscientists would disagree with this statement. The conceptual nervous systems generated to help explain sensory (Helmholtz 1852), motor (Sherrington 1906), and associative (Pavlov 1927) processes were all inferred from behavior, and each has served a valuable heuristic role in subsequent work on the neural aspects of behavior. To deny the value of such models is to dismiss the basis for substantial progress in the neurosciences.

Skinner also rejects the notion that behavior can be completely understood by understanding the brain and nervous system. Instead, he has argued that the goal of neuroscience (he calls it the promise of physiology) is to describe how the nervous system mediates the contingencies between a discriminative stimulus, a response, and a reinforcer. In doing this, Skinner has argued that it is behavior that neuroscientists must strive to explain. It is this adherence to the notion that behavior is the phenomenon that neuroscientists must consider focal that forms Skinner's most valuable contribution to the study of the brain. Through this argument he has suggested that a theory of brain function can be meaningful only if it is posited in the context of behavior.

Consider, for example, how neuroscientists study memory. One approach is to understand the anatomy, physiology, and pharmacology of the nervous system with the hope of eventually understanding how various neuronal processes combine to code memory. The goal here is to uncover mechanisms of plasticity that *might* be responsible for coding memory (see, for example, Swanson, Teyler, & Thompson 1982). As those working in this field recognize, much of the work using this approach is both elegant and important. Yet because it divorces itself from behavior, I doubt that Skinner would favor it. Skinner's approach is better reflected in the model systems approach to studying neural mechanisms of learning and memory (see Kandel 1976; Thompson 1976). Here the beginning point, the incontrovertible evidence which must always be considered, is the behavior of the organism. All attempts to understand possible mechanisms of memory must stem from and be consistent with a particular learned behavior. This seemingly simple point that many of us studying brain–behavior relationships now take for granted has its foundations in the work of Skinner and other behaviorists.

In "Selection by Consequences" Skinner has built bridges between the often separated approaches of behaviorists and biopsychologists. This is especially true in his treatment of language and biological constraints. There still appears to be some tension between radical behaviorism and the neuroscience community concerning the relationship between brain and behavior. Yet behavioral neuroscientists in particular should take note of Skinner's basic contention: Behavior is the starting point for studying brain function, and any final understanding of brain function must be commensurate with the behavior it is evoked to explain.

BFS: Solomon quotes my statement that vocal responses can be modified through operant conditioning "apparently only with respect to the occasions upon which they occur or their rate of occurrence." The statement was about species below the human level. The human species became preeminent when its vocal musculature could be much more readily modified, particularly with respect to its topography. I have not changed my position on language. Certainly no one will argue that there is an innate disposition to use a particular set of speech sounds; languages differ far too much to make that plausible. As to the universals of grammar, they are, I believe, merely the universal uses of verbal behavior by language communities. In all languages people give orders, ask questions, describe situations, and so on, and different languages work out different ways of doing so.

I have answered Solomon's other criticisms in Skinner (1983b). The Garcia effect is punishment, not reinforcement, and operates precisely as I described punishment in *Science and Human Behavior* in 1953. When I said "pigeon, rat, monkey, which? It doesn't matter," I was referring to schedule performances, not to entire repertoires. I doubt that the conceptual nervous systems constructed to explain sensory, motor, and associative processes have a valuable heuristic role. Instead, they have generally led the neurologist to look for the wrong thing – for example, the supposed copies or representations which are said to be constructed in the nervous system when a person perceives a situation or remembers it later.

Selection misconstrued

Stephen C. Stearns

Biological Laboratories, Reed College

Skinner makes at least three claims that attract the attention of an evolutionary biologist: (a) that conditioning works on individual behavior in a manner strictly analogous to the operation of natural selection in evolution; (b) that this analogy sheds light on the evolution of learning and on the impact of learning on evolution; and (c) that more attention needs to be paid to the process of selection and less to the objects selected. How far do these insights take us, and are they new?

Lewontin (1970) stated quite clearly that as long as things vary in a heritable manner and undergo differential survival and reproduction, those things will evolve, whether they be organisms, ideas, or cultures. Dawkins (1976) has taken the consequences of that idea much farther, and it is now a familiar, if not universally accepted, part of evolutionary biology. Thus Skinner's first claim is not new.

I question his repeated presentation of natural selection as designing traits for the benefit of species. Skinner seems to be unaware of the controversy over group selection, individual selection, and gene selection that has occupied the attention of evolutionary biologists for the last 20 years. It has considerably clarified the way we think about natural selection (see Maynard Smith 1964; Price 1972; Wade 1978; Williams 1966). Although the debate is not over, it seems safe to say that only under special circumstances could one conclude that a trait had evolved for the benefit of the species. In nearly all cases, traits have evolved because they increased the fitness of genes, individual organisms, or both. There is some persuasive evidence that certain behavioral traits have evolved because they increased the inclusive fitness of individuals, that is, fitness gained through relatives (Hamilton 1972; Sherman 1977), and some evidence indicates that certain traits, such as female-biased sex ratios (Colwell 1981; Hamilton 1967) and recombination itself (Maynard Smith 1978), have evolved in part through group selection. However, biologists continue to produce alternative explanations based on individual selection or gene selection (e.g., Felsenstein 1974; Hamilton 1980; Rice 1983) for even those traits, such as recombination, for which the evidence is most consistent with group selection. Skinner also seriously underestimates the rapidity of evolutionary change. Significant changes can occur in ecological time, on the order of tens of generations (Kettlewell 1961; Stearns 1983). Skinner's view of natural selection is badly out of date.

Skinner's most constructive point is to call attention to the interaction of selection and learning. I particularly appreciated his description of how the evolution of learning could lead to nonadaptive or even to maladaptive behavior. However, he again falls disappointingly short of the sort of analysis that would be suggested by recent developments in evolutionary biology. Learning is a sophisticated form of developmental plasticity. Ashby (1956) has suggested that plasticity in some traits may buffer other traits against the force of selection, and Caswell (1983) has developed this idea in the context of the evolution of reproductive traits. Charnov and Bull (1977) have argued that labile sex determination is favored by natural selection when an individual's fitness – as male or female – is strongly influenced by environmental conditions and when the individual has little control over which environment it will experience. Stearns and Crandall (1983) have extended this argument to traits and environments that can vary continuously. These analyses of nonbehavioral traits provide a prototype for a biologically based analysis of the evolution of learning. Cavalli-Sforza and Feldman (1981) have recently published an extensive discussion of the interaction between genetic and cultural evolution. In all these biological discussions there are many more concrete points for departure and suggestive hypotheses about the evolution of learning and the impact of learning on evolution than are suggested by Skinner's straightforward analogy. What things are easy to learn, what things are hard to learn, and why did that distinction evolve? Skinner passes that essential question by.

Skinner's final notable point is that selection processes are blind mechanisms, and that too much attention has been paid to the object selected and not enough to the process of selection. I completely agree with his denial that organisms can be construed as initiating the process of adaptation, and with his plea that more attention be paid to the process of selection, but I cannot countenance his decision to treat the organism as a black box and to concentrate solely on the external circumstances affecting the organism. We must understand enough of the internal structure of organisms to explain how they interact with their external circumstances. That internal structure can make a critical differences to the predictions one would make both about the direction of evolution and about the development of behavior.

In summary, Skinner's analogy between evolution and learning is apt but hardly new, and his picture of evolution errs in its details. The questions Skinner states explicitly do not seem likely to lead to productive new lines of research, but the questions he states implicitly are loaded with significance: How does learning evolve? Once evolved, what implications does learning have for subsequent evolution? Does it uncouple phenotype and genotype, as suggested by Huxley (1942)? What things are hard to learn and what things are easy to learn? Biology and psychology can interact productively in these areas (see Kamil & Sargent 1981). Skinner enters a final plea for an objective assessment of the causes of human behavior. Although I do not think his scheme of selection by consequences is adequate to represent causation. I do agree that we must understand the biological basis of human behavior and the limits it sets – if any – on what can be learned. That knowledge would make it easier to solve problems caused by our own behavior.

BFS: I am not an evolutionary biologist, but I have been at least aware of most of the issues Stearns brings up. Many of them have parallels in the field of operant conditioning, but a consideration would have taken far too much space. I do not think that a more accurate account of the present position on natural selection would have made much of a difference for the point of my paper, the four kinds of concepts which have usurped the role played by selection. Evolutionary theorists may not appeal to concepts like life, mind, and zeitgeist, but behavioral scientists, in the sense that includes economists, political scientists, and anthropologists, do so, and so do philosophers, theologians, and many others who have an effect on what is happening in the world today. Creation science may be easily dismissed by the evolutionary theorist, but something very much like it is a problem for the behavioral scientist. Even biologists are not free from the misuse of the concept of purpose, and the role of values is still widely debated. These are the main issues in my paper, and my lack of expertise in evolutionary theory is not, I think, a serious threat to the validity of my argument.

Selection by consequences: A universal causal mode?

William Timberlake

Psychology Department, Indiana University, Bloomington

For some time it has been customary to attribute human behavior to a combination of the effects of biology, individual learning, and society. Though it is clear that these determinants are related, experience has taught most of us to consider them separately rather than to ignore divisions between disciplines and suffer the cross-fire of individuals defending their turf. Skinner has frequently crossed such disciplinary boundaries, in the present case by arguing that selection by consequences is the key causal mechanism in all three areas. Though I admire his bravery and have sympathy for his goal of integration, I think the resemblances Skinner sees are overstated and his emphasis on a common causal mechanism interferes with rather than facilitates analysis of the relations among natural selection, individual learning, and culture.

What Skinner calls attention to is that changes in evolution (new species), individual learning (new behaviors), and culture (new societies) typically occur in the context of some alteration of the environment. On the basis of this resemblance Skinner argues that the changes are based on the common causal mechanism of selection by consequences. The fundamental problem with this argument is that a consequence is by definition an outcome that follows necessarily from a set of conditions. By this definition only operant learning can be a product of selection by consequences; examples of natural selection and cultural evolution do not follow from any set of prior conditions that can be specified. I develop and add to this argument below. Since Skinner considers operant learning a microcosm of the other two phenomena, I consider it first.

In operant learning selection is judged by a change in probability of responding that occurs when an environmental contingency links responses and outcomes. Though this statement seems simple enough, there are critical qualifications on the nature of contingencies and outcomes. Selection of a particular response occurs when:

1. there is a contingency relation that produces temporal and spatial conditions that support the development of a representation of the relation among environment, behavior, and outcome (such a representation need not be "cognitive" or complete, but it must be present in some form; without the linkage provided by this representation there is no consequence);
2. the contingency relation involving a particular response produces a stronger representation than any other one related to the same outcomes;
3. the outcome is a reinforcer (that is, an event or circumstance capable of producing learned changes in responding); and
4. the reinforcer is the most important one available at that time.

What constitutes a reinforcer has been a point of contention, and Skinner initially settled for a definition in terms of its effect, later arguing for a basis in natural selection. However, it appears that a reinforcer is most reasonably seen not as an event, but as a circumstance produced by a challenge imposed by the contingency on the regulatory systems underlying behavior (e.g., Hanson & Timberlake 1983).

Not only are contingencies and outcomes subject to qualifications, but the nature of selection also has particular qualities. First, the level of responding under a contingency is functionally related to characteristics of the outcome (e.g., quality of reward), and the relation prescribed by the contingency (e.g., fixed-ratio schedule). Second, selection is conditional in that it applies primarily within a particular stimulus setting. Third, selection can be reversed (at least partially) by omitting the outcome.

In short, the key elements in selection by consequences in operant learning are:

1. an environmentally based linkage between behavior and outcome that supports the development of a representation of the relation among the specific stimulus environment, the behavior to be changed, and the outcome;
2. an outcome (circumstance) that contributes to this linkage and motivates its expression in performance;
3. a comparator that determines which of the available behaviors and linkages to pursue; and
4. the possibility of removing the environmental linkage and reversing the selection effect.

In biology, selection occurs as alterations of the gene pool when genetic or environmental change results in differential survival of individuals. Presuming that it is possible to treat the gene pool as analogous to the potential repertoire of individual behaviors, there are still major problems in applying the concept of selection by consequences. The most fundamental difficulty is that the contingency or link between selection and outcome is not defined before the fact. The absence of an a priori linkage means there are no characteristic relations between the gene pool and survival that produce selection; in the language of operant conditioning, one cannot specify reinforcing circumstances, or relations between reinforcing circumstances and changes. Even after the fact of survival is established, the changes in the gene pool are complex. Genes both relevant and irrelevant to survival will meet a common fate because they are grouped by individuals. This is a fundamental fact in biology, and only a side issue in the case of learning and behavior. Essentially, the absence of linkage means there are no specifiable consequences, just events that change the gene pool by eliminating some of it. This removal is neither conditional in the sense of occurring only for particular stimulus conditions, nor reversible.

Further, there is no integration of possibilities of action in natural selection. If conditions are generally appropriate for the gene pool to be depleted in two ways, it will be depleted in two ways. In learning, if conditions are generally appropriate for behavior to be altered in two ways, it is more likely that only one way will occur. This need not imply a homunculus decision maker, but simply a mechanism for integrating possible behaviors that compete for a final common path. Finally, although evolutionary change has a functional "memory" of past successes in terms of the elements available in the gene pool, this memory is quite different from what occurs in learning. In learning, the animal learns not to emit a particular unsuccessful response in particular stimulus circumstances, but the response is still available in other situations. In evolution, if genes of a type that have been selected against are gone from the pool, they are not available in any situation, and if a few examples remain in the pool, they will be expressed independently of their failure to produce survival in a particular circumstance the last time.

In short, in natural selection there is no a priori environmental linkage of gene pool and survival and thus no representation of the relation among particular stimulus environments, genes, and survival. Since consequences as used in operant learning require an environmentally defined linkage, it follows that natural selection is simply selection, not selection by consequences. Changes that occur in the gene pool are not conditional, reversible, or functionally related to characteristics of the outcome or the contingency. Outcomes are not remembered conditionally. Furthermore, much of a given change in the gene pool is completely unrelated to the particular circumstances of individual death or survival. Finally, there is no momentary integration of possibilities in terms of efficiency or importance.

In the case of culture, Skinner's focus varies between social reinforcers of individual behavior and the role of selection by consequences in the survival of cultures; however, the last seems to be the most important to his argument. Skinner treats cultures as combinations of elements in a sort of cultural gene pool. Changes in the pool occur as a consequence of differential survival of cultures. Most of the objections raised to viewing natural selection as selection by consequences apply here as well. Again there are no consequences, just effects. Skinner seems to see that in terms of selection by consequences the interesting phenomenon is the way in which individuals contribute to culture through learning and innovation, but this interaction is more illustrated than analyzed.

Skinner has contributed uniquely to the continuing struggle to develop models of learning and behavior largely free from stultifying concerns with imaginary causal agents. I believe he is right in his concern that we not slip back into inventing causal concepts that depend almost exclusively on our private models of how we behave. However, in the present case I think his concern with general mechanisms has led him to ignore critical differences among phenomena. He has generated parallels among natural selection, learning, and cultural selection that, although initially thought provoking, are without much long-term heuristic value. His insistence on a common causal mode has not promoted a more complete analysis of these phenomena or their relations. In some ways this work is a mirror image of recent sociobiological explanations of behavior. Sociobiologists attempt to explain everything at the level of gene survival; Skinner attempts to explain everything at the level of a common abstract mechanism. What is needed at present is an approach that captures, expands, and integrates these levels of explanation.

The beginning of an integrative approach lies in the assumption of evolutionary biology that all behavior, including learning and elements of culture, is based on the differential survival of genes promoting these phenomena. However, the local basis for an integrative approach must be in terms of local mechanisms. An analogy may be useful in clarifying the situation. Suppose that we have a large computer that has the single function of assembling chess-playing programs from a pool of program elements. (The assembly actually takes place probabilistically by sampling without replacement from smaller subpools of the program elements, so that individual programs may have similar elements and all programs are complete.) Periodically the computer puts together a new group of programs and sends them through a series of tournaments before returning the elements to the pool. The elements of the most successful program are doubled, and the elements of the least successful program are removed. This process is roughly analogous to natural selection. There is no a priori linkage between particular aspects of the gene pool and survival, and there is no conditional memory for success or failure. Given that the elements remain in the pool, the same unsuccessful program can be assembled again.

To add learning by consequence we must allow the programs to profit from experience with local successes and failures in each game. To facilitate learning it will be useful to provide a representation of the relation between stimulus conditions, behavior, and outcome, to evaluate the importance of any outcome in the context of the game, and to allow the representation to be conditional and reversible. Finally, to add culture we must allow some of the programs to have access to past relations between behavior and outcomes compiled by previous programs of a similar sort. Competition between cultures would be based on survival of particular kinds of elements in the pool. A simulation of such a system might provide further insight into the relations among the levels and effects of biology, individual learning, and culture in determining behavior.

BFS: Timberlake's paper is in many ways a puzzle. First of all, there is its terminology. I found it hard to think of "a contingency relation that produces temporal and spatial conditions that support the development of a representation of the relation among environment, behavior, and outcome" or to see "a reinforcer...as a circumstance produced by a challenge imposed by the contingency on the regulatory systems underlying behavior." But more puzzling was Timberlake's apparent belief that evolution occurs because of variations in the environment rather than the organism: "Changes in evolution (new species), individual learning (new behaviors), and culture (new societies) typically occur in the context of some alteration of the environment." "In the context of" does not mean "because of," but Timberlake writes as if it did. Thus, "in operant learning selection is judged by a change in probability of responding that occurs when an environmental contingency links responses and outcomes." I should have said that it occurs when some variation occurs in the behavior of the organism, quite possibly in a stable environment. Evolution may be accelerated by environmental changes, but the essence of evolution is variation and reproduction in whatever environment presents itself.

Having misunderstood operant conditioning, Timberlake naturally cannot see the parallel with natural selection. He seems to suggest, though here the language is difficult, that nothing in natural selection corresponds to stimulus control in operant conditioning. But if the long neck of the giraffe, to use an outworn example, was selected in terrains in which there was an advantage in being able to eat leaves high on trees, the trait is adaptive only when tall trees are available. Timberlake also suggests that there is nothing in natural selection corresponding to extinction, but I should have supposed that the legs of the whale would qualify as an example.

Timberlake says that I "initially" defined the reinforcer in terms of its effect but "later" argued for a basis in natural selection. I still do both. A susceptibility to reinforcement by a given substance or event is an evolved trait.

Although Timberlake says that a representation of the relation among environment, behavior, and outcome need not be cognitive, he does say that it must be present in some form. "Without the linkage provided by this representation there is no consequence." But all one needs to say is that the organism is changed by the relation; the change need not be a representation of the relation. What is wrong with cognitive science is not dualism but the internalization of initiating causes which lie in the environment and should remain there.

Giving up the ghost

William Vaughan, Jr.

Department of Psychology and Social Relations, Harvard University

We may construe the history of science in part as consisting of three major revolutions which have radically altered man's view of himself. Prior to the Copernican revolution, the fusion of Christianity and Aristotle taught that the earth was the center of the universe, that we had been created in the image of an omnipotent and omniscient being, and that, governed by reason, we could act to save our immortal souls. The work of Copernicus led inexorably to the view we now hold of the universe: Our sun is a star of a fairly common variety, situated about two-thirds of the way from the center of one of many spiral galaxies; our local group of galaxies is in turn part of a larger grouping, the Virgo cluster. The universe at large is indifferent to mankind.

Darwin ushered in the second revolution, arguing that we were not created by an omniscient being. Rather, by means of the joint action of variation and selection, plants and animals had, over millions of years, gradually become better adapted to their environments. We were the product of that adaptation. Dawkins (1976) gives us a contemporary picture of where Darwin's position led. Constructed by genes, we are machines that tend to act in such a manner that more of the genes that created us are in turn created. Other organisms within our environment are not indifferent to us, but rather act to bend us to their aims.

Selection by consequences is one step in the third, Skinnerian, revolution, which will have far-reaching implications regarding our very identities. Previous revolutions left basically intact our assumptions that we are moral, responsible beings, free to choose a course of action, justly punished if we make the wrong choice. The main thrust of Skinner's position, exemplified in "Consequences," is that voluntary behavior is not. Various forms of behavior arise, some are strengthened and some not, and we are left with some subsequent distribution of behavior.

The parallel between evolution and behavior allows the derivation of a number of strong conclusions. Ernst Mayr (1976a, p. 28) contrasted the view that a species consists of a fixed type with the more scientific view that a species consists of a distribution of organisms:

> The ultimate conclusion of the population thinker and of the typologist are precisely the opposite. For the typologist, the type (eidos) is real and the variation an illusion, while for the populationist the type (average) is an abstraction and only the variation is real. No two ways of looking at nature could be more different.

Following up the parallel with regard to human behavior could lead to a profound change in our views of individuals. What we call our identity may more properly be described as an average form of behavior maintained by a relatively constant environment. Although it may be painful to give up the position that each of us is, or has, an integrated self or identity, in the long run the closer we are to the true state of affairs the better off we will be.

BFS: Vaughan accepts the general argument of "Consequences" but adds a useful point about the individual and his place in population studies. The individual is distinguished as such by the variations that have occurred at all three levels, and these are his potential contribution to the future of the species or the culture.

Natural selection and operant behavior

Wanda Wyrwicka

Brain Research Institute and Department of Anatomy, University of California School of Medicine, Los Angeles

Skinner's article "Consequences" offers the reader a fascinating intellectual adventure. In a few pages which contain enough material for several large volumes, the author presents his complete concept of the origin and maintenance of behavior of animals including, specifically, humans. The "selection by consequences," as Skinner calls his concept, operates on three levels: natural selection, individual behavior, and evolution of cultures. As the phenomena of at least two of these levels cannot be directly or easily observed, the concept must, nolens volens, be based on suppositions and simplifications. This gives the reader an opportunity to ask questions. Here are some of them. Does the development of behavior really resemble the process of natural selection? Are the consequences in each case of the same nature?

Let me concentrate first on natural selection. According to Darwin's theory, only those individuals and species survive that have a genetic ability to cope with the changing environmental conditions. This results in the development of new variations and new species, in other words, in evolution by natural selection, a process characterized by Skinner as "selection by consequences." This process, completely passive, occurs without any interaction from the individual organism. But the inborn features critical to survival are transferred to the next generations.

The evolution of the animal world does not seem to be a straight-line process. Insects, for instance, are admittedly much lower in the evolutionary hierarchy than vertebrates, but their central nervous system, although different from that of vertebrates, is quite extensive, and their motor abilities (relative to the size of the body) and the sensitivity of certain sensory systems (such as olfaction), at least in some species (e.g., ants), surpass those in vertebrates. And, among vertebrates, birds (for instance) have better vision than mammals. Birds also have a differently developed muscular system. The pectoral muscles supporting the action of the wings are enormous compared to corresponding muscles in mammals. Humans, who consider themselves as being at the top of the evolutionary scale, not only have poorer vision than birds, but also a poorer muscular system than other mammals of similar size. In fact, humans would not be able to defend themselves against predators if they were not equipped with more efficient brains. The development of the large cerebral hemispheres with their associative cortex compensated for the deficiencies of other systems of the body, and not only resulted in the survival of humans but also secured them the highest position among living beings.

Let me turn now to individual behavior consisting, for the most part, of operant behavior (using Skinner's terminology). Does the development of operant behavior in an individual resemble the evolution of life over millions of years? It has been asserted that the successive stages of ontogenetic development roughly approximate the successive stages of phylogenetic development (Gould 1977). This process occurs mostly during the prenatal period and continues for some limited time after birth. Then operant behavior starts to develop in response to environmental conditions.

The development of operant behavior and the evolutionary process are similar in that they are both based on selection by consequences and both become gradually more and more complex. But there are also big differences between them. By contrast with natural selection,

1. operant behavior is an active process capable of producing permanent changes in inborn reactions and complicating their patterns;
2. its development seems to be quite a straight-line process unless slowed by adverse conditions (including aging); and
3. it is not genetically transferable to later generations.

But there is still another important difference between natural selection and operant behavior. Although in both cases selection by consequences is the basic principle, the consequences are different in each case. In natural selection the consequence is survival. But is it also that in operant behavior? Let us take, for instance, feeding behavior. It has been reported that 6–7-day-old rat pups prefer nonnutritional 0.1% saccharin solution in water to 2.8% lactose solution corresponding to the sweetness of mother's milk (Jacobs & Sharma 1969). Adult rats, even when hungry, prefer nonnutritive 0.25% saccharin solution to nutritive 3% glucose solution (Valenstein 1967). Other experiments have shown that hungry rats, offered a choice between food and intracranial self-stimulation, prefer to self-stimulate, although this leads to death from starvation (Routtenberg & Lindy 1965). Excellent examples of behavior contrary to survival are also provided by drug addiction and dangerous sports. It seems, then, that the consequences of operant behavior must be not so much survival as sensory gratification. It can be supposed that what is called "reinforcement" in operant behavior is sensory satisfaction or, in other words, improvement in sensory state resulting from the presence of unconditioned stimuli in approach behavior, or from the absence of unconditioned stimuli in avoidance behavior (Wyrwicka 1975; 1980).

So far, there is no objective and direct evidence that improvement in sensory state is the main causal factor in operant behavior. Still, can we be sure that animals living in their natural environment do not care about the taste of food and eat only in order to survive? Or that they mate only in order to produce progeny (that way securing the survival of the species), and not in order to get sensory satisfaction from mating? Of course, there exist behaviors where survival is at stake. These include fights with competitors for territory, food, or mates. But is survival the real "purpose" of the fight? It may be so, but on condition that survival means experiencing sensory gratification.

If the above supposition is correct, this means that the survival of the species is secured only when sensory satisfaction obtained from operant behavior goes together with survival. On the other hand, in cases in which it works against survival, the whole species can perish. This especially applies to humans, who have developed such a variety of means to provide sensory satisfaction.

BFS: Wyrwicka has misunderstood the parallel I drew between natural selection and operant conditioning. Operant conditioning is an evolved process. Part of it includes an evolved susceptibility to reinforcement by foodstuffs. We, too, have dangerous susceptibilities to reinforcement – for example, by sweets. Until very recently, most sweet things were in short supply but highly nutritious. With the discovery of sugar cane and other sources of sugar, not to mention saccharin, we have constructed a world in which there are altogether too many sweet things to reinforce our behavior. We do not die of starvation; we grow fat.

The effects of operant conditioning are "transferred" only to the same organism at a later date, not, of course, to the species.

I think we can decide whether "animals living in their natural environment...care about the taste of food [or] eat only in order to survive." We have only to discover whether the taste of food is a reinforcer. I suspect that in many simple organisms eating given foodstuffs is little more than reflex, but if a susceptibility to reinforcement has evolved, then redundant support for eating comes from operant conditioning.

2 Methods and theories in the experimental analysis of behavior

Abstract: We owe most scientific knowledge to methods of inquiry which are never formally analyzed. The analysis of behavior does not call for hypothetico-deductive methods. Statistics, taught in lieu of scientific method, is incompatible with major features of much laboratory research. Squeezing significance out of ambiguous data discourages the more promising step of scrapping the experiment and starting again. As a consequence, psychologists have taken flight from the laboratory. They have fled to Real People and the human interest of "real life," to Mathematical Models and the elegance of symbolic treatments, to the Inner Man and the explanatory preoccupation with inferred internal mechanisms, and to Laymanship and its appeal to "common sense." An experimental analysis provides an alternative to these divertissements.

The "theories" to which objection is raised here are not the basic assumptions essential to any scientific activity or statements that are not yet facts, but rather explanations which appeal to events taking place somewhere else, at some other level of observation, described in different terms, and measured, if at all, in different dimensions. Three types of learning theories satisfy this definition: physiological theories attempting to reduce behavior to events in the nervous system; mentalistic theories appealing to inferred inner events; and theories of the Conceptual Nervous System offered as explanatory models of behavior. It would be foolhardy to deny the achievements of such theories in the history of science. The question of whether they are necessary, however, has other implications.

Experimental material in three areas illustrates the function of theory more concretely. Alternatives to behavior ratios, excitatory potentials, and so on demonstrate the utility of rate or probability of response as the basic datum in learning. Functional relations between behavior and environmental variables provide an account of why learning occurs. Activities such as preferring, choosing, discriminating, and matching can be dealt with solely in terms of behavior, without referring to processes in another dimensional system. The experiments are not offered as demonstrating that theories are not necessary but to suggest an alternative. Theory is possible in another sense. Beyond the collection of uniform relationships lies the need for a formal representation of the data reduced to a minimal number of terms. A theoretical construction may yield greater generality than any assemblage of facts; such a construction will not refer to another dimensional system.

The point of view of an experimental analysis of behavior has not yet reached very far afield. Many social sciences remain untouched, and among natural scientists there is almost complete ignorance of the promise and achievement of the scientific study of behavior. Neils Bohr (1958), the distinguished physicist, discussed certain issues in psychology as follows:

> Quite apart from the extent to which the use of words like "instinct" and "reason" in the description of animal behavior is necessary and justifiable, the word "consciousness," applied to oneself as well as to others, is indispensable when describing the human situation. . . . The use of words like "thought" and "feeling" does not refer to a firmly connected causal chain, but to experiences which exclude each other because of different distinctions between the conscious content and the background which we loosely term ourselves. . . . We must recognize that psychical experience cannot be subjected to physical measurements and that the very concept of volition does not refer to a generalization of a deterministic description, but from the outset points to characteristics of human life. Without entering into the old philosophical discussion of freedom of the will, I shall only mention that in an objective description of our situation the use of the word "volition" corresponds closely to that of words like "hope" and "responsibility," which are equally indispensable to human communications.

These terms and issues would have been at home in psychological discussions 50 years earlier. (Indeed the similarity of Bohr's views to those of William James has been noted.)

How shocked Bohr would have been if a distinguished psychologist had discussed modern problems in physical science in terms which were current at the beginning of the century! Psychology in general, and experimental psychology in particular, is still a long way from providing a conception of human behavior which is as readily accepted by those who deal with people as the views of physics are accepted by those who deal with the physical world. And psychologists themselves are not doing much about it.

Fortunately, the problem can be attacked with a better brand of behavioral engineering. I propose to analyze the behavior of psychologists. Why are they not currently developing the pure science of human behavior from which such tremendous technological advances would certainly flow? How are we to explain the continuing flight from the experimental field? Where have the experimental psychologists gone, and what are they doing instead? And why? And, above all, what steps can be taken to remedy the situation?

So stated, the problem has an analogy in a type of experiment which is growing in importance in the experimental analysis of behavior. When we have studied the performances generated by various contingencies of reinforcement in a single arbitrary response, we can move on to two or more concurrent responses. Instead of one lever to be pressed by a rat or one key to be pecked by a pigeon, our experimental space now frequently contains two or three levers or keys, each with its own set of reinforcing contingencies. In the present experiment, we are to account for the fact that psychologists have stopped pressing the experimental lever and have turned to other available manipulanda. To explain this two questions must be asked: (1) What has happened to the reinforcing contingencies on the experimental lever? and (2) What contingencies compete so effectively elsewhere? Once these questions have been answered, we can proceed to the engineering task of increasing the relative effectiveness of the experimental contingencies. It would probably be unfair to do this by attacking competing conditions, for any source of scientific zeal should be respected, but it is possible that some of the reinforcements responsible for activity on other levers can be made contingent upon the response in which we are primarily interested.

The flight from the laboratory

All sciences undergo changes in fashion. Problems lose interest even though they remain unsolved. In psychology many green pastures have been glimpsed on the other side of the experimental fence. The very success of a science may force it to become preoccupied with smaller and smaller details, which cannot compete with broad new issues. The philosophical motivation of the pioneers of a "mental science" has been lost. Although idealism is evidently still a fighting word in some parts of the world, dualism is no longer a challenging issue in American psychology. Classical research on the relation between the psychic and the physical has been transmuted into the study of the physiological and physical actions of end organs. This is a scientific step forward, but an important source of inspiration has been left behind.

Some of the most effective rewards contingent upon experimental practice have been inadvertently destroyed in another way. We owe most of our scientific knowledge to methods of inquiry which have never been formally analyzed or expressed in normative rules. For more than a generation, however, our graduate schools have been building psychologists on a different pattern of Man Thinking. They have taught statistics in lieu of scientific method. Unfortunately, the statistical pattern is incompatible with some major features of laboratory research. As now taught, statistics plays down the direct manipulation of variables and emphasizes the treatment of variation after the fact. If the graduate students' first results are not significant, statistics tells them to increase the size of their samples; it does not tell them (and, because of self-imposed restrictions on method, it cannot tell them) how to achieve the same result by improving their instruments and their methods of observation. Bigger samples mean more work, the brunt of which the young psychologists may have to bear. When they get their degrees (and grants), they may pass the labor on to others, but in doing so they themselves lose contact with the experimental organisms they are studying. What statisticians call experimental design (I have pointed out elsewhere that this means a design which yields data to which the methods of statistics are appropriate) usually generates a much more intimate acquaintance with a calculating machine than with a behaving organism. One result is a damaging delay in reinforcement. An experiment may "pay off" only after weeks of routine computation. Graduate students who design experiments according to accepted statistical methods may survive the ordeal of the calculating room by virtue of their youthful zeal, but their ultimate reinforcement as scientists may be so long deferred that they will never begin another experiment. Other levers then beckon.

Psychologists who adopt the commoner statistical methods have at best an indirect acquaintance with the "facts" they discover – with the vectors, factors, and hypothetical processes secreted by the statistical machine. They are inclined to rest content with rough measures of behavior because statistics shows them how to "do something about them." They are likely to continue with fundamentally unproductive methods, because squeezing something of significance out of questionable data discourages the possibly more profitable step of scrapping the experiment and starting again.

Statistics offers its own brand of reinforcement, of course, but this is often not contingent upon behavior which is most productive in the laboratory. One destructive effect is to supply a sort of busy work for the compulsive. In the early stages of any inquiry, investigators often have to weather a period of ignorance and chaos during which apparent progress is slight, if not lacking altogether. This is something they must be taught to endure. They must acquire a kind of faith in the ultimate value of ostensibly undirected exploration. They must also learn to be indifferent to the criticism that they are not getting anywhere. If they have accepted funds in support of their research, they must learn to tolerate a gnawing anxiety about the annual report. At such times statistics offers consoling comfort and, what is worse, an all-too-convenient escape hatch. How simple it is to match groups of subjects, devise a crude measure of the behavior at issue, arrange for tests to be administered, and punch the scores into IBM cards! No matter what comes of it all, no one can say that work has not been done. Statistics will even see to it that the result will be "significant" even if it is proved to mean nothing.

The intention of statisticians is honorable and generous. They want experimental scientists to be sure of their results and to get the most out of them. But, whether or not they understand the essence of laboratory practice, their recommendations are often inimical to it. Perhaps against their will, they have made certain essential activities in good laboratory research no longer respectable. The very instrument which might have made an experimental science more rewarding has, instead, all but destroyed its basic features. In the long run, psychologists have been deprived of some of their most profitable, and hence eventually most reinforcing, achievements.

The resulting flight from the laboratory can be stopped by pointing to alternative methods of research. If all psychologists are to be required to take courses in statistics, they should also be made familiar with laboratory practices and given the chance to behave as scientists rather than as the robots described by scientific methodologists. In particular, young psychologists should learn how to work with single organisms rather than with large groups. Possibly with that one step alone we could restore experimental psychology to the vigorous health it deserves.

But it will be worthwhile to examine the competing contingencies.

Psychologists have fled from the laboratory, and perhaps for good reason. Where have they gone?

The flight to real people. Laboratories can be dull places, and not only when furnished with calculating machines. It is not surprising that psychologists have been attracted by the human interest of real life. The experimental subject in the laboratory is only part of a person and frequently an uninteresting part, whereas the whole person is a fascinating source of reinforcement. Literature flourishes for that reason. Psychologists have long since learned to borrow from the literary domain. If a lecture flags, or a chapter seems dull, one has only to bring in a case history and everything literally "comes to life." The recipe is so foolproof that the lecture or text which consists of nothing but case histories has been closely approximated. But in resorting to this device for pedagogical or therapeutic effect psychologists have themselves been influenced by these reinforcers; their courses of action as scientists have been deflected. They often recognize this and from time to time have felt the need for a special theory of scientific knowledge (based, for example, on empathy or intuition) to justify themselves. They seldom seem to feel secure, however, in the belief that they have regained full citizenship in the scientific commonwealth.

The reinforcement which flows from real people is not all related to, on the one hand, an intellectual conviction that the proper study of mankind is man or, on the other, the insatiable curiosity of a Paul Pry. In a world in which ethical training is widespread, most people are reinforced when they succeed in reinforcing others. In such a world personal gratitude is a powerful generalized reinforcer. We can scarcely hold it against psychologists that, like other people of good will, they want to help their fellows – either one by one in the clinic or nation by nation in, say, studies of international goodwill. We may agree that the world would be a better place if more people would concern themselves with personal and political problems. But we must not forget that the remedial step is necessarily a short-term measure and that it is not the only step leading to the same goal. The lively prosecution of a science of behavior, applied to the broad problem of cultural design, could have more sweeping consequences. If such a promising alternative is actually feasible, anyone who is capable of making a long-term contribution may wisely resist the effect of other consequences which, no matter how important they may be personally, are irrelevant to the scientific process and confined to short-term remedial action. A classical example from another field is Albert Schweitzer. Here is a brilliant man who, for reasons we need not examine, dedicated his life to helping others – one by one. He has earned the gratitude of thousands, but we must not forget what he might have done instead. If he had worked as energetically for as many years in a laboratory of tropical medicine, he would almost certainly have made discoveries which in the long run would help – not thousands – but literally billions of people. We do not know enough about Schweitzer to say why he took the short-term course. Could he not resist the blandishments of gratitude? Was he freeing himself from feelings of guilt? Whatever his reasons, his story warns us of the danger of a cultural design which does not harness some personal reinforcement in the interests of pure science. The young psychologist who wants above all to help other people should be made to see the tremendous potential consequences of even a small contribution to the scientific understanding of human behavior. It is possibly this understanding alone, with the improved cultural patterns which will flow from it, which will eventually alleviate the anxieties and miseries of the human species.

The flight to mathematical models. The flight from the experimental method has sometimes gone in the other direction. If subjects studied in the laboratory have been too drab and unreal for some, they have been just the opposite for others. In spite of our vaunted control of variables, experimental subjects too often remain capricious. Sometimes they are not only warm but, as baseball players say, too hot to handle. Even the "average person," when captured in the statistical net, may be unpleasantly refractory. Some psychologists have therefore fled to an ivory image of their own sculpturing, mounted on a mathematical pedestal. These Pygmalions have constructed a Galatea who always behaves as she is supposed to behave, whose processes are orderly and relatively simple, and to whose behavior the most elegant of mathematical procedures can be applied. She is a creature whose slightest blemish can be erased by the simple expedient of changing an assumption. Just as political scientists used to simplify their problems by talking about an abstract Political Man, and the economists theirs by talking about Economic Man, so psychologists have built the ideal experimental organism – the Mathematical Model.

When I return later to the need for theory, I consider in more detail the effect of this practice on so-called learning theory. Early techniques available for the study of learning – from the nonsense syllables of Ebbinghaus, through the problem boxes of Thorndike and the mazes of Watson, to the discrimination apparatuses of Yerkes and Lashley – always yielded learning curves of disturbing irregularity. In experiments with these instruments an orderly change in the behavior of a single organism was seldom seen. Orderly processes had to be generated by averaging data, either for many trials or many organisms. Even so, the resulting "learning curves" varied in a disturbing way from experiment to experiment. The theoretical solution to this problem was to assume that an orderly learning process, which always had the same properties regardless of the particular features of a given experiment, took place somewhere inside the organism. A given result was accounted for by making a distinction between learning and performance. Though the performance might be chaotic, the psychologist could continue to cherish the belief that learning was always orderly. Indeed, the mathematical organism seemed so orderly that model builders remained faithful to techniques which consistently yielded disorderly data. An examination of mathematical models in learning theory will show that no degree of disorder in the facts has placed any restriction on the elegance of the mathematical treatment.

The properties which (to drop to a two-dimensional figure of speech) make a paper doll more amenable than a living organism are crucial in a scientific account of behavior (the reference, of course, is to the song by J. S. Black, in which the lyricist expresses his preference for "a paper doll to call his own" rather than a "fickle-minded real live girl"). No matter how many of the formulations derived from a study of a model eventually prove useful in describing reality (remember wave mechanics!), the questions to which answers are most urgently needed concern the correspondence between the two realms. How can we be sure that a model is a model of *behavior*? What *is* behavior, and how is it to be analyzed and measured? What are the relevant features of the environment, and how are they to be measured and controlled? How are these two sets of variables related? The answers to these questions cannot be found by constructing models. (Nor is a model likely to be helpful in furthering the necessary empirical inquiry. It is often argued that some model, hypothesis, or theory is essential because the scientist cannot otherwise choose among the facts to be studied. But there are presumably as many models, hypotheses, or theories as facts. If the scientific methodologist will explain how he proposes to choose among them, his answer will serve as well to explain how one may choose among empirical facts.)

What sort of behavioral engineering will reduce the rate of responding to the mathematical lever and induce distinguished psychologists to get back to the laboratory? Two steps seem to be needed. First, it must be made clear that the formal properties of a system of variables can be profitably treated only after the dimensional problems have been solved. The detached and essentially tautological nature of mathematical models is usually frankly admitted by their authors, particularly those who come into experimental psychology from mathematics, but for the psychologist these disclaimers are often lost among the integral signs. Second, the opportunity to be mathematical in dealing with factual material should be clarified. To return to the example of learning theory, the psychologist should recognize that with proper techniques one can *see learning take place*, not in some inner recess far removed from the observable performance of an organism, but as a change in that performance itself. Techniques are now available for the experimental analysis of very subtle behavioral processes, and this work is ready for the kind of mathematical theory which has always been productive at the proper stage in the history of science. What is needed is not a mathematical model, constructed with little regard for the fundamental dimensions of behavior, but a mathematical treatment of experimental data. Mathematics will come into its own in the analysis of behavior when appropriate methods yield data which are so orderly that there is no longer any need to escape to a dream world.

The flight to the inner man. Experimental psychology has suffered perhaps its greatest loss of manpower because competent investigators, beginning with a *descriptive* interest in behavior, have passed almost immediately to an *explanatory* preoccupation with what is going on inside the organism. In discussing this flight to the inner man I should like to believe that I am whipping a dead horse, but the fact remains that human behavior is still most commonly discussed in terms of psychic or physiological processes. A dualistic philosophy is not necessarily implied in either case for it may be argued, on the one hand, that the data of physics reduce at last to the direct experience of the physicist or, on the other, that behavior is only a highly organized set of biological facts. The nature of any real or fancied inner cause of behavior is not at issue; investigative practices suffer the same damage in any case.

Sometimes, especially among psychoanalysts, the inner men are said to be organized personalities whose activities lead at last to the behavior of the organism we observe. The commoner practice is to dissect the inner man and deal separately with his traits, perceptions, experiences, habits, ideas, and so on. In this way an observable subject matter is abandoned in favor of an inferred. It was Freud himself who insisted that mental processes could occur without "conscious participation" and that, since they could not always be directly observed, our knowledge of them must be inferential. Much of the machinery of psychoanalysis is concerned with the process of inference. In the analysis of behavior we may deal with *all* mental processes as inferences, whether or not they are said to be conscious. The resulting redefinition (call it operational if you like) conveniently omits the mentalistic dimension. At the same time, however, the explanatory force is lost. Inner entities or events do not "cause" behavior, nor does behavior "express" them. At best they are mediators, but the causal relationships between the terminal events which are mediated are inadequately represented by traditional devices. Mentalistic concepts may have had some heuristic value at one stage in the analysis of behavior, but it has long since been more profitable to abandon them. In an acceptable explanatory scheme the ultimate causes of behavior must be found *outside* the organism.

The *physiological* inner man is, of course, no longer wholly inferential. New methods and instruments have brought the nervous system and other mechanisms under direct observation. The new data have their own dimensions and require their own formulations. The behavioral facts in the field of learning, for example, are dealt with in terms appropriate to behavior, whereas electrical or chemical activities occurring at the same time demand a different conceptual framework. Similarly, the effects of deprivation and satiation on behavior are not the same as the events seen through a gastric fistula. Nor is emotion, studied as behavioral predisposition, capable of being analyzed in terms appropriate to pneumographs and electrocardiographs. Both sets of facts, and their appropriate concepts, are important – but they are *equally* important, not dependent one upon the other. Under the influence of a contrary philosophy of explanation, which insists upon the reductive priority of the inner event, many brilliant researchers who began with an interest in behavior, and might have advanced our knowledge of that field in many ways, have turned instead to the study of physiology. We cannot dispute the importance of their contributions; we can only imagine with regret what they might have done instead.

If we are to make a study of behavior sufficiently reinforcing to hold the interest of young people in competition with inner mechanisms, we must make clear that behavior is an acceptable subject matter in its own right, and that it can be studied with acceptable methods and without an eye to reductive explanation. The responses of an organism to a given environment are physical events. Modern methods of analysis reveal a degree of order in such a subject matter which compares favorably with that of any phenomena of comparable complexity. Behavior is not simply the result of more fundamental activities, to which our research must therefore be addressed, but an end in itself, the substance and importance of which are demonstrated in the practical results of an experimental analysis. We can predict and control behavior, we can modify it, we can construct it according to specifications – and all without answering the explanatory questions which have driven investigators into the study of the inner man. The young psychologist may contemplate a true science of behavior without anxiety.

The flight to laymanship. Experimental psychology has also had to contend with what is in essence a rejection of the whole scientific enterprise. In a review of a study of the psychological problems of aging, the reviewer comments upon

> a tendency in psychological thought which is returning to prominence after some years of relative disfavor. The statements have a certain refreshing directness and "elegance" in their approach to the study of human behavior. The sterile arguments of so-called "learning theory," the doctrinaire half-truths of the "schools," the panacea treatments of "systems" and the high-sounding, empty technical terms often found in psychological writings are conspicuous by their absence.

No one will want to defend "*sterile* arguments," "half-truths," "panaceas," or "*empty* technical terms," no matter what their sources, but the force of the passage is more than this. The author is rejecting all efforts to improve upon the psychology of the layman in approaching the problems of the aged. And many psychologists agree with him. "Enough of the lingo of the laboratory!" the argument runs. "Enough of clinical jargon! Enough of frightening equations! A plague on all your houses! Let us go back to common sense! Let us say what we want to say about human behavior in the well-worn but still useful vocabulary of the layman!" Whether this is a gesture of fatigue or impatience, or the expression of a desire to get on with practical matters at the expense of a basic understanding, it must be answered by anyone who defends a pure science. It would be easier to find the answer if experimental psychology had moved more rapidly toward a helpful conception of human behavior.

Some progress has been made in proving the superiority of scientific concepts over those of traditional usage. Consider, for example, two psychological accounts written in the vulgar tongue. First, a sample in the field of emotional behavior:

> The emotional temper of the type of juvenile delinquent just mentioned is as extraordinary as it is well-known. Far from being naturally peaceful, sympathetic, or generous, men who are excluded from the society of their fellow men become savage, cruel, and morose. The wanton destructiveness of the delinquent is not due to sudden bursts of fury, but to a deliberate and brooding resolve to wage war on everything.

The second has to do with intellect. It is an explanation of how a child learns to open a door by depressing a thumb latch and pushing against the door with his legs.

> Of course the child may have observed that doors are opened by grownups placing their hands on the handles, and having observed this the child may act by what is termed imitation. But the process as a whole is something more than imitative. Observation alone would be scarcely enough to enable the child to discover that the essential thing is not to grasp the handle but to depress the latch. Moreover, the child certainly never saw any grownup push the door with his legs as it is necessary for the child to do. This pushing action must be due to an originally deliberate intention to open the door, not to accidentally having found this action to have this effect.

Both passages make intelligible points and would conceivably be helpful in discussing juvenile delinquency or the teaching of children. But there is a trap. Actually the heroes of these pieces were not human at all. The quotations are slightly altered passages from Romanes's *Animal Intelligence*, published late in the last century (1892). The first describes the behavior of the prototype of all delinquents – the rogue elephant. The "child" of the second was a cat – possibly the very cat which set Thorndike to work to discover how animals do, indeed, learn to press latches.

The experimental analysis of behavior has clearly shown the practical and theoretical value of abandoning a commonsense way of talking about behavior and has demonstrated the advantages of an alternative account of emotion and intelligence. That is to say, it has done this for cats, rats, pigeons, and monkeys. Its successes are only slowly reaching into the field of human behavior – not because we any longer assume that people are fundamentally different but in part because an alternative method of analysis is felt to be available because of the scientist's membership in the human species. But the special knowledge resulting from self-observation can be given a formulation which preserves intact the notion of the continuity of species. Experimental methods can be applied first to the behavior of the Other One, and only later to the analysis of the behavior of the scientist himself. The value of this practice is demonstrated in the consistency of the resulting account and the effectiveness of the resulting technological control.

It is not difficult to explain the strength of traditional concepts. Many of those who discuss human behavior are speaking to laymen and must adapt their terms to their audience. The immediate effect of the lay vocabulary also gains strength from its deep entrenchment in the language. Our legal system is based on it, and the literature of ideas is couched in it. Moreover, from time to time efforts are made to rejuvenate the philosophical systems from which it came. Aristotle, through Thomas Aquinas, still speaks to some students of behavior. The very fact that Aristotle's psychology, scarcely modified, can be seriously championed in behavioral science today shows how little it has done to advance our understanding. Aristotelian physics, chemistry, and biology have enjoyed no such longevity. We may look forward to the early demise of this sole survivor of Greek science.

A return to the lay vocabulary of behavior cannot be justified. The move is a matter of motivation, competence, or the accessibility of goals. These are all irrelevant to the long-term achievement of a scientific account of behavior. No doubt, many pressing needs can still be most readily satisfied by casual discussion. In the long run, however, we shall need an effective understanding of human behavior – so that, in the example cited, we shall know the nature of the changes which take place as men and women grow old and shall, therefore, be in the most favorable position to do something about them. To reach that understanding we must recognize the limitations of the remedial patchwork which emerges from commonsense discussions and must be willing to resort to experiments which quite possibly involve complicated techniques and to theoretical treatments quite possibly expressed in difficult terms.

We have glanced briefly at four divertissements in the growth of a science of human behavior. Real Men, Mathematical Men, Inner Men, and Everyday Men – it would be a mistake to underestimate their seductive power. Together they constitute a formidable array of rival suitors, and to groom the Experimental Organism for this race may seem a hopeless enterprise. But it has a chance, for in the long run it offers the greatest net reinforcement to the scientist engaged in the study of behavior. An adequate theory of behavior, in the sense in which any empirical science leads eventually to a theoretical formulation, is possible and has enormous technical potential. The science of behavior has already seen physiological theories, mentalistic theories, and theories of the Conceptual Nervous System. These too may be divertissements of a sort. Let us now compare them with what the Experimental Organism has to offer.

Are theories of learning necessary?

Certain basic assumptions, essential to any scientific activity, are sometimes called theories. That nature is orderly rather than capricious is an example.

Certain statements are also theories simply to the extent that they are not yet facts. A scientist may guess at the result of an experiment before the experiment is carried out. The prediction and the later statement of result may be composed of the same terms in the same syntactic arrangement, the difference being in the degree of confidence. No empirical statement is wholly nontheoretical in this sense because evidence is never complete, nor is any prediction probably ever made wholly without evidence. The term *theory* will not refer here to statements of these sorts but rather to any explanation of an observed fact which appeals to events taking place somewhere else, at some other level of observation, described in different terms, and measured, if at all, in different dimensions.

Three types of theory in the field of learning satisfy this definition. The most characteristic is to be found in the field of physiological psychology. We are all familiar with the changes which are supposed to take place in the nervous system when an organism learns. Synaptic connections are made or broken, electrical fields are disrupted or reorganized, concentrations of ions are built up or allowed to diffuse away, and so on. In the science of neurophysiology statements of this sort are not necessarily theories in the present sense. But in a science of behavior, where we are concerned with whether or not an organism secretes saliva when a bell rings, or jumps toward a gray triangle, or says *bik* when a card reads *tuz*, or loves someone who resembles his mother, all statements about the nervous system are theories in the sense that they are not expressed in the same terms and could not be confirmed with the same methods of observation as the facts for which they are said to account.

A second type of learning theory is in practice not far from the physiological, although there is less agreement about the method of direct observation. Theories of this type have always dominated the field of human behavior. They consist of references to "mental" events, as in saying that an organism learns to behave in a certain way because it "finds something pleasant" or because it "expects something to happen." To the mentalistic psychologist these explanatory events are no more theoretical than synaptic connections to the neurophysiologist, but in a science of behavior they are theories because the methods and terms appropriate to the events to be explained differ from the methods and terms appropriate to the explaining events.

In a third type of learning theory the explanatory events are not directly observed. The suggestion in *The Behavior of Organisms* (Skinner 1938) that the letters CNS be regarded as representing not the Central Nervous System but the Conceptual Nervous System seems to have been taken seriously. Many theorists point out that they are not talking about the nervous system as an actual structure undergoing physiological or biochemical changes but only as a system with a certain dynamic output. Theories of this sort are multiplying fast, and so are parallel operational versions of mental events. A purely behavioral definition of expectancy has the advantage that the problem of mental observation is avoided and with it the problem of how a mental event can cause a physical one. But such theories do not go so far as to assert that the explanatory events are identical with the behavioral facts they purport to explain. A statement about behavior may support such a theory but will never resemble it in terms or syntax. Postulates are good examples. True postulates cannot become facts. Theorems may be deduced from them which, as tentative statements about behavior, may or may not be confirmed, but theorems are not theories in the present sense. Postulates remain theories to the end.

It is not the purpose of this paper to show that any of these theories cannot be put in good scientific order, or that the events to which they refer may not actually occur or be studied by appropriate sciences. It would be foolhardy to deny the achievements of theories of this sort in the history of science. The question of whether they are necessary, however, has other implications and is worth asking. If the answer is no, then it may be possible to argue effectively against theory in the field of learning. A science of behavior must eventually deal with behavior in its relation to certain manipulable variables. Theories – whether neural, mental, or conceptual – talk about intervening steps in these relationships. But instead of prompting us to search for and explore relevant variables, they frequently have quite the opposite effect. When we attribute behavior to a neural or mental event, real or conceptual, we are likely to forget that we still have the task of accounting for the neural or mental event. When we assert that an animal acts in a given way because it expects to receive food, then what began as the task of accounting for learned behavior becomes the task of accounting for expectancy. The problem is at least equally complex and probably more difficult. We are likely to close our eyes to it and to use the theory to give us answers in place of the answers we might find through further study. It might be argued that the principal function of learning theory to date has been, not to suggest appropriate research, but to create a false sense of security, an unwarranted satisfaction with the status quo.

Research designed with respect to theory is also likely to be wasteful. That a theory generates research does not prove its value unless the research is valuable. Much useless experimentation results from theories, and much energy and skill are absorbed by them. Most theories are eventually overthrown, and the greater part of the associated research is discarded. This could be justified if it were true that productive research requires a theory – as is, of course, often claimed. It is argued that research would be aimless and disorganized without a theory to guide it. The view is supported by psychological texts which take their cue from the logicians rather than empirical science and describe thinking as necessarily involving stages of hypothesis, deduction, experimental test, and confirmation. But this is not the way most scientists actually work. It is possible to design significant experiments for other reasons, and the possibility to be examined is that such research will lead more directly to the kind of information which a science usually accumulates.

The alternatives are at least worth considering. How much can be done without theory? What other sorts of scientific activity are possible? And what light do alternative practices throw upon our present preoccupation with theory?

It would be inconsistent to try to answer these questions at a theoretical level. Let us therefore turn to some experimental material in three areas in which theories of learning now flourish and raise the question of the function of theory in a more concrete fashion.

The basic datum in learning. What actually happens when an organism learns is not an easy question to answer. Those who are interested in a science of behavior will insist that learning is a change in behavior, but they tend to avoid explicit references to responses or acts as such. "Learning is adjustment or adaptation to a situation." But of what stuff are adjustments and adaptations made? Are they data, or inferences from data? "Learning is improvement." But improvement in what? And from whose point of view? "Learning is restoration of equilibrium." But what is in equilibrium and how is it put there? "Learning is problem solving." But what are the physical dimensions of a problem – or of a solution? Definitions of this sort show an unwillingness to take what appears before the eyes in a learning experiment as a basic datum. Particular observations seem too trivial. An error score falls; but we are not ready to say that this is learning rather than merely the result of learning. An organism meets a criterion of 10 successful trials; but an arbitrary criterion is at variance with our conception of the generality of the learning process.

This is where theory steps in. If it is not the time required to get out of a puzzle box which changes in learning, but rather the strength of a bond, or the conductivity of a neural pathway, or the excitatory potential of a habit, then problems seem to vanish. Getting out of a box faster and faster is not learning; it is merely performance. The learning goes on somewhere else, in a different dimensional system. And although the time required depends upon arbitrary conditions, often varies discontinuously, and is subject to reversal of magnitude, we feel sure that the learning process itself is continuous, orderly, and beyond the accidents of measurement. Nothing could better illustrate the use of theory as a refuge from the data.

But we must eventually get back to an observable datum. If learning is the process we suppose it to be, then it must appear so in the situations in which we study it. Even if the basic process belongs to some other dimensional system, our measures must have relevant and comparable properties. But productive experimental situations are hard to find, particularly if we accept certain plausible restrictions. To show an orderly change in the behavior of the *average* rat or ape or child is not enough, since learning is a process in the behavior of the individual. To record the beginning and end of learning of a few discrete steps will not suffice, since a series of cross-sections will not give complete coverage of a continuous process. The dimensions of the change must spring from the behavior itself; they must not be imposed by an external judgment of success or failure or an external criterion of completeness. But when we review the literature with these requirements in mind, we find little justification for the theoretical process in which we take so much comfort.

The energy level or work output of behavior, for example, does not change in appropriate ways. In the sort of behavior adapted to the Pavlovian experiment (respondent behavior) there may be a progressive increase in the magnitude of response during learning. But we do not shout our responses louder and louder as we learn verbal material, nor does a rat press a lever harder and harder as conditioning proceeds. In operant behavior the energy or magnitude of response changes significantly only when some arbitrary value is differentially reinforced – when such a change is what is learned.

The emergence of a right response in competition with wrong responses is another datum frequently used in the study of learning. The maze and the discrimination box yield results which may be reduced to these terms. But a behavior ratio of right versus wrong cannot yield a continuously changing measure in a single experiment on a single organism. The point at which one response takes precedence over another cannot give us the whole history of the change in either response. Averaging curves for groups of trials or organisms will not solve this problem.

Attention has been given to latency, the relevance of which, like that of energy level, is suggested by the properties of conditioned and unconditioned reflexes. But in operant behavior the relation to a stimulus is different. A measure of latency involves other considerations, as inspection of any case will show. Most operant responses may be emitted in the absence of what is regarded as a relevant stimulus. In such a case the response is likely to appear before the stimulus is presented. It is no solution to escape this embarrassment by locking a lever so that an organism cannot press it until the stimulus is presented, since we can scarcely be content with temporal relations which have been forced into compliance with our expectations. Runway latencies are subject to this objection. In a typical experiment the door of a starting box is opened and the time which elapses before a rat leaves the box is measured. Opening the door is not only a stimulus, it is a change in the situation which makes the response possible for the first time. The time measured is by no means as simple as a latency and requires another formulation. A great deal depends upon what the rat is doing at the moment the stimulus is presented. Some experimenters wait until the rat is facing the door, but to do so is to tamper with the measurement being taken. If, on the other hand, the door is opened without reference to what the rat is doing, the first major effect is the conditioning of favorable waiting behavior. The rat eventually stays near and facing the door. The resulting shorter starting time is due not to a reduction in the latency of a response, but to the conditioning of favorable preliminary behavior. Latencies in a single organism do not follow a simple learning process.

Another datum to be examined is the rate at which a response is emitted. Fortunately the story here is different. We study this rate by designing a situation in which a response may be freely repeated, choosing a response (for example, touching or pressing a small lever or key) which may be easily observed and counted. The responses may be recorded on a polygraph, but a more convenient form is a cumulative curve from which rate of responding is immediately read as slope. The rate at which a response is emitted in such a situation comes close to our preconception of the learning process. As the organism learns, the rate rises. As it unlearns (for example, in extinction) the rate falls. Various sorts of discriminative stimuli may be brought into control of the response with corresponding modifications of the rate. Motivational changes alter the rate in a sensitive way. So do those events which we speak of as generating emotion. The range through which the rate varies significantly may be as great as of the order of 1,000:1. Changes in rate are satisfactorily smooth in the individual case, so that it is not necessary to average cases. A given value is often quite stable: In the pigeon a rate of 4,000–5,000 responses per hour may be maintained without interruption for as long as 15 hours.

Rate of responding appears to be the only datum which varies significantly and in the expected direction under conditions which are relevant to the "learning process." We may, therefore, be tempted to accept it as our long-sought-for measure of strength of bond, excitatory potential, and the like. Once in possession of an effective datum, however, we may feel little need for any theoretical construct of this sort. Progress in a scientific field usually waits upon the discovery of a satisfactory dependent variable. Until such a variable has been discovered, we resort to theory. The entities which have figured so prominently in learning theory have served mainly as substitutes for a directly observable and productive datum. They have little reason to survive when such a datum has been found.

It is no accident that rate of responding is successful as a datum because it is particularly appropriate to the fundamental task of a science of behavior. If we are to predict behavior (and possibly to control it), we must deal with *probability of response*. The business of a science of behavior is to evaluate this probability and explore the conditions which determine it. Strength of bond, expectancy, excitatory potential, and so on, carry the notion of probability in an easily imagined form, but the additional properties suggested by these terms have hindered the search for suitable measures. Rate of responding is not a "measure" of probability, but it is the only appropiate datum in a formulation in these terms.

As other scientific disciplines can attest, probabilities are not easy to handle. We wish to make statements about the likelihood of occurrence of a single future response, but our data are in the form of frequencies of responses which have already occurred. These responses were presumably similar to each other and to the response to be predicted. But this raises the troublesome problem of response instance versus response class. Precisely what responses are we to take into account in predicting a future instance? Certainly not the responses made by a population of different organisms, for such a statistical datum raises more problems than it solves. To consider the frequency of repeated responses in an individual demands something like the experimental situation just described.

This solution of the problem of a basic datum is based upon the view that operant behavior is essentially an emissive phenomenon. Latency and magnitude of response fail as measures because they do not take this into account. They are concepts appropriate to the field of the reflex, where the all but invariable control exercised by the eliciting stimulus makes the notion of probability of response trivial. Consider, for example, the case of latency. Because of our acquaintance with simple reflexes we infer that a response which is more likely to be emitted will be emitted more quickly. But is this true? What can the word *quickly* mean? Probability of response, as well as prediction of response, is concerned with the moment of emission. This is a point in time, but it does not have the temporal dimension of a latency. The execution may take time after the response has been initiated, but the moment of occurrence has no duration. In recognizing the emissive character of operant behavior and the central position of probability of response as a datum, we see that latency is irrelevant to our present task.

Various objections have been made to the use of rate of responding as a basic datum. For example, such a program may seem to bar us from dealing with many events which are unique occurrences in the life of the individual. People do not decide upon a career, get married, make a million dollars, or get killed in an accident often enough to make a rate of response meaningful. But these activities are not responses. They are not simple unitary events lending themselves to prediction as such. If we are to predict marriage, success, accidents, and so on, in anything more than statistical terms, we must deal with the smaller units of behavior which lead to and compose these unitary episodes. If the units appear in repeatable form, the present analysis may be applied. In the field of learning a similar objection takes the form of asking how the present analysis may be extended to experimental situations in which it is impossible to observe frequencies. It does not follow that learning is not taking place in such situations. The notion of probability is usually extrapolated to cases in which a frequency analysis cannot be carried out. In the field of behavior we arrange a situation in which frequencies are available as data, but we use the notion of probability in analyzing and formulating instances or even types of behavior which are not susceptible to this analysis.

Another common objection is that a rate of response is just a set of latencies and hence not a new datum at all. This is easily shown to be wrong. When we measure the time elapsing between two responses, we are in no doubt as to what the organism was doing when we started our clock. We know that it was just executing a response. This is a natural zero – quite unlike the arbitrary point from which latencies are measured. The free repetition of a response yields a rhythmic or periodic datum very different from latency. Many periodic physical processes suggest parallels.

We do not choose rate of responding as a basic datum merely from an analysis of the fundamental task of a science of behavior. The ultimate appeal is to its success in an experimental science. The material which follows is offered as a sample of what can be done. It is not intended as a complete demonstration, but it should confirm the fact that when we are in possession of a datum which varies in a significant fashion, we are less likely to resort to theoretical entities carrying the notion of probability of response.

Why learning occurs. We may define learning as a change in probability of response, but we must also specify the conditions under which it comes about. To do this we must survey some of the independent variables of which probability of response is a function. Here we meet another kind of learning theory.

An effective classroom demonstration of the Law of Effect may be arranged in the following way. A pigeon, reduced to 80% of its ad lib weight, is habituated to a small, semicircular amphitheater and is fed there for several days from a food hopper, which the experimenter presents by closing a hand switch. The demonstration consists of establishing a selected response by suitable reinforcement with food. For example, by sighting across the amphitheater at a scale on the opposite wall, it is possible to present the hopper whenever the top of the pigeon's head rises above a given mark. Higher and higher marks are chosen until, within a few minutes, the pigeon is walking about the cage with its head held as high as possible. In another demonstration the bird is conditioned to strike a marble placed on the floor of the amphitheater. This can be done in a few minutes by reinforcing successive steps. Food is presented first when the bird is merely moving near the marble, later when it looks down in the direction of the marble, later still when it moves its head toward the marble, and finally when it pecks it. Anyone who has seen such a demonstration knows that the Law of Effect is no theory. It simply specifies a procedure for altering the probability of a chosen response.

But when we try to say *why* reinforcement has this effect, theories arise. Learning is said to take place because the reinforcement is pleasant, satisfying, tension reducing, and so on. The converse process of extinction is explained with comparable theories. If the rate of responding is first raised to a high point by reinforcement and reinforcement is then withheld, the response is observed to occur less and less frequently thereafter. One common theory explains this by asserting that a state is built up which suppresses the behavior. This "experimental inhibition" or "reaction inhibition" must be assigned to a different dimensional system, since nothing at the level of behavior corresponds to opposed processes of excitation and inhibition. Rate of responding is simply increased by one operation and decreased by another. Certain effects commonly interpreted as showing release from a suppressing force may be interpreted in other ways. Disinhibition, for example, is not necessarily the uncovering of suppressed strength: It may be a sign of supplementary strength from an extraneous variable. The process of spontaneous recovery, often cited to support the notion of suppression, has an alternative explanation, to be noted in a moment.

Level of motivation is one variable to be taken into account. Level of hunger determines the slope of the extinction curve but not its curvature. Another variable, difficulty of response, is especially relevant because it has been used to test the theory of reaction inhibition (Mowrer & Jones 1943), on the assumption that a response requiring considerable energy will build up more reaction inhibition than an easy response and lead, therefore, to faster extinction. The theory requires that the curvature of the extinction curve be altered, not merely its slope. Yet there is evidence that difficulty of response acts like level of hunger simply to alter the slope. A pigeon is suspended in a jacket which confines its wings and legs but leaves its head and neck free to respond to a key and a food magazine. Its behavior in this situation is quantitatively much like that of a bird moving freely in an experimental box, but the use of the jacket has the advantage that the response to the key can be made easy or difficult by changing the distance the bird must reach. The change from one position to another is felt immediately. If repeated responding in a difficult position were to build a considerable amount of reaction inhibition, we should expect the rate to be low for some little time after returning to an easy response. Contrariwise, if an easy response were to build little reaction inhibition, we should expect a fairly high rate of responding for some time after a difficult position is assumed. Nothing like this occurs. The "more rapid extinction" of a difficult response is an ambiguous expression.

One way of considering the question of why extinction curves are curved is to regard extinction as a process of exhaustion comparable to the loss of heat from source to sink or the fall in the level of a reservoir when an outlet is opened. Conditioning builds up a predisposition to respond – a "reserve" – which extinction exhausts. This is perhaps a defensible description at the level of behavior. The reserve is not necessarily a theory in the present sense, since it is not assigned to a different dimensional system. It could be operationally defined as a predicted extinction curve, even though, linguistically, it makes a statement about the momentary condition of a response. But it is not a particularly useful concept, nor does the view that extinction is a process of exhaustion add much to the observed fact that extinction curves are curved in a certain way.

There are, however, two variables which affect the rate, both of which operate during extinction to alter the curvature. One of these falls within the field of emotion. When we fail to reinforce a response which has previously been reinforced, we not only initiate a process of extinction, we set up an emotional response – perhaps what is often meant by frustration. The pigeon coos in an identifiable pattern, moves rapidly about the cage, defecates, or flaps its wings rapidly in a squatting position which suggests treading (mating) behavior. This competes with the response of striking a key and is perhaps enough to account for the decline in rate in early extinction. It is also possible that the probability of a response based upon food deprivation is directly reduced as part of such an emotional reaction. Whatever its nature, the effect of this variable is eliminated through adaptation. Repeated extinction curves become smoother, and in some schedules there is little or no evidence of an emotional modification of rate.

A second variable has a much more serious effect. Maximal responding during extinction is obtained only when the conditions under which the response was reinforced are precisely reproduced. A rat conditioned in the presence of a light will not extinguish fully in the absence of the light. It will begin to respond more rapidly when the light is again introduced. This is true for other kinds of stimuli. The pitch of an incidental tone or the shape of a pattern, if present during conditioning, will to some extent control the rate of responding during extinction. Let us suppose that all responses to a key have been reinforced and that each has been followed by a short period of eating. When we extinguish the behavior, we create a situation in which responses are not reinforced, in which no eating takes place, and in which there are probably new emotional responses. The very conditions of extinction seem to presuppose a growing novelty in the experimental situation. Is this why the extinction curve is curved?

Some evidence comes from the data of "spontaneous recovery." Even after prolonged extinction an organism will often respond at a higher rate for at least a few moments at the beginning of another session. One theory contends that this shows spontaneous recovery from some sort of inhibition, but another explanation is possible. No matter how carefully an animal is handled, the stimulation coincident with the beginning of an experiment must be extensive and unlike anything occurring in the later part of an experimental period. Responses have been reinforced in the presence of, or shortly following, this stimulation. In extinction it is present for only a few moments. When the organism is again placed in the experimental situation the stimulation is restored; further responses are emitted. The only way to achieve full extinction in the presence of the stimulation of starting an experiment is to start the experiment repeatedly.

Other evidence of the effect of novelty comes from the study of periodic reinforcement. The fact that intermittent reinforcement produces bigger extinction curves than continuous reinforcement is a troublesome difficulty for those who expect a simple relation between number of reinforcements and number of responses in extinction. But this relation is actually quite complex. One result of periodic reinforcement is that emotional changes adapt out. This may be responsible for the smoothness of subsequent extinction curves but probably not for their greater extent. The latter may be attributed to the lack of novelty in the extinction situation. Under periodic reinforcement many responses are made without reinforcement and when no eating has recently taken place. The situation in extinction is therefore not wholly novel.

Periodic rather than aperiodic reinforcement, however, is not a simple solution (what was here called "periodic reinforcement" has since come to be known as the fixed-interval schedule, and "aperiodic reinforcement" as the variable-interval schedule of reinforcement). If we reinforce on a regular schedule – say, every minute – the organism soon forms a discrimination. Little or no responding occurs just after reinforcement, since stimulation from eating is correlated with absence of subsequent reinforcement. The discrimination yields a pause after each reinforcement. As a result of this discrimination the bird is almost always responding rapidly when reinforced. This is the basis for another discrimination. By responding the pigeon creates a stimulating condition previously optimally correlated with reinforcement.

Further study of reinforcing schedules may or may not answer the question of whether the novelty appearing in the extinction situation is entirely responsible for the curvature. It would appear to be necessary to make the conditions prevailing during extinction identical with the conditions prevailing during conditioning. This may be impossible, but in that case the question is academic. The hypothesis, meanwhile, is not a theory in the present sense, since it makes no statements about a parallel process in any other universe of discourse. It is true that it appeals to stimulation generated in part by the pigeon's own behavior. This may be difficult to specify or manipulate, but it is not theoretical in the present sense. So long as we are willing to assume a one-to-one correspondence between action and stimulation, a physical specification is possible.

The object of the study of extinction is an economical description of the conditions prevailing during reinforcement and extinction and of the relations between them. In using rate of responding as a basic datum we may appeal to conditions which are observable and manipulable and we may express the relations between them in objective terms. To the extent that our datum makes this possible, it reduces the need for theory. When we observe a pigeon emitting 7,000 responses at a constant rate without reinforcement, we are not likely to explain an extinction curve containing perhaps a few hundred responses by appeal to the piling up of reaction inhibition or any other fatigue product. Research which is conducted without commitment to theory is more likely to carry the study of extinction into new areas and new orders of magnitude. By hastening the accumulation of data, we speed the departure of theories. If the theories have played no part in the design of our experiments, we need not be sorry to see them go.

Complex learning. A third type of learning theory is illustrated by terms like *preferring*, *choosing*, *discriminating*, and *matching*. An effort may be made to define these solely in terms of behavior, but in traditional practice they refer to processes in another dimensional system. A response to one of two available stimuli may be called choice, but it is commoner to say that it is the result of choice, meaning by the latter a theoretical prebehavioral activity. The higher mental processes are the best examples of theories of this sort; neurological parallels have not been well worked out. The appeal to theory is encouraged by the fact that choosing (like discriminating, matching, and so on) is not a particular piece of behavior. It is not a response or an act with specified topography. The term characterizes a larger segment of behavior in relation to other variables or events. Can we formulate and study the behavior to which these terms would usually be applied without recourse to the theories which generally accompany them?

Discrimination is a relatively simple case. Suppose we find that the probability of emission of a given response is not significantly affected by changing from one of two stimuli to the other. We then make reinforcement of the response contingent solely upon the presence of one. The well-established result is that the probability of response remains high under this stimulus and reaches a very low point under the other. We say that the organism now discriminates between the stimuli. But discrimination is not itself an action, or necessarily even a unique process. Problems in the field of discrimination may be stated in other terms. How much induction obtains between stimuli of different magnitudes or classes? What are the smallest differences in stimuli which yield a difference in control? And so on. Questions of this sort do not presuppose theoretical activities in other dimensional systems.

A somewhat larger segment must be specified in dealing with the behavior of choosing one of two concurrent stimuli. This has been studied in the pigeon by examining responses to two keys differing in position (right or left) or in some property like color randomized with respect to position. By occasionally reinforcing a response on one key or the other without favoring either key, we obtain equal rates of responding on the two keys. The behavior approaches a simple alternation from one key to the other. This follows the rule that tendencies to respond eventually correspond to the probabilities of reinforcement. Given a system in which one key or the other is occasionally connected with the magazine by an external clock, then if the right key has just been struck, the probability of reinforcement via the left key is higher than that via the right since a greater interval of time has elapsed during which the clock may have closed the circuit to the left key. But the bird's behavior does not correspond to this probability merely out of respect for mathematics. The specific result of such a contingency of reinforcement is that changing to the other key and striking is more often reinforced than striking the same key a second time. We are no longer dealing with just two responses. To analyze "choice" we must consider a single final response, striking, without respect to the position or color of the key, and in addition the responses of changing from one key or color to the other.

Quantitative results are compatible with this analysis. If we periodically reinforce responses to the right key only, the rate of responding on the right will rise while that on the left will fall. The response of changing from right to left is never reinforced while that of changing from left to right is reinforced occasionally. When the bird is striking on the right, there is no great tendency to change keys; when it is striking on the left, there is a strong tendency to change. Many more responses come to be made to the right key. The need for considering the behavior of changing over is clearly shown if we now reverse these conditions and reinforce responses to the left key only. The ultimate result is a high rate of responding on the left key and a low rate on the right. By reversing the conditions again the high rate can be shifted back to the right key. The mean rate shows no significant variation, since periodic reinforcement is continued on the same schedule. The mean rate shows the condition of strength of the response of striking a key regardless of position. The distribution of responses between right and left depends upon the relative strength of the responses of changing over. If this were simply a case of the extinction of one response and the concurrent reconditioning of another, the mean rate would not remain approximately constant since reconditioning occurs much more rapidly than extinction.

What is called "preference" enters into this formulation. At any stage of the process preference might be expressed in terms of the relative rates of responding to the two keys. This preference, however, is not in striking a key but in changing from one key to the other. The probability that the bird will strike a key regardless of its identifying properties behaves independently of the preferential response of changing from one key to the other.

These formulations of discrimination and choosing enable us to deal with what is generally regarded as a much more complex process – matching to sample. Suppose we arrange three translucent keys, each of which can be illuminated with red or green light. The middle key functions as the sample, and we color it either red or green in random order. We color one of the two side keys red and the other green, also in random order. The "problem" is to strike the side key which corresponds in color to the middle key. There are only four three-key patterns in such a case, and it is possible that a pigeon could learn to make an appropriate response to each pattern. This does not happen. If we simply present a series of settings of the three colors and reinforce successful responses, the pigeon will strike the side keys without respect to color or pattern and be reinforced 50% of the time. This is, in effect, a schedule of "fixed ratio" reinforcement which is adequate to maintain a high rate of responding.

Nevertheless it is possible to get a pigeon to match to sample by reinforcing the discriminative responses of striking red after being stimulated by red and striking green after being stimulated by green while extinguishing the other two possibilities. The difficulty is in arranging the proper stimulation at the time of the response. The sample might be made conspicuous – for example, by having the sample color in the general illumination of the experimental box. In such a case the pigeon would learn to strike red keys in a red light and green keys in a green light (assuming a neutral illumination of the background of the keys). But a procedure which holds more closely to the notion of matching is to induce the pigeon to "look at the sample" by means of separate reinforcement. We may do this by presenting the color on the middle key first, leaving the side keys uncolored. A response to the middle key is then reinforced (secondarily) by illuminating the side keys. The pigeon learns to make two responses in quick sucession – to the middle key and then to one side key. The response to the side key follows quickly upon the visual stimulation from the middle key, which is the requisite condition for a discrimination. Successful matching was readily established in all 10 pigeons tested with this technique. Choosing the opposite is also easily set up. The discriminative response of striking red after being stimulated by red is apparently no easier to establish than striking red after being stimulated by green. When the response is to a key of the same color, however, generalization may make it possible for the bird to match a new color. (Subsequent research has shown that such generalization is difficult to demonstrate with pigeons.)

Even when matching behavior has been well established, the bird will not respond correctly if all three keys are now presented at the same time. The bird does not possess strong behavior of looking at the sample. The experimenter must maintain a separate reinforcement to keep this behavior in strength. In monkeys, apes, and human subjects the ultimate success in choosing is apparently sufficient to reinforce and maintain the behavior of looking at the sample. It is possible that this species difference is simply a difference in the temporal relations required for reinforcement.

The behavior of matching survives unchanged when all reinforcement is withheld. An intermediate case has been established in which the correct matching response is only periodically reinforced. In one experiment one color appeared on the middle key for one minute; it was then changed or not changed, at random, to the other color. A response to this key illuminated the side keys, one red and one green, in random order. A response to a side key cut off the illumination to both side keys, until the middle key had again been struck.

Pigeons which have acquired matching behavior under continuous reinforcement have maintained this behavior when reinforced no oftener than once per minute on the average. They may make thousands of matching responses per hour while being reinforced for no more than 60 of them. This schedule will not necessarily develop matching behavior in a naive bird, for the problem can be solved in three ways. The bird will receive practically as many reinforcements if it responds to (1) only one key or (2) only one color, since the programming of the experiment makes any persistent response eventually the correct one.

These experiments on a few higher processes have necessarily been very briefly described. They are not offered as proving that theories of learning are not necessary, but they may suggest an alternative program in this difficult area. The data in the field of the higher mental processes transcend single responses or single stimulus–response relationships. But they appear to be susceptible to formulation in terms of the differentiation of concurrent responses, the discrimination of stimuli, the establishment of various sequences of responses, and so on. There seems to be no a priori reason why a complete account is not possible without appeal to theoretical processes in other dimensional systems.

Conclusion. Perhaps to do without theories altogether is a tour de force which is too much to expect as a general practice. Theories are fun. But it is possible that the most rapid progress toward an understanding of learning may be made by research which is not designed to test theories. An adequate impetus is supplied by the inclination to obtain data showing orderly changes characteristic of the learning process. An acceptable scientific program is to collect data of this sort and to relate them to manipulable variables, selected for study through a commonsense exploration of the field.

This does not exclude the possibility of theory in another sense. Beyond the collection of uniform relationships lies the need for a formal representation of the data reduced to a minimal number of terms. A theoretical construction may yield greater generality than any assemblage of facts. But such a construction will not refer to another dimensional system and will not, therefore, fall within our present definition. It will not stand in the way of our search for functional relations because it will arise only after relevant variables have been found and studied. Though it may be difficult to understand, it will not be easily misunderstood, and it will have none of the objectionable effects of the theories here considered.

We do not seem to be ready for theory in this sense. At the moment we make little effective use of empirical, let alone rational, equations. The data from the original version of this paper could have been fairly closely fitted. But the most elementary preliminary research shows that there are many relevant variables, and until their importance has been experimentally determined, an equation which allows for them will have so many arbitrary constants that a good fit will be a matter of course and cause for very little satisfaction.

Some afterthoughts

In 1950 I asked the question, Are theories of learning necessary?, and suggested that the answer was no. I soon found myself representing a position which has been described as a Grand Anti-Theory (Westby 1966). Fortunately, I had defined my terms. The word *theory* was to mean "any explanation of an observed fact which appeals to events taking place somewhere else, at some other level of observation, described in different terms, and measured, if at all, in different dimensions" – events, for example, in the real nervous system, the conceptual system, or the mind. I argued that theories of this sort had not stimulated good research on learning and that they misrepresented the facts to be accounted for, gave false assurances about the state of our knowledge, and led to the continued use of methods which should be abandoned.

A reputation as an antitheorist is easily acquired by anyone who neglects hypothetico-deductive methods. When a subject matter is very large (for example, the universe as a whole) or very small (for example, subatomic particles) or for any reason inaccessible, we cannot manipulate variables or observe effects as we should like to do. We therefore make tentative or hypothetical statements about them, deduce theorems which refer to accessible states of affairs, and by checking the theorems confirm or refute our hypotheses. The achievements of the hypothetico-deductive method, where appropriate, have been brilliant. Newton set the pattern in his *Principia*, and the great deductive theorists who followed him have been given a prominent place in the history of science.

Their significance has nevertheless probably been exaggerated, and in part for rather trivial reasons. Unlike direct observation and description, the construction of a hypothesis suggests mysterious intellectual activities. Like those who are said to be capable of extrasensory perception, the hypothesis makers seem to display knowledge which they cannot have acquired through ordinary channels. That is not actually the case, but the resulting prestige is real enough, and it has had unfortunate consequences.

For one thing, the method tends to be used when it is not needed, when direct observation is not only possible but more effective. To guess who is calling when the phone rings seems somehow more admirable than to pick up the phone and find out, although it is no more valuable. The extrasensory procedure is similar: To guess the pattern on a card and then turn the card over and look at the pattern is to make and confirm a hypothesis. Such performances command attention even when the results are trivial. Like those body builders who flex their muscles in setting-up exercises or handstands on the beach, hypothesis makers are admired even though their hypotheses are useless, just as extrasensory perceivers are admired even though they never make practical predictions of the movements of armies or fluctuations in the stock market. (Like that third specialist in unproductive behavior, the gambler, both are sustained by occasional hits – and by very rare hits, indeed, if they have been reinforced on a variable-ratio schedule favorably programmed.)

The hypothetico-deductive method and the mystery which surrounds it have been perhaps most harmful in misrepresenting ways in which people think. Scientific behavior is possibly the most complex subject matter ever submitted to scientific analysis, and we are still far from having an adequate account of it. Why does a scientist examine and explore a given subject? What rate of discovery will sustain his behavior in doing so? What precurrent behaviors improve his chances of success and extend the adequacy and scope of his descriptions? What steps does he take in moving from protocol to general statement? These are difficult questions, and there are many more like them. The scientist is under the control of very complex contingencies of reinforcement. Some of the more obvious ones have been analyzed, and a few rules have been extracted, particularly by logicians, mathematicians, statisticians, and scientific methodologists. For a number of reasons these rules apply mainly to verbal behavior, including hypothesis making and deduction. Students who learn to follow them no doubt behave in effective and often indispensable ways, but we should not suppose that in doing so they display the full range of scientific behavior. Nor should we teach such rules as if they exhausted scientific methods. Empirical surveys (for example, *An Introduction to Scientific Research* by E. Bright Wilson, 1952) show a better balance in representing the contingencies under which scientists actually work, but a functional analysis which not only clarifies the nature of scientific inquiry but suggests how it may be most effectively imparted to young scientists still lies in the future.

Behavior is one of those subject matters which do not call for hypothetico-deductive methods. Both behavior itself and most of the variables of which it is a function are usually conspicuous. (Responses which are of very small magnitude or difficult to reach are notable exceptions, but the problems they pose are technical rather than methodological.) If hypotheses commonly appear in the study of behavior, it is only because the investigator has turned his attention to inaccessible events – some of them fictitious, others irrelevant. For Clark Hull (1943) the science of behavior eventually became the study of central processes, mainly conceptual but often ascribed to the nervous system. The processes were not directly observed and seemed therefore to require hypotheses and deductions, but the facts were observable. Only so long as a generalization gradient, for example, remained a hypothetical feature of an inner process was it necessary to determine its shape by making hypotheses and confirming or disproving theorems derived from them. When gradients began to be directly observed, the hypothetico-deductive procedures became irrelevant.

Cognitive psychologists have promoted the survival of another inaccessible world to which deductive methods seem appropriate. An introspectionist may claim to observe some of the products and by-products of mental processes, but the processes themselves are not directly perceived, and statements about them are therefore hypothetical. The Freudian mental apparatus has also required a deductive approach, as have the traits, abilities, and factors derived from "mental measurements." We can avoid hypothetico-deductive methods in all these fields by formulating the data without reference to cognitive processes, mental apparatuses, or traits. Many physiological explanations of behavior seem at the moment to call for hypotheses, but the future lies with techniques of direct observation which will make them unnecessary.

Some of the questions to which a different kind of theory may be addressed are: What aspects of behavior are significant? Of what variables are changes in these aspects a function? How are the relations among behavior and its controlling variables to be brought together in characterizing an organism as a system? What methods are appropriate in studying such a system experimentally? Under what conditions does such an analysis yield a technology of behavior and what issues arise in its application? These are not questions to which a hypothetico-deductive method is appropriate. They are nevertheless important questions, for the future of a science of behavior depends upon the answers.

POSTSCRIPT

Two papers published in 1950 and 1961 can scarcely be presented as a review of current methods, and "Methods" is certainly not to be read as such. What, then, is it? I would call it a defense of the experimental method in the analysis of behavior and a formulation of behavior based as closely as possible on experimental results, as contrasted with the traditional formulations inherent in most languages and derived from historical processes primarily of historical interest only. I was objecting to the use of traditional terms and principles on the part of otherwise distinguished figures and complaining that psychologists had turned to fields of human behavior or methods which were not primarily experimental. Statistics had its place but, particularly at the time I was writing, it was being strongly promoted in ways which I thought replaced possibly more effective experimental methods.

I am not against applying the terms and principles taken from the laboratory to the problems of people at large. In fact, I think the experimental analysis of behavior has made a greater contribution in that direction than other fields of psychology. And I still believe that even a modest improvement in the kind of understanding of human behavior that follows from laboratory research could help far more people than can be helped face to face by a therapist in one lifetime.

I regard methematical model building as an enjoyable intellectual exercise but, again, it is a threat if it draws young people away from laboratory research. Even in the laboratory much depends upon the questions being asked. The effort to understand the mental life responsible for behavior has directed research away from the environmental variables which make a simpler account possible. The second half of "Methods" supplies many examples. The afterthoughts were published later – in 1969 – and I would not change them substantially today.

In summary, the target article pleads with psychologists not to abandon an experimental method determined as far as possible by a subject matter rather than by theories about a subject matter. It asserts the priority of experimentation even when, as in physics, the great achievements seem to be theories. It opposes speculation about inner causes and cautions against those blandishments of gratitude which come from helping some people here and now rather than the much larger numbers who will appear in the future.

COMMENTARIES AND RESPONSES

Real people, ordinary language, and natural measurement

Samuel M. Deitz

Educational Foundations Department, Georgia State University

It is difficult to argue with the major points of Professor Skinner's "Methods." How could one disagree with the statement that a scientific psychology demands a careful, complete, experimental analysis of the variables responsible for the behavior of individual organisms? An accurate account of the effects of those variables is required if psychologists are to understand, let alone predict and control, the important or trivial activities of humans or other animals. Whether such an analysis provides all the answers is at this point an irrelevant question. Until those variables are investigated thoroughly, speculations about physiological, mental, or conceptual variables are at best premature and at worst, as Skinner says, a hindrance.

Such premature and possibly unnecessary speculations are what Skinner argues against when discussing theory. He calls for theory that closely parallels the data of psychology, data that are always some form of human verbal or nonverbal behavior. This form of theory is tied to the variables investigated and is, if nothing else, verifiable, possibly a restriction for some theorists but one that should be welcome and cherished. Such theory may not be as exciting as speculating about mental or physiological events, but it also lacks jumps, gaps, and flights of fancy.

The flights Skinner discusses are not ones of fancy, however, and deserve some comment. First of all, I'm not sure he should even be talking of flights at all. Psychologists have not actually left the laboratory; many were never there in the first place. Consistently throughout the history of psychology, psychologists have devoted their time to real people, mathematical models, and inner man. The cognitive science of today, for example, with minor exceptions, is not entirely unlike the cognitive psychology at the turn of the century and generally does not reflect a new point of view.

What is most interesting to me about the actual flights from the laboratory is that they have been taken by many expermental analysts of behavior. I could speculate as to the misguided reasons that led these behaviorists to flee to inner man or mathematical models, but it is difficult to surpass the explanations Skinner provided. On the other hand, I think I can supply some legitimate reasons, at least for the other two flights.

Although I strongly support laboratory analyses of human behavior, I disagree that the flight to real people is necessarily harmful to a scientific psychology. There exist educational, business, and psychotherapeutic technologies (among others) that have no solid data base on the variables responsible for their effectiveness. There is a need for an experimental analysis of these technologies, and such an analysis cannot be done in a laboratory. As I have explained elsewhere (Deitz 1978; 1982), research in applied settings *can* provide useful, scientific information although it does not always do so. Carefully conducted applied research can answer some of the questions about some behaviors or some experimental variables. Problems only arise when the limits of applied research are neither understood nor respected. Laboratory investigations either of these technologies or of other issues, such as more complicated human action, can only be the sometimes unsatisfactory analogues of their real world counterparts.

The flight to laymanship can also be defended. The questions psychology seeks to answer were at least originally phrased in ordinary language; for example, Should teachers spank children? can lead to investigations of punishment. But if the ordinary meaning of punishment is changed or transformed (see Harzem & Miles 1978, pp. 113–14) into a new scientific term, the answers from studies on this variable as redefined may not fit well with the question as originally asked (see Deitz & Arrington, 1983). In that case, the flight *from* laymanship has made it more difficult to understand the world as we experience it.

There is also a second advantage to the flight to laymanship. Ordinary language about "mental" events may not be referring to the mysterious, at all. Although cognitive psychologists (e.g., Fodor 1981a) would disagree, as would many current behaviorists, philosophers such as Wittgenstein (1953), Ryle (1949), and Malcolm (1977) have eloquently explained the nonmentalistic basis of mind, reason, thought, feelings, hope, responsibility, and other terms that Skinner criticizes in the opening section of "Methods." It may be, if these philosophers are right, that cognitive rather than behavioral psychologists are the ones doing injustice to these expressions. Not only would this argument strengthen Skinner's position against the flight to a peculiar form of inner man, it would place behaviorists in the best position to investigate these more interesting and complicated aspects of human action.

The current interest in studying these complex parts of human action by both cognitive and behavioral psychologists leads to my final point of disagreement with Skinner's article. This point concerns the statement that rate of response is "the basic datum in learning." I would not argue that behavior is not "emissive" or that it is not "continuously changing." I will argue that rate of response does not reflect some of the important dimensions of complex, human behavior. Skinner (1969, p. 81) stated that trial by trial measures are "a practice derived from accidental features of early psychological research"; similarly, rate measures are a practice derived from purposeful features of research in an operant chamber. In both cases, different features of complex human behavior that deserve measurement may not be detected.

This is most noticeable in the area of operant research called stimulus control, or the control of behavior by antecedent events. It is this area, as Sidman (1978; 1979) has so carefully explained, that behaviorists study what can be called cognition. A common behavioral measure of stimulus control is the rate of behavior in the presence or absence of a particular stimulus. But to what is that analogous in the real world? In terms of complex human behavior (or simple human behavior, for that matter), the only parallel I can think of could be called "incomplete" understanding or knowledge.

Suppose, for example, that my three-year-old son Joshua is asked to bring a diaper so I can change his younger sister, Celia. He does so, and I praise his performance and thank him for his help. If on this or another occasion the same request (stimulus) is present, but he begins to go back and forth bringing me many diapers, I would conclude he was performing incorrectly because of excessive responding. Here, rate of response (in excess of one) in the presence of the stimulus does not show "correct" stimulus control; instead it reflects some inadequacy. With more complex action, such as behavior in the presence of How much is 6 × 6?, rate becomes even less appropriate. As Baer (1982, p. 2) noted, for behaviors that are "opportunity-bound, rate is an unpragmatic way of displaying the probability of responding to opportunities." It also does not reflect complex action as we see it occur everyday.

In spite of my reservations about Skinner's statements about problems in the flights to real people and laymanship or those in favor of the exclusive use of rate as a measure, I think "Methods" provides much evidence of the value of Skinner's radical behaviorism. The call for an experimental analysis of human activity should interest all experimental psychologists since it is so fundamentally necessary to progress in the field. That such an analysis might restrict theorizing to variables of which an account can be made is equally necessary but a possible reason that the call is so often ignored.

BFS: Deitz is right in saying that not everyone has flown from the laboratory and that those who have have often done so for good reason and with good results, but I am uneasy about some of his examples. While a more technical analysis of punishment may not provide an immediately effective answer to the question of whether teachers should spank their students, I think in the long run it is more likely to give a better evaluation and suggest better improvements than a lay analysis. Rate of responding is a basic *experimental* datum because of its close association with probability of response, but the fact that reinforcement may be contingent upon rate (as in the differential reinforcement of high or low rates) is a difficult complication, as are contingencies in which one instance of a response is reinforced but a second is not.

Some overt behavior is neither elicited nor emitted

Wayne Hershberger

Department of Psychology, Northern Illinois University

Skinner's canon that the overt behavior of organisms comprises merely elicited and/or emitted responses appears strangely provincial in view of the fact that practitioners in the hard sciences deal routinely with mechanisms whose overt behavior is of neither type. A closed-loop control system that monitors the value of a variable/parameter in its environment and uses negative feedback to drive the controlled value into correspondence with a reference value is a case in point. The household thermostat/furnace system is a commonplace example. Setting the thermostat of such a system specifies the temperature its thermocouple is intended to sense, not the amount of heat the furnace is going to emit. Having set the thermostat, one can predict the indoor temperature but not the fuel bill. The latter varies with the weather. The indoor temperature, however, is the mechanism's doing. What these mechanisms do at our command is control the value of their own sensed input, which, of course, is also one of ours: sensed room temperature. Their response to our command is, hence, a particular, self-controlled value of input rather than any particular value of output, either emitted or elicited. This is not to say that the furnace does not *emit* heat nor that cold weather does not *elicit* compensatory emissions of heat from the furnace, but only that the control system does not itself control those heat emissions. That is not what *it does*! What it does, at our command, is control sensed temperature.

Since organisms such as ourselves are replete with exteroceptors, it is eminently conceivable that at least occasionally we too control our inputs so that at least some of *our* responses are neither emitted nor elicited, but rather are self-controlled inputs. Skinner's reluctance to acknowledge even the possibility of this type of intentional behavior, on the grounds that to do so would be to invoke entelechies, is quixotic. Because it involves reference values (intended values or intentions), an organism's control of its inputs, just as a mechanism's control of its inputs, is an admittedly purposive type of overt behavior, but is overt behavior nonetheless, and well within the scope of any psychology devoted to the experimental analysis of behavior. Indeed this analysis is already well begun (Powers 1973; 1978). However, apparently few behaviorists of B. F. Skinner's persuasion can be expected to lend a helping hand, and therein lies a tragic irony, because they, above all others, have a vested interest in its successful outcome. Surely, if behaviorism is to survive Skinner, behaviorists have got to try to explain purposive behavior and stop trying to explain it away.

BFS: When a room grows hot, I turn the furnace off; when it grows cold, I turn the furnace on. I do so because I am a biochemical system that operates in that way – with heat sensors, muscles, and a nervous system. A thermostat turns the furnace off when the room grows hot and on when it grows cold, and it does so because it is built that way – with sensors, electromagnetic switches, and wires. The resulting change in temperature does not affect the behavior of either of us. We do not show purpose in the sense of being affected by any future event. The difference between us is not so much in how we are built as in why we were built that way.

Some of the behavior with which I control my temperature is the product of natural selection. When I am cold, I reduce the surface of my body by wrapping my arms around me, and when I am hot, I sweat. I do so, not because I am then warmer or colder, but because variations in behavior which had those effects were selected by their contribution to the survival of the human species. Much more of what I do is operant. I cool myself by taking off my jacket and warm myself by putting it on. I do both these things, not because of the consequences which then follow, but because of what followed when I did so in the past. Thermostats are built in given ways, not because of what they will now do, but because of what they have done when built that way.

Hershberger overlooks the important fact that only living things exhibit variation and selection. Feedback, in its original cybernetic sense, is a form of guidance. A feedback loop, as Hershberger says, is a "monitor." It lacks the strengthening effect of reinforcement. It is not true that "the indoor temperature...is the mechanism's doing," unless "mechanism" includes the furnace. It is only the value of the temperature that is its doing.

Biologists now rarely misuse the term purpose. The human hand is not designed in order to grasp things; hands grasp things well because variations in structure which have enabled them to do so were selected by that consequence and transmitted to later members of the species through reproduction. Psychologists are not yet as careful. I do not grasp a cup in a given way because I then hold it better; I grasp it in that way because when I have done so I have held it better. A variation having reinforcing consequences was "transmitted" to my subsequent behavior through processes commonly called memory.

A guided missile reaches its target because it is affected by radiation from the target. I reach the door of my office because I am similarly affected by radiation from the door. But neither the missile as a physical system nor I as a biochemical one is affected by this instance of reaching the target or the door. We respond as we have been built to respond, in our separate ways.

Behavior theory: A contradiction in terms?

R. Duncan Luce

Department of Psychology and Social Relations, Harvard University

Skinner's major thesis in "Methods" is that theory is not needed in the study of behavior, where "theory" refers to "any explanation of an observed fact which appeals to events taking place somewhere else, at some other level of observation, described in different terms, and measured, if at all, in different dimensions." To flesh this out, he discusses in some detail what he means both by the study of behavior and by theory in this domain.

The basic datum of behavior is rate of responding. To be sure, this is not the only thing one can observe about behavior, but it is the one that, to date, has provided the most striking regularities. "Once in possession of an effective datum, however, we may feel little need for any theoretical construct" such as strength of bond or excitatory potential. "It is no accident that rate of responding is successful as a datum because it is particularly appropriate to the fundamental task of a science of behavior. If we are to predict behavior (and possibly to control it), we must deal with *probability of response*." Of course, probability is not an observable in the same sense as is rate. Moreover, "rate of responding is not a 'measure' of probability, but it is the only appropriate datum in a formulation in these terms." If I understand this correctly, Skinner is contrasting, on the one hand, the time series of discrete events that he observes – key presses, bar pushes, and the like, which he reports as a cumulative record – with, on the other hand, an underlying mechanism of what he calls response probability, which itself is not observable. (In statistics, such a probabilistic rate function, which has none of the usual properties of probability as such, goes by the name of hazard or intensity function, not response probability, which is used for static probability structures.) Many view the unobservable intensity function as a theoretical construct, designed to relate discrete events that can be observed to the hypothetical concept of an underlying, continuous disposition to respond. Apparently, theory at this level is acceptable, and the time series of behavioral events and the underlying intensity function are viewed as being measured on the same dimension.

Yet when it comes to choice, Skinner seems to feel that theory, at what seems to me a comparable level, is unacceptable. For example, we find:

> An effort may be made to define [choosing] solely in terms of behavior, but in traditional practice [it] refer[s] to processes in another dimensional system....The appeal to theory is encouraged by the fact that choosing...is not a particular piece of behavior. It is not a response or an act with specified topography.

Neither, of course, is response rate or "response probability." I fail to grasp why a stochastic intensity function is acceptable but a choice probability is not; they seem cut from the same cloth, the one having to do with a process that unfolds in time and the other with the behavior at a prescribed instant when the subject is required to make a choice.

Skinner's major objections, however, are reserved for modeling of a more substantive character. He divides models into three classes. The first consists of purely behavioral ones that formulate empirical generalizations in terms of behavioral and experimental observables. Because these observables are all viewed as arising from the same dimensional system – exactly what this means is never specified clearly – such theory is acceptable, and Skinner believes it will arise when an adequate amount of orderly behavioral data are in hand. And, indeed, in the past few years, long after this material first appeared, such modeling has become a prominent development in operant research (e.g., Prelec 1982). To my knowledge, Skinner has not commented publicly on such models.

Skinner's second and third categories both involve reductive models that attempt to account for behavior in terms other than behavioral and experimental variables. In the first, the attempt is to reduce behavior to physiological observations. Here he says there are two systems of dimensions, not one, and one tries to account for the details of the behavior in terms of measurable brain activity. At the present time such modeling is almost always carried out by postulating hypothetical mechanisms that are assumed to operate on physiological variables we can currently observe and measure. For this reason, these models are not greatly different from the second class, which consists of those that attempt to reduce behavior to hypothetical mental processes. It is the hypothetical mechanisms invoked in both types that draw Skinner's fire, leading to constructions that he says are worthless or worse. The central objection is: "When we attribute behavior to a neural or mental event, real or conceptual, we are likely to forget that we still have the task of accounting for the neural or mental event."

When one reads this, what comes to mind? One reading, suggested to me by R. J. Herrnstein, has to do with studies that demonstrate a correlation between a behavioral and a physiological event, and the reader is asked to accept, without a carefully worked out argument as to how, that the latter event explains the former. Often in these cases one neither understands how the physiological event arises nor what, if any, causal relation it has to the behavior. A second reading, suggested to me by S. M. Kosslyn, is that even if an explanatory theory is provided, one must still account, in behavioral terms, for the origins of that particular physiological state. To me, a third reading seems more natural. It involves something like a homunculus, located somewhere in the brain, who manages to "read" the output of the retina, to "hear" the resonances of the basilar membrane, to have drives, and the like. If that is Skinner's meaning, then few will disagree with the objection. But that really is not very typical of the modeling of the past few decades. Usually the mechanisms discussed are far more mechanistic and their properties are specified in some detail. For example, a matrix system of memory, such as the one developed by Anderson (1973), which is a simple model of distributed memory, will be justified by finding a physiological system that is functionally such a matrix. It is not a question of accounting for it so much as finding its physiological embodiment.

An analogy, which seems to me to be close, is the theoretical development in biology of the (originally hypothetical) construct of the gene and its ultimate detailed investigation at a level of observation far different from those to be explained. It is not obvious to me why such theory in biology (and there are numerous similar examples in othr sciences) has proven useful – nay, essential – and yet analogous constructions will necessarily fail in the study of behavior. To be sure, there is not yet an example of a highly successful, reductive behavior theory, else there would be no issue to debate. Nonetheless, I fail to see the ways in which behavior is so inherently different from other scientific questions that one can be certain, as Skinner seems to be, that modeling in terms of constructs at a different level of discourse is a sterile activity. It is difficult to imagine that research in genetics would have been better off had it not been driven by a theory of the (then) hypothetical gene, just as I find it hard to believe that current high-energy physics is being greatly distracted by theories having to do with complex, hypothetical particles. Saying this does not preclude the existence of successful theory that is not reductive in character – relativity theory is a case in point. It does, however, lead me to question the wisdom of asserting – with little detailed argument as to why in this particular field and in sharp contrast to other fields – that harm necessarily follows from the study of the consequences of hypothetical mechanisms that relate concepts at two different observational levels.

BFS: In writing that "when we attribute behavior to a neural or mental event, real or conceptual, we are likely to forget that we still have the task of accounting for the neural or mental event," I was not talking about sophisticated neurological or even cognitive work. Perhaps I was not untouched by the folk neurology of addled brains and taut nerves or the folk psychology of striking because one is angry or getting up late because one thought it was Sunday, but I could have found instances in profusion in, let us say, introductory textbooks in psychology, or for that matter often enough in journals published by the American Psychological Association.

I am willing to accept the parallel with genetic theory. In fact, I have said that a science of behavior stands in about the position of genetic theory prior to the discovery of the role of DNA. The facts in an experimental analysis of behavior correspond to the relations among the traits of successive generations, where the major operation is breeding and cross-breeding. T. H. Morgan and others could add additional information about chromosomes and to some extent group traits accordingly. That information might be said to correspond to established neurological facts, such as end organs, effectors, and the gross anatomy of the brain insofar as its relations with the facts of behavior have been established. We are waiting, of course, for the discovery of an equivalent of DNA. The mentalistic, neurological, and conceptual theories I criticized are concerned with supposed DNA equivalents.

The challenge to Skinner's theory of behavior

Brian Mackenzie

Department of Psychology, University of Tasmania, Australia

Skinner does have a theory, and it's much like the ones he criticizes; it "appeals to events taking place somewhere else, at some other level of observation, . . . and measured, if at all, in different dimensions." These are not faults of the theory, but characteristics of almost any theory. The faults of the theory are first, that it is unacknowledged and covert, and second, that in consequence it has been insulated from criticism. As a result, although the theory has been under increasingly serious challenge over the past 10 to 15 years, few people have commented on the fact and even fewer have tried to do anything about it.

Skinner's is a theory about the acquisition and control of behavior: of all behavior in all organisms, but with special reference to birds and mammals, including human beings. Its fundamental precept (or postulate?) is that the descriptive language of schedules of reinforcement, discriminative stimuli, and the like, which is useful in helping us manipulate some particular kinds of behavior in the operant laboratory, provides an adequate account of behavior generally, both in the laboratory and out of it. This theory is much more than a generalization to the outside world of the "principles of behavior" discovered in the operant laboratory. It involves that too, of course, but the crucial first step is to declare (or assume) that the terms used in describing an operant conditioning experiment *are* principles of behavior. The theory requires us to accept that these terms are adequate to describe *how the behavior of the animal in the operant chamber is structured and controlled*, rather than merely *the particular techniques that we use to control the animal's behavior*. Thus, reinforcement (for instance) is taken to refer, not merely to the administration of grain following key pecks in this experiment or rat chow following bar presses in that one, but to the administration generally of response-contingent events that increase the probability or rate of responding. Specification of the response and the reinforcer thus becomes secondary, a mere technical detail in the application of the "principle of reinforcement." Once we accept that crucial theoretical point, the generalization to the wider world naturally follows. The question about person *A*'s behavior becomes not, Why did she act the way she did?, but, What were the reinforcement contingencies that led her to act the way she did? As soon as we ask that question, we are committed to the theory.

Here is an extreme example of the use of Skinner's theory to account for some real life behavior. The unscientific description comes first; the scientific reformulation is in parentheses.

> Consider a young man whose world has suddenly changed. He has graduated from college and is going to work, let us say, or has been inducted into the armed services. Most of the behavior he has acquired up to this point proves useless in his new environment. The behavior he actually exhibits can be described, and the description translated, as follows: he lacks assurance or feels insecure or is unsure of himself (*his behavior is weak and inappropriate*); he is dissatisfied or discouraged (*he is seldom reinforced, and as a result his behavior undergoes extinction*); he is frustrated (*extinction is accompanied by emotional responses*);. . . there is nothing he wants to do or enjoys doing well, he has no feeling of craftsmanship, no sense of leading a purposeful life, no sense of accomplishment (*he is rarely reinforced for doing anything*). (Skinner 1971 [1973], p. 144)

These explanations of the observed facts appeal to events taking place somewhere else (in the operant laboratory, where the language of reinforcement contingencies has experimental applications), at some other level of observation (of discrete, separable operant responses), and measured in different dimensions (of key presses and readings from a cumulative recorder). The appeal is not made in the same way as it is in the physiological or mentalistic theories that Skinner criticizes, but it is as necessary for Skinner's theory as it is for the others. The events are not, however, "described in different terms." This is the one feature in Skinner's list of criticisms of other theories that is absent from his own. The language of reinforcement contingencies and the like is used to account for the behavior of the young man in despair as confidently as for that of the pigeon in the operant chamber. It is because Skinner's theory of behavior uses the same words as the technology of operant conditioning that he can sometimes maintain that he doesn't have a theory at all. But of course he does; there is nothing in the technology itself to suggest that the particular techniques of control it uses (rather than any others) can be mapped onto a general description of when or under what circumstances any particular piece of behavior will be emitted. That mapping is a bold theoretical leap, and once we have made it, the solution to the young man's difficulties is, in principle, straightforward: "It is the contingencies which must be changed if his behavior is to be changed" (Skinner 1971 [1973], p. 145).

Since the leap that makes operant conditioning methods into a theory of behavior occurs inside the laboratory, it is likewise inside the laboratory that we should look for evidence that challenges it. Such evidence is not hard to find. There is clear experimental evidence of situations in which the reinforcement contingencies are inadequate to control behavior, and in which knowledge of the reinforcement history of the organism does not enable us to predict behavior. Much of this evidence comes from studies of "biological boundaries of learning" (Seligman & Hager 1972); a single example will illustrate the approach here. It is very easy to condition a pigeon to peck at a lighted key with grain as the reinforcer, and almost as easy to condition it to flap its wings with shock avoidance as the reinforcer. However, it is less easy to condition it to flap its wings with grain as the reinforcer, and very difficult to condition it to peck at a lighted key with shock avoidance as the reinforcer. Grain and shock avoidance are both reinforcing to the pigeon, but each can be associated with some responses more easily than with others. Seligman and Hager suggest that this kind of differential conditionability results from the inborn, biologically adaptive, behavioral propensities of the animal: Pigeons in the wild regularly peck for food and flap their wings to escape danger, but rarely do the converse. The point here is that the language of reinforcement contingencies no longer provides an adequate account or description of the organism's behavior. Making a salient reinforcer contingent on an available response no longer suffices to bring about that response; it has to be the "right" response for the particular reinforcer. The language of reinforcement contingencies has to be supplemented (at best) or replaced (at worst) with language that belongs to a completely different account, an account that owes more to ethology than to the experimental analysis of behavior.

In an insightful review of Seligman and Hager (1972), Schwartz (1974, p. 191) remarked that the interdependence of stimuli, responses, and reinforcers raises "profound problems with respect to the set of definitions and premises on which the operant conditioning edifice is built." It does that and more; it challenges the fundamental precept of Skinner's theory of behavior. Because that theory is widely regarded as something other than a theory, however, the challenge is implicitly relegated by most operant psychologists to the level of abstract debate, with no implications for their ongoing experimental work and its interpretation. This attitude is a mistake. Unless the biological boundaries of learning can be successfully incorporated into operant psychology, the work of operant psychologists risks being devoid of any significance beyond the limitations of their particular experimental manipulations.

BFS: I would ask Mackenzie where the science of genetics would be today if the principles demonstrated in garden peas by Mendel and in fruitflies by T. H. Morgan had never been used to "explain" the genetics of any other species? "The theory of the gene" was another matter. It appealed to "events taking place somewhere else, etc." and proved to be a good theory, confirmed with techniques appropriate to the "somewhere else." I gave my reasons for objecting to mentalistic, physiological, and conceptual theories of behavior and said that fortunately we could dispense with them and still have a science of behavior.

Before making a scientific analysis of a different species, or even a different setting, one must look at relevant details. I do not know in advance that food will reinforce the behavior of a hungry pigeon. I make sure that it will do so before using it as a reinforcer. I do not know what will reinforce the behavior of a psychotic patient. I discover useful reinforcers by asking the patient to choose among a number of items which may serve. Certainly there are genetic reasons why many events are reinforcing. I published a paper at about the same time as the major part of the target article in which I gave a phylogenic explanation of the powerful human susceptibility to reinforcement by salt and sugar – a "biological constraint," in a popular contemporary usage.

The use of the principles of operant conditioning to interpret behavior which takes place under conditions which are not suitable for exact prediction and control is perhaps "theoretical," but still, as Mackenzie says, the appeal is not made in the same way as in physiological and mentalistic theories. My *Verbal Behavior* (Skinner 1957) was an example of interpretation of this kind, as is the paragraph cited by MacKenzie.

The role of the statistician in psychology

F. H. C. Marriott

Department of Biomathematics, University of Oxford, England

Any science is based on hypotheses or "laws" that can be investigated, and falsified or modified, by experiments. Any science that is not strictly deterministic must rely on statistics for the interpretation of experimental results.

The first requirement for the statistician is that he should understand the purpose of a proposed experiment and the practical constraints that limit the design. When he has done so, he may be able to make valuable suggestions. Sometimes the design may be unsound because the results – whatever they are – will be open to ambiguous interpretations; possible biases, unsuspected by the experimenter, may be obvious to someone more experienced in experimental design. Sometimes quite small modifications may make it possible to compare results much more accurately, without increasing the experimental work involved. Finally, the statistician may be able to help with the arithmetical work, perhaps quite complex but essentially trivial, of interpreting the results.

This is very far from the process of "squeezing something of significance out of questionable data" that is criticized by Skinner in "Methods." Yet the criticism is pertinent, and too often justified. What has happened to turn statistics from an essential aid in the interpretation of experimental results into a prop for dubious scientific theories?

A major factor is the attitude of editors and examiners. A "significant" result is regarded as a contribution to knowledge, something publishable. However obvious a result may be, the author must insert ($P < .05$) before it is acceptable; however meaningless, that parenthesis converts it to scientific truth.

This attitude is encouraged – "reinforced" is perhaps the right word – by elementary statistics textbooks. Significance tests have been used, to excellent effect, for more than 100 years. About 50 years ago, Neyman and Pearson (1967) worked out a mathematical formulation of the process, a technical and formal statement that led to valuable results in the theory of mathematical statistics. Unfortunately, this description is repeated as if it were an account of how scientists interpret, or should interpret, their results. They are supposed to decide on a "significance level," define a "critical region," and, according to whether their result falls in this region, "accept" or "reject" a null hypothesis.

What nonsense! The null hypothesis is usually entirely implausible, and the experiment is designed to investigate the way in which it breaks down. A nonsignificant result means that the results give no useful information about that question, not that the hypothesis is true. A larger departure, whether or not it reaches the magic $P < 0.05$, suggests a definite answer, and the need for futher experiments to confirm the conclusion and quantify the discrepancy. Occasionally, a very low significance probability may leave no doubt about the direction of the effect, and give a clear idea of its size.

Finally, package programs enable the psychologist to analyse his data without any understanding of statistics. Many different programs will accept the same data – surely one of them will make it significant? Or perhaps a sufficiently sophisticated technique will make the work publishable as a contribution to methodology?

This a deplorable situation. It is widely recognized by professional statisticians. Some have suggested that significance tests should disappear from statistical methods; others would restrict statistical analysis to fully trained professionals. There is a vast and self-perpetuating problem; a particular type of syllabus has been taught to a whole generation of scientists, who devise syllabi for the next generation, examine their theses, and referee their papers.

To break this chain requires a great effort, by both scientists and statisticians. Much can be done. Confidence intervals are far more informative than significance tests. Where tests are used, exact P values should be given: $P = 0.051$, $P = 0.049$, $P = 0.015$ tells more than $P > 0.05$, $P < 0.05$. Simple exploratory methods can often profitably replace difficult and sophisticated techniques – how many psychologists really understand factor analysis? The complexities of "multiple comparison tests," with the associated questions about what constitutes an experiment and what the experimenter was thinking about when he planned it, are largely irrelevant and should at least be dropped from elementary teaching. If all those concerned realize the problems, perhaps we shall no longer be asked, "Can you make this significant?"

BFS: I welcome Marriott's sophisticated support of my unskilled protest against the misuse of statistics by psychologists. I wish I had had a copy of his commentary many years ago when I was trying to do something about the statistics examination in the Department of Psychology at Harvard.

Cognitive science: A different approach to scientific psychology

Richard Millward

Walter S. Hunter Laboratory of Psychology, Brown University

The fact that Skinner has so little to add to his canonical papers must be a surprise to many. Has all that has happened in psychology over the past 25 to 50 years had no impact on Skinner's position? Skinner was influenced by logical positivism, the philosophy of the 1930s. But few accept that analysis of science, even those who originally espoused it (Hempel 1980, for example). The Kuhnian influence has changed our view of the hypothetico-deductive method to which Skinner reacted so strongly. Psychology itself has broadened to such an extent that rigorous studies of language, thinking, memory, and perception swamp our journals. The computer revolution and its associated attempts to make machines behave intelligently have provided us with new questions. Neuroscience is a discipline in its own right and delivers us facts to be integrated into our philosophy of mind, facts that few can ignore. Taken together, these changes constitute the information-processing revolution of cognitive science. Has none of this dented the armor of Skinner's behaviorism?

Cognitive science is a philosophy diametrically opposed to Skinner's, and its current popularity must be disheartening to him. It represents what he would call a massive "flight from the laboratory." Cognitive scientists consider philosophical issues, ask about innate propensities, construct computer models as well as mathematical models, try to relate neurological facts to cognitive facts, build artificial intelligence systems of mental events, and, perhaps worst of all, construct theories. Cognitive scientists almost perversely seem to do all the things Skinner told us we should not do. Most experimental work in cognitive science, and there is still plenty of that, does not follow Skinner's "experimental analysis," by which he means recording the frequency of a free operant under different stimulus conditions. Instead, the experiments are aimed at testing some hypothesis, or demonstrating the adequacy of some theory, using whatever response measure seems appropriate – reaction time, probability, errors, or verbal protocols – but rarely rate of response.

The fact that the field has changed cannot, of course, be held against a researcher. With luck, it will happen to all of us. Skinner shaped the nature of psychological research for over 25 years; only a few researchers have been so influential. We should perhaps evaluate Skinner in terms of what his program accomplished. No one would deny that he discovered a way to control the behavior of animals in a laboratory setting. That these principles are viable outside the laboratory is attested to by their extensive use by animal trainers. Punishment is often included in the animal trainer's bag of tricks, and innate factors enter into behavior in inextricable ways (as the Brelands 1961 have convincingly demonstrated), but operant conditioning principles are still a fundamental contribution to our knowledge of learning. Can these principles be generalized to complex human behavior? Chomsky's (1959) review of Skinner's *Verbal Behavior* answered that question clearly. Attempts to revolutionize education with teaching machines were a dismal failure. Opinions vary, and perhaps all the facts are not yet in; however, many believe that behavior modification programs are not very successful, because they treat symptoms and do not attempt to explain causes. I do not object to applying knowledge gained in the laboratory to real problems, and I certainly appreciate the fact that in the real world the necessary control of variables may be difficult to attain. However, I believe that the application of operant conditioning to real problems has failed, not because of inadequate stimulus control, but because operant conditioning has not characterized the psychological processes involved in a theoretical way that can be extrapolated to more complex problems.

One of the curious aspects of Skinner's influence on psychology is that he did not have a theory of psychology. Instead, he had strong opinions on how psychology should – and should not – be studied. We should eschew theories and mathematics, study only operants, use only rate of response as a dependent variable, and make scientific decisions by experimental control and not through statistical means. Given the emphasis on being scientific during the first half of this century, the acceptance of Skinner's extreme prescription is understandable. Some of what he said was justifiable, and we certainly must guard against false explanations and unnecessary mentalistic theorizing. But, all in all, it seems to me that his view of science is fundamentally flawed.

First, Skinner's emphasis on control is wrong. When a phenomenon is understood and technology provides the means for controlling relevant variables, then control will follow. We knew what was required to go to the moon long before we could even imagine accomplishing it. The emphasis should be on understanding, not control, though control can be of help by allowing us to manipulate variables in sensible ways.

Second, Skinner's position that theories are unnecessary is a disaster for our science – and for any science. Science is not simply a compendium of facts and observations. It is a classification of observations, a model of the world designed to explain relationships and phenomena observed in the world, a theory of what objects and events are noteworthy and how they interrelate. We turn to the laboratory, not merely to collect data but to make observations about the world which can confirm or disconfirm our hypotheses. It is the current "view" of a subject, the theory about it, that indicates the success of a science, its level of sophistication, its generality. Raw facts from the laboratory do not easily tell us what we know.

Does cognitive science have a philosophy? Well, it does not have one that is simple to express and probably not one that every cognitive scientist would profess. But this is part of the new spirit of eclecticism – or anarchy, depending on one's opinion. Three ideas seem to fit together to spell out a kind of philosophy of science of the mind from a cognitive scientist's point of view. One is the distinction made by Chomsky (1965) between performance and competence. Another is Newell's (1981) distinction among the device, symbol, and knowledge levels. Finally, Marr (1982) suggests three levels of analysis of psychological processes: the implementation level, the algorithmic level, and the computational level. Whether these three sets of distinctions are parallel, or to what extent they are, is of theoretical interest but cannot be entered into here. What is pertinent is the fact that all three postulate a distinction between an abstract and a performance level of analysis. Chomsky refers to the knowledge we have of the rules of grammar as *tacit* knowledge since it governs behavior but is not explicitly known to the speaker. Newell uses the term *rationality* for his top level. Marr calls his the *computational level*. The laws of cognition for this level would be laws for any intelligent system. Chomsky suggests a set of constrained rewrite rules as the primary component of competence. These are simple and universal so that invoking them limits the set of possible worlds a child has to consider. Newell assumes that the knowledge level consists of an agent, a body of knowledge, and a set of goals. The principle of rationality states simply that "if an agent has knowledge that one of its actions will lead to one of its goals, then the agent will select that action" (Newell 1981, p. 8). Marr, making more of a methodological point than a psychological distinction, looks at the computational level as specifying the goals of the computation – a mapping of one kind of information onto another.

The second methodological level of these theorists generally encompasses what most psychologists mean when they talk about information-processing models, that is, the mechanisms or algorithms used by the system to perform the abstract operations specified by the top level. Here we have such concepts as parallel versus serial processing, short-term memory buffers, semantic nets, and the like. Performance is critical for specifying the details of such systems. Finally, at the implementation level, one brings the details of hardware and wetware into account. This is where biological constraints have explicit effects, although obviously the characteristics of the other two levels are also biologically determined.

Our job as scientists, then, is to put these levels together into a coherent whole. Consider a clock as a system to be analyzed. At the top level, we want to specify what constitutes a clock and what its purpose is. It must be temporally regular, it must include a general concept of succession, it must have some kind of a dial to announce one of its finite states, and it must cycle through the states repetitively. One can realize an algorithm for a clock in a number of ways – in an analog manner as with a sundial or hourglass, in a digital way as with a grandfather clock or a digital clock. The dial can vary in numerous ways, the base rate can be fast or slow, and so on. The ultimate implementation obviously interacts with the algorithm and this is where the constraints of the implementation become important; for example, it is rather difficult – although not impossible – to think of a digital sundial.

How does Skinner's "science of human behavior" fit into this scheme? In brief, it doesn't. And that is the point. Yet to understand what a clock is, one must understand something about its nature and purpose. (The purpose is required for clocks since they are human artifacts. No one would expect a statement of purpose for a cat, for example. However, to understand how a visual system works, purpose may once again be part of its abstract characterization.) For some questions, the abstract description of a clock is sufficient. For other questions, such as why clocks look so different or perform with varying reliability, one wants to consider the algorithm or the mechanism involved. Finally, if one must build or repair the clock, it is necessary to know how it is implemented in hardware. When some clocks are manipulated in certain ways, they perform badly. Recording such facts for all possible manipulations, but not asking why they perform the way they do, or how they are built, or what their purpose is, is a mindless task. I can understand why Skinner's experimental analysis is not pursued very vigorously by scientists, since there is really nothing to reinforce such behavior. Skinner's experimental analysis doesn't help us fix clocks, or build them, or tell us how they work – which is the ultimate knowledge that we need to be scientific about clocks. Can the knowledge we need about human minds be any less well described?

BFS: I should indeed be "disheartened" if things were as bad as Millward portrays them – if the viability of operant principles was attested to by their extensive use by animal trainers, if Chomsky had proved that those principles cannot be generalized to complex behavior, if "attempts to revolutionize education with teaching machines were a dismal failure," if "behavior modification programs [were] not very successful, because they treat symptoms and do not attempt to explain causes," and so on. Millward apparently thinks that the rejection of logical positivism has some bearing upon my position, that I "eschew theories and mathematics," that by "experimental analysis" I mean nothing more than "recording the frequency of a free operant under different stimulus conditions," and so on. Under these circumstances I am not surprised by his cognitive euphoria, even when tempered by the admission that cognitive science does not have a philosophy that is simple to express or one that every cognitive scientist would profess.

Should we return to the laboratory to find out about learning?

J. M. E. Moravcsik

Department of Philosophy, Stanford University

"Problems lose interest" writes Skinner in "Methods," but it is not clear how the conceptual framework articulated in this paper accounts for the notion of *interest*. Of two equally intelligent and hard-working students, one becomes interested in a subject and the other does not. Of two equally intelligent and dedicated teachers one loses interest in teaching and the other does not. Why? No answer is provided by talk of enjoyment and positive reinforcement. For one might become or remain interested in a subject but not enjoy it. Furthermore, the burned-out teacher did not lose interest because he stopped enjoying teaching; rather he stopped enjoying teaching because he lost interest.

This simple puzzle shows one of the disadvantages of starting out with pigeons. The distinction between enjoying or not enjoying versus being interested and not being interested does not make sense when applied to pigeons. What would it be like to have a pigeon that is interested in pecking at something but is not enjoying it? Yet this distinction is crucial for any adequate explanation of why learning takes place, and can continue.

Although the pertinent material in Skinner's "Methods" fails to help with this problem, common sense suggests that the person who can maintain interest can detect constantly new features in the objects that he deals with. How would the framework elaborated in Skinner's paper deal with the creativity involved in detecting new features of familiar situations?

The work with pigeons that Skinner refers to concerns stimuli that share salient perceptual elements. This is not involved in the typical human learning situation. Let us consider, for example, a child learning how to perform calculations involving the number 2. This requires coming to understand the common denominator between the groups of, say, 2 tables, 2 birthdays, 2 rules, and 2 kinds of pain. In this case there is no common perceptual denominator. Skinner talks of seeing learning taking place in seeing changes in performance. But in our case there is no one performance that is changing. Rather, the child learns how to generate new performances that involve, from a perceptual point of veiw, a totally new environment. Skinner can record the new performances, but how does he explain these?

At this point Skinner might object that I am taking the wrong unit of behavior. He says that simple units of behavior underlie the complex events labeled by the vernacular of English, German, and so on. Thus he is committed to the conceptual reduction of events like calculation to simpler units. There is no sign, however, that such a conceptual program can achieve real progress.

The very tenor of this commentary might seem inappropriate to Skinner, since it uses shamelessly such everyday conceptions as interest, boredom, creativity, calculation, and the like. But in rejecting any close link with this framework Skinner goes against what has been successful in the history of science. In physics and chemistry, we start out with commonsense notions like those of body, force, compound, and mixture, and then go on to refine them, and to develop new terms in order to conceptualize underlying elements posited to explain what we observe on the commonsense level. (Technology also allows us to carry observation beyond common sense, but that is irrelevant to the point at issue.) Eventually, the physicist and the chemist return to the level of everyday observation and can account for the questions that got the inquiry started in the first place. Skinner wants to remove psychology from everyday language and observation both with respect to the observational and with respect to the theoretical vocabulary. What arguments can he adduce in support of such a radical departure from the way other sciences developed? Is it not the case that the flight from Skinner's laboratory is partly a flight to a pattern that has been successful in other sciences?

Skinner's psychology merely correlates and predicts behavior. To the charge that he avoids looking for underlying causes Skinner would reply that these underlying causes will be developed in physiology, chemistry, and the like.

But the assertion that such a rendezvous will occur remains simply an article of faith for Skinner. As of now, there are very few indications that such a program will be successful. Skinner is surprisingly dogmatic on this issue, as he is concerning the death of dualism, the demise of the view that humans differ from animals in some basic way, and the eventual disappearance of Aristotelian psychology. As a pragmatist, I will take as my explanatory schemes whatever will work. Choices between materialism and dualism, or between a human–animal dichotomy and a human–animal continuum are empirical issues; why be dogmatically for or against any one of these options?

Skinner offers as an alternative for psychologists a theory in which "we can predict and control behavior," and he wonders why more persons do not opt for this. But in astronomy, too, practices of describing and predicting planetary motions were quite well developed before people had even the vaguest ideas of what the planets were. Curiosity motivated scientists to move from mere observation, correlation, and prediction to attempts to explain what the agents involved really were, and what caused the movements. Is it so surprising if an analogous movement is now taking place in psychology?

The following is a standard pattern of explanation in many of the empirical sciences. First, one posits a law that governs entities under various idealizations. Then one adds a number of variables and parameters. The conjunction of these two steps should yield an explanation and prediction of what we actually observe. This is the pattern to which cognitive science and linguistics is turning. On what grounds does Skinner deem it inappropriate for psychology?

BFS: Let me explain my use of the word "interest" by paraphrasing what Moravcsik says about physics and chemistry:

In psychology we start out with commonsense notions like those of mind, idea, interest, personality, and so on, and then go on to refine them and to develop new terms in order to conceptualize underlying elements posited to explain what we observe on the commonsense level. (Technology also allows us to carry observation beyond common sense, but that is irrelevant to the point at issue.) Eventually, the psychologist returns to the level of everyday observation and can account for the questions that got the inquiry started in the first place.

To write "Methods" using nothing but terms carefully defined according to the concepts and principles of an experimental analysis of behavior would probably have been impossible and certainly impracticable.

I used the word "interest" as part of a lay vocabulary, but I now return to it to answer Moravcsik's complaint. Different kinds of behavior have multiple consequences, and this can be shown in pigeons as well as in people. There is a well-known experiment in which a pigeon will peck a key to turn off an experiment, though in the absence of that key it will not stop responding to the prevailing contingencies. I am not suggesting that is a strict parallel with the burned-out teacher who nevertheless enjoys teaching, but I am simply answering Moravcsik's question, "What would it be like to have a pigeon that is interested in pecking at something but is not enjoying it?" Pigeons can also "abstract" the response "two" and apply it to new situations. They come "to understand the common denominator" between groups of two objects of different kinds by making a common response (for example, pecking a key marked "2" rather than "1" or "3") determined only by the number of objects. A child, of course, would say "two" but would come to do so under comparable contingencies. There is no "reduction" in such an analysis.

I readily agree that the appeal to neurology is at the moment pretty much an article of faith. I do not have any way of observing the nervous system or its action, but I have reasonable "confidence" (which I have defined behaviorally elsewhere; Skinner 1974) that we shall eventually know much of what we need to know about the underlying "explanation" of behavior.

Skinner's philosophy of method

R. J. Nelson

Department of Philosophy, Case Western Reserve University

Although there is no denying the first importance of Professor Skinner's experimental research in animal behavior (which I have the greatest admiration for), his philosophy of method strikes me as very intolerant and singularly barren. Leaving it to others to comment on his negative views of models and unbridled statistics in "Methods," I want to offer some remarks on the extreme austerity of what he conceives to be right method, particularly on his total eschewal of inner causes. I believe he rejects these for the wrong reasons, and, moreover, that there is a fruitful way of understanding "inner cause" that is unobjectionable on Skinner's very own grounds.

Consider the question of changes of response illustrated by the levels of a pigeon's head in certain experiments. In general, suitable reinforcements illustrate the law of effect: A pigeon holds its head higher and higher as food is presented to it in successive, reinforcing stages. According to Skinner one might answer the question, Why? in operational terms, but not in terms of inner causes such as "excitations," as these "must be assigned to a different dimensional system"; nor in terms of intervening variables ("mediators"), which are otiose in behavioral descriptions. Familiar examples of terms of different dimensional systems are those of neuroscience or of mentalistic psychology – terms like "pleasure" or "pain" used to explain the law of effect. All such are to be ruled out of laboratory-oriented behavioral psychology.

Suppose you do eliminate all such mentalistic, irrelevant (i.e., neuroscientific), and vacuous (i.e., intervening variable) concepts. You still do not get rid of all types of putatively useful notions of inner cause. For instance, a computational theory of behavior can quite possibly contribute answers to why questions and do so without (a) going to a different level or dimension of terms, (b) appealing to intervening variables, or (c) introducing mentalistic terms. Computationalism, as I am about to partially characterize it, is perhaps a species of what Skinner calls a "conceptual nervous system" theory.

(a) A computational in contrast to an operant-reinforcement model introduces entities called "states" in the technical sense of discrete state machine theory. Reinforcements (as an example) are then conceived to depend on both stimulations (S) and inner states (Q). S and Q might reinforce a subject's operant behavior while S and Q^1 might not, just as a quarter might produce a bottle of pop from a dispensing machine when the machine is in a certain state, and might not when it is in another. This model is no more "mathematical" than the operant-reinforcement paradigm in any serious sense of the word.

True, these entities are "hypothetical," but not in the meaning that they are of a different dimension or level of description. In fact, just as responses and reinforcements are space-time, physical events, so are inner states physical events. And although a physiological or other nonbehavioral language would put one in a "wrong" or "some other" place for dealing with the behavioral, the same holds for inner states. They do not have to be couched in or reduced to the physiological. If "some dimension" can be made clear in terms of the formal idea of a vocabulary, then what I am saying is that terms for states are of the *same* vocabulary as "operant," and so forth. They are *not* part of any mentalistic or neuroscientific vocabulary. I will complete this section of my remarks in (c).

(b) Internal states are not intervening variables or mediators (Nelson 1969). The state is not linearly caused by the stimulation or operant response, nor is response behavior linearly changed or enhanced in turn by the state – in short, states do not play the same roles as mediators under Skinner's own characterizations. In the previous simple analogy, if a state were an intervening variable, a quarter would *always* produce a Coke *via* the state.

(c) In principle state expressions are definable explicitly in terms of observables (Bealer 1978). With regard to Skinner's conceptual repertoire, this means in terms of operant behavior, reinforcing events, and the like. In practice this might be very difficult to achieve since explicit definitions are forthcoming only if one has a complete hypothesis covering the state space (Nelson 1982). So the fact of definability does not entail that the state concept is otiose. Nevertheless, the proper conclusion here is that inner causes qua states are strictly operational as they reduce to manipulable variables. One's hypothesis about a computational system, animal or otherwise, can be settled by empirical means.

I should not want to argue that Skinner's distinctive approach to the science of behavior in terms of operant conditioning is strengthened in any appreciable way using inner states in this mechanical sense, although it does point to a way of explaining response differences or frequencies, for example, in terms of the internal without the vacuous introduction of mediators, without appealing to "something else," namely, the neurophysiological or the mentalistic, and without, I might add, hunting for side conditions in an environment that is known to be stable and fixed.

Suppes (1975) has termed an approach to behavioral psychology using internal state concepts "neobehaviorism" and has discussed the power of such an approach in some detail, especially with regard to learning theory. I myself have argued (Nelson 1982) that a method augmented in this manner can account for language acquisition and use (in a way, I believe, that satisfies even Chomsky's demands), gestalt perception, and other cognitive phenomena, including the intentional. Adoption of computationalism by the inquirer does not have to be accounted for by a search for special reinforcing contingencies. Those that reinforce Skinner will do.

BFS: One of my first papers (Skinner, 1932a) was on the state of hunger (or "drive"), and I have been interested in states off and on ever since. The organism we observe and possibly study can certainly be said to be in a given state at a given time. The state will eventually be directly observed by those who have the proper instruments and methods – namely, anatomists and physiologists. They will complete the account offered by an experimental analysis of behavior, which necessarily has temporal and spatial gaps. Let us say that I deprive an organism of food for 24 hours and that as a result it eats ravenously; I am quite willing to say that the state produced by the deprivation is relevant to the ravenous behavior. Or let us say that I reinforce a response one day and find it more likely to occur the next day; I am willing to say that reinforcement changed a state of the organism which survived for 24 hours. As a behavioral scientist I can accept those facts without assigning any additional property to "hunger" or "memory," and

I see no reason to say that either one is "in contrast to an operant-reinforcement model." They are in principle "definable explicitly in terms of observables." If Nelson really believes what I think he is saying, I see no reason for calling my position "intolerant and singularly barren." And if he can indeed not go beyond the computational model as he presents it and still account for language acquisition, gestalt perception, and intention, I shall be the first to welcome him to the operant camp.

Lessons from the history of science?

John M. Nicholas

Departments of Philosophy and History of Medicine and Science, University of Western Ontario, Canada

There is a historical irony to Professor Skinner's polemic against learning theories. His operationalism and conviction that the role of theories is to codify economically facts disclosed by experiment were, as far as the available record goes, espoused by him from the beginning of his intellectual career in the late 1920s. The influence of the physicists was fairly direct. Skinner has reported making considerable use of Mach's *Science of Mechanics* in his dissertation years and had prolonged discussions on operationalism with a physicist friend, Cutbert Daniel, who was working under Percy Bridgman at the time (Gudmondsson 1983; Skinner 1931; 1972; 1979). The firmness of Skinner's conviction seems unshaken with the passage of time as the methodological message comes through clearly still. But although the voice is his, the message is from the 19th century, prior to the massive transformations in the physical and chemical sciences which were being consolidated at the time that Skinner was writing his thesis at Harvard. If the message is anybody's, it is Ernst Mach's; it may have been plausible in the 1880s perhaps, but it scarcely survives the assimilation of the new atomic theory and statistical mechanics, both inextricably bound up with quantum mechanics. These are, arguably, the best theories ever devised on almost every factor by which they can be ranked, one being that they are firmly engaged with a great array of experiments of historic caliber.

"Phenomenological" thermodynamics, confining itself to characterizing constraints on idealized macroscopic systems, and refraining from discussing microsystems on another "dimension," provided a putative example of science à la Mach (Skinner). Einstein, also influenced strongly by Mach, was sufficiently impressed by the theory to view the special theory of relativity in the same methodological light, seeing, as he did, the light postulate as similar in function to the impossibility of the *perpetuum mobile.* That did not prevent him, however, from making foundational contributions to statistical mechanics.

The irony is that at the time when scientific behaviorism was a tentative program in psychology, reinforced and legitimated by operationalistic and narrowly empiricist trends in the physical sciences of two or three decades before, those sciences shrugged off those very constraints and plunged into microphysics. The new theories were by no means generalizations simply abstracted from observational laws. So at the time that Skinner and other behaviorists had picked up the conventional methodological wisdom that went with the physics of the 1880s, physics itself had moved on to embrace theories that required the denial of the narrow view of the function of theories.

The point is this: Good science, when its time has come, simply cannot be tied by the constraints Skinner has consistently laid down. If science had been so constrained, the extraordinary contributions of Boltzmann, Planck, Einstein, Bohr, and Born would have to have been set aside. For their theories fundamentally relied upon the characterization of "events taking place somewhere else," clearly "at some other level of observation" (and beyond!), "described in different terms," and definitely measured in "different dimensions" from the experimental setup. With Skinner's rule book, we would not be permitted the best science available to date.

From this perspective, Skinner's doubts about physiological, mentalistic, and other theories which have been touted as offering explanations in the domain of human and animal behavior seem almost perverse, for he is castigating those who employ them on the grounds that those theories share certain characteristics with the best empirical theories ever known.

Apart from these very general considerations about what should count as admissible scientific theories, Skinner also recites a number of the hazards that generally threaten the users of theories. If we begin with a puzzle in behavior and attribute it to, say, a neural event, we merely substitute for one (perhaps tractable) problem another problem which in all likelihood will be more complex and more difficult. We will have forgotten that we must account for the neural event. But, surely, two matters are conflated here. One is the bitter fact that any explanation will appeal to "explainers" which are, in the instance, unexplained, and which invite scrutiny for their explanation in turn. It has to stop somewhere, I presume, on pain of regress; there will have to be some basic, unexplained laws of nature that are, as it were, definitive of this world. It might indeed be the case that some of the primitive not-to-be-explained laws are laws correlating behavior with behavior, and behavior with other observables. To insist at the outset that this is the case would, of course, be the cardinal scientific sin; it denies Nature her important prerogative of teaching us.

The second aspect of this alleged hazard is the heuristic one of whether, at risk of being embroiled with more variables, problematic calculations, and considerable complexity one should ascend to a higher theoretical level to assist in the tracking down of the lower level laws. Current cancer research probably gives a striking example of how in a domain where it is not clear what the facts are research progresses not by focusing on the hard grind of laboratory exploration to the exclusion of theory, but sometimes by working "top down." Skinner's behaviorism applied to cancer research would foreclose some of the important heuristic and by all accounts increasingly productive lines of research now available. Indeed, it strikes me as an intriguing problem for Skinner, arguing as he does on the basis of very *general* claims about the nature of good science, to extricate himself from arguing by parity that cancer researchers would do better to drop their interest in the cellular level and the subcellular biochemistry of oncogenes in favor of a molar treatment of macroscopic individuals. There certainly are differences between the cases, but they don't seem to be of the sort that would undermine the parallelism. Why isn't the cancer victim an "empty organism"?

Wastefulness, too, is a vice Skinner attributes to researchers with a theoretical bent. But then he does not tell us, in the spirit of scientific "control," just how wasteful theory-free research is. It may be that, in general, research is like Madame Curie's pitchblende. Most of it has to be thrown away.

Methodological debates between scientists are frequently not disinterested inquiries into methods as such. That is to say, methodological claims tend to be simply sticks with which to beat scientific opponents' substantive scientific claims. And perhaps that is forgivable, since the scientist qua scientist has as his domain nature, not methods. The danger in trying to carry off a material scientific debate by appealing to *general* higher-order claims about what it is to be scientific is that one ends up with unanticipated consequences outside one's own scientific patch of ground. And I suspect that this is a problem that faces Skinner's critique of learning theories. Better that he should have argued simply that those theories are not particularly good ones when it comes to offering staple fare: explanatory power (showing precisely why one phenomenon occurs rather than others, and not just offering promissory notes for success down the road), predictive power (the anticipation of nature!), and interpretive success (the role of theory as a guide to instrumentation). It is this last factor most of all which will, in all probability, serve to bring back to the laboratory those researchers tempted by the vices described by Professor Skinner. (Skinner's setting up mere hypothetico-deductive methods as the opposition is gratuitous. A quick look at the range of theory-laden procedures available for fixing, say, the Avogadro number, gives the lie to the idea that strictly unobservable properties are only grasped by such weak means. An insightful antidote has been provided by Glymour, 1979.)

BFS: To Nicholas I am the grand antitheorist referred to at the beginning of "Some Afterthoughts." But I was criticizing a special kind of theory, and I did not "exclude the possibility of theory in another sense." I also agreed that "the achievements of the hypothetico-deductive method, where appropriate, have been brilliant. Newton set the pattern in this *Principia*, and the great deductive theorists who follow him have been given a prominent place in the history of science." I nevertheless reminded my readers that the great theorists would not have got far without experimental science. It is true that Boltzmann, Planck, Einstein, Bohr, and Born theorized about "'events taking place somewhere else,' clearly 'at some other level of observation..., described in different terms' and definitely measured in different dimensions' from the experimental setup," but take the experiments away and they could not have done so. As Nicholas says, "the best theories ever devised on almost every factor by which they can be ranked" were "firmly engaged with a great array of experiments of historic caliber." It is perhaps equally true that there would be no research without theories in the fields represented by scientists of that kind; they are dealing with a world beyond the reach of direct observation. It is also worth asking whether Einstein, Planck, Bohr, and the others discovered a new kind of scientific thinking or whether their science had reached the stage at which a new method could be invoked. If the latter is the case, we have to ask whether a science of behavior has reached that stage or whether cognitive science is premature in pretending to have reached it.

Are Skinner's warnings still relevant to current psychology?

Marc N. Richelle

Laboratoire de Psychologie Expérimentale, University of Liège, Belgium

The two papers combined in "Methods" are the best known of Skinner's writings, and they have certainly contributed an important part to the representation of Skinner's approach in the scientific community. When he is accused of rejecting statistical guidelines in experimental methodology, or of ignoring the fact that organisms have brains, or of naively believing that laboratory results on pigeons are more relevant to human happiness than straightforward attention to real-life problems, or, above all, of advocating a science without theories, these are typically the texts referred to. Reading them again more than 20 or 30 years after they were first published might seem to have but historical interest, especially to those who feel that we have reached "the end of the long and boring behaviorist night" (Bunge 1980).

It is, indeed, interesting, from the point of view of the history of psychology, to look at these papers at a distance and ask the question, Did they really contain the arguments for grounding the familiar accusations recalled above? Skinner's thinking, as I have shown elsewhere (Richelle 1976; 1977) has been misrepresented and distorted by his opponents of all persuasions to an extent unusual in science, or even in philosophy. Insofar as such distortions are the result of classical tactics in controversy – building a straw man, selecting phrases and sentences according to one's thesis, ignoring the original text and condemning it "second hand" (most people who judge *Verbal Behavior* [1957] have not read it; they are echoing Chomsky's destructive 1959 review), and the like – we cannot expect to find in the text any objective ground for the attacks. This is the point Skinner made in his "Afterthoughts," written in 1969, apropos of his reputation as an antitheorist. He emphasizes the fact that he used the term *theory* in a very restrictive sense – meaning "any explanation of an observed fact which appeals to events taking place somewhere else, at some other level of observation," and everyone can verify this to be true.

However, some part, at least, of what a reader derives from a text has its origin in the phrasing of the text itself, not in the past history or the biases of the reader. A detailed textual analysis would take us too far afield, but it would show that Skinner's formulations have in some cases contributed to maintaining ambiguities. For instance, while clearly addressing himself to the uselessness of theories as defined above, he occasionally insists on *data* speaking for themselves, and "speeding the departure of theories." The argument would have been more persuasive had he opposed theories at the same level, that is behavioral theories proper, to theories appealing to some other level of observation, as becomes obvious only in the 1969 afterthoughts. The crude positivist position that facts, without theories, can make science, was, of course, no longer tenable when Skinner's papers were written.

Another way to read "Methods" is to ask the question, Is it still of some relevance to psychology today? Of course, the world has changed, and so has the study of behavior. For one thing, largely because of the impetus given by Skinner's ingenious experimental technique, our understanding of many behavioral phenomena has increased enormously, and the experimental illustrations (curves and graphs have been deleted in the present condensation) invoked by Skinner look almost simplistic compared with the sophistication of current research. Second, our age is marked by an integrative effort in the biological sciences, and especially in those disciplines concerned with brain and behavior. The idea that the "universe of discourse" of behavioral science should be kept apart from the universe of brain science(s), which already seemed shocking 25 years ago to many of Skinner's otherwise well-disposed readers, has become incompatible with the zeitgeist. Even if we admit that such a deliberate isolation was once justifiable for methodological reasons (we need good behavioral data and theory if we want to describe and analyze brain functions correctly), parallel progress in all the fields of neuroscience has made it impossible to maintain artificial separations between them. In any case, crossing borders between areas of knowledge has always been a rewarding enterprise, which has proved of particular heuristic value in the realm of biology, to which psychology belongs – as Skinner has repeatedly emphasized. He, in fact, never refrained from crossing borders himself; the core of his own theory – possibly the most valuable concept he contributed to psychology – that is, the selective action of the environment, is essentially an extension (by analogy) to individual behavior of a kind of causal relation that has demonstrated its success in biology. It is nonetheless true that, in some cases, adopting another universe of discourse may be a way of avoiding a real confrontation, however difficult, with a subject matter. Such cases have been frequent in psychology.

With these reservations, and if one is not blinded by a widespread prejudice against Skinner's view, one is struck by the very current relevance of some of his remarks. Let me take a few examples.

No doubt, the passage of Bohr (1958), showing how easily nonspecialists indulge in authoritative statements on psychology with terms and issues that "would have been at home in psychological discussions 50 years earlier" could have been replaced, in the present reprint, by any one of a wide choice of similar quotations from many contemporaries, including people like Monod (1970), Chomsky (1968), and Changeux (1983) to mention but a few. Another practice consists in discussing important psychological issues without even referring to central contributions of prominent psychologists. A case in point is Popper writing dozens of pages on a view of knowledge that would fit in the frame of general evolutionary theory, and not even mentioning Piaget, whose lifelong endeavor has been devoted to exactly that problem (Popper & Eccles 1977). The flight to real people and to laymanship is still with us, and it is still true that "experimental psychology has. . .to contend with what is in essence a rejection of the whole scientific enterprise" – a rejection that is, indeed, extending its effects far beyond the frontiers of psychology (think of creationism!). More than ever, apparently generous remedial action is preferred to basic research and training, on the ground that people need help right now. Skinner's scientific faith, on this issue, has always been on the side of those who work hard in the laboratory to discover a vaccine rather than on the side of the practitioners who use their skills to save a small minority of desperate cases. Skinner might be disappointed by the fact that fundamental knowledge of behavior has not had a large hand in shaping practical action, but still more disappointing is the ineffectiveness of remedial action to solve the problems of human conduct.

What about the inner man, mental or physiological? It is fair to note that modern experimental psychology, engaged in highly sophisticated experiments, be it under the official flag of cognitive psychology or in the operant conditioning laboratory using animal subjects, no longer indulges in loose inference as a way to elude the problems; on the contrary, it makes precise and qualified inferences, which generally can be tested further by an appropriate experiment. Similarly, physiological research is more and more intimately intermingling with behavioral description and explanation. However, there is a strange revival of reductive explanations or of dualistic accounts on the part of influential neuroscientists. Eccles (1979) presents an extreme case of a recent dualistic conception; he resorts to fanciful immaterial mental entities responsible for reading all the stuff marvelously processed by the columnar modules. A no less extreme case of "neuronal reductionism" is offered by Changeux (1983) whose account of mental events – percepts and concepts identified with more or less complex cell assemblies (Hebb's 1979 influence is duly acknowledged) – leaves little, if any room for the interactive process that, for many psychologists (and not necessarily just behaviorists), is the essence of behavior. Our problem, says Changeux, is to look for the *cellular mechanisms* that account for "mental objects." How we describe these mental objects is not a matter of concern to him, since they *are* the cellular mechanisms themselves. There is no doubt that certain cognitivist psychologies give support to this sort of approach. (Changeux's view has many facets, some of which would be worth examining in connection with Skinner's theory. His concept of selective stabilization [Changeux & Danchin 1976] in neuronal development certainly offers more suggestive similarities with Skinner's notion of learning as a selective process than with Mehler's [1974] paradoxical idea of *learning by losing*.

Partial oppositions between theories should not mask interesting convergences and complementarities.)

A last word on another aspect of the flight to laymanship: Skinner, as a typical example, refers to a psychologist rejecting "all efforts to improve upon the psychology of the layman in approaching the problems of the aged." He has been through the personal experience of aging in the last few years, and this has not dissuaded him from the hope of improving the difficulties of real life by resorting to an analysis of behavior, nor from the conviction that simple principles, when applied correctly, can help a lot. This has turned up in a small nontechnical book for his fellow men and women, inviting them to "enjoy old age" (Skinner & Vaughan 1983). This is no revolution. It is just like claiming that it might be worthwhile to apply simple rules of hygiene (such as doctors washing their hands before obstetrical or surgical work) without waiting for the discovery of the general treatment for cancers. Simple ideas have always been disturbing.

BFS: I agree with Richelle that "the idea that the 'universe of discourse' of behavioral science should be kept apart from the universe of brain science ...has become incompatible with the zeitgeist," but only because a brain science has come into existence to replace the hypothetical neurology which was current at the time I wrote "Methods." The use of operant techniques in the brain science laboratory is the best demonstration I can offer of the contribution of an independent science of behavior in making the task of brain science clear. Valid facts about behavior are not invalidated by discoveries concerning the nervous system, nor are facts about the nervous system invalidated by tacts about behavior. Both sets of facts are part of the same enterprise, and I have always looked forward to the time when neurology would fill in the temporal and spatial gaps which are inevitable in a behavioral analysis.

Richelle's commentary is useful in counseling moderation, and I have no other observations to make about it.

What then should we do?

Seth Roberts

Department of Psychology, University of California, Berkeley

Among other things, Skinner seems to be saying (1) something is wrong with the way experimental psychologists are studying animal behavior, and (2) here are some suggestions for improvement. I would like to comment on both of these points, and make some suggestions of my own.

1. Something is wrong. That was 1950 (when something was wrong with current learning theories) and 1960 (when psychologists were leaving the laboratory). It is still true, I think, in the sense that things have been much better than they are now. Interest in the laboratory study of animal behavior reached a peak at about the time of Hull, and has subsided ever since. Concretely, there are far fewer people in the field. Interest may or may not be declining at this very moment, but the long-term trend is very clear. Perhaps Skinner will be seen as the prophet of this decline.

There is less interest, I think, because there is less excitement. The earlier excitement (Pavlov, Watson, Hull) was of course based on a promise, the promise that animal-learning experiments would reveal very important things. The promise has not been kept. There has not been either (a) substantial understanding (i.e., detailed description) of underlying mechanisms or (b) widespread applications. If we could describe the steps involved in learning the way biologists can describe the steps involved in photosynthesis, that would be substantial understanding; but current learning theories are, at best, only a little more detailed than when the whole enterprise began (compare the 1972 Rescorla–Wagner model with learning models from the fifties). As for applications of non-Skinnerian work, some exist – predator control (Gustavson, Garcia, Hankins, & Rusiniak 1974), perhaps treatment of drug addiction (Siegel 1979) – but they have not changed the world of most of us. Skinner made different promises, some of which are mentioned in "Methods." They were exciting to many. Behavior modification is an important application that came from Skinner's promise, but there do not seem to be any others in the offing, and, again, behavior modification does not affect the lives of most of us. Of course, a promise can be exciting only when it is fresh. Future excitement, I think, will have to be based on results (a detailed description of mechanism or widespread applications) rather than promises. In other words, the future number of psychologists studying animals will probably depend on the rate and importance of applications that are found, and the rate of progress toward the description of mechanism.

2. *Suggestions for improvement.* Some of Skinner's suggestions for improvement are:

1. Do not use hypothetico-deductive methods. Do not strive for "reductive explanation." "Acquire a...faith in the ultimate value of ostensibly undirected exploration."
2. Do not place much weight on statistical methods.
3. Do not rely on "commonsense" psychological concepts.
4. Measure rate of response rather than other dimensions of behavior.
5. Find (more) relevant variables and study their effects.

I doubt that these will help produce results of the sort I think are necessary to keep the field from shrinking even more. In general, suggestions 2–5, and other suggestions not on the list, seem small compared to the size of the problem (the need to rely on results rather than promises). Suggestion 1 would be fatal to a search for mechanism. To describe a mechanism in detail requires, among other things, choosing among a vast number of possibilities; to do this without a step-by-step method of narrowing the possibilities is about as likely to succeed as trying to telephone someone by dialing random numbers. Perhaps these suggestions would help in a search for applications, but I see no empirical reason to think so. I suspect that widespread applications are usually found in two ways: (a) by searching for an animal model of a widespread problem (e.g., the drug research that led to tranquilizers); or (b) by basic research whose goal is a detailed description of mechanism (e.g., the medical promise of recent discoveries in biology). Both ways require a search much more focused than Skinner's suggestions seem to imply.

3. *Alternative suggestions.* The goal of many animal psychologists is a detailed description of mechanism, yet progress is very slow (relative to sciences dealing with

more concrete things). Our problems *are* very difficult, but I think that two features of our search make progress slower than it has to be. We do experiments, and any experiment involves changing something and measuring something. Two features of our search that limit progress are:

(a) The set of changes used is small (compared, say, to human experimental psychology). For example, almost all classical-conditioning experiments are built around changes in a few parameters (e.g., timing, probability) of a small number of external events (e.g., lights, sounds, food). It is as if we are trying to describe something using very few words. A related problem is that the changes used to explain a result (to describe the mechanism) are not very different from the changes used to produce the result. Skinner might see this as a virtue; it seems to me like tryng to build something out of wood using only wooden tools. The solution, of course, is to use a richer set of changes. The manipulations of physiological psychology (drugs, lesions, brain stimulation, etc.) are one possibility. The work of Meck (1983) shows how a drug study can answer questions of interest to a psychologist.

(b) The usual measures provide only a little information. In most cases, the real information in an experiment – the information that helps us choose between different mechanisms – is merely whether one number is larger or smaller than another number. This is the case, for example, in most Conditioned-Emotional-Response experiments. Experiments usually take weeks. At best, then, we gather information at the rate of a few bits per month, and the true rate is probably much less. This can hardly be very productive. There is a need not so much to collect more numbers at once, but rather a need to collect more numbers that *are uncorrelated* – that measure different parts of the mechanism producing the behavior. The peak procedure, for example, was designed to provide two independent measures of performance in a time-discrimination task (Roberts 1981), and the procedure has made it easier to learn about the mechanisms that produce time discrimination (e.g., Roberts 1982; Roberts & Holder, 1984). There is also a need for experiments that provide so much data that the end result is a *picture* rather than, say, a bar graph or a learning curve. Many experiments of Blough (e.g., 1963; 1972; 1978; 1982) meet this criterion.

BFS: I am afraid I must question Roberts's authority as a historian. He says that "the laboratory study of animal behavior reached a peak at about the time of Hull, and has subsided ever since." Hull was active in the thirties and forties. In the fifties almost all the large pharmaceutical companies opened operant laboratories for the assessment of drug effects. In 1957 the Society for the Experimental Analysis of Behavior was founded and the *Journal of the Experimental Analysis of Behavior* began publication. During that decade, meetings of a Conference on the Experimental Analysis of Behavior grew to the point at which by 1964 they led to the founding of Division 25 of the American Psychological Association (the only division, I believe, representing a single scientific position). The *Journal of Applied Behavior Analysis* began publication in 1968. The Association of Behavior Analysis is now in its 10th year, and separate state branches have been founded. Annual conferences are held in many Latin American countries, and the first European Conference on the Experimental Analysis of Behavior, held in 1983 in Liège, attracted people from 27 countries. Not all of this is concerned with *animal* behavior, but animal research is still prominent.

The dark side of Skinnerian epistemology

William W. Rozeboom

Department of Psychology, University of Alberta, Canada

One of the larger tragedies in psychology's intellectual history is its recent repudiation of the behaviorist program for our discipline. I have said elsewhere that we need a resurrection of behaviorism. Not of specific mid-century behavior theories whose simplicities are clearly obsolete. And certainly not of the largely mythological positivistic behaviorism that proscribed theories of the inner organism as idle fancy. The behaviorist ideal which takes seriously the old-fashioned tried-and-true scientific distinction between evidence and hypothesis, which seeks to shape our models of psychonomic mechanism by toughminded inference from sceptically hardened data on which mentalistic interpretations have not been imposed at the outset, *that* is the doctrine whose revival to counterbalance current cognitive science's runaway aprioricism has become urgent.

What has gone wrong? Essentially, it is that behaviorism became prevailingly viewed as a perverse, stultifying suppression of concern for what goes on within us. It takes little attentive reading of the neobehaviorist classics, notably Hull and Tolman, to perceive that image's malign inaccuracy. But it does fairly characterize behaviorism's radical splinter for which Skinner has been the latter-day spokesman. And because moral outrage is both emotionally gratifying and a labor-saving surrogate for tight thinking, extremist views are what outsiders love to hate. It is ironic that the same Skinner who has so powerfully enriched the technology of behaviorist research should also have contributed so much to its demise as an active intellectual force.

The issue here – the scope and practical methodology of human knowledge – could scarcely be larger. We can surely agree that the main task of any empirical science is to work out credible conclusions about its chosen topic by plausible inference from firm evidence. And let us not dispute that psychology's most reliable evidence is behavioral. But then we must ask, What can be inferred from such data, and how? One might suspect this to be a question of considerable depth and intricacy, on which responsible opinion should be accompanied by some thoughtfully articulate theory of knowledge acquisition. But Skinner has never voiced more than intuitive fiats on this matter, nor has he shown much interest in probating these in the court of debate on the detailed praxis of data interpretation. His aversion to the licentiousness of hypothetico-deductive reasoning is indeed amply justifiable by arguments I have developed elsewhere (Rozeboom 1970; 1972; 1982). But although it is important to expose textbook hypothetico-deductivism for the epistemic fraud it is, Skinner offers no principles of practical inference to replace this, only loose positivistic slogans that would be intellectually impossible to live by even were it not foolish to try.

Skinner urges that we eschew attempts to explain "an observed fact which appeals to events taking place somewhere else, at some other level of observation, described in different terms, and measured, if at all, in different dimensions." But *why* should we abstain from this? Because events of nonobservational kinds do not exist at all (ontological positivism)? Because we cannot meaningfully conceive of what we cannot observe (semantic positivism)? Because observational data can never confer high credibility upon assertions containing nonobservational constructs (epistemological positivism)? You don't believe any of those things, and neither on pain of incoherence can Skinner: His response probabilities and even momentary response rates are prime examples of conjectured causes of overt behavior that we never observe directly but only infer from past and present performance. (Skinner will retort that these are "measured in the same dimensions" as observed responding, but that is just not so.) The operative problem of scientific inference is not *whether* we should try for conclusions about the hidden sources of overt events, but by what patterns of reasoning in what real-life circumstances this becomes epistemically feasible.

What Skinner and his opposition in the many philosophers and some scientists who extoll hypothetico-deductive theorizing as the quintessence of scientific method have alike failed to appreciate is that there exist determinate forms of *explanatory induction* by which in practice we discover and progressively refine our understanding of hidden causes. These are patterns of inferential disclosure which, at levels of confidence often approaching the force of commonsense perception, transform observed local regularities into inductive conclusions about how these are due to underlying source factors of which the local data parameters are diagnostic. There is far more to say about such inductions than what is covered in my previous accounts (Rozeboom 1961; 1966; 1972), but here I can only note once again that their most primitively compelling version is the logic by which we acquire dispositional concepts. Skinner has made plain his disdain for the explanatory value of the latter (e.g., "the term [viscosity] is useful in referring to a characteristic of a fluid, but it is nevertheless a mistake to say that a fluid flows slowly because it is viscous or possesses a high viscosity. A state or quality inferred from the behavior of a fluid begins to be taken as a cause"; Skinner 1974, p. 161; see also Skinner 1953, pp. 202ff.). But even disregarding my own realist arguments for the causal efficacy of dispositions (Rozeboom 1973; 1984), there is a large technical literature (see, e.g., Tuomela 1978) to attest how ingenuous is Skinner's understanding in this matter. And dispositions are merely the bottom rung of hidden mechanisms to which iteration of explanatory induction gives us epistemic access.

Because explanatory induction is data driven, its practice strongly endorses Skinner's call to search out empirical regularities, the cleaner the better, described in terms from which all problematic theoretical presumptions have been expunged. But Skinner's refusal to see the explanatory import of these also blinds him to the more intricate behavioral regularities that manifest central states deeper than surface dispositions. As a major case in point, I give you conditioned generalization (Rozeboom 1958), which is the empirical underlay of the "what is learned?" controversies that so greatly exercised mid-century mainstream behavior theory, and for which Skinnerian behavior principles have made no provision.

Suppose that organism *o*'s rate of operant *R* has been intermittently reinforced to high strength by a stimulus S^r which has become secondarily rewarding for *o* through its discriminative cuing of primary reward. (Say, *R* is bar pressing which occasionally produces a tone that signals delivery of a food pellet.) If, in the absence of *R*-doing, S^r's reinforcement value for *o* is now reconditioned from positive to negative (say, the bar is removed and *o* is repeatedly presented with the tone followed by shock instead of food), to what extent does this reconditioning of S^r suppress *o*'s responding when *R*'s availability to *o* is renewed on a straight extinction schedule that no longer yields S^r? That is, once *R* has been established by its production of reward S^r, does subsequent altering of S^r's reinforcement value correspondingly modify the strength of *R* prior to new contingencies of S^r upon *R*? Or does the curve of *R*-extinction begin instead at the level (adjusted for complicating factors such as aversive conditioning of the background stimuli) to which *R* was terminally reinforced by S^r, as Skinner would have it? Commonsensically, it seems evident that if *o* learns to expect S^r from doing *R*, then *o*'s *R*-emissions should fall off abruptly if S^r is switched for *o* from attractive to aversive. And conversely, although response shifts so induced can have many explanations other than mentalistic ideation, they *are* strong evidence for the involvement in *o*'s postconditioning *R*-output of *some* internal mediator, whatever its nature, that is functionally rather like a cognitive representation of S^r.

Hard evidence for conditioned generalization, which has many varieties beyond the one just described, is still meager at the infrahuman level. (For me, loss of innocence was discovery from my early research on this paradigm that rats and pigeons just don't seem to think like people do.) But it is clearly demonstrable in human learning (Rozeboom 1967) – which is to say that this phenomenon is strongly local at least across species and probably even more so with variation in the parameters of training and testing. How local degrees of conditioned generalization covary with other simple or data-structurally complex observables remains a seminal issue for behavioral research that seeks to chart the subtler contours of organismic adaptability to change. But Skinnerians find it difficult to acknowledge such higher-level regularities, not because these are any less observational than the basic reinforcement phenomena that operant conditioning research has worked out in such instructive local detail, but because they are incompatible with the simplistic overgenerality in which operant reinforcement *theory* has been orthodoxly formulated.

To summarize: Soft theoretical speculations, if astutely analyzed, can guide us to the discovery of complex empirical phenomena whose theory-free descriptions instruct us by explanatory induction about the central mechanisms behind overt behavior even though, in all likelihood, this confirms only fragments of the theories instigating the inquiry and may well cast doubt on their remainders. The inevitable practical consequence of Skinner's doctrinaire insensitivity to this interplay between theory and data is inflation of local regularities into sweepingly rigid laws that prejudge many significant operational questions about the management of behavior. In short, Skinnerian psychology, too, remains largely bogus, despite its enormous power in those special circumstances to which its generalities legitimately apply. For it has worded its findings to claim a universality vastly beyond the scope supported by their data base, and thereby implies closure on complex empirical issues that in fact remain fascinatingly unresolved.

BFS: Rozeboom has not convinced me of the causal efficacy of his position or of "hidden mechanisms to which iteration of explanatory induction gives us epistemic access." W. H. Morse and I did an experiment something like the one Rozeboom describes (Morse & Skinner, 1958). A naive hungry pigeon was placed in a box illuminated by a colored light. The box was illuminated or dark for various periods of time. When it was illuminated, a food dispenser operated on a variable-interval schedule. In the dark, the food dispenser was never operated. Subsequently, in white light, responses to a key were reinforced for several days until stable rates appeared. During a test session no food was given, and responses to the key went unreinforced. Many more responses were emitted when the colored light was turned on, although the response had not been reinforced with food in its presence. The experiment throws additional light on the nature of the control exerted by stimuli. Eventually a physiological explanation will be available. Meanwhile, I do not see that anything is gained by referring to a hidden mechanism. On the contrary, representing a datum with a hidden mechanism makes it harder to integrate with other data from other experiments, which could also be done without postulating a hidden mechanism.

Current questions for the science of behavior

Kenneth M. Sayre

Department of Philosophy, University of Notre Dame

Skinner is probably best known today as a polemicist for behaviorism. If so, this is unfortunate; by rights he should be known instead as the primary founder of an experimental method that has met with more success than any other method this uncertain discipline has yet to offer. For, talk of "fads" and "isms" and "paradigm shifts" aside, there *is* an experimental science of operant behavior, and Skinner more than anyone else has made it so.

In candor, however, the unbiased contemporary observer must hasten to add that there are broad areas of human activity (e.g., language and thought) that appear beyond the reach of Skinner's methods, and that there are other methods (e.g., computer modeling) that show distinct promise in the study of such activities. Despite Skinner's monumental achievements, the future of psychology does not lie with operant analysis alone. More likely, it lies with an approach that can integrate the methods of behavioral analysis with those of neuroscience and computer modeling.

A disappointing feature of "Methods" is that it consists largely of excerpts from polemical writings of past decades. From one point of view, the selection is understandable. Skinner has reason to feel that his arguments against the misuse of statistics and other forms of mathematics in the study of behavior have never been adequately answered, and that his advocacy of rigorously applied experimental techniques has been paid too little heed by contemporary researchers. Rather than reissue challenges of the past, nonetheless, it would have been more productive and interesting if he had taken the opportunity to bring us up to date on his thinking about the current status of the science of behavior, and the direction it might be expected to take as it continues to mature.

"Methods" does in fact contain a number of provocative remarks bearing on the future of psychology, specifically regarding (1) the appropriate use of mathematics in the experimental study of behavior, and (2) the eventual merger of the science of behavior with the neurosciences. I would like to draw attention to some issues under each heading, hoping to hear more about them in the author's response.

1. The use of mathematics in the study of behavior. One unpromising alternative to the laboratory study of behavior cited in "Methods" is the statistical analysis of large sample sets of data; another is the use of "mathematical models" (Skinner's stylization). The troubles Skinner finds with the first are reasonably clear. Such techniques emphasize "the treatment of variation after the fact"; and given sufficient sample size one can find significance in almost any combination of empirical data. His problems with mathematical models are less clear, but include at least (a) their resistance to falsification by empirical data, and (b) their tendency to take shape before it is clear what "properties of a system of variables" might profitably be formalized.

As of 1961 at least, Skinner was not happy with any of the mathematical techniques that had begun to be used in the study of behavior. Yet at the same time he suggests that the experimental analysis of behavior has reached a point where it "is ready for the kind of mathematical theory which has always been productive at the proper stage in the history of science. What is needed is...a mathematical treatment of experimental data."

What kind of mathematical treatment, specifically? If the treatment needed is not that of mere statistical analysis, nor of mathematical modeling (presumably of the sort surveyed in Bush 1960), nor that of information theory or cybernetics (disclaimed in Skinner 1969, p. 104), then what is left? As the science of behavior approaches maturity, what contribution specifically should be expected from mathematics?

2. *The science of behavior and the neurosciences.* Theory, in the sense Skinner finds objectionable, appeals to events "at some other level of observation" (like those of introspection), events "measured...in different dimensions" (perhaps via microscopes and microprobes), or events "taking place somewhere else" (like concepts and intentions) and neither observed nor measured. Put very simply, the problem with such events is that they have the status at best of intermediate steps in the production of the behavior to be explained, and thus (*pace* the nativist) require explanation themselves in terms of their environmental determinants. An optimal experimental method, accordingly, might be one that bypasses these intervening "internal" steps entirely and undertakes explanation of an organism's responses in terms of correlations with publicly observable antecedents.

Neat and elegant as this may be as a methodological ideal, it suffers limitations in application that have long been apparent. To put it baldly, there are just too many forms of behavior we consider appropriate for empirical investigation that cannot be correlated with specific classes of environmental antecedents. For example, a memory of having been mistreated by a human being obviously might influence an organism's behavior, and would presumably do so as a state or process of its nervous system. Yet this memory could be produced in turn by such a wide variety of environmental circumstances, occurring throughout the organism's lifetime, that it would be quite impractical to hope to find an explanatory correlation between the behavior produced *by* a memory state and the environmental circumstances that *produced* the memory state in turn. In such cases, some form of reference to "internal" states seems essential to an adequate explanation. An adequate experimental design would thus appear to require some sort of access to the neuronal states or processes by which the behavior in question is more immediately determined – in other words, to the memory itself.

Another type of behavior obviously beyond the scope of Skinner's methods is that produced by genetically based factors which cannot be traced back to environmental determinants at all. To explain such behavior in terms of its causal antecedents again would seem to require access to states and structures of the nervous system. And this at least seems (*pace* some cognitivists) to call for a merger of experimental resources between the science of behavior and the neurosciences.

It is much to Skinner's credit as a scientist that, despite the displeasure expressed in "Methods" with efforts "to reduce behavior to events in the nervous system" (whatever that might mean), he seems to anticipate such a merger in other less polemical writings. In Skinner (1969, p. 282), for instance, he foresees the time when we will have "a complete account of a behaving organism – of both the observable behavior and the physiological processes occurring at the same time," and when accordingly the "organism would be seen to be a unitary system, its behavior clearly part of its physiology."

There are two questions I wish to pose in this regard:

1. Given recent advances of experimental technique in the neurosciences, are we any closer to a fruitful merger between physiology and psychology?
2. When the time of merger arrives, how specifically might we expect the laboratory techniques of neuroscience to augment those of operant analysis?

BFS: Sayre has, I think, put the central issue of "Methods" in its clearest terms, but I am unhappy about his example of a memory that seems to require a reference to an internal state.

Let us say that I am cheated by a used car dealer. He has an ethnic name, wears a lapel button indicating his membership in a veterans organization, and operates from a used car lot marked by strings of colored flags. Henceforth, let us say that when I hear a name of the same ethnic group, see someone wearing a similar button, or pass a used car lot marked by colored flags, I observe changes in my body, presumably resulting from the activity of my autonomic nervous system, which I have been taught to call anger. I avoid or escape from people with such names or wearing such buttons, and whenever possible I use routes which do not pass used car lots. Must we say that the ethnic name, the lapel button, and the flag-marked lot produce a memory state and that the memory state in turn produces the responses in my autonomic and central nervous systems? Or can we not simply say that the cheating episode changed me in such a way that certain responses now occur in certain circumstances? Of course the change took place in my nervous system, which at any given time is in a "state" – a state that will eventually be described in other terms. I would say more or less the same thing about the "states" arising from genetic factors. Until more is known about neurology and genetics, our only access to states is via the history that produced them.

Theories and human behavior

Morton L. Schagrin

Faculty for Arts, Eduction and Humanities, State University of New York, Fredonia

Professor Skinner's behavior disconfirms his own views on human behavior: With little positive and much negative reinforcement, he continues to publish his views on scientific method and the proper analysis of human behavior. I would like to argue that his conceptions of scientific theories and of human behavior are too narrow, and, consequently, his research program, even if successful, will not lead to much progress in the science of psychology.

There are two sorts of theory on Skinner's account. The first sort "appeals to events taking place somewhere else, at some other level of observation, described in different terms, and measured, if at all, in different dimensions." The reference point for contrast is the event to be explained. Skinner believes this sort of theory is not useful, and that the pursuit of such theories is a waste of time and resources.

The second sort of theory does not appeal to other dimensions. It consists in stating orderly, functional relations among items in the same dimension. In psychology in particular these theories relate observable behavior to observable environmental variables and changes in observable behavior to observable changes in the environment. Theories of this sort have usually been called "laws" by philosophers of science, and Skinner has no difficulty in accepting theories of this second sort. In what follows, I refer to theories in this sense as laws, and theories of the first sort as theories.

For Skinner, the aim of science is to predict and control events studied by the science. For psychology, it is to predict and control behavior. Laws are sufficient for this purpose, Skinner claims, and explanations of events by means of theories are not needed.

I shall not argue that theories (even erroneous ones) are needed to discriminate and describe the relevant observables – the "theory ladenness" of observation. In his discussion on "preference," Skinner himself notes that it is not the (behavior of) striking a key, but the (behavior of) changing from one key to another that is relevant. Theories can guide us in describing phenomena, yet I shall not argue this case.

One can grant that the prediction and control of events can be accomplished by empirical laws. Consider the technology that produced Damascus steel, or the long history of breeding horses and dogs. (It is probably more accurate to say these technologies were based on erroneous theories than to say they were based on no theory at all.) Surely, the explanatory power of theories in chemistry and metallurgy and of the theory of genes has led to greater successes in technology in these fields. Examples can be multiplied, of course. Indeed, the history of science and technology in all fields reveals that, first, until about 1870, a technology of prediction and control preceded explanatory theories, and, second, these technologies were subsequently greatly improved by these more adequate theories. Moreover, I hasten to add, theories did not arise, in a Baconian fashion, as generalizations of the empirical laws – an observation made long ago by Whewell (1967). Thus, contrary to Skinner's position, theories have, without exception, been useful in perfecting the prediction and control of events, and, in some branches of science, have been necessary conditions for progress.

Turning to my second point of disagreement with Skinner, I would argue that items of human behavior are not observable in physical or motor terms. I recall an experiment a few years ago, where children at an orphanage were conditioned to choose whole-wheat bread over white bread in a cafeteria line. Conditioning was accomplished by having each child select one of two items such as a pair of new, clean brown gloves, or else a pair of torn, ragged white gloves. Positive reinforcement followed the choice of the darker item. The experiment was successful to some degree: Consumption of whole-wheat bread increased during the experiment.

I wonder, however, how one would "condition" the children not to steal. Would one condition them not to pick up green colored pieces of paper? Learning not to steal requires the student to acquire the concept of possession, of mine and thine. Nothing physical or observable marks a thing as mine and not yours. One cannot describe the human behavior called "stealing" solely in physical or motor terms, although surely physical movements are occurring.

Consider kosher food. What marks, or identifies, an item of food as kosher is not, in general, a purely physical or observable aspect of the food. The behavioral reaction to the stimulus is mediated by knowledge (or beliefs) about the history and preparation of the dish, and cannot be controlled by reinforcement of responses to the physical environment alone.

My point is that animal behavior, and some human behavior, can be conditioned, a result that Skinner and his followers have demonstrated. But what is most interesting and important about human behavior cannot be reduced to bodily movements as Skinner's program requires. Understanding (and predicting and controlling) human behavior is a project that goes well beyond controlling physical movements cued by the physical environment.

BFS: It is a trivial point, but I do not disconfirm my own views in continuing to publish "with little positive and much negative reinforcement." Schagrin presumably means the social reinforcements of approval and emulation. I am perfectly happy with those I have received (see my replies to other commentaries), but the primary reinforcer of scientific behavior is the clarification which follows, even if apparent only to oneself.

I am not sure what Schagrin means by "without exception" when he says "theories have, without exception, been useful in perfecting the prediction and control of events, and, in some branches of science, have been necessary conditions for progress." Does he mean that theories have *always* helped predict and control events, or that all successful prediction and control have involved theories, even though masses of theories have been thrown away as useless? I certainly agree that in some branches of science theories of a particular kind have been necessary.

I also agree that Schagrin has not succeeded in analyzing stealing or the knowledge or belief that food is kosher in such a way that a behavioral analysis will apply. But can they not be so analyzed? And I was not aware that my program requires that "what is most interesting and important about human behavior...be reduced to bodily movements."

The question: Not *shall* it be, but *which* shall it be?

Charles P. Shimp

Department of Psychology, University of Utah

In "Methods" Skinner is instructing us on how to discriminate between good and bad theories. I first describe the criteria by means of which Skinner proposes we can do this, then discuss where the criteria apparently come from, and finally examine their general suitability as tools for the evaluation of behavioral theories.

Skinner has consistently favored a cumulative-growth version of science, in which empirical generalizations of ever increasing scope are built up inductively. He favors this over a version in which progress depends on the development and evaluation of theory. Accordingly, one should perhaps not be too dismayed at finding little guidance from Skinner on how to sort good theories from bad. Still, in "Methods" Skinner is trying to instruct us on how to do just that, and in sorting good from bad theories evaluative criteria are essential. What are Skinner's evaluative criteria?

First, a good theory should not involve a "level of observation" other than that of behavior itself, and should instead be stated in terms of the "fundamental dimensions of behavior." What are "the fundamental dimensions of behavior"? We are actually given only one, the discovery of which, according to Skinner, is the most scientifically significant contribution of his career (Skinner 1966b). This dimension is the "rate or probability of response." Second, a good theory should summarize the observed facts "solely in terms of behavior" and should do so with a "minimal number of terms." These two criteria seem to be the chief ones Skinner proposes to separate good from bad theories.

Where do these criteria come from? Skinner implicitly assumes a particular relation between empirical method and data on the one hand and theory on the other. He strongly emphasizes differences between empirical things, methods and data, and theories. The former are "objective" and involve such things as "empirical facts" and "observed facts." It is clear that Skinner considers his methodology to be objective and empirical. Such attributions about the nature of method and data are more controversial and less widely accepted now than they were when Skinner began to make them. Philosophical analyses by Wittgenstein (1953), Hanson (1969), and Rorty (1979), and psychological research on top–down processing in perception, where what one sees depends on what one knows, both suggest that scientific seeing, rather than being the sort of thing Skinner assumes it to be, is theory laden. From this perspective, the empirical methodology of science is theory laden in the sense that the use of an empirical method can be shown to translate into a commitment to a theory in terms of which the method makes sense. In contrast to Skinner's position where facts come first and theories only come later, this alternative position holds that facts are facts only in the context of a theory.

The particular underlying theory in Skinner's case turns out to be easily identifiable. It is a common form of early association theory inherited from the epistemology of the British empiricists. The justification for this claim is provided in detail elsewhere (Shimp 1975; 1976). Briefly, the justification is that most of Skinner's empirical methods, or schedules of reinforcement, involve the repeated pairing of reinforcement with an essentially instantaneous behavior (one that is "freely repeated" and has a "moment of emission" that "is a point in time"). Skinner notes that such a brief response is selected because it is "easily observed," but it also enters ideally into the empiricist idea of a causal relation or chain. This chaining idea even appears as part of recent demonstration of behavioral approaches to language (Epstein, Lanza, & Skinner 1980), despite Chomsky's famous criticism of it (Chomsky 1959). In any event, Skinner's methods are clearly theory laden.

Is there a relation between this theoretical position and the two criteria he proposes for the evaluation of theories? The first criterion seems unexceptionable and is little more than a classic appeal to parsimony. Virtually everyone would agree that, everything else being equal, the theory that has fewer terms is better. But the second criterion seems directly relevant to Skinner's theoretical position deriving from classic British empiricism and associationism. It is well known that this epistemology motivates Skinner's kind of conceptual and linguistic dichotomization between empirical and theoretical matters (Hanson 1969; Rorty 1979). Skinner's assumption that the "behavioral facts" and "observable facts" and the "fundamental datum" can be obtained and identified without an appeal to "some other dimensional system" is part and parcel of this questionable epistemological position. In general, we may say that his criteria for evaluating theories are themselves theory laden.

We can now consider how effective Skinner's recommended criteria for distinguishing between good and bad theories are. The first criterion is virtually inapplicable except in rare cases where competing theories can be judged to be equally preferable on all matters except the number of terms they include (Hanson 1969). The second criterion requires us to accept Skinner's claims that he knows what the "observable facts" are. But it can be argued that in principle facts are not observable. Instead, facts are certain kinds of linguistic propositions (Hanson 1969; Wittgenstein 1953). One can neither validate nor invalidate the claim, according to Skinner the factual claim, that mean response rate is a dimension of behavior outside the context of a theory that explains why mean response rate is a dimension of behavior. One does not determine the dimensions of behavior simply through direct observation. Nor can one interpret the phrase "levels of observation" outside the context of a theory that tells us what observation is, what its different levels are, and so on.

That Skinner's views on the fundamental unit of behavioral analysis are theory laden becomes clearer when alternatives are explicitly described. One alternative attributes significant temporal duration to it, even though this makes its direct observation more difficult or impossible (Shimp 1975; 1976). Such analyses, which attribute significant temporal duration and temporal patterning to the fundamental behavioral unit of analysis, have been part of a molecular approach to behavioral analysis (Shimp 1975; 1976a). This approach typically involves a hierarchical rather than linear picture of the structure of knowledge (Anderson & Bower 1973) and links up much more easily than does Skinner's with contemporary work on behavioral patterning (Hulse & O'Leary 1982; Straub, Seidenberg, Bever, & Terrace 1979). In terms of these approaches, the "fundamental datum" has not yet been discovered, nor are the chief dimensions of behavior yet known. Thus, in terms of the criteria of Hanson (1969), Rorty (1979), and others, we do not yet know what behavior is. As a concept we do not know what it means.

Skinner's criteria for theory evaluation are consistent with his empirical methodology, forms of data analysis, and metatheoretical statements about the fundamental datum. But a change in any of the elements of his conceptual system causes a major breakdown in the whole. Reject mean response rate as the fundamental datum, or dimension of behavior, and one is left not knowing what behavior is. Reject his empiricist epistemology separating data from theory, and one is left not knowing what a behavioral fact is. Reject his inductionist approach in favor of mathematical theories (Gibbon 1977) or computer models (Shimp, 1984a; 1984b), and his criteria become simply arbitrary or irrelevant.

Whereas Skinner considers an important problem to be *whether* one should or should not develop a theory having variables in terms other than the dimensions of behavior, an alternative position considers the important problem to be *which* such theory one should develop. To pretend one has the choice Skinner examines is to consider an option we do not have; it also prolongs the time a scientific community will implicitly subscribe to a theoretical alternative it would reject if it were made explicit.

BFS: Shimp is strong on theory. He says one must have a theory in order to see a rat in a box (seeing is theory laden). One must have a theory to say that the rat presses a lever (propositions are theory laden). One must have a theory to say that after pressing a lever the rat eats the bit of food that is dispensed (sequencing or chaining is theory laden). One must have a theory to say that, in the absence of further reinforcement, the rat then presses the lever more often than would otherwise be the case ("One can neither validate nor invalidate the claim...that mean response rate is a dimension of behavior outside the context of a theory that explains why mean response rate is a dimension of behavior.")

Shimp's effort to associate my position with "early association theory inherited from the epistemology of the British empiricists" resembles that of current theorists who try to explain operant conditioning in terms of Pavlovian conditioning, which is much closer to associationism. Shimp seems to miss entirely the notion of selection by consequences and the parallel between operant conditioning and natural selection.

The chaining to which Chomsky (1959) objects (and which I have never proposed) is not exemplified in the demonstrations to which Shimp refers. If the organisms in the demonstration had been people rather than pigeons, their behavior could have been described in the following way:

In order to operate a machine dispensing candy bars, Jack must press just that one of three buttons the color of which corresponds to a sample color which only Jill can see. He says to Jill:

"What is the color?"

Jill looks at the hidden color and says, "Red."

"Thank you," says Jack, thus making it more likely that Jill will do similar favors in the future. He presses the red button and receives a candy bar.

Is Shimp suggesting that that is not a *chain* in the sense that each step is linked to the preceding? Behaviorists are supposed to use a very different sort of chaining to explain complex behavior, verbal or nonverbal. They are accused of saying that the successive responses of a skilled pianist are triggered one by one by the preceding responses, which, of course, is absurd.

Evidently, Shimp and others have reached a position in which "we do not yet know what behavior is. As a concept we do not know what it means." So much for the usefulness of theory.

Behavior, theories, and the inner

Ernest Sosa

Department of Philosophy, Brown University

Against Hume's associationism Karl Popper (1969) urges a refutation no less damaging to the behaviorism of B. F. Skinner. Indeed, a very similar objection is used by Noam Chomsky (1959) for his widely known critique of Skinner. I first expound and consider these objections, and then discuss Skinner's rationale.

Here is Popper on Hume's associationism:

> The central idea of Hume's theory is that of *repetition, based upon similarity* (or "resemblance")....But we ought to realize that in a psychological theory such as Hume's, only repetition-for-us, based upon similarity-for-us, can be allowed to have any effect upon us....This apparently psychological criticism has a purely logical basis which may be summed up in the following simple argument....The kind of repetition envisaged by Hume can never be perfect; the cases he has in mind cannot be cases of perfect sameness; they can only be cases of similarity. Thus *they are repetitions only from a certain point of view*. (What has the effect upon me of a repetition may not have this effect upon a spider.) But this means that, for logical reasons, there must always be a point of view – such as a system of expectations, anticipations, assumptions, or interests – *before* there can be any repetition; which point of view, consequently, cannot be merely the result of repetition. (Popper 1969, sec. 4)

No isolated exception, this objection appears also in the appendix to Popper's *Logic of Scientific Discovery*, as follows:

> Generally, similarity, and with it repetition, always presuppose the adoption of a *point of view*: some similarities of repetitions will strike us if we are interested in one problem, and others if we are interested in another problem. But if similarity and repetition presuppose the adoption of a point of view, or an interest, or an expectation, it is logically necessary that points of view, or interests, or expectations, are logically prior, as well as temporally (or causally or psychologically) prior, to repetition. (Popper 1961, pp. 421–22)

According to Popper's critique: (a) there is no repetition independent of a point of view, and (b) only repetition-for-us based upon similarity-for-us can be allowed to have any effect upon us. In that case Skinner's program to go beyond mentalism (and freedom and dignity) would get nowhere. For the main concepts and principles of such behaviorism require the possibility of objective (nonmentalistic) repetition. Positive reinforcement of operant behavior in bar-pressing experiments, for example, is understood as increase of "operant strength," defined in turn by the rate of response during extinction. And secondary reinforcers develop through *repeated* association with primary reinforcers. If Popper is right then, ironically, the multiple dependence of Skinner's theories on the notion of repetition makes them multiply mentalistic. There is hence no logical possibility that such theories would enable us *either* to explain all beliefs (expectations, assumptions, etc.) by association à la Hume, *or* to be rid of all mentalistic concepts in favor of behaviorist replacements.

Popper goes on to elaborate his critique of Hume and to propose his own psychology and logic of discovery as a matter of conjectures and refutations. But his own summary above shows up Popper's refutation as a non sequitur. A beach and a rocky cliff are affected differently by the waves. Repeated stretchings will permanently stretch a rubber band before a steel spring. Must we therefore appeal to difference in point of view – in expectations, anticipations, assumptions, or interests – in order to explain such differences? And if we need not do so there, why is it logically required in accounting for difference in effects on a spider and a human? Perhaps *at present* no hypothesis (beyond "there must be some intrinsic difference") is plausible which is free of any mentalistic content. The absence of any plausible hypothesis is far from a logical proof that no hypothesis is at all possible, however, nor does Popper provide any other proof.

Chomsky makes a similar argument from a different angle. Here he is on Skinner's behaviorism (parenthetical page references are to Skinner 1957):

> A typical example of *stimulus* control for Skinner would be the response to a piece of music with the utterance *Mozart* or to a painting with the response *Dutch*. These responses are asserted to be "under the control of extremely subtle properties" of the physical object or event (108). Suppose instead of saying *Dutch* we had said *Clashes with the wallpaper, I thought you liked abstract work, Never saw it before, Tilted, Hanging too low, Beautiful, Hideous, Remember our camping trip last summer?* or whatever else might come into our minds when looking at a picture (in Skinnerian translation, whatever other responses exist in sufficient strength). Skinner could only say that each of these responses is under the control of some other stimulus property of the physical object. If we look at a red chair and say *red*, the response is under the control of the stimulus *redness*; if we say *chair*, it is under the control of the collection of properties (for Skinner, the object) *chairness* (110), and similarly for any other response. This device is as simple as it is empty. Since properties are free for the asking (we have as many of them as we have nonsynonymous descriptive expressions in our language, whatever this means exactly), we can account for a wide class of responses in terms of Skinnerian functional analysis by identifying the *controlling stimuli*. But the word *stimulus* has lost all objectivity in this usage. Stimuli are no longer part of the outside physical world; they are driven back into the organism. We identify the stimulus when we hear the response. It is clear from such examples, which abound, that the talk of *stimulus control* simply disguises a complete retreat to mentalistic psychology. (Chomsky 1959, sec. 3)

Chomsky objects that stimuli are "driven back into the organism" which implies "a complete retreat to mentalistic psychology." But it is not clear what the objection amounts to: For example, what kind of retreat to mentalism is charged? Is it that since we can't identify a stimulus independently of the response by the subject, therefore the stimulus must be inside the subject and mentalistic? That is a non sequitur. Is it that since we can't identify a stimulus independently of the response by the subject, therefore it is somehow illegitimate to explain the response by the stimulus thus identified? But exactly why is that illegitimate? (Compare our inability to identify or characterize the start of our known universe independently of its later states, which such a start must presumably help explain: our inability, that is, to know about such a start and its character without inference from later states which it may still in turn help to explain.) Is it rather that properties like chairness are unlikely to figure in a Peircean millenary science (Peirce 1878, esp. sec. 4)? That is true, but irrelevant to social and behavioral science as it is today. (Other main themes in Chomsky's critique do, however, seem right: e.g., that even today we are at a loss to predict or control verbal behavior except in highly artificial and special situations. But this proves neither behaviorism's retreat to mentalism nor its driving of stimuli back into the organism. The foregoing defends behaviorism's *possibility* against Chomsky's charge of a retreat to mentalism. It does not dispute Chomsky's detailed argument that, at least with regard to verbal behavior, it is as yet little more than a *mere* possibility.)

Skinner's advocacy of behaviorist methodology highlights the practical objectives of prediction and control:

> The objection to inner states is not that they do not exist, but that they are not relevant in a functional analysis. We cannot account for the behavior of any system while staying wholly inside it; eventually we must turn to forces operating upon the organism from without. Unless there is a weak spot in our causal chain so that the second link is not lawfully determined by the first, or the third by the second, then the first and third links must be lawfully related. If we must always go back beyond the second link for prediction and control we may avoid many tiresome and exhausting digressions by examining the third link as a function of the first. Valid information about the second link may throw light upon this relationship but can in no way alter it. (Skinner 1953, p. 35)

In other words: Any procedure for the prediction or control of behavior would require observable inputs. Even if in fact there really are intervening variables in the brain or in the mind, therefore, these can be bypassed; for our only access to them must in turn be observable. Since intervening variables can be thus bypassed, finally, any behavioral science that holds prediction and control paramount can safely ignore the inner. Such behavioral science must rather focus on functional relationships between outer stimuli and behavioral responses.

Though Skinner's argument has great surface plausibility, and though it has served as the official rationale for behaviorist methodology, it will not hold up under scrutiny. After all, it is by *not* ignoring the inner that physical science has provided our astonishing ability to predict and control nature. How then can it be held that prediction and control of behavior are best attained by ignoring the inner? Surely Skinner's a priori argument for bypassing the inner is refuted by the plain success of inner-focused physical science in attaining precisely the desiderata of prediction and control.

This is not at all to say what sort of data or theories behavioral science should aim for at any given stage. In fact, it can obviously be the best early strategy to gather what functional relationships one can at the surface level, with or without a view to the later formulation of explanatory hypotheses, which may *or may not* themselves take the form of such functional relationships. Many behaviorists must have had nothing more than this in mind. Skinner's official rationale has been more ambitious, however, but it cannot be sustained.

In the final section, "Some Afterthoughts," of "Methods" Skinner offers a new argument against hypothetico-deductive theories in behavioral science:

> When a subject matter is very large (for example, the universe as a whole) or very small (for example, subatomic particles) or for any reason inaccessible, we cannot manipulate variables or observe effects as we should like to do. We therefore make tentative or hypothetical statements about them, deduce theorems which refer to accessible states of affairs, and by checking the theorems confirm or refute our hypotheses. . . . Behavior is one of those subject matters which do not call for hypothetico-deductive methods. Both behavior itself and most of the variables of which it is a function are usually conspicuous. . . . If hypotheses commonly appear in the study of behavior, it is only because the investigator has turned his attention to inaccessible events – some of them fictitious, others irrelevant.

That behavior *can* be studied without hypothetico-deduction seems trivially indisputable. But if the claim is more ambitious, then is it really the case that "behavior itself and most of the variables of which it is a function are usually conspicuous"? How can we be confident in the absence of any powerful and wide-ranging science of behavior? For instance, what reason is there to regard verbal behavior as a function of variables "most" of which are "usually" conspicuous? And even if it does turn out that way (for some specification of "most" and of "usually"), what would that really show? If even just a few such variables are always or sometimes inconspicuous – and inaccessible to surface methods – might not behavior then after all call for hypothetico-deduction? Would not "inaccessible" events after all turn out not to be "irrelevant"?

What is more, even if behavior itself and certain variables of which it is *completely* a function are *always* conspicuous, what could that show? According to results of W. Craig (1953; 1956), theories that satisfy certain requirements can be replaced by alternative theories whose vocabulary is all *observational* (apart from the mathematical or logical) and which free us from all theoretical baggage at no cost in observational content. But there is no guarantee that such replacement theories would be equally suitable for explanation, prediction, or control by limited humans, since, for one thing, nothing restricts them to finitely many basic laws. Nor does the history of science to date offer any reason to suppose successful theories in practice are thus replaceable. Even if behavior were *completely* a function of surface variables, therefore, that would not show other dimensions (e.g., the inner) to be negligible without detriment to explanation, prediction, or control.

BFS: I agree with much of Sosa's evaluation of Popper. I dealt with the question of repetition some 50 years ago in a paper called "The Generic Nature of Stimulus and Response" (Skinner 1935a). It is not a point of view that enables us to speak of repetition but the orderliness of the results which follow when we accept a certain set of defining properties. The passage Sosa quotes is typical of Chomsky's criticism. The utterance "Mozart to a piece of music" or "Dutch to a painting" is an example of what I call a tact, but we do not *say* "Mozart" whenever we hear the music or "Dutch" whenever we see the painting. There is usually a listener present, and a past history with respect to that listener is relevant. Neither the music nor the picture is a sufficient explanation of the response; the presence of the listener is needed to explain the addition of an "autoclitic." Similarly, the control exercised by a single property of a stimulus under contingencies which are probably exclusively verbal is not "'as simple as it is empty.'" Stimuli are not "'driven back into the organism'"; they are operating in predictable ways because of a special kind of contingency easily demonstrated even with lower organisms.

Once again, I am not "ignor[ing] the inner." The plain success of inner-focused physical science is not due to practices which resemble those to which I object in "Methods."

Psychology: Toward the mathematical inner man

James T. Townsend

Department of Psychological Sciences, Purdue University

I start with the indisputable if somewhat vague premise that psychologists are interested in things "psychological" concerning individual organisms, most especially humans. To keep terminology simple I will assume we are talking about human beings, although most of my statements would pertain to any organism. Not only is there a pervading concern with observable behavior, but an increasing number of scientists are reopening old questions of phenomenology of the individual's consciousness. In what follows, I briefly outline my own perspective on psychological theorizing and then attempt to view B. F. Skinner's stance as given in "Methods" from that perspective. We must skirt a number of philosophical niceties in this terse rendition.

First, a general postulate that almost all would accept: Theories are good. Even Skinner apparently would accept some type of theory; the question is, Is the type acceptable to him the best kind? Most of us believe a good theory should (a) explain and enhance understanding, (b) predict, (c) be falsifiable as well as verifiable, (d) economize in terms of theoretical structure relative to phenomena explained. Other less precise criteria such as simplicity and elegance can often be interpreted in terms of the above stipulations.

Now, what is the best way to go about putting together such a theory? It is my thesis that a good psychological theory should be systemic, mathematical, physiological, and behavioral.

1. Systemic. I mean systemic in a system sense rather than as simply orderly or systematic. The only way to approach the most interesting questions concerning human psychology is by viewing a person as a *system*, which can in principle be formally specified by a set of subsystems operating in real time. The deeper the psychological phenomena, the more important it is to depart from the surface level of behavior and depict psychological events in terms of internal processes operating through the functioning of the various subsystems and their interactions. Associated with the subsystems as well as with the global system at any moment will be a *state*, which, along with the input and time, will specify an output and therefore an input–output "correlation" or rule. The level of the subsystems will depend on the phenomena under scrutiny. For instance, the appropriate subsystems and pertinent states will be different in studying: (a) eye movements in reading, (b) learning a list of foreign words, or (c) entering a meditative trance.

2. Mathematical. As with the other theoretic goals stated here, the specification that the theory be mathematical is meant to be "insofar as is feasible and fruitful" rather than categorical. All science depends on measurement and order, although measurement may not always be in terms of numbers. Certainly, one would not quibble that certain qualitative principles of great merit have been discovered in Skinner's school as well as, for instance, through more or less pure observation by the ethologists. Nevertheless, mathematics is of profound value, not only in the theory and methodology of measurement and statistics, but also in the formulation and testing of the type of black-box theory alluded to above; it is, in fact, indispensable.

3. Physiological. In my estimation, the physiological goal is somewhat less important than the others. However, it would seem myopic to fail to take account of physiological determinants when they are available. Suppose, for instance, that there existed two opposing theories, one predicting that a behavior segment is produced by an open-loop system and the other that the behavior segment is produced by a closed-loop feedback system. We may further suppose that the two theories are mathematically identical (which is in fact true for a broad spectrum of control processes). Now let us pretend that psychobiologists have discovered a neural loop from the cerebellum to cortical areas likely to be involved in the presumed behavior segment. Other things being equal, this might well offer convincing support for the closed-loop theory. Obviously, some areas of psychology are by their nature closer to physiology than others, and we expect these to take more account of physiology than the others. We would also hope that those in cognate physiological disciplines might make themselves aware of psychological phenomena and laws.

4. Behavioral. The behavioral goal is not last because it is less important but rather because its value is self-evident. Behavior is the output of the aforementioned black box and therefore indispensable in building the input → internal state → output theory. However, the behavior may be more subtle than sometimes envisioned. Introspection is no longer an object of scorn ("verbal behavior" is the more voguish term); brain waves and nonverbal signals are also acceptable forms of behavior, in the broad sense.

As far as I can ascertain, Skinner's version of an acceptable theory is a pale simulacrum of either the epistemological precepts mentioned first in this commentary or the goals brought up thereafter. I believe that Skinner's "formal representation" which reduces the data to a minimal number of terms and yields greater generality than an assemblage of facts will either (a) provide only an inelegant and noneconomical reduction with little reward in the way of generality or (b) force him to recant his aversion to certain of his bugbears, in particular "inner man" and "mathematical man." Both of the latter may be made rigorous within the context of my earlier requirements for a good theory.

One cannot procure a psychologically interesting general and economical representation without implementation of a formal theory stated in psychological terms and axioms, some critical subset of which refers to empirical events or measurements and the like. "Psychologically interesting" is contained here because in some situations one may gain at least a modicum of economy and generality by simply making the induction that, say, all the observed curves fall within a given family (e.g., the power law of S. S. Stevens 1957). However, unless regularity or a family of structures is related to an underlying theory it cannot be very psychologically valuable, and it is unlikely to be very elegant, simple, or general. When one insists on remaining quite close to the surface structure of data, it is impossible to attain great economy and generality; one is forced to use more descriptors, and the theoretical purview will be superficial.

At this point, I should make one remark concerning the mutual mimicking that can occur between two models representing quite distinct real systems (see, e.g., Townsend 1972; Townsend & Ashby 1983). When one is engaged in black-box modeling or theorizing, there will virtually always exist some canonical set of models (and therefore systems) all of which produce the same input–output behavior. As pointed out earlier, physiology may occasionally (but perhaps rarely) help in resolving such issues. Otherwise, the best we can hope for is to narrow down the candidate theories by insightful behavioral experimentation.

This dilemma is not avoided by the Skinnerian approach. If scientists are content, say, only to notice and collate regularity in behavior functions, without deigning to resort to a deeper theoretical treatment, they will simply have no idea what kinds of psychological systems could have produced the systematic behavior; they may not even notice some of the systematic aspects in the absence of such a theory. In a subjective sense, almost all systems are then possible – no falsification of some and partial verification of others has occurred. If one is satisfied with that state of affairs, so be it; I am not.

In a final tribute, I should like to say that B. F. Skinner has made an inestimable contribution to psychology, science, and society. Although I disagree with his views most vigorously, it is apparent that many of his and his colleagues' discoveries have considerable scientific worth and practical value. His provocative and ingenious writings will excite the intellect for a long spell to come.

BFS: I agree with Townsend that "deep" psychological theories are more satisfying (reinforcing?) than "superficial" ones; perhaps that is why they have been so popular for so many centuries. But is it a question of whether the facts are deep or superficial? What do we really know about the "things 'psychological'" in which psychologists are said to be interested? To start with what one observes about oneself – one's feelings and one's states of mind – has been the established practice for more than 2,000 years. I do not think that very much improved methods of self-observation have been developed, and the cognitive field of brain science is in large part a move of desperation. Some time we will know about deep psychological phenomena. Until then, the main result of the depth is to encourage theory rather than observation.

Townsend apparently believes in an input–output theory in which one must have an internal state to make the connection. It is not that I do not "deign" to resort to a deeper theoretical treatment. I simply do not see the need for one if we stick to our observations. A subsystem in which the role of an internal state is to convert input to output neglects the important element of selection by consequences.

In general, I accept Townsend's criteria for a good theory. I think we differ only in our understanding of the data available for theorizing at the present time.

Behavioral and statistical theorists and their disciples

Leroy Wolins

Department of Psychology, Iowa State University

According to Skinner, "the point of view of an experimental analysis of behavior has not yet reached very far afield." In this regard, it is instructive to look at the *Social Science Citation Index* and the *Science Citation Index*. In the former are five columns of citations to B. F. Skinner for 1982 and in the latter more than one. Those who cite him report results of laboratory research as well as applied research, and they originate from Japan, Soviet bloc countries, and elsewhere. Not all who cite him agree with his approach to the study of behavior, but all of this attests to the fact that Skinner and his experimental analysis of behavior have made a large and far-reaching impact.

I do not believe psychologists have fled the laboratory so much as they have been ejected from it. Those interested in basic research have not been able to find support there, but they have found support in clinics, rehabilitation centers, pharmaceutical firms, and educational enterprises. In these settings psychologists have dealt effectively with behavioral problems involving many different species, using, in part, the devices and ideas developed by Skinner from observing the behavior of rats and pigeons in a laboratory setting. There can be no doubt that Skinner's approach has led to "a helpful conception of human behavior." Skinner's ideas have been spread by those who fled or were ejected from the laboratory.

On the other hand, C. L. Hull, a modeler whose ideas Skinner deprecates, gets only a single column of citations in the 1982 *Social Science Citation Index* and one-fourth of a column in the *Science Citation Index*, and those who cite him do not appear to be as diverse in location or interest as those who cite Skinner. This evidence, plus general knowledge of the psychological literature, does not support the notion that modeling of behaviors is flourishing. I regret this, because I regard Hullian theory and Freudian theory as speculations of well-informed people, and such speculations have been fun, interesting, controversial, and, above all, heuristic. Unlike Skinner, I would not want to restrict the way in which we theorize. The negative heuristic value of such speculative theories stems from "true believers," disciples who ignore results derived in contexts other than the one that they espouse.

Skinner does not appear to distinguish between behavioral and statistical models. However, statisticians have presented ideas about substantive models closely related to those of Skinner. Apropos the hypothetico-deductive system, Bridgman's (1945b) statement, "The scientific method, as far as it is a method, is nothing more than doing one's damnedest with one's mind, no holds barred," is quoted in a statistics textbook published in 1956 (Wallis & Roberts 1956, p. 5). Tukey (1980) states, "Finding the question is often more important than finding the answer. Exploratory data analysis is an attitude, a flexibility, and a reliance on display, NOT a bundle of techniques and should be so taught." In that same issue of the *American Statistician*, which contains other relevant discourse, Hooke (1980) states,

> Clearly the whole scientific world may not yet be ready to admit that statisticians have become the custodians of the scientific method,. . .so we [the statisticians] are inheriting the scientific method because we care about it, we write about it and we do something about it, and no one else seems to do all those things.

Statisticians would often regard the question of the truth of statistical models as irrelevant. Rather they would advise researchers to impose statistical models tentatively, to gain experience from using them in order to evaluate whether the summarizations they provide are meaningful. Statistical models should provide guidance in analysis that enhances the viewing of data. The fact that some researchers are blinded by such models, attempt to use models that they do not understand, and relegate the responsibility of model development and evaluation to statisticians, reflect badly on the education or acumen of those researchers and not on modeling.

Psychology, in the main, should study the behavior of individual organisms. It is also clear that many conditions obtaining between individuals can be important determiners of individuals' behaviors. Therefore psychologists should be interested in comparing species, incentives, environments, physiological states. There appears to be no way to do this except by aggregation over individuals' behaviors that occur in each condition even when these individual behaviors are derived from individual-subject designs. The question of how and what to aggregate requires both forms of modeling in order to be answered. However, one important concern of the psychologist should be the deviations from such models. I agree that it is wrong to regard such deviations as merely error or chance, although that is one appropriate way to regard them.

Formal behavioral models are not just fun, but some people do enjoy them. The appreciative audience may be small, as is surely the case for abstract mathematics where there is no pretense of scientific meaning. The Hullian system (Hull 1943) does have this pretense, and it would be difficult for many researchers to persevere in the face of the huge amount and diversity of research results without the hope that some such model will some day be credible. The only way we can learn about when we are ready for behavioral models is through continuous effort in developing them.

I perceive that much of Skinner's philosophy is accepted by many psychologists, statisticians, and other scientists, although this was not the case in the past. The technology he instigated is widely applied and is developing rapidly in diverse fields and locations. Laboratory research continues at a high rate, but is diminishing, more as a result of our poor economy and the associated withdrawal of support for basic research than anything else.

Finally, the optimists who develop behavioral theory and statistical models should be encouraged and taken seriously – but not literally.

BFS: Unlike Wolins I do not think that my view of science takes the joy out of it. I have agreed that theories are fun, but I have not cautioned moderation in theory to spoil the fun. Indeed, I have pointed out that much statistically designed animal research often means a delay in learning about the results and takes most of the joy out of the work. In an operant laboratory you flip a switch and watch the behavior change, often in a highly reinforcing way. But I accept the need for statistics when the data require them. I accept the possibility that models may be useful, but I am less sanguine about the need for them. I still think there is a negative correlation between the precision of data and the proliferation of models or theories. One looks for order somewhere – if not in the data then in a theory that seems to explain the data. I myself prefer orderly data whenever possible. I do not claim that they are always available.

3 The operational analysis of psychological terms

Abstract: The major contributions of operationism have been negative, largely because operationists failed to distinguish logical theories of reference from empirical accounts of language. Behaviorism never finished an adequate formulation of verbal reports and therefore could not convincingly embrace subjective terms. But verbal responses to private stimuli can arise as social products through the contingencies of reinforcement arranged by verbal communities.

In analyzing traditional psychological terms, we need to know their stimulus conditions ("finding the referent"), and why each response is controlled by that condition. Consistent reinforcement of verbal responses in the presence of stimuli presupposes stimuli acting upon both the speaker and the reinforcing community, but subjective terms, which apparently are responses to private stimuli, lack this characteristic. Private stimuli are physical, but we cannot account for these verbal responses by pointing to controlling stimuli, and we have not shown how verbal communities can establish and maintain the necessary consistency of reinforcement contingencies.

Verbal responses to private stimuli may be maintained through appropriate reinforcement based on public accompaniments, or through reinforcements accorded responses made to public stimuli, with private cases then occurring by generalization. These contingencies help us understand why private terms have never formed a stable and uniform vocabulary. It is impossible to establish rigorous vocabularies of private stimuli for public use, because differential reinforcement cannot be made contingent upon the property of privacy. The language of private events is anchored in the public practices of the verbal community, which make individuals aware only by differentially reinforcing their verbal responses with respect to their own bodies. The treatment of verbal behavior in terms of such functional relations between verbal responses and stimuli provides a radical behaviorist alternative to the operationism of methodological behaviorists.

Operationism may be defined as the practice of talking about (1) one's observations, (2) the manipulative and calculational procedures involved in making them, (3) the logical and mathematical steps which intervene between earlier and later statements, and (4) *nothing else*. So far, the major contribution has come from the fourth provision and, like it, is negative. We have learned how to avoid troublesome references by showing that they are artifacts which may be variously traced to history, philosophy, linguistics, and so on. No very important positive advances have been made in connection with the first three provisions because operationism has no good definition of a definition, operational or otherwise. It has not developed a satisfactory formulation of the verbal behavior of the scientist.

Operationists, like most contemporary writers in the field of linguistic and semantic analysis, are on the fence between logical "correspondence" theories of reference and empirical formulations of language in use. They have not improved upon the mixture of logical and popular terms usually encountered in causal or even supposedly technical discussions of scientific method or the theory of knowledge (e.g., Bertrand Russell's *An Inquiry into Meaning and Truth*, 1940). *Definition* is a key term but is not rigorously defined, Bridgman's (1928; see also 1945a) original contention that the "concept is synonymous with the corresponding set of operations" cannot be taken literally, and no similarly explicit but satisfactory statement of the relation is available. Instead, a few roundabout expressions recur with rather tiresome regularity whenever this relation is mentioned: We are told that a concept is to be defined "*in terms of*" certain operations, that propositions are to be "based upon" operations, that a term denotes something only when there are "*concrete criteria for its applicability*," that operationism consists in "*referring any concept for its definition to*. . .concrete operations," and so on. We may accept expressions of this sort as outlining a program, but they do not provide a general scheme of definition, much less an explicit statement of the relation between concept and operation.

The weakness of current theories of language may be traced to the fact that an objective conception of human behavior is still incomplete. The doctrine that words are used to express or convey meanings merely substitutes "meaning" for "idea" (in the hope that meanings can then somehow be got outside the skin) and is incompatible with modern psychological conceptions of the organism. Attempts to derive a symbolic function from the principle of conditioning (or association) have been characterized by a very superficial analysis. It is simply not true that an organism reacts to a sign "as it would to the object which the sign supplants" (Stevens 1939). Only in a very limited area (mainly that of autonomic responses) is it possible to regard a sign as a simple substitute stimulus in the Pavlovian sense. Modern logic, as a formalization of "real" languages, retains and extends this dualistic theory of meaning and can scarcely be appealed to by the psychologist who recognizes his own responsibility in giving an account of verbal behavior.

The operational attitude, in spite of its shortcomings, is a good thing in any science, but especially in psychology because of the presence there of a vast vocabulary of ancient and nonscientific origin. It is not surprising that the broad empirical movement in the philosophy of science, which Stevens has shown to be the background of operationism, should have had a vigorous and early representation in the field of psychology – namely, behaviorism. In spite of the differences which Stevens claimed to find, behaviorism has been (at least to most behaviorists) nothing more than a thoroughgoing operational analysis of traditional mentalistic concepts. We may disagree with some of the answers (such as Watson's disposition of images), but the *questions* asked by behaviorism were strictly operational in spirit. I also cannot agree with Stevens that American behaviorism was "primitive." The early papers on the problem of consciousness by Watson, Weiss, Tolman, Hunter, Lashley, and many others, were not only highly sophisticated examples of operational inquiry, they showed a willingness to deal with a wider range of phenomena than do current streamlined treatments, particularly those offered by logicians (e.g., Carnap 1934) interested in a unified scientific vocabulary. But behaviorism, too, stopped short of a decisive positive contribution – and for the same reason: It never finished an acceptable formulation of the "verbal report." The conception of behavior which it developed could not convincingly embrace the "use of subjective terms."

A considerable advantage is gained from dealing with terms, concepts, constructs, and so on, quite frankly in the form in which they are observed – namely, as verbal responses. There is then no danger of including in the concept the aspect or part of nature which it singles out. One may often avoid that mistake by substituting *term* for *concept* or *construct*. Meanings, contents, and references are to be found among the determiners, not among the properties, of response. The question. What is length? would appear to be satisfactorily answered by listing the circumstances under which the response "length" is emitted (or, better, by giving some general description of such circumstances). If two quite separate sets of circumstances are revealed, then there are two responses having the form "length," since a verbal response class is not defined by phonetic form alone but by its functional relations. This is true even though the two sets are found to be intimately connected. The two responses are not controlled by the same stimuli, no matter how clearly it is shown that the different stimuli arise from the same "thing."

What we want to know in the case of many traditional psychological terms is, first, the specific stimulating conditions under which they are emitted (this corresponds to "finding the referents") and, second (and this is a much more important systematic question), why each response is controlled by its corresponding condition. The latter is not entirely a genetic question. The individual acquires language from society, but the reinforcing action of the verbal community continues to play an important role in maintaining the specific relations between responses and stimuli which are essential to the proper functioning of verbal behavior. How language is acquired is, therefore, only part of a much broader problem.

We may generalize the conditions responsible for the standard "semantic" relation between a verbal response and a particular stimulus without going into reinforcement theory in detail. There are three important terms: a stimulus, a response, and a reinforcement supplied by the verbal community. (All of these need more careful definition than are implied by current usage, but the following argument may be made without digressing for that purpose). The significant interrelations between these terms may be expressed by saying that the community reinforces the response only when it is emitted in the presence of the stimulus. The reinforcement of the response "red," for example, is contingent upon the presence of a red object. (The contingency need not be invariable.) A red object then becomes a discriminative stimulus, an "occasion" for the successful emission of the response "red."

This scheme presupposes that the stimulus act upon both the speaker and the reinforcing community; otherwise the proper contingency cannot be maintained by the community. But this provision is lacking in the case of many "subjective" terms, which appear to be responses to *private* stimuli. The problem of subjective terms does not coincide exactly with that of private stimuli, but there is a close connection. We must know the characteristics of verbal responses to private stimuli in order to approach the operational analysis of the subjective term.

The response "My tooth aches" is partly under the control of a state of affairs to which the speaker alone is able to react, since no one else can establish the required connection with the tooth in question. There is nothing mysterious or metaphysical about this; the simple fact is that each speaker possesses a small but important private world of stimuli. So far as we know, responses to that world are like responses to external events. Nevertheless the privacy gives rise to two problems. The first difficulty is that we cannot, as in the case of public stimuli, account for the verbal response by pointing to a controlling stimulus. Our practice is to *infer* the private event, but this is opposed to the direction of inquiry in a science of behavior in which we are to predict a response through, among other things, an independent knowledge of the stimulus. It is often supposed that a solution is to be found in improved physiological techniques. Whenever it becomes possible to say what conditions within the organism control the response "I am depressed," for example, and to produce these conditions at will, a degree of control and prediction characteristic of responses to external stimuli will be made possible. Meanwhile, we must be content with reasonable evidence for the belief that responses to public and private stimuli are equally lawful and alike in kind.

But the problem of privacy cannot be wholly solved by instrumental invasion. No matter how clearly these internal events may be exposed in the laboratory, the fact remains that in the normal verbal episode they are quite private. We have not solved the second problem of how the community achieves the necessary contingency of reinforcement. How is the response "toothache" appropriately reinforced if the reinforcing agent has no contact with the tooth? There is, of course, no question of whether responses to private stimuli are possible. They occur commonly enough and must be accounted for. But why do they occur, what is their relation to controlling stimuli, and what, if any, are their distinguishing characteristics?

There are at least four ways in which a verbal community with no access to a private stimulus may generate verbal behavior in response to it:

1. It is not strictly true that the stimuli which control the response must be available to the community. Any reasonably regular accompaniment will suffice. Consider, for example, a blind man who learns the names of a trayful of objects from a teacher who identifies the objects by sight. The rein-

forcements are supplied or withheld according to the contingency between the blind man's responses and the teacher's visual stimuli, but the responses are controlled wholly by tactual stimuli. A satisfactory verbal system results from the fact that the visual and tactual stimuli remain closely connected.

Similarly, in the case of private stimuli, one may teach a child to say "That hurts" in agreement with the usage of the community by making the reinforcement contingent upon public accompaniments of painful stimuli (a smart blow, tissue damage, and so on). The connection between public and private stimuli need not be invariable; a response may be conditioned with intermittent reinforcement and even in spite of an occasional conflicting contingency. The possibility of such behavior is limited by the degree of association of public and private stimuli which will supply a net reinforcement sufficient to establish and maintain a response.

2. A commoner basis for the verbal reinforcement of a response to a private stimulus is provided by collateral responses to the same stimulus. Although a dentist may occasionally be able to identify the stimulus for a toothache from certain public accompaniments as in (1), the response "toothache" is generally transmitted on the basis of responses which are elicited by the same stimulus but which do not need to be set up by an environmental contingency. The community infers the private stimulus, not from accompanying public stimuli, but from collateral, generally unconditioned, and at least nonverbal responses (hand to jaw, facial expressions, groans, and so on). The inference is not always correct, and the accuracy of the reference is again limited by the degree of association.

3. Some very important responses to private stimuli are descriptive of the speaker's own behavior. When this is overt, the community bases its instructional reinforcement upon the conspicuous manifestations, but the speaker presumably acquires the response in connection with a wealth of additional proprioceptive stimuli. The latter may assume practically complete control, as in describing one's own behavior in the dark. This is very close to the example of the blind man; the speaker and the community react to different, though closely associated, stimuli.

Suppose, now, that a given response recedes to the level of covert or merely incipient behavior. How shall we explain the vocabulary which deals with this private world? (The instrumental detection of covert behavior is again not an answer, for we are interested in how responses to private stimuli are normally, and noninstrumentally, set up.) There are two important possibilities. The surviving covert response may be regarded as an accompaniment of the overt one (perhaps part of it), in which case the response to the private stimulus is imparted on the basis of the public stimulus supplied by the overt responses, as in (1). On the other hand, the covert response may be *similar to*, though probably less intense than, the overt one and hence supply the *same* stimulus, albeit in a weakened form. We have, then, a third possibility: A response may be emitted in the presence of a private stimulus, which has no public accompaniments, provided it is occasionally reinforced in the presence of the same stimulus occurring with public manifestations. Terms falling within this class are apparently descriptive only of behavior, rather than of other internal states or events, since the possibility that the same stimulus may be both public and private (or, better, may have or lack public accompaniments) seems to arise from the unique fact that behavior may be both covert and overt.

4. The principle of transfer or stimulus generalization supplies a fourth explanation of how a response to private stimuli may be maintained by public reinforcement. A response which is acquired and maintained in connection with public stimuli may be emitted, through generalization, in response to private events. The transfer is based not on identical stimuli, as in (3), but on coinciding properties. Thus, we describe internal states as "agitated," "depressed," "ebullient," and so on, in a long list. Responses in this class are all metaphors (including special figures like metonymy). The term *metaphor* is not used pejoratively but merely to indicate that the differential reinforcement cannot be accorded actual responses to the private case. As the etymology suggests, the response is "carried over" from the public instance.

In summary, a verbal response to a private stimulus may be maintained in strength through appropriate reinforcement based upon public accompaniments or consequences, as in (1) and (2), or through appropriate reinforcement accorded the response when it is made to public stimuli, the private case occurring by generalization when the stimuli are only partly similar. If these are the only possibilities (and the list is here offered as exhaustive), then we may understand why terms referring to private events have never formed a stable and acceptable vocabulary of reasonably uniform usage. This historical fact is puzzling to adherents of the "correspondence school" of meaning. Why is it not possible to assign names to the diverse elements of private experience and then to proceed with consistent and effective discourse? The answer lies in the process by which "terms are assigned to private events," a process we have just analyzed in a rough way in terms of the reinforcement of verbal responses.

None of the conditions which we have examined permits the sharpening of reference which is achieved, in the case of public stimuli, by a precise contingency of reinforcement. In (1) and (2) the association of public and private events may be faulty; the stimuli embraced by (3) are of limited scope; and the metaphorical nature of those in (4) implies a lack of precision. It is, therefore, impossible to establish a rigorous scientific, vocabulary for public use, nor can the speaker clearly "know himself" in the sense in which knowing is identified with behaving discriminatively. In the absence of the "crisis" provided by differential reinforcement (much of which is necessarily verbal), private stimuli cannot be analyzed. (This has little or nothing to do with the availability or capacity of receptors.)

The contingencies we have reviewed also fail to provide an adequate check against fictional distortion of the relation of reference (e.g., as in rationalizing). Statements about private events may be under control of the deprivations associated with reinforcing consequences rather than antecedent stimuli. The community is skeptical of statements of this sort, and any attempt to talk about one's private world (as in psychological system making) is fraught with self-deception.

Much of the ambiguity of psychological terms arises from the possibility of alternative or multiple modes of reinforcement. Consider, for example, the response "I am hungry." The community may reinforce this on the basis of the history of ingestion, as in (1), or on the basis of collateral behavior associated with hunger, as in (2), or as a description of behavior with respect to food, or of stimuli previously correlated with food, as in (3). In addition the speaker has (in some instances) the powerful stimulation of hunger pangs, which is private since the community has no suitable connection with the speaker's stomach. "I am hungry" may therefore be variously translated as "I have not eaten for a long time" (1), or "That food makes my mouth water" (2), or "I am ravenous" (3) (compare the expression "I was hungrier than I thought" which describes the ingestion of an unexpectedly large amount of food), or "I have hunger pangs." While all of these may be regarded as synonymous with "I am hungry," they are not synonymous with each other. It is easy for conflicting psychological systematists to cite supporting instances or to train speakers to emit the response "I am hungry" in conformity with a system. Using a stomach balloon, one might condition the verbal response exclusively to stimulation from stomach contractions. This would be an example of either (1) or (2) above. Or speakers might be trained to make nice observations of the strength of their ingestive behavior, which might recede to the covert level as in (3). The response "I am hungry" would then describe a tendency to eat, with little or no reference to stomach contractions. Everyday usage reflects a mixed reinforcement. A similar analysis could be made of all terms descriptive of motivation, emotion, and action in general, including (of special interest here) the acts of seeing, hearing, and other kinds of sensing.

When public manifestations survive, the extent to which the private stimulus takes over is never certain. In the case of a toothache, the private event is no doubt dominant, but this is due to its relative intensity, not to any condition of differential reinforcement. In a description of one's own behavior, the private component may be much less important. A very strict external contingency may emphasize the public component, especially if the association with private events is faulty. In a rigorous scientific vocabulary private effects are practically eliminated. The converse does not hold. There is apparently no way of basing a response entirely upon the private part of a complex of stimuli. *Differential reinforcement cannot be made contingent upon the property of privacy*. This fact is of extraordinary importance in evaluating traditional psychological terms.

The response "red" is imparted and maintained (either casually or professionally) by reinforcement which is contingent upon a certain property of stimuli. Both speaker and community (or psychologist) have access to the stimulus, and the contingency can be made quite precise. There is nothing about the resulting response which should puzzle anyone. The greater part of psychophysics rests upon this solid footing. The older psychological view, however, was that the speaker was reporting, not a property of the stimulus, but a certain kind of private event, the sensation of red. This was regarded as a later stage in a series beginning with the red stimulus. The experimenter was supposed to manipulate the private event by manipulating the stimulus. This seems like a gratuitous distinction, but in the case of some subjects a similar later stage could apparently be generated in other ways (by arousing an "image"), and hence the autonomy of a private event capable of evoking the response "red" in the absence of a controllable red stimulus seemed to be proved. An adequate proof, of course, requires the elimination of other possibilities (e.g., that the response is generated by the procedures which are intended to generate the image).

Verbal behavior which is "descriptive of images" must be accounted for in any adequate science of behavior. The difficulties are the same for both behaviorist and subjectivist. If the private events are free, a scientific description is impossible in either case. If laws can be discovered, then a lawful description of the verbal behavior can be achieved, with or without references to images. So much for "finding the referents"; the remaining problem of how such responses are maintained in relation to their referents is also soluble. The description of an image appears to be an example of a response to a private stimulus of class (1) above. That is to say, relevant terms are established when the private event accompanies a controllable external stimulus, but responses occur at other times, perhaps in relation to the same private event. The deficiencies of such a vocabulary have been pointed out.

We can account for the response "red" (at least as well as for the "experience" of red) by appeal to past conditions of reinforcement. But what about expanded expressions like "I *see* red" or "I am *conscious* of red"? Here "red" may be a response to either a public or a private stimulus without prejudice to the rest of the expression, but "see" and "conscious" seem to refer to events which are by nature or by definition private. This violates the principle that reinforcement cannot be made contingent upon the privacy of a stimulus. A reference cannot be narrowed down to a specifically private event by any known method of differential reinforcement.

The original behavioristic hypothesis was, of course, that terms of this sort were descriptions of one's own (generally covert) behavior. The hypothesis explains the establishment and maintenance of the terms by supplying natural public counterparts in similar overt behavior. The terms are in general of class (3). One consequence of the hypothesis is that each term may be given a behavioral definition. We must, however, modify the argument slightly. To say "I see red" is to react, not to red (this is a trivial meaning of "see"), but to one's reaction to red. "See" is a term acquired with respect to one's own behavior in the case of overt responses available to the community, but according to the present analysis it may be evoked at other times by *any private accompaniment* of overt seeing. Here is a point at which a nonbehavioral private seeing may be slipped in. Although the commonest private accompaniment would appear to be the stimulation which survives in a similar covert act, as in (3), it might be some sort of state or condition which gains control of the response as in (1) or (2).

The superiority of the behavioral hypothesis is not merely methodological. That aspect of seeing which can be defined behaviorally is basic to the term as established by the verbal community and hence most effective in public discourse. A comparison of cases (1) and (3) will also show that terms which recede to the private level as overt behavior becomes covert have an optimal accuracy of reference, as responses to private stimuli go.

The additional hypothesis follows quite naturally that being conscious, as a form of reacting to one's own behavior, is a social product. Verbal behavior can be distinguished, and conveniently defined, by the fact that the contingencies of reinforcement are provided by other organisms rather than by a mechanical action upon the environment. The hypothesis is equivalent to saying that it is only because the behavior of the individual is important to society that society in turn makes it important to the individual. One becomes aware of what one is doing only after society has reinforced verbal responses with respect to one's behavior as the source of discriminative stimuli. The behavior to be described (the behavior of which one is to be aware) may later recede to the covert level, and (to add a crowning difficulty) so may the verbal response. It is an ironic twist, considering the history of the behavioristic revolution, that as we develop a more effective vocabulary for the analysis of behavior we also enlarge the possibilities of awareness, so defined. The psychology of the other one is, after all, a direct approach to "knowing thyself."

The main purpose of this discussion has been to define a definition by considering an example. To be consistent, psychologists must deal with their own verbal practices by developing an empirical science of verbal behavior. They cannot, unfortunately, join logicians in defining a definition, for example, as a "rule for the use of a term" (Feigl 1945); they must turn instead to the contingencies of reinforcement which account for the functional relation between a term, as a verbal response, and a given stimulus. This is the "operational basis" for their use of terms; and it is not logic but science.

Philosophers will call this circular. They will argue that we must adopt the rules of logic in order to make and interpret the experiments required in an empirical science of verbal behavior. But talking about talking is no more circular than thinking about thinking or knowing about knowing. Whether or not we are lifting ourselves by our own bootstraps, the simple fact is that we *can* make progress in a scientific analysis of verbal behavior. Eventually we shall be able to include, and perhaps to understand, our own verbal behavior as scientists. If it turns out that our final view of verbal behavior invalidates our scientific structure from the point of view of logic and truth value, then so much the worse for logic, which will also have been embraced by our analysis.

Some afterthoughts on methodological and radical behaviorism

In the summer of 1930, two years after the publication of Bridgman's *The Logic of Modern Physics*, I wrote a paper called "The Concept of the Reflex in the Description of Behavior" (Skinner 1931), later offered as the first half of a doctoral thesis. Although the general method, particularly the historical approach, was derived from Mach's *The Science of Mechanics* (1893), my debt to Bridgman was acknowledged in the second paragraph. This was, I think, the first psychological publication to contain a reference to *The Logic of Modern Physics* (1928), and it was the first explicitly operational analysis of a psychological concept.

Shortly after the paper was finished, I found myself contemplating a doctoral examination before a committee of whose sympathies I was none too sure. Not wishing to wait until an unconditional surrender might be necessary, I put out a peace feeler. Unmindful or ignorant of the ethics of the academy, I suggested to a member of the Harvard department that if I could be excused from anything but the most perfunctory examination, the time which I would otherwise spend in preparation would be devoted to an operational analysis of half a dozen key terms from subjective psychology. The suggestion was received with such breathless amazement that my peace feeler went no further.

The point I want to make is that at that time – 1930 – I could regard an operational analysis of subjective terms as a *mere exercise in scientific method*. It was just a bit of hackwork, badly needed by traditional psychology, which I was willing to engage in as a public service or in return for the remission of sins. It never occurred to me that the analysis could take any but a single course or have any relation to my own prejudices. The result seemed as predetermined as that of a mathematical calculation.

I am of this opinion still. I believe that the data of a science of psychology can be defined or denoted unequivocally, and that some one set of concepts can be shown to be the most expedient according to the usual standards in scientific practice. Nevertheless, these things have not been done in the field which was dominated by subjective psychology, and the question is, Why not?

Psychology, alone among the biological and social sciences, passed through a revolution comparable in many respects with that which was taking place at the same time in physics. This was, of course, behaviorism. The first step, like that in physics, was a reexamination of the observational bases of certain important concepts. But by the time Bridgman's book was published, most of the early behaviorists, as well as those of us just coming along who claimed some systematic continuity, had begun to see that psychology actually did not require the redefinition of subjective concepts. The reinterpretation of an established set of explanatory fictions was not the way to secure the tools then needed for a scientific description of behavior. Historical prestige was beside the point. There was no more reason to make a permanent place for terms like "consciousness," "will," or "feeling" than for "phlogiston" or "*vis anima.*" On the contrary, redefined concepts proved to be awkward and inappropriate, and Watsonianism was, in fact, practically wrecked in the attempt to make them work.

Thus it came about that while the behaviorists might have applied Bridgman's principle to representative terms from a mentalistic psychology (and were most competent to do so), they had lost all interest in the matter. They might as well have spent their time in showing what an 18th-century chemist was talking about when he said that the Metallic Substances consisted of a vitrifiable earth united with phlogiston. There was no doubt that such a statement could be analyzed operationally or translated into modern terms, or that subjective terms could be operationally defined, but such matters were of historical interest only. What was wanted was a fresh set of concepts derived from a direct analysis of the newly emphasized data, and this was enough to absorb all the available energies of the behaviorists. Besides, the motivation of the *enfant terrible* had worn itself out.

I think the Harvard department would have been happier if my offer had been taken up. What happened instead was the operationism of Boring and Stevens. This has been described as an attempt to climb onto the behavioristic bandwagon unobserved. I cannot agree. It is an attempt to acknowledge some of the more powerful claims of behaviorism (which could no longer be denied) but at the same time to preserve the old explanatory fictions. It is agreed that the data of psychology must be behavioral rather than mental if psychology is to be a member of the Unified Sciences, but the position taken is merely that of "methodological" behaviorism. According to this doctrine the world is divided into public and private events; and psychology, in order to meet the requirements of a science, must confine itself to the former. This was never good behaviorism, but it was an easy position to expound and defend and was often resorted to by the behaviorists themselves. It is least objectionable to the subjectivist because it permits him to retain "experience" for purposes of "nonphysicalistic" self-knowledge.

The position is not genuinely operational because it shows an unwillingness to abandon fictions. It is like saying that although the physicist must admittedly confine himself to Einsteinian time, it is *still true* that Newtonian absolute time flows "equably without relation to anything external." It is a sort of *E pur si muove* in reverse. What is lacking is the bold and exciting behavioristic hypothesis that what one observes and talks about is always the "real" or "physical" world (or at least the "one" world) and that "experience" is a derived construct to be understood only through an analysis of verbal (not, of course, merely vocal) processes.

It may be worthwhile to consider four of the principal difficulties which arise from the public–private distinction.

1. The relation between the two sets of terms which are required has proved to be confusing. The pair most frequently discussed is "discrimination" (public) and "sensation" (private). Is one the same as the other, or reducible to the other, and so on? A satisfactory resolution would seem to be that the terms belong to conceptual systems which are not necessarily related in a point-to-point correspondence. There is no question of equating them or their referents, or reducing one to the other, but only a question of translation – and a single term in one set may require a paragraph in the other.

2. The public–private distinction emphasizes the arid philosophy of "truth by agreement." The public, in fact, turns out to be simply that which can be agreed upon because it is common to two or more agreers. This is not an essential part of operationism; on the contrary, operationism permits us to dispense with this most unsatisfying solution of the problem of truth. Disagreements can often be cleared up by asking for definitions, and operational definitions are especially helpful, but operationalism is not primarily concerned with communication or disputation. It is one of the most hopeful of principles precisely because it is not. The solitary inhabitant of a desert isle could arrive at operational definitions (provided he had previously been equipped with an adequate verbal repertoire). The ultimate criterion for the goodness of a concept is not whether two people are brought into agreement but whether the scientist who uses the concept can operate successfully upon his material – all by himself if need be. What matters to Robinson Crusoe is not whether he is agreeing with himself but whether he is getting anywhere with his control over nature.

One can see why the subjective psychologist makes so much of agreement. It was once a favorite sport to quiz him about intersubjective correspondences. "How do you know that *O*'s sensation of green is the same as *E*'s?" And so on. But agreement alone means very little. Various epochs in the history of philosophy and psychology have seen wholehearted agreement on the definition of psychological terms. This makes for contentment but not for progress. The agreement is likely to be shattered when someone discovers that a set of terms will not really work, perhaps in some hitherto neglected field, but this does not make agreement the key to workability. On the contrary, it is the other way round.

3. The distinction between public and private is by no means the same as that between physical and mental. That is why methodological behaviorism (which adopts the first) is very different from radical behaviorism (which lops off the latter term in the second). The result is that whereas the radical behaviorist may in some cases consider private events (inferentially, perhaps, but nonetheless meaningfully), the methodological operationist has maneuvered himself into a position where he cannot. "Science does not consider private data," says Boring (1945). I contend, however, that my toothache is just as physical as my typewriter, though not public, and I see no reason why an objective and operational science cannot consider the

processes through which a vocabulary descriptive of a toothache is acquired and maintained. The irony of it is that, whereas Boring must confine himself to an account of my external behavior, I am still interested in what might be called Boring-from-within.

4. The public–private distinction apparently leads to a logical, as distinct from a psychological, analysis of the verbal behavior of the scientist, although I see no reason why it should. Perhaps it is because the subjectivist is still not interested in terms but in what the terms used to stand for. The only problem a science of behavior must solve in connection with subjectivism is in the verbal field. How can we account for the behavior of talking about mental events? The solution must be psychological, rather than logical, and I have tried to suggest one approach in my present paper.

The confusion which seems to have arisen from operationism – a principle which is supposed to eliminate confusion – is discouraging. But upon second thought it appears that the possibility of a genuine operationism in psychology has not yet been fully explored. With a little effort I can recapture my enthusiasm of some years ago. (This is, of course, a private event.)

POSTSCRIPT

When I was asked to participate in the symposium for which this paper was written, I was at work on a manuscript that would be published 12 years later under the title *Verbal Behavior* (Skinner 1957). It was an interpretation of the field of language which avoided "ideas," "meanings," "information," and all the other things said to be expressed by a speaker or communicated to a listener. Although I had lost interest in the operationism of the thirties, I still called myself an operationist and thought that certain parts of the manuscript were suitable for the symposium. They concerned the place of private events in the analysis of verbal behavior, in particular the privacy of "sensations" and "feelings," which were still important to psychologists at the time, particularly E. G. Boring, who had organized the symposium.

In traditional terms the question I addressed was this: How is it possible to learn to refer to or describe (and I would say know) things or events within our own bodies to which our teachers do not have access? How can they tell us that we are right or wrong when we describe them?

I used as an example a special type of verbal response called (in my manuscript and later in my book) the *tact*. The term refers to the probability of occurrence of a verbal response (say, *chair*) as it is affected by a stimulus (say, a chair or chairlike object). At any given moment a native speaker of English possesses the verbal operant *chair* in some strength (where "in strength" means "with a given probability of emission"). During a quiet walk in the woods it is weak. In a furniture store, it is strong even though not being actually emitted.

The response *chair* in its relation to a chair as a controlling stimulus is a tact (and the chair is then said to be tacted); it is *not* a "reference to a chair," or a "statement about chairs," nor does it "express the idea of a chair," or "denote a chair," or "name a chair." It is simply a probability of emission of *chair* as a function of a particular kind of stimulus. Tacts sometimes occur alone, but they are usually parts of larger samples of verbal behavior. They can be, but need not be, explicitly taught, as when a child is taught to name objects.

(The response *chair* is not always a tact. If it occurs because it has often been followed by the appearance of a chair as a reinforcing consequence, it is a *mand*, a "request for a chair." If, because it often occurs in expressions like *table and chair* or *sitting in a chair*, it is strengthened when *table and* or *sitting in a* is read or heard, it is an *intraverbal response*. If it is strong because someone else has just said *chair*, it is an echoic response. If the speaker is simply reading the word, it is a textual response. These kinds of verbal responses are not important for the present response.)

Speakers acquire and emit tacts under many different states of deprivation and aversive stimulation and when many different kinds of reinforcing consequences follow. The reinforcements are mediated by other people. There are no important nonsocial consequences of saying *chair*, at least until the speaker himself becomes a listener. The question I raise in "Terms" is this: How can we tact private stimuli inaccessible to the verbal community which arranges the necessary contingencies of reinforcement? For *chair*, substitute *pain*, and one reaches the problem of "the operational definition of a psychological term."

My paper argues that there are only four ways in which we can learn to tact private stimuli:

1. The verbal community can base its reinforcements on associated public stimuli.
2. It can use public responses made to the same stimuli.
3. Some private stimuli are generated by covert behavior to which responses can be learned when the same behavior is overt.
4. The tact can be metaphorical and acquired when made to similar public stimuli.

Now, nearly 40 years later, I do not see any other possibilities. There are, however, some common misunderstandings:

1. I was not trying to bring *sensations* back into behaviorism. By toothache, I mean only the stimulation arising from a damaged tooth. We must wait for physiology to supply further details.
2. Although private stimuli are often salient, the public accompaniments used by the verbal community often continue to contribute to the strength of a tact. I may say, "I am hungry" mainly because I see myself eating voraciously, a public stimulus.
3. A tact, once established or in the process of being established, usually figures in larger samples of verbal behavior to which terms

like reference, denotation, and description are often applied, but the term is not itself correctly thus used.

4. A tact may have the form of a sentence if it is acquired as such. The whole expression "I'm hungry as a bear" may be a single response and useful as such upon a given occasion. On a different occasion it may be composed as a sentence of which the tact *hungry* is only a part.
5. Verbal contingenciës bring responses under the control of single properties of stimuli. Only by looking at a number of instances can we identify the property that is functioning in a tact. *Chair* is, in this sense, an abstract response, but the issue is clearer when the defining property is more often found with other properties, as in the tact *red*, to the probability of which the size and shape of red objects contribute very little.

COMMENTARIES AND RESPONSES

Stimulus–response meaning theory

Jonathan Bennett

Department of Philosophy, Syracuse University

Skinner's account of how subjective psychological terminology gets its meaning relies on his views about meaning in general. Though not extensively laid out in "Terms," their general outline emerges clearly enough to show how radically mistaken they are. So there must be a lot wrong also with Skinner's account of the meanings of psychological terms, but I shall not follow out those consequences; my topic is the underlying stimulus–response approach to meaning in general.

To evaluate Skinner's views about meaning we must first cleanse them of their most unrealistic assumption, namely that the basic linguistic performance is the uttering of a single word. When Skinner speaks of "the circumstances under which the response 'length' is emitted" he is not discussable. Apart from certain highly specialized circumstances, such as helping with a crossword puzzle, or displaying reading skills, there are no circumstances under which that one word is uttered in isolation. And when he implicitly contrasts "I see red" with "red," calling the former an "expanded expression," he puts the cart before the horse. Although we grasp sentences only through understanding their constituent words, the notion of meaning attaches primarily to whole sentences and only derivatively to smaller units such as words. Our primary concept of meaning is that of something's meaning *that P*, and the notion of word meaning must be understood through the idea of the effect on a sentence's meaning of replacing this word in it by that. Try to imagine a tribe that has a word for trees, a word for sand, a word for fire, and so on, but that does not use these words in sentences to say anything about trees, sand, or fire. The supposition makes no sense: If the noises in question are not used to say anything, to express whole "that-P" messages, there is nothing to make it the case that the noises are *words* at all.

However, when Skinner and other stimulus–response meaning theorists focus on the single word, perhaps they are really thinking not of the word "red," say, but rather of the one-word sentence "Red!," meaning something like "That thing (in front of me) is red." Let us suppose this, and forget that it still makes no sense of "the response 'length.'"

The activity of labeling whatever public or private item one is presented with is a rare event. Even if we allow for it to be done in normal sentences with several words each – for example. "This is a chair" or "That is a Ming vase" – it does not happen often, and there is no reason to take it as paradigmatic of linguistic behavior, or as central or basic in it.

Let us set that fact aside also, and attend to the tiny fragment of linguistic behavior that does fit this pattern. Still there is trouble for Skinner's theory of meaning. I am confronted by something red; it is a stimulus, to which I respond by saying "(That is) red." In calling these items a "stimulus" and a "response" respectively, Skinner is implying that the former causes the latter: Like most stimulus–response meaning theorists, he is apparently attracted by the idea that the meanings of our utterances are determined by the very same items that cause them. In his own words, the "referents" of what we say "control" our saying it, and he ties control to prediction, speaking of a "science of behavior in which we are to predict response through, among other things, an independent knowledge of the stimulus."

The phrase "among other things" is needed in that sentence. Without it, Skinner would be implying that linguistic behavior is vastly more predictable than it really is, in the manner of the stimulus–response meaning theorist who once wrote: "If you want a person to utter the word chair, one of the best ways is to let him see an unusual chair" (Miller 1951, p. 166). That is plainly false, of course, and no one would write it who was not in thrall to a bad theory. In a large range of situations we can predict something about the world from a fact about what is said – for example, someone's saying "This is a chair" is evidence that he is probably in the presence of a chair – but predictions running the other way are nearly always quite hopeless (this point is made by Ziff 1970, p. 73; see also Ziff 1960, secs. 46 and 54). But Skinner says "among other things." We are to suppose that the causally sufficient conditions for a person's uttering "(That is) red" consist in (i) a red stimulus in conjunction with (ii) a set of circumstances *C* which always mediates between a stimulus and an utterance whose meaning is somehow given by the stimulus. If the theory is not that there is a single value of *C* such that someone who undergoes a red stimulus in *C* circumstances says something like "That is red," someone who sees a chair in *C* circumstances says "That is a chair," and so on, then there is no theory. The aim is to say something *systematic* about how the meanings of utterances relate to their causes, and that requires a *general rule* enabling us to read off the meaning of an utterance from the facts about the causal chain that produced it. We shan't get that merely by learning that in each case the causal chain includes, together with a lot of other stuff, something constitutive of the meaning of the utterance. We need a systematic way of filtering out the "other stuff" in order to isolate the element that gives the meaning; and so, as I said, we need a single value of *C* that tells us in each case which part of the causal chain gives the meaning and which part belongs to the all-purpose "other stuff." (For a fuller defense of this, see sec. 6 of Bennett 1975.)

That is the project of Skinner's kind of stimulus–response meaning theory. (There is another kind – no better but different – according to which meaning is determined not by the stimuli to which an utterance is a response but rather by the responses to the utterance considered as stimulus. For more on this, and on relations between the two, see secs. 7–9 of Bennett 1975.) As a project, it has no hope of success: There is no reason to think there is anything remotely resembling a general truth of the form "Whenever anyone encounters an *F* item in *C* circumstances he utters something meaning that the item is *F*." Let *C* be somewhat vague and tattered around the edges; let it also be less than perfectly unitary, consisting perhaps of about 17 disjuncts; lower your sights by looking only for a rule that applies about 20% of the time; help yourself to two or three further indulgences as well. Still the project will have no chance of success. It assumes a world-to-meaning relationship that simply doesn't exist.

This is not to deny that when a person says something meaning "That is an *F*," the odds are that he is confronted by an *F*, that he has been in perceptual contact with it, and that this contact is part of the causal history of his making that utterance. That much is true, and is presumably the launching pad from which Skinner and the other stimulus–response meaning theorists have embarked on their theory. But it is a truth that brings no comfort to stimulus–response meaning theory, as can be seen by seeing *why* it is true. The explanation is as follows.

When a person utters something that means that a certain thing *x* is *F*, he is likely to have some one of a certain cluster of intentions (intending to get someone else to think that *Fx*, or intending to fix in his own memory his belief that *Fx*, or the like); if he has such an intention, he probably believes that *Fx*; and if he believes that *Fx* then the odds are that *x* is *F*-like and that the person has been caused to believe it is *F* by a perceptual transaction with it. And so someone who says "That is red" has probably been acted upon perceptually by something red.

This involves several probabilities each falling short of certainty; multiply them all together and the upshot is a long way below certainty. Still, it provides an inference from "He has just uttered 'That is a chair'" to "He has recently encountered a chair" which has some cogency: If I had to bet on whether someone had recently seen a chair, I would be interested to learn that he had recently said "That is a chair." But for obvious reasons it provides a vastly less secure basis for inferring the utterance from the perception. Granted that when the utterance occurred it was partly as a result of the perception, there is no systematic and manageable way in which it could have been predicted with as much as 1% probability, except in special cases where the perception is accompanied by a threat or a bribe. Furthermore, there is good reason to think that it is not a strictly causal flow from the perception through the belief to the utterance, and that the causal explanation of the utterance will run along physiological channels and not psychological ones. For a lot of argument to this effect, see Fodor (1980). The best argument, in a nutshell, is as follows. It seems reasonable to think that

(i) any item of linguistic behavior admits of a correct causal explanation in physiological terms, and that
(ii) *there is no systematic mapping between facts about mental content and associated facts about physiological states*, and that
(iii) there is a systematic mapping between any two correct causal explanations of the same phenomenon.

Thus, my suggested route from the perceptual encounter through to the utterance, as well as failing to support a prediction, also fails to be strictly causal. How then can I offer it as a replacement for, or improvement on, what Skinner is trying to get?

Well, useless as this relation between world and meaning is for Skinner's purposes, it is the nearest thing to his theory that is anywhere near true. What is most striking about it is that it depends essentially upon two of the concepts – intention and belief – that belong to that "subjective psychology" that Skinner thinks he can safely disregard as being of merely antiquarian interest, like phlogiston and *vis anima*. Now, quite a lot of philosophers of psychology these days are also inclined to drop the concepts of intention and belief or to look forward to the day when we shall be able to do so (see Churchland 1981), and for all I know they are right. I am not contending that a good scientific account of behavior must involve those concepts, but only that they are required for any semblance of a systematic link between meaning and circumstance of utterance. Like some others, I think that the *very notion of meaning* depends essentially on intention and belief, and cannot stand if they fall (see Armstrong 1971; Bennett 1976; Grice 1957; Schiffer 1972), but I do not insist on that either. All I need is the much securer thesis that any *systematic bridge between meanings and circumstances of utterance* must involve intention and belief.

Incidentally, once that fact has been faced we can liberate ourselves from the restriction to utterances such as "That is a chair" and "This is red" and "I feel a pain." Skinner's attempt to explain the meanings of psychological terms depends essentially on his taking that kind of utterance as paradigmatic, but it obviously isn't, and now we can break free from it. Instead of the restricted thesis "When someone utters something meaning that some present thing *x* is *F*, it is fairly likely that the thing is *F*-like and the speaker has recently had perceptual contact with it," we have the much more widely applicable thesis "When someone utters something meaning that *P*, it is fairly likely that there is evidence that *P* and the speaker has recently had perceptual contact with some of it." In this statement, of course, we must understand "evidence" as "what would count as evidence for the person whose utterance is in question," and so the notion of evidence we are using here further involves the concept of belief: what counts for a person as evidence that *P* is, roughly, what inclines him to believe that *P*. But that is not a further trouble for Skinner's program, because even within the tiny area to which the program is confined it doesn't work – doesn't achieve the beginnings of an approximation to the truth – except with help from the concepts of intention and belief.

BFS: I do not think that Bennett is right in saying that by calling one thing a stimulus and another a response I am "implying that the former causes the latter" or that "like most stimulus–response meaning theorists, [I am] apparently attracted by the idea that the meanings of our utterances are determined by the very same items that cause them." That is precisely what I am not saying. I am saying that the presence of an object (call it a stimulus) increases the probability that a response will be emitted. This can be fairly easily demonstrated and can indeed be used in predicting a speaker's behavior. Of course, "other things" enter into the actual speaking of a word, and I have dealt with them in detail in *Verbal Behavior*. I cannot agree with Bennett that the statement "If you want a person to utter the word 'chair,' one of the best ways is to let him see an unusual chair" (Miller 1951, p. 166) is "plainly false." Let someone scaling Mt. Everest arrive at the summit and find a chair, and the word "chair" will be pronounced with alacrity. (Incidentally, the reader should not infer that George Miller, from whose book the sentence is taken, is in thrall to a stimulus–response theory of meaning; he is one of its sharpest critics.)

It would be unfair of me to refer to my book, published 12 years after "Terms," if Bennett were devoting his commentary to my paper. But a critic of my theory of meaning must look at my book, where I appeal to much more than a stimulus in accounting for a verbal response. I do not suggest "that the causally sufficient conditions for a person's uttering '(That is) red' consist in (i) a red stimulus in conjunction with (ii) a set of circumstances *C* which always mediates between a stimulus and an utterance whose meaning is somehow given by the stimulus." What must be taken into account "among other things" is (1) a setting which includes a listener and (2) a long history in which speaking in similar settings has been followed by the reactions of similar listeners. The listeners have supplied the reinforcers which built the functional control exercised by the stimulus.

Typical of modern philosophers. Bennett replaces a history of reinforcing consequences with a currently felt or at least active "intention." His expression "intending to get someone else to think that *Fx*, or intending to fix in his own memory his belief that *Fx*, or the like" is an effort to find a current entity to replace the speaker's relation to the listener and the kinds of effects he has had on listeners, especially the effects described in detail in *Verbal Behavior*.

(Far from disregarding intention and belief as "of merely antiquarian interest" I am at the moment involved with a colleague, Dr. Pere Julià, a linguist, in reviewing the use of those words in current philosophy. Bennett's best effort to supply an alternative theory depends, he says, essentially upon intention and belief. From my point of view, it depends upon the personal histories which lead to verbal behavior, histories for which intention and belief stand as current surrogates.)

In "Terms" I compare those who teach the meanings of words referring to private events which they themselves cannot see to a blind man teaching someone the names of colors. Obviously the blind man must have collateral information before he can do so successfully. A solution by Bennett of the problem of the blind man with the concepts of belief and intention would be a useful contribution to this discussion.

An experiment might be helpful. Let us undertake to explain to a bright 10-year-old boy what intentions and beliefs are. When we have finished, the boy must be able to tell us when he has an intention and when he holds a belief. What things shall we point to as we tell him what those words mean? What things must he know about himself to report correctly that he has an intention or holds a belief? I think we shall find that we have taught him to mention actions and to mention or imply their consequences. These are parts of the contingencies of reinforcement of which his behavior is a function. As states of mind, intentions and beliefs are current surrogates of the contingencies. As a behaviorist, I dispense with the surrogates but take the contingencies quite seriously.

Waiting for the world to make me talk and tell me what I meant

Richard P. Brinker and Julian Jaynes

Educational Testing Service, Princeton, New Jersey (RPB) and Department of Psychology, Princeton University (JJ)

Like so much of Professor Skinner's work, "Terms" separates him from the main thrust of operationism and from the main body of behaviorism. Yet history rarely sees subtle differences. For example, Piaget and Inhelder (1969) miss such distinctions when they brand Skinner a "copy theorist" indistinguishable from other behavioral associationists such as Pavlov or Hull. Why have such criticisms, or those of Chomsky (1959), been so lasting when in fact Skinner's use of terms such as operant discriminative stimulus, and reinforcement could be used to refer to and "explain" many phenomena treated by cognitive psychologists (Catania 1979)? Perhaps the reason that Skinner has been a focal target of criticism from cognitively oriented psychologists is that the differentiation of himself from other behaviorists and other operationists has never culminated in the promised program of research in human behavior that would demonstrate the differences between the old and the new operationism. That is the main point of this commentary, in which we are trying to stay within Skinner's purview, refraining from discussion of that purview itself.

What are the distinctions whereby Skinner differentiates himself from previous operationists? He offers a "definition of definition" rather than mere correspondences between concepts and the operations by which they are defined or between terms and the criteria for their application. The definition of definition is a statement of the social community's contingency of reinforcement for a term. Thus, psychologists must develop

> an empirical science of verbal behavior. They cannot . . . join logicians in defining a definition, for example as a "rule for the use of a term" (Feigl 1945); they must turn instead to contingencies of reinforcement which account for the functional relation between a term, as a verbal response, and a given stimulus. That is the "operational basis" for their use of terms.

Since it has previously been concluded that there is no basis for differential reinforcement of private events – no "inner" reinforcing – public verbal responses are the only admissible data for operationism. The promise of this 1945 paper, then, is that an analysis of reinforcement contingencies from the verbal community for verbal behavior will lead to truly operational definitions of terms and therefore to a complete behaviorism.

Twenty-four years later, Skinner seems to have rescinded this promise of operationism. In 1969, he insisted that an observer of contingencies, even the simple contingencies in an operant conditioning chamber, will not be able to describe the contingencies.

> Over a substantial period of time he has seen various stimuli, responses, and reinforcers appear and disappear. The fact remains that *direct observation, no matter how prolonged, tells him very little about what is going on . . . if he could not see what was happening in a relatively simple experimental space, how can we expect him to understand the behavior he sees in the world around him?* . . . It is only when we have analyzed behavior under known contingencies of reinforcement that we can begin to see what is happening in daily life. (Skinner 1969a, pp. 9–10, italics in original)

Thus, operationism really requires the demonstration of behavioral control. But how and over what? Is the verbal behavior that is to be "operationalized" the specific words spoken, the inflection, the intensity pattern, the temporal pattern, other features of how words are spoken, or the entire class of synonymous ways that the same thing could be said, or all of these, or something still more? And how, for example, would we operationalize the term *had* in the sentence from a grammar lesson "Mary, where Jane had *had*, had *had had*; *had had* had the teacher's approval." Such examples exert enough control (in Skinner's terms) upon most of us out here in the language community that we express our acceptance of the grammatical nature of the statement and acknowledge the independence of the grammatical rule from the specific stimulus words.

Although Skinner did not seem to follow through on the distinction between his use of operational definition and his behaviorist predecessors' use of that term, others have explored with other vocabularies what Skinner knows as the verbal community's contingencies for verbal and vocal behavior (Bruner 1975; Wells 1981). However, this endeavor has culminated in a framework that includes consideration of the active "intentions" of both the language community and the speaker. Words and word combinations have different meanings in the language community depending upon the conditions under which they are emitted. The stimuli are not the sounds uttered or even such utterances in the environmental context. Aspects of both must be intentionally selected by an active language community attempting to reconstruct messages from the environmental context and the sounds uttered (Brinker 1982). This active process occurs even when infants emit sounds that could not possibly by words: Adults behave as if these sounds meant something (Bruner 1975).

Even when research on the semantic and pragmatic development of language contains the data that could be relevant to "Terms" (see Segal 1975), a successful analysis of this language data from an operational point of view seems unlikely, given Skinner's 1969 rejection of the possibility of making sense of such observations. Moreover, although organisms freely emit behavior (Skinner 1938), the structure of behavioral repertoires and the probabilities as to which of several behaviors would be emitted – surely prolegomena for such an analysis – were never seriously studied within the operant framework. Nor was the impact of a history of learning upon an organism's performance in a new contingency ever seriously examined.

The Skinnerian picture seems to be of a passive individual who brings nothing to contingencies of reinforcement. He waits for referents to talk about. When a referent comes along he uses terms that are or have been positively reinforced. Thus, he learns the appropriate verbal behavior to talk about public and ultimately private things. It is this passive view of human nature in Skinner's later writings that was *not* necessary on the basis of his early theoretical distinctions (1935a; 1938), but *was* necessary to be consistent with Skinner's operationism. Moreover, this passive view reduces the possibility of a serious and complete contingency analysis of verbal behavior.

Skinner's sense of operational definition in "Terms" then, promises a program of research in which natural contingencies of reinforcement by the verbal community for verbal behavior provide the concept of definition. Yet it has fallen to others to study such contingencies from a standpoint quite removed from either traditional or radical behaviorism (Bates 1976; Bruner 1975; Greenfield & Smith 1976). Skinner (1969a) seems to have moved away from his 1945 position and abandoned the possibility of understanding any behavior, verbal or otherwise, based on an analysis of natural contingencies. The later position is that understanding is equivalent to experimental control. It is this position, rather than the 1945 one, that is very poorly suited to an analysis of verbal behavior. It is the requirement for experimental control of verbal behavior that has produced the anti-Skinnerian position reviewed by Herrnstein (1977). Skinner (1977) himself feels that such criticism does not apply to his own verbal behavior.

What all this shows perhaps is the power of derivative fashions over the best of 20th-century psychology. The fashion here is operationism which, after the disillusionments of World War I and the ensuing fever for pure objectivity, had grown out of the logical positivism of the Vienna Circle into a promise of a "Unity of Science" for all who would accept its simple rules of initiation. And psychology, weakened with the ineptness of its earlier misguided attempts at a science of consciousness (Fechner, Wundt, Titchener, et al.), wearily climbed on the bandwagon and tried to behave like physics.

But operationism was soon cast off by physicists themselves. It contained logical contradictions (e.g., a "thing" measured or observed in two ways is really two things) and regressions (e.g., how do we operationally define the operationally defining measuring instruments?), and was an insensitive bull in the china shop of psychology with nowhere to go (e.g., how do we operationally define dreams?). As Skinner himself points out in "Terms," Bridgman's (1928) formulation "cannot be taken literally." We note also that in his last sentences some of Professor Skinner's earlier enthusiasm for operationism seems to have become attenuated. For the sake of his own important theorizing, we wish he had never had any enthusiasm for it at all.

BFS: Brinker and Jaynes seem to misunderstand my saying that a casual observer can tell very little about what is going on in an operant experiment in spite of its supposed oversimplification. The experimenter sees what is going on in the experimental space much more clearly than the casual observer because he has additional information about the history of the organism – its deprivational state, its history of reinforcement, possibly something about its genetics, and so on. To understand behavior, one must know the history of the organism as well as the present "structure" of the behavior. I do not see how admitting that necessity "rescind[s] [the] promise of operationism." It simply recognizes the need for a closer study of controlling variables.

I think the same thing can be said about casual encounters between people. If the listener "makes sense of what the speaker is saying," both must be members of the same language community (i.e., have had much the same verbal history) and sense will be made more effectively if this particular speaker and listener have shared other verbal experiences. (It often takes a certain amount of time to be clear about what a stranger is saying.)

I agree in general with Brinker and Jaynes's dismissal of operationism as that term is most often used, but behaviorism, when applied to the definition of psychological terms, the subject of the symposium to which "Terms" was contributed, is very close to the spirit of operationism, and I submitted the paper on that understanding. I, too, regret that more work has not been done in line with my analysis in *Verbal Behavior*, particularly in the behavior of young children. The field is only slowly recovering from the developmentalism of Piaget and others, in which the appearance of verbal behavior is followed with little or no attention paid to the contingencies of reinforcement responsible for it.

Skinner on the verbal behavior of verbal behaviorists

Arthur C. Danto

Department of Philosophy, Columbia University

Skinner's scenario for fixing the reference of psychological terms has the structure of a Greek tragedy, in which the verbal community acts as chorus, instructing the tragic subject in how to name his agonies. The ancients left unexplained the manner in which choruses came by their knowledge, and it is no less a puzzle how the verbal community in Skinner's semantical story comes by its cognitions, all the more so if the story is true. For the question then is how anyone ascends from such basic verbal reports as "toothache" in the presence of toothache, or "red" in the presence of red, as emitted by the well-conditioned subject, to the rich, dense metalanguage of the story itself. The unwritten program of the paper is to show how so exiguous an input gets processed to yield an output as rich as the paper that presupposes the program, if its author began the way its subject does. It is Skinner's belief that we shall, by procedures scarcely more complex than those through which the meaning of "toothache" gets transmitted to otherwise inchoate agonizers, arrive at an understanding of the verbal behavior of scientists. Self-understanding must after all be an aim of psychology, psychologists being human; and if "knowing oneself" is limited even in the case of simple names of simple pains, how likely is it that reflexive knowledge – knowledge *de se* – can be attained of science at the level of science? The question is whether *Verbal Behavior* would have been possible if verbal behavior at large is analyzable as it is said to be here. This I shall show reason to doubt. But I must first applaud Skinner's recognition that science itself cannot be left outside science, and that what he fears may look like circularity – characterizing a practice in the language of the practice characterized – is not an obstacle to but a condition for the validity of any analysis that pretends to adequacy. *Quis custodiet ipsos custodes* – Who shall guard the guardians? – a problem for the implementation of Skinner's utopia, has its methodological counterpart here.

The genius of tragedy is inseparable from the genius of comedy, Socrates observed after a legendary night of drinking, and it is comic that the conditions for instructing in the reference of psychological predicates immediately gives rise to the Problem of Other Minds, as well as the lesser possibility of malingering pretense on the subject's part. For the collateral accompanying stimuli – "hand to the jaw, facial expressions, groans, and the like" – can be present in the absence of the pain. *Logical* behaviorism, which seeks to define psychological terms through what for Skinner are merely collateral accompaniments, is a radical effort to abort skepticism by making it linguistically inexpressible. But Skinner's native radicalism is tempered by a certain realism: It is "a simple fact" that private stimuli occur and that a (humanly) important class of psychological terms take them as their primary referenda. Besides, logical behaviorism is dogged by the circumstance that at best disjunctive definientia leave psychological terms ultimately ambiguous, neat translations being hard to come by. If this is so for toothaches, think how much more true it is as we rise to such civilized feelings as gratitude to M. Swann for his gift to the family of a case of Asti, which the narrator's aunts, in *Du côté de chez Swann*, report with such obliquity that even those who know them best, let alone the intended beneficiary of their thanks, are left unclear as to what is said and what is felt. Feelings like gratitude, pride, jealousy, and love typically occur within networks of other feelings as well as beliefs and other propositional attitudes, and it may often take the omniscient powers of a chorus to know what is really going on in alien breasts, as readers of Proust know. And matters are complicated by the intentional structure of many important feelings, which enables them to occur in the absence of stimuli correspondent with their contents – as when someone is grateful to his god (when there is none) for his many blessings (when there aren't any). Toothache is minimally intentional, but even "toothache" requires the user to know something about teeth and appreciate that pains have location. Yet even here, in this minimal case, collateral reference is sufficiently dilating as to foreclose, on Skinner's view, precision of reference.

Now my problem is less with whether his account of the reference of psychological terms is adequate than with whether his analysis of the emission of "Red!" in the presence of red gives an adequate model of the verbal behavior of scientists, though the two problems are deeply connected. The implicit semiotics is this: A verbal report is reinforced only when it is emitted in the presence of the stimulus that the emitted term denotes when the emission is correct. The burden of the paper concerns those cases in which the stimulus, though real, is inaccessible to the agents of reinforcement, in contrast to the standard case where it is accessible to emitter and reinforcer equally. But the terms I regard as central to science are not of this latter sort, but denote things and events inaccessible to anyone, and only loosely connected via definitional ties to "stimuli" themselves interpretable only against a background of typically complex theory. Now there are very familiar programs of analysis that maintain programmatically that all such theoretical terms may be defined without remainder in the idiom of terms that refer merely to what Skinner will call stimuli. Since Skinner has been realist enough to resist logical behaviorism, it is difficult to see how he can consistently yield, strongly tempted as his paper implies he is, to logical empiricism. But once one admits into the language of science terms as loosely tied to stimuli as theoretical terms are, the schedules of reinforcement will be no more stable here than they are with psychological terms. But if this means, in the latter case, that "it is...impossible to establish a rigorous scientific vocabulary for public use," well, it should be so in the former case as well, which means it is impossible, unless one yields to one form or another of radicalism, to establish a rigorous scientific vocabulary at all!

If, in the case of private stimuli, the lack of precision in referring terms makes it impossible for the speaker to know himself, in the case of null stimuli it must equally follow from the correspondent lack of precision for theoretical terms, that we cannot know the real world the terms refer to either. A theory of the semantics of scientific terms that makes it impossible for science to attain its cognitive aims had better be carefully considered, and this certainly must hold for a theory of verbal behavior that makes it impossible to understand the language of science. The symmetries suggest, however, that if we are to make knowledge possible by relaxing the demand for sharpness of reference in the one case, we have no logical basis for not relaxing it in the other direction as well, enabling self-knowledge to arise together with the possibility of knowledge of the world. But as these demands are symmetrically loosened, the picture of verbal behavior limned in "Terms" seems decreasingly adequate to the language of science. In compensation, I would propose that the relevance of immediate inner experience to self-understanding is probably as circumscribed as the relevance of immediate outer experience to understanding the deep realities of the world. Our representations of either must be considerably more complex than mere constellations of verbal reports. The creative individual, in science as in sensibility, will often have to teach the verbal community a thing or two.

BFS: I agree that an *analysis of my toothache* will not get us very far toward explaining a Greek tragedy or the works of Marcel Proust. Physics is a much more advanced science, but it has not got very far toward explaining the present condition of the universe. Biology and biochemistry are advanced sciences, but they have not got very far toward explaining that rite of spring in which molecules work their way up through the branches of trees and take their appointed places in leaves and flowers and fruit. Nor has philosophy or religion offered alternative accounts of any of this that satisfy the critical thinker. Let us be content with beginnings.

Danto summarizes the point of my paper quite accurately, and I agree that the "terms...central to science are not of this...sort." I would also be interested in a further analysis of those terms which are "as loosely tied to stimuli as theoretical terms are." I have had something more to say about that in "Problem Solving." I do not believe that we must in any sense relax a demand for sharpness of reference.

Wishful thinking

Daniel C. Dennett

Department of Philosophy, Tufts University

Even bearing in mind that "Terms" is a "theoretical" paper, not a report of experimental work, I am struck by how totally *ideology driven* the claims in it are. There is no glimmer of brute empirical fact cited to motivate or support the claims expressed. In particular, no puzzling or recalcitrant or otherwise inexplicable facts about human behavior are shown to succumb nicely to the theory proposed (always a persuasive theme in selling a way of doing science). Instead what we have here is the extrapolation of a creed: working out the details of what the devout behaviorist *has to say*, figuring out the kosher categories into which all facts must be cast, *no matter how the facts come out*. Skinner's role in "Terms" is thus analogous to the theologian's role in codifying, extending, and proselytizing for a system of dogmas.

Skinner, foe of ideology that he is, may take this observation as a particularly shrill criticism, but that is not how I intend it. Every scientific "school" I know anything about has its theologians, and they perform a singularly useful – perhaps even indispensable – service. They clarify the "position," showing what one is committed to if one does science in that way, and this not only sharpens the edges of the theories so that they can better be put to empirical test for confirmation and disconfirmation, it also generates new questions and problems for the theorists and experimentalists to explore.

There is good scientific theology and bad scientific theology, however; one of the benchmarks of excellence is forthrightness and explicitness of claims – leading with one's chin and giving the skeptics and critics an unmistakable target to challenge. Skinner, however, feints and weaves. We get bold declarations ("The significant interrelations between these terms may be expressed by saying that the community reinforces the response only when it is emitted in the presence of the stimulus"), but then discover that they don't mean what they seem at first to mean, since the host of obvious counterinstances one could cite does not count against the claim, for one reason or another.

It is an interesting exercise to go through the sentences of "Terms" one at a time and ask oneself: What would it be, *exactly*, to disagree with this claim? One of Skinner's favorite auxiliaries is "may," which occurs with great frequency in "Terms." Here are just a few examples: "the surviving covert response may be regarded as," "a response may be emitted in the presence of," "we may understand why terms referring to private events have never formed a stable and acceptable vocabulary of reasonably uniform usage." "Statements about private events may be under control of the deprivations associated with reinforcing consequences rather than antecedent stimuli." "'I am hungry' may therefore be variously translated."

A further review of the text shows variations on the theme: "Might" and "could" and "possible" are high-frequency items. What is frustrating about these terms is that they have several quite distinct dictionary meanings, and it is often not clear from context which way the reader is intended to go. Sometimes it seems to be the "may" of doctrinal permission ("The communicant may take the wafer on the tongue or in the hand"), and since it's a free country, who could argue with that? Sometimes it seems to be the "may" of mere logical possibility ("It may rain tomorrow, and then again it may not"), and who in his right mind would quarrel with that? Sometimes there is a hint that much more is being asserted: that what *may* be regarded as such and such may *correctly* be regarded as such and such; that when a response *may* be under the control of x or y or z, it *cannot* have any other explanation, it *must* be under the control of exactly one of x, y, and z, and so on. But these stronger claims are not forthrightly made. So who knows what doctrine is being asserted? There is a way of reading almost every sentence of "Terms" so that the staunchest, most radical "mentalist" could agree with it. But we know that that would be a misreading; we are meant to understand that this is a behaviorist manifesto, but exactly which manifesto it is has been left to the intuition of the reader.

There is a reason, I think, for the high frequency of what Skinner would probably call the "may" response in "Terms." What Skinner was proposing at the time was a certain brand of wishful thinking that *might* have worked – but didn't. Every science must simplify, and even oversimplify, its phenomena in search of tractable ways of manipulating, and conceiving of, the "basic" forces, processes, principles. As investigators in artificial intelligence would say, you have to find a "toy problem" you can master first, and no one can give rules or "criteria" for a "good" simplification. "Terms" is a paper about behaviorism's proposed simplifications, and while in the cold light of retrospect we can see that they were not good choices, they were probably well worth a try. "Maybe," Skinner is saying, "we can get away with this crude version of 'translation,' this tractably simple substitute for 'meaning,' this theoretically easy way with reference and consciousness." It is not that Skinner and other behaviorists were oblivious to the ravishing complexities of human behavior, but that they hoped – not unreasonably – to bootstrap their way to some manageably doable science of human behavior with the aid of a little wishful (or even willful) thinking. There is probably no alternative to that basic strategy; today's cognitive scientists just as willfully propose their own oversimplifications. One of these years those defenders of mysterious complexity who hang around waiting to say "I told you so" will be silenced by success.

BFS: If I have neglected brute facts, as Dennett claims, it is only because I have no reason to rehearse them. The role of the discriminative stimulus in controlling the probability of emission of a response was already well established when I wrote "Terms" and has since been abundantly confirmed. The point of my paper concerned a procedure through which a private stimulus could play the usual role in spite of its inaccessibility to the verbal community which maintains the necessary contingencies. There were no "puzzling or recalcitrant or otherwise inexplicable facts" to be accounted for. The facts were well known to everyone.

My paper was not theoretical. It was an interpretation. Through what fairly obvious ways could the verbal community circumvent privacy? I cannot see any theory in my exposition of four ways in which it could be done or the conclusion that none of these ways leads to a very precise control by private stimuli.

Dennett, along with other commentators, accuses me of dogmatism. I am "extrapolat[ing] a creed: working out the details of what the devout behaviorist *has to say*, figuring out the kosher categories into which all facts must be cast, *no matter how the facts come out*." And yet he complains at length of my use of "may" and "might," terms which, in all the "dictionary meanings" he cites, suggest far from a dogmatic stance. In order to have it both ways, Dennett says that I am feinting and weaving and that when I say "may" I really mean "must." (The only "bold declaration" that he offers as a sample of my dogmatism occurs in a paragraph in which I say that "we may generalize the conditions responsible for the standard 'semantic' relation between a verbal response and a particular stimulus without going into reinforcement theory in detail." The paragraph is little more than a definition of "contingency of reinforcement" – a key term borrowed from the experimental analysis of behavior. Dennett gives no example of the "host of obvious counterinstances" that he could cite, but if he means instances in which the community reinforces a response under other circumstances, they are instances I was excluding from the present discussion.)

"Terms" makes a fairly simple point about a kind of verbal behavior – behavior that Dennett would perhaps say "refers to" events inaccessible to those who teach us to speak. I believe the technical terms it uses are consistent with each other and with other terms in the work in progress to which I repeatedly referred. The point was relevant to the symposium because it shows how difficult it is to validate a system of mentalistic psychology which calls for introspection by trained observers. The theological violence of Dennett's commentary suggests that it must raise particularly troublesome difficulties for his own discipline.

Private reference

K. R. Garrett

Department of Philosophy, Brandeis University

This commentary elaborates the theory of reference implicit in B. F. Skinner's canonical paper, "The Operational Analysis of Psychological Terms" in an effort to further distinguish Skinner's radical behaviorism from the logical or philosophical behaviorism of Ludwig Wittgenstein's *Philosophical Investigations* (1953). Wittgenstein rejects the notion that we refer to private stimulation (i.e., "sensations") or at least rejects the notion that we do so in the very same way we refer to people or parades. I argue that, in a Skinnerian analysis, there is no essential difference between the way we "refer" to public things and events and private stimulation.

Our elaboration of Skinner's analysis of reference may begin with Skinner's *Verbal Behavior* (1957), in which he discusses the reference of *tacts*. Tacts are, roughly, verbal operants evoked by some particular object or event. Generally, their referent is the object or event evoking them; for example, the referent of "That animal is a lion" might be a lion or (in the event of an error) some large dog whose presence prompted the remark. Sometimes, however, a tact may be evoked by an object or event that is not the referent itself, but only causally linked with the referent in some way; for example, "That bear stole our food again" in response to a bear track found near an empty picnic table. Nonetheless, in these cases too, the referring response and the referent may be said to be causally linked; that is, the bear referred to may be said to have caused the prompting stimulus, the bear track. *Generalizing, we may say that referents or objects or events causally linked with referents are responsible for the referring response.*

Although Skinner does not consider reference in contexts other than tacts, it is possible to do so. What Skinner calls *echoics* is an example. Roughly, an echoic is a verbal operant evoked by another verbal operant of the *same form*. Suppose a wife says to her husband over the phone, "A skunk got in the basement" and the husband turns to his secretary and repeats, "A skunk got in the basement." The wife's response is a tact, the husband's an echoic; yet husband and wife refer to the same thing, namely, to the skunk. This same analysis also applies to what Skinner classifies as *intraverbals* or verbal operants evoked by other verbal responses having a *different form*. Thus, suppose instead of merely repeating the wife's report, "A skunk got in the basement," the husband had said, "There is a polecat in my cellar." In that case, his remark would have been an intraverbal. Nonetheless, it still would have referred to the same skunk. Generalizing we may say that the referents of intraverbals and echoics are the same as the referents of the tacts to which they may be traced. Since the referent or some object or event causally linked with the referent is responsible for the tact and the tact in turn is responsible for the echoic or the intraverbal, the referent or some object or event causally linked with it is ultimately responsible for the echoic or intraverbal, too.

When we turn from public objects or events to private stimulation, the same essential causal or functional relations exist between referent and referring response. When I say, "The pain is in my neck," I am emitting a tact evoked by the private stimulation in my neck and this is precisely what I am referring to as well. Another person cannot be said to emit a tact *directly* under the control of that very same stimulation for the simple reason that the stimulation is only in my body and not in the other person's body as well. For this reason, the stimulation evoking the tact and the referent of the tact are distinct. Another may, nonetheless, emit a tact ("Richard is in pain") under the control of an object or event causally linked with the painful stimulation occurring in my body; he may, for example, see me holding my neck and moaning and take that as "evidence" that painful stimulation is occurring in my neck. In both cases (whether I or another describes my pain), the referent (the painful stimulation) is what is ultimately responsible for the verbal response. Had the other person's tact ("Richard is in pain") been emitted at the sight of blood, then we could still say that the evoking stimulus is a condition (damaged tissue) causally linked with the referent (the painful stimulation). Thus, the essential causal or functional relationships are no different from cases in which the referent is a public object or event. Nor is there any cause to exaggerate the importance of the fact that only I can *directly* tact the painful stimulation. There are parallel situations that can arise even when we are dealing with public objects or events. If, for example, I am the only one who witnesses a certain event, say the eruption of a volcano, then I alone am in a position to emit the relevant tacts (e.g., "The dust of the volcano went miles into the air") in a "direct" way. Indeed, each of us is in a position to emit very few tacts of this "direct" sort with respect to most of the things to which we nonetheless refer.

A great many of our statements referring to the private stimulation of others are emitted as intraverbals. That is, for the most part we rely upon the tacts of the person in whose body the stimulation occurs. (Obviously, this is not the case when we are establishing such tacts in the young. In those cases, we rely upon the measures noted by Skinner in "Terms.") In any case, when intraverbals are emitted, the painful stimulation is responsible for both the tact of the person in pain and ultimately, therefore, for the intraverbal as well. And in these cases, moreover, that very same private stimulation is what both tact and intraverbal refer to. Thus, if someone says, "The discomfort is in Richard's neck" upon hearing my report, "The pain is in my neck," both responses refer to and are the result of the painful stimulation in my body. Similar consideration would apply when a parent echoes his child's pain report, "The pain is in Margaret's tummy." Here, too, the parent's echoic and the child's tact refer to and are the result of the very same painful stimulation occurring in the child's body.

In conclusion, then, it has been argued that there is no essential difference between public and private reference in a Skinnerian analysis. In both cases, the very same sort of functional relations may be seen to obtain between referent and referring response. This is, I believe, a very great advance over Wittgenstein's notion that there is some essential difference between the two cases – a suggestion that only mystifies us, since it is never spelled out in a clear or detailed way.

BFS: Garrett's paper is a useful interpretation of the relation called reference, particularly with respect to Wittgenstein's insistence that we do not refer to private events. As Garrett points out, such references are no more "direct" than references to other kinds of events. Private events are exclusive, but so are other events with which we alone are in contact. Privacy raises a problem only for those who teach us how to refer. Garrett's analysis of the reference function of intraverbal and echoic behavior is also useful. I have only one criticism to make of his analysis of the tact. Saying "bear" in response to a bear track found near an empty picnic table is a metonymical tact. Saying "A bear has been here" is much more. In a normal occurrence "That animal is a lion" is also more than a tact. The expression contains two tacts: *animal* and *lion*. It also contains additional material serving a function that I call in my book "autoclitic." It includes what linguists call syntax or grammar. If we are to stick closely to demonstrated behavioral processes, only the increased probability of saying *lion* in the presence of a lion is the relation called a tact. The sentence as a whole is controlled by other features of the situation, especially the presence of a listener who is likely to reinforce behavior that proves useful to him in the setting to which the speaker is responding. Short sentences are sometimes learned as units under the control of stimuli in connection with which they can be called tacts, but sentences are usually to some extent composed. Primordial verbal materials (tacts, intraverbals, echoics, etc.) are put together with the help of autoclitic devices so that the listener reacts in a more effective way.

Sensation and classification

George Graham

Department of Philosophy, University of Alabama at Birmingham

The aspect of Skinner's canonical target article on psychological terms on which I want to focus attention is that of the role of stimuli and responses in the classification of sensations. On Skinner's view, when subjects report certain private stimuli, sensation classification takes place. Something is called a pain rather than an ache, and a sharp pain rather than a dull one. These classifications involve as prime movers both the previous stimuli for the sensations and the consequent responses; that is, the surrounding community operantly conditions subjects to classify sensations in terms of the stimuli that produce them and the responses that they produce. Stimuli and responses may vary, and there may also be publicly unobservable stimuli and responses. Thus, classifications are pegged by conditioning to a tangled skein of stimuli and responses.

If we consider Skinner's view of sensation classification in the light of the currently regnant philosophy of mind – functionalism or the causal theory of mind (e.g., Churchland & Churchland 1981; Lycan 1981) – we see immediately that Skinner's account bears a striking resemblance to the functionalist or causal account. On the functionalist or causal account, sensations are classified in terms of their causal roles. If there is a difference between one kind of sensation and another, there is a difference in their causes and effects.

Resemblance between Skinner's and the functionalist account is no accident. Skinner is a kind of functionalist, for he has always found it necessary to interpret behavior as standing in functional relations with environmental and physiological events. But his psychology tends to concentrate on three sorts of behavioral relata or effects: (1) movement of a joint or limb in service of the *creature as a whole* such as kisses and key pecks; (2) locomotor acts such as walking and jumping; and (3) speech acts (Skinner 1957) such as *tacting* (roughly, stating) and *manding* (roughly, commanding and requesting). What "Terms" contains is atypical: a glimpse of Skinner's view of sensory experience below the level of joint or limb movements, locomotor acts, and speech. Here, I think, is where confusion in interpreting Skinner arises. Malcolm (1964), in a widely read discussion, called attention to Skinner's view of sensation classification. But he argued that the view implied that introspection does not occur, that reports of sensations by subjects of the sensations are based on observations of their movements and locomotor acts.

Contrary to Malcolm's interpretation, Skinner argues that classification by subjects is immediate, in the direct report of sensations under the aspect of the stimuli that produce them and the responses they produce. Subjects do not observe movements and then classify. They immediately respond to their sensations – both "feel" and report them – as typed according to their causes and effects. A person knows what it is like to have a sharp pain as a result of having conditioned responses of the sharp pain sort – where sharp pain sort is defined in terms of stimuli and responses associated with sharp pains.

"Terms" and sections of *Verbal Behavior* (pp. 130ff.) explain, on my reading, how such conditioned responses are possible. The key idea is that reinforcement by outside observers fixes or pegs certain overt responses (introspective reports, e.g.) and covert responses (introspections) to sensations by virtue of their associated stimuli and responses. Subjects learn to "feel" or perceive what is distinctively sharp about sharp pains. This is what their typical stimuli and responses consist of. For example, a sharp pain is a pain felt to be the sort one usually gets from knives and tacks. A burning pain is a pain perceived to be like those produced by contact with fire or hot surfaces. An adjective such as "blinding" reported of a sensation suggests that the character of the sensation has something about it that makes a subject close his eyes or shuts off his vision. Each of these ways of characterizing sensations involves reference to the typical stimuli–responses of the sensation. For Skinner, subjects are taught to make such discriminations or classifications by the surrounding verbal community, which makes reinforcement for introspective reports (and by generalization for introspections) contingent upon whether the subject of the sensation classifies sensations by reference to their typical stimuli–responses.

My reading welcomes Skinner as a contributor to current debate on sensations. There are several ways to make this point. It seems promising, for example, to consider how Skinner would respond to the inverted qualia objection to functionalism (e.g., Block 1978). The heart of the objection is that it is possible for sensations to remain the same (in kind) on introspection when their roles change. But Skinner should retort that this is not possible. The operant conditioning of introspections to sensations as-classified-by-stimuli–responses means that if stimuli–responses or roles change, introspections would change also. What sort of sensation a person has – or what it is like to have a certain sensation – cannot be detached from the stimuli and responses associated with the sensation.

Another point worth mentioning is that Skinner's account of sensation classification makes for symmetry between classifications by subjects and outside observers. Both subjects in *introspection* and observers through inference from associated stimuli and responses classify sensations the same way for Skinner: in terms of their associated stimuli and responses. Introspective classifications are pegged to stimuli and responses by the mechanism of operant conditioning. A recurrent problem for functionalism is to explain the introspective classification of sensations without appeal to exclusively introspectible qualities or so-called intrinsic properties. The importation of the mechanism of operant conditioning from Skinnerian psychology might be the solution to this problem.

In summary, reflection on "Terms" should serve to locate Skinner in the center of current debate on the classification of sensations. When he discusses certain private stimuli, he is discussing sensations. And his view, like that of the currently regnant philosophy of mind, is that types of sensations are defined by their causal roles. The distinctive contribution of Skinner to the debate in question is the postulation of operant conditioning as the mechanism whereby subjects classify sensations in terms of their causal roles.

BFS: I am not familiar enough with "functionalism or the causal theory of mind" to do justice to Graham's commentary, but if for "sensation classification" we may read "stimulus classification" then so far as I can see the comparison is correct. I am not sure, however, that Graham would accept that substitution of terms. One may speak of the cause of a stimulus by distinguishing between the object (for example, a red light) and its stimulating effect (the arousal of nerve impulses in the retina), but I think it is the latter that Graham would want to call the cause of a sensation.

There are different kinds of "painful" stimuli. We classify them with terms like sharp and dull which we take from the objects which cause the pain. As a behaviorist I can say that a sharp object causes the kind of stimulation that evokes the response *sharp pain*, but Graham, I suppose, would want to say that it is the sensation which, in turn, is reported as a sharp pain.

I allowed for that possibility in a passage in "Terms" that I am surprised has gone unnoticed by those who are critical of behaviorism. The passage reads as follows:

> "See" is a term acquired with respect to one's own behavior in the case of overt responses available to the community, but according to the present analysis it may be evoked at other times by *any private accompaniment* of overt seeing. Here is a point at which a nonbehavioral private seeing may be slipped in.

The point is relevant to Malcolm's (1964) contention that I must deny that introspection is possible. I agree with Graham in saying that Malcolm is wrong, and so are all those who take the operation to be identical with the thing it is said to define. So far as I am concerned, whatever happens when we *in*spect a public stimulus is in every respect similar to what happens when we *intro*-spect a private one. "Terms" is concerned only with the problems which arise in learning to do so. What people eventually "'feel' [as] distinctively sharp about sharp pains" may contain no vestige of the stimuli which were needed when they were taught to call them sharp.

Operationism, smuggled connotations, and the nothing-else clause

Peter Harzem

Department of Psychology, Auburn University

Scientific language contains two types of words: those that are also used in the ordinary language of the scientist, and those that have been specially developed for specific use in the science. The latter, that is, the technical terms, are generally more precise than ordinary words in the sense that there is little ambiguity about the phenomena to which they refer. This is simply because an *a priori* agreement exists in the scientific community as to exactly how a given technical term shall be used. Some technical terms are coined for the purpose: for example, *neutron, haemoglobin, trigonometry*, and *bacillus*. In some sciences, notably psychology, however, a different practice is common. Selected words of ordinary language are used *as if* they were technical terms. This has resulted, as we shall see, in considerable confusion. It is important, therefore, to note that the sort of terms discussed in "Terms," that is verbal responses to "private" stimuli, are not, as Skinner's title implies, psychological ones. They are words of ordinary language.

The characteristics of words in ordinary languge are quite different from those of technical terms. Ordinary words do not have predetermined meanings because they do not come into use as a result of prior deliberation. Moreover, as any good dictionary will show, there is no word that has only a single meaning. Ordinary language functions perfectly well, however, for two main reasons. First, the context in which a word is used makes clear its meaning on that occasion. The word "reinforcement," for example, has very different (but not unconnected) meanings when it is used in discussions of military strategy, architecture, and psychology. Second, the sort of accuracy generally necessary in science is not demanded in ordinary discourse. The statement "Jane smiled," for example, does not invite questions as to the extent and direction of Jane's facial movements, or about the precise criteria by which the smile was distinguished from a grimace or a laugh.

When a word is considered apart from context there is nothing to indicate what meaning should be given to it. For example, despite the fact that a false belief to the contrary is common, the question, What is "mind"? is not answerable because it does not make clear which of a multitude of usages is in question; for example, "my mind is on other things," "mind that child," "have you lost your mind," "he has a good mind," and "my mind is made up." None of these statements calls for the speaker to subscribe to any "theory" of mind, dualist or otherwise, and the word "mind" presents no difficulties when, in Wittgenstein's terms, it is used in its "original home," namely "everyday usage" (1953, sec. 116). Confusion occurs only when *the* definition is sought for a word such as "mind."

Operationism has been the most influential attempt in psychology to deal with this difficulty. In essence it seeks to institute a single (operational) definition for a term that has numerous uses. These uses must be eliminated if a single definition is to stand. For this reason the nothing-else clause in Skinner's definition of operationism is crucially important. As Skinner notes, however, operationism has failed – though not because the nothing-else clause is negative, but because it has not been observed.

In the first place, it has proved impossible to eliminate the ordinary-language connotations of a word. For example, operationally defining "stress" as immobilizing a rat for 48 hours has not prevented the same psychologist from making assertions about job stress, marital stress, and the like. Indeed, operational definitions have been used to *smuggle* into scientific statements claims that are unwarranted by data. The confusion is made worse by the impossibility of legislating a single operational definition for a term. Different individuals have used different operational definitions for the same term, and the same individual has used different operational definitions from time to time. Thus, the very purpose of operationism in psychology has been thwarted.

Skinner offers an entirely different approach to the problem that operationism failed to resolve. I shall term this the "special theory" of verbal behavior, as it is a specific application to the issue at hand of his "general theory" of verbal behavior. This theory is a monumental contribution to our understanding of language. It is also a curiosity of the intellectual history of this century because, for various reasons – none of them sound – it has been neglected in favor of linguistic theories of no lasting value. Nevertheless the special theory does not effectively deal with the problems of scientific discourse. This is because these problems are conceptual whereas the theory is empirical. In fact Skinner noted this distinction, some years after the first publication of "Terms," as follows: "Behaviorism is not the science of human behavior; it is the philosophy of that science" (1974, p. 3). By the same token, the special theory of verbal behavior is a scientific theory, whereas issues concerning the language of science are problems of philosophy of science. Only the theory of verbal behavior depends upon empirical evidence whereas the philosophy of science entails conceptual analysis (cf. Harzem & Miles 1978).

Consider, for example, a child (or for that matter, an adult) saying "Mama!" when in pain. Merely to assert that here "Mama" is associated with pain stimuli does not render it any the less correct that "Mama" refers to the individual's mother. Moreover, "Mama" may also be uttered under a variety of other stimulus conditions; when one is unhappy, wistful, over-joyed, and so on. And this, of course, again entails the problem of ambiguity that operationism failed to remedy. For a different example, consider the words used by Skinner in his definition of operationism: "observation," "procedure," "step," "intervene," and so on. Knowing the stimulus conditions prevailing at the time he wrote them will help us to comprehend neither the words nor the definition. What is needed is a conceptual analysis. The techniques of conceptual analysis, mostly developed by Wittgenstein (1953), Ryle (1949), Austin (1946), and other "linguistic" philosophers, in the years following the first publication of "Terms," constitute a major support for behaviorism as the philosophy of the science of behavior (see Harzem & Miles 1978 for a detailed discussion). These techniques provide significant new insights concerning, for example, "mentalistic" terms. It is high time that they were recognized and used in contemporary behaviorism. For without them many of the puzzles of the language of a science of behavior will remain unsolved.

BFS: There is nothing in Harzem's commentary to which I can seriously object. It summarizes a philosophy of human behavior which, as Harzem points out, was shared by Wittgenstein, Ryle, and Austin. (It is often forgotten that Wittgenstein called for animal research to answer some of the questions he raised.) I wish, however, that Harzem had spent more time on the problem of privacy, which is not quite identical with that of mentalism. It is worth emphasizing that an analysis of verbal behavior and of "how words become attached to their meanings" raises what seems to me an insuperable obstacle in the path of any kind of rigorous science of mental life.

What, then, is Skinner's operationism?

Philip N. Hineline

Department of Psychology, Temple University

Although much of Professor Skinner's essay, "Terms," is a critique of ways in which operationist notions are commonly applied and understood, he clearly identifies his own work with an operationist position. What sort of operationism, then, is his? "Terms" offers no direct statement of this except through example; it provides only clues as to the role of operationist principles in behavioral analysis considered as a whole theory. Since those clues provide an indistinct and perhaps misleading impression of Skinner's operationism, they bear examination in relation to some of his other work.

A salient clue appears toward the end of the first section of "Terms," when Skinner asserts that contingencies of reinforcement provide the proper operational basis for analyzing psychologists' use of terms. One might infer from this, as critics have inferred from other of his writings, that for Skinner contingencies of reinforcement are the only admissible operations in a scientific accounting of behavior. Indeed, he places these among the most fundamental of interpretive principles. However, Skinner's approach to behavioral science also includes, at the very least, elicitation as the defining relation of reflexive behavior. After all, Skinner was the first to distinguish clearly control of behavior by elicitation from control by consequences (1935b; 1937), and two of his early papers (1931; 1935a) provide some of the most astute analyses of elicitation that are to be found anywhere. But these do not exhaust the range of behavioral processes that Skinner entertains. In "Selection by Consequences" (1981 and this volume), he asserts the validity of selective consequences other than the reinforcement principle. And in a recent exchange with Herrnstein (Skinner 1977a), it became clear that Skinner is willing to entertain additional formulations for dealing with "phylogenic behavior," which seems to be maintained neither through elicitation nor through reinforcement.

A key feature of Skinner's operationism, while implicit in his many positive contributions, is explicitly identified mainly by exclusion. Part of the exclusion is specified in "Terms" when he questions the usefulness of operationalizing mentalistic terms. He uses similar arguments to put aside less mentalistic terms that are also derived from vernacular explanations of behavior. In such cases, as illustrated here for "being conscious" and for "matters of reference or definition," Skinner accounts for domains of phenomena in which vernacular or mentalistic terms are commonly invoked, but he does not use such labels to shape his enterprise. Examining his rationale still further, one finds him in a later paper, "Are Theories of Learning Necessary?" (Skinner 1950), putting aside not only mentalistic and vernacular terms as useful foci for operational definition, but also rejecting certain technical terms – those that appeal to "events taking place somewhere else, at some other level of observation, described in different terms, and measured, if at all, in different dimensions" (Skinner 1950, p. 193). Thus his enterprise is not a pursuit of engrams, or of the nature of an association, as could be said of other behaviorists. Nor is it an attempt to give scientific legitimacy to psychological terms from ordinary language, as could be said of much of the current fashion in psychology. Rather, Skinner's behavior analysis is a conceptual fabric in which operations are themselves the very warp and weft.

Further, it is a bona fide theory, monistically construed, of "the 'real' or 'physical' world (or at least the 'one' world)." Skinner's specification of operations, then, is an attempted characterization of features of the world as they affect behavior. The theory is an attempt to describe efficiently the effective environment in interactions between behavior and environment.

With hindsight, it seems unfortunate to have asserted this position was "nontheoretical," for this appears often to have led to its being misunderstood. Skinner's assertions that the causes of behavior are in the environment are read by his critics as logical howlers, or even as claims to metaphysical truth. If one clearly identifies such assertions as stating an assumption of a theory – the key axiom in a "bold and exciting behavioristic hypothesis" – philosophically trained readers are obliged to entertain the assumption while reading on, whether or not the statement violates commonly held assumptions.

An additional issue is the place of logic within Skinner's system. An explicit message of the essay is that logic is neither the starting point in his approach nor the ultimate source of its validity. In elaborating the rubric of discriminandum, response, and consequence, Skinner provides an interpretive account of the scientist's working – and of what it means to be discriminating and aware, as indeed a scientist may be. "It is not logic, but science," in that these relationships efficiently characterize the phenomena whereby scientific activity is effective, and thus valid. The reader might conclude that for Skinner, "logic is out," for "Terms" gives no hint of the fact that the circumstances in which we ordinarily speak of logic do have a place within his system. The interpretation that handles them resembles the one he presents here, but the discriminanda are not mainly one's own behavior, as in the case of awareness, but rather are special products of behavior – rules and algorithms. Most of this elaboration came later than "Terms" and is worked out in "An Operant Analysis of Problem Solving" (Skinner 1966a and this volume). Thus, logic is still in, but not in a keystone position. One finds it instead as a category under rule-governed behavior, in an exposition that clarifies a basic fact that is obscured in everyday usage: Only part of the behavior described as logical is functionally attributable to formal logic. So, contrary to a likely inference from "Terms," rules of formal logic do play a role in Skinner's system. Still, deemphasis of that role is appropriate to Skinner's present article, for within behavior analysis the role of what we commonly call logic is not a definitive one that justifies either theory or scientific practice.

BFS: Hineline's commentary is a better reply than my own to some of the points made in the other commentaries. His references to my analysis and use of logic are particularly helpful. I am always surprised, however, when it is said that I have *only very recently* acknowledged the role of natural selection in the shaping and maintaining of behavior, although the fact that I am willing to yield some of the place of operant conditioning to its rival is worth repeating (see "Consequences" and "Phylogeny"). I am also glad that Hineline clarifies my objection to theory. I do not object to mentalistic theories of behavior so much because of the mentalism as because of the irrelevance, an irrelevance which also applies at the present time to neurological theories. In the paper on theory to which Hineline refers (Skinner 1950; here, part of "Methods"), I questioned the use of theories that appeal to "events taking place somewhere else, at some other level of observation, described in different terms, and measured, if at all, in different dimensions," but I called for a theory of behavior of a different kind.

Skinner on sensations

Max Hocutt

Department of Philosophy, University of Alabama

What does the word *toothache* mean? In the view of a mentalist, it means a personal experience, a private sensation; in the view of an operationist, it means the public moaning and grasping of the jaw containing an abscessed tooth. As his 1945 paper, "Terms," indicates, Professor Skinner is an operationist. For him, the word *toothache* means not the private stimulus that elicits its use but the public stimuli that control reinforcement of its use. Furthermore, Skinner resists the moderate suggestion that *toothache* means both private sensation and public accompaniments. He prefers the more provocative thesis that its meaning is exhausted by talking about the latter. No fence sitting for him. Radical behaviorism or none at all. Toothache is to be defined solely in terms of its dental causes and behavioral manifestations.

What, exactly, is Skinner saying here? Definitions properly so called are equations, assertions of identity. They have the form "$a = b$," and they mean "a is the same thing as b." By saying that *toothache* is to be defined in terms not of private sensations but of public accompaniments, does Skinner mean either to deny that there is such an experience as toothache or to assert that it consists in moaning and grasping of the jaw of an abscessed tooth? Such is the usual interpretation of his views, but I do not think it will fit "Terms." As I read him, Skinner is saying here that *toothache* denotes neither a private sensation nor its public accompaniments but an *unknown bodily condition* normally caused by an abscessed tooth and normally manifesting itself in moaning and grasping of the jaw. To say that we can only define this condition by talking about its public causes and symptoms is to say not that it is identical with these but that we know how to identify it only by referring to these

If Skinner is often taken as denying the very view that I have here attributed to him, part of the reason may be that he does deny a superficially similar view. This view, which he attributes to such "methodological behaviorists" as E. G. Boring, is the doctrine that toothache is that *unobservable experience* normally caused by an abscessed tooth and normally manifested in moaning and grasping of the jaw. Skinner certainly rejects this doctrine, which sounds very much like the one I have attributed to him. However, there is a considerable difference between the two. On Boring's view, nobody can know what another's toothache feels like, or tell someone else what his own toothache feels like. To know what a toothache feels like, one must have it; and no one can have anyone else's toothache. By contrast, Skinner says that one can know what someone else's toothache is like in two ways. First, one can know that it is the sort of experience that people have under certain conditions; for it is defined by reference to those conditions. Thus, one can know that a piercing toothache is like the ache one feels when one's skin is pierced by a knife; for that is its definition. Second, one can learn what another person's toothache is like by discovering its physiological properties; thus, we might one day discover that someone's having a toothache consists in his brain being in a certain state.

The distinction just stated will be clearer if I explain it by means of an analogy. In front of a room two people are in clear view. *X* says; "Behind the screen between those two people is a person whom you do not see but whose voice you hear. We do not know what he looks like, but we could find out if we could get behind the screen." By contrast, *Y* says, "Behind the screen between those two people is an invisible and intangible person. We do not know what he looks like, and we never shall; but we know he is there because we can hear him." *X* is Skinner; *Y* is Boring (at least as Skinner sees him). What *X* and *Y* say will sound identical to those who detect no important difference between an unseeable person and one that is merely unseen. Similarly, those who uncritically and incoherently assume (as Boring apparently did) that an unobservable experience could be identical with an observable state of the body will see no important difference between the doctrine I have attributed to Skinner and the doctrine he attributes to Boring and repudiates as untenable. However, they are worlds apart. Boring has postulated an unknowable; Skinner has not.

It is true that, at the present moment, both Boring's and Skinner's toothache are unknown in the sense that we lack knowledge of their intrinsic properties. We know toothache only as that organic condition, whatever it may be, typically caused by an abscessed tooth and typically causing moaning and grasping of the jaw. We do not know whether toothache is a brain state or a muscular condition or both. For this reason, Skinner often says that there is little profit in talking about this undetermined state. Doing so is rather like trying to say what the person behind the screen looks like ("He is tall and has brown hair") before we have seen him. It would be better, thinks Skinner, to wait until we can have a look – especially since the thing making the sounds might be not a person but a record player or two persons talking alternately. Similarly, it would be better, thinks Skinner, to wait until we have independent information about the intrinsic properties of such states as toothache – especially since, so far as we know, there may be not one but many different physiological conditions answering to the one word *toothache*. Skinner's cautions against postulating unobserved states may be unjustified, but they do not amount to denials that such states exist.

In summary, I read Skinner as arguing in "Terms" not that toothache just is its overt accompaniments, but that it is the physiological state or states that these usually accompany. His claim that we can only define *toothache* in terms of abscess and moaning and grasping of the jaw, I take to mean not that toothache just is abscess plus moaning and grasping of the jaw but that, lacking ability to specify the physiological properties of toothache, we are able to identify it only by talking about its usual causes and symptoms. Doing so may not provide us with the best kind of identification, but for the moment it provides us with all the definition we have.

BFS: Hocutt raises the question of meaning. The colloquial statement that a person "uses a word to express a meaning" appears to be an explanation of the occurrence of the word, but what and where is the meaning? To the mentalist, as Hocutt says, toothache means a personal experience. To a methodological behaviorist it means the setting which is said to give rise to such an experience. To the crude operationist it means the operation from which the experience is inferred. I do not accept any of those views. As a radical behaviorist I would say that if the term "meaning" has any meaning at all, it is the setting which gives rise to the response of the speaker or the subsequent action of the listener with respect to that setting.

I am glad to accept Hocutt's paraphrase that "*toothache* denotes neither a private sensation nor its public accompaniments but an *unknown bodily condition* normally caused by an abscessed tooth and normally manifesting itself in moaning and grasping of the jaw." But that is not what he says when he writes "for [Skinner], the word *toothache* means not the private stimulus that elicits its use but the public stimuli that control reinforcement of its use." The trouble arises from the words "denote" and "mean." When a person says, "My tooth aches," stimulation from the tooth is in control, but it does not "elicit" the response as in a reflex. It makes a contribution to its strength. "Public accompaniments," such as a cry of pain or a hand to the jaw, play no part at the time. They were important to the verbal community in setting up the response at some earlier date, but this instance of the response is now under the control of private stimulation. With the rest of Hocutt's commentary I generally agree.

Social traits, self-observations, and other hypothetical constructs

Douglas T. Kenrick and Richard C. Keefe

Department of Psychology, Arizona State University

In returning to read Skinner's original writings, one is struck with the contrast between the much maligned and simplistic "Skinnerian" position and Skinner's own work. Whatever one's theoretical stance, it is hard to read more than a few pages of Skinner and not find a compelling logical argument. Likewise, one is reminded in "Terms" of the characteristic that marks so much of Skinner's work, and that is most responsible for his position within and outside the discipline of psychology: Skinner has never been content to apply his functional approach exclusively to limited problems of the laboratory, but has, throughout his career, grappled with crucial philosophical issues. It is this great breadth that is, more than anything else, the basis of Skinner's important contribution to contemporary thought.

In "Terms," Skinner introduces issues that continue to be of great interest to those studying personality and social psychology. For instance, the abundant research on "self-perception" owes much of its impetus to Bem's (1967) radical behaviorist analysis of "cognitive dissonance" research. In fact, 35 years after Skinner's paper appeared in the *Psychological Review*, one of us published a paper there dealing with the issue of self-observation of one's own "traits" (Kenrick & Stringfield 1980), and the lines of reasoning there can be traced directly through Daryl Bem (Bem 1967; Bem & Allen 1974) to Skinner.

From the vantage point of the recent research on trait measurement, we wish to make two points regarding Skinner's analysis. One is that Skinner may yet be making too much of the distinction between public events and private events as they occur in natural (nonlaboratory) settings. The other is that people can be taught to make the important and useful discrimination between those covert events with public concomitants and those without such accompaniments, and this distinction is a useful one for psychology.

With regard to the first point, public language may not be as closely discriminating as Skinner implies, but may instead approach the imprecision of describing private events. Nevertheless, both may still have a rough utility. In learning to apply terms to publicly available events, one is not usually dealing with phenomena as stable and reliable as a "red" ball. Many of the interesting (and survival relevant) discriminations have to do with applying social labels (e.g., "aggressive," "friendly," "seductive") to overt behavior. Unfortunately, such behavior is often subtle and transient. Consider, for instance, the case of aggressive behavior, which occurs infrequently, briefly, and which is, except in rare instances, modified and attenuated by situational constraints. In addition, a given instance of overt behavior may not look the same to (or even be processed by) observers at different vantage points. Behavior that looks like a friendly pat on the back to one observer may appear to be an aggressive and competititive act to another, and may not even be processed by a third observer. Thus, the "sharpening of reference that is achieved, in the case of public stimuli, by a precise contingency of reinforcement" may not be possible in many important cases of overt social behavior. Even so, recent research has demonstrated that our reports about the "traits" of those we know well, for all the ambiguity and complexity of their basis, are well corroborated by other familiar observers. These findings have gone contrary to the expectations of many social psychologists who, focusing on all the potential sources of unreliability in trait ascription, came to believe that traits existed mainly in the "eye of the beholder" (see Kenrick & Dantchik 1983). With all their problems, social-trait terms do nevertheless have utility, and the same case may be extended to reports of private events. If we were to disregard descriptions of private events solely because they are often inexact or ambiguous to the outside observer, we would by the same reasoning have to discard descriptions of overt social behavior. Rather than do this, however, we would argue that the evidence from the social realm should encourage us to give more credibility to actors' reports about their internal states. Not only are such states frequently salient and easily discriminable, but they may be no more subject to bias than reports about overt behavior, and like such reports, they may nevertheless have an important utility.

A related point regards Skinner's contention that "differential reinforcement cannot be made contingent upon the property of privacy." This statement can be interpreted in two ways. If we take it to mean that the community cannot differentially reinforce two covert events, it is true, but rather obvious. If, however, we interpret it in its literal sense, to imply that the community cannot provide feedback that will allow for a discrimination between those internal events that have public concomitants and those that do not, it is false. For instance, if I say "I feel anxious," an observer may respond, "Yes, you're shaking like a leaf" or "That's funny, you look calm." The self-observer's ability to make such a distinction is, in fact, of practical utility to the personality researcher. Subjects in the Kenrick and Stringfield (1980) study were able to provide such information successfully, and this proved useful in enhancing the strength of the correlations between self-reported trait standing and criterion ratings (made by others). Neither parents nor friends could accurately gauge the emotionality experienced by people who describe their emotion as private, while parents and friends could reliably assess the emotionality of those who described their emotionality as public. This finding was recently corroborated in a more intensive investigation by Cheek (1982).

A final point we wish to make is that while there is some utility in dealing with constructs "in the form in which they are observed," this analysis of overt verbal responses can take us just so far. Skinner is to be lauded for showing the limitations of the earlier operationism, but he does not go far enough in making the case for inference-based approaches to science. After all, the elements of the periodic table were placed by Dalton's inference, and Mendel established the existence of "genes" by inference. In the behavioral realm, there is some utility in performing a functional analysis of the verbalizations of schizophrenics, in the interest of modifying their utterances to bring them into an acceptable range for social discourse. However, no amount of such proximate functional analysis would by itself have led one to suspect a genetic involvement in the disorder, a discovery that could ultimately prove useful in understanding and treating the disorder. Similarly, a functional analysis might be useful in understanding the circumstances surrounding the complaints of a conversion hysteric, but an operant approach to modifying the verbal behavior of such an individual might be misplaced indeed, given the research indicating that the majority of individuals so diagnosed actually had serious physical symptoms (Slater & Glithero 1965; Whitlock 1967).

In summary:

1. Skinner's functional analysis of psychological terms continues to have diverse ramifications throughout the field.
2. He may have overstated the differential accuracy with which words describing public and private events are used in normal language.
3. The usefulness of a functional approach does not negate the use of approaches relying upon hypothetical constructs (provided that these are ultimately verifiable).

BFS: I am glad that Kenrick and Keefe bring up the relevance of "Terms" to self-perception and Bem's (1967) analysis of cognitive dissonance, and I agree that there are problems of reference with respect to public stimuli as well as private. That, indeed, was the principal contention of physical operationism. What are time, length, force, and so on? I should want to see the same kinds of answers given with respect to psychological traits. Should we try to discover exactly what a trait *is*, or should we look at the facts from which the trait *is*, as Kenrick and Keefe put it, inferred. The operational answer to Newton's time and space was not to solve the problem by improving the process of inference but to question whether the things Newton thought he was talking about existed. Is there any point in trying to "sharpen the reference" of the word "aggression"? It seems to me much more useful to examine the many instances to which the term has been applied and see whether any single term will prove useful with respect to all of them. It is true that terms from the vernacular can often be redefined scientifically, but they are usually found to acquire different definitions under different circumstances.

It seems to me that Kenrick and Keefe have misunderstood my contention that "differential reinforcement cannot be made contingent upon the property of privacy." I did not mean that a person cannot distinguish between the public and private attributes which underlie the use of a term. I can understand why self-description of the wholly private aspects of an emotion is probably less useful than self-descriptions of their public accompaniments. I was referring to the problem of psychological entities which were by definition exclusively private. The essence of consciousness was once said to be its privacy. But I do not think that is a useful definiens if it means there are no public accompaniments.

The flight from human behavior

C. Fergus Lowe

Department of Psychology, University College of North Wales, Wales

"Terms" is undoubtedly one of the most important papers that Skinner has written. It is also one of the most neglected. Thereon hangs a tale of misrepresentation, misunderstanding, or simply confusion on the part of behaviorists and non behaviorists alike; a tale, moreover, that reveals a strange reluctance by behaviorists to grapple with the central problems of human psychology.

In his book *The Behavior of Organisms* (1938) Skinner wrote that the importance of his science of behavior, then based upon research with animals, lay in the possibility of its eventual extension to human affairs. He speculated that the only differences existing between the behavior of rat and man – apart from differences of complexity – might be in the area of verbal behavior (p. 442). His paper on operationism pursues the direction he had earlier signalled and is an attempt to extend his account of animal behavior to humans, and in particular to verbal behavior. Implicit throughout "Terms" is the recognition of something special about human behavior – the salient characteristic being that not only can humans like rats "see objects," but also that they can "see that they are seeing them." That is, humans become aware or conscious of their own behavior, and in a way that is true of no other animal species. The great achievement of "Terms" is that it shows that "consciousness," which has long been ignored or denied in both behaviorist and nonbehaviorist sectors of psychology, is, after all, amenable to scientific analysis. Far from being forever locked away in the purely private domain of an individual's "mind," it has its origin (and therefore its decipherment) in the most public of arenas – the "verbal community." We learn from our parents and others how to use words to describe the environment and our own overt behavior, and we also learn to describe stimuli and behavior that are not directly observable by the verbal community, such as our "having a toothache" and our "seeing red." Over time, much of this verbal commentary on our own behavior itself becomes covert and elliptical in form, but it remains behavior nonetheless, and as such is subject to a behavioral analysis.

This analysis, dealing as it does with the role of covert stimuli and covert behavior, contrasts with the approach of methodological behaviorism which maintains that, since there can be no public agreement about unobservable events, they cannot be included in a scientific account. Skinner, never one to balk at a lack of public agreement, cogently argues that this is an outmoded view of science and that there should be no aspect of human activity left out of account on the grounds that it is not publicly observable or that it has to be inferred from other events. It is this concern with the role of "private events" in human behavior that distinguishes his approach and is, indeed, at the heart of his radical behaviorism (Skinner 1974, p. 212).

Thus it is surely a strange irony of contemporary psychology that an approach which, as far back as 1945, established its identity on the basis of its recognition of the "inner life" of humans should so often be charged with the error of ruling it out of court. It is widely asserted, for example, that Skinner's is a "black box" account of human behavior, that it does not deal with consciousness and cognitive processes, that it eschews the analysis and modification of private events, and that it shuns inferential accounts of behavior because they are unparsimonious (see Chomsky 1975; Harré & Secord 1972; Kendall & Hollon 1979; Koestler 1967; Ledgwidge 1978; Locke 1979; Mahoney 1977; Wilson 1978). Recently, for example, a new movement within clinical psychology, known as *cognitive behavior therapy* has found it necessary to adopt the conceptual apparatus of cognitivism apparently out of a mistaken belief that the behavioral approach cannot deal with the modification of people's covert behavior (see Lowe & Higson 1981; Zettle & Hayes 1982). It may be partly the responsibility of behaviorists themselves that such misconceptions about radical behaviorism are so widespread. For, unhappily, despite the clear theoretical lead given by Skinner in this paper, radical behaviorists have been reluctant to investigate the role of language in human learning. Although Skinner's account of the development of human "consciousness" is similar in many respects to that of Vygotsky (1962) and Luria (1961), it has not had anything like a comparable impact on psychological research. Whereas Vygotsky's ideas inspired valuable research on the way in which self-descriptive verbal behavior develops and interacts with other behavior (cf. Luria

1961; Sokolov 1972), there has been little empirical investigation of the ideas that Skinner outlines in "Terms" and goes on to elaborate in subsequent publications (e.g., Skinner 1953; 1957; 1963; 1974). Instead, radical behaviorist research has been concerned almost exclusively with animal behavior or with human behavior treated as if it did not differ significantly, in terms of controlling variables, from the key peck of the pigeon or the lever press of the rat.

One can only speculate about the factors responsible for behaviorists' neglect of the complexities of human behavior. From the start what was attractive for many about the Skinnerian system was the new methodology and techniques that it introduced for the prediction and control of animal behavior, together with the basic conceptual apparatus within which the effects of the environment on behavior could be expressed. On the other hand, "Terms," together with Skinner's other writings on the philosophy of science and on the development of human, as opposed to animal, consciousness, was perhaps not known, and certainly was not widely appreciated. Instead, earlier notions, dating from Watson, of what behaviorism was about and the prevailing zeitgeist of positivism overshadowed behaviorism's principal theoretical innovation. Thus, for many aspiring behavior analysts, it became almost a matter of ideological purity to deny the existence or efficacy of any event that could not be publicly and directly observed and measured. Watson's (1913) ban on introspection, although no longer justified by Skinnerian theory, continued to hold sway and had particularly bad effects. If, as Skinner argues, what is unique about humans is their capacity to reflect upon their own behavior, then not allowing subjects to report such behavior served only to distance it from behavioral analysis.

So it is that almost 40 years have elapsed since "Terms" was written and yet its challenge to contemporary psychology remains. For example, Skinner's hypotheses that "being conscious, as a form of reacting to one's own behavior, is a social product" and that "one becomes aware of what one is doing only after society has reinforced verbal responses with respect to one's behavior as the source of discriminative stimuli" have not yet been systematically investigated. Moreover, little is known about the ways in which the rest of human behavior is affected when this form of consciousness develops. Could it be the case, as recent evidence suggests, (i) that the effects of reinforcement are altered qualitatively when subjects acquire the skill of generating verbal descriptions (of whatever accuracy) of their own behavior and its consequences, and (ii) that human performance that is free of this "interfering" consciousness is indistinguishable from that of animals? (see Lowe 1979; 1983; Lowe, Beasty, & Bentall 1983). How much of our behavior is conscious in the sense that Skinner posits, and, finally, is it possible within the context of an overall behavioral analysis to alter "consciousness," thereby enabling humans to control more effectively their own behavior and their conditions of existence? Radical behaviorism offers a coherent conceptual system and methodology which, as this paper of Skinner's demonstrates, can be applied to human as well as to animal behavior. It would seem, then, a particularly suitable approach to adopt in the investigation of such questions, and it is issues such as these that should surely be central to any human psychology.

BFS: Lowe has, predictably, summarized my position correctly, and I am happy to join him in calling for the next step: research on self-knowledge and self-management and their possible effects on human behavior in general. I would formulate his questions in a rather different way, however. I doubt whether "the effects of reinforcement are altered qualitatively when subjects acquire the skill of generating verbal descriptions" of their own behavior and its consequences. When they do so, they generate other controlling variables which play a part in controlling subsequent behavior. That is why it is so hard to do research on operant behavior in human subjects who have learned to analyze the contingencies to which they are exposed. Their analyses (whether or not they are correct) enter into the control of their behavior as self-generated rules (see "Problem Solving"). Research on human behavior which compares favorably with animal research is most successful in small children and retarded persons or when the contingencies are concealed. My answer to Lowe's second question (Is "human performance that is free of this 'interfering' consciousness...indistinguishable from that of animals") is yes, although the data Lowe (1983) cites may prove me wrong.

Radical behaviorism and mental events: Four methodological queries

Paul E. Meehl

Department of Psychiatry, University of Minnesota at Minneapolis/St. Paul

This somewhat neglected paper, "Terms," is one of the most important theoretical articles that Skinner ever wrote, and his arguments are as worthy of attention today as they were in 1945. The paper is Skinner at his consistent best (or worst, for nonbehaviorists) and this friendly critic puts four questions to the author:

1. In his initial definition, legitimate (cognitive) operations are "the logical and mathematical steps that intervene between earlier and later statements, *and... nothing else*." Are these confined to deductive (algorithmic) steps? And even if the mathematics is like that, is its embedding interpretive text reductive, all such "intervening" (theoretical) terms being explicitly defined by means of stimulus, response, and S–R dispositions? If a looser, conjectural relation – as in normal scientific theorizing about postulated entities – is allowed, just what does this kind of behaviorism forbid?

2. Skinner's brilliant analysis of why verbal operants reporting inner events are imprecise shows why the introspectionist program degenerated. If the discriminations and shapings had been precise, so that a high degree of reproducibility existed in the domain of self-report about inner events, what then would have been the thrust of the behaviorist thesis? If most verbal accounts by naive subjects concerning inner events had the high predictability and order of, say, a naive sophomore's lab report on his negative afterimage, would behaviorism have been a significant methodological proposal? Now of course it was the way it was; but the contemporary cognitive psychologist, whether experimental or clinical, will argue that certain subdivisions of that subject matter do have the scientific reproducibility of the negative afterimage, and that, given Skinner's analysis, there is no good methodological reason to exclude them. That puts us on a slippery slope, because reproducibility, consistency, clarity, and the like are matters of degree. More complicated properties of the visual field less replicable than, say, shadow caster experiments, or "fuzzy" clinical events, like the Isakower phenomenon (Hinsie & Campbell 1970, p. 334) in psychoanalytic therapy (uncanny sensations of equilibrium and space, unclear objects rotating or rhythmically approaching and receding, crescendo–decrescendo sensations localized in mouth, skin, and hands), might have enough consistency, as rough but complex patterns, to be admissible. It is not clear what Skinner can say as a matter of *principle* rather than a matter of *varying degrees*

of reliability against such "subjective" reports. But does he want to? Intimately associated with that problem is the question of how much inner structure is to be attributed to such an entity as a visual image when it appears to play the same role that an external stimulus does with respect to the verbal operant describing it. Consider the eidetiker who cannot tell us how many teeth the crocodile had in the picture we showed him earlier but who can, on request, "call up the image" and then proceed to count the teeth off his crocodile image and get it right. I can imagine Skinner saying here, "Well, but we do not *have* to say that there is an image which. . .," a locution recurring frequently in his writings. That brings me back to my first question about operations, because the fact that we do not *have* to speak a certain way about an inner event, that the behavioral data do not *coerce* us to say that, is of course not equivalent to saying that it is unreasonable to say it, or that it wouldn't be good scientific strategy to allow ourselves to say such things. Inductive (ampliative) inference about the empirical world is just not the same as strict deduction, and it is not a fatal objection to a theoretical concept's introduction to point out that no observational datum compels you to infer it.

3. Can state variables like emotions and drives (postulation of which was beautifully justified in Skinner's 1938 book despite his subsequent distaste for them) play the role of private stimuli? As I understand his position they cannot, but the model as presented in "Terms" is that of discriminative stimulus, and the examples used (like toothache) make it easy to think of them as stimuli. Does that mean that we do not believe that people, having acquired language, should be able to report on inner states if these lack the usual "stimulus" properties, such as a structure, reference to a sensory modality, or being "events" rather than "states"?

4. Why does Skinner want to reduce the logical and epistemological concepts of truth and validity to behaviorese? It is not necessary for the coherency of his position, and it gets him into trouble with the logicians. We do not reduce the *concepts* of geometry, analysis, or number theory to the behavior of mathematicians, and in fact we could not operate in these disciplines if we did because our knowledge of mathematical behavior is too primitive, as I'm sure Skinner would agree. Why, then, is it necessary to behaviorize logic? Deducibility as norm – distinguished from inference as (psychological) fact, as an empirical transition in discourse – is part of mathematics, and of logic. Suppose no mathematician succeeds in proving Goldbach's Conjecture (every even number is a sum of two primes) before the sun burns out. Nobody will have been reinforced for emitting such a valid chain of mathematical operants. Does Skinner want to say that in that case the Goldbach Conjecture would be neither true nor false? Logic and mathematics being more advanced and rigorous than the science of behavior, isn't it an undoable (and needless) task to reduce the former to the latter? Similarly, if a rat that is suddenly shifted from continuous reinforcement to a fixed ratio schedule requiring 192 responses per food pellet starves, the truth of the matter is that the pellets are objectively available, whatever the rat knows or does. The objective truth of the proposition "food available" does not depend on the rat's behaving and being reinforced. Why should it depend on the psychologist's asserting it? As Skinner's radical behaviorism differs from "methodological behaviorism" partly in its consistently physicalist ontology, his insistence on psychologizing all concepts of logic and epistemology is puzzling and, I suggest, not defensible.

BFS: Meehl poses four hard questions. My tentative replies:

1. The first question concerns my opening definition of operationism, which was not very relevant to the rest of the paper. How we formulate rules as descriptions of the contingencies of reinforcement encountered in nature and society, and how logicians manipulate those rules and derive from them

other rules descriptive of contingencies not yet experienced by anyone (and, possibly, never to be experienced by anyone) form too big a field to be characterized accurately with terms as general as deduction, induction, reduction, and so on. I pass.

2. If an accurate introspective vocabulary were available. I should be an ardent introspectionist (as I am, personally, with a far from accurate one). But I regard introspection, like all other forms of "spection," as behavior.

3. I think clinicians sometimes get useful information, from which they can infer something of their clients' histories, from answers to the question "How do you feel about that?" But I am not sure what private stimuli are involved or how many of the stimuli are public. In general, I have said that we cannot introspect cognitive *processes* because we do not have nerves going to the right places. Such nerves would be useful, but verbal behavior and hence introspection arose too late in the history of the species to have made the evolution of such nerves possible.

4. I should not want logicians to use behaviorese, but if I am to analyze the behavior of logicians, I must use my terms, not theirs. Theirs appear among the subject matter. I am willing to use "true" and "false" in logic and mathematics, where they can be defined reasonably well. If the sun burns out before Goldbach's Conjecture has been proved, no one will have been able to say that the conjecture is true or false. In what sense could its truth or falsity exist prior to a proof? If Goldbach had conjectured that where there is smoke there is fire, a very different account of the "truth or falsity" of the behavior would be needed, and those terms would have a very different meaning.

On Skinner's radical operationism

J. Moore

Department of Psychology, University of Wisconsin–Milwaukee

Professor Skinner's contribution to the 1945 Symposium on Operationism is a landmark paper in the development of behavioristic epistemology and philosophy of science. During the decade immediately preceding the Second World War, logical positivism and operationism as interpreted by Stevens (1939), Boring (1936), and Bergmann and Spence (1941) had established in psychology an intellectual position that Skinner terms "methodological behaviorism." According to methodological behaviorists, science should be restricted to publicly observable, intersubjectively verifiable phenomena. As Skinner acknowledges, this restriction was not without some virtue, but the problem was that methodological behaviorists nearly always conceded the existence and importance of mental events as distinct from physical or behavioral events at the same time that they ruled mental events out of scientific consideration. This practice was perhaps most conspicuous in the "science of science," when scientists analyzed their own scientific behavior. Scientists simply took it for granted that mental events taking place in "immediate experience" constituted the essential basis for science; the issue was how to deal respectably with the events from the mental dimension. In brief, operationism came to imply the symbolic representation of the scientist's mental events by means of a set of measurements, so that agreement could be reached about the concepts involved. Accordingly, operationism became the cornerstone of the new scientific epistemology.

As certain passages in "Terms" indicate, Skinner had clearly had enough of this interpretation and the mentalism upon which it was predicated. The symposium offered a formal opportunity to challenge the conventional practices, and challenge them he did. The article itself mixes Skinner's critical assessment of conventional practices with his revolutionary, constructive proposals derived from the behavioristic perspective. Running throughout his critique is the attack upon the mentalistic, if not dualistic, bifurcation of nature into physical and nonphysical (i.e., "mental") ontological realms. Thus, perhaps the most central of his criticisms is that the conventional interpretation of operationism implicitly assumes that the scientists' language is a logical activity, taking place in some other dimension, which is related in some causal way to a nonphysical copy – imperfect, transformed, or otherwise – of reality called immediate experience. As Skinner asked later, Why was it supposed that there were two dimensions? Who sees the copy in the other dimension? Moreover, if meaning in language is essentially a referential or symbolic activity that links entities, concepts, or categories from immediate experience with reality, what is the origin of the entities, concepts, and categories in the first place? Where do they come from? Do they come from the pineal gland, Broca's area, or an Apperceptive Mass? Are they learned? If so, what processes are involved in their acquisition? What terms apply to the analysis of this activity, those from the presumed mental dimension or those from the physical dimension?

A second criticism, following from the first, concerns the general conception of human beings with regard to matters of epistemology. Given that behavioral matters are physical matters, and physical matters are observable, does it follow that something unobserved is something unobservable, that unobservable implies nonphysical, and nonphysical further implies mental, which in turn means that the whole business has to be dealt with in a different way by science, if science can deal with it at all? Skinner's argument, in "Terms" and subsequently, is that although private events aren't "observed" by more than one person, they need not be construed as nonphysical, that is, as mental, such that they need be dealt with in a special way. Thus, they are indeed amenable to scientific analysis. Moreover, private events have no special causal status; in particular, they do not produce knowledge. Rather, they are behavioral matters. From this perspective, truth follows from a consideration of pragmatic utility in behavior, rather than from a consideration of public status vis-à-vis private status.

A third criticism is that by failing to speak plausibly of private events and embracing instead every variety of explanatory fiction, one is in fact operating counterproductively. One is insulating private events from analysis by assuming that they are actually ineffable and therefore not amenable to scientific analysis. Thus, most methodological operationists assume an ironic posture: They implicitly acknowledge private events as causal, if only for themselves, but then they state their laws only in terms of publicly observable variables. In effect, methodological operationists regard introspective reports of their own immediate experience as incorrigible, but at the same time mistrust introspective reports of their subjects' immediate experience, a curious inconsistency at best.

The major portion of "Terms" is in fact constructive and concerns how private events can be approached from the fresh perspective provided by a behavioral viewpoint. Of course such private phenomena as descriptions of toothaches, images, and thinking must be accommodated in any adequate science of behavior, but that assertion doesn't mean that some measurement must be taken to symbolize what the scientist is talking about. Rather, private events have to do with the discriminative control by private stimuli over subsequent operant behavior, generally verbal behavior. As is stated in another section of the original symposium, Skinner was indeed filled with his unwritten book – Skinner's contribution was extracted from the work that was to become *Verbal Behavior* (1957). Private events may therefore be approached from that direction. How do private stimuli gain control given the problem of privacy? Skinner notes that they are present when the verbal community differentially reinforces responses on the basis of public stimuli (ways 1 and 2, and, through generalization, way 4), or that they supply a weaker form of the same stimulation as does the public response (way 3). Thus, Skinner was perfectly willing to talk about the relation between covert phenomena and verbal behavior, but he was unwilling to grant the mentalistic premises (a) that anyone's language, including the scientist's, was essentially descriptive of private, mental entities or logical relations among them, or (b) that the causal analysis of behavior essentially involved specifying the nature of any affective or effective, prebehavioral neurophysiological activity that occurred when organisms came into contact with their environment. The subjective verbal report and the process by which covert behavior exercises discriminative control over subsequent operant behavior must be dealt with, but these two processes are the ones that need to be assessed in connection with the relation between private phenomena and language. In particular, the whole business of language as logical symbols describing the contents of immediate experience was simply the wrong way to go. Boring should have been frightened; Skinner was rejecting his entire worldview.

Now, both Skinner and a methodological behaviorist might agree that one can't scientifically analyze a "mental event," but the bases for their positions are entirely different. Skinner would say that "mental events" are explanatory fictions – neural, psychic, or conceptual creations empowered with precisely the characteristics necessary to explain what needs to be explained. Skinner calls instead for some assessment of what the person is talking about when talking about images and the like, not so that some measurement can be taken, but so that the controlling contingencies can be examined, if only by the single person involved. In contrast, the methodological behaviorist declines to comment on mental events, but for another reason: They aren't intersubjectively verifiable. One can have a science only about things that can be agreed upon, for example, by being measured. One must specify what measured behavior serves as the index for and gives evidence of the operation of the underlying mental event. It follows that all sorts of nonsense can be pursued under such a program, and Skinner felt obliged to repudiate the position. Thus, to call Skinner "a practising operationist," as does Boring, requires considerable clarification as to what kind of operationism Skinner was practising. Skinner's repeated emphasis on the observability of behavioral processes should certainly not be taken to mean that he endorsed the practice of reifying the "mental" in terms of the "physical" through taking measurements, which is the all-too-frequent but erroneous interpretation of Skinner's operationism. In fact, it is to just that interpretation that Skinner has spent much of his professional life objecting.

"Terms" is now over 35 years old, and its message is as timely today as then. In a way, its continued timeliness is tragic, because it means that despite the availability of this remarkable article for those 35 years, we have failed to act upon its message as we should and move forward. Perhaps the most appropriate step to take at this point is finally to implement the operational program as Skinner envisioned it, on the basis of a functional analysis of verbal behavior. To do so requires in part the recognition that the explanatory verbal behavior of scientists be dealt with at a single level of observation, rather than as an indicant of things going on somewhere else, in some other dimension, to be described, if at all, in different terms. Whether scientists will see the mentalism inherent in their ways, given that they have not done so for the preceding 35 years, is questionable.

BFS: Moore's commentary is useful because it summarizes the argument of my paper in fresh terms and brings it into line with some of the other things that were being said about the operational definition of psychological terms at the time. It also calls attention to an important related problem. Privacy has caused trouble to psychologists and philosophers struggling to exchange views about their mental life. It has also caused trouble, unnecessarily it would seem, to the physical scientist who insists that science is personal knowledge. Polanyi (1960) argued that, and I spent many hours, to no avail, discussing the point with P. W. Bridgman, whose operationism failed him when it came to his own behavior. The scientist first interacts with the world, like everyone else, in contingency-shaped behavior. He becomes a scientist when he begins to describe the contingencies and to design experiments which make them clearer. The ultimate product, the "laws" of science, governs scientific behavior as a corpus of rules to be followed. The behavior of the scientist in following them is reinforced by the same consequences as the original contingency-shaped behavior, but the controlling stimuli are different (see "Problem Solving"). I take it that Moore is saying that they are free of private stimuli and that those science philosophers who insist that science is personal knowledge only create problems for themselves by returning to contingency-shaped behavior.

Logic, reference, and mentalism

Ullin T. Place

Department of Philosophy, University of Leeds, England

While there is much in this paper that seems to me entirely right, I shall confine my discussion to three points where in my view Skinner has got it wrong.

Logic. Skinner draws a distinction between "logical theories of reference" on the one hand and an account of reference based on a "scientific analysis of verbal behavior" on the other, and envisages that the latter will ultimately supersede the former.

Although it is difficult to be certain what Skinner is actually saying in these passages, he seems to think that the only arguments recognised as valid by logicians are those that conform to the explicitly stated rules of an existing logical calculus. In fact logicians are well aware that human beings who have never heard of logic or still less of a logical calculus have been giving valid arguments in support of their conclusions and detecting fallacies in the arguments of others long before the first treatise on logic was ever written.

Reasoning in accordance with the principles of logic, like all verbal skills, is, as Skinner himself (1969a, chap. 6) puts it, "contingency shaped" rather than "rule governed" behaviour. The principles of logic formulated by the logician are an abstraction from the intuitive contingency-shaped inferential practice of thinkers, not a set of verbally formulated rules which the thinker is obliged to follow if he is to reason correctly.

The logician's concern is to give formal expression to the principles whereby we relate the truth value of one statement to the truth value of another. It is therefore a reasonable criticism of the accounts of language and its meaning given by logicians that they concentrate on those aspects of an indicative sentence and its utterance that determine its truth value and ignore imperatives and interrogatives (Skinner's "mands") where the concept of "truth value" has no obvious application. However, to talk, as Skinner does, as if questions of truth value are irrelevant from the standpoint of an empirical science of verbal behaviour is equally unbalanced.

As I have suggested elsewhere (Place 1981b) Skinner's cavalier attitude towards truth in his account of verbal behaviour (Skinner 1957) stems from his preoccupation with verbal behaviour from the standpoint of the speaker whose interest, *qua* speaker, lies in the effectiveness of verbal behaviour as a device for manipulating the behaviour of the listener. He ignores the standpoint of the listener from whom the truth value and hence the reliability of what is communicated by others is of vital concern.

Reference. The effect of Skinner's preoccupation with verbal behaviour viewed from the standpoint of the speaker to the exclusion of that of the listener is also apparent in the account of reference which he offers as an empirical scientific alternative to "logical theories of reference." This leads him to concentrate on the case in which the speaker names an object when confronted by an instance of objects of that kind as his paradigm case of the referring function of verbal behaviour, whereas the problem of reference, when viewed from the standpoint of the listener, is the problem of how verbal behaviour emitted by the speaker can prepare a listener to encounter a situation that is not only *not* impinging on his sense organs at the time, but never has done in that precise form in the past. Reference is not, as Skinner supposes, a matter of the stimulus control exercised by nonverbal stimuli over the verbal behaviour of the speaker. It is a matter of the stimulus control exercised by verbal behaviour emitted by the speaker over the verbal and nonverbal behaviour of the listener.

Mentalism. As Skinner conceives it, the problem about our ordinary psychological vocabulary is that the controlling stimuli to which, on his account, these words refer are accessible only to the individual to whom the words in question apply. For him "being in pain" is the paradigm case of a psychological expression. What he fails to appreciate is that "being in pain" is one of a very small number of expressions in our very extensive psychological vocabulary whose primary use is indeed in the context of first-person sentences that report the occurrence of a private event of which the listener would not otherwise be aware. As Ryle (1949) points out, the majority of the psychological terms we use in everyday life occur primarily in the context of the third-person sentences that we use to describe, explain, and predict the public behaviour of other people, especially verbs like "knowing," "believing," "thinking," "wanting," and "intending," which comprise what behaviourists like Skinner dismiss as "mentalistic" explanations. To say of someone that he knows, believes, or thinks that so and so is the case, that he wants or intends to do something, is not to assert the occurrence of a private event or indeed the existence of a private mental state; it is simply to say something about what the individual in question would publicly say and do if certain broadly specifiable contingencies were to arise. More recent work (Place 1981a) on the intensionality of the grammatical objects of these psychological verbs suggests that what we are dealing with here is a device whereby the individual's behavioural dispositions are specified in terms of how he would describe the situation and his objectives with respect to it. This in turn suggests that the use of mentalistic terms in the explanation of behaviour involves the assumption that the behaviour in question is governed by a verbal formula or "rule" that "specifies" the contingencies involved (Skinner 1969a, pp. 146–52) and hence that the use of such explanations for scientific purposes is not, as Skinner believes, objectionable in every case, but only insofar as this assumption of a consistent rational and causal connection between what is said and what is otherwise done fails to hold.

BFS: I have not said that reasoning in accordance with the rules of logic is "'contingency shaped' *rather than 'rule governed' behaviour*" (italics added). All behavior is, I believe, contingency shaped. We take advice and follow rules because of reinforcing consequences which have followed when we have done so in the past. But the behavior referred to by the advice or the rules has other consequences. Thus, if a friend advises me to take one route rather than another on a journey I do so because of what has happened in the past when I have taken advice from him or others like him. In addition, I enjoy a shorter, smoother, or pleasanter journey – the consequences specified in the advice. I obey the laws of government not because I have disobeyed them and been punished but because I was taught to obey them. In addition, I avoid the contingent punishments specified in the laws. One behaves logically by following rules which describe contingencies; at other times one might behave in the same way after having been exposed to the contingencies. The business of the logician is deriving new roles from old and arriving at descriptions of contingencies to which no one has necessarily yet been exposed.

I don't believe my attitude toward "truth" is cavalier. I accept the tautological truth of logic, but I do not think that science, including behavioral science, can be true or false in the same sense – or in any useful sense. Some verbal responses are controlled by sharply defined stimuli which have acquired their power from the part they play in very consistent contingencies. They are as close as one can come to being true. Beyond that I do not think we can go.

Place's concern for the listener seems to me irrelevant. My book *Verbal Behavior* was different from most linguistic material of the time in emphasizing the behavior of the speaker. I did not think that the behavior of the listener called for any special treatment beyond the role played in reinforcing the behavior of speakers. The behavioral processes involved when a person responds to "It is raining" do not differ significantly from those involved in responding to a few drops of rain on the skin or a particular noise on the roof. All three "mean" rain. The "meaning" of a verbal response for the speaker is not the same as its "meaning" for the listener. That is what is wrong with "communication" as making something common to both parties.

Place speaks of "being in pain" when I speak of the stimuli generated by a carious tooth. I chose some such response as "My tooth aches" as a simple example, not as a "paradigm case of a psychological expression." I do not agree that "it is one of a very small number of expressions in our very extensive psychological vocabulary." I agree with Ryle that we are usually talking about behavior when we speak of knowing, believing, thinking, wanting, and intending (I would not be much of a behaviorist if I did not!), but that is not what the psychologists of 1945 were saying. The editor of the symposium (E. G. Boring), a student of Titchener and, through Titchener, Wundt, believed in a world of mental life in which mental events obeyed mental laws observed by "trained observers." These were the things of which I was offering an operational definition.

Mental, yes; private, no

Howard Rachlin

Department of Psychology, State University of New York, Stony Brook

Skinner's most valuable contribution to psychology (so far) is the concept of the *operant*. This concept, pursued consistently, provides a psychology of the whole organism independent of physiology, neurology, endocrinology, and the like. There is no room in such a psychology for consideration of private, internal events.

An operant is a class of behavior defined by its consequences rather than by its antecedents. Thus, a rat's bar press as an operant may be defined in terms of the closure of a microswitch but not in terms of the neural events inside the rat that precede and, in a physiological sense, cause and control the bar press. Such internal physiological events undoubtedly occur, but they are irrelevant to operant conditioning. The history of reinforcement of the bar press is both necessary and sufficient to explain (i.e., predict and control) bar presses.

The other behavioral class in Skinner's science of behavior is the class of *respondents*. A respondent is indeed defined according to its antecedents. But these antecedents must be external. Otherwise, one could consider a rat's bar press, controlled as it must be by internal physiological events, to be a respondent. If no external stimuli are found that reliably elicit a response such as a rat's bar press, Skinner does not ask you to look for stimuli inside the rat. It is always possible to discover or invent such stimuli. That is the path that Watson and Hull took (and on which they lost their way). To look inside the rat for the cause of a bar press is to assume that the bar press is a respondent (and to abandon the search for the cause of the bar press in the contingencies of its reinforcement). Skinner, instead, considers a response with no apparent eliciting stimulus to be an operant which may be more or less manipulable by contingencies of reinforcement.

It is inconsistent with this notion of the operant to say, as Skinner does in "Terms," that a toothache is a private event. In a (truly) Skinnerian science of psychology, a toothache must be a respondent or an operant (or some combination of the two). If the stimulus is considered to be the diseased tooth and the diseased tooth is supposed to be part of the person who has the toothache, then the toothache is an operant and consists of the class of *overt* behavior to which the label "toothache" is given. Alternatively, for the sake of analysis, one may want to consider the diseased tooth apart from the person with the toothache. In that case a toothache may be a respondent consisting of whatever behavior is elicited by that tooth (as determined by laws of the reflex). The operant toothache may well consist of a different, even nonoverlapping, class of behavior from the respondent toothache. In either case, however, the toothache is overt, public behavior.

In the case of thoughts, feelings, and other mental events, there is usually no apparent objective cause like a tooth that may be alternately considered inside or outside the organism. There is (usually) no apparent external antecedent stimulus that can be said (by the laws of the reflex) to elicit these mental events. Such events are thus operants – overt actions controlled by their consequences. Nothing in "Terms," nothing Skinner has written, and nothing in nature contradicts this idea. The main difference between a rat's hope and a rat's bar press is not that one is private and internal (even partially) and the other is public and external. Both are wholly external and (at least potentially) public, but one takes longer to occur than the other.

In "Terms" Skinner suggests that mental terms are used in ordinary speech to refer to private events and that, because it is so difficult for the verbal community to control such events, any analysis of mental terms as operants and respondents would be strained at best and ultimately futile. But Skinner gives unnecessary ground to his critics by this suggestion. As he indicates, in teaching people to use the mentalistic vocabulary, it must be overt behavior that society observes and then rewards or punishes. It would seem to follow that a person who uses that vocabulary to refer to private events must be using it incorrectly. Thus, a boy who says he is hungry just after he has eaten a big meal is either ignored or punished. Hunger pangs are not relevant here. In general, the use of mental or emotional terms without (eventual) support by overt behavior ("I love you," being perhaps the most egregious example of such use) is frowned upon. When we use those terms we are in much the same position as the boy who cried wolf. People will respond only so many times without confirmation. And it is not to private but to public events that they look for confirmation.

It would seem to be an important task for psychology to determine what the (overt behavioral) criteria are for the use of mental terms, how they change with circumstances, how they interact with one another. Before doing this job, it may be necessary to widen the conception of the operant, as originally advanced by Skinner, from a single discrete event (such as a lever press) to a complex pattern of events that may occur over days or weeks and (consequently) to alter the notion of reinforcement from contiguity between a pair of discrete events (response and reward) to more complex correlations that have meaning only over an extended period (see Commons, Herrnstein, & Rachlin 1982). When the important variables of such molar behaviorism are discovered, the mentalistic vocabulary will, I believe, come nicely to hand.

To the extent that mental terms refer to the overt behavioral context of immediate behavior it is possible to use them in a behavioral science. To the extent that mental terms refer to the covert or internal context of immediate behavior they have no place in behavioral science, because such use of mental terms converts observable operants into hypothetical respondents.

BFS: I found Rachlin's paper puzzling. He evidently uses the term "toothache" for all the behavior elicited or evoked by a carious tooth, where I was using it to mean only the stimulation arising from such a tooth. He also speaks of thoughts, feelings, and other mental events and argues that they must be operants because they have "no apparent external antecedent stimulus." But one point of "Terms" was that a substantial amount of behavior that would be called operant was indeed under the control of private stimuli; that was the problem I was discussing. I can't imagine what Rachlin means by a rat's hope or how he knows that it takes longer than a bar press.

I do not see why it follows from the fact that "in teaching people to use the mentalistic vocabulary, it must be overt behavior that society observes and then rewards or punishes" that "a person who uses that vocabulary to refer to private events must be using it incorrectly." To the extent that the private event correlates with the public evidence, terms will be used correctly. Rachlin later makes that point by saying that "to the extent that mental terms refer to the overt behavioral context of immediate behavior it is possible to use them in a behavioral science." But since we do not know the extent to which they do so, any such use is questionable.

B. F. Skinner's operationism

Jon D. Ringen

Philosophy Department, Indiana University at South Bend

"Terms" represents a brilliant and powerful innovation in the development of behaviorism. The paper presents Skinner's conception of operationism and outlines a framework and set of problems for a radical behaviorist analysis of verbal behavior. Skinner (1957) develops the program further.

Skinner's operationism is quite different from the operationism of the logical positivists (Hempel 1965b; 1965c). Skinner rejects the aim of providing complete, explicit (behavioristic) definitions of (psychological) terms from ordinary language. He also rejects any form of operationism that requires a statement of logically necessary or sufficient conditions for the correct application of technical scientific terms. Like the positivists, Skinner does acknowledge the influence of Mach (1919) and Bridgman (1928), and he clearly draws the term operational definition from the latter. Unlike the positivists, Skinner limits himself to endorsing Mach's historical method and the procedure Bridgman ascribes to himself, namely, observing what people (e.g., scientists) do with the terms they use. As construed by Skinner, Bridgman's procedure makes the task of the logician and philosopher of science a task for psychology. The type of "psychological" investigation Skinner proposes is an experimental analysis of the contingencies of reinforcement under which those verbal *responses* ordinarily classified as verbal reports are acquired and maintained. Skinner's operationism is, thus, one part of the radical behaviorist program for the experimental analysis of verbal behavior.

Skinner explicitly requires that his operationism solve the problem of explaining how verbal responses are brought under the control of private stimuli (i.e., stimuli that only the responder can discriminate and respond to). This requirement marks a distinction between radical behaviorism and methodological behaviorism, since methodological behaviorism presupposes that private stimulation lies outside the realm of scientific investigation.

The program Skinner proposes escapes the standard objections to methodological behaviorism and the operationism of the logical positivists (contra Boden 1972; Koch 1964; Scriven 1956). In addition, the program provides principled reasons for behaviorists' long-standing suspicion of scientific use of commonsense psychological terms and for the behaviorist conclusion that introspection is an inappropriate method of investigation in science.

Serious attempts to evaluate Skinner's program must begin with a clear appreciation of how radical a program it is. Like his contemporary Quine (1960), Skinner rejects the use of the "intentional idiom" in scientific descriptions and explanations of verbal behavior. For example, verbal behavior ordinarily classified as first-person reports of concurrent psychological states (e.g., "My tooth aches," "I am depressed.") are not to be treated as reports or statements at all, much less as reports or statements that are accurate, reliable, true, or correct. (For discussion of the difference this makes see Ringen 1977; 1981.) Explanations of these verbal responses are to be given in terms of the contingencies of reinforcement by which they are shaped and maintained. Explanatory reference to meanings, intentions, or psychological states of the speaker is prohibited.

Recent work in the history and philosophy of science (e.g., Kuhn 1970) has emphasized that the more radically the commitments embodied in a given research program diverge from those of whoever attempts to assess it, the greater the difficulties objective assessment presents. For all of us whose customary ways of speaking and thinking embody western cultural traditions, considerable difficulty attends objective assessment of Skinner's program. The intentional idiom, which Quine and Skinner proscribe, constitutes an absolutely fundamental feature of our customary ways of describing and explaining all human action, and especially action that involves language. It is hard to imagine anything more radical or revolutionary than the attempt to describe and explain human verbal behavior without the concepts the intentional idiom embodies. Indeed, without this idiom it is difficult to find anything coherent to say about verbal behavior.

When faced with such difficulties, it is only prudent to ask whether there is any reason to pursue Skinner's program or even to make the considerable effort required to understand what the program involves. It is instructive to reflect on the reasons Skinner suggests. Quite clearly his reasons do not include a commitment to the operationism logical positivists recommend. Rather, Skinner's own statements (e.g., 1931; 1959b) suggest that his rejection of the intentional idiom derives from two sources: an interpretation of the history of science according to which scientific progress occurs only after anthropomorphic conceptions have been rejected, and suspicion that reference to psychological states will be problematic in putative explanations of behavior because these states are not identified independently of the behavior or functional relations they are to explain. Evidence of successful development of the program aside, Skinner's commitment to operationism is linked to its promise in eliminating anthropomorphism and explanatory vacuity from a scientific study of behavior.

Chomsky (1959) and others provide considerable reason for Skinner to be concerned about explanatory vacuity in existing radical behaviorist accounts of verbal behavior. (Major criticisms are directed at explanatory references to unobserved covert behavior – "Terms" – as providing stimuli for verbal responses – see point 3 in Terms" – and to unspecified dimensions of generalization in accounts of responses occurring under public stimulus conditions which differ from those under which the response has previously been conditioned – see point 4.) Hence, there is reason to conclude that Skinner's operationism has not, in fact, served one of the functions it was designed to serve. In addition, strong arguments have been given (e.g., Hempel 1965a; Taylor 1964; Woodfield 1976; Wright 1976) that explanatory use of concepts embodied in the intentional idiom need not be vacuous in any sense that concerns Skinner. Thus, we are free to wonder whether anthropomorphism really is misplaced in a scientific study of human (verbal) behavior. Whether it is misplaced or not can be determined only by comparing the results of serious attempts to provide a scientific analysis of behavior without the use of concepts embodied in the intentional idiom with the results of attempts in which those concepts occur essentially. The radical behaviorism of Skinner and the contemporary cognitivism inspired by Chomsky provide an opportunity for such a comparison. Both programs have been defended and elaborated in work subsequent to Chomsky's (1959) well-known critique of Skinner (1957). Quine (1970), MacCorquodale (1970), Fodor, Bever, and Garrett (1974), and Winokur (1976) provide a place to begin comparing the results of pursuing the programs. Lacey (1974) provides some useful guidance.

BFS: It would be ungrateful of me to complain of Ringen's excellent summary of my position, and the only remark I have to make is not a complaint. Ringen extends the argument of my paper to cover the behavioristic contention that anthropomorphism, in particular "the cognitivism inspired by Chomsky," is "misplaced in the scientific study of human (verbal) behavior." I would have been willing to make the extension at the time I wrote "Terms" (and indeed was making it in the manuscript from which the paper was essentially taken), but I would put it rather differently today. The explanatory terms which have been used for more than 2,000 years to explain human behavior are troublesome not because they raise questions about dimensions but because they assign the initiation of behavior to the person rather than to that person's genetic and personal history. The problem is centrism rather than anthropomorphism. The terms I hoped to dispense with in my analysis of verbal behavior (terms like meaning, idea, information, and knowledge) represent supposed possessions of the speaker. So far as I am concerned they are inconvenient surrogates of the speaker's history. Their dimensions (physical, mental, conceptual?) are not really at issue. What causes trouble is the usurpation of the initiating role of the environment.

There is more than one way to access an image

Lynn C. Robertson

Veterans Administration Medical Center, Martinez, California

For Professor Skinner, science depends on operationalism. He argues that private stimuli cannot be operationally defined; only the verbal response to a private stimulus can be so defined. One could dismiss this argument as outdated, since mainstream psychology abandoned its obsession with operationalism in the 1940s and has since migrated toward the philosophy of critical realism. However, to disregard "Terms" on this basis would be to miss some of the compelling differences between modern behaviorism and cognitive psychology that are relevant today.

The most important issue that Skinner addresses is the question of how and why people respond to private stimuli. This is indeed one of the current concerns of experimental psychology. There is a search for the nature of internal representations (private stimuli) and cognitive processes (private events). Skinner predates, and is in agreement with, some contemporary arguments that it is impossible to know the nature of an internal representation (Anderson 1978; Palmer 1978). However, current controversy is based on mathematical analyses and pertains only to internal representations in isolation and not to the processes (one could call them behaviors) that operate upon them.

Skinner believes that "internal representations" and "mental processes" are fictions, yet private stimuli and private events are not. He agrees that there are "images" but disagrees that they can be studied. His basic premise is that we can only study a verbal response like "red" in the context of a history of verbal responses to some public red. We cannot study the private stimulus to which it may refer. In other words, we cannot find the reference to "red" in the internal event (except physiologically, which is not relevant to the issue), so we must find it in the contingencies of reinforcement that correlate with, or, as Skinner would say, control the verbal response.

This line of thought can be extended to any response that is symbolic of the private stimulus red. If subjects were asked to press a key whenever they imagined the word red, the evaluation of the response would not lie in inferences of processing strategies and comparative analyses of internal representations. It would, rather, be possible to examine only the contingencies of reinforcement that lead to the key response. In this case the key response and the verbal report "red" presumably refer to the same stimulus – the color red. If we compared the verbal report "red" to the manual key response in the same experiment, I suspect we would find that the conditions under which the key response and the verbal response were emitted would be the same. For one moment, let's accept Skinner's operationalism and analyze the history of reinforcement contingencies for saying "red" and of reinforcement contingencies for pressing keys. It is probable that the two histories would be very different (except by the greatest coincidence), yet it is clear that the responses have the same referent. It is not the functional analysis of key pressing and verbally saying "red" that will reveal how the same referent can result in two diverse responses (responses that have different reinforcement histories). Rather, the question is how reorganization (an internal process) occurs to form a new relationship between a referent and a response. Knowing how verbal reports to private stimuli are shaped does not answer this question.

A second, somewhat related, problem is that parametric variations in the response seem to be of little importance in "Terms." The verbal response "red" may be said with greater intensity and more rapidly when a traffic signal turns red than when one is asked the color of a dress. Contingencies of reinforcement could presumably explain a part of the differences in intensity, since the effect of ignoring a red light may be much greater than that of ignoring the color of clothing. Reinforcement contingencies, however, are not sufficient to explain all the factors contributing to parametric variations in response patterns.

When Shepard and Metzler (1971) presented two figures in different orientations and found that reaction time increased linearly with the degree of difference, the contingencies of reinforcement that contribute to faster and slower responses are not obviously relevant. Shepard interpreted these data in terms of images and internal referents, and his subjects verbally reported the experience of "seeing" a rotating image. It is true that Shepard may be wrong about the nature of the private event, just as a behaviorist could be wrong about the contingencies of reinforcement that contribute to the response. Yet, as I understand Skinner's view, we would have to regard the differences in reaction time in Shepard and Metzler's study as responses that must be analyzed in themselves. It appears that Skinner would deemphasize the reaction-time data and analyze the contingencies of reinforcement that "control" reporting the experience of having an image, including the reference to images by Shepard and Metzler and the rest of the scientific community.

This approach leads Skinner to argue that the verbal reports of scientists should be analyzed in the same way as their subjects' verbal responses. It is an interesting question how words function in the thinking and behavior of scientists. Skinner's orientation, however, leads to an infinite regress.

Suppose we decide to define operationally the concept "red" according to Skinner's recipe of operationalism. We seek the contingencies of reinforcement that have shaped the verbal report "red," and we look at the contingencies in the present use of the word "red." As noted above, a person may yell "red" when the driver of a car is about to run a traffic signal, and say "red" more softly when commenting on the color of a dress. Privately, the two verbal reports of "red" refer to two very different meanings. So we must operationalize two instances of "red," the intense verbal report of red and the less intense verbal report of red. Now we have a new task – to define intensity operationally. According to Skinner, "intensity" consists of the conditions under which the word "intensity" is used. Thus, the use of the phrase "intense red" now is the verbal report of the person who defines intensity. We have louder "red" and softer "red" referring to the contingencies of reinforcement surrounding the response "intense" combined with the contingencies of reinforcement surrounding the response "red." We now need a verbal report of the person who is reporting the difference between these two responses. This verbal report, in turn, needs analysis in the form of another verbal report. Something is surely amiss.

BFS: Robertson raises the question of sensations and images as representations of stimuli. Do we see red as a property of an object, as a retinal response to a given frequency of radiation, as nerve impulses in the optic tract, or as activity in the occipital cortex? As a behaviorist, I must reply that what is happening in retina, optic tract, and occipital cortex are part of seeing red. As a behaviorist, I leave that to the physiologist, who has more appropriate instruments and methods. As a behaviorist, I am concerned only with the way in which a discriminative response (whether it be key press, saying "red," or stepping on the brake of a car) is brought under the control of red objects.

Also as a behaviorist, I am concerned with how a person learns to say "I see red" in both the presence and absence of red objects. It is the word "see" that causes trouble. We teach a child to answer questions like, "Do you see that animal?" or, "Can you see the clock?," but we do so successfully only if we have evidence that the child's responses are correct. The evidence we use usually consists of subsequent behavior, as in answering the question. "What is it?" or, "What time is it?" Certain private events are part of that behavior, and the private events take over control when the child is eventually told to "think of an elephant" or "imagine a clock." We have no evidence that copies of elephants or clocks exist inside the child at any time. Whatever is happening when we see an elephant or a clock does not require a representation.

B. F. Skinner's theorizing

Douglas Stalker and Paul Ziff

Department of Philosophy, University of North Carolina at Chapel Hill

In 1938 (the year of *The Behavior of Organisms*) B. F. Skinner began developing a technology of behavior. He has worked at it over the years. His achievement has been awesome, inspiring: It has yet to be rivaled.

But even the best of technologists, and the best of engineers, can succumb to a lust for philosophic theorizing, and Skinner has been no exception.

By 1945 ("Terms") Skinner had other things in mind beside technology. Though he would talk (albeit in passing) about this technology and our need for it, Skinner had become more and more concerned with theorizing. He proceeded from describing operant behavior and how to shape it all the way to theorizing about every feature of human life willy nilly, behavioral or not. By 1974 (*About Behaviorism*) Skinner was openly pursuing an elusive weltanschauung: Philosophy had replaced technology. With fast talk from a strategic armchair, Skinner extended his theory of behavior by definition and redefinition, rather than by experiment.

Consider, for example, what has happened to Skinner's conception of behavior over the years. In 1938 it was clear and in line with his practical aim: immediate, overt, and observable behavior was the relevant datum to describe and control. There was no need to explain or deny the existence of other forms of behavior, let alone mental states, events, or processes. But by 1974 that conception had been expanded beyond all belief: Any sort of matter became behavioral in all sorts of ways; so knowing that something is so became a form of behavior, and so did thinking a thought. How could these count as immediate, overt, and observable? A new label was created: "covert behavior." Covert behavior is minuscule and after the fact, in truth, is it behavior at all? And scurrying along with covert behavior, in *About Behaviorism*, came current behavior, probable behavior, perceptual behavior, past behavior, future behavior, and, certainly, whatever behavior was needed to fill the bill of a technological bird fishing for philosophic frissons in Plato's wordy meander.

When reading Skinner, one must ask oneself, Is this the technologist or a philosopher speaking? Early on he is almost exclusively the first; by 1974 he is the second. The first is more intriguing than the second, and so are his position and its value. It is a technology, and its value is that of a technology – a way of changing the ways in which humans (and nonhumans) behave; to have these means available, Skinner needed only modest means – his unvarnished definition of behavior and his notions of operant and respondent conditioning. If these means were to need supplementation, the reasons would be technological: The results, being unsatisfactory, could only be aberrant. In "Terms" Skinner, perhaps in passing, says the only criterion for the utility of a notion is whether it helps one get anywhere in controlling things. That is the great technological Skinner speaking, and espousing the criterion of a technology. What replaces it, or supplants it, when the philosopher king speaks? Large gestures about science and what is prescientific; there are motions made to scientific revolutions in physics, breakthroughs here and there, and how all the dross – the phlogiston and ether and élan vital – has gone by the boards. Somewhere in all this there is supposed to be a lesson for psychology, but the lesson is lost at the level of slogans we can all agree to: Do we all agree to accept no explanatory fictions? How do we now tell a fiction from a fact, decoy from a duck? When Skinner was a behavioral engineer, he knew what his criterion was: utility. In his philosophic period, which seems to have afflicted him even as early as 1945, Skinner lacked a criterion for discriminating between psychological phlogiston and the daydreams of cognitive psychologists. He gestures and promises and displays high ideals, which serves merely to turn behaviorism into a posture – defiant and quixotic.

Some will wonder at Skinner's "operational" definitions. We wonder at the attempt. Why did he feel the need?

Even a genius can be seduced by philosophy.

BFS: Stalker and Ziff have assumed that beyond science and technology there lies only philosophy. I have found something else: interpretation. I would define it as the use of scientific terms and principles in talking about facts about which too little is known to make prediction and control possible. The theory of evolution is an example. It is not philosophy; it is an interpretation of a vast number of facts about species using terms and principles taken from a science of biology based upon much more accessible material and upon experimental analyses and their technological applications. The basic principle, reproduction with variation, can be studied under controlled conditions, but its role in the evolution of existing species is a mere interpretation.

Plate tectonics is another example. It is not philosophy but an interpretation of the present state of the crust of the earth, using physical principles governing the behavior of material under high temperatures and pressures established under the conditions of the laboratory, where prediction and control are possible.

Laboratory analyses of the behavior of organisms have yielded a good deal of successful prediction and control, and to extend the terms and principles found effective under such circumstances to the interpretation of behavior where laboratory conditions are impossible is feasible and useful. I do not think that it is properly called philosophy. The human behavior we observe from day to day is unfortunately too complex, occurs too sporadically, and is a function of variables too far out of reach to permit a rigorous analysis. It is nevertheless useful to talk about it in the light of instances in which prediction and control have proved to be possible. It is true that I was in contact with philosophers in the thirties and forties and I believe to my benefit. In particular, I discussed the point of "Terms" with Herbert Feigl, a distinguished member of the Vienna Circle. But I was not "pursuing an elusive weltanschauung." I have not "succumb[ed] to a lust for philosophic theorizing."

My book *Verbal Behavior* was an interpretation of the field. Early on I had removed a few sections that could be said to present facts (about word associations, alliteration, guessing, and so on) just in order to make the nature of the book clearer. The book differed from what might have been called the philosophy of language that was then current in linguistics, semantics, and books like *The Meaning of Meaning* (Ogden & Richards 1938). In turning to the history of the speaker rather than to the presumed current endowments of speech, I could avoid saying that a speaker uses words to refer to things, to express ideas, or to communicate meanings. I questioned the existence of these things in their traditional sense. I could, however, have defined them behaviorally, although the resulting expressions would not have been convenient.

Stalker and Ziff had some difficulty in finding the new kinds of behavior I am said to have used to "fill the bill of a technological bird fishing for philosophic frissons in Plato's wordy meander." The essential dependent variable in the behavioral analysis is the probability of behavior, rather than the behavior itself, and why should I not refer to past, current, and future behavior? I agree that perceptual behavior is difficult, but philosophers have found it so, too. The term is not to be dismissed as a slogan. The expression "covert behavior" was current long before my time, and its referent is familiar to anyone who has talked silently to himself.

A behavioral theory of mind?

H. S. Terrace

Department of Psychology, Columbia University

How timely it is to reread "The Operational Analysis of Psychological Terms," a remarkable gem of Skinner's prodigious output of seminal publications. Especially during this age of cognitive psychology, many readers may be surprised to discover Skinner's idiosyncratic but carefully reasoned analysis of "private events." They may be equally surprised by the unusual metaphysical and epistemological positions that Skinner assumed in his first detailed treatment of mentalism.

The uninviting and misleading title of this important article has undoubtedly contributed to its neglect. Instead of revealing Skinner's distaste for operationism, it suggests yet another arid exercise in deriving operational definitions of psychological phenomena. It also seems likely that the more alluring titles of some of Skinner's other well known articles, such as "Are Theories of Learning Necessary?" and "Why I Am Not a Cognitive Psychologist," have led many psychologists to conclude that Skinner is antitheoretical and that he denies the existence of mental events.

The truth of the matter is that Skinner has a theory of behavior, that he acknowledges the existence of an inner mental life, but that he also argues forefully against the Cartesian dualism implied by traditional (operational) definitions of cognitive phenomena (see Terrace 1970). In short, Skinner's 1945 classic is an appeal to psychologists to regard thoughts, beliefs, perceptions, memories, feelings, and so on, as bona fide subject matter for psychology, a subject matter that, from Skinner's point of view, obeys the same laws as those that govern overt behavior.

It is important to recognize that Skinner's penetrating analysis of private events occurred well in advance of the rise of modern cognitive psychology. It is widely recognized that the metaphor of the computer revolutionized the study of cognition by showing how complex processes can be conceptualized as material phenomena that obey mechanical laws and how cognitive phenomena can be studied meaningfully without reducing them to the electrical activity of the computer's hardware. Solely on the basis of his careful analysis of behavior. Skinner provided his own monistic alternative to the dualistic mentalism inherent in traditional definitions of cognitive events. He also argued convincingly that psychologists need not concern themselves about the locus of private events in the nervous system (Skinner 1950). Thus, long before the paradigms of modern cognitive psychology began to take root, Skinner insisted on a materialistic and nonreductionistic approach to its subject matter.

Skinner parts company with most other psychologists concerned with private events by his unwillingness to regard them as introspective givens. Statements such as "I feel or think *X*" prompt Skinner to ask what variables are responsible for the occurrence of a particular feeling or thought. That question is seldom asked because, by their very nature, private events seem to be insulated from external influences. Skinner nevertheless maintains that the experience of a private event presupposes public intervention, at some earlier time, by other members of the "verbal community." According to Skinner, we "know ourselves" only because others direct our attention to what we think, feel, or do. Children, for example, learn what it is appropriate to say "I think," or "My stomach aches," or "I had a bad dream" only after listening to innumerable comments or queries such as, "You look deep in thought. Are you thinking about *X*?" or "Are you upset because you have a stomach ache?" or "What were you dreaming about when you woke up crying?"

Skinner's view of the ontogeny of private events is consistent with a wide range of psychological theorizing. Skinner himself reminds us of Freud's belief that it is our natural condition to be unconscious of our actions, thoughts, feelings, and so on, and that mental activity does not presuppose consciousness (see Skinner 1969a, p. 225). Piaget commented extensively about the kinds of training needed by his daughter to understand that she was thinking and that her head was the locus of her thoughts (e.g., Piaget 1929, p. 44). At least one social psychologist (Bem 1967) has noted the similarity between the logic of Skinner's analysis of how we come to know about private events and the logic of attribution theory, a theory that claims that particular kinds of social interactions determine how we describe our thoughts and feelings. It is also of interest to note that Jaynes's review of early history led him to conclude that consciousness is a relatively recent development, a development that Jaynes claims occurred after the invention of writing (Jaynes 1976). Jaynes hypothesized that, prior to the appearance of man's sense of consciousness, his language made reference only to objects and events of the external environment and that man had no vocabulary with which to refer to his mental life – or, for that matter, to himself. When, on occasion, he heard "inner voices," they were interpreted as the voices of gods or as hallucinations. Only as a result of violent upheavals did early societies develop the cultural practice of teaching their members to identify their inner thoughts and feelings and to attribute those thoughts and feelings to themselves.

Skinner's counterintuitive hypothesis about private events (that they owe their existence to the public efforts of others who teach us how to respond verbally to internal stimuli) was an effective reply to Boring, Stevens, and other like-minded operationists who argued that the study of private (and, therefore, scientifically inaccessible) events should be limited to their public manifestations. Skinner not only revealed the dualistic flaw of such operational definitions but also defined a radically new view of private events.

For a variety of reasons that view has not received the attention it deserves. One problem stems from some unexplored ramifications of Skinner's analysis of private events. Another is Skinner's reluctance to consider private events other than those he so insightfully defined. Ironically, Skinner does not appear to have recognized that the struggle against mentalism or, more specifically, dualism, has been won. Thanks, in large part, to his own efforts, modern studies of human and animal cognition need not concern themselves with the ghost in the machine.

Before reviewing the import of recent developments in cognition, let us consider the following implications of Skinner's hypothesis about private events: (1) Private events are conscious, (2) consciousness presupposes language, and (3) only human beings experience consciousness.

Since so much of Skinner's view of consciousness hinges on the verbal labels we have been taught to apply to internal stimuli, it is important to ask whether a verbal label is a necessary or sufficient condition for consciousness. That we are conscious of unlabeled images suggests that verbal labeling is neither necessary nor sufficient (see Skinner's examples of "operant seeing," 1953, pp. 270ff.). Even if one wanted to argue that verbal labels were a necessary or a sufficient condition for consciousness, we would still need to know why we label certain internal stimuli and not others. Skinner's suggestion (1969a, pp. 157ff.) that consciousness functions to help us cope with difficult situations (i.e., situations in which the cause of the problem is behavior of which we are unaware) is a promising start. I doubt, however, that Skinner would argue that such situations are the only cause of consciousness.

A moment's thought should reveal why the basic objection to Skinner's explanation of consciousness is one of those he raised against mentalistic explanations in general. Skinner notes that to say that John did *X* because he thought *Z* is to beg the question, Why did John think *Z*? To answer that question by asserting that John thought *Z* because he applies verbal response *Z* to internal stimulus *z'* is to beg the question. Why the occurrence of verbal response *Z*?

Skinner's insistence that all mental activity be characterized as private (conscious) events, under the control of particular internal stimuli, would seem to deny the existence of unconscious private events. So extreme a position is understandable in a zeitgeist in which reference to mental processes of any sort implied a dualistic view of psychology's subject matter (in "Terms" Skinner writes that "the distinction between public and private is by no means the same as that between physical and mental"). However, Skinner's more recent publications (1974; 1977b) suggest that he has yet to acknowledge that the study of cognitive phenomena does not presuppose dualism.

Skinner also doesn't appear to recognize that much of human and animal behavior can no longer be explained by reference to the three-term contingency (a discriminative stimulus, a response, and a reinforcer) that he applied so imaginatively to a large variety of examples of human and animal behavior. A basic problem arises when organisms respond appropriately in the *absence* of any relevant environmental stimulus (see Hunter 1913; Terrace 1983a). This state of affairs has motivated the study of representations of environmental stimuli, in both human and animal subjects (e.g., Bousfield & Bousfield 1966; Bower 1972; Mandler 1967; Olton & Samuelson 1976; Roitblat 1980; Shepard 1975; Shimp 1976b; Terrace 1983b). The study of representations in animals is of especial interest because of their nonverbal nature (Terrace 1982).

What separates Skinner from the modern study of cognitive processes is his reluctance to acknowledge that the study of representations does not imply a regression to mentalism. Indeed, the study of representations can be regarded profitably as an extension of the study of stimulus control (Terrace 1983a). Asking about the nature of a representation is simply to pose the questions. What features of an environmental stimulus are coded by the organism and how does the organism represent those features to itself when it must respond in the absence of the environmental stimulus?

An instructive example of the need to include representations of environmental stimuli in the experimental analysis of behavior can be seen in a pigeon's performance on a matching-to-sample task (Skinner 1950). In the original version of this paradigm, the pigeon was shown a sample stimulus (either red or green). A few seconds later, two choice stimuli (red and green) were added, one on each side of the sample. The subject was rewarded if and only if it selected a choice stimulus that matched the color of the sample stimulus.

Subsequent research showed that Skinner's description of the pigeon's behavior as "matching" was a misnomer. When confronted with novel samples (in conjunction with appropriate novel choices), performance fell to chance (Cumming & Berryman 1965). What the pigeons seemed to have learned was to respond to the left choice when confronted with stimulus configuration 1 and to the right choice when confronted with stimulus configuration 2, and so on.

A variety of recent studies has shown that it is possible to obtain generalization of matching-to-sample (Premack 1976; Zentall 1983). Accordingly, it is necessary to ask how one might characterize the stimulus that results in matching. It cannot be the physical identity that exists between the sample and the choice stimuli. The experimental literature indicates that physical similarity *per se* fails as often as it succeeds in producing generalization of matching. The only alternative is to postulate some internal response, generated by the organism, which yields an internal "same" stimulus. That stimulus, in turn, leads to the correct choice. In short, successful generalization of matching must mean that the subject makes a judgment of "sameness" before responding to the correct choice. Specifically, the subject must transform the environmental stimuli provided by the experimenter into an intermediate cue that indicates which choice it should select.

The importance of taking into account the subject's contribution to the stimulus complex that results in accurate matching-to-sample performance is especially apparent when a delay is interposed between the presentation of the sample and the presentation of the choices (Grant 1983; Roberts & Kraemer 1982; Roitblat 1980).

Accurate responding under those circumstances suggests that the subject has access to a representation of the sample when the choice stimuli are made available.

Skinner should be heartened by these and other demonstrations of the feasibility of studying complex processes in humans and animals from a monistic and a materialistic point of view. Rather than regard such developments as contrary to the tenets of radical behaviorism, Skinner should welcome them as significant extensions of the approach to cognitive events that he introduced in "Terms."

BFS: Although I do not deny "the existence of mental events," I do not believe they exist. There is an inner behavioral life including private stimuli and private responding. Traditional expressions referring to mental events I regard as surrogates of histories of reinforcement. Thus, for me, the bona fide subject matters are

> not thoughts, but what is happening as one thinks and the history of reinforcement responsible for it;
> not beliefs, but behavior with respect to controlling stimuli and the histories responsible for that control;
> not perceptions, but the current control exercised by stimuli as the result of earlier contingencies of reinforcement;
> and so on.

It is true that "modern studies of human and animal cognition need not concern themselves with the ghost in the machine," but it is equally important that they dispense with the internal origination of behavior.

Terrace begins a review of "recent developments in cognition" with three supposed implications of my hypothesis about private events. I should want to state them in a very different form:

1. "Private events are conscious." The percentage of which we are conscious must be very small. We seldom say we are conscious of interoceptive or proprioceptive stimulation or of much of the exteroceptive stimulation which can be shown to have an effect on our behavior. "Terms" dealt with responses which are brought under the control of private events by a verbal community.
2. "Consciousness presupposes language." Self-knowledge requires verbal contingencies.
3. "Only human beings experience consciousness." The verbal communities which generate such responses have until very recently generated them for human beings only.

With these translations, I do not see the import of the paragraphs which follow in Terrace's commentary. A few remarks: I would certainly not say that "all [the behavior contributing to] mental activity [should] be characterized as private (conscious) events, under the control of particular internal stimuli." We "think" about public stimuli and talk about private ones.

I agree that "the study of cognitive phenomena does not presuppose dualism," but I insist it presupposes inner determination, which is the heart of the matter when one says that one acts because one feels like acting or takes a particular course because one thinks it will succeed.

This is not the place to argue with Terrace about "representations" (but see "Behaviorism-50"). It is the essence of behaviorism to argue that one does not take in the world or make copies of it in any form and that behavior which appears to require an internal representation must be explained in other ways. A complete account of an alternative explanation in neurological terms is, so far as I know, still out of reach, but that is also out of my reach as a behaviorist.

On the operational definition of a toothache

Colin Wright

Department of Philosophy, University of Exeter, England

Psychology was in its most formative stage in the 1930s, when the philosophy of science was in its heyday. Many of its elements are to be found in Professor Skinner's paper "Terms": the fictionalism of Mach, the physicalism and the problems of the public and the private of the Vienna Circle, and the operationism of Einstein and Bridgman. The psychologists wanted to know how a science of man was possible, and they turned to the philosophers as the only authorities they knew for guidance; for the acknowledged scientists, qua scientists, of course did not understand the principles of their own subject, no matter how skillfully they might use them. But the philosophers of science did not understand them either, and they led the psychologists up the garden path.

In "Terms" Skinner tells us that experience is "a derived construct to be understood only through an analysis of verbal...processes." But one always supposed that verbal processes reported experience, whether "inner" or "outer," or at least reported the content of experience, what was experienced; and if so, experience can hardly be a construct out of verbal behavior. Words themselves, we are told, are not signs or symbols used to express or convey meanings. Words are responses to stimuli resulting from reinforcement by the verbal community. In other words, *all words* are meaningless physical effects caused by specific kinds of physical stimuli – including this paper by Skinner, what I am writing now, and the various verbal *effects, caused* in you, the reader. If this is so, there is no meaning, no understanding, no judgment – and no science. Or shall we suppose that we are in some God-given privileged position in our investigations, possessing in ourselves faculties that we deny in those we study, like the spiritually enlightened in Plato's allegory of the cave? Well, apparently we are, right up to the end: Then, however, "we shall be able to include, and perhaps to understand, our own verbal behavior as scientists." To do this, of course, we would have to treat our own verbal behavior as meaningful in order to prove that it wasn't. In fact, there would be nothing to explain. There is nothing to explain insofar as people think rationally, and since science is supposed to be, par excellence, a rational activity, there shouldn't be much to explain in it; and if it wasn't very largely rational there wouldn't be much point in listening to its explanations as to why it wasn't! Psychology must, on pain of otherwise cutting off its own head, presuppose that human discourse is very largely rational – that *it isn't caused by stimuli.*

One had supposed that the methodological and radical behaviorists agreed that science was, by definition, concerned with the publicly observable and publicly testable world, and that the real difference between them was that the former accepted and the latter denied that there was a private mental world – a difference that would appear to be of no material consequence. Skinner, however, denies this. It meant for a start that the methodological behaviorists were soft on those old explanatory fictions, consciousness, feeling, and the will, and looked for behavioral manifestations that could be given operational definitions. Of course, our intuitive concepts will not do for scientific – or indeed for philosophical – purposes. Our intuitive concepts of truth and knowledge, as Carnap (1962) pointed out, need explication. But that does not mean that they should be abandoned. Some scientific concepts have not proved very fruitful: The medieval concept of impetus (which, until it was finally dissipated like the heat in a poker, was supposed to keep a projectile in motion) was abandoned in favour of the concept of momentum; and the concept of phlogiston, one of Skinner's examples, was abandoned in favour of that of oxygen. But the concepts of electricity, heat, velocity, and so on, have simply been modified. And it was empirical science that was the judge in each case.

But Skinner is still right in rejecting the program of methodological behaviorism. Suppose for the moment that consciousness, feelings, and the will are real. Surely the manifestations in behavior of these intentional states can only be intelligibly described in terms of the intentional states themselves. If so, the program is self-defeating. The solution might be to abandon the notion that psychology cannot be a science unless it restricts its subject matter to what is publicly observable, and so to abandon behaviorism with it. Skinner, of course, does not abandon behaviorism; indeed he reaffirms his credo. But, incredibly, he drops the requirement of publicity. Or does he? He, too, he says, has a toothache, and a toothache is a private event. But it is private only in the sense that the only system that is directly "wired up" to the tooth in question is the physical system called "Skinner": the toothache is a purely physical event, just like the radioactive event that is manifested in the click in the Geiger counter. Skinner, it seems, does not suffer from toothache like ordinary mortals, he just displays the kinds of behavior one usually associates with a toothache – play acting, some would call it.

What is wrong with operationism is not that no explicit statement of the relation between concept and operation has been provided. It is that the very character of the relation has been misconceived. One's actions are not defined by one's bodily movements but the reverse – in order to know what sort of operation a person is performing one must know what he is trying to achieve – one must know what velocity is before one can set out to measure it. Newton was well aware that there was no operation by which he could measure velocity as he understood it, that is, motion relative to God's Sensorium (I ignore his bucket experiment), and he used the "fixed" stars as a surrogate framework instead. The concept determines the operation, the operation does not define the concept. There may, of course, be something wrong with the concept, something that a consideration of the operation determined by it may reveal. Philosophical analysis is required to reveal such deficiencies and decide where the fault lies. Unfortunately the scientist rarely has the philosophical training for the job – or the philosopher the necessary conceptual background.

BFS: Wright goes far beyond the scope of "Terms" to a criticism of what is essentially the argument of the book (*Verbal Behavior*) from which it was in a sense taken. It is true that I was attempting to account for verbal behavior without formulating it as a "report of experience," as "the expression or communication of meaning," or as necessarily involving "understanding" or "judgment," as those terms were traditionally defined. The account worked in a very different way, and if successful it should have included the behavior of scientists if not some essence of "science" as knowledge. I could answer Wright only by reviewing the whole book, and that would be irrelevant here. I may point out, however, that he is wrong in characterizing my position as that "*all words* are meaningless physical effects caused by specific kinds of physical stimuli." The selective action of operant conditioning establishes a controlling relation among *three* things – stimuli (the setting), behavior (in this case, verbal), and the reinforcing consequences (in this case, arranged by a verbal community).

The argument that "psychology must, on pain of otherwise cutting off its own head, presuppose that human discourse is very largely rational – that *it isn't caused by stimuli*" – raises a different point. Apart from the last phrase, with which of course I agree, I make a very different point about rationality. Prior to the advent of verbal behavior (which required the evolution of physiological changes bringing the vocal musculature under operant control), all behavior must have been shaped and maintained by natural selection or operant conditioning. It is true that some linguists and cognitive psychologists have asserted that contingencies of reinforcement *contain* rules, where I would say rather that rules are descriptions of such contingencies, but something else happened when descriptions became possible and rules could be formulated. A different kind of behavior then emerged which needed to be distinguished (see "Problem Solving"). Once people could talk about their behavior and the circumstances under which it occurred, they could begin to give each other reasons for acting in given ways. An early form must have been the command, describing an action and at least implying a consequence of failure to act. Advice and warnings presumably followed in turn. They described behavior and at least implied consequences. The laws of religion and government more explicitly specified behavior and consequences. Behavior that is called taking advice, heeding a warning, or obeying a law, or behavior that follows rules composed upon occasion by an immediate analysis of contingencies can be called rational. The behaver can be said to have "knowledge of the consequences." Nevertheless I doubt that it is true that human behavior is "very largely rational" in that sense. Would that it were!

The point of my paper could have been made in traditional terms. How do we learn the meanings of words? And how do we do so when the things the words mean are not accessible to those who teach us? Why did I not make the point that way? Because I was composing a different account of verbal behavior in which meanings in some Platonic sense did not exist in words but were to be sought among the variables of which verbal behavior was a function (colloquially, the situations in which words are used). For the purpose of "Terms," I chose a very simple functional relation, the discriminative control exercised by a private stimulus.

Radical behaviorism and theoretical entities

G. E. Zuriff

Department of Psychology, Wheaton College, Norton, Massachusetts

After nearly four decades, "Terms" retains its significance and its brilliance. But along with its liberating impact on behaviorist thought, it is also the source of certain ambiguities and confusions persisting to the present. I address two of these.

1. Ironically, commentators on the history of behaviorism commonly ignore the historical context of this article. "Terms" was presented as part of a symposium on operationism in psychology. Skinner was concerned with distinguishing his approach from the operationism of his Harvard colleagues S. S. Stevens and E. G. Boring. The latter was not a behaviorist, and the former only marginally so. Certainly neither was part of the behaviorist mainstream devoted to the study of conditioning and learning and to the development of a science of behavior. Yet over the next 40 years, the distinction between the position of Skinner on the one hand and the operationism of Boring and Stevens on the other hand came to be regarded as a major distinction between Skinner's "radical" behaviorism and all other forms of behaviorism. It is commonly thought that only radical behaviorism admits private events into the science of behavior, while all forms of methodological behaviorism are restricted to publicly observable entities and events. While this distinction may differentiate Skinner from Boring and Stevens, it does not distinguish him from nearly any other major behaviorist. Watson, Weiss, Tolman, Guthrie, Hull, and Spence all included private events, such as "implicit," "covert," and "incipient" responses, in their behavioral systems. Furthermore, they suggested that these unobserved events can serve as stimuli for verbal responses, including reports of emotions, pains, and images. What distinguishes Skinner from these other behaviorists is not his legitimization of private events but the fact that he provides the most coherent account of how these events come to function as stimuli for verbal behavior. Thus, contrary to common opinion, the admission of private events into a behavioral science does not distinguish radical behaviorism from other forms. In sophisticated methodological behaviorism, scientific data are derived by observation, and private events are postulated as hypothetical constructs. This hypothetical nature of private events leads to my second point.

2. In "Terms" Skinner states: "Our practice is to *infer* the private event." Similarly, he speaks of considering private events "inferentially." This implies that private stimuli, as inferred events, are theoretical entities as opposed to observables. On the other hand, Skinner (1969a, p. 242; 1974, p. 17) at times writes as if private events are observed rather than inferred because they are observed by the person in whose body they occur and whose verbal behavior they control. Contemporary researchers in behavior therapy have extrapolated this position to an extreme in some cases. Ignoring Skinner's cautionary attitude toward the reliability of reports of private events, they treat the patient's first-person reports about covert events as genuine data reports observed by a "public of one."

I believe that private events must be considered inferred entities (i.e., theoretical) for two reasons. First, if psychology is to be the "psychology of the other one" in Meyer's (1921) felicitous phrase, then even if a subject may be said to be observing a private event, the experimenter, representing the science, must be said to infer the private event. Second, Skinner's statement that private events are discriminative stimuli for certain verbal responses is, at present, no more than a plausible hypothesis. No evidence is currently available to show that verbal responses enter into causal relationships with private events as required by the hypothesis, or that these private events are stimuli in the sense of conforming to the same laws as their overt counterparts. Therefore, the existence of private stimuli controlling verbal behavior is an inference. Even the subject's verbal reports provide no observational evidence for the hypothesis since they are in the form "I have a toothache" rather than "Private stimulus X is controlling my verbal behavior." It must be concluded that the scientific status of private stimuli is that of a hypothetical construct.

BFS: Zuriff's first point is very important. Methodological behaviorists also talked about private events that serve as stimuli and also about private (covert) behavior. The part of methodological behaviorism I rejected was the argument that science must confine itself to events accessible to at least two observers (the position of logical positivism) and that behaviorism was therefore destined to ignore private events. (Hence the still current popular view that behaviorists confine themselves only to the behavior they can see.) It was Stevens and Boring, not Watson, Weiss, Tolman, Guthrie, or Hull who then continued to believe in the existence of mental life.

But Zuriff misreads my view of the role of the private stimulus. It is true that the practice of the verbal community is to infer the private event in arranging instructional contingencies, but the person who thereby learns to describe the event is responding to it directly, not by inference. It is no doubt wrong of behavior therapists to assume that self-descriptive statements are correct (as it is wrong of Freudian or other kinds of therapists to do the same thing), but within the limits of accuracy of such reports, something can be learned about a person's history by asking how he feels.

The listener who responds to "I am depressed," by acting henceforth as he usually reacts to a depressed person is using inference only to the extent that a person who hears someone say "It is raining" then takes an umbrella. If doing either of these things is using a hypothetical construct, so be it.

4 An operant analysis of problem solving

Abstract: Behavior which solves a problem is distinguished by the fact that it changes another part of the solver's behavior and is strengthened when it does so. Problem solving typically involves the construction of discriminative stimuli. Verbal responses produce especially useful stimuli, because they affect other people. As a culture formulates maxims, laws, grammar, and science, its members behave more effectively without direct or prolonged contact with the contingencies thus formulated. The culture solves problems for its members, and does so by transmitting the verbal discriminative stimuli called rules. Induction, deduction, and the construction of models are ways of producing rules. Behavior which solves a problem may result from direct shaping by contingencies or from rules constructed either by the problem solver or by others. Because different controlling variables are involved, contingency-shaped behavior is never exactly like rule-governed behavior. The distinction must take account of (1) a system which establishes certain contingencies of reinforcement, such as some part of the natural environment, a piece of equipment, or a verbal community; (2) the behavior shaped and maintained by these contingencies; (3) rules, derived from the contingencies, which specify discriminative stimuli, responses, and consequences, and (4) the behavior occasioned by the rules.

Behavior which solves a problem is distinguished by the fact that it changes another part of the solver's behavior and is reinforced when it does so. Two stages are easily identified in a typical problem. When hungry we face a problem if we cannot emit any of the responses previously reinforced with food; to solve it we must change the situation until a response occurs. The behavior which brings about the change is properly called problem solving and the response it promotes a solution. A question for which there is at the moment no answer is also a problem. It may be solved by performing a calculation, by consulting a reference work, or by acting in any way which helps in recalling a previously learned answer. Since there is probably no behavioral process which is not relevant to the solving of some problem, an exhaustive analysis of techniques would coincide with an analysis of behavior as a whole.

Contingencies of reinforcement

When a response occurs and is reinforced, the probability that it will occur again in the presence of similar stimuli is increased. The process no longer presents any great problem for either organism or investigator, but problems arise when contingencies are complex. For example, in Thorndike's experiment the probability that the cat would turn the latch was at first quite low. The box evoked conditioned and unconditioned escape behavior, much of it incompatible with turning the latch, and emotional responses which may have made the food less reinforcing when it was eventually reached. The terminal performance which satisfied the contingencies was a chain of responses: orienting toward and approaching the latch, touching and turning the latch, orienting toward and passing through the opened door, and approaching and eating the food. Some links in this chain may have been reinforced by the food and others by escape from the box, but some could be reinforced only after other reinforcers had been conditioned. For these and other reasons the box presented a problem – for both the cat and Thorndike.

Thorndike thought he solved *his* problem by saying that the successful cat used trial-and-error learning. The expression is unfortunate. "Try" implies that a response has already been affected by relevant consequences. A cat is "trying to escape" if it engages in behavior which either has been selected in the evolution of the species because it has brought escape from comparable situations or has been reinforced by escape from aversive stimulation during the life of the cat. The term "error" does not describe behavior, it passes judgment on it. The curves for trial-and-error learning plotted by Thorndike and many others do not represent any useful property of behavior – certainly not a single process called problem solving. The changes which contribute to such a curve include the adaptation and extinction of emotional responses, the conditioning of reinforcers, and the extinction of unreinforced responses. Any contribution made by an increase in the probability of the reinforced response is hopelessly obscured.

Even in Thorndike's rather crude apparatus it should be possible to isolate the change resulting from reinforcement. We could begin by adapting the cat to the box until emotional responses were no longer important. By opening the door repeatedly (while making sure that this event was not consistently contingent on any response), we could convert the noise of the door into a conditioned reinforcer which we could then use to shape the behavior of moving into a position from which the latch would be likely to be turned. We could then reinforce a single instance of turning the latch and would almost certainly observe an immediate increase in the probability that the latch would be turned again.

This kind of simplification, common in the experimental analysis of behavior, eliminates the process of trial and error and, as we have noted, disposes of the data which are plotted in learning curves. It leaves no problem and, of course, no opportunity to solve a problem. Clearly it is not the thing to do if we are interested in studying or in teaching problem solving.

Constructing discriminative stimuli

Consider a simple example not unlike Thorndike's puzzle box. You have been asked to pick up a friend's suitcase from an airport baggage claim.

You have never seen the suitcase or heard it described; you have only a ticket with a number for which a match is to be found among the numbers on a collection of suitcases. To simplify the problem let us say that you find yourself alone before a large rotary display. A hundred suitcases move past you in a great ring. They are moving too fast to be inspected in order. You are committed to selecting suitcases essentially at random, checking one number at a time. How are you to find the suitcase?

You may, of course, simply keep sampling. You will almost certainly check the same suitcase more than once, but eventually the matching ticket will turn up. If the suitcases are not identical, however, some kind of learning will take place; you will begin to recognize and avoid cases which do not bear the matching number. A very unusual case may be tried only once; others may be checked two or three times, but responses to them will eventually be extinguished and the corresponding suitcase eliminated from the set.

A much more effective strategy is to mark each case as it is checked – say, with a piece of chalk. No bag is then inspected twice, and the number of bags remaining to be examined is reduced as rapidly as possible. Simple as it seems, this method of solving the problem has some remarkable features. Simply checking cases at random until the right one is found is of no interest as a behavioral process; the number of checks required to solve the problem is not a dimension of behavior. It is true that behavioral processes are involved in learning not to check cases which have already been marked because they bear nonmatching numbers, but the time required to find the right case throws no useful light on them. Mathematicians, showing perhaps too much confidence in psychologists, often take this kind of learning seriously and construct theoretical learning curves and design learning machines in which probabilities of responding change in terms of consequences; but the changes actually occurring as extinction and discrimination can be studied much more directly.

It is the use of the chalk which introduces something new. Marking each suitcase as it is checked is a kind of precurrent behavior which furthers the reinforcement of subsequent behavior – by reducing the number of samplings needed to find the right suitcase. Technically speaking, it is constructing a discriminative stimulus. The effect on the behavior which follows is the only reinforcement to which making such a mark can be attributed. And the effect must not be neglected, for it distinguishes the chalk marks from marks left by accident. One could "learn" the Hampton Court maze after a fresh fall of snow simply by not entering any path showing footprints leaving it (more precisely, in a maze with no loops – i.e., where all wrong entrances are to culs-de-sac – the right path is marked after one successful passage through the maze by any odd number of sets of prints); it is only when footprints have been found useful and, hence, when any behavior which makes them conspicuous is automatically reinforced that we reach the present case. A well-worn path over difficult terrain or through a forest is a series of discriminative stimuli and hence a series of reinforcers. It reinforces the act of blazing or otherwise marking the trail. Marking a path is, technically speaking, constructing a discriminative stimulus. The act of blazing or otherwise marking a trail thus has reinforcing consequences.

It is much easier to construct useful discriminative stimuli in verbal form. Easily recalled and capable of being executed anywhere, a verbal response is an especially useful kind of chalk mark. Many simple "statements of fact" express relations between stimuli and the reinforcing consequences of responses made to them. In the expression *red apples are sweet* for example, the word *red* identifies a property of a disciminative stimulus and *sweet* a property of a correlated reinforcer; red apples are "marked" as sweet. The verbal response makes it easier to learn to discriminate between sweet and sour apples, to retain the discrimination over a period of time, and, especially when recorded, to respond appropriately when the original discrimination may have been forgotten. (Whether one must describe or otherwise identify contingent properties in order to form a discriminaton is not the issue. Other species discriminate without responding verbally to essential properties, and it is unlikely that the human species gave up the ability to do so. Instead, the additional value of constructing descriptive stimuli which improve the chances of success was discovered.)

Transmission of constructed stimuli

A constructed external mark has another important advantage; it affects other people. Strangers can follow a well-worn path almost as well as those who laid it down. Another person could take over the search for the suitcase using our marks – either after being told to ignore cases marked with chalk (that is, after the chalk mark has been made an effective discriminative stimulus through verbal instruction), or after learning to ignore marked cases – in a process which would still be quicker than learning to ignore some cases when all have remained unmarked. Two people could also search for the same case using each other's marks. Something of the sort happens when, for example, a team of scientists is said to be "working on a problem."

The stimuli constructed in solving problems can be helpful to other people precisely because the variables manipulated in self-management are those which control the behavior of people in general. In constructing *external* stimuli to supplement or replace *private* changes in our behavior we automatically prepare for the transmission of what we have learned. Our verbal constructions become public property as our private discrimination could not. What we say in describing our own successful behavior (*I held the base firmly in my left hand and turned the top to the right*) can be changed into a useful instruction (*Hold the base firmly in your left hand and turn the top to the right*). The same variables are being manipulated and with some of the same effects on behavior.

The role of a public product of problem solving in the accumulation and transmission of folk wisdom is exemplified by a formula once used by blacksmith's apprentices. Proper operation of the bellows of a forge was presumably first conditioned by the effects on the bed of coals. Best results followed full strokes, from wide open to tightly closed, the opening stroke being swift and the closing stroke slow and steady. Such behavior is described in the verse:

> Up high, down low,
> Up quick, down slow –
> And that's the way to blow. (Salaman 1957)

The first two lines describe behavior, the third is essentially a social reinforcer. A blacksmith might have composed the poem for his own use in facilitating effective behavior or in discussing effective behavior with other blacksmiths. By occasionally reciting the poem, possibly in phase with the action, he could strengthen important characteristics of his own behavior. By recalling it upon a remote occasion, he could reinstate an effective performance. The poem must also have proved useful in teaching an apprentice to operate the bellows. It could even generate appropriate behavior in an apprentice who does not see the effect on the fire.

Much of the folk wisdom of a culture serves a similar function. Maxims and proverbs describe or imply behavior and its reinforcing consequences. *A penny saved is a penny earned* may be paraphrased *Not spending, like earning, is reinforced with pennies. Procrastination is the thief of time* describes a connection between putting things off at the moment and being unpleasantly busy later. Many maxims describe social contingencies. The reinforcing practices of a community are often inconsistent or episodic, but contingencies which remain relatively unchanged for a period of time may be described in useful ways. *It is better to give than to receive* specifies two forms of behavior and states that the net reinforcement of one is greater than that of the other. (The golden rule is a curious instance. No specific response is mentioned, but a kind of consequence is described in terms of its effect on those who use the rule. In the negative form one is enjoined not to behave in a given way if the consequence would be aversive to oneself. In the positive form one is enjoined to behave in a given way if the consequences would be reinforcing to oneself. The rule may have been discovered by someone particularly sensitive to effects on others, but once stated it should have proved generally useful.) Maxims usually describe rather subtle contingencies of reinforcement, which must have been discovered very slowly. The maxims should have been all the more valuable in making such contingencies effective.

The formal laws of governmental and religious institutions also specify contingencies of reinforcement involving the occasions upon which behavior occurs, the behavior itself, and the reinforcing consequences. The contingencies were almost certainly in effect long before they were formulated. Someone who took another's property, for example, would often be treated aversively. Eventually people learned to behave more effectively under such contingencies by formulating them. A public formulation must have had additional advantages; with its help authorities could maintain the contingencies more consistently and members of the group could behave more effectively with respect to them – possibly without direct exposure. The codification of legal practices, justly recognized as a great advance in the history of civilization, is an extraordinary example of the construction of discriminative stimuli.

A well-known set of reinforcing contingencies is a language. For thousands of years men spoke without benefit of codified rules. Some sequences of words were effective, others were less so or not at all. The discovery of grammar was the discovery of the fairly stable properties of the contingencies maintained by a community. The discovery may have been made first in a kind of personal problem solving, but a description of the contingencies in the form of rules of grammar permitted people to speak correctly by applying rules rather than through long exposure to the contingencies. The same rules became helpful in instruction and in maintaining verbal behavior in conformity with the usages of the community.

Scientific laws also specify or imply responses and their consequences. They are not, of course, obeyed by nature but by those who deal effectively with nature. The formula $s = \frac{1}{2}gt^2$ does not govern the behavior of falling bodies, it governs those who correctly predict the position of falling bodies at given times.

As a culture produces maxims, laws, grammar, and science, its members find it easier to behave effectively without direct or prolonged contact with the contingencies of reinforcement thus formulated. (We are concerned here only with stable contingencies. When contingencies change and rules do not, rules may be troublesome rather than helpful.) The culture solves problems for its members, and it does so by transmitting discriminative stimuli already constructed to evoke solutions. The importance of the process does not, of course, explain problem solving. How do people arrive at the formulas which thus prove helpful to themselves and others? How do they learn to behave appropriately under contingencies of reinforcement for which they have not been prepared, especially contingencies which are so specific and ephemeral that no general preparation is possible?

Problem-solving behavior

The question, Who is that just behind you? poses a problem which, if the person is known by name, is solved simply by turning around and looking. Turning and looking are precurrent responses which generate a discriminative stimulus required in order to emit a particular name. One may also generate helpful stimuli by looking more closely at a stimulus which is not yet effectively evoking a response even though it is already in the visual field, and beyond "looking more closely" lie certain problem-solving activities in which a vague or complex stimulus is tentatively described or characterized. A stimulus is more likely to be seen in a given way when it has been described, and may then even be "seen in its absence." A crude description may contribute to a more exact one, and a final characterization which supports a quite unambiguous response brings problem solving to an end. The result is useful to others if, in public form, it leads them to see the same thing in the same way. The reactions of others which are reinforcing to those who describe vague situations may shape their descriptions, often exerting a control no less powerful than the situations themselves.

Behavior of this sort is often observed as a kind of running comment on contingencies of reinforcement to which one is being exposed. Children learn to describe both the world to which they are reacting and the consequences of their reactions. Situations in which they cannot do this become so aversive that they escape from them by asking for words. Descriptions of their own behavior are especially important. The community asks: *What did you do? What are you doing? What are you going to do? And why?* and the answers describe behavior and relate it to effective variables. The answers eventually prove valuable to the children themselves. The expression *I grabbed the plate because it was going to fall* refers to a response (grabbing) and a property of the occasion (it was going to fall) and implies a reinforcer (its falling would have been aversive to the speaker or others). It is particularly helpful to describe behavior which fails to satisfy contingencies, as in *I let go too soon* or *I struck too hard*. Even fragmentary descriptions of contingencies speed the acquisition of effective terminal behavior, help to maintain the behavior over a period of time, and reinstate it when forgotten. Moreover, they generate similar behavior in others not subjected to the contingencies they specify. As a culture evolves, it encourages running comments of this sort and prepares its members to solve problems most effectively. Cultures which divert attention from behavior to mental events said to be responsible for the behavior are notably less helpful.

It is possible to construct discriminative stimuli without engaging in the behavior. A piece of equipment used in the study of operant behavior is a convenient example of a reinforcing system. One may arrive at behavior appropriate to the contingencies it maintains through prolonged responding under them and in doing so may formulate maxims or rules. But the equipment itself may also be examined. One may look behind the interface between organism and apparatus and set down directions for behaving appropriately with respect to the system there discovered. The environment is such a reinforcing system, and parts of it are often examined for such purposes. By analyzing sample spaces and the rules of games, for example, we compose instructions which evoke behavior roughly resembling the behavior which would be generated by prolonged responding under the contingencies they maintain. Science is in large part a direct analysis of the reinforcing systems found in nature; it is concerned with facilitating behavior which will be reinforced by them.

(When prescriptions for action derived from an analysis of a reinforcing system differ from prescriptions derived from exposure to the contingencies maintained by the system, the former generally prevail. There are many reasons for this. A system is usually easier to observe than a history of reinforcement. The behavior summarized in a running comment may not be the terminal behavior which most adequately satisfies a given set of contingencies. A terminal performance may be marked by permanent though unnecessary features resulting from coincidental contingencies encountered en route. And so on.)

Contingencies are sometimes studied by constructing a model of a reinforcing environment. One may react to the model in simpler ways (for example, verbally) and acquire appropriate behavior more quickly. If rules derived from exposure to the model are to prove helpful in the environment, however, the contingencies must be the same, and a model is helpful therefore only if the reinforcing system has already been described. It is helpful simply in facilitating exposure to the contingencies and in studying the resulting changes in behavior.

Many instances of problem-solving behavior would be called *induction*. The term applies whether the stimuli which evoke behavior appropriate to a set of contingencies are derived from an exposure to the contingencies or from inspection of the reinforcing system. In this sense induction is not deriving a general rule from specific instances but constructing a rule which generates behavior appropriate to a set of contingencies. Rule and contingency are different kinds of things; they are not general and specific statements of the same thing.

Deduction is still another way of constructing discriminative stimuli. Maxims, rules, and laws are physical objects, and they may be manipulated to produce other maxims, rules, and laws. Second-order rules for manipulating first-order rules are derived from empirical discoveries of the success of certain practices or from an examination of the contingency-maintaining systems which the first-order rules describe. In much of probability theory first-order rules are derived from a study of reinforcing systems. Second-order rules are discovered inductively when they are found to produce effective first-order rules or deductively (possibly tautologically) from an analysis of first-order rules or of the contingencies they describe.

Many rules which help in solving the problem of solving problems are familiar. "Ask yourself 'What is the unknown?'" is a useful bit of advice which leads not to a solution but to a modified statement to which a first-order rule may then be applied. Reducing the statement of a problem to symbols does not solve the problem, but, by eliminating possibly irrelevant responses, it may make first-order problem solving more effective. Second-order, "heuristic" rules are often thought to specify more creative or less mechanical activities than the rules in first-order (possibly algorithmic) problem solving, but once a heuristic rule has been formulated, it can be followed as "mechanically" as any first-order rule (Skinner 1968).

Solving a problem is a behavioral event. The various kinds of activities which further the appearance of a solution are all forms of behavior: The course followed in moving toward a solution does not, however, necessarily reflect an important behavioral process. Just as there are almost as many "learning curves" as there are things to be learned, so there are almost as many "problem-solving curves" as there are problems. Logic, mathematics, and science are disciplines which are concerned with ways of solving problems, and the histories of these fields record ways in which particular problems have been solved. Fascinating as this may be, it is not a prime source of data about behavior. Strategies and instances in which strategies have actually been used have the same status whether a problem is solved by an individual, a group, or a machine. Just as we do not turn to the way in which a machine solves a problem to discover the electrical, mechanical, optical, or chemical principles on which it is constructed, so we should not turn to the way in which an individual or a group solves a problem for useful data in studying individual behavior, communication, or coordinated action. This does not mean that we may not study individual, group, or machine behavior in order to discover better ways of solving problems or to reveal the limits of the kind of strategies which may be employed or the kinds of problems which may be solved.

Contingency-shaped versus rule-governed behavior

The response which satisfies a complex set of contingencies, and thus solves the problem, may come about as the result of direct shaping by the contingencies (possibly with the help of deliberate or accidental programming), or it may be evoked by contingency-related stimuli constructed either by the problem solver or by others. The difference between rule-following and contingency-shaped behavior is obvious when instances are pretty clearly only one or the other. The behavior of a baseball outfielder catching a fly ball bears certain resemblances to the behavior of the commander of a ship taking part in the recovery of a reentering satellite. Both move about on a surface in a direction and with a speed designed to bring them, if possible, near a falling object at the moment it reaches the surface. Both respond to recent stimulation from the position, direction, and speed of the object, and they both take into account effects of gravity and friction. The behavior of the baseball player, however, has been almost entirely shaped by contingencies of reinforcement, whereas the commander is simply obeying rules derived from the available information and from analogous situations. As more and more satellites are caught, it is conceivable that an experienced commander, under the influence of successful or unsuccessful catches, might dispense with or depart from some of the rules thus derived. At the moment, however, the necessary history of reinforcement is lacking, and the two cases are quite different.

Possibly because discriminative stimuli (as exemplified by maxims, rules, and laws) are usually more easily observed than the contingencies they specify, responses under their control tend to be overemphasized at the expense of responses shaped by contingencies. One resulting mistake is to suppose that behavior is always under the control of prior stimuli. Learning is defined as "finding, storing, and using again correct rules" (Clark 1963), and the simple shaping of behavior by contingencies which have never been formulated is neglected. When the brain is described as an "organ for the manipulation of symbols," its role in mediating changes in behavior resulting from reinforcement is not taken into account.

Once the pattern has been established, it is easy to argue for other kinds of prior controlling entities such as expectancies, cognitive maps, intentions, and plans. We refer to contingency-shaped behavior alone when we say that an organism behaves in a given way with a given probability because the *behavior has been followed by a given kind of consequence in the past*. We refer to behavior under the control of prior contingency-specifying stimuli when we say that an organism behaves in a given way because *it expects a similar consequence to follow in the future*. The "expectancy" is a gratuitous and dangerous assumption if nothing more than a history of reinforcement has been observed. Any actual formulation of the relation between a response and its consequences (perhaps simply the observation, "Whenever I respond in this way such and such an event follows") may, of course, function as a prior controlling stimulus.

The contingency-specifying stimuli constructed in the course of solving problems never have quite the same effects as the contingencies they specify. One difference is motivational. Contingencies not only shape behavior, they alter its probability; but contingency-specifying stimuli, as such, do not do so. Though the topography of a response is controlled by a maxim, rule, law, or statement of intention, the probability of its occurrence remains undetermined. After all, why should a person obey a law, follow a plan, or carry out an intention? It is not enough to say that people are so constituted that they automatically follow rules – as nature is said, mistakenly, to obey the laws of nature. A rule is simply an object in the environment. Why should it be important? This is the sort of question which always plagues the dualist. Descartes could not explain how a thought could move the pineal gland and thus affect the material body; Adrian (1928) acknowledged that he could not say how a nerve impulse caused a thought. How does a rule govern behavior?

As a discriminative stimulus, a rule is effective as part of a set of contingencies of reinforcement. A complete specification must include the reinforcer which has shaped the topography of a response and brought it under the control of the stimulus. The reinforcers contingent on prior stimulation from maxims, rules, or laws are sometimes the same as those which directly shape behavior. When this is the case, the maxim, rule, or law is a form of advice (Skinner 1957). *Go west, young man* is an example of advice when the behavior it specifices will be reinforced by certain consequences which do not result from action taken by the adviser. We tend to follow advice because previous behavior in response to similar verbal stimuli has been reinforced. When maxims, rules, and laws are commands, they are effective only because special reinforcers have been made contingent upon them. Governments, for example, do not trust to the natural advantages of obeying the law to ensure obedience. Grammatical rules are often followed not so much because the behavior is then particularly effective as because social punishers are contingent upon ungrammatical behavior.

Rule-governed behavior is obviously unmotivated in this sense when rules are obeyed by machines. A machine can be constructed to move a bellows up high, down low, up quick, and down slow, remaining forever under the control of the specifying rules. Only the designer and builder are affected by the resulting condition of the fire. The same distinction holds when machines follow more complex rules. A computer, like a mechanical bellows, does only what it was constructed and instructed to do. Mortimer Taube (1961) and Ulric Neisser (1963) are among those who have argued that the thinking of a computer is less than human, and it is significant that they have emphasized the lack of "purpose." But to speak of the purpose of an act is simply to refer to its characteristic consequences. A statement of purpose may function as a contingency-specifying discriminative stimulus. Computers merely follow rules. So do people at times – for example, the blacksmith's apprentice who never sees the fire or the algorithmic problem solver who simply follows instructions. The motivating conditions (for machines and people alike) are irrelevant to the problem being solved.

Rules are particularly likely to be deficient in the sovereignty needed for successful government when they are derived from statistical analyses of contingencies. It is unlikely that anyone will ever stop smoking simply because of the aversive stimulation associated with lung cancer, at least not in time to make any difference. The actual contingencies have little effect on behavior under the control of contingency-specifying facts or rules. A formal statement of contingencies (*cigarette smoking causes lung cancer*) needs the support of carefully engineered aversive stimuli involving sanctions quite possibly unrelated to the consequences of smoking. For example, smoking may be classified as shameful, illegal, or sinful and punished by appropriate agencies.

Some contingencies cannot be accurately described. Old family doctors were often skillful diagnosticians because of contingencies to which they had been exposed over many years, but they could not always describe these contingencies or construct rules which evoked comparable behavior in younger doctors. Some of the experiences of mystics are ineffable in the sense that all three terms in the contingencies governing their behavior (the behavior itself, the conditions under which it occurs, and its consequences) escape adequate specification. Emotional behavior is particularly hard to bring under the control of rules. As Pascal put it, "the heart has its reasons which reason will never know." Nonverbal skills are usually much harder to describe than verbal ones. Verbal behavior can be reported in a unique way by modeling it in direct quotation (Skinner 1957). Nonverbal behavior is modeled so that it can be imitated but not as precisely or as exhaustively.

Rule-governed behavior is in any case never exactly like the behavior shaped by contingencies. Golf players whose swing has been shaped by its effect on the ball are easily distinguished from players who are primarily imitating a coach, even though it is much more difficult to distinguish between people who are making an original observation and those who are saying something because they have been told to say it; but when topographies of response are very similar, different controlling variables are necessarily involved, and the behavior will have different properties. When operant experiments with human subjects are simplified by instructing the subjects in the operation of the equipment (Skinner 1963b), the resulting behavior may resemble that which follows exposure to the contingencies and may be studied in its stead for certain purposes, but the controlling variables are different, and the behavior will not necessarily change in the same way in response to other variables – for example, under the influence of a drug.

The difference between rule-following and contingency-shaped behavior may be observed as one passes from one to the other in "discovering the truth" of a rule. We may have avoided postponing necessary work for years either because we have been taught that *procrastination is the thief of time* and therefore avoid procrastination as we avoid thieves, or because we dutifully obey the injunction *do not put off until tomorrow what you can do today*. Eventually our behavior may come under the direct influence of the relevant contingencies – in doing something today we actually avoid the aversive consequences of having it to do tomorrow. Though our behavior may not be noticeably different (we continue to perform necessary work as soon as possible) we now behave for different reasons, which must be taken into account. When at some future time we say *procrastination is the thief of time*, our response has at least two sources of strength; we are reciting a memorized maxim and emitting a contingency-specifying statement of fact.

The eventual occurrence of a planned event works a similar change. Plans for a symposium are drawn up and followed. Eventually, almost incidentally it may seem, the symposium is held and certain natural consequences follow. The nature of the enterprise as an instance of behavior and, in particular, the probability that similar behavior will occur in the future have been changed. In the same way those half-formed expectancies called "premonitions" suddenly become important when the premonitored events occur. A similar change comes about when actors, starting with memorized words and prescribed actions, come under the influence of simulated or real reactions by other members of the cast, under the shaping effect of which they begin to "live" their roles.

The classical distinction between rational and irrational or intuitive behavior is of the same sort. The "reasons" which govern the behavior of rational people describe relations between the occasions on which they behave, their behavior, and its consequences. In general we admire intuitive people, with their contingency-shaped behavior, rather than mere followers of rules. For example, we admire those who are "naturally" good rather than the merely law abiding, the intuitive mathematician rather than the mere calculator. Plato discusses the difference in the *Charmides*, but he confuses matters by supposing that what we admire is speed. It is true that contingency-shaped behavior is instantly available, whereas it takes time to consult rules and examine reasons; but irrational behavior is more likely to be wrong and therefore we have reason to admire the deliberate and rational person. We ask the intuitive mathematician to behave like one who calculates – to construct a proof which will guide others to the same conclusion even though the intuitive mathematician did not need it. We insist, with Freud, that the reasons people give in explaining their actions should be accurate accounts of the contingencies of reinforcement which were responsible for their behavior.

The objectivity of rules

In contrasting contingency-shaped and rule-governed behavior we must take account of four things:

1. A system which establishes contingencies of reinforcement, such as some part of the natural environment, a piece of equipment used in operant research, or a verbal community.
2. The behavior which is shaped and maintained by these contingencies or which satisfies them in the sense of being reinforced under them.
3. Rules derived from the contingencies, in the form of injunctions or descriptions which specify occasions, responses, and consequences.
4. The behavior evoked by the rules.

The topography of (4) is probably never identical with that of (2) because the rules in (3) are probably never complete specifications of the contingencies in (1). The behaviors in (2) and (4) are also usually under the control of different states of deprivation or aversive stimulation.

Items (2) and (4) are instances of behavior and as such, ephemeral and insubstantial. We observe an organism in the act of behaving, but we study only the records which survive. Behavior is also subjective in the sense that it is characteristic of a particular person with a particular history. In contrast, (1) and (3) are objective and durable. The reinforcing system in (1) exists prior to any effect it may have upon an organism, and it can be observed in the same way by two or more people. The rules of (3) are more or less permanent verbal stimuli. It is not surprising, therefore, that (2) and (4) often take second place to (1) and (3); (1) is said to be what a person acquires "knowledge about" and (3) is said to be possessed as "knowledge."

Map. In finding one's way about a complex terrain, the relation between the behavior and its reinforcing consequences can be represented spatially, and "purposive" comes to mean "goal directed." A special kind of rule is then available – a map. A city is an example of item (1). It is a system of contingencies of reinforcement: When one proceeds along certain streets and makes certain turns, one arrives at certain points. One learns to get about in a city when behavior (2) is shaped by these contingencies. This is one way in which, as we say, one "acquires knowledge of the city." Whenever the reinforcement associated with arriving at a given point is relevant to a current state of deprivation, one behaves in ways which lead to arrival at that point. A map on which a route is marked is an example of (3) and the behavior of following a map (4) may resemble getting about the city after exposure to the contingencies (2), but the topographies will probably be different, quite apart from the collateral behavior of consulting the map in the former case. Since the map (3) appears to be a kind of objective "knowledge" of the city, it is easy to infer that (2) itself involves a map – Tolman's cognitive map, for example. It has been pointed out (Skinner 1966d) that almost all the figures which describe apparatus in Tolman's *Purposive Behavior in Animals and Men* are maps. Terrain (1) is not only what is learned, it is what knowledge (3) is about. Learning then seems to be the discovery of maps. But a map is plausible as a kind of rule only when contingencies can be represented spatially. It is true that other kinds of psychological space have been hypothesized (for example, by Kurt Lewin 1936) in order to account for behavior which is not an example of moving toward a goal or getting out of trouble, but the notion of a map and the concept of space are then strained.

The extent to which behavior is contingency shaped or rule governed is often a matter of convenience. When a trail is laid quickly (as at Hampton Court after a fresh fall of snow), there is no need to learn the maze at all; it is much more convenient simply to learn to follow the trail. If the surface leaves no mark, the maze must be learned as such. If the trail develops slowly, the maze may be learned first as if no path were available and the path which is eventually laid down may never be used. If the maze is difficult, however – for example, if various points in it are very much alike – or if it is easily forgotten, a slowly developing path may take over the ultimate control. In that case one eventually "discovers the truth" in a trail as one discovers the truth of a maxim.

It is the contingencies, not the rules, which exist before the rules are formulated. Behavior shaped by the contingencies does not show knowledge of the rules. One may speak grammatically under the contingencies maintained by a verbal community without "knowing the rules of grammar" in any other sense, but once these contingencies have been discovered and grammatical rules formulated, one may upon occasion speak grammatically by applying rules.

Concepts. The items on our list which seem objective also tend to be emphasized when reinforcement is contingent upon the presence of a stimulus which is a member of a set defined by a property. Such a set, which may be found in nature or explicitly constructed, is an example of (1). Behavior is shaped by these contingencies in such a way that stimuli possessing the property evoke responses while other stimuli do not. The defining property is named in a rule (3) extracted from the contingencies. (The rule states that a response will be reinforced in the presence of a stimulus with that property.) Behavior (4) is evoked by stimuli possessing the property, possibly without exposure to the contingencies. The "concept" is "in the stimulus" as a defining property in (1) and it is named or otherwise specified in the rule of (3). Since the topography of the response at issue is usually arbitrary, it is quite likely that the behaviors in (2) and (4) will be similar, and it is then particularly easy to suppose that one responds to (1) because one "knows the rule" in (3).

Other kinds of problems

To define a problem, etymologically, as something explicitly put forth for solution (or, more technically, as a specific set of contingencies of reinforcement for which a response of appropriate topography is to be found) is to exclude instances in which the same precurrent activities serve a useful function although the topography of a response is already known. The distinction between contingency-shaped and rule-following behavior is still required. When the problem is not *what* to do but *whether* to do it, problem-solving behavior has the effect of strengthening or weakening an already identified response. Conflicting positive and negative consequences, of either an intellectual or ethical nature, are especially likely to raise problems of this sort – for example, when a strongly reinforced response has deferred aversive consequences or when immediate aversive consequences conflict with deferred reinforcers.

A relevant problem-solving practice is to emit the questionable response in tentative form – for example, as a *hypothesis*. Making a hypohesis differs from asserting a fact in that the evidence is scantier and punishment for being wrong more likely to follow. The emitted response is nevertheless useful, particularly if recorded, because it may enter into other problem-solving activities. For rather different purposes one acts verbally before acting in other ways when one makes a *resolution*. It is easier to resolve than to act, but the resolution makes the action more likely to take place. (A *promise* specifies a response and creates social contingencies which strengthen it, and contingencies of social origin are invoked when one "promises oneself" to do something in making a resolution.) A *statement of policy* is also a description of action to be taken. (Resolutions and statements of policy are often made because action itself is at the moment impossible, but they are relevant here only when the action they strengthen or weaken is not under physical constraint.) A joint secret statement of policy is a *conspiracy*; it describes cooperative action to be undertaken by a group.

Like the rules and plans appropriate to problems in which the topography of the solution is not known, hypotheses, statements of policy, and so on, are not to be inferred in every instance of behavior. People act without making resolutions or forming policies. Different people or groups of people (for example, "capitalists" in socialist theory) act in the same way under similar contingencies of reinforcement, even cooperatively, without entering into a conspiracy. The conclusion to which a scientist comes at the end of an experiment was not necessarily in existence as a hypothesis before or during the experiment.

Sometimes the problem is to decide which of two or more responses to emit, the topographies of all alternatives being known. The concepts of choice and decision making have been overemphasized in psychological and economic theory. It is difficult to evaluate the probability that a single response will be made, but when two or more mutually exclusive responses are possible, the one actually emitted is presumably stronger than the others. For this reason early psychological research emphasized situations and devices in which only relative strength was observed (the rat turned right rather than left or jumped toward a circle rather than a square). Efforts to assess the separate probabilities of the competing responses were thus discouraged. Single responses were treated only as decisions between acting and not acting, within the time limits set by a "trial." The notion of relative strength is then practically meaningless, and "choose" simply means "respond." The problem of whether to act in one way or another differs from the problem of whether or not to act only because one of the aversive consequences of acting in one way is a loss of the opportunity to act in another. The same problem-solving activities are relevant. A decision announced before acting is essentially a resolution or statement of policy. The mere emission of one response rather than another, however, does not mean that a decision has been formulated.

The notion of a problem as something set for solution is even less appropriate when neither the topography of the behavior strengthened by precurrent activity nor its consequences are known until the behavior occurs. Artists, composers, and writers, for example, engage in various activities which further the production of art, music, and literature. (Sometimes they are required to produce works meeting quite narrow specifications, and their behaviors then exemplify explicit problem solving, but this is by no means always the case.) The artist or composer explores a medium or a theme and comes up with an unforeseen composition having unforeseen effects. A writer explores a subject matter or a style and comes up with a poem or a book which could not have been described or its effects predicted in advance. In this process of "discovering what one has to say," relevant precurrent behavior cannot be derived from any specification of the behavior to follow or of the contingencies which the behavior will satisfy. The precurrent behavior nevertheless functions by virtue of the processes involved in solving statable problems. For example, crude sketches and tentative statements supply stimuli leading to other sketches and statements, moving toward a final solution. Here again, it is a mistake to assume that the artist, composer, or writer is necessarily realizing some prior conception of the work produced. The conditions under which Renoir was reinforced as he painted *The Boating Party* must have been as real as those under which a mathematician or scientist is reinforced for solving a set problem, but much less could have been said about them in advance.

Problem solving is often said to produce knowledge. An operant formulation permits us to distinguish between some of the things to which this term has been applied. What is knowledge, where is it, and what is it about? Michael Polanyi (1958; 1960) and P. W. Bridgman (1952; 1959) have raised these questions with respect to the apparent discrepancy between scientific facts, laws, and theories (as published, for example, in papers, texts, tables of constants, and encyclopedias) and the personal knowledge of the scientist. Objective knowledge transcends the individual; it is more stable and durable than private experience, but it lacks color and personal involvement. The presence or absence of "consciousness" can scarcely be the important difference, for scientists are as "conscious" of laws as they are of the things laws describe. Sensory contact with the external world may be the beginning of knowledge, but contact is not enough. It is not even enough for "conscious experience," since stimuli are only part of the contingencies of reinforcement under which an organism distinguishes among the aspects and properties of the environment in which it lives. Responses must be made and reinforced before anything can be seen.

The world which establishes contingencies of reinforcement of the sort studied in an operant analysis is presumably "what knowledge is about." A person comes to know that world and how to behave in it in the sense of acquiring behavior which satisfies the contingencies it maintains. Behavior which is exclusively shaped by such contingencies is perhaps the closest one can come to the "personal knowledge" of Polanyi and Bridgman. It is the directed "purposive" behavior of the blacksmith who operates his bellows because of its effect on the fire.

But there is another kind of behavior which could be called knowledge of the same things – the behavior controlled by contingency-specifying stimuli. These stimuli are as objective as the world they specify, and they are useful precisely because they become and remain part of the external world. Behavior under their control is the behavior of the apprentice who never sees the fire but acts as he instructs himself to act by reciting a poem. So far as topography goes, it may resemble behavior directly shaped by contingencies, but there remains an all important difference in controlling variables. (To say that the behaviors have different "meanings" is only another way of saying that they are controlled by different variables; Skinner 1957).

The distinction which Polanyi (1960) in particular seems to be trying to make is between contingency-shaped and rule-governed behavior rather than between behaviors marked by the presence or absence of "conscious experience." Contingency-shaped behavior depends for its strength upon "genuine" consequences. It is likely to be nonverbal and thus to "come to grips with reality." It is a personal possession which dies with the possessor. The rules which form the body of science are public. They survive the scientist who constructed them as well as those who are guided by them. The control they exert is primarily verbal, and the resulting behavior may not vary in strength with consequences having personal signficance. These are basic distinctions, and they survive even when, as is usually the case, the scientist's behavior is due both to direct reinforcement and to the control exercised by the contingency-specifying stimuli which compose facts, laws, and theories.

Differences between contingency-shaped and rule-governed behavior

We may play billiards intuitively as a result of long experience, or we may determine masses, angles, distances, frictions, and so on, and calculate each shot. We are likely to do the former, of course, but there are analogous circumstances in which we cannot submit to the contingencies in a comparable way and must adopt the latter. Both kinds of behavior are plausible, natural, and effective; they both show "knowledge of the contingencies," and (apart from the precurrent calculations in the second case) they may have similar topographies. But they are under different kinds of stimulus control and hence are different operants. The difference appears when we examine our behavior. In the first case we *feel* the rightness of the force and direction with which the ball is struck; in the second we feel the rightness of calculations but not of the shot itself (Skinner 1963a).

It is the control of nature in the first case with its attendant feelings which suggests to Polanyi and Bridgman a kind of personal involvement characteristic only of direct experience and knowledge. The point of science, however, is to analyze the contingencies of reinforcement found in nature and to formulate rules or laws which make it unnecessary to be exposed to them in order to behave appropriately. What one sees in watching oneself following the rules of science is therefore different from what one sees in watching oneself behave as one has learned to do under the contingencies which the rules describe. The mistake is to suppose that only one of these kinds of behavior represents knowledge. Polanyi argues that "tacit knowing is...the dominant principle of all knowledge, and...its rejection would therefore automatically involve the rejection of any knowledge whatever" (Polanyi 1960). It is true that an apprentice blacksmith may not know why he is operating the bellows as he does – he may have no "feel" for the effect on the fire – but the rule, together with its effect on his behavior, is still a "form of knowledge."

Rogers (1961) and Maslow (1962) have tried to reverse the history of psychological science and return to a kind of knowledge generated by personal contingencies of reinforcement. They presumably do not question the effectiveness of the rules and prescriptions drawn from a consideration of the circumstances under which people behave or can be induced to behave, but they give preference to personal knowledge which has the feeling of contingency-shaped behavior. It is not too difficult to make this feeling seem important – as important as it seemed to Polanyi and Bridgman in attempting to evaluate what we really know about the world as a whole.

Rogers and Maslow feel threatened by the objectivity of scientific knowledge and the possible absence of personal involvement in its use; but the personal and social behavior shaped by social contingencies has, except in rare instances, been as cold, scheming, or brutal as the calculated behavior of a Machiavelli. We have no guarantee that personal involvement will bring sympathy, compassion, or understanding, for it has usually done just the opposite. Social action based upon a scientific analysis of human behavior is much more likely to be humane. It can be transmitted from person to person and epoch to epoch, it can be *freed* of personal predilections and prejudices, it can be constantly tested against the facts, and it can steadily increase the competence with which we solve human problems. If need be, it can inspire in its devotees a feeling of rightness. Personal knowledge, whether contingency shaped or rule governed, is not to be judged by how it feels but by the help it offers in working toward a more effective culture.

POSTSCRIPT

I have no particular comment on this paper except to emphasize that rules are statements about facts. The blacksmith does not discover the *rule* that a certain way of operating the bellows gives him the best fire in his forge; a way of operating the bellows is simply strengthened by its effect on the fire. But the blacksmith gains by describing the behavior and its effect if the description then functions as a rule to be followed in behaving more effectively, possibly by himself and certainly by the apprentice, who may not see the fire.

COMMENTARIES AND RESPONSES

On the depth and fit of behaviourist explanation

L. Jonathan Cohen

The Queen's College, Oxford University, England

To a relatively dispassionate philosopher of science two interconnected weaknesses in Professor Skinner's account of problem solving are particularly apparent. These weaknesses are certainly much more important than the account's characteristic disregard for the subjective aspect of consciousness. Questions about what it feels like to face, tackle, and solve a problem of such or such a kind are no better dealt with (see Fodor 1981b, chap. 3; Nagel 1974) by computationalist accounts. And nothing is gained by rejecting an otherwise useful theory just because it fails to deal with facts that no rival theory deals with either. Nor is it a point of universal cogency that an altruistic moralist would not accept the interpretation of "it is better to give than to receive," or of the golden rule, that is implicit in Skinner's suggestion that such a maxim can be learned by reinforcement.

The first weakness in Skinner's account is rather that it fits the facts that it claims to fit only by ignoring the difference between a rule's form and its content. The chalk marks that may operate as a negatively discriminative stimulus in the search for a wanted suitcase in Skinner's paradigm problem are tokens of a particular form. As such they are also physical objects, and their occurrence on a suitcase within the view of the searcher can be observed to be correlated with the searcher's not checking that suitcase. Analogously, utterances of rules, such as notices on the workshop wall, printed instructions in the workshop copy of a user's manual, or oral reminders by the foreman, are tokens that might operate as discriminative stimuli for the blacksmith's apprentice. But rules themselves, like maxims and laws, are not physical objects at all, pace Skinner's explicit assertion that they are: They are saying types and, as such, are individuated by their content, not their form. A fortiori they are not tokens and cannot function as stimuli. So the apprentice who has learned to solve a problem about the bellows by deliberately applying a rule has learned much more than just to utter recitals of the rule on occasions on which this recital will function as an appropriate stimulus. He has also learned to recognise what he has done wrong when he accidentally forgets to follow the rule; he has learned how he could sabotage his own work by deliberately not following the rule; he has learned what to tell other people about the solution of his problem; and so on. In all these respects he responds to the content of the rule that he has learned, not to its form. If he has not learned those other things, then he has learned to solve his problem not by applying a rule but by acquiring the contingency-shaped habit of reciting some doggerel that happens to stimulate a response appropriate to the problem, much as a shy and timid language teacher might solve the problem of how to face his class of inner-city pupils by learning to recite to himself a piece of ungrammatical and meaningless doggerel that one of these pupils once produced, the recital of which goads him to face his ignorant young tormenters once again. So the behaviourist account here is open to the standard criticism that it cannot establish the simple correlation between observable events that it seeks, because the actual patterns of human behaviour are very much more complex.

The second important weakness in Skinner's account is that, as we can see better now than 20 years ago, it offers no explanation of how or why reinforcements operate in the way that they are supposed to do. The account does not tell us how it is possible for exposure to contingencies to shape behaviour or how it is possible to translate rules into action. It is like telling an enquirer from a prescientific culture who asks how light comes to be emitted from our lamp bulbs that this always happens when the relevant switches are on. The enquirer wants an explanation of the obvious in terms of the nonobvious: He might be satisfied by being told something about electricity, but not by being referred to other events that are of the same order of observable obviousness. He wants to be told how such emissions of light are possible, not just what triggers them off on particular occasions. Similarly, the psychologist of chess playing wants to know not just what kinds of moves are followed by reinforcing results, but also how it is possible for chess players' moves to be thus guided. Accordingly, whatever the faults of this or that computationalist model as an explanation of how humans solve a particular kind of problem, such models at least attempt to resolve a suitably deep question. Their existence measures a substantial advance in the subject – like any other science's advance beyond the point at which it is concerned only with shallow correlations between surface observables. Of course, behaviorists may well object to the metaphysical glosses that some philosophers (e.g., Fodor 1975; 1980) impose on computationalist methodology – doctrines about a language of thought, about mental operations on the forms of internal representations, and the like. But these ontological extravagances are not essential to the users of the methodology, who are better construed more austerely (Cohen, 1986) as just hypothesising about how neuronal activity, if conceived as the working of a digital computer, could account for experimentally detectable patterns of problem solving and similar achievements.

The two shortcomings in Skinner's account are closely connected. Indeed they both have a common ancestor in the philosophy of Hume (1739). Crudely empiricist in outlook, and choosing his paradigm from the study of motion, Hume analysed all statements about causal connections as statements about sequential uniformities between one observable kind of event and another. He thus misrepresented the scientific situation in two main ways. First, he implied that the familiar causal explanations of everyday life rest on actually known uniformities of observable occurrence, which is rarely if ever the case: We say that the white billiard ball's impact caused the red one to move even though we know well that the latter would not have moved if it had been glued, nailed, or whatever to the table. And by ignoring this he obscured the fact that one main task of science is to search for the real uniformities that underlie the untidy approximations and multiformities that are directly observable. Second, Hume held it quite impossible to discover any of the deeper causal explanations that Bacon (1620) had desiderated and that, when found, have in fact contributed so much to the progress of science and technology (explanations of light, heat, magnetism, chemical properties, diseases, etc.). In most of science it is only at this level of explanation that genuine uniformities are established and apparently disparate phenomena are unified.

Classical behaviorism thus inherits its main weaknesses from its Humean ancestry. Because it refers only to observable events and processes, it cannot claim to find the simple correlations that it seeks without ignoring important differences; at the same time it cuts itself off from offering the deeper kind of explanation that scientific progress requires.

BFS: Judging from Cohen's commentary, I would say that the only "particularly apparent" weakness in my account of problem solving seems to be the failure to make my position clear. Behaviorism does not neglect the meaning or content of terms or propositions nor does it neglect feelings, but its treatments of those matters are not traditional.

Meaning or content is not a current property of a speaker's behavior. It is a surrogate of the history of reinforcement which has led to the occurrence of that behavior, and that history is physical. I have developed the point at length in *Verbal Behavior* (1957). The crucial question about feeling is "What is felt?" So far as I am concerned, the answer is "our bodies." We may feel feelings in the sense in which we see sights, but the feelings and the sights are objects not processes. In the case of feelings the objects are often private, and we learn to talk about them (and hence, perhaps, feel them more clearly) in ways discussed in my "Terms."

I am sure that a person who is solving a problem usually feels himself doing so. He also responds to other private events not called feelings. For example, he may talk to himself about the problem, and what he says may prove useful. So far as I am concerned, however, all that is physical. I do not think anyone has shown that it is anything else.

The Golden Rule advises all who follow it to examine how they would respond to a proposed action, and how it would feel, and to use what they then observe in deciding whether or not to act. The Rule can be learned as doggerel and perhaps most often is, but it can also be learned from interactions with other people, as it must have been learned before the Rule was formulated. Once formulated, a rule becomes a physical object – say, marks on paper. Before formulation, its role was played by the contingencies of reinforcement it describes. Both are objects.

Cohen has tried to flesh out the apprentice's action in following a rule by listing other things he might do. I accept them all but insist that they are the products of other contingencies and would have little or nothing to do with the operation of a bellows, which was the point of my example. If operating the bellows was affected, if it had "acquired other content," it was only in the sense of coming under the control of histories of reinforcement.

It is rather an anticlimax to say behaviorism "cannot establish the correlation between observable events which it seeks, because the actual patterns of human behavior are very much more complex." They are indeed complex, but let us not therefore dismiss a partial analysis by calling it "oversimplified."

I am as anxious as anyone to learn "wnat is really going on" in problem solving in the sense of what is happening in the nervous system, but I don't expect to learn it in my lifetime. Meanwhile, the experimental analysis of behavior offers, I believe, the most rigorous analysis of the facts which neurology will someday explain. The situation is analogous to that of genetics prior to the discovery of the structure of DNA: Genetics was a respectable science before anyone knew "what was really going on."

Can we analyze Skinner's problem-solving behavior in operant terms?

P. C. Dodwell

Department of Psychology, Queen's University, Canada

For Skinner problem-solving behavior is the emitting of responses that lead consistently to reinforcement. We can agree with him that this definition is too wide to be helpful; what is needed is some way of capturing the distinctive nature of problem solving. Skinner does not address this problem; he merely cites examples of what most reasonable people would agree are instances of problem solving. His distinction between contingency-maintained and rule-governed behavior is important, and obviously necessary if one is to give an account of the more interesting classes of problem-solving behavior. There is no doubt a continuum from simple to complex, and all the interesting cases lie at the latter end.

The acquisition of simple skills, whether under the control of reinforcement contingencies or the following of simple rules, can be explained in operant terms and is not contentious. However, the important question is, Can *all* problem solving, including that involving long-range planning, appreciation of possible consequences, abstract solutions, scientific discovery, and the like, be so explained? This question is crucial to Skinner, given the comprehensive nature of his theorizing. It is not enough to show that his analyses are plausible in some – possibly even in most – instances. He is claiming that, in principle, *all* problem-solving behavior can be explained in terms of his two categories of behavior control.

The examples Skinner gives in "Problem Solving" tend to come from the low end of the continuum, where the relevant contingencies and rules of procedure are either known or relatively easy to discover. A look at what would be involved in analyzing an example from the other end is instructive, and points up the major weakness in Skinner's position. Let us take the example of Skinner's own attempt to develop a theory of problem solving on the basis of operant principles, surely a good example of high-level scientific problem solving, by most psychologists (including Skinner's) criteria.

To give a convincing account of the theory's development (or indeed of the general theory of which this is a specific application) it would be necessary to identify, at least in principle:

(a) the sources of motivation for undertaking such a complex chain of behavior.
(b) either the reinforcement contingencies that shaped or maintained that behavior, or the maxims, precepts, and rules of behavior that spawned it, and
(c) the history of the individual's development that led to his acceptance of those maxims, precepts, and rules (i.e., the history of reinforcements that led Skinner to become a behavioral scientist).

It would also be necessary for completeness and consistency to explain via such a history why Skinner came to espouse *this* theory, rather than *that*. Questions of truth, parsimony, generality, and other scientific criteria do not appear to arise, except insofar as these affected Skinner's own experience of reinforcements as a developing scientist. (Looked at from this point of view, the fact that he developed *this* theory rather than *that* is, in the exact philosophical sense, a contingent matter. A different set of reinforcements would have led him to a different set of conclusions about the analysis of behavior.)

Can we, even in principle, give an account of the development of a scientific theory in such contingent terms? And if so, does it constitute a sufficient and adequate explanation of this piece of problem-solving behavior? I would argue that the answer to both questions is no, and for good scientific reasons. One is reminded forcefully of Popper's (1963) description of how two other theories claiming universality of application, Marx's theory of economic determinism and Freud's theory of personality, led him to formulate the principle of falsifiability as the hallmark of a genuine and substantive scientific theory. Adherents to those theories, or doctrines, will never admit the possibility of a situation or experience that cannot be analyzed and explained in their terms. Apparently negative instances can always be explained away by new and ad hoc applications of a supposedly universal principle. What on first acquaintance may appear to be a negative piece of evidence can always be accounted for by searching further for previously hidden factors in the situation. When does this search stop? Only when those previously hidden factors have been identified, thereby adding further "confirmation" to the universality of the theory.

Attempting to give an account of Skinner's development as a scientist in terms of the items (a), (b), and (c) above would clearly be laborious and inconclusive.

Suppose one identified a situation in which the reinforcement contingencies should apparently predict the development of some concept or rule other than the one that in fact developed. Would a Skinnerian be bothered? Assuredly not. This would be a case of misidentification of the relative contingencies and reinforcements. Further search would certainly reveal the correct ones. Unfortunately, however, there is no criterion for deciding when such a search should be initiated or terminated, except the criterion of conformity to the theory. Thus there are no circumstances under which a statement of Skinnerian theory could be conclusively refuted. However plausible the account of any particular instance of problem solving may be, if no genuine empirical tests of the theory are available, or even criteria for such tests, it cannot claim the status of being scientific.

The principles one espouses in judging the merits of scientific theory are not themselves usually handled in the same terms used to evaluate such theory. Thus the principle of verification of the logical positivists is not itself verifiable (Wisdom 1938), and the principle of falsifiability is not itself falsifiable. To grant Skinner an important point, one might say that such principles are useful in guiding scientific research to the extent that they are successful and reinforcing, and this is determined by the cultural milieu within which the principles are applied. This point applies to the acceptance of canons of scientific procedure, not to the theories that such procedures generate. As I hinted earlier, the criteria for this evaluation are quite different and not contingent in the technical sense.

Thus I think that there is a fundamental flaw in Skinner's proposed theory of problem solving. The procedures followed in developing scientific theories (for instance) are subject to the reinforcement contingencies Skinner identifies, although I think that it would be difficult to prove that such contingencies fully determine the procedures, but the theories themselves have to be, and generally are, judged on a quite different set of criteria (Bunge 1968; Dodwell 1977). The latter do not in any important sense rely on contingencies of reinforcement or rule following of the sort discussed by Skinner. To attempt to prove that they do involves the sort of indeterminate and doctrinaire ad hoc reasoning discussed above.

No one would doubt that Skinner has made fundamental contributions to understanding the conditions under which many sorts of behavior are developed and maintained. When it comes to a question of the necessity and universality of his principles, whether applied to problem solving or some other category of behavior, one has to face the question of scientific accountability. At the very least it will be necessary to set criteria for testing the empirical validity of Skinner's theories. By what process of contingent reinforcement, I wonder, did I arrive at that conclusion?

BFS: Of course I cannot explain "*all* problem-solving," especially "long-range planning, appreciation of possible consequences, abstract solutions, scientific discovery, and the like," but it is the complexity and not the fact that different behavioral processes are involved that causes trouble. Beyond a certain point, one can do no more than offer an interpretation of problem solving, using principles which have been more clearly established in simpler examples. Falsification is presumably the opposite of the establishment of truth, and I make no claim there even in simple cases. So far as I am concerned, science does not establish truth or falsity; it seeks the most effective way of dealing with subject matters. The theory of evolution is not true or false; it is the best possible interpretation of a vast range of facts in the light of principles which are slowly coming to be better known in genetics and related sciences. I have been rash enough to suggest, for example, that a careful analysis of modern physical theory using terms from the experimental analysis of behavior would expose some of the sources of its present troubles (e.g., Skinner 1983d, p. 395). Unfortunately, I do not have the competence to undertake such an analysis myself. I do not think that those who have tried to solve the problem of problem solving by looking at larger samples have done very well, although they have been at it for more than 2,000 years.

Learning from instruction

Jerome A. Feldman

Department of Computer Science, University of Rochester

There is one aspect of "Problem Solving" that is very bothersome. There appears to be no way at all, in Skinner's view, for rule-governed behavior to directly affect contingency-directed behavior. This not only rules out the teaching of skills, but also appears to eliminate the possibility of learning by imitation. Surely one must assume a fairly rich chain of inferences (rule applications) between light striking the eye and the realization that one could produce behavior similar to that which is being observed. There is a way out of this problem (in Skinner's terms) but it involves hypothesizing that internal states of the brain, such as percepts, can serve as stimuli and consequences and thus shape behavior. It would be interesting to see Skinner's current view of this issue.

BFS: As Feldman says, I do not see how rule-governed behavior can affect contingency-directed behavior directly, but by following a rule a person comes under the control of the contingencies the rule describes. We learn to drive a car by sitting at the wheel and following rules – the advice and instructions of the person who is teaching us. As the car moves, starts, turns, and stops, these consequences affect our behavior, and are responsible for our final performance on the highway. By then we have completely forgotten the rules.

I myself once shared Feldman's doubt that organisms possess imitative behavior in the sense that the sight of another organism behaving in a given way evokes similar behavior. Nevertheless, many species imitate in that sense, and the behavior is due to natural selection rather than "a fairly rich chain of inferences."

The microscopic analysis of behavior: Toward a synthesis of instrumental, perceptual, and cognitive ideas

Stephen Grossberg

Center for Adaptive Systems, Department of Mathematics, Boston University

As founder of one of the great experimental movements and conceptual systems of twentieth-century psychology, Professor Skinner can justly be proud that his concepts are useful in the analysis of many types of behavior. It is also natural and proper for a scientist of his stature to seek a unifying theoretical synthesis of the broadest possible range of experimental data. Complex problem-solving behavior, including culturally maintained language utterances and creative scientific and artistic endeavors, are thus subjected to an instrumental analysis in "Problem Solving." Such an analysis emphasizes several important aspects of these behaviors; notably, that they are dynamic activities whose generation and maintenance depend upon their adaptive value for the individual learning subjects who employ them. This emphasis provides a challenging alternative to thinkers who view these human capabilities as static primitives that are given a priori.

It is ironic that thinkers who start from similar premises at different times can arrive at opposing conclusions about major issues. Skinner has, for example, reached his conclusions from a moment-by-moment analysis of an individual subject's adaptive behavior. Such an analysis has led him to conclusions such as "The 'expectancy' is a gratuitous and dangerous assumption" and "The concepts of choice and decision making have been overemphasized in psychological and economic theory." During a period in history when data about expectancies and choices were hard to find, one might wish to support these opinions if only to prevent untestable hypotheses from being entertained. Since 1966, however, a great deal of data has been collected that directly implicates expectancy mechanisms in goal-directed behavior, notably data concerning event-related potentials such as the N200, P300, and contingent negative variation (Näätänen, Hukkanen, & Järvilechto 1980; Squires, Wickens, Squires, & Donchin 1976; Tecce 1972) and neurophysiological data concerning perceptual coding (Freeman 1979). A large neurophysiological literature has also implicated inhibitory interactions as mechanistic substrates of many behavioral choice situations. Even within the community of experimentalists who specialize in instrumental learning, concepts about expectancies, competition, and choice have increasingly been invoked to explain data about such phenomena as partial reward, peak shift, and behavioral contrast (Berlyne 1969; Bloomfield 1969; Fantino, Dunn, & Meck 1979; Hinson & Staddon 1978; Killeen 1982). Thus at the present time, the greatly expanded data base about the role of expectancies and choice mechanisms in behavior suggests that Skinner's 1966 formulation was incomplete.

This lack of completeness also becomes apparent when one considers how Skinner analyzes the behavioral units out of which behavior sequences are formed and shaped by reinforcement. For example, he writes "we must change the situation until a response occurs"; he considers "a chain of responses: orienting toward and approaching the latch,. . .and approaching and eating the food"; he notes that "in constructing *external* stimuli to supplement or replace *private* changes in our behavior we automatically prepare for the transmission of what we have learned. Our verbal constructions become public property"; and he claims that "the question, Who is that just behind you?. . .is solved simply by turning around and looking." Throughout these discussions, concepts such as stimulus, response, orienting, approaching, eating, verbal construction, turning around, and looking are accepted as behavioral atoms. They are, in a sense, used as static primitives that are given a priori. Skinner's dynamic analysis of the moment-by-moment unfolding of individual behavior does not consider how the individual stimuli and responses of his analysis are themselves dynamically synthesized and maintained. His analysis of individual behavioral units is essentially classical. The irony is that a more microscopic analysis of an individual's moment-by-moment adaptive behavior, including how behavioral units are synthesized and maintained, leads to principles and mechanistic instantiations that embody the types of expectancy and choice concepts that Skinner deplores (Grossberg 1978a; 1978b; 1980; 1982c; 1983a). Moreover, because of the fundamental nature of the behavioral unit issue, these principles and mechanisms play a central role in explaining difficult data about instrumental conditioning per se (Grossberg 1975; 1982a; 1982b; 1983b).

Why should a more microscopic analysis of individual behavior lead to such a different viewpoint about the relationship of cognitive and perceptual processes to instrumental processes? Let me illustrate why this profound change is not surprising by citing two examples.

How one defines one's behavioral units will influence how one thinks about sequences of these units unfolding through time. An organism that has not yet built up its behavioral units is exposed to a continuous stream of sensory patterns, to a veritable "blooming buzzing confusion." Most, or even all, possible subsequences of this data stream could, in principle, be synthesized or grouped into behavioral units. When one frontally attacks the problem of how all these subsequences are processed through time by a behaving organism, it becomes apparent that reinforcement, no matter how consistent, cannot act selectively on the correct subsequences unless they undergo adequate preprocessing. Reinforcement can act selectively only at the level of preprocessed internal representations. Unless these representations are self-organized according to appropriate principles, it is not even possible to conclude that all extant representations will not be hopelessly biased or degraded by every future environmental fluctuation. No such problems arise in discussions of contemporary computers, because the architectures of these machines are prewired.

The principles that have been used to overcome these sequencing problems lead to mechanisms for generating temporal order information in short-term memory and in long-term memory; for bottom–up adaptive filtering, as in feature extraction and chunking; for competitive masking, matching, and choice within multiple spatial frequency channels; and for top–down expectancy learning. Such concepts are traditionally more at home in studies of perception, cognition, and motor control, but they are also needed to synthesize the sequences of behavioral units that are influenced by reinforcements during instrumental conditioning.

One of the great strengths of Skinner's approach is its emphasis on the dynamic nature of behavior. Concerning the issue of how individual behavioral units are formed, a dynamic approach leads one to ask: Once a learned behavioral representation is synthesized, how is it maintained? What prevents it from being eroded by the sheer flux of experience? This question leads one to analyze how an organism learns the difference between relevant and irrelevant cues, and how irrelevant cues are prevented from eroding the representations of relevant cues. Part of the answer depends upon an analysis of how reinforcements help to characterize what cues become relevant to each organism. Reinforcement questions aside, however, one must also analyze how learned representations can maintain their stability for years against the flux of irrelevant cues, yet can be rapidly modified when their use generates unexpected consequences even in the absence of external reinforcers (Epstein 1977; Harris 1980; Held 1961; Wallach & Karsh 1963). A frontal analysis of this stability–plasticity issue again leads to testable hypotheses about learned expectancy and choice mechanisms.

These examples only hint at how pervasive a shift in emphasis is caused by a dynamic analysis of how behavioral units are self-organized. Because many of the design issues that arise, notably the stability issues, are of a general nature, many of the same mechanisms that instantiate these principles in dealing with instrumental phenomena are also used to help explain perceptual and cognitive phenomena. Different specialized networks are needed for the different applications, but all of the networks are built up from a small number of dynamic equations.

In summary, the dynamic analysis of individual behavior that Skinner pioneered has begun to generate a synthesis of instrumental, perceptual, and cognitive approaches that have often previously been discordant. The classical Skinnerian position must pay a price to be included in this synthesis. Reinforcement no longer exists at the center of the behavioral universe. It modulates and is modulated by perceptual, cognitive, and motor processes that, only taken together, enable humans to successfully mold their behaviors in response to complex environmental contingencies.

BFS: I too have moved beyond my 1966 position, but not in the same direction as Grossberg. The crucial issue in behaviorism was not dualism; it was origin. Operant ("instrumental") conditioning is a kind of selection by consequences, and like natural selection it replaces a creator by turning to a prior history. With his insistence upon perceptual and cognitive functions, Grossberg is returning to the ancient Greek view of the inner determination of behavior. I look for antecedent events in the history of the individual to account for the origin of behavior, as Darwin looked for antecedent events to account for the origin of species. Of course it matters how an organism "perceives a situation," but perceiving is behaving, and what an organism sees is the product of past contingencies of reinforcement. Of course it matters how an organism cognizes facts about its world, but the facts *are* contingencies of reinforcement. The organism does not take them in; it is changed by them. The "preprocessing" which is involved in a current act of reinforcement is affected by changes which have occurred in previous reinforcements.

Exciting things are no doubt happening in the study of the nervous system, but cognitive psychologists have put those who are studying them on the wrong track. Eventually we shall know how the lawful relations shown in the behavior of an individual are indeed mediated by the nervous system. The relations will not be proved wrong; indeed, they will have given students of the brain their assignments.

Grossberg offers two examples to illustrate why it is not surprising that a "profound change" has occurred, thanks to neuroscience, but later we learn that the examples "only hint at how pervasive [the] shift in emphasis is." May we not ask for an example that *shows* what neuroscience is so commonly said to be doing?

Psychology as moral rhetoric

Rom Harré

Sub-Faculty of Philosophy, Oxford University, England

Any student of the works of B. F. Skinner must struggle with two enigmas. First, there is the great difficulty in understanding the text. There is a special Skinnerian terminology, the difficulties with which I discuss in some detail. Once this hurdle has been cleared the second enigma presents itself. What would explain the adoption of such a special and opaque terminology? In answering that question I hope to bring out very clearly the source of the moral consternation that many people find accompanies their reading of the Skinnerian corpus. In some way, we feel, human life is being devalued and human beings degraded. And yet it is quite difficult to say exactly how the moral element appears.

The enigma of the terminology: One notices first how few concepts Skinner deploys. There are "contingency of reinforcement," "reinforcer," "discriminative stimulus," "control," and of course "behavior." The main difficulty in understanding Skinner's writing comes, I believe, from the fact that these terms are used in such a way as to encompass their opposites, so to speak. Thus, in "Problem Solving," "the codification of legal practices" which is the result of a very high order of theoretical work, involving jurisprudential theorizing, is described as "the construction of discriminative stimuli." But a legal code is just exactly *not* a stimulus, discriminative or otherwise. It is in contrast to a tot of brandy, a prod with a stick, or the sudden presentation of a novel object in the visual field. There is another example involving the notorious term "behavior." "Solving a problem," says Skinner, "is a behavioral event." How can this possibly make sense, one asks, when many problems are solved by reflection and ratiocination, for example, problems in geometry, in textual criticism, or in the discrimination of moral wickedness? Such problem solvings as these stand in contrast to behavioral events. They are precisely *not* behavioral events. It is not as if Skinner is unaware of this sort of distinction. He distinguishes in another section of the text between the case of a baseball fielder who takes a catch and the case of the ship's captain who organizes the recovery of a returning spacecraft. In the latter case the cognitive solution of the problem is sharply distinguished from the moving about of ships and helicopters in the behavior of which that solution is realized. This curious semantic feature can be found in the way Skinner uses his other key terms, such as "control" and "reinforcer." We see very clearly *how the terms* are used, that is in such a way as to encompass their formal complements, but this makes the problem of trying to discern what concepts they express even more intractable.

One solution, proposed by G. Pelham (1982) in his monumental study of the Skinnerian corpus, is that the meaning of such terms is determined and exhausted by their relation to the Skinner box. Their meaning is to be explained in terms of the structure of that apparatus and the way it works. It follows from Pelham's analysis that these terms have no psychological content and bear no relation to their etymological ancestors "stimulus," "behavior," and the like. There is no puzzle to be solved in analyzing the text under discussion, it is just one enormous muddle. It is strictly meaningless since it requires one to apply a terminology outside its defined range or extension. It is comparable to trying to describe numerical differences in the vocabulary of colors. Attractive though Pelham's solution is in many ways, it does not seem to me to go deep enough. The question of why such a terminology should have been used must be addressed.

First, however, we must try to catch a glimpse of the empirical content of "Problem Solving." In discussing the difference between rule-governed and contingency-shaped behavior Skinner does not refer to the results of a program of scientific experiments, but draws on the presumption of the shared understanding of an anecdote *told in ordinary English*. The rules he discusses are items of practical wisdom conveyed in a common and everyday terminology. Without exception the empirical content of each section of the text is available to us as commonsense psychology by virtue of the necessity we are under to have a working knowledge of just that psychology and our grasp of ordinary English. Skinner's paper then takes the form of a series of anecdotes or illustrated statements of various principles of commonsense psychology, followed by redescription in his special terminology. What is achieved by this redescription? In the twelfth paragraph of the section entitled "Contingency-Shaped versus Rule-Governed Behavior," we have the exercise of the natural capacities and skills of "intuitive" people redescribed as "contingency-shaped behavior." A verbal community becomes "a system which establishes certain contingencies of reinforcement." Thus the encouragement of growing success in catching a ball, for example, is brought under the same term (Skinnerian category) as, say, being praised for one's insight into the psychological problems of a friend. Unlike any other scientific terminology of which I am aware this terminology is used to "lump" existing categories, to wash out distinctions that are routinely maintained in commonsense psychology because they are routinely maintained in life.

But why wash out these distinctions? Looking over the examples again with the foregoing in mind the answer is plain. The Skinnerian terminology is not a scientific vocabulary at all, and it does not serve to present empirical matters in terms of a coherent theory. Skinner is a moralist, and his terminology works as part of the moral assessment of actions. A typical lumping operation occurs when Skinner says that "to speak of the purpose of an act is simply to refer to its characteristic consequences." But all acts have characteristic consequences, whether purposed or not. Thus the terminology washes out the distinction between acts for which the actor considers the possible consequences before he acts and those acts for which he does not. But there is a close relation between the purposiveness of acts and the moral responsibility of actors. So in the end the lumping operation has had the effect of eliminating moral responsibility from the discussion of human action. The elimination of the distinction between acts for which one is responsible and those for which one is not, is not, however, based upon a scientific discovery. It is achieved by a rhetorical transformation of the descriptions under which such acts were morally distinguished and psychologically diverse. It is itself a bit of moralizing.

The question as to whether the text under discussion should count as a scientific paper offering a substantial contribution to the psychology of rule following and problem solving cannot very well be answered. As a moral commentary on the distinction between agentive and automatic or habitual action it is not a part of empirical science. The only empirical element in the text is a reiteration of Wittgenstein's well-known observation that rule-following explanations must terminate somewhere in a "That's how I do it!" exclamation, which marks the boundary between a hierarchy of cultural imperatives and some natural human endowment. For my part I find the moral stance implicit in the Skinnerian terminology not just unacceptable but demeaning since it cuts at the root of that which distinguishes human societies from all other forms of organic association, namely the willingness of men and women to take moral responsbility for their actions.

BFS: Harré has trouble with my terms because he insists upon using them in his own, obsolescent way. A stimulus, he says, must be a prod, a sudden presentation; it cannot be a text. (In a sense that I do not understand, a text is somehow the "opposite" of a prod.) I myself wish that the action of stimuli was better understood, but I do not see how the matter is improved by referring to givens, to experience versus reality, to perception as the grasping of reality, or to the input of information. For Harré what is done in solving a problem in geometry is "precisely" not behavior. I disagree, and I see no great gain in speaking of reflection or rationalization until those processes are better understood. There is no doubt a "very high order of theoretical work, involving jurisprudential theorizing" in the codification of legal practices, but the result is the construction of verbal discriminative stimuli with the help of which citizens avoid legal punishment and legal authorities administer punishment consistently.

If it is "strictly meaningless...to apply a terminology outside its defined range or extension," then cosmology, plate tectonics, and evolution come off as badly as behavior. They are interpretations of uncontrollable and unpredictable events using terms and concepts derived from research where control and prediction are possible.

In "lumping" purpose with selection by consequences, I may have "eliminated moral responsibility" from the discussion of human action. Darwin did the same thing in lumping the purpose of the anatomy and physiology of the species with natural selection. Harré is quite right in saying that I am a moralist, but so was Darwin, and it does not follow that our terminologies are therefore "not. . .scientific vocabular[ies] at all."

On choosing the "right" stimulus and rule

Robin M. Hogarth

Graduate School of Business, University of Chicago

On summarizing why linear models are so effective in decision making, Dawes and Corrigan (1974) remark: "The whole trick is to decide what variables to look at and then to know how to add" (p. 105). For someone interested in the effectiveness of problem-solving activities, this sentence captures much of the content of Skinner's stimulating paper. That is, Skinner emphasizes the need first to construct discriminative stimuli, then to follow a rule (broadly defined) in using such stimuli. In this commentary, I wish to elaborate on issues concerning the construction of discriminative stimuli and rules. However, my emphasis differs from that of Skinner. I am principally concerned with how well people solve problems as opposed to describing the process. In a nutshell, I want to stress the difficulties inherent in constructing discriminative stimuli and the conflict implicit in choosing rules.

It is relatively trivial to assert that effective problem solving depends on constructing discriminative stimuli. It is quite a different matter to do this when faced with a particular problem. The major reason is that the appropriate contingencies in the environment are often far from evident. Consider, for instance, the fact that the problem solvers' own acts can affect the very environmental contingencies they wish to discover prior to taking action. That is, to use Skinner's language, the problem solvers are themselves part of the system of contingencies. An illuminating, not to say horrific, example is provided by Lewis Thomas (1983) in describing the diagnostic activities of an early 20th-century physician:

> This physician enjoyed the reputation of a diagnostician, with a particular skill in diagnosing typhoid fever, then the commonest disease on the wards of New York's hospitals. He placed particular reliance on the appearance of the tongue, which was universal in the medicine of that day (now entirely inexplicable, long forgotten). He believed that he could detect significant differences by palpating that organ. The ward rounds conducted by this man were, essentially, tongue rounds; each patient would stick out his tongue while the eminence took it between thumb and forefinger, feeling its textures and irregularities, then moving from bed to bed, diagnosing typhoid in its earliest stages over and over again, and turning out a week or so later to have been right, to everyone's amazement. He was a more effective carrier, using only his hands, than Typhoid Mary. (p. 22)

Although this is a striking example, I don't believe that it illustrates a rare problem. Self-fulfilling and self-defeating prophecies are not uncommon and are usually accompanied by lack of awareness on the problem solvers' part of their role in the process. Indeed, in a controlled laboratory experiment, Camerer (1981) showed how easy it was to induce in adult subjects the feeling that they understood a complex prediction task, when in fact outcomes were largely generated by their own judgments.

Information about environmental contingencies can mislead in several ways. Consider, in particular, situations in which the taking of an action prohibits one from seeing the outcomes of actions that are not taken (Einhorn & Hogarth 1978). For example, when firms select among job candidates they rarely check later to see how rejected candidates fared in other jobs. Instead, the contingencies between characteristics of *selected* candidates and outcomes become the only information used to assess applicant–outcome correlations. However, by restricting information to only 2 of the 4 cells of a contingency table, one cannot assess environmental contingencies accurately. Moreover, few firms wish to face the short-term economic costs of gathering the data necessary to assess the contingencies accurately since this would require hiring candidates who were believed unsuitable a priori. Einhorn (1980) has discussed these kinds of situations in greater detail, even inventing the acronym OILS (outcome irrelevant learning situations) to emphasize the fact that environmental contingencies are often so structured that we cannot learn through experience. Indeed, the rewards of experience can be quite contrary to developing accurate perceptions of problem-solving environments.

In attempting to comprehend our environment, it is well known that we attend to cues other than contingencies per se. For example, when seeking the unknown causes of observed effects, we may be struck by some similarity between effect and possible cause (Nisbett & Ross 1980), by temporal or spatial contiguity (Michotte 1946), or by the fact that the causal candidate preceded the effect in time. Such "cues to causality" (Einhorn & Hogarth 1982; 1983) can only be imperfect indicators of any "true" causal relation and do not, by themselves, eliminate other causal candidates. Indeed, we may often describe some observed correlations as "spurious" to remind ourselves that the contingencies so designated have little real significance. As emphasized by Brunswik (1952), the probabilistic nature of cue–criterion relations also makes the discovery of behavioral rules particularly difficult. On the other hand, given that the variation in environmental stimuli is far greater than our ability to make unique responses, we are forced into adopting a probabilistic, and thus error-prone mode of knowing. In this respect, therefore, I have some difficulty in comprehending Skinner's dismissal of the term "trial-and-error" learning. If not by trial, how else can one ever generate and test *new* responses?

Finally, let me comment on the issue of choosing the appropriate rule for behavior (however learned) assuming that we have made the appropriate discrimination of the stimulus. Skinner correctly points out how society neatly codifies experience in the form of maxims, proverbs, and so on, which can be passed on from generation to generation. What he fails to illustrate, however, is that the advice implicit in one proverb may often be contradicted by another. Moreover, we all have considerable liberty in deciding which maxim to follow. For example, do "too many cooks spoil the broth" or do "many hands make light work"? Most legal systems, the ultimate form of codification, are also beset by contradictions and conflicts between principles and precedents. Thus, an important issue in the psychological analysis of problem solving is to explain how people resolve the conflicts inherent in the different rules available to them. Are such conflicts always resolved via the perception of environmental contingencies, or can and do other principles apply?

BFS: I do not disagree with most of what Hogarth says, and I am surprised that he feels that he is disagreeing with me. I certainly agree that contingencies are often "far from evident," and that "the discovery of behavioral rules [is] particularly difficult." Thousands of papers have been published simply on the subtleties of scheduled reinforcements, and traditional efforts to understand just one example (the "variable ratio" schedule in all gambling systems) have ranged from mathematical treatises to hunches and rules of thumb. I do not think it is trivial, however, "to assert that effective problem solving depends on constructing discriminative stimuli"; several of the other commentators show how far from trivial the point is.

One can define "try" and "error" in such a way that "trial-and-error learning" makes sense, but the first emission of a response that soives a problem is not something one has necessarily *tried*. The history of science contains many obvious exceptions. And I agree that maxims, governmental and religious laws, and even scientific laws may conflict with one another. There has been a Newton to say "too many cooks spoil the broth" for every Einstein who says "many hands make light work."

A case study of how a paper containing good ideas, presented by a distinguished scientist to an appropriate audience, had almost no influence at all

Earl Hunt

Department of Psychology, University of Washington

B. F. Skinner's "Operant Analysis of Problem Solving" first appeared in 1966 as a paper presented to the First Annual Carnegie Symposium on Cognition. Among those in attendance were Herbert Simon, Allen Newell, Adrian de Groot, Donald Taylor, and D. E. Berlyne, every one of them already an influential figure in the study of cognition. Some of the papers presented to the symposium (most notably Paige & Simon 1966) were going to be cited frequently in the next few years. Skinner's contribution passed and was forgotten. I do not recall ever having seen it cited. Why? Was it because the paper had poor ideas, or because the ideas were quickly refuted by experiment, or because the paper was poorly presented? Given Skinner's well-deserved reputation, it is difficult to believe that any one of these explanations could be right. I think one of them is, and that it is instructive to discover which one it is.

Skinner's major point was, predictably, that the responses emitted by a problem solver must be evoked by the stimulus situation, and not teleologically drawn out by the desired goal. Therefore it is not correct to say that a problem solver is trying to do something; problem solvers are always responding to something. What they are responding to, though, are not the physical characteristics of an external problem. They are responding to their internal representation of that problem. The words "internal representation" are my own, and are part of the jargon of cognitive science, rather than that of operant conditioning. The idea, however, is clearly stated in Skinner's paper, when he speaks of "discriminative stimuli." These are simply labels that are placed upon a problem, and that then serve as guides to future problem-solving activity. Somewhat more obliquely (although right at the start of his paper), Skinner points out that one of the labels that can be applied is one indicating that reinforcement-achieving behaviors are to be emitted. In other words, a goal state may be one of the internal, discriminative labels of a problem. And once that label is there, it can be used as a guide to behavior.

Has this idea dropped out of modern studies of problem solving? Hardly. Virtually all problem-solving simulations being written today assume that the basic step in cognition is the execution of a "production." A production is defined as a pattern–action rule; if pattern *P* can be detected in the internal representation of a problem, then take action *A*. Because the internal representation can contain a symbolic statement (i.e., a discriminative label) of the goal state, production systems can appear to be teleologically driven toward a goal. In fact, they are evoked by our statement of a problem and its goal. The learning theorists of the 1940s and 1950s (and Skinner) had the impoverished notion that problem solving could be stated in terms of an S → R notation. Modern cognitive psychologists find that $P \rightarrow A$ is more appropriate. Skinner could justly claim that his paper had the essentials of the modern idea!

Skinner assigned an extremely important role to the discriminative stimulus. He pointed out that a problem solver must learn to respond directly to an external problem by examining it in such a way that certain aspects of the problem will be highlighted. The method of examination is itself a learned response. The aspects the examination highlights serve as cues to evoke labeling responses that produce (often verbal) discriminative stimuli, that are themselves the cues for further responses, with more discriminative stimuli, and so on. Today's slogan is that the problem solver manipulates a physical symbol system. And the difference is...?

What is more to the point, research subsequent to Skinner's paper, and apparently not derived from it, has shown that one of the most important steps in problem solving is learning to make appropriate labeling responses. The spate of recent research on the contrast between expert and novice behavior illustrates this dramatically (Chi, Glaser, & Rees 1982; Larkin, McDermott, Simon, & Simon 1980). The expert surpasses the novice in the ability to label problems as "appropriate for a particular solution method," and, once the label has been assigned, the expert is able to rattle off a sequence of stimulus-evoked problem-solving responses. Skinner certainly did not anticipate the details of the expert–novice studies. The conclusions from those studies were not framed in Skinnerian terms by their authors. Far from it! But there is no reason why Chi, Larkin, and their colleagues could not have used Skinner's language instead of terms borrowed from computer science.

Finally, Skinner makes a sharp distinction between problem-solving behavior that is "rule governed" and behavior that is governed by experiences with the reward contingencies in a problem-solving situation. The former is conceptualized as a slow process guided by a sequence of (usually verbal) discriminative stimuli. In fact, the appropriate rules for producing the appropriate stimuli could be acquired by tuition, instead of by experience, providing that the problem solver had previously learned how to learn from tuition. Because the rule-governed stimuli were controlled by a sequence of verbal labels, a problem solver could typically report "why" particular responses were made by simply recalling the labeling sequence and the rules associated with it.

Skinner's distinction between rule-governed and contingency-governed behavior bears more than a superficial resemblance to the 1980s' distinction between controlled and automatic processing (Schneider & Shiffrin 1977). There are two aspects to this distinction. From the viewpoint of an observer, automatic processing is said to be rapid, established by direct experience with the stimulus situation, and relatively effortless. Controlled processing is slower and conscious. These descriptions clearly fit Skinner's two categories of behavior. From a theoretical point of view, Skinner's ideas are still somewhat in advance of today's, for we still lack a detailed theoretical account of the automatic- and controlled-processing distinction. Some of my own thoughts on the topic are close to Skinner's position (Hunt 1981; Hunt & Pixton 1982). I have suggested that the theoretical distinction is between behavior that, in theory, is governed by the execution of productions and behavior that is produced by the automatic activation of semantic associates. Although my own ideas were developed without any conscious reliance on Skinner's paper, they could be looked upon as an elaboration of his distinctions, presented in a different terminology.

To summarize, Skinner's "Problem Solving" contains a number of ideas. The ideas have not been contradicted by subsequent research. If anything, they have been confirmed. It is not too far off the mark to say that it took about ten years for the ideas contained in Skinner's 1966 paper to develop, independently, in cognitive psychology. Now that they have developed they are guiding principles of the field. Presumably a good deal of effort could have been saved if Skinner's paper had been read more carefully by the information-processing psychologists. Why was it ignored?

The problem was in the presentation. My criticism is certainly not directed at Skinner as a writer – both here and in other papers he has established himself as clear, literate, and even elegant. His presentation violated several of the cognitive constraints on communication that we are just now beginning to appreciate. First and foremost, Skinner used the wrong metaphor for thought. Although the word "pigeon" does not appear in the paper, Skinner's reputation and the terminology he used made it clear that he proposed that principles useful in the analysis of animal learning should be applied to the analysis of human thought. For Skinner, such a position was so taken for granted that he saw no need to defend it. His audience felt quite differently. By and large, the proposers of embryonic cognitive psychology, as it existed in 1965, were more than a little disenchanted with the animal model. This is especially clear in Berlyne's (1966) discussion of Skinner's paper. Berlyne felt obliged to defend the general learning model from attack, whereas Skinner had not even acknowledged the existence of an attack.

Skinner presented his ideas. He made no attempt to relate them to the spate of theoretical and experimental papers on cognition that had been published in the years 1955 to 1965. Newell and Simon were not cited. The only reference to observations of problem solving was to Thorndike's studies of cats, more than 30 years earlier. Skinner's discussion of the role of language in problem solving was carried forward at the level of anecdotes. Only two years before, Newell and Simon had published an account of explicit, goal-oriented behavior in the General Problem Solver program. At the same conference at which Skinner spoke, Paige and Simon (1966) presented a paper describing a computer program that extracted meaning from algebra word problems. These were the sorts of observations that cognitive psychologists wanted to understand. On the surface, Skinner's arguments seemed archaic and almost irrelevant.

They were not. Beneath the surface structure there was an important deep structure. It was ignored.

There is a lesson here. The laws of cognition apply to cognitive psychologists. One of those laws is the "given–new" contract in communication (Clark & Haviland 1977). Every message should first connect itself to an idea that the receiver already has and then amplify it in the way the sender wants the idea to be amplified. Skinner failed to provide a given, so the audience ignored the new. This is not surprising. Skinner's listeners knew how to survive the information explosion. Time is finite; do not waste it meditating on irrelevant papers. I do not know whether ideas ever sold themselves, but they certainly do not in the hyperactive academic world of the 20th century. Skinner's listeners, the cognitive psychologists, can hardly be blamed for being subject to psychological laws. It is hard to fault Skinner for not being familiar with new research in a field outside his own. But communication did fail.

BFS: Hunt asks a question that has bothered me for a long time. At least a dozen of my books have been directly concerned with presenting a scientific position, yet as these papers show all too clearly, the position is still widely misunderstood. Obviously I have not made my point. Why? Where Harré blames my style as a writer, Hunt at least finds me "clear, literate, and even elegant." The fault, he says, is rather a question of my choice of model. But the pigeon is more than a model. The research it has come to symbolize is carried out in hundreds of laboratories throughout the scholarly world and with a rather unusual unanimity of results. It has supplied terms and principles of great practical value and, I believe, of equal value in *interpreting* human behavior observed under less favorable circumstances outside the laboratory.

It was not wrong of me to choose that work as a model; it was wrong of psychology to ignore it. And Hunt points to one explanation: Psychologists are always looking for help outside their own field, and at the time I wrote this paper the vogue of information processing was at its height. The computer was coming into its own as a model of human behavior that avoided any charge of dualism. But I think the rise of computer science is only a "surface structure" explanation. The "deep structure" contains the real reason my analysis was rejected: it moves the origin of problem solving from a central nervous system to the environmental history of the problem solver. It is an issue I dealt with five years later in *Beyond Freedom and Dignity* (Skinner 1971).

Contingencies, rules, and the "problem" of novel behavior

Pere Julià

Department of d'Ensenyament Universitati, Generalitat de Catalunya, Barcelona, Spain

A frequent criticism of an operant analysis runs as follows: If behavior must first occur to be reinforced, there necessarily remain, *ex hypothesi*, important aspects of human behavior outside the scope of the formulation. How can we possibly account, for example, for novelty, generality, or creativity? Dennett (1978a), who acknowledges that the law of effect is here to stay, diagnoses the problem as a reluctance to bring terms like "want," "believe," "intend," "think," "feel," "expect," and the like, into the explanatory picture. Without intentional idioms no account of rationality or intelligence is possible; the "use" of these terms, it turns out, presupposes intelligence or rationality, which, Dennett contends, holds the answer to our original question.

The prescription is mentalism in a new guise – theoretical models and computer simulation for the time being, to be validated by neurophysiology some distant future day. The program is thus physicalistic in principle and likely to allay, in some quarters at least, possible fears of reintroducing age-old dualisms.

But is there any reason to suppose that the relevant processes have been identified? Can we assume that simulation is synonymous with explanation, or that broad categories such as intentionality will give neurophysiology useful clues as to how the organism is changed, at every step, in its interaction with the environment?

The "insufficiency argument" fails to appreciate: (1) the probabilistic nature of operant behavior; (2) the complexity and diversity of contingencies of reinforcement; and (3) the interaction of verbal and nonverbal behavior in the human organism.

1. Operant behavior is shaped and maintained by contingencies of reinforcement. Several contingencies can be effective at a given time: Most behavior is indeed multiply caused. As the contingencies change so does the behavior, and novel forms are selected by their consequences: Overall changes in probability of occurrence follow.

New settings often share relevant properties with old; unless there are competing variables, behavior previously reinforced is thereby bound to be automatically strong. This interplay between behavioral history and current settings is often dismissed, however, as ad hoc or trivial (e.g., Chomsky 1959; Dennett 1978a; Taylor 1964). One important source of generality is consequently ruled out. It would appear that the extensive experimental literature on stimulus control is pure fancy.

2. Imitation is another important source of novel behavior. Probably drawing on a strong genetic substratum, imitative contingencies soon play a significant role in the environment of the young child and continue to do so throughout the lifetime of the individual faced with novel behavioral requirements (cf. contemporary research on "observational learning"). The fact that they involve at least another individual enlarges the scope of the formulation to include social behavior. (This is obviously not to suggest that all social and verbal behavior is imitative in nature.)

3. Once a verbal repertoire has been "acquired" we can describe the contingencies and bring this description to bear on other behavior, nonverbal or verbal. Rules are not in the contingencies of the speaker, but once formulated they can become part of the contingencies of the listener, who can then behave in ways which have never been reinforced before. Like all verbal behavior, the formulation of rules – ranging from an incidental bit of advice to the generality of scientific laws – must be accounted for in terms of its effects upon the listener. An often neglected, though crucial fact, is that the speaker eventually becomes his own listener (Skinner 1957). Much self-descriptive behavior has this rulelike effect; self-knowledge has a social origin.

The contingency–rule distinction permits an analysis of the interaction between verbal and nonverbal behavior, as in making plans, decisions, efforts to recall, and the like; or in the formulation of resolutions, hypotheses, and so on. Although no single behavioral process will cover them all, some traditional forms of "reasoning" can be analyzed as the formulation and manipulation of rules. All these activities are geared to the production of novel behavior or behavior that, though perhaps not entirely new, is at the moment too weak to appear. This is the essence of problem solving – the archetypal field of novelty and creativity.

Perhaps a final word about the "intentional stance" is in order. Presumably, the intelligence or rationality postulated by Dennett and others has to do with the verbal activity involved in complex sets of contingencies of the sort just mentioned. But surely verbal intervention is not as ubiquitous as is usually implied by philosophers and many psychologists? Much if not most of what we do merely shows the effects of the contingencies, nonverbal or verbal, past or present.

The "use" of intentional idioms is an effort to capture observed or inferred probabilities of action. When we say that individuals behave in a certain way because they "know that...," the *that*-clause points to the contingencies. The invoked knowledge is an internal surrogate for the history responsible for the current strength of the behavior as well as possibly related verbal or perceptual behavior in the present setting. A similar analysis applies to the rest of intentional idioms. So-called intentional states are derivative, not causal – hence the basic methodological objection to bringing them into the explanatory picture.

Intentionality is too broad a notion to be instructive. Wants, beliefs, thoughts, feelings, and the like are very different behavioral events, bound to have different effects on the living organism. Machines are not sensitive to the law of effect; they merely "follow rules." At issue are not the waxing and waning probabilities of ongoing behavioral repertoires but the accuracy of the analyst's guesses about putative data. The "generate-and-test" strategy common to artificial intelligence, cognitive simulation, and much psycholinguistic theorizing makes this all too clear (Julià 1983). Behavior, verbal or nonverbal, does not occur in vacuo: It occurs at specific places and times for good functional reasons. Until the intentionalist comes to appreciate the basic principle that each instance of behavior must be interpreted in terms of the functional class of which it is a member, attempts to simulate behavior (and therefore, in his terms, "explain" it) will necessarily remain question begging.

BFS: I find Julià's opening point surprising, but of course he is right. Problem solving is part of the problem of the First Instance. Where does the behavior come from that is taken over by contingencies of reinforcement? Genetic examples are not very important in the human species; indeed, they are particularly hard to modify through operant reinforcement. Fortunately, the species possesses a large pool of uncommitted behavior available for quick shaping. But another substantial corpus of behavior is generated, as Julià makes clear, by the individual with problem-solving practices which need to be much more extensively analyzed as such.

Can Skinner define a problem?

Geir Kaufmann

Department of Cognitive Psychology, University of Bergen, Norway

Skinner attempts to capture the territory of human problem solving armed with the weapons of purely nonintentional concepts. I would argue that even for a scientific warrior as eminent as Skinner, this is an impossible task.

In the first place, Skinner's exposition is replete with intentional idioms. When solving problems, people are said to "construct models," "rules," and "plans," to "frame hypotheses," and so on. No serious attempt is made to demonstrate convincingly that such intentional concepts can be translated into behavioral equivalents without significant loss in predictive power or referential accuracy. It is strange that Skinner takes this task so lightly, since his enterprise stands and falls with the feasibility of achieving such a translation. I would argue for the necessity of adopting the "intentional stance" (Dennett 1978a) in our study of human problem solving by claiming that it is not even possible to achieve a satisfactory definition of what a problem is in purely nonintentional terms. If we are committed to using intentional terms in our basic conceptual point of departure, a theory that rests exclusively on nonintentional concepts cannot even get off the ground.

Skinner explores a range of problems that may all be said to fall in the category of what I will call *presented problems*. The individual is faced with a difficulty that has to be handled. Such a situation may be well structured (initial conditions, goal conditions, and operators are clearly definable). At the other pole is the unstructured problem situation, as in the artist example given by Skinner, where the number of unknowns is at a maximum, and where the problem may lie in constructing a new composition and the like. But these are not the only problems people deal with. There is also a class of problems that may be called *foreseen problems*; that is, the individual anticipates that a problem (serious pollution, a massive traffic jam, etc.) will result if present developmental trends continue. Evasive action may then be taken.

Perhaps even more interesting in the context of my argument is the class of problems that may be called *constructed problems*. The initial condition may here be a consistently reinforcing, satisfactory state of affairs. Nevertheless, a problem may arise when an individual compares the existing situation to a future, hypothetical state of affairs that could represent an improvement over the present situation. An example would be the present TV technology which may be said to be quite satisfactory. Yet an individual might see a problem here in that there is no TV set with an adjustable-sized screen. The problem may be solved by constructing a new TV set with a small transformer unit and an adjustable-sized monitor unit.

How, then, are we to define a problem in such a way that it encompasses the whole range of problem-solving activities that people do in fact engage in? As far as I can see, the only defensible options would have to include intentional terms. A satisfactory solution would be to define a problem as a discrepancy between an existing situation and a *desired* state of affairs (see Pounds 1969).

One might attempt to externalize the concept of a problem, for instance by stating that a problem is a situation that needs to be changed. But this will clearly not do. The TV situation mentioned above does not need to be changed *in itself*. It is a rational agent with a definite purpose in mind who desires to change it. Another strategy might be to define a problem as a verbal statement of a discrepancy between an existing situation and a new, improved situation. But now we are thrown back into the category of presented problems, and no account can be given of how the problem *originated*, that is, out of an individual's *desire* to reach a new situation.

If we cannot avoid using intentional concepts in the very definition of what a problem is, it seems that we are committed to theories that posit internal representations.

Skinner's dismay with much of existentialist–humanist psychology may be justified. However, the arguments and evidence favoring the top-down research strategy of cognitive psychology over the bottom-up psychology advocated by Skinner seem entirely convincing to me.

With its functionalist philosophical underpinning cognitive psychology also steers clear of a problematic dualism (see Block 1981). And, even more important in the present context, the functional explanations of cognitive psychology are *genuine* explanations and may even eventually be replaced by purely mechanistic explanations. And – as Dennett (1978a) has cleverly and convincingly pointed out – there will always be a central place for a version of the law of effect.

BFS: Kaufmann raises essentially three problems:

1. The need for intentional explanations. But I can give an alternative version of each of Kaufmann's sentences in which intention is replaced by a history of reinforcement. The field of operant behavior is the field of intention as well as purpose, but it replaces these current surrogates of the history of the individual with the history itself.

2. Complex problems, particularly those having to do with a predicted future, are not only harder to solve but harder to bring into a formulation of problem solving. Apparently Kaufmann accepts as givens the key terms in "it is a rational agent with a definite purpose in mind who desires to change it." I ask for a definition of "rational," "agent," "purpose," "mind," and "desire." Only with those in hand can I attempt to answer.

3. By "genuine" solution, Kaufmann appears to mean a current one. There is inevitably a temporal gap in the account given by the experimental analysis of behavior, and it must eventually be filled by physiology. But for that purpose, the formulation given by an experimental analysis will be of much greater help than a cognitive psychology which is leading physiologists to look for the wrong things. The nervous system mediates the relations studied in an experimental analysis of behavior. Neurology will not discover the current surrogates constructed for the same purpose by cognitive psychology.

Problem solving as a cognitive process

Manfred Kochen

Mental Health Research Institute, University of Michigan

If solving a problem is a "behavioral event," then a non-behavioral event could not be problem solving. Yet in the writing of this commentary I am solving several problems. A major one is providing a clear analysis of my thoughts, reflecting on my own problem-solving patterns. By the time I exhibit writing behavior, most of my problem solving is done. Moreover, I respond to writing behavior by rethinking what is written. I think, or reflect, despite lack of differential reinforcement. Even if I perceive my conclusions or the step-by-step process of reaching them to be reinforcing, I must still justify my arguments and beliefs.

Are we to stretch the concept of behavior to include reflection? Or are we to exclude reflection from problem solving? The phrase quoted above stimulates me to decide whether I believe it. If I can reach and justify a decision one way or the other, I understand the phrase, and according to Skinner, I have solved a problem. But no one could directly observe me contemplating that question. It would take operations other than the inputs and outputs that behaviorism considers relevant to ascertain those mental processes of whose existence I, and only I, am certain.

The concepts of "behavior," "response," and "reinforcement" appear to be used so broadly that, given a suitable interpretation, there is hardly anything they do not seem to encompass. Skinner has stretched these notions as far as he faults Kurt Lewin (1936) for stretching the notion of "space" – which has, incidentally, proved to be very fruitful and prescient. It is therefore paradoxical that Skinner's explication of problem solving seems to me to miss the essence of that process, at least as I understand it. If I were asked to pick a simplified prototypical problem, it would be the tennis tournament problem or the Tower of Hanoi puzzle (a standard problem in artificial intelligence). Skinner's example problem of locating a friend's suitcase at an airport by means of its baggage claim number only, *without a description*, does not capture the essence of a problem. It is a standard sequential file-access task which is not considered problem solving by a computer. Moreover, the important question is how, of all possible actions, that of marking suitcases that have been inspected with chalk in order to avoid reinspecting them would ever be selected. The generation of "all possible actions" and selection are important to problem solving. Problem solving is not merely following an algorithm, but rather selecting or constructing one. Even more important, it is formulating and reformulating the problem. In the tennis tournament problem, the question is to determine how many single-elimination matches (with no ties) must be played for a final winner of 1,024 contestants to emerge. It is unclear what "response" or "behavioral process" is relevant to working on this problem. Possibly, to a person so trained, the miscue that 1,024 = 2^{10} may be regarded as a "similar" stimulus, and lead to the conclusion that 10 rounds must be played. Since that was not the question, the problem solver can now reason that in the first round, with 2 players per match, 1024/2 = 512 matches were played; 256 in the second round; 128 in the third. Though this awkward, nongeneralizable method yields the correct answer, 512 + 256 + 128 + ... + 1 = 1,023, it is not a good solution. Generalizability is centrally important, as is elegance of method. Probability does not enter. Neither does "strength of behavior" nor "reinforcement." The problem solver does not generate responses that are not the results of a computation, by which I do not mean a behavioral process but a series of internal state-transitions. The *idea* or *hypothesis* that in each match there must be one loser implies immediately that the number of matches is equal to the number of losers, or the number of contestants less 1.

The formation of hypotheses prior to their expression is hardly behavior. If we could only respond in situations of perceived need or opportunity, or act (behave) as part of the problem-solving process, the range and complexity of problems with which we cope would be more limited than they are. And if operant conditioning were the sole mechanism by which we extend our problem-solving skills, then our rate of learning would be slower than it is. Just marking or constructing discriminative stimuli is as far less effective as seeing alone is inferior to imagining. We cannot see four-dimensional surfaces, but because we can imagine or construct them, we can solve important problems involving such mental constructs.

The implicit claim that operant analysis is the best or the only scientific approach may be in error. The essence of problem solving in my view is to generate a new idea. Persons, not behaviors, solve problems, as implied in the seventh sentence of the abstract of "Problem Solving." Perhaps problem solving is to coping as decision making is to deciding. Coping and deciding are behavior. They are manifestations of phenotypes. A person can cope with a task without formulating it as a problem and planning as well as justifying a chain or algorithm of actions. Problem formulation, problem recognition, and problem solving are mental operations governed by the behavior of neuronal circuits, as are coping and deciding, but biochemical and neurophysiological processes underlying the two types of activity almost certainly differ. These are actions or behavioral events, but at different categorical levels. Failure to distinguish between levels diminishes the power of the operant approach. So does interpreting behavior so very broadly. It becomes difficult to select what is to be reinforced. Forcing problem solving into a framework of operant analysis does not seem to apply or provide a fruitful scientific approach to explicating or describing how it is possible to solve interesting, complex, and important problems.

BFS: In his first two paragraphs, Kochen uses seven key words (think, reflect, rethink, perceive, justify, decide, understand) which have never been defined in ways which satisfy all those who use them. No definitions are given by Kochen, presumably on the understanding that every educated person knows what the words mean. That is the kind of problem that behaviorism attacks, and in one place or another (e.g., Skinner 1953; 1957; 1974) I have offered alternative definitions of all those words. I have not done so, however, in terms of input and output or by referring only to publicly observable events. (Kochen seems to have accepted the popular view that behaviorism deals only with observables, and with observables confined to stimuli or input and responses or output.)

My definitions would be a kind of interpretation. Most instances of human behavior are functions of too many variables or of variables of which we have too little knowledge to be understood in any scientific sense. Behavioral science studies simpler instances under conditions in which some degree of prediction and control is possible. Terms and principles drawn from such research are then used to interpret more complex instances. Philosophers use their own experiences in the same way, as psychologists like James and Freud used happy accidents in their personal experiences.

I am glad to know that computers have reached the stage at which they "consider" a task to be problem solving, and "consider" is a term we might add to the list. Whether or not finding the right bag in the baggage claim is a problem for a computer, it was a problem for those who invented computers.

I should not want to undertake a behavioral solution to the problems Kochen poses, but I should certainly take Kochen's behavior in solving them as something requiring interpretation. A child who can add a column of figures does not thereby understand what adding means, and those who learn to manipulate the rules of logic and mathematics may be quite successful without understanding the behavioral processes involved.

Is there such a thing as a problem situation?

Kjell Raaheim

Department of Cognitive Psychology, University of Bergen, Norway

Human problem solving may be looked upon as a means whereby individuals attempt to deal with their partly unfamiliar present in terms of their better-known past (Raaheim 1961; 1974). Failure to describe precisely the types of tasks called "problems," however, has probably served to reduce the scientific value of a number of approaches in the psychology of thinking. Almost all kinds of difficult tasks have been referred to as problems; hence there is little chance of discovering basic principles of adjustment on the behavioral side.

Now, Skinner seems to go even further in complicating the analysis by even omitting "difficulty" as a defining characteristic of a problem. However, his description of differences between behavior shaped and maintained by certain contingencies of reinforcement and behavior occasioned by rules derived from the contingencies can be seen as a means of making a distinction between problem situations (in which, at least for some time, you do not know what to do) and situations that are *un*-problematic (in the sense that someone has already formulated appropriate rules of behavior).

We should not be confused by the fact that we may still be left with *some* (other) problems, such as, for example, whether to follow that rule now or later. Problems may also be seen to vary considerably with regard to both the nature and the severity of the challenge.

Skinner presents some excellent examples of difficulties met with in describing contingencies and constructing rules to be followed by others later on. Both the old family doctor and the person with mystical experiences have difficulties, since the two kinds of "knowledge" to be reported "escape adequate specification," to use Skinner's own terms. Theorists in the field of human thinking face the same difficulties. Human experience regularly escapes the categories proposed by psychologists and rule followers, be they humans or computers.

To advance as a science psychology needs its own proper units of analysis. In physics the development of theories and progress can be seen as based upon new units of analysis: Now there are molecules, now there are atoms and elementary particles. Within psychology we seem to decide on units in a somewhat arbitrary way. "The object" is often seen to represent the more complex unit, at least as far as some experimental and theoretical studies are concerned. And so we have smaller objects like "apples" (red and sweet) and bigger ones, like "suitcases" and "rotary displays." However, a proper description of the behavior of Skinner's man at the airport cannot perhaps be made unless we take a more complex experiential unit as our point of departure.

The word "situation" is used in "everyday speech" and also by theorists in psychology (and even by Skinner in the section "Problem-Solving Behavior") to refer to the "circumstances" under which an individual finds himself on a given occasion. But what is the situation of the man going to pick up his friend's suitcase at the airport? Must the task be performed quickly (to allow his friend to catch a train)? Is it necessary to avoid any action that would make other passengers believe that he is after other people's property?

At the risk of being misunderstood I would add that marking other people's property with a piece of chalk might in any case not be a reasonable way of proceeding. Even when you are in a hurry it would perhaps pay to wait a few minutes to let other people remove *their* suitcases. What I mean to say is that we in psychology must have a proper framework for describing human beings in situations outside the laboratory. Nor do I think that the experiences of the old family doctor must elude the grasp of the young doctor. If we do not take the shortcomings of our present categorical systems seriously, much of what should rightly belong to the domain of psychological research will remain within the field of mysticism.

A clearer view of the factors of problem solving can be gained by taking the "particular person with a particular history" as the point of departure and as a factor in determining the experiential units that form the basis of problem-solving behavior (Raaheim 1974). It is possible to argue that a "problem *situation*" is best defined as a situation experienced by the individual as *a deviant member of a series of familiar situations* (Raaheim 1961). This point has recently been discussed at some length by Sternberg (1982).

We are not left, then, with an easily detectable, objective, and durable reinforcing system that "exists prior to any effect it may have upon an organism." What we may hope for, on the other hand, is that there is more to be said about problem-solving behavior than that "it changes another part of the solver's behavior."

With some knowledge of the individual's history, surprisingly good predictions may sometimes be made as to behavior in a problem situation. The reason for this seems to be that human beings follow relatively simple *general* rules of behavior in intelligently using past experience to change the problem situation into a more easily mastered, familiar one.

BFS: I do not see why difficulty must be a defining characteristic of a problem. There are easy problems and there are hard ones, and they are both problems. I agree that we must look at the contingencies of reinforcement under which people follow rules, and they are usually not the contingencies described by the rules. As Raaheim points out, the man going to the airport to pick up his friend's suitcase is affected by many things. Raaheim suggests two – technically speaking, the schedule effect, called *drh* (the differential reinforcement of high rates), and avoidance (of attack for theft). As to letting other people pick up their suitcases first, I had assumed that no one else was there (an unlikely but not inconceivable eventuality in commercial aviation). While I think we must eventually deal with a "particular person with a particular history," that may not be the best point of departure in determining the units of an analysis. The experimental analysis of behavior has been concerned with units from the very beginning.

Except for the terms in which it is expressed, it seems to me that Raaheim has correctly summarized my paper by saying that "human beings follow relatively simple *general* rules of behavior in intelligently using past experience to change the problem situation into a more easily mastered, familiar one." But in doing so, problem-solving behavior "changes another part of the solver's behavior," a formulation Raaheim rejects as inadequate.

Questions raised by the reinforcement paradigm

Anatol Rapoport

Institute for Advanced Studies, Vienna, Austria

The fundamental role of reinforcement in the evolution of behavior patterns during the lifetime of an individual organism is a principal theme in Professor Skinner's writings, and "Problem Solving" is no exception. Should this be taken as a discussion issue? I once read a facetious review of one of Skinner's books, in which a refutation of the reinforcement hypothesis was offered. A man accosted by a gunman, who demands his money or his life, surrenders his wallet but hardly because of his previous experiences with being dead. Clearly, such a literal interpretation of reinforcement theory is not a contribution to a constructive criticism. On the other hand, if the theory is to be interpreted on a more general level, it stands in danger of becoming unfalsifiable. If mental operations, for example, are acceptable as substitutes for past concrete experiences, *any* choice of action can be attributed to differential reinforcement. The modern behaviorist, abandoning the old orthodoxy, can certainly accommodate "mental operations" (for example, remembering what a chalk mark on a suitcase means) among behavior patterns. Add a tacit identification of a behavior pattern with an appropriate *class* of patterns, and the reinforcement theory becomes impervious to any assault. Consider, for example, the objection based on the "logical" grammatical mistakes made by small children ("two sheeps," "I knowed," etc.), which apparently cannot be attributed to reinforcement by the language community. If, however, "generalization" is assumed to be a reinforced behavior pattern, the counterexample becomes an example.

So the prospects for a "constructive" interaction between "Skinnerians" and "non-Skinnerians" on the reinforcement issue are not bright. More promising is the juxtaposition of rule-guided and contingency-shaped behavioral adaptation. The difference manifests itself in a great variety of contexts and can serve as an integrating concept. In system engineering, for instance, a distinction is made between "open loop" and "closed loop" control. Open-loop control can be applied without monitoring the trajectory of the system. The optimal control function is calculated once for all on the basis of assumptions about how the behavior of the system is determined (e.g., by known physical laws). Clearly, any discrepancy between the postulated model and reality or any accidental deviation of the system from its prescribed trajectory can lead to quite large departures from the optimal course, especially if optimization is to be made over a long period. In a closed-loop device, the control is a function not only of time but also of the current state of the system; hence this form of control is based on continual monitoring, and deviations can be corrected as they occur.

Analysis of each type of control is theoretically instructive and so not only provides a solution for some practical problem of engineering but also a stimulus for further development of control theory. Moreover, points of contact can be expected between this theory and a theory of behavior developed along analogous lines – shaped by rules (open-loop control) or by contingencies (closed-loop control). Connections to sociological contexts also suggest themselves, where bureaucratic or ideologically guided practices are compared with pragmatically oriented ones; to ethical contexts – decisions governed by categorically stated principles or by anticipated consequences. Also in the study of problem solving occurring in expert chess play, distinctions can be discerned between "playing the board" (following established strategic and tactical principles) and "playing the opponent" (taking into account the latter's previously noted idiosyncrasies or predilections). All these approaches are clearly related to the distinction brought out by Skinner between rule-governed and contingency-governed behavior.

It is instructive to note also the relativity of these two concepts. For example, from one point of view, the chess player who "plays the board" can be said to be guided by contingencies, because he makes his decisions in situations as they occur instead of following an a priori formulated optimal strategy (which can be formally proved to exist, but which is inaccessible to any human mind or machine). On the other hand, the situations he encounters are seldom identical with previously encountered situations, so he must be guided by some sort of rules, even though he might find it difficult or impossible to state them.

In short, the key concept in the problem of explaining problem-solving behavior is that of generalization. No two stimuli, no two situations are identical. A learning organism, whether it learns by classical, instrumental, or operant conditioning, *must* generalize, that is, organize stimuli, situations, and responses into classes. On our own level of cognition, we call this process concept formation. It seems to me that to explain concept formation by postulating reinforcement schedules borders on evading the fundamental problem of cognition: How are concepts (classifications of stimuli, etc.) formed in the first place? The possibility cannot be excluded that here too reinforcement plays a part, but the problem remains of showing not just *that* it operates but exactly *how* it operates. This problem suggests an analogous one in the context of evolution. A formal analogy between natural selection and incremental learning has been repeatedly noted. [See Skinner's "Consequences," this volume.] Is there an analogue of "problem solving" in biological evolution, where adaptation can be said to "goal directed" but nevertheless explainable by (generalized) natural selection mechanisms?

In rejecting the reinforcement paradigm, the "holistic" or "humanistic" psychologists (who, perhaps, can be regarded as representative non-Skinnerians) have also evaded the fundamental problem of cognition. Here I find myself in full agreement with the implications of Professor Skinner's closing remarks. To remedy inadequacies of analysis, we need not the abandonment of analysis in favor of intuitively or ethically attractive concepts but more penetrating analysis. Scientific objectivity can and should be used as a bulwark against abuses of power, that is, in defense of human dignity and autonomy. Human involvement is unavoidable in creative behavioral science, but it should be regarded as a problem to be dealt with by designing appropriate methods of research, not as an antidote against allegedly "dehumanized" science.

BFS: I agree with Rapoport more closely than he thinks, because there are features of an operant analysis which he does not fully take into account. A few issues:

1. Do we need a mental operation called "remembering"? I pick up an easily distinguished suitcase and examine the number on the ticket. It is not the number I am looking for. When the suitcase comes by again, I do not pick it up. We can say either that I now remember that I examined it and found it to be the wrong suitcase, or that when I found it to be the wrong suitcase my behavior with respect to it was changed so that I no longer pick it up. What is remembered in the sense of what survives is a changed organism, not an internal copy or memory of the event that changed it.

2. The grammatical mistakes of children are due to reinforcement of their verbal responses, but not reinforcement item by item. Generalization is a well-established process in operant conditioning.

3. While the distinction between contingency-shaped and rule-governed behavior is important, it must not be forgotten that people formulate and use rules only because their behavior in doing so is shaped by other contingencies.

4. I do not evade "fundamental problems of cognition" by postulating reinforcement schedules. Rapoport's question "How are concepts (specifications of stimuli, etc.) formed in the first place?" seems to me to be easily answered. Reinforcements are contingent not only on behavior but upon the setting in which the behavior occurs. In a well-known experiment by Herrnstein, Loveland, and Cable (1976), pigeons quickly learned to distinguish colored slides in which people were present from slides in which they were absent. Had the pigeon formed a concept? No, the experimenter formed it when he made reinforcement contingent upon a property of stimuli. No internal copy of those contingencies in the head of the pigeon is needed to explain the behavior.

Response classes, operants, and rules in problem solving

Jan G. Rein

Department of Social Sciences, University of Tromsoe, Norway

In this commentary the definition of response classes and operants and Skinner's conception of rule-governed behavior are considered.

According to Skinner, problem-solving behavior can be contingency shaped or rule governed. Rules are extracted from contingencies of reinforcement which define operants. Thus, "operant" is the fundamental concept in functional analyses of problem solving. An operant is a class of responses shown to be modifiable (Skinner 1938, p. 433) and which is defined by a set of contingencies of reinforcement (Skinner 1969, p. 131), that is, the interrelations among discriminative stimuli, responses, and reinforcing stimuli (Skinner 1969, p. 23).

To decide whether certain responses occur with increased probability because of the introduction of a reinforcer, it must be shown that the generated responses are of the same kind as those on which the reinforcer is contingent. Skinner (1969, p. 7) writes that "the class of responses upon which a reinforcer is contingent is called an operant, to suggest the action on the environment followed by reinforcement." This seems to mean that all responses producing a certain reinforcer belong to the same class. However, as pointed out by several authors (e.g., Rein & Svartdal 1979; Schick 1974) circularity may arise when behavior is identified by a reinforcer and a reinforcer cannot be identified until a change in the probability of a certain *kind* of behavior has been demonstrated.

The reason for this apparent circularity seems to be a failure to distinguish clearly between a consequence and a reinforcing consequence (Stinessen 1983). Skinner (1953, p. 65) writes that "the consequences define the properties with respect to which responses are called similar." This seems to mean that all responses producing a certain consequence belong to the same class, a class that is then submitted to experimental manipulation. Nothing is so far said about operants and reinforcers. Consequence is then used to determine when responses of this same kind occur at later occasions. Instances of the response class that are now occurring with increased probability because of the earlier presentation of the consequence can now be assigned to the same operant, and to the consequence can be added the property of being reinforcing.

Although definitional circularity may be avoided, several problems remain.

A certain consequence *defines* particular responses as belonging to the same class. How, then, can this same consequence be used to *explain* an increased rate of responding for members of this class?

During extinction the consequence found to reinforce instances of a certain response class is withdrawn, and during intermittent reinforcement it is presented only on some of the occasions on which a response occurs. How are particular responses to be identified when the reinforcing consequence is not presented?

It is possible to argue that during both extinction and intermittent reinforcement a response may have other consequences than the one that is reinforcing. One of these may be selected to classify the behavior emitted. However, this will require that a consequence of the same kind has already been used to define the behavior on which a consequence was contingent that turned out to be a reinforcer. What determines which among several consequences is to be selected as the *defining* one?

When a consequence is shown to be a reinforcer, knowledge of which aspects of this consequence actually control behavior is not acquired in an all-or-none fashion but increases gradually through functional analysis. How are we to decide when to terminate the search for these critical features? Moreover, it may be difficult to state the criteria for determining when two consequences are so similar or so different that they will necessitate classification of preceding responses as same or different.

Since rules are extracted from contingencies of reinforcement, the problems inherent in Skinner's definition of response class and operant will also apply to rules.

Rules are objective and physical verbal descriptions of contingencies of reinforcement and may function as (contingency-specifying) discriminative stimuli. According to Skinner in "Problem Solving," behavior is under the control of prior contingency-specifying stimuli when it is said that an organism behaves in a given way because it expects a certain consequence to follow.

From a person's knowledge of a certain rule no particular behavior follows. For a particular behavior to occur the person must believe that the rule is true; that is, he must expect that the behavior prescribed will produce the stated consequence. Explaining behavior in terms of rules therefore implies that intentions are ascribed to persons. According to Skinner, intentional expressions such as "he believes that" and "he expects that" do not refer to mental events, but have to be analyzed in terms of an earlier history of reinforcement, that is, in terms of extensional concepts.

However, it may be argued that intentional sentences have different logical properties from extensional sentences and cannot be logically reduced to extensional sentences (Gauld & Shotter 1977). One cannot substitute for the sentence "he believes that by doing *X* the problem will be solved" the sentence "by doing *X* the problem will be solved." The former may be true and the latter false. If descriptions of beliefs and expectations cannot be reduced to descriptions of contingencies of reinforcement, it may be difficult to explain rule-governed behavior in purely extensional terms.

BFS: I agree "that all responses producing a certain reinforcer" do not "belong to the same class." Reinforcement of pressing a lever does not strengthen sitting on the lever. But once one has specified the setting (the lever), a rough specification of topography (pressing), and a consequence (e.g., receipt of food if the organism is hungry), the topography will be more and more sharply determined by its effect in producing a consequence. At issue is not a definition of the response but its probability of emission. It is in this sense that, as I have said, "the consequences define the properties with respect to which responses are called similar." If we include the setting and the topography of the responses as part of a definition, there is no problem in identifying the responses which occur when reinforcement does not follow, and we have no reason to try to find other consequences which will serve in an alternative definition.

Rein agrees that "since rules are extracted from contingencies of reinforcement, the problems inherent in Skinner's definition of response class and operant will also apply to rules." (It is a mistake to say "extracted from" since the rules are not in the contingencies. They are descriptions of contingencies.) And it is true that "no particular behavior follows from a person's knowledge of a certain rule." Whether a rule is followed depends not upon whether "the person believes that the rule is true" but upon past experiences in using the rule or other rules offered by the same authority. The person need not *expect* that the behavior prescribed will produce the stated consequence any more than he needs to expect the consequence when the behavior has been directly shaped by contingencies. Of course "He believes that by doing *X* the problem will be solved" means more than "By doing *X*, the problem will be solved." Belief refers to probability of behavior due to earlier contingencies in which the rule or something like it has already figured.

New wine in old glasses?

Joseph M. Scandura

Interdisciplinary Studies in Structural Learning and Instructional Science, University of Pennsylvania

To my mind, and undoubtedly to the minds of many other cognitive theorists, Skinner is contemporary behaviorism personified. One might therefore wonder whether Skinner has had anything significant to say about problem solving despite his long and illustrious career in psychology.

Frankly, I was somewhat surprised at the extent to which Skinner's ideas on problem solving find parallels in contemporary cognitive theory – especially since the essence of his paper was originally published in 1966, when only a few of us were seriously pursuing the study of problem solving.

A tremendous amount of work on problem solving has been done since that early period. Hence, it is of some interest to consider the extent to which Skinner anticipated more current developments, as well as where his ideas appear lacking.

One of the first things I noticed was that Skinner's description of the problem-solving situation is reminiscent of more recent information-processing representations. Specifically, Skinner refers to a problem as a situation in which we cannot emit any (previously learned) responses. Compare this with "problem situations which cannot be solved via any previously learned rule" (Scandura 1971, p. 35).

Skinner's distinction between first- and second-order rules is also more than just a bit reminiscent of my own distinction between higher- and lower-order rules (e.g., Roughead & Scandura 1968; Scandura 1970; 1971; 1973, pp. 205–13). It should be emphasized in this regard, however, that the order of a rule is a function of its level of use in solving particular problems, not a characteristic of the rules themselves (e.g., see Scandura 1977). Certainly, the elements on which higher-order rules operate must include rules, but whether elements are considered rules or atomic entities is a function of the level of detail expressed in the cognitive representation. More refined analysis is always possible, and may indeed be necessary, depending on the experimental subjects whose behavior is to be explained.

Most contemporary problem-solving researchers would undoubtedly find self-evident many other remarks made by Skinner. For example, Skinner's remark to the effect that "second-order, 'heuristic' rules. . .can be followed as 'mechanically' as any first-order rule" has been demonstrated empirically in a long line of studies on rule learning beginning in the early 1960s (e.g., Roughead & Scandura 1968; Scandura 1964; 1969).

Other similarities are less direct but, I think, equally real. Skinner makes a major distinction between rule-governed behavior and contingency-shaped behavior, largely, it would appear, to justify his continued commitment to behavioral contingencies. This distinction too is commonplace in modern theories of cognition but for quite different reasons. It corresponds rather directly to what is often referred to as the distinction between nonexpert and expert knowledge and behavior. The nonexpert's behavior is largely rule governed (based on procedural knowledge) whereas the expert's is more automatic (based on structural or more holistic knowledge).

Given this degree of overlap, one might wonder what the last 15–20 years of work on cognitive processes has accomplished. Perhaps the old behaviorist had it right from the beginning. Ignoring the obvious benefits of talking about new problems in familiar terms (albeit only familiar to Skinnerian behaviorists), Skinner's proposals have a fundamental limitation. They gloss over or ignore important considerations and simply are not sufficiently precise to allow prediction of behavior on nontrivial problems, much less the control that Skinner himself would seem to demand.

One of the major contributions of modern cognitive theory over the past 20 years is the development of precise languages that make it possible to represent cognitive processes in great detail. Although there are differences of opinion as to what kind of language to use, and even whether it makes any difference which language is used or how to derive such representations in the first place (Scandura 1982), most cognitive theorists are agreed on the need for some such language. Most would also agree on the need for general purpose control mechanisms, although again there are major differences of opinion.

Skinner's formulation says nothing about these matters. This would not be a serious omission if Skinner could predict or control complex problem-solving behavior using contingencies and the like. But to my knowledge this has never been done empirically. (It is also true that many contemporary cognitive theorists have not done so either, but that is another matter.)

Ironically, just as Skinner criticizes Thorndike's explanation of problem solving in terms of "trial and error" behavior, so cognitive theorists can criticize Skinner. For one thing, Skinner gets so involved in predicting specific responses that he rarely (if ever) gets around to explaining why humans routinely learn simultaneously to perform entire classes of totally different responses (e.g., Scandura 1970; see Scandura 1976 for a series of early papers on the relative merits of using associations versus rules as the basic unit of behavioral analysis by Suppes, Arbib, Scandura, and others). For another thing, it is certainly true that Thorndike's trial and error explanations derive from empirical results based on multiple measures of different subjects on a variety of problems. Yet, Skinner's goal of predicting probabilities of individual problem-solving responses (which to my knowledge has never been done successfully with nontrivial problems) is also limiting. Some contemporary cognitive theorists have shown how individual instances of complex human problem solving can be explained deterministically (e.g., Newell & Simon 1972; Scandura 1971; 1977). Moreover, Scandura (1971; 1977) has demonstrated empirically that under idealized conditions it is also possible to predict such problem-solving behavior (i.e., individual behavior on specific problems) ahead of time.

There are many further instances of this sort, but for present purposes let me just mention two that strike a personal note. In attempting to reconcile the problem of motivation from a "structural learning" perspective (i.e., what rule to use when more than one might do), I originally considered various general selection principles, including behavioral contingencies, that would explain selection in all cases. I even obtained empirical evidence that strongly favored one such hypothesis (Scandura 1971; 1973). The probability of selecting the more specific (less general) of two applicable rules was generally much higher than that of selecting the more general one (e.g., Scandura 1969). Shortly thereafter, however, it became apparent that a more deterministic alternative was necessary (Scandura 1971; 1973). Ironically, the introduction of higher-order selection rules for this purpose not only increased the internal consistency of the overall theory but provided a cognitive explanation for behavioral contingencies (e.g., Scandura 1973, pp. 262–71).

Another parallel in my own work which came to mind in reading Skinner's paper corresponds directly to Skinner's major distinction between rule-governed (procedural) and contingency-shaped (structural) behavior. Although I do not claim to have convinced other cognitive theorists of this, recent research strongly suggests that the very same mechanism that underlies problem solving is also responsible for the process of automatization (e.g., Scandura 1981; Scandura & Scandura 1980). Specifically, procedures of the rules used by nonexperts appear to be gradually transformed via higher-order rules into the structurally more complex rules (which are observed during practice) characteristic of experts. (Results from Scandura and Scandura [1980] further suggest that rules must be automated before they can serve to define higher-order problems, which explains why it may be difficult to train children at one stage of development in tasks at a higher level.) In effect, procedural complexity, corresponding to Skinner's rule-governed behavior, is transformed into structural complexity, corresponding to Skinner's contingency-shaped behavior. Given Skinner's lifelong emphasis on analyzing behavior qua behavior it is not surprising that he has overlooked this potentially fundamental relationship between the two types.

BFS: Scandura, like Hunt, acknowledges my early appearance in the field of cognitive problem solving, but proposes to move me out of it by saying that I have glossed over or ignored some important aspects. The things he lists as ignored or glossed over, however, seem to me to be merely awkward alternative formulations of points that are more accurately made in operant terms. What really are "general purpose control mechanisms?" In a world of what physical dimensions are "cognitive processes [represented] in great detail"?

I do not emphasize the distinction between rule-governed and contingency-shaped behavior "largely. . .to justify [my] continued commitment to behavioral contingencies." The distinction is an important one, and contingencies of reinforcement are present in both. The contingencies which control the behavior of following a rule are usually not the contingencies specified in the rule, but they exist and must not be ignored. They are not adequately replaced by speaking of the belief of a person using a rule or his faith in the person formulating it.

Scandura does not fully take advantage of what is known about contingencies of reinforcement. There is nothing *automatic* about behavior reinforced by its direct consequences, although something else is involved when the same behavior occurs in following a rule.

I do not think that an analysis of problem-solving behavior is the same as solving problems in general, nor do I think that a test of such an analysis is found in solving particular problems. It may be true that "under idealized conditions" it has been demonstrated empirically that it is possible to predict problem-solving behavior, but I doubt whether a cognitive analysis has gone any further in that direction than an operant analysis, although the "idealized conditions" of the latter are a common target of criticism.

Scandura makes an appeal to structure that is typical of cognitive psychologists when they do not want to consider functional relations, and he says: "In effect, procedural complexity, corresponding to Skinner's rule-governed behavior, is transformed into structural complexity, corresponding to Skinner's contingency-shaped behavior. Given Skinner's lifelong emphasis on analyzing behavior qua behavior it is not surprising that he has overlooked this potentially fundamental relationship between the two types." But I submit that my analysis of the two types is much simpler and closer to the facts than Scandura's and that, quite apart from overlooking it, my paper was concerned with emphasizing it.

Rule-governed behavior in computational psychology

Edward P. Stabler, Jr.

Centre for Cognitive Science, University of Western Ontario, Canada

Skinner argues that psychologists who define learning as the acquisition of rules or as some other sort of symbolic process cannot take into account changes in behavior that result directly from reinforcement; they are forced to treat all cases of learning as if they were theoretically indistinguishable from the learning of rules and maxims in English or some other natural language. This is incorrect. Furthermore, none of the distinctions that Skinner mentions coincides with the distinction between rule-following and rule-governed behavior as it has been drawn in recent philosophy and psychology. This last distinction is clear in the "symbolic" or "representational" approaches but cannot be made out in a behaviorist program like Skinner's. I first quickly sketch a symbolic approach to learning that is not susceptible to Skinner's criticisms and then show how this account, unlike Skinner's, can make sense of the recent controversy about rule-conforming versus rule-governed behavior.

Skinner points out that a machine can be constructed to obey the instructions of a program, but he does not note that the mere fact that an instruction is encoded does not imply that it will ever be executed. The instruction might only be copied from one part of memory to another, for example, or it might just be printed out. Thus the machine cannot be seen as blindly executing every instruction in its memory; it will use the various symbols in its memory in various ways depending on the particulars of its operation. So all we can say is that the machine is built to execute an instruction only when it stands in a particular sort of relation to that instruction (or, more precisely, to a particular representation of that instruction). In human psychology, similarly, we assume that people are so constituted that they automatically follow rules only if and when they stand in a special sort of relation to them. There is nothing particularly problematic in this. The special relation might be brought about by consistent reinforcement of some behavior or by some other means. We want our psychology to provide a substantive account of this, just as Skinner wants a psychology that will provide a substantive account of how certain kinds of stimulation will reinforce behavior that depends on certain discriminative stimuli. As Dennett (1978b) has pointed out, it is easy enough to sketch out roughly how the respective accounts will go, but the real empirical support for these approaches will come from the formulation of detailed theories that can do some work in predicting and explaining the facts.

Skinner argues that "rule-governed behavior is in any case never exactly like the behavior shaped by contingencies." What Skinner points out is that behavior shaped directly by contingencies is not like behavior shaped by a rule or maxim expressed in English: Even when the behaviors are overtly similar, as in the case of an original verbal pronouncement and a pronouncement made according to instructions, "different controlling variables are necessarily involved"; "we. . .behave for different reasons." Of course this is true, but it poses absolutely no problem for the symbolic account of learning. Obviously, according to the representational account the causes of any particular behavior (like an utterance of some sentence) can involve relations to different symbolic states on different occasions, and these different causes may be differentially affected, so in Skinner's terms they would have different "controlling variables." The point is perfectly clear when any of the proposed examples are considered. It would be absurd to suppose that what one learns in the course of experience with financial matters is only some simple maxim like "a penny saved is a penny earned." And so of course behavior that results from blindly following the implicit recommendation of this maxim will differ from the (perhaps overtly similar) behavior of one experienced in financial matters. This is no obstacle to accounting for both as rule-governed behavior, since different rules would presumably be involved, and in any case they would certainly be rules that bore different sorts of relations to other material in memory, and consequently they would have "different controlling variables."

Another point to note in this connection is that it would be a mistake to suppose in general that the rules that are psychologically relevant will have a natural expression in English. Even the instructions of computing languages cannot be expressed in familiar English (though they might be expressible in the jargon of an English-speaking computer scientist); for example, some instructions deal with changing the states of particular, theoretically important internal states of the computing device.

So it is natural to suppose that at least some of the rules relevant to human psychology may be similarly removed from our pretheoretical vocabulary. This underlines the point that the rules governing a subject's behavior, like the rules governing a computing machine, need not be rules that can be expressed by the subject (or computing device); the subject need not be, and typically is not, aware of or able to report the rules guiding his behavior. Thus, not only the heart but also the mind has its reasons, which reason may never know, unless some clever psychologist discovers them.

So both sorts of cases that Skinner contrasts, his cases of "contingency-shaped" and "rule-governed" behavior, may be treated alike as rule-governed behavior with this approach; the cases are distinguished by what are, in effect, their "controlling variables." Not *all* behavior is to be treated as rule governed with this approach, though, and not all cases of what is pretheoretically regarded as learning are likely to turn out to involve the acquisition of new rules to govern behavior. For example, Skinner's case of the golf swing may turn out to be one in which the relevant adjustments in the behavior are not mediated by the acquisition of rules, and Chomsky (1969, pp. 154–55) suggests that learning to ride a bicycle may not involve rules. But in any case, in recent discussions the issue of whether or not a particular sort of behavior is rule governed concerns features of the causation of behavior that Skinner does not recognize. In this literature, behavior is said to be rule governed only if it is caused or guided by an actual representation of rules (Chomsky 1969; Fodor 1975). Obviously, this is just the sort of issue that is naturally framed within the symbolic or representational accounts of cognition, but it cannot make any sense in the behaviorist program.

According to the symbolic account, it is clearly an empirical question whether any particular sort of behavior is rule governed. Recent theory suggests that linguistic behavior is surely governed by rules, at least in part. There is controversy about whether the rules of grammars formulated by linguists play this governing role (Chomsky 1980b); Fodor, Bever & Garrett 1974; Stabler 1983), but there are no serious proposals about linguistic abilities that do not suppose that internally encoded representations are playing an important causal role. The hypothesis that behavior is rule governed is most plausible in cases in which the behavior is variable or "plastic" in a certain respect (Pylyshyn 1980).

One final point worth noting, since it concerns a central methodological strategy of recent cognitive psychology, is Skinner's curious suggestion that problem-solving strategies are not particularly relevant to psychology. He provides no good reason for adopting this view. When we discover that an organism is computing a certain sort of solution to a certain sort of problem, then it makes perfect sense to try to characterize precisely the sorts of computing systems that can perform that computation and to look for natural realizations of these systems in the organism. Work in low-level sensory processing seems to be a clear case in which this strategy has been used with some real success (e.g., Marr 1982; Ullman 1979); the strategy is also clearly at the foundation of a good deal of the recent work in cognition and some of that in neurophysiology as well (e.g., Arbib & Caplan 1979). The human child faces a problem of formidable proportions in attempting to become linguistically competent. There has been a good deal of fruitful investigation of how the child solves the problem (Wanner & Gleitman 1982). Human problem-solving strategies for more mundane, everyday sorts of problems are more difficult to untangle, but there has been much suggestive work even here (e.g., Nisbett & Ross 1980). Skinner's suggestion that the same strategies can be used equally well by any organism, machine, or social group is obviously incorrect, and one does not need to explore the depths of comparative psychology to discover this, although the digger wasp's ways of dealing with its reproductive tasks are a favorite example of clear limitations specific to a species (Woolridge 1963).

BFS: So far as I can tell, what Stabler characterizes as the "distinction between rule-following and rule-governed behavior as it has been drawn in recent philosophy and psychology" is the distinction between rule-governed (as I use the term) and contingency-shaped behavior. Philosophers and cognitive psychologists have insisted that the rules are *in* the contingencies (with the exception, according to Chomsky, of learning to ride a bicycle). The blacksmith who operates a bellows because of the effect the behavior has had on the fire is not following, being directed by, or governed by, a rule. But he can use a description of the effective contingencies (to strengthen his own effective behavior as well as to tell an apprentice what to do) as a rule. There were presumably no rules in the world prior to the evolution of verbal behavior; there were only orderly contingencies which shaped and maintained appropriate behavior. I not only note that "the mere fact that an instruction is encoded does not imply that it will ever be executed"; I repeatedly say that following a rule must be due to contingencies of reinforcement – though usually not the contingencies mentioned in the rule. These contingencies explain Stabler's assumption "that people are so constituted that they automatically follow rules only if and when they stand in a special sort of relation to them."

Stabler promises us a brief sketch of a symbolic approach to learning that is not susceptible to my criticisms. I am said not to recognize that behavior is rule governed only if it is caused or guided by an actual representation of rules. "This is just the sort of issue that is naturally framed within the symbolic or representational accounts of cognition, but it cannot make any sense in the behaviorist program." I should say rather that it does not make sense in any program. The "actual representation of rules" is at best an inference. It is a hypothetical current surrogate of a history of reinforcement. Among linguists and psycholinguists it may be true that "there are no serious proposals about linguistic abilities which do not suppose that internally encoded representations are playing an important causal role," but my own proposal (about linguistic *behavior*, not *abilities*) was serious and is taken seriously by an increasing number of people in the experimental analysis of behavior.

I do not see anything curious about my "suggestion that problem-solving strategies are not particularly relevant to psychology." They are part of the subject matter of psychology, not the science. If you express that subject matter in problem-solving terms ("the human child faces a problem of formidable proportions in attempting to become linguistically competent"), it may be true, but a behavioral account of the acquisition of verbal behavior is not necessarily an account of problem-solving strategies. I did not say that all strategies can be used equally well by any organism, machine, or social group. Machines can be designed to follow rules, and organisms and social groups can be taught to do so. Being changed by contingencies of reinforcement is another matter, and it comes within my definition of problem solving.

Operant analysis of problem solving: Answers to questions you probably don't want to ask

Robert J. Sternberg

Department of Psychology, Yale University

By now, it has become a commonplace that changes in paradigms for understanding scientific phenomena represent at least as much changes in the questions asked as changes in the answers proposed: If the answers change, it is in part because they are answers to questions no longer being asked. Nowhere has this commonplace been more striking to me, at least in the past several years, than in my reading of Skinner's piece on the operant analysis of problem solving.

When I first read the original version of "Problem Solving" as an undergraduate, I viewed it as an analysis to be refuted, at that time, by what I believed to be the white knight of information-processing psychology. On rereading the piece, my reaction was quite different. I think Skinner has provided an ingenious analysis of problem solving that just happens to address relatively few of the issues that I and many others view as our primary concerns today. This is not to say that our concerns are right and Skinner's wrong – simply that they are addressed to different aspects of the phenomena of problem solving. Consider, for example, Skinner's definition of induction as applying "whether the stimuli which evoke behavior appropriate to a set of contingencies are derived from an exposure to the contingencies or from inspection of the reinforcing system." This view may be correct, but it tells me little of what I want to know about induction: How do people decide to project certain regularities rather than others? What are the mental processes involved in the inductive "leap?" What kinds of strategies do individuals use to make inductive inferences? How do they decide upon these strategies? And so on. Skinner's definition of deduction is equally uninformative with respect to the questions I would most like for myself or someone else to answer.

Skinner not only does not answer the questions that interest me – he purposively dismisses or redefines them in a way that begs the questions that I hope to see answered. Thus, for example, he states that "to speak of the purpose of an act is simply to refer to its characteristic consequences," that "the motivating conditions (for machines and people alike) are irrelevant to the problem being solved," and perhaps most significantly, that "solving a problem is a behavioral event." I do not believe that goals can be subsumed by characteristic consequences, that motivation is irrelevant to the way in which a problem is posed or solved, or that an understanding of problem solving is possible without an understanding of the mental mechanisms that underlie observable behavior. Skinner's answers may well satisfy someone whose interest is purely in observables; they do not satisfy me.

Although this sense of irrelevance returned to me throughout my reading of his text, I did find Skinner dealing with questions that I think were often too quickly shoved aside in the first flush of enthusiasm with information-processing research. For example, Skinner shows quintessential sensitivity to the effects of the situation upon behavior; information-processing psychologists have often treated tasks as though they occur in isolation, without reference to a variety of situational constraints. Moreover, Skinner shows a concern with issues of learning that have often been ignored or explained away by information-processing psychologists, most recently, by claims that experts differ from novices in, it seems, little else but the knowledge they bring to bear on the problems they solve. Certainly it was their superior learning strategies that helped them acquire their enormous knowledge; I suspect Skinner would have more to say about how this learning took place than would those who start their analysis only after the learning has taken place.

Skinner's analysis of problem solving gives way, at the end of his paper, to a flight of speculation, one might even say fancy, regarding the social uses to which scientific knowledge of behavior can be put. Skinner believes that "social action based upon a scientific analysis of human behavior is much more likely to be humane...it can be *freed* of personal predilections and prejudices, it can be constantly tested against the facts, and it can steadily increase the competence with which we solve human problems." It is curious to compare this optimism of the 1960s regarding the social use of scientific knowledge to the pessimism and even cynicism that characterize the early 1980s. If we have learned anything in the almost two decades since this piece was first published, it is that scientific knowledge, like any other knowledge, can be used for social harm just as readily as it can be used for social good. It is difficult to be ingenuous in the 1980s regarding the undesirable, if not evil, uses to which scientific information about human behavior as well as about other things has been put. The very same information that can be used for good can be used for propaganda, brainwashing, racist quotas on immigration, and a host of other ills of our current society. If we come away from reading Skinner's article with anything, it perhaps should be a renewed remembrance of our capacity to cause, in the name of science, harm as well as good. We can never free ourselves of the burden of this fact.

BFS: I certainly did not intend to give an adequate account of induction or deduction, but I think I indicated the kind of terms in which an account could be written. It would have been better not to use the traditional terms. I have had trouble with a perhaps simpler issue: abstraction. Is abstraction one of the higher mental processes, or is it simply the result of verbal contingencies of reinforcement which alone can bring a response under the control of a single property of a stimulus? When one reviews the literature of the field of abstraction the latter definition seems ridiculously trivial, but I believe that it is one of the essential points about verbal behavior and its dependence upon reinforcement by a verbal community.

With the exception of a reference to those whose interest is purely in observables (a very much out-of-date definition of a behaviorist), I cannot take exception to the rest of Sternberg's paper. I myself am much more pessimistic about the future of the world than when I wrote "Problem Solving," but I still think that our only chance of solving our problems is to look at the variables of which our behavior is a function rather than at the mental events which serve as current surrogates of those variables. Science is no doubt being misused in many ways, but I believe that only science will save us if we are to be saved.

The egg revealed

William S. Verplanck

Department of Psychology, University of Tennessee at Knoxville

"I'm afraid you've got a bad egg, Mr. Jones."
"Oh no, my Lord, I assure you! Parts of it are excellent!"

"Problem Solving" needs either a brief and summary appraisal or an extended one – too long for the space likely to be allotted. Written lucidly and persuasively, it demonstates that Dr. Skinner can define and analyze a broad set of behaviors using a limited set of behavioral terms and concepts. Believers will find it convincing, even brilliant. Behaviorists who have worked on problem solving, who have observed their subjects carefully, and who have collected data analytically – especially those who have also labored to clarify the technical terminology of behaviorism operationally – will find it a good deal less than persuasive. Glib, superficial, and misleading are more appropriate terms. Closely argued and exemplified points are followed by one liners, such as: "But to speak of the purpose of an act is simply to refer to its characteristic consequences." *That* cannot survive critical examination.

The difficulties arise from two sources: First, the definitions of "stimulus," "reinforcement," and "contingencies" are so broad, so flexible, and so loosely used that they can be, and are, applied to anything whatsoever. More precisely defined, more unequivocally applicable behavioral concepts are required if they are to be used fruitfully. We are past the stage of talking about *Stoff*. We can distinguish among solid, liquid, and gaseous states. We need to start thinking at the level of elements and their properties in isolation and in compounds with others.

The second difficulty lies in the absence of a substrate of observational data that would require Skinner to write and think more realistically about his subject matter. When you know little of your topic but have thought about it a great deal without actually looking, then it is easy to analyze the area with broad beguiling strokes.

In the author's terminology, this paper is an excellent example of rule-governed behavior, but the rules are those of logic and grammar, applied to India-rubber concepts. They are not rules derived from the contingencies of reinforcement and of observation that function when a behaviorist carries out research on people faced with, and solving, problems.

Skinner is to be congratulated on his belated discovery that subjects must "construct" or find discriminative stimuli if they are to solve problems, and for his rediscovery of what I term "notates," "notants," and "monents" (Verplanck 1962). The distinction between "contingency-shaped" behaviors (conformances) and "rule-governed behaviors" (compliances) is appropriately drawn, although the former are inadequately described, and would seem to exclude imitating (contingency polished, perhaps, but not shaped), which often appears in problem solving, and cannot be excluded from either consideration or research by labeling it "innate" or "instinctive." Missing, too, is molding, or being "put through," which problem solvers often request. But perhaps these, too, are covered by the "contingency" tent.

The analysis, then, is incomplete, vague to the point of total imprecision and unfalsifiability. Hence it is not likely to discomfit "cognitive" psychologists, much less persuade them.

In sum, this is an exercise in the use of language. It is not a scientific contribution but an interpretive one, contributing little that is new (except to Skinner's own thinking); nor will it stimulate the research that will be needed if a less literary and more searching behavioral analysis of problem solving is to be done.

BFS: I agree with Verplanck that "Problem Solving" is not a scientific contribution. It is an interpretation, and that is all it pretends to be. The facts I report contribute "little that is new" – even in my own thinking.

I have dealt with the concept of purpose in greater detail in "Consequences," where, I think, it survives any "critical examination" that Verplanck has to offer. I thank Verplanck for his congratulations on my "belated discovery that subjects must 'construct' or find discriminative stimuli if they are to solve problems," but if he means my "rediscovery" of a paper of his written in 1962, I must add that the main point was covered (on pages 246–52) of my *Science and Human Behavior*, published in 1953.

Negation in Skinner's system

N. E. Wetherick

Department of Psychology, University of Aberdeen, Scotland

Skinner makes two very important points in "Problem Solving." One concerns the universality of problem-solving behaviour since "an exhaustive analysis of [problem solving] techniques would coincide with an analysis of behavior as a whole"; the other, the need to postulate two levels of responding (in the human case at least), one with responses shaped directly by the personal reinforcement history of the organism and the other with responses dependent on rules, maxims, laws of nature, and the like, which may have been derived from the reinforcement history of the organism or (via language) from that of some other organism or from someone's analysis of the reinforcement contingencies implicit in a given reinforcing system. Both points are widely accepted, except among experimental psychologists outside the Skinnerian tradition.

In my view, however, the evidence requires Skinner to go further in his analysis of the second level than he does, in order to accommodate the mammalian organism's capacity for negation. If he does so, however, his analysis appears to lose many of its distinctive features and becomes difficult to distinguish from the commonsense view.

I look first at behaviour near the lower end of the scale of complexity. Suppose (to adapt one of Skinner's own examples) that all apples are either sweet or sour but that in fact small apples are sweet and large ones sour, irrespective of colour. An organism might here learn that colour is irrelevant by eating red and green apples and finding that each colour was equally likely to prove reinforcing or aversive. Unfortunately most reinforcers are not linked in this direct fashion with an aversive property; more frequently the reinforcer is simply either present or absent. An organism can clearly learn from the presence of a reinforcer, but how does it learn from its absence? What is not present cannot function as a stimulus. It can hardly be that absence of a reinforcer makes a stimulus configuration aversive since then the majority of states of the real world would be aversive! The organism can only learn from the absence of a reinforcer if it has an expectation that the reinforcer will be present; thus, far from "expectancy" being "a gratuitous and dangerous assumption," it is a *necessary* assumption for organisms at or above the level of the rat. This is shown, for example, by observations of Bitterman (1975).

Bitterman presented a black and white discrimination in which black was reinforced 70% of the time and white, 30%. Submammalian organisms matched their responding to the probability of reinforcement and thus received 58% reinforcement ($0.7 \times 0.7 + 0.3 \times 0.3$). These organisms learned only from the presence of the reinforcer, and both black and white were sometimes reinforced; no expectancy need be postulated. Rats, however, learned to respond to black only and thus received 70% reinforcement. Response to white appears to have been extinguished because nonreinforcement was more frequent than reinforcement; the organism was therefore capable of learning from nonreinforcement which, I submit, requires the postulation of an expectancy. For an organism like the fish that finds its food by serendipity in the course of random movement, any stimulus that has ever been associated with reinforcement is worth investigation – but learning to search in some places and not in others, as the rat does, is a more efficient strategy.

Skinner asserts that behaviour at the other (human) end of the scale of complexity is often dependent on maxims, rules, laws of nature, and the like, and that such behaviour differs from behaviour directly dependent on the organism's own reinforcement history. It may, for example, be affected differently by drugs, but, more important, the probability of its occurrence remains undetermined, unlike that of behaviour shaped directly by reinforcement. However, in his view, behaviour is ultimately determined by a "set of contingencies of reinforcement," of which the rules form only part, so the principle of behavioural determinism is saved. This, in my view, raises a further difficulty. Suppose that a rule has been established by a psychologist as one governing the behaviour of a specified organism and that this organism becomes aware that the rule exists and governs its behaviour; can it not then, in principle, negate it? Often this may prove extremely difficult (e.g., if the rule governs a phobic response), and manipulation of the reinforcement contingencies may be required to break the link between stimulus and response. But in principle we can surely negate any rule at will. We are all acquainted with rules (of physics, physiology, etc.) that we only negate at our peril; nevertheless an individual under the influence of drugs will sometimes jump out of a high window in the conviction that the law of gravity does not apply to him. Surely we do also sometimes negate rules purporting to govern our behaviour? The mere fact that a psychologist is known to be predicting our behaviour may be sufficient to persuade us to do so.

It might be possible to maintain that knowledge of the fact that my behaviour is being predicted merely constitutes another element in the set of stimuli eliciting my behaviour and that the new set elicits behaviour opposite to that elicited by the old. But if I did not wish to offend the psychologist I *might* go on as before. The postulation of new stimulus sets for each hitherto unpredicted response begins to look more like metaphysics than science. I know of no ground for the assertion that, either directly or indirectly (via rules, etc.), *all* responses are *a priori given* as elicited by a set of stimuli, all that needs to be done being to enumerate the set. Indeed the assertion seems to me to be false since once any new set of stimuli has been enumerated the resulting rule can in its turn be negated by the organism to whom it is supposed to apply.

There is nothing mysterious about the capacity to negate. It is in continuity with a demonstrably useful capacity possessed by mammalian organisms down at least to the level of the rat. Whether or not we exercise the capacity in a particular case may be determined by factors newly perceived by us as relevant (in which case a post hoc Skinnerian analysis will be possible) or it may be determined by chance. Either way the resulting behaviour originates in us not in our stimulus environment. Much of the rest of our behaviour may also be presented post hoc as determined in the Skinnerian sense, but the analysis can be only contingently true – things might in principle have been otherwise.

BFS: There is a subtle error in saying, that an organism "learn[s] that colour is irrelevant." "Colour is irrelevant" is a partial description of the contingencies in Wetherick's example. When the organism learns, the contingencies do not pass into its head in the form of knowledge. The only observed fact is that contingencies in which color is irrelevant bring about no change in behavior with respect to color. When a sweet taste is contingent upon biting a red apple and a sour taste upon biting a green one, the organism does not "learn that red apples taste sweet and green apples sour" (that is a description of the contingencies); it simply continues to eat red apples and neglect or avoid green ones. A person would no doubt be "surprised" if a red apple then tasted sour, but not because of an expectation that it would taste sweet. A change has occurred in the contingencies, and the old behavior is maladaptive. Suppose now, that the person has simply been told that red apples taste sweet and green ones sour. A sour red apple would then change not only the future behavior of eating red apples but the person's tendency to respond to advice from a similar source.

I am sure that people learn not to follow rules when the consequences have that effect, including the consequences of messing up the experiment of someone who is "known to be predicting [your] behaviour." It is only because one assumes a "capacity" to negate that a change of this sort can be said to "originate in the individual." Capacities are ad hoc surrogates of probabilities of responding in given settings.

5 Behaviorism at fifty

Abstract: Each of us is uniquely subject to certain kinds of stimulation from a small part of the universe within our skins. Mentalistic psychologies insist that other kinds of events, lacking the physical dimensions of stimuli, are accessible to the owner of the skin within which they occur. One solution often regarded as behavioristic, granting the distinction between public and private events and ruling the latter out of consideration, has not been successful. A science of behavior must face the problem of privacy by dealing with events within the skin in their relation to behavior, without assuming they have a special nature or must be known in a special way.

The search for copies of the world within the body (e.g., the sensations and images of conscious content) has also had discouraging results. The organism does not create duplicates: Its seeing, hearing, smelling, and so on are forms of action rather than of reproduction. Seeing does not imply something seen. We know that when we dream of wolves, no wolves are actually there; it is harder to understand that not even representations of wolves are there.

Mentalistic formulations create mental way stations. Where experimental analyses examine the effects of variables on behavior, mentalistic psychologies deal first with their effects on inferred entities such as feelings or expectations and then with the effects of these entities on behavior. Mental states thus seem to bridge gaps between dependent and independent variables, and mentalistic interpretations are particularly attractive when these are separated by long time periods. The practice confuses the order of events and leads to unfinished causal accounts.

Behaviorism, with an accent on the last syllable, is not the scientific study of behavior but a philosophy of science concerned with the subject matter and methods of psychology. If psychology is a science of mental life – of the mind, of conscious experience – then it must develop and defend a special methodology, which it has not yet done successfully. If it is, on the other hand, a science of the behavior of organisms, human or otherwise, then it is part of biology, a natural science for which tested and highly successful methods are available. The basic issue is not the nature of the stuff of which the world is made, or whether it is made of one stuff or two, but rather the dimensions of the things studied by psychology and the methods relevant to them.

Mentalistic or psychic explanations of human behavior almost certainly originated in primitive animism. When a man dreamed of being at a distant place in spite of incontrovertible evidence that he had stayed in his bed, it was easy to conclude that some part of him had actually left his body. A particularly vivid memory or hallucination could be explained in the same way. The theory of an invisible, detachable self eventually proved useful for other purposes. It seemed to explain unexpected or abnormal episodes, even to the person behaving in an exceptional way because he was thus "possessed." It also served to explain the inexplicable. An organism as complex as man often seems to behave capriciously. It is tempting to attribute the visible behavior to another organism inside – to a little man or homunculus. The wishes of the little man become the acts of the man observed by his fellows. The inner idea is put into outer words. Inner feelings find outward expression. The explanation is satisfying, of course, only so long as the behavior of the homunculus need not be explained.

Primitive origins are not necessarily to be held against an explanatory principle, but the little man is still with us in relatively primitive form. He was the hero of a television program called "Gateways to the Mind," one of a series of educational films sponsored by Bell Telèphone Laboratories and written with the help of a distinguished panel of scientists. The viewer learned, from animated cartoons, that when a man's finger is pricked, electrical impulses resembling flashes of lightning run up the afferent nerves and appear on a television screen in the brain. The little man wakes up, sees the flashing screen, reaches out, and pulls a lever. More flashes of lightning go down the nerve to the muscles, which then contract, as the finger is pulled away from the threatening stimulus. The behavior of the homunculus was, of course, not explained. An explanation would presumably require another film. And it, in turn, another.

The same pattern of explanation is invoked when we are told that the behavior of a delinquent is the result of a disordered personality, or that the vagaries of a man under analysis are due to conflicts among his superego, ego, and id. Nor can we escape from primitive features by breaking the little man into pieces and dealing with his wishes, cognitions, motives, and so on, bit by bit. The objection is not that these things are mental but that they offer no real explanation and stand in the way of a more effective analysis.

It has been about 50 years since the behavioristic objection to this practice was first clearly stated, and it has been about 30 years since it has been very much discussed. A whole generation of psychologists has grown up without really coming into contact with the issue. Almost all current textbooks compromise: Rather than risk a loss of course adoptions, they define psychology as the science of behavior and mental life. Meanwhile the older view has continued to receive strong support from areas in which there has been no comparable attempt at methodological reform. During this period, however, an effective experimental science of behavior has emerged. Much of what it has discovered bears on the basic issue. A restatement of radical behaviorism would therefore seem to be in order.

Explaining the mind

A rough history of the idea is not hard to trace. An occasional phrase in classic Greek authors which seemed to foreshadow the point of view need not be taken seriously. We may also pass over the early bravado of a La Mettrie who could shock the philosophical bourgeoisie by asserting that man was only a machine. Nor were those who, for practical reasons, simply preferred to deal with behavior rather than with less accessible, but nevertheless acknowledged, mental activities close to what is meant by behaviorism today.

The entering wedge appears to have been Darwin's preoccupation with the continuity of species. In supporting the theory of evolution, it was important to show that man was not essentially different from the lower animals – that every human characteristic, including consciousness and reasoning powers, could be found in other species. Naturalists like Romanes began to collect stories which seemed to show that dogs, cats, elephants, and many other species were conscious and showed signs of reasoning. It was Lloyd Morgan, of course, who questioned this evidence with his Canon of Parsimony. Were there not other ways of accounting for what looked like signs of consciousness or rational powers? Thorndike's experiments, at the end of the 19th century, were in this vein. He showed that the behavior of a cat in escaping from a puzzle box might seem to show reasoning but could be explained instead as a result of simpler processes. Thorndike remained a mentalist, but he greatly advanced the objective study of behavior which had been attributed to mental processes.

The next step was inevitable: If evidence of consciousness and reasoning could be explained in other ways in animals, why not also in man? And in that case, what became of psychology as a science of mental life? It was John B. Watson who made the first clear, if rather noisy, proposal that psychology be regarded simply as a science of behavior. He was not in a very good position to defend the proposal. He had little scientific material to use in his reconstruction. He was forced to pad his textbook with discussions of the physiology of receptor systems and muscles, and with physiological theories which were at the time no more susceptible to proof than the mentalistic theories they were intended to replace. A need for "mediators" of behavior which might serve as objective alternatives to thought processes led him to emphasize subaudible speech. The notion was intriguing because one can usually observe oneself thinking in this way, but it was by no means an adequate or comprehensive explanation. He tangled with introspective psychologists by denying the existence of images. He may well have been acting in good faith, for it has been said that he himself did not have visual imagery, but his arguments caused unnecessary trouble. The relative importance of a genetic endowment in explaining behavior proved to be another disturbing digression.

All this made it easy to lose sight of the central argument – that behavior which seemed to be the product of mental activity could be explained in other ways. In any case, the introspectionists were prepared to challenge it. As late as 1883 Francis Galton could write: "Many persons, especially women and intelligent children, take pleasure in introspection, and strive their very best to explain their mental processes." But introspection was already being taken seriously. The concept of a science of mind in which mental events obeyed mental laws had led to the development of psychophysical methods and to the accumulation of facts which seemed to bar the extension of the principle of parsimony. What might hold for animals did not hold for men, because men could *see* their mental processes.

Curiously enough, part of the answer was supplied by the psychoanalysts, who insisted that although a man might be able to see some of his mental life, he could not see all of it. The kind of thoughts Freud called unconscious took place without the knowledge of the thinker. From an association, verbal slip, or dream, it could be shown that a person must have responded to a passing stimulus although he could not tell you that he had done so. More complex thought processes, including problem solving and verbal play, could also go on without the thinker's knowledge. Freud had devised, and he never abandoned faith in, one of the most elaborate mental apparatuses of all time. He nevertheless contributed to the behaviorist argument by showing that mental activity did not, at least, *require* consciousness. His proofs that thinking had occurred without introspective recognition were, indeed, clearly in the spirit of Lloyd Morgan. They were operational analyses of mental life – even though, for Freud, only the unconscious part of it. Experimental evidence pointing in the same direction soon began to accumulate.

But that was not the whole answer. What about the part of mental life which one can see? It is a difficult question, no matter what one's point of view, partly because it raises the question of what "seeing" means and partly because the events seen are private. The fact of privacy cannot, of course, be questioned. Each of us is in special contact with a small part of the universe enclosed within our own skin. To take a noncontroversial example, each is uniquely subject to certain kinds of proprioceptive and interoceptive stimulation. Though two people may in some sense be said to see the same light or hear the same sound, they cannot feel the same distension of a bile duct or the same bruised muscle. (When privacy is invaded with scientific instruments, the form of stimulation is changed; the scales read by the scientist are not the private events themselves.)

Mentalistic psychologists insist that there are other kinds of events uniquely accessible to the owner of the skin within which they occur which lack the physical dimensions of proprioceptive or interoceptive stimuli. They are as different from physical events as colors are from wavelengths of light. There are even better reasons, therefore, why two people cannot suffer each other's toothaches, recall each other's memories, or share each other's happiness. The importance assigned to this kind of world varies. For some, it is the only world there is. For others, it is the only part of the world which can be directly known. For still others, it is a special part of what can be known. In any case, the problem of how one knows about the subjective world of another must be faced. Apart from the question of what "knowing" means, the problem is one of accessibility.

Public and private events

One solution, often regarded as behavioristic, is to grant the distinction between public and private events, and rule the latter out of scientific consideration. This is a congenial solution for those to whom scientific truth is a matter of convention or agreement among observers. It is essentially the line taken by logical positivism and physical operationism. Hogben (1957) has redefined "behaviorist" in this spirit. The subtitle of his *Statistical Theory* is "An Examination of the Contemporary Crises in Statistical Theory from a Behaviorist Viewpoint," and this is amplified in the following way:

> The behaviorist, as I here use the term, does not deny the convenience of classifying *processes* as mental or material. He recognizes the distinction between personality and corpse: But he has not yet had the privilege of attending an identity parade in which human minds without bodies are by common recognition distinguishable from living human bodies without minds. Till then, he is content to discuss probability in the vocabulary of *events*, including audible or visibly recorded assertions of human beings as such.

The behavioristic position, so defined, is simply that of the publicist and "has no concern with structure and mechanism."

This point of view is often called operational, and it is significant that P. W. Bridgman's (1959) physical operationism could not save him from an extreme solipsism even within physical science itself. Though he insisted that he was not a solipsist, he was never able to reconcile seemingly public physical knowledge with the private world of the scientist. Applied to psychological problems, operationism has been no more successful. We may recognize the restrictions imposed by the operations through which we can know of the existence of properties of subjective events, but the operations cannot be identified with the events themselves. S. S. Stevens (1935) has applied Bridgman's principle to psychology, not to decide whether subjective events exist, but to determine the extent to which we can deal with them scientifically.

Behaviorists have from time to time examined the problem of privacy, and some of them have excluded so-called sensations, images, thought processes, and so on, from their deliberations. When they have done so not because such things do not exist but because they are out of reach of their methods, the charge is justified that they have neglected the facts of consciousness. The strategy is, however, quite unwise. It is particularly important that a science of behavior face the problem of privacy. It may do so without abandoning the basic position of behaviorism. Science often talks about things it cannot see or measure. When a man tosses a penny into the air, it must be assumed that he tosses the earth beneath him downward. It is quite out of the question to see or measure the effect on the earth, but an effect must be assumed for the sake of a consistent account. An adequate science of behavior must consider events taking place within the skin of the organism, not as physiological mediators of behavior but as part of behavior itself. It can deal with these events without assuming that they have any special nature or must be known in any special way. The skin is not that important as a boundary. Private and public events have the same kinds of physical dimensions.

Self-descriptive behavior

In the 50 years which have passed since a behavioristic philosophy was first stated, facts and principles bearing on the basic issues have steadily accumulated. For one thing, a scientific analysis of behavior has yielded a sort of empirical epistemology. The subject matter of a science of behavior includes the behavior of scientists and other knowers. The techniques available to such a science give an empirical theory of knowledge certain advantages over theories derived from philosophy and logic. The problem of privacy may be approached in a fresh direction by starting with behavior rather than with immediate experience. The strategy is certainly no more arbitrary or circular than the earlier practice, and it has a surprising result. Instead of concluding that man can know only his subjective experiences – that he is bound forever to his private world and that the external world is only a construct – a behavioral theory of knowledge suggests that it is the private world which, if not entirely unknowable, is at least not likely to be known well. The relations between organism and environment involved in knowing are of such a sort that the privacy of the world within the skin imposes more serious limitations on personal knowledge than on accessibility of that world to the scientist.

An organism learns to react discriminatively to the world around it under certain contingencies of reinforcement. Thus, a child learns to name a color correctly when a given response is reinforced in the presence of the color and extinguished in its absence. The verbal community may make the reinforcement of an extensive repertoire of responses contingent on subtle properties of colored stimuli. We have reason to believe that the child will not discriminate among colors – that he will not see two colors as different – until exposed to such contingencies. So far as we know, the same process of differential reinforcement is required if a child is to distinguish among the events occurring within his own skin.

Many contingencies involving private stimuli need not be arranged by a verbal community, for they follow from simple mechanical relations among stimuli, responses, and reinforcing consequences. The various motions which comprise turning a handspring, for example, are under the control of external and internal stimuli and are subject to external and internal reinforcing consequences. But the performer is not necessarily "aware" of the stimuli controlling his behavior, no matter how appropriate and skillful it may be. "Knowing" or "being aware of" what is happening in turning a handspring involves discriminative responses, such as naming or describing, which arise from contingencies necessarily arranged by a verbal environment. Such environments are common. The community is generally interested in what a person is doing, has done, or is planning to do, and why, and it arranges contingencies which generate verbal responses which name and describe the external and internal stimuli associated with these events. It challenges his verbal behavior by asking, "How do you know?" and the speaker answers, if at all, by describing some of the variables of which his verbal behavior was a function. The "awareness" resulting from all this is a social product.

In attempting to set up such a repertoire, however, the verbal community works under a severe handicap. It cannot always arrange the contingencies required for subtle discriminations. It cannot teach a child to call one pattern of private stimuli "diffidence" and another "embarrassment" as effectively as it teaches him to call one stimulus "red" and another "orange," for it cannot be sure of the presence or absence of the private patterns of stimuli appropriate to reinforcement or lack of reinforcement. Privacy thus causes trouble first of all for the verbal community. The individual suffers in turn. Because the community cannot reinforce self-descriptive responses consistently, a person cannot describe or otherwise "know" events occurring within his own skin as subtly and precisely as he knows events in the world at large.

There are, of course, differences between external and internal stimuli which are not mere differences in location. Proprioceptive and interoceptive stimuli may have a certain intimacy. They are likely to be especially familiar. They are very much with us: We cannot escape from a toothache as easily as from a deafening noise. They may well be of a special kind: The stimuli we feel in pride or sorrow may not closely resemble those we feel in sandpaper or satin. But this does not mean that they differ in physical status. In particular, it does not mean that they can be more easily or more directly known. What is particularly clear and familiar to the potential knower may be strange and distant to the verbal community responsible for his knowing.

Conscious content

What *are* the private events which, at least in a limited way, a man may come to respond to in ways we call knowing? Let us begin with the oldest and in many ways the most difficult kind, represented by "the stubborn fact of consciousness." What is happening when a person observes the conscious content of his mind, when he looks at his sensations or images? Western philosophy and science have been handicapped in answering these questions by an unfortunate metaphor. The Greeks could not explain how a man could have knowledge of something with which he was not in immediate contact. How could he know an object on the other side of the room, for example? Did he reach out and touch it with some sort of invisible probe? Or did he never actually come into contact with the object at all but only with a copy of it inside his body? Plato supported the copy theory with his metaphor of the cave. Perhaps a man never sees the real world at all but only shadows of it on the wall of the cave in which he is imprisoned. (The "shadows" may well have been the much more accurate copies of the outside world in a camera obscura. Did Plato know of a cave at the entrance of which a happy superposition of objects admitted only the thin pencils of light needed for a camera obscura?) Copies of the real world projected into the body could compose the experience which one directly knows. A similar theory could also explain how one can see objects which are "not really there," as in hallucinations, afterimages, and memories. Neither explanation is, of course, satisfactory. How a copy can arise at a distance is at least as puzzling as how a man can know an object at a distance. Seeing things which are not really there is no harder to explain than the occurrence of copies of things not there to be copied.

The search for copies of the world within the body, particularly in the nervous system, still goes on, but with discouraging results. If the retina could suddenly be developed, like a photographic plate, it would yield a poor picture. The nerve impulses in the optic tract must have an even more tenuous resemblance to "what is seen." The patterns of vibrations which strike our ear when we listen to music are quickly lost in transmission. The bodily reactions to substances tasted, smelled, and touched would scarcely qualify as faithful reproductions. These facts are discouraging for those who are looking for copies of the real world within the body, but they are fortunate for psychophysiology as a whole. At some point the organism must do more than create duplicates. It must see, hear, smell, and so on, and the seeing, hearing, and smelling must be forms of action rather than of reproduction. It must do some of the things it is differentially reinforced for doing when it learns to respond discriminatively. The sooner the pattern of the external world disappears after impinging on the organism, the sooner the organism may get on with these other functions.

The need for something beyond, and quite different from, copying is not widely understood. Suppose someone were to coat the occipital lobes of the brain with a special photographic emulsion which, when developed, yielded a reasonable copy of a current visual stimulus. In many quarters this would be regarded as a triumph in the physiology of vision. Yet nothing could be more disastrous, for we should have to start all over again and ask how the organism sees a picture in its occipital cortex, and we should now have much less of the brain available in which to seek an answer. It adds nothing to an explanation of how an organism reacts to a stimulus to trace the pattern of the stimulus into the body. It is most convenient for both organism and psychophysiologist if the external world is never copied – if the world we know is simply the world around us. The same may be said of theories according to which the brain interprets signals sent to it and in some sense reconstructs external stimuli. If the real world is, indeed, scrambled in transmission but later reconstructed in the brain, we must then start all over again and explain how the organism sees the reconstruction.

An adequate treatment at this point would require a thorough analysis of the behavior of seeing and of the conditions under which we see (to continue with vision as a convenient modality). It would be unwise to exaggerate our success to date. Discriminative visual behavior arises from contingencies involving external stimuli and overt responses, but possible private accompaniments must not be overlooked. Some of the consequences of such contingencies seem well established. It is usually easiest for us to see a friend when we are looking at him, because visual stimuli similar to those present when the behavior was acquired exert maximal control over the response. But mere visual stimulation is not enough; even after having been exposed to the necessary reinforcement, we may not see a friend who is present unless we have reason to do so. On the other hand, if the reasons are strong enough, we may see him in someone bearing only a superficial resemblance to him, or when no one like him is present at all. If conditions favor seeing something else, we may behave accordingly. If, on a hunting trip, it is important to see a deer, we may glance toward our friend at a distance, see him as a deer, and shoot.

It is not, however, seeing our friend which raises the question of conscious content but "seeing that we are seeing him." There are no natural contingencies for such behavior. We learn to see that we are seeing only because a verbal community arranges for us to do so. We usually acquire the behavior when we are under appropriate visual stimulation, but it does not follow that the thing seen must be present when we see that we are seeing it. The contingencies arranged by the verbal environment may set up self-descriptive responses describing the *behavior* of seeing even when the thing seen is not present.

If seeing does not require the presence of things seen, we need not be concerned about certain mental processes said to be involved in the construction of such things – images, memories, and dreams, for example. We may regard a dream not as a display of things seen by the dreamer but simply as the behavior of seeing. At no time during a daydream, for example, should we expect to find within the organism anything which corresponds to the external stimuli present when the dreamer first acquired the behavior in which he is now engaged. In simple recall we need not suppose that we wander through some storehouse of memory until we find an object which we then contemplate. Instead of assuming that we begin with a tendency to *recognize* such an object once it is found, it is simpler to assume that we begin with a tendency to *see* it. Techniques of self-management which facilitate recall – for example, the use of mnemonic devices – can be formulated as ways of strengthening behavior rather than of creating objects to be seen. Freud dramatized the issue with respect to dreaming when asleep in his concept of dreamwork – activity in which some part of the dreamer played the role of a theatrical producer while another part sat in the audience. If a dream is, indeed, something seen, then we must suppose that it is wrought as such, but if it is simply the behavior of seeing, the dreamwork may be dropped from the analysis. It took us a long time to understand that when we dreamed of a wolf, no wolf was actually there. It has taken us much longer to understand that not even a representation of a wolf is there.

Eye movements which appear to be associated with dreaming are in accord with this interpretation, since it is not likely that the dreamer is actually watching a dream on the undersides of his eyelids. When memories are aroused by electrical stimulation of the brain, as in the work of Wilder Penfield, it is also simpler to assume that it is the behavior of seeing, hearing, and so on which is aroused than that it is some copy of early environmental events which the subject then looks at or listens to. Behavior similar to the responses to the original events must be assumed in both cases – the subject sees or hears – but the reproduction of the events seen or heard is a needless complication. The familiar process of response chaining is available to account for the serial character of the behavior of remembering, but the serial linkage of stored experiences (suggesting engrams in the form of sound films) demands a new mechanism.

The heart of the behavioristic position on conscious experience may be summed up in this way: Seeing does not imply something seen. We acquire the behavior of seeing under stimulation from actual objects, but it may occur in the absence of these objects under the control of other variables. (So far as the world within the skin is concerned, it always occurs in the absence of such objects.) We also acquire the behavior of seeing-that-we-are-seeing when we are seeing actual objects, but it may occur in their absence, as well.

To question the reality or the nature of the things seen in conscious experience is not to question the value of introspective psychology or its methods. Current problems in sensation are mainly concerned with the physiological function of receptors and associated neural mechanisms. Problems in perception are, at the moment, less intimately related to specific mechanisms, but the trend appears to be in the same direction. So far as behavior is concerned, both sensation and perception can be analyzed as forms of stimulus control. The subject need not be regarded as observing or evaluating conscious experiences. Apparent anomalies of stimulus control which are now explained by appealing to a psychophysical relation or to the laws of perception can be studied in their own right. It is, after all, no real solution to attribute them to the slippage inherent in converting a physical stimulus into a subjective experience.

The experimental analysis of behavior has a little more to say on this subject. Its techniques have been extended to what might be called the psychophysics of lower organisms. Blough's (1956; Blough & Schrier 1963) adaptation of the Békésy technique – for example, in determining the spectral sensitivity of pigeons and monkeys – yields sensory data comparable with the reports of a trained observer. Herrnstein and van Sommers (1962) developed a procedure in which pigeons "bisect sensory intervals." It is tempting to describe these procedures by saying that investigators have found ways to get nonverbal organisms to describe their sensations. The fact is that a form of stimulus control has been investigated without using a repertoire of self-observation or, rather, by constructing a special repertoire the nature and origin of which are clearly understood. Rather than describe such experiments with the terminology of introspection, we can formulate them in their proper place in an experimental analysis. The behavior of the observer in the traditional psychophysical experiment can then be reinterpreted accordingly.

Mental way stations

So much for "conscious content," the classical problem in mentalistic philosophies. There are other mental states or processes to be taken into account. Moods, cognitions, and expectancies, for example, are also examined introspectively, and descriptions are used in psychological formulations. The conditions under which descriptive repertoires are set up are much less successfully controlled. Terms describing sensations and images are taught by manipulating discriminative stimuli – a relatively amenable class of variables. The remaining kinds of mental events are related to such operations as deprivation and satiation, emotional stimulation, and various schedules of reinforcement. The difficulties they present to the verbal community are suggested by the fact that there is no psychophysics of mental states of this sort. That fact has not inhibited their use in explanatory systems.

In an experimental analysis, the relation between a property of behavior and an operation performed upon the organism is studied directly. Traditional mentalistic formulations, however, emphasize certain way stations. Where an experimental analysis might examine the effect of punishment on behavior, a mentalistic psychology will be concerned first with the effect of punishment in generating feelings of anxiety and then with the effect of anxiety on behavior. The mental state seems to bridge the gap between dependent and independent variables, and a mentalistic interpretation is particularly attractive when these are separated by long periods of time – when, for example, the punishment occurs in childhood and the effect appears in the behavior of the adult.

The practice is widespread. In a demonstration experiment, a hungry pigeon was conditioned to turn around in a clockwise direction. A final, smoothly executed pattern of behavior was shaped by reinforcing successive approximations with food. Students who had watched the demonstration were asked to write an account of what they had seen. Their responses included the following: (i) the organism was conditioned to *expect* reinforcement for the right kind of behavior; (ii) the pigeon walked around, *hoping* that something would bring the food back again; (iii) the pigeon *observed* that a certain behavior seemed to produce a particular result; (iv) the pigeon *felt* that food would be given it because of its action; (v) the bird came to *associate* its action with the click of the food dispenser. The observed facts could be stated, respectively, as follows: (i) the organism was reinforced *when* its behavior was of a given kind; (ii) the pigeon walked around *until* the food container again appeared; (iii) a certain behavior *produced* a particular result; (iv) food was given to the pigeon *when* it acted in a given way; and (v) the click of the food dispenser was *temporally related* to the bird's action. These statements describe the contingencies of reinforcement. The expressions "expect," "hope," "observe," "feel," and "associate" go beyond them to identify effects on the pigeon. The effect actually observed was clear enough: The pigeon turned more skillfully and more frequently. But that was not the effect reported by the students. (If pressed, they would doubtless have said that the pigeon turned more skillfully and more frequently *because* it expected, hoped, and felt that if it did so food would appear.)

The events reported by the students were observed, if at all, in their own behavior. They were describing what *they* would have expected, felt, and hoped for under similar circumstances. But they were able to do so only because a verbal community had brought relevant terms under the control of certain stimuli, and this had been done when the community had access only to the kinds of public information available to the students in the demonstration. Whatever the students knew about themselves which permitted them to infer comparable events in the pigeon must have been learned from a verbal community which saw no more of their behavior than they had seen of the pigeon's. Private stimuli may have entered into the control of their self-descriptive repertoires, but the readiness with which they applied these repertoires to the pigeon indicates that external stimuli had remained important. The extraordinary strength of a mentalistic interpretation is really a sort of proof that, in describing a private way station, one is to a considerable extent making use of public information.

The mental way station is often accepted as a terminal datum, however. When a man must be trained to discriminate between different planes, ships, and so on, it is tempting to stop at the point at which he can be said to *identify* such objects. It is implied that if he can identify an object he can name it, label it, describe it, or act appropriately in some other way. In the training process he always behaves in one of these ways; no way station called "identification" appears in practice or need appear in theory. (Any discussion of the discriminative behavior generated by the verbal environment to permit a person to examine the content of his consciousness must be qualified accordingly.)

Cognitive theories stop at way stations where the mental action is usually somewhat more complex than identification. For example, a subject is said to *know* who and where he is, what something is, or what has happened or is going to happen, regardless of the forms of behavior through which this knowledge was set up or which may now testify to its existence. Similarly, in accounting for verbal behavior, a listener or reader is said to understand the *meaning* of a passage although the actual changes brought about by listening to or reading the passage are not specified. In the same way, schedules of reinforcement are sometimes studied simply for their effects on the *expectations* of the organism exposed to them, without discussion of the implied relation between expectation and action. Recall, inference, and reasoning may be formulated only to the point at which an experience is remembered or a conclusion is reached, behavioral manifestations being ignored. In practice the investigator always carries through to some response, if only a response of self-description.

On the other hand, mental states are often studied as causes of action. A speaker thinks of something to say before saying it, and this explains what he says, although the sources of his thoughts may not be examined. An unusual act is called "impulsive," without further inquiry into the origin of the unusual impulse. A behavioral maladjustment shows anxiety, but the source of the anxiety is neglected. One salivates upon seeing a lemon because it reminds one of a sour taste, but why it does so is not specified. The formulation leads directly to a technology based on the manipulation of mental states. To change a man's voting behavior we change his opinions, to induce him to act we strengthen his beliefs, to make him eat we make him feel hungry, to prevent wars we reduce warlike tensions in the minds of men, to effect psychotherapy we alter troublesome mental states, and so on. In practice, all these ways of changing a man's mind reduce to manipulating his environment, verbal or otherwise.

In many cases we can reconstruct a complete causal chain by identifying the mental state which is the effect of an environmental variable with the mental state which is the cause of action. But this is not always enough. In traditional mentalistic philosophies various things happen at the way station which alter the relation between the terminal events. The effect of the psychophysical function and the laws of perception in distorting the physical stimulus before it reaches the way station has already been mentioned in the discussion (see page 287). Once the mental state is reached, other effects are said to occur. Mental states alter each other. A painful memory may never affect behavior, or it may affect it an unexpected way if another mental state succeeds in repressing it. Conflicting variables may be reconciled before they have an effect on behavior if the subject engages in mental action called "making a decision." Dissonant cognitions generated by conflicting conditions of reinforcement will not be reflected in behavior if the subject can "persuade himself" that one condition was actually of a different magnitude or kind. These disturbances in simple causal linkages between environment and behavior can be formulated and studied experimentally as interactions among variables, but the possibility has not been fully exploited, and the effects still provide a formidable stronghold for mentalistic theories designed to bridge the gap between dependent and independent variables in the analysis of behavior.

Methodological objections

The behavioristic argument is nevertheless still valid. We may object, first, to the predilection for unfinished causal sequences. A disturbance in behavior is not explained by relating it to felt anxiety until the anxiety has in turn been explained. An action is not explained by attributing it to expectations until the expectations have in turn been accounted for. Complete causal sequences might, of course, include references to way stations, but the fact is that the way station generally interrupts the account in one direction or the other. For example, there must be thousands of instances in the psychoanalytic literature in which a thought or memory is said to have been relegated to the unconscious because it was painful or intolerable, but the percentage of instances in which even the most casual suggestion is offered as to why it was painful or intolerable must be very small. Perhaps explanations *could* have been offered, but the practice has discouraged the completion of the causal sequence. A second objection is that a preoccupation with mental way-stations burdens a science of behavior with all the problems raised by the limitations and inaccuracies of self-descriptive repertoires. We need not take the extreme position that mediating events or any data about them obtained through introspection must be ruled out of consideration, but we should certainly welcome other ways of treating the data more satisfactorily. Independent variables change the behaving organism, often in ways which persist for many years, and such changes affect subsequent behavior. The subject may be able to describe some of these intervening states in useful ways, either before or after they have affected behavior. On the other hand, behavior may be extensively modified by variables of which, and of the effect of which, the subject is never aware. So far as we know, self-descriptive responses do not alter controlling relationships. If a severe punishment is less effective than a mild one, this is not because it cannot be "kept in mind." (Certain behaviors involved in self-management, such as reviewing a history of punishment, may alter behavior, but they do so by introducing other variables rather than by changing a given relation.)

Perhaps the most serious objection concerns the order of events. Observation of one's own behavior necessarily follows the behavior. Responses which seem to be describing intervening states alone may embrace behavioral effects. "I am hungry" may describe, in part, the strength of the speaker's ongoing ingestive behavior. "I was hungrier than I thought" seems particularly to describe behavior rather than an intervening, possibly causal, state. More serious examples of a possibly mistaken order are to be found in theories of psychotherapy. Before asserting that the release of a repressed wish has a therapeutic effect on behavior, or that when one knows why he is neurotically ill he will recover, we should consider the plausible alternative that a change in behavior resulting from therapy has made it possible for the subject to recall a repressed wish or to understand his illness.

These attempts to short-circuit an experimental analysis can no longer be justified on grounds of expedience, and there are many reasons for abandoning them. Much remains to be done, however, before the facts to which they are currently applied can be said to be adequately understood. Behaviorism means more than a commitment to objective measurement. No entity or process which has any useful explanatory force is to be rejected on the ground that it is subjective or mental. The data which have made it important must, however, be studied and formulated in effective ways. The assignment is well within the scope of an experimental analysis of behavior, which thus offers a promising alternative to a commitment to pure description on the one hand and an appeal to mentalistic theories on the other.

POSTSCRIPT

My paper contains many instances of what one commentator noted as the "royal 'we.'" In a democratic country, perhaps we should say the "editorial 'we.'" For example, I speak of "the stimuli we feel in pride or sorrow," "we may not see a friend who is present," "We need not suppose that we wander through some storehouse of memory," "We learn to see things with ease, but it is hard to learn that we are seeing them," and so on. At times the "we" is presumably the behavioral scientist; at other times it is the behaving organism. Only in paraphrase is it some inner homunculus.

In *Science and Human Behavor* (1953) I developed the notion of a self as a repertoire of behavior. A given individual contains many selves, which may work together or in conflict. In self-control there is a set of controlling behaviors generated largely by society, which is concerned with suppressing the asocial effects of another self. The "we's" in "Behaviorism-50" are selves in this sense. I ask my readers to join me as observers looking at human behavior, as individuals reflecting upon their own behavior as it might be observed by a behavioral scientist, and so on. All these "we's" – all these selves – are to be interpreted as the product of explicit contingencies of reinforcement. Many are social; others arise from the nonsocial environment. The repertoires of scientists derive from both sources – from the materials they have observed and from what they have read or heard.

The following issues are, I think, to some extent clarified by this discussion:

1. The distinction between seeing and observing that one is seeing. (I agree that seeing that we are seeing is an unfortunate expression. The inner eye has a different structure.)
2. The distinction between representation and perception.
3. The distinction between contingency-shaped and rule-governed behavior. That was a central issue of "Problem Solving," but some broader implications are discussed in connection with "Behaviorism-50." A computational analysis of the relations prevailing among the elements in a given setting (of a sample space) looks like an analysis of thinking about that setting. But it is not an analysis; it is an example.

COMMENTARIES AND RESPONSES

A defense of ignorance

Jonathan E. Adler

Department of Philosophy, Brooklyn College, City University of New York

Professor Skinner promises that the "science of behavior" will be able to explain, albeit by reinterpreting, many of our mentalistic concepts, while doing away with such illusions as freedom. He is not, as many philosophers disposed to physicalism are, an *eliminativist* with regard to the mental (Dennett 1978b). Skinner also differs from these philosophers in that he urges the adoption of his austere science as a guide to understanding ourselves and designing our social institutions. Refusals to follow him are attributed to ignorance and antiscientific bias.

Although there is unclarity as to what aspects of our mental life will find a safe home in operant conditioning terms, it seems likely that concepts like resentment, anger, and love, which describe vast areas of human experience, will be preserved. P. F. Strawson (1968) groups these and related concepts together as "reactive attitudes" – attitudes we form in response to the actions of others toward ourselves. He argues that our reactive attitudes presuppose ascriptions of freedom, and that whatever the truth of hard determinism, it is inconceivable that our social life could survive the forsaking of our reactive attitudes.

Let us focus on anger, as one specific instance, though any of the other reactive attitudes could be substituted in the argument. When you are angry at someone for insulting you, evidence that the person did not act freely or responsibly undermines your anger. If you discover that the insult was unintentional, that the person was not in his right state, that he had been drinking too much, or whatever, then to varying degrees the lessened responsibility of that person lessens your anger *at* him.

It is not simply that the language of freedom permeates our explanations of the action of others. Rather, assumptions of freedom appear to be integrated into the very constitution of our understanding of the actions of ourselves and others. Thus, we cannot hope to preserve our reactive attitudes shorn of their connection to freedom. Although examples like the one above are the most convincing, it is also worth noting the judgmental components of our reactive attitudes – to be angry with someone for insulting you is to judge his action wrong.

There is a further kind of general threat to our reactive attitudes – one that Strawson unfortunately neglects – which involves our knowledge of something like the history of reinforcements under various contingencies. There is always some causal – environmental, genetic – history which, if heard, will weaken our reactive attitude to particular actions. The hard determinist's accounts of the antecedents of a person's actions seem forceful in diminishing our ascription of agency (Hospers 1958). However flawed they are as arguments, they nonetheless carry exculpatory force. Familiarity with such accounts, or with social scientific tracings of the roots of a particularly heinous criminal act, is widespread. So is the sense that these are apologies necessitating a reminder that "to explain is not to condone." The need for this litany is due, I suspect, to the fact that – as a matter of psychological response, at least – to explain in this way does indeed condone.

Thus I claim that the ubiquitous availability of such causal histories is well known, and second, that this knowledge sufficiently approximates an understanding of the mechanisms of conditioning to infer from our evaluation of the former to our judgment of the latter. Finally, I have intimated that the effect of such histories is always a flattening of reactive attitude.

The reasons for this flattening are complex. I would conjecture, though, that any account will find a conflict between the ascription of freedom and such detailed knowledge of the antecedents of action. In particular, such histories indicate an inevitability to an action – either in bringing us step-by-step to the particular event or in suggesting the many ways in which anyone else in similar circumstances would have acted similarly.

The final part of my argument is to observe that, though we know that such causal histories are always available, and though they do offer us a type of determinate knowledge for the action, we usually choose to ignore them. The anger I direct to the person who insulted me does not welcome – in fact, resents – various hints about why the person really acted that way.

This rejection is justified emotionally and morally by the very nature of the general threat to our emotional life and our moral sense. But it is also justified cognitively since the ready availability of such histories always leading to the same conclusion is informationally irrelevant; that is, without special reason we expect that they will tell us nothing new.

Of course the coexistence of general knowledge and its denial in specific instances shows a fragility in our reactive attitudes. We often do not know whether our refusal to hear more about why the person acted that way is dogmatic or reasonable. So our reactive attitudes can have the awkward qualities of staging and negotiation studied by sociologists like Goffman (1959).

To admit the problematic nature of our reactive attitudes in the face of our admitting the claims of an allegedly more scientific view is just to admit a tension and conflict that are themselves part of our social world. Any understanding of human behavior claiming completeness must accommodate this fact, not dismiss it.

The following conclusions emerge. There is little hope for a position between eliminativism and some mentalism. Eliminating freedom, while *attempting* to reduce other mentalistic language, fails its purpose. To simply accept freedom in some new behavioristically acceptable sense reduces the proposals to triviality. It is now what is mentalistically valued that dictates what is behavioristically accepted.

False is Skinner's reiterated claim that it is owing to ignorance that we reject radical behaviorism as a science of behavior and as a tool for setting social policy. The fact is, we often remain *willfully* ignorant of environmental determinants of specific actions just because we know and reject the general effect such an understanding appears to offer.

BFS: Adler brings up an excellent example of the distinction between a behavioristic and a mentalistic account. Strawson's (1968) "reactive attitudes" are personal possessions. Let us instead move outside, treating anger not as an attitude but as a tendency to attack, physically or verbally, a d to withhold reinforcers from those with whom we are angry. Many of the sources are no doubt genetic, having to do with the survival of the individual promoted by attacking, driving off, weakening, or killing enemies. Other sources are environmental – angry behavior often suppresses further damaging behavior in those with whom one is angry. None of this demands the "ascription of freedom" to those who harm us. It demands only that our measures will be effective in changing behavior. No judgmental component need be involved. We act not because others are wrong but because we are injured. All of this is made much more complex, of course, by the cultura practices with which the group controls angry behavior and by the possibly individual discovery of other ways of changing those who behave in harmful ways.

Our tendency to behave in angry ways and the circumstances under which we do so, of course, can be felt, described, and discussed, and a thorough survey of the behavior not only of those who harm us but of our own reactions may change what we feel in ways called "flattening."

Although I have no doubt accused those who reject radical behaviorism of not understanding it, I have explained its rejections precisely as Adler does. It requires that some cherished concepts be abandoned. That was the point of *Beyond Freedom and Dignity* (1971).

The fruitful metaphor, but a metaphor, nonetheless

Marc Belth

School of Education, Queens College, City University of New York

Behaviorism takes seeing as an act, thinking as an act, and the quest for truth as an act of finding or constructing. For modern science even objects in space are acts in various phases, some very rapid, some slowed down to a hover. When objects are complete, solid, and inert, it is because we have ceased to act, or have reduced that act to a state of inert receptivity. In short, the table is solid at the point at which I have ceased the act of exploring or penetrating into its inner dynamics. I no longer see the myriad molecules whirling around at varying rates of speed, and have allowed myself to behave like a camera, producing images at rest.

My report of this, however, is not altogether my own willful doing. My verbal community has reinforced me in this, and rewarded me for this splendid achievement.

Now, all of this is quite reasonable (I hesitate to say "true"), but there are a number of matters that I cannot seem to escape.

Arguments on behalf of behaviorism take on the character of religious zeal, and its disciples are so obdurate that they display a sense of outrage at any challenge. (Apparently this does not apply to Skinner, certainly not in the target essay, for Skinner seems to have avoided becoming his own disciple, much the way Freud and Marx declared themselves not Freudians and not Marxians when they read later extrapolations of their theories.)

It has long been known that science replaced religion when it demonstrated it had better access to "truth" than religion did. Thus, science replaced religious myths, beliefs in immaterial phenomena of a supernatural nature, spirits, ethereal "creatures," and the like. But its quest is borrowed from religion, and it replaces religious myths with its own mythic forms. The awesome truths of nature and of man remain its quest. And when they are found, we must submit to them with humility, quiver with respect, build new Pantheons to its priests. Only a pagan or an intellectual anarchist would be irreverent before its verities.

But the myths of science are transformed into metaphors and analogies, and it is these that we must be on guard against, for there is always the fear that they may come to be treated as realities. So metaphors and analogies are always called *mere*, more misleading than helpful, and we must destroy them when they are found, and replace them with genuine realities.

The trouble, however, is that people are at their best in this very pursuit when they are inventing those metaphors and analogies, for their capacities to act, to "see," depend upon the contexts created by them. The regions between the external world and "the world within the skin" which must be crossed if ever a unitary vision of human beings in nature is to be achieved, can only be bridged by analogies and metaphors. (An analogy is, after all, one among a number of types of metaphors.) People invent what they can only partially demonstrate to make this bridge between those worlds, and then they seek to demonstrate how this invention makes it possible to fit all the elements together into a whole. People's explanations, from this context, are also inventions, for they must posit the existence of what they either cannot see, or cannot, even in principle, ever see. Nevertheless, they sense that when they come upon a metaphor they must work to replace it as quickly as possible with some literal statement of observation.

And yet, to do away with metaphor is to do away with the organizing principle by means of which intellectual inventions are achieved. If a metaphor is ungainly, or unfortunate, awkward or misleading, people seem to be able to do nothing better than replace it with a more graceful, more fortunate, or more predictably heuristic metaphor which will bring together in a more consistent and harmonious way the momentary conclusions of the universe of experience and the universe of discourse. It is all right, for example, to be impatient with Neurath's (1970, p. 47) metaphor of philosophy as a ship whose planks are rotting, but which can be replaced only while the ship is afloat, unable to beach itself anywhere first to make the repairs. But impatience is no answer. Only a better metaphor would be. In this, behaviorism, either as a science or as a philosophy, finds itself in the same dilemma.

Privacy (of thought or of feeling) is, indeed, best understood when it is given public form. But to recognize that such privacies must take on physical dimensions, must be *given* physical dimensions, is to be at the point of inventing metaphors. I will, whatever I say next, be working with the form of "I 'see' *X* as *Y*." "I 'construe' *X* as *Y*." "I 'see' the content of the mind as a copy of external things" (unfortunate metaphor). "I 'see' the mind as comprised of a little man who is performing a series of mechanical activities on proper request" (even more unfortunate metaphor). "I 'see' private events as having the same physical dimensions as physical events" (fortunate metaphor).

This is not, in its propositional form, different from saying that "I 'see' this hard table as a swarm of molecules." or Socrates saying to Meno, when he had been offered a number of definitions of virtue: "I ask for one, and you give me a 'swarm of them'." Each of these is a good deal more, as Black (1962) has argued, than just ornamental speaking or writing.

But once I accept that fortunate metaphor, the remainder of my task is marked out for me. I must first assure myself that the metaphor is apt. (The procedures for this are much too extensive to present in this short commentary.) After that, my problem is to construct the completed picture out of the otherwise fragmentary data at hand until I have developed a causally complete picture which comes to be the explanation I am seeking – in this case, the explanation of human behavior, public and private. I must be sure to give an account, within this metaphor, of dreams, illusions, eye movements during sleep, visual errors; I must translate definitions of reality, meaning, evidence, organic functions, differences between levels and orders of living species into terms that are coherent with one another. If it sounds as if I am about the business of developing a metaphysic, on which my physical explanations rest, or, as Quine (1953) holds, an empirical epistemology, it is because that is what I am now doing.

Further, I must now take into account all of the lacunae, the inconsistencies, the ripples of disturbance that impinge upon me, but for which I have no name (being prepared to build a catachresis in such cases) until the metaphor has become accommodating to them. And when accommodation is no longer possible (as Kuhn 1970 has pointed out), I must be prepared to bolt or to revolt. At that point, the whole metaphor is thrown out and a new one is constructed that will do a better job organizing the whole mass of received agreements.

As congenial as I find the behaviorist metaphor to be, I am reasonably sure that it is not the ultimate metaphor. No metaphor ever is, except for those who have given up on the act of thinking.

It is undoubtedly a disturbing notion, this one, that all of our sciences are rooted in metaphor. For it does away with the premise of uncontrovertible truths, upon which we build, stone by stone, until a complete edifice of perfect truths is attained.

In sum, then, Skinner is about the business of positing a complete conceptual scheme, and fitting sensible data and data to which he *ascribes* physical status, prevailing theories, and fundamental concepts into a unitary model, from which all future behaviors can be described and explained. If there are claims being made for which he finds no place (intention, dignity, etc.), why, these are but lingering verbal vestiges of old superstitions, or decayed communities.

Now, the fact is that I may have misread Skinner altogether. I find that I often misread. And I discover, too, that I deliberately misread (though without too much embarrassment) because I already have a thesis in mind that *I* want to support. So I read into a present essay all the inadequacies I want it to have. My intentions are very clear, at least to me. When I am put to it, I can even develop interpretations of sections, phrases, sentences, whole paragraphs of that essay that will not altogether outrage the dictionary, though they may make it wince a bit. Moreover, I recognize that I do this to maintain the dignity of my resistance to behaviorist reductionism, and needless parsimony. (I sometimes think it is better identified as "miserliness" in the face of what we are able to say of the way we think about our thinking.) How is all of this to be explained in such reduced terms? Danto (1983) has commented that Skinner is a walking counterinstance against his own insistences. So, in fact, are we all, but not to be dismissed for all that. Bolter (1984) in his *Turing's Man* offers some tender insights even for the toughest of us of gain and loss in this mechanistic-turned-computer metaphor.

BFS: I assume that Belth will agree that the sentence "All of our sciences are rooted in metaphor" is itself a metaphor. In the sense that the settings in which we acquire language are never exactly repeated, all our verbal behavior shows some metaphorical extension, as I defined that expression in *Verbal Behavior* (1957), but in the nature of things, it is the best we can do. I agree that there are many problems about privacy and private events which have not been solved, by me or anyone, but I do not think that behaviorism has reached the point at which it must "bolt or revolt." It seems to me to be doing as well as any philosophy of human behavior with these difficult questions.

Skinner as conceptual analyst

Lawrence H. Davis

Department of Philosophy, University of Missouri–St. Louis

Skinner doubts that the inner events of ordinary mentalistic discourse have any explanatory role to play in a proper science of behavior. But he concedes their existence, and assumes a responsibility to explain what they are. What he calls "seeing," for example, is behavior. But he equivocates as to whether this "behavior" really occurs "within the skin," or is overt. (If the former, couldn't it properly be cited in – partial – explanation of introspective reports?) Taking him the first way, one can interpret his position as a form of philosophical functionalism (Block 1980c; Davis 1982). "Seeing" would then be defined as a state having such-and-such causal relations with sensory "inputs," behavioral "outputs," and other mental states. The residual truth in Skinner's dictum that "seeing is behavior" would lie in the fact that the sensory "input" is not itself part of the seeing. Seeing is a *reaction* of the organism *to* (visual) sensory input – and it is a reaction in the arena where beliefs, desires, and other mental items interact to determine behavior. Skinner is right that so long as the package of visual information – the "image," if you please – is still merely being transmitted or (re)constructed, seeing has not yet occurred.

At what point does "seeing" occur? I would say, not before the information becomes generally available for influencing the organism's beliefs and other mental goings-on. Jerry Fodor (1983) has recently defended a sharp distinction between "input systems" and "central processes." The former are "informationally encapsulated" and relatively inaccessible to the latter; the latter interact holistically in ways Fodor despairs of understanding. If this is correct, it strikingly corroborates Skinner's view that "trac[ing] the pattern of the stimulus into the body" is irrelevant to explaining what it is to see. The mental event of "seeing" is to be associated with the central processes. What happens in the visual input system is no more mental than what happens in the cornea.

How is "seeing" related to what Skinner calls "seeing that we see"? If the latter is also interpreted as a functionally defined state, the dominant impression emerging from Skinner's discussion is that it is a state distinct from and typically caused by "seeing." In turn, it can cause introspective remarks such as "I see my friend" and "As I see him now, he looks well." But in places Skinner's thought seems to be that "seeing that one sees," understood as an inner event, is *not* distinct from the "seeing" itself. In an organism that has undergone appropriate linguistic training, "seeing one's friend," for example, can cause introspective remarks directly. A distinct state of awareness or consciousness of the "seeing" need not be postulated. On this second interpretation, consciousness and its private objects are identical, not causally related – and certainly not related as are "seeing" and "thing seen." (Even on the first interpretation, it is misleading to view the relation as like that of "seeing" and "thing seen." I suppose Skinner is using the phrase "seeing that we see" ironically.)

Skinner should favor the second interpretation. It involves commitment to fewer inner events. Our linguistic community is ill-placed to have taught us to distinguish between distinct states of "seeing" and "seeing that we see." And it does not seem that we can distinguish them even in imagination. To understand this last point, note that if they are distinct states, we should be able to imagine one occurring in the absence of the other – as with a person who "sees that he sees his friend," but does not in fact "see his friend." Perhaps such a person will believe he sees his friend, say so, and describe his visual experience? But, by hypothesis, he does not see his friend, even in the sense we have been using, in which "seeing one's friend" is compatible with the absence of all visual stimuli. He will have no tendency to smile, say "Hi!," or behave in any other way that typically manifests sight of one's friend; with the sole exception of his introspective remarks, he will seem to have no visual beliefs about his friend. Shall we credit his claim to see his friend? Will he himself credit it, in the face of his other behavioral tendencies? The situation is anomalous. (Cf. Dennett's description, 1978a, p. 44, of the difficulty in surgically implanting in an only child the belief that he has a brother in Cleveland.) Eliminative materialists may say the anomaly bespeaks incoherence in the concepts of "seeing" and "seeing that one sees" (viz. conscious experience), which perforce should be banished from the domain of psychology. But the more cautious course is to conclude that an account of these concepts as other than coextensive (at least in us) cannot be motivated.

I have followed Skinner in supposing that consciousness arises from appropriate inguistic training, so I will conclude by pointing out that consciousness might exist in some nonlinguistic creatures. There are suggestions nowadays that our understanding of others as having mental states is at least partly innate, and so our understanding of our*selves* as having them might also be so. That is, maybe human infants have, or can develop, the capacity to "see that they see" without special linguistic training. And if that is conceivable, it is also conceivable that a nonlinguistic creature be born with, or develop, this capacity. Such a creature's seeing a predator, for example, would also be a case of its seeing that it sees a predator. What would make it so, given that this creature cannot manifest its alleged consciousness in linguistic communication with others? Well, in us, there is such a thing as silent thinking, and there could be something worthy of that name in some nonlinguistic creatures. If so, the creature could tell itself, so to speak, that it sees a predator. The main problem with this sort of speculation is in imagining what use the creature might have for the information, beyond its use for the information that a predator is present. Why would such an innate capacity for consciousness have evolved (cf. Dennett 1979, p. 171)? But there are possibilities worth exploring. Some kinds of self-control, for example, might be useful capacities to have, and require consciousness but not language. Skinner may have been right to regard consciousness as exclusively a product of linguistic training. But we do not know that, nor could he have known it when he wrote "Behaviorism at fifty."

BFS: Davis points to an important issue: Can a nonlinguistic creature be born with the capacity to see that it sees? Animals are "conscious" in the sense that they hear, see, and so on, and we may treat them compassionately because we believe that they feel pain. But do they see that they are seeing or know that they are feeling pain?

What happens when you first ask a boy, "Do you see that chair?" If the chair is conspicuous and if you point to it, there is little difference between that question and "Do you call that a chair?" But suppose the object is not clear. "Do you see the bird in that tree?" Under what conditions will the boy say yes? I believe that it depends upon what has followed the response in the past. I suggest that the boy will say yes if he is ready to answer other questions, such as, "What kind of bird is it?," "What color is it?," or "How big is it?" These are the kinds of questions which have been asked after he has reported seeing other things. I see (observe, believe, know) that I am seeing something if I can respond to it in other ways. I observe that it is exerting sensory control over my behavior.

Treading the primrose path of dalliance in psychology

B. A. Farrell

Corpus Christi College, University of Oxford, England

In his Herbert Spencer lecture at Oxford, Skinner – to use his own words – "railed" at "dalliance," and called on psychologists "to forsake the primrose path" which "diverted" them from the scientific study of behaviour (Skinner 1975b). The studies at which he is railing appear to include "information theory, cybernetics, systems analysis, mathematical models and cognitive psychology" (p. 64). Skinner accepts that the behavior of organisms "will eventually be described and explained by the anatomist and physiologist" (p. 59). Therefore, the neurophysiological study of behaviour is a legitimate enterprise. The only psychological enterprise that Skinner appears to accept as scientific, and therefore legitimate, is his "own speciality, the experimental analysis of behavior." He appears to express the same, or a similar, point of view in "Behaviorism-50" and other places (Skinner 1953; 1971). What reasons does Skinner produce in support of this view? And how good are they?

Skinner claims that it is the relation of the organism to the environment that is the important matter on which psychologists should concentrate. For it is environmental stimulation that controls the behaviour of the organism; and it is just this with which the psychologist is concerned in the experimental analysis of behaviour. But how does Skinner know that the environment has the very important, indeed exclusive, role he assigns to it? He asserts that "it was *the relation of the organism to the environment* that mattered in evolution." Similarly, it is the relation to the environment that matters in the "ontogeny of behaviour" (Skinner 1975b, p. 65).

This argument from analogy is very weak. No doubt the environment did matter in evolution. But to say this alone is utterly simplistic in view of what we know today about the important contributions made by the biological equipment of organisms. The environment was not the only thing that mattered, and it had the consequences it did via its interactions with the internal biological states and processes of organisms. If, therefore, Skinner is to rely on the analogy with evolution, he has to say the same about the ontogeny of behaviour. But to say this is to legitimize the study of internal states and processes in organisms, and to give up the claim that the experimental analysis of behaviour has a monopoly of virtue in psychology. In any case, however, even if the environment was very important in evolution, it does not follow at all that it is therefore also very important in the description and explanation of behaviour. It is quite possible that behaviour could turn out to be the outcome in large measure of the internal states of the organism, and only in some small degree the outcome of environmental stimulation.

But here Skinner would probably reply that this possibility is not realised in actual fact. For the experimental analysis of behaviour – by its use of operant concepts and methods – has shown that the behaviour of organisms is controlled in very subtle and complex ways by contingencies of reinforcement. This has been shown for behaviours over a sufficiently wide front to constitute a considerable advance in the scientific study of behaviour – an advance that gives us sufficient grounds to believe that the same is true over the whole behavioural front – hence the importance of the environment for psychology, and the unimportance, indeed the irrelevance, of the supposed internal states of the organism.

This probable reply from Skinner is very weak, for most psychologists would simply deny that contingencies of reinforcement, and related generalizations, have been established over a sufficiently wide range of functioning for Skinner's argument to hold. After all, there do seem to be very large ostensible differences between the feeding behaviour of a pigeon and the verbal behaviour of, say, Skinner himself. So we have good reason to doubt whether Skinner is justified in generalizing – as confidently as he does – from the pecking behaviour of pigeons, the (apparently) successful treatment of some disorders by operant methods, and the like, to *all* behaviours whatever. At this point it is natural for psychologists to claim that they can only get at the complexities of function involved in attention, perception, memory, emotional conflicts, and the rest, by *not* confining themselves to the experimental analysis of behaviour; and by going on to use other scientific methods to explore the roles played by the internal states of the individual.

Skinner objects to this natural move in his second chief reason for "railing" at branches of psychology other than his own. He maintains that they suffer from a "diverting preoccupation with a supposed or real inner life." Ordinary people, with their "feelings," "thoughts," and so on, or the introspective psychologist or model builder do not explain behaviour, and cannot do so. For the inner determiners (or "mental way stations") they refer to have themselves to be explained. Skinner implies that such explanation can never logically be forthcoming – hence the futility of turning to the internal states of the individual.

This argument will not do either. Broadbent (1958) explained certain behaviours of his naval ratings as revealing and being due (in part) to their "limited channel capacity." If Skinner asks, "How can this inner determiner be explained?," Broadbent has a knock-down answer: "We are built in this way, and this fact is open in turn to further explanation." Obviously, what Skinner is up to here is simply to *presuppose* that the *only* legitimate type of explanation is that which specifies the controlling stimulus. And this begs the whole issue in his favour. Skinner's strictures may have applied to traditional introspective psychology. But they do not apply to contemporary studies of the man beneath the skin.

What is more, Skinner's argument lays him wide open to a countercharge: It is *his* program that cannot do much to explain behaviour. At most it can explain by reference to a history of reinforcement. But his regularities leave it unexplained how the controlling stimulus issues in the behaviour in question. Moreover, if Jones knows how to play chess and Smith does not, and we ask for an explanation of this difference, it is *not sufficient* to resort to a history of reinforcement and the different behaviours Jones and Smith will exhibit *if* confronted by a chessboard and pieces. For we *also* want to be told what it is about Jones *here and now* that makes him different from Smith. Skinner cannot logically tell us. Worst of all, it is difficult to see how he can explain the very regularities that operant work has itself uncovered. For example, can he explain the relative effectiveness of intermittent reinforcement? Presumably he can only do so by reference to the machinery of the organism and to models of it.

So Skinner's case for railing at other branches of psychology is not justified. Moreover, it is inappropriate and invites ridicule. Naturally, he is concerned to emphasise the present-day importance of operant psychology. I have the impression, however, that contemporary psychologists appreciate very well the present-day role of operant concepts and methods. They appreciate that these are indispensable in certain areas, and complementary to, and in need of supplementation by, work in other branches of the subject. Therefore, in railing at these other branches, Skinner is behaving in a way that is logically and practically unfortunate. He is tilting at windmills – windmills that, I suspect, are conjured into being by his own narrow and inadequate view of the nature of science.

BFS: It is a given organism at a given moment that behaves, and it behaves because of its "biological equipment" at that moment. Eventually neurology will tell us all we need to know about the equipment. Until then we can do other things:

1. So far as possible, we can trace the origins of the equipment. The behavior we observe at a given moment is a product of a possibly long process of selection by consequences. The theory of evolution, now powerfully supported by genetics, is part of the story; the experimental analysis of individual behavior is another part.
2. We can try to observe the biological equipment directly – by introspection (for limitations on introspection, see "Terms").

3. We can infer states and processes from the behavior, applying information theory, building models, and so on.

I have argued that the second and third courses of action have shown more promise than achievement. We do not observe thought processes directly; we observe only the occasions and the results, because we have no sensory nervous systems going to the structures involved. Introspection is a social product that arose long after the pattern of the nervous system had been laid down and it was laid down for other reasons. Inferences from current behavior cannot be legitimately used to explain the same behavior. Broadbent's (1958) limited channel capacity is an example; what evidence for overloading have we except the facts which the concept is used to explain? Information processing was devised for, and is useful in formulating, systems which are not analogous to the human organism. That some copy of the contingencies is taken into the organism to be used at a later date is a fundamental "cognitive" mistake. Organisms do not store the phylogenic or ontogenic contingencies to which they are exposed; they are changed by them.

Undifferentiated and "mote–beam" percepts in Watsonian–Skinnerian behaviorism

John J. Furedy and Diane M. Riley

Department of Psychology, University of Toronto (JJF) and Addiction Research Foundation, Toronto, Ontario, Canada (DMR)

Behaviorism, like most influential "isms," requires qualification by proper names to differentiate between its many forms. The behaviorism whose 50th birthday was celebrated in the target article is obviously different from the approaches of other behaviorists such as Hull (who used beneath-the-skin, internal hypothetical explanatory constructs) and Tolman (who was both mentalistic and teleological in his approach). Watsonian–Skinnerian behaviorism is radical in its rejection of many of the assumptions of approaches such as those of Hull and Tolman. That is, radical behaviorism not only rejects teleological explanations, it also rejects "internal" hypothetical constructs, especially mentalism. However, approaches that seek to cleanse us root and branch tend to offer judgments that are undifferentiated in that there is no attention paid to some critical distinctions. Another feature of such approaches is that the flaws that appear writ large in the opposition are ignored in the favored approach; this selectivity results in (in reference to the biblical phrase) "mote–beam" percepts. We briefly discuss two undifferentiated distinctions. The first is between teleological and mechanistic mentalism, the second between knowledge and ability. Finally, a case of "mote–beam" perception of explanatory circularity is presented.

Regarding mentalism, it is true that in an approach such as that of Tolman, there was a link between teleology (the inclusion of purpose as an intervening variable) and mental events (the inclusion of the concept of the cognitive map as an intervening variable). The link between teleology and mentalism, however, is historical rather than logical. Instances of mechanistic (ateleological) mentalist positions are available even from Tolman's era (see, e.g., the attack on teleology in the concept of homeostasis by Maze 1953). Moreover, many current cognitive experimental psychologists are not teleological inasmuch as their basic analogy – the computer – does not involve purposes but only mechanistically determined programs. Finally, specific issues under current investigation involve examining a form of cognitivism that is not teleological but mechanistic. For example, the claim that awareness of the CS–US relationship is necessary, but not sufficient, for autonomic conditioning (see, e.g., Dawson 1973; Dawson & Furedy 1976; Furedy 1973) is a position that involves no talk of purposes whatsoever.

Skinner's "Behaviorism-50" does not appear to make this important distinction between teleology and mentalism. For example, in the discussion of "mental way stations," the account of the student explanations or "responses" lumps together the mechanistic and teleological forms of mentalism, in that it does not differentiate between explanations in terms of the organism's mechanistic knowledge and its purposive intentions. It bears emphasis that, especially because Skinner's main charge against mentalism is that its explanatory constructs are circular, the distinction between teleological and mechanistic mentalism is of more than mere scholastic significance. Teleogical concepts have a built-in circularity as explanations, because any contrary-to-prediction outcome can be explained away as a result of a change in purpose of the (implicit) agent (see, e.g., Maze 1953).

This is not to imply that mentalism when used in explanations is without problems – numerous difficulties arise over issues such as the nature of representation. However, these problems are not as intractable as those of teleological explanations. The problem with ateleological, mentalist explanations is that they appear to be less parsimonious than those of radical behaviorism. However, to the extent that one seeks to account for what complexly occurs, it is necessary to recognize that the feeling of striving appears to be a real feature of human mental activity. This feature then requires explanation, rather than excision by Ockham's razor. And the ateleological mentalist would argue that such explanation has the virtue of providing some account of events that do, in fact, occur. By analogy, and related to Skinner's discussion of representation, it may seem more parsimonious to explain moving pictures in terms only of the events that are actually visible on the screen, and to dismiss references to movie projectors as constituting unnecessary mysticism. However, in terms of the way things, in their complexity, are, accounts of the process that include reference to movie projectors are more appropriate, because they are more accurate. Such accounts are more complex than those of the radical-behaviorist form, and may require reference to "a new mechanism," but this is because the phenomena require it, and not just because theorists do.

The other distinction that the target article appears to neglect is that between knowing propositions and having the ability to perform responses, or knowing that and "knowing" (in quotes, because, strictly speaking, only propositions can be known) how (Ryle 1949). The running together of this distinction occurs most obviously in Skinner's discussion of the acrobat. In this account, it is suggested that not only the performance (handsprings) but also the account of that performance (propositions concerning the important actions needed to produce successful performance) are all responses, the latter sort of expressions being "verbal responses" which "arise from contingencies...arranged by a verbal community." However, on this account, we would not be able to discriminate between so-called verbal responses that state false propositions (i.e., a champion handspringer who, however, is a poor coach inasmuch as he is cognitively unaware of the nature of good handspringing) and those that state true ones (i.e., one who can cognitively teach as well as produce correct performance responses). The reason this discrimination cannot be made is because responses are not propositional, being expressions that it would be a "category mistake" (Ryle 1949) to speak of as either true or false (see also Furedy & Riley 1982; Furedy, Riley & Fredrikson 1983). In Ryle's terms, knowing that and knowing how are different processes, and neither can be reduced to the other without a serious loss of the ability to make factually, and therefore scientifically, relevant distinctions.

Concerning the "mote–beam" perception of circularity in explanatory concepts, we have already noted that "Behaviorism-50" roundly condemns positions opposed to radical, Watsonian–Skinnerian behaviorism for such concepts, and therefore charges their theories with being untestable. "Mentalism," with its "way stations," is portrayed as the main villain in the piece, but behaviorisms like those of Hull would also be suspect, because they make use of internal, within-the-skin constructs instead of sticking to the presumably noncircular external, environmental concepts like various "schedules of reinforcement," the "verbal environment," and past reinforcement history.

Because in the target article the focus is on mentalism rather than nonradical behaviorist systems, we restrict the discussion to the comparison between mentalism and radical behaviorism. The circularity in mentalism is less problematic or more motelike than Skinner would have it, because, as indicated above, it is only in the teleological form of mentalism that circularity is inherent in the explanations, and the theory is hence untestable. The beamlike perception, we suggest, is due to a commonly made error of not recognizing the teleological-mechanistic distinction (discussed above) in the unfavored mentalist camp and that at least some mentalist accounts are not teleological but mechanistic.

On the other hand, radical behaviorists have continued to appear quite insensitive to the beam of circularity in their own eyes when it comes to explanations. The point is that, contrary to certain metaphysical prejudices, circularity is determined not by the "stuff" of which the explanatory concept is made, but by the extent to which theorists specify their explanatory constructs so that they can be assessed independently of the effects they are supposed to explain. So the gravity and libido constructs are equally intangible, but gravity theory is more testable than the Freudian libido theory. The former theory (asserting that all physical objects are influenced by gravity) is vulnerable to specifiable, disconfirming events such as hovering 10 feet above the ground without any mechanical aids in a way that the latter theory (asserting that all human behavior is influenced by the sex drive) is not, because there is no specifiable behavior that would, if it did occur, falsify the libido hypothesis. This is because Freudian theory has constructs like "repression" in it that are not specifiable independently of the (apparently asexual) behavior that they, in conjunction with the libido, are taken to explain.

However, the environmental, "tangible" constructs used in "Behaviorism-50" appear to be no more adequately specified than the libido and repression. What behavioral outcome would it take to produce a disconfirmation of the explanatory concept of "various reinforcement schedules"? Again, is there any conceivable verbal utterance that would, if it did occur, require Skinner to give up the radically environmentalist explanation that the utterance was caused by "the verbal community"? To the extent that no such outcomes (even were they to be hypothetical rather than actual) can be specified, it would seem that the circularity in the eye of radical behaviorism's modes of explanation is, indeed, beamlike in proportions.

In discussing the problem of circularity, we have deliberately used the scientifically low-status Freudian system. Our reason for doing so is to reinforce our contention (not argued for in detail here) that the problem of explanatory circularity must be dealt with by adequately specifying the explanatory constructs, rather than by thinking that a move from internal to external referents is sufficient for the task.

BFS: The teleological side of Furedy and Riley's commentary could have found a more appropriate place in "Consequences." What they call mecha-

nism seems to be the current state of the organism described in the language of physics and biology. The organism behaves as it does because of its present state. What they find missing is intentionality. Others might have spoken of purpose, expectation, and anticipation. These are not aspects of the present state of the organism but of its selective phylogenic and ontogenic history. Behavior seems to be directed toward future consequences, but only because it is a product of past consequences. The hand is not made for the purpose of holding things; it has evolved in a given way because it has held things well. A boy does not go to the cookie jar with the purpose of getting a cookie; he goes because he has got cookies in the past. (If he goes because he has been told that there are cookies there, a different set of selective contingencies must be invoked, as discussed in "Problem Solving." The contingencies will be much more complex but nevertheless only contingencies.)

In common use, knowledge refers to a personal possession resulting from exposure to environmental contingencies. To use it only for propositions is in violation of tradition and common sense. Most people would say that a boy who learns to ride a bicycle well knows how to ride. But does he possess knowledge or has his behavior simply been well shaped by the contingencies maintained by a bicycle? When a hungry rat presses a lever, receives food, and as a result presses the lever more rapidly, many cognitive psychologists say that it has "learned (and hence knows) that pressing the lever brings food." "Pressing the lever brings food" is a description of the contingencies. Somehow or other a version is said to pass into the head of the rat. A human subject could, of course, describe the contingencies and know them in the sense in which a person knows a poem.

Has anyone shown that there is an advantage in creating these internal simulacra of environmental contingencies? We "impart knowledge" through environmental means. We test for its existence through environmental measures. We determine its essential properties by examining what the supposed possessor does. If there is any circularity it is in the eye of the cognitive psychologist, as a hypothetical internal knowledge inferred from behavior is used to explain the behavior.

Consciousness, explanation, and the verbal community

Gordon G. Gallup, Jr.

Department of Psychology, State University of New York, Albany

Skinner uses the terms "explanation," "explain," or "explanatory" almost 30 times in "Behaviorism-50." He asserts that mental events "offer no real explanation and stand in the way of a more effective analysis," but at no point is the reader told what would constitute an adequate explanation.

Skinner argues correctly that "a disturbance in behavior is not explained by relating it to felt anxiety until the anxiety has in turn been explained." But, by the same token, a change in behavior is not explained by relating it to reinforcement until reinforcement has been explained. What do all reinforcers have in common, aside from the effect they produce on behavior? What makes a reinforcing stimulus reinforcing? Until reinforcement has been defined independently of the behavior it is supposed to explain, an "experimental analysis of behavior" begs the question of explanation.

Skinner manages to beg other questions as well. He contends that consciousness is a by-product of language. According to him "we learn to see that we are seeing only because a verbal community arranges for us to do so," and "knowing" is a consequence of the verbal community. But, does that mean that prior to the advent of language humans were unconscious? Are all nonhuman species unconscious? At what point during the emergence of language did we become conscious? How did verbal communities ever acquire conscious knowledge in the first place? Since Skinner feels that "there are no natural contingencies for such behavior," either language is not governed by natural contingencies or it fails to provide an adequate account of consciousness.

We now know that, in stark contrast with Skinner's position, chimpanzees, lacking the benefit of a verbal community, are aware of being aware in pretty much the same sense as you or I, as evidenced by their ability to use their experience to model the experience of others (e.g., Premack & Woodruff 1978; de Waal 1982).

In the last analysis the question of consciousness and mental events is a question of evidence. I have recently developed a conceptual framework and methodology for dealing with these issues in animals at an empirical level, and the data show that consciousness may be a by-product of reproductive rather than environmental contingencies (Gallup 1983).

It seems to me that the real advantage of cognitive interpretations of behavior is that they can have heuristic value.

BFS: Why should a reinforcer have to be defined independently of the behavior it is supposed to explain" ? I teach my nine-month-old daughter to raise her hand by turning a table lamp on and off whenever she makes a series of gradually more extensive movements. Do I need independent evidence that the light is a reinforcer? To explain *why* it is a reinforcer I must look to the evolution of the species. It is reasonable to assume that the species gained an advantage when, through some variation, changes worked in the environment by its behavior began to strengthen that behavior. I suppose that food is reinforcing to a hungry organism for a similar reason. I do not think it reinforces because it is "drive reducing." It has been important for organisms to be reinforced by food when hungry. (Why most foods are reinforcing only when the organism is hungry must be explained by further evolutionary advantages. Eating regardless of hunger would cause trouble.)

I believe that all nonhuman species are conscious in the sense in which the word conscious is being used here, as were all humans prior to the acquisition of verbal behavior. They see, hear, feel, and so on, but they do not observe that they are doing so. I believe I have given a reasonable explanation of why a verbal community asks the individual such questions as "What are you doing?," "Do you see that?," "What are you going to do?,' and so on, and thus supplies the contingencies for the self-descriptive behavior that is at the heart of a different kind of awareness or consciousness

I have not seen any behavior that resembles this in chimpanzees, though it is conceivable.

The heuristic value of an interpretation is to be judged by the *quality* of the theory and research to which it leads. I believe that cognitive interpretations have burdened the literature with an immense amount of useless data.

In search of a theory of learning

Alison Gopnik

Department of Psychology and Linguistics, University of Toronto, Canada

Most of the points Skinner raises in "Behaviorism-50" seem curiously irrelevant to the concerns of modern mentalistic psychologists. In particular, the distinctions Skinner draws between "private" and "public" events and between "representation" and "action" don't really apply to contemporary theories. The mental entities proposed by these theories are not private experiences with some special epistemological status. They are not even "unconscious" or "repressed" versions of such experiences. No one supposes that people have privileged, private, direct experiences of phonemes, object-permanence rules, or semantic networks. These are theoretical constructs designed to explain a variety of different kinds of evidence, primarily behavioral evidence. They never have been and probably never could be directly experienced. The distinction between private and public events does present interesting philosophical problems, but they don't impinge on our construction of mentalistic psychological theories.

Similarly, the distinction between representation and action seems irrelevant to modern theories, particularly theories that employ the computational metaphor. A set of instructions to print a series of dots may be a representation of an object in the same way that a photograph or a picture is a representation. We can move back and forth with ease between representations that are phrased in terms of entities and representations that are phrased in terms of instructions for action.

Moreover, we needn't prefer representations that are phrased in terms of action simply because we want to explain human action. We don't necessarily need to explain actions in terms of actions or even in terms of dispositions to act. If we wanted to explain how a computer performed a certain calculation we would talk in terms of actions (it added) and in terms of entities (it doubled the sum of the addition). We choose the description that accounts for the greatest variety of evidence in the most economical way, not the description that resembles the evidence most closely.

The one part of Skinner's argument that does seem relevant to contemporary concerns is his claim that mentalistic accounts don't provide a complete causal explanation of behavior. This claim reflects a genuine and important problem in psychology. Mentalistic theories have provided us with clear and interesting accounts of what our mental structures are like and how they are related to our behavior. They have not provided an account of the genesis of those structures. We have almost no idea how human beings construct the concepts, rules, and beliefs that underlie their behavior. Skinner is quite right in claiming that this is a serious flaw in mentalistic accounts.

It is tempting to try to fill this gap in our knowledge. And it is particularly tempting when we discover that a theory can explain *some* kind of behavioral development, even if it doesn't directly explain human cognitive development. When Skinner discovered that principles of operant conditioning could explain how pigeons learn to peck levers it was tempting to apply those principles to humans learning language. Similarly, Chomsky (1980b) takes the fact that behavioral changes like learning to walk or fly are the consequences of maturation and tries to apply this principle to humans learning language. Scientists, particularly philosophically minded scientists, abhor a vacuum as much as nature does.

It is significant, however, that neither Skinner nor Chomsky has ever studied the phenomena they are trying to explain. We don't need expeditions or microscopes or laboratories to observe the genesis of mental structures. It takes place a few feet under our noses all the time, in the heads of our children. Moreover, children are obliging enough to produce all sorts of fascinating and bizarre behaviors that allow us to make inferences about their cognitive processes. When we actually look at how real children really develop we are much less tempted by theories that explain other kinds of development.

In particular, operant conditioning principles simply cannot explain the overwhelming majority of changes in children's behavior. To take just one example, in "Behaviorism-50" Skinner states that "a child learns to name a color correctly when a given response is reinforced in the presence of the color and extinguished in its absence." Skinner never looked at a child learning color names, but he is in good company. Philosophers since Augustine have made similar claims on the basis of similarly little evidence. It is only in the past eight years that someone got around to seeing how children really do learn color names (Carey 1978).

The results of these studies suggest that learning color names is a much more complex and obscure business than any of the philosophers supposed. However, they do eliminate some explanations, particularly the account Skinner advances here. Children can learn a new color term after hearing the term used once, with no reinforcement of their own use of the term, and even without using the term themselves at all. Moreover, children apply a color term to the wrong colors (for example, they apply "red" to yellow, green, and blue) even when they are given clear and repeated negative reinforcement. A rat would learn.

Those psychologists who have actually examined children's cognitive and linguistic development, a Piaget or a Bruner, a Roger Brown or a Dan Slobin, have had to reluctantly abandon apparently plausible theories, theories like operant conditoning or maturation that might yield a causal account of behavior.

Developmental psychologists are left staring at the vacuum at the center of their discipline. The darkness is not complete, however. We are beginning to get a glimpse of some of the contours of the beast. For my part, I prefer to have an incomplete theory that may be right than a complete theory that is almost certainly wrong.

BFS: Gopnik's first three paragraphs are an excellent example of what cognitive psychologists think they have achieved. She is talking about rule-governed rather than contingency-shaped behavior (see "Problem Solving"). Once the contingencies are put into words and the words manipulated, one may believe that there is no distinction between private and public and need not distinguish between representations and reality (not "action!"). We can talk about computers in the same way.

It is when Gopnik turns to what is left out that she comes to the heart of "Behaviorism-50." How do people acquire the behavior with respect to complex stimuli that we attribute to the formation of concepts? How do they adjust to contingencies of reinforcement in ways which lead us to suppose that they have discovered rules or acquired beliefs? This is the "serious flaw in mentalistic accounts" that I was talking about.

In speaking of pigeons "pecking levers" and in confusing negative reinforcement with punishment, Gopnik demonstrates unfamiliarity with operant conditioning. I don't know where she has learned that I have never studied the color-naming behavior of children or that I have neglected the contributions of maturation to human behavior. When Gopnik says that "operant conditioning principles simply cannot explain the overwhelming majority of changes in children's behavior," I cannot believe that she is referring to my book *Verbal Behavior* (1957). Perhaps, like so many others, she has read only Chomsky's review. The contingencies of reinforcement do not need to be arranged by a teacher, but they can be identified in the behavior of the language community when children reach a stage at which they can be told the name of a color and will use the word correctly thereafter. This again is rule-governed behavior, and although reinforcing contingencies are involved in the acquisition and use of rules, the result is different from the contingencies which can bring the identifying responses of very young children or other nonverbal organisms under the control of colored objects. The mistaken generalization of red to yellow, green, and blue has exact parallels in the behavior of pigeons. (A rat would *not* learn, because it does not have color vision.) I am sorry that those who have "actually examined children's cognitive and linguistic development" (Piaget, Bruner, Brown, and Slobin) have not understood operant conditioning well enough to see its relevance.

A causal role for "conscious" seeing

Robert M. Gordon

Department of Philosophy, University of Missouri–St. Louis

The kind of "mentalistic psychology" that Professor Skinner attacks is for the most part *Cartesian* mentalism: It is incompatible with either materialism or behaviorism. Recent formulations of "mentalism" or "neomentalism" (e.g., Paivio 1975) are compatible with, and typically favorable to, materialism. And they are avowedly "behavioristic," in the generous sense of the term which Skinner explicates in the last paragraph of "Behaviorism-50."

Today most advocates of *non*Cartesian mentalism would probably endorse Skinner's position on the problems of privacy and conscious content. The relevant data are not the alleged givens of "immediate experience" but the fact that we acquire the behavior of "reporting what we see." We report – and if sincere, "see" – that we see, for example, a light. We learn that we may report this even though we acknowledge that no light is really there to be seen. Yet it should not be supposed that in "seeing that we see a light" we have a special window on the states or processes that intervene between visual stimulation and behavior. Even those who allow "mental" states and processes to intervene between stimulation and behavior would grant that these are no more "visible" to the subject than to observers. Our sincere first-person reports might be *manifestations* of certain inner states, but they do not report privileged *glimpses* at them.

There is a complication, however, that is overlooked both by Skinner and by the new mentalists. Granted that "seeing that I see a light" involves no *look* into the mechanisms that underlie visually guided behavior, might it not have important behavioral consequences *in its own right?* Isn't it possible that visually guided behavior, at least in adult human beings, depends on what we can (sincerely) report we see? To approach "conscious" seeing as "part of behavior itself," as Skinner urges, surely should not rule out approaching it *also* as a "mediator" of other behavior.

But is there any evidence that visually guided behavior depends, as common sense would have it, on "conscious" seeing? One might think there is not. A great deal of visual processing goes on without any "seeing" for the subject to report. Indeed, some visually guided *behavior* goes on without any reportable "seeing." The most dramatic example of "sightless" visually guided behavior occurs in hemianopic "blindsight." As a result of lesions in the visual cortex, subjects deny *seeing* objects within a corresponding region of the visual field. Yet, to their own astonishment, these subjects are to a remarkable degree successful when asked only to "guess" the location, shape, and orientation of these objects (Weiskrantz, Warrington, Sanders & Marshall 1974). (Since hemianopic blindsight involves a lesion in the striate cortex, there is, not surprisingly, a considerable loss of visual acuity.) "Seeing" – in such a way that one can sincerely report that one sees – thus proves unnecessary for (more or less) reliable responses to visual stimuli. It is not needed to *guide* visually guided behavior.

And yet the very same findings show the great importance of "conscious" seeing to visually guided behavior, for without it, the blindsight subjects evidently fail to trust their own responses. They can put them forward only as "guesses." For why should they trust their responses to objects they are unable to see? The same lack of trust, we may presume, would tend to inhibit any blindsight-guided behavior, outside the laboratory as well as in.

I think Skinner is right to emphasize the role of linguistic training in "seeing that we see." But the evidence is that such training leads to something more than mere verbal behavior. For "see" is at least potentially a justificatory term:

> What reason do you have for saying there's a light over there?
> I can see it.

Lacking such epistemological justification, the blindsighted have let their remarkable ability go to waste.

The "need" for epistemological justification restores plausibility to our naive assertions of causal dependency:

> I wouldn't have pointed at the light if I hadn't (consciously) *seen* it.
> I pointed in that direction because I (consciously) *saw* the light there.

If this is correct, then our commonsense intuitions can be explained, and "saved," without resort to Cartesianism. One can endorse common sense on this point and remain, in a broad sense, a behaviorist.

BFS: I am never very happy about eponymous categories. I do not know whether I am Cartesian or anti-Cartesian. Except for that, there is much in Gordon's commentary that I like. There are several kinds of evidence that one has seen something and yet cannot say "I saw it." Freudians have their examples, and the blindsight subject is a dramatic instance. But there are reasons why the something is not seen. The Freudian may say that seeing has been repressed; what was seen was to some extent aversive. The blindsight subject does not see at the moment for a different reason. But whether behavior is guided by what is not seen depends upon the reasons it is not seen. In the Freudian examples, something a person says or does is offered as proof that a given stimulus must have been seen and must have guided the behavior.

I should want to translate the last few paragraphs of Gordon's commentary, replacing the "need" for epistemological justification with practical consequences. When I am asked whether I see something, my reply is usually some kind of report of my readiness to respond in other ways to what I see.

Leibnizian privacy and Skinnerian privacy

Keith Gunderson

Department of Philosophy and Minnesota Center for Philosophy of Science, University of Minnesota at Minneapolis/St. Paul

I recall that by 1963, the year in which "Behaviorism-50" was first published, behaviorist theories of mind were running nip and tuck with Cartesian ones in the most popular metaphysical scapegoat contest, and that most aspiring philosophers of mind, whatever else they disagreed about, shared the desire to avoid either positing the colorless ghost of Cartesianism or restricting themselves to the data amenable to the black box S–R tactics of behaviorism. Something both less and more seemed to be required. Having harbored such a desire myself, I find it instructive as well as chastening to reexamine some of the things Skinner actually wrote, as distinct from some still vivid caricatures I once thought representative of his views.

What strikes me most forcefully about "Behaviorism-50" is its refusal to soft-pedal the problem of subjectivity or privacy ("events within the skin") for a science of behavior. Skinner is not tempted to deny or eliminate the existence of private mental events, nor is he content to admit that although such events may be knocking at the door, they simply can't be let into the party. As far as I can tell – and this is where I've felt instructed – there is a sense in which he is quite hospitable to all the seemingly intractable lived-through data of consciousness that give rise to the problem of "other minds" and its partner in confusion, the mind–body problem. The question thus becomes whether such "personalized" data must remain sequestered in some exquisite epistemic (-ontic?) niche beyond the reach of the experimental psychologist, or whether no fixed boundary separates the private world within our skins from the presumably public world outside of them. Skinner's answer to that, elaborated in *Science and Human Behavior* (1953) and rearticulated in "Behaviorism-50" is: "The boundary shifts with every discovery of a technique for making private events public" (1953, p. 282) and "The skin is not that important as a boundary. Private and public events have the same kinds of physical dimensions" [target article]. It is this conception of a *shifting* boundary between the private mental world and the public physical-behavioristic one that I wish to digress on. And I must emphasize that it *is* a digression, and hardly an attempt at assessing the still-provocative remaks contained in "Behaviorism-50" on self-descriptive behavior and copy theories of conscious content.

With respect to the boundary, I heartily agree with Skinner that it's not the skin that's important. (But that's because I believe it to be a rather different sort of boundary.) And it may even be that "private and public events have the same kinds of physical dimensions." But what would count as demonstrating this is another issue and, I think, an ambiguous one. The ambiguity turns on what I take to be two different kinds of privacy. One I'll label *Leibnizian*, and the other *Skinnerian*.

In The Monadology (1714, p. 228) Leibniz writes:

> And supposing there were a machine, so constructed as to think, feel, and have perception, it might be conceived as increased in size, while keeping the same proportions, so that one might go into it as into a mill. That being so, we should, on examining its interior, find only parts which work one upon another, and never anything by which to explain a perception.

It's as if Leibniz is imagining an Age of Utopian Neurological (and Behavioral) Science and concluding that even then the thoughts, feelings, or perceptions of another would not be exhibited in any outward or public manner, which is another way of saying he believed they must always remain sequestered inward, which is in turn a way of saying they are to us only indirectly or inferentially knowable, and hence private. (Recall that his monads are "windowless.") This kind of privacy I am labeling *Leibnizian privacy*.

In the case of *Leibnizian privacy* my perceptions are known only by me. What a perception *is* involves, to a significant extent, what it is like *for me* to be having one, and this is never something that can be displayed outwardly.

A quite different way of looking at the privacy of the mental, however, first assimilates the mental to the behavioral, as Skinner does in "Behaviorism-50" when he claims that "an adequate science of behavior must consider events taking place within the skin of the organism, not as physiological mediators of behavior but as part of behavior itself." What is then viewed as most private is whatever behaviors ("within the skin") seem least accessible to our investigational techniques. Thus covert behaviors of small magnitude are viewed as more private than overt behaviors of larger and more easily measurable magnitudes. Here there is a shifting boundary between the private and the public akin to what one would experience by moving from motel rooms with thick walls to motel rooms with thin walls. This kind of privacy I shall label *Skinnerian privacy*.

Now if even some of our mental life can be seen as behaviorally saturated, as I think it can – consider thinking out loud, or learning to tie one's shoe – then the notion of Skinnerian privacy and a shifting boundary between the private and the public has a use. (Cf. the subsection "The Private Made Public" in *Science and Human Behavior*, 1953, p. 282, and the remark that "deafmutes who speak with their fingers behave covertly with their fingers and the movements may be suitably amplified.") But what I wish to focus on here is that a shifting boundary between Skinnerian privacy and the publicly observable does nothing to budge the boundary between Leibnizian privacy and the publicly observable. For the latter kind of privacy, unlike the former, derives from a fundamental qualitative difference in epistemological basis between first- and third-person psychological statements. And to assimilate the noninferential basis for the one ("I know I'm in pain") to the inferential basis for the other ("I know Waldo's in pain") is what, even in imagination, it seems impossible to do. When I know I'm in pain or thinking something or viewing this or that, the way in which I know any of these psychological facts about myself is through my indulging in them directly, immediately, noninferentially, whereas any comparable knowledge I might come by with respect to Waldo will, necessarily, be garnered in a nondirect, nonimmediate, inferential manner. To abrogate the difference in epistemologica basis between my knowledge of my pain, thought, or perception, and my knowledge of Waldo's pain, thought, or perception – or make the difference just a shifting matter of degree – would necessitate my being able to be in a position (more or less) to fee Waldo's pain, think his thoughts, or be privy to his visual field. And this, it seems, is something I couldn't do without to some significant extent becoming Waldo. That this is so can be made more vivid by considering the following example which I have elsewhere called the Cinematic Solution to the Other Minds Problem (Gunderson 1971, pp. 307–8). Suppose a film director wishes to treat us to the perceptua experiences of Waldo as he stares into his fifth martini while ruminating on the gloomy fact that Wilma has jilted him. How is this best done? Not, to be sure, by simply showing us Waldo staring at a martini. For this would not be the same as being privy to Waldo's perceptual experience. Instead what is (characteristically) done is that Waldo's body (or at least the better part of it) is somehow (gradually or suddenly) subtracted from the screen such that we, without being made aware of it, are insinuated into roughly whatever space Waldo is occupying and made party to the visual field containing martini cum olive et al. that we can safely presume Waldo would from the same vantage point be seeing. We cannot literally, of course, occupy exactly the same space that Waldo does – a prerequisite to having his visual experience – but the tricks of the cinematic trade permit us to enjoy a simulation of such an occupancy.

What the foregoing example helps to illustrate, I think, is that the high price for sharing the perspective or point of view of another is nothing less than the coalescence of the payer with the payee. And because such a price is too high – that is, impossibly high – to pay, a liberal amount of ongoing Leibnizian privacy is guaranteed to all of us as well as any cognitive-sentient bats or robots that might come along.

Such a circumscription of privacy – Leibnizian privacy – may seem to reduce to the unilluminating tautology that we're always only who we are, and never someone else. But even tautologies can have interesting implications. As John Wisdom in his *Other Minds* (1952, p. 194) writes:

> For it's not merely that a condition fulfilled in the case of inference from the outward state of a house or a motor car or a watch to its inward state is not fulfilled in the case of inference from a man's outward state to his inward state, it is that we do not know what it would be like for this condition to be fulfilled, what it would be like to observe the state of the soul which inhabits another body.

And in this respect mental events that enjoy Leibnizian as distinct from Skinnerian privacy are in an epistemologically different category from unobservable (theoretical) entities in science (cf. "Behaviorism-50"). This does not mean they are graced by some special metaphysical status – a remark I am sure Skinner would concur with – but it does mean they are known in a "special way" – a remark I believe Skinner would and does take issue with (cf. "Behaviorism-50").

BFS: I agree with much that Gunderson says, though I see no reason to call the private events I observe in myself "mental," if that term implies that they are made of a different kind of stuff. The way in which I observe them "introspectively" is not the way neurologists would observe them if they could, and until they can observe them as they would like to do, their neurology will remain "only indirectly or inferentially knowable." I know about presumably the same events directly and without inference, though in an almost certainly limited and faulty way. The "thinking" that one does out loud is clearly behavior rather than thought processes said to be responsible for behavior. I can observe the same kind of thinking silently when t has little if any muscular involvement.

I should also want to modify the statement that "the way in which I know any of these psychological facts about myself is through my indulging in them directly, immediately, noninferentially." Surely one must "indulge" in a psychological fact before observing it, but one of the main points of "Behaviorism-50" is: self-observation is more than mere indulgence. It is a special kind of behavior mainly of social origin. When it comes to "knowing another mind" we are unable both to engage in the behavior observed and for an additional reason to observe it. We cannot observe the Parthenon or observe that we are observing it unless we are in Athens.

I've got you under my skin

John Heil

Department of Philosophy, Virginia Commonwealth University

Philosophers seem most often to regard behaviorism as a special doctrine about the mind, one that envisages a conceptual link between descriptions of mental events and descriptions of behavior. In "Behaviorism-50," however, Skinner contends that behaviorism is best understood as a philosophy of science, or at any rate as a view about explanation. Indeed, the doctrine that philosophers associate with behaviorism is taken up by Skinner and rejected (see iii, below). Why, then, all the fuss? It stems, perhaps, from the fact that Skinner and his sympathizers have held, in addition to their views about explanation, a certain conception of mind, a conception bound to produce disagreements in theory even when "methodology" is not at issue. If behaviorism is just a philosophy of science then this conception of mind may be one that behaviorists would be willing to abandon. Were that to happen, many of the sharpest differences between behaviorists and nonbehaviorist cognitive psychologists would simply vanish or dwindle into insignificance. This, however, brings us back to our starting point: What is distinctive about behaviorism in psychology is, after all, its concept of mind.

Skinner mentions three accounts of mental events that are at odds with his own.

i. Mental events do not exist at all (materialism).
ii. Mental events exist, but, owing to their private character, cannot be studied scientifically (positivism).
iii. Mental events exist and can be studied scientifically so long as they can be characterized "operationally," by reference to behavior (operationism).

Skinner rejects each of these conceptions, however, and suggests a fourth:

iv. Mental events exist as private, interior stimuli on a par with external stimuli. We respond to these no less than to our surroundings, although, because they are private, patterns of reinforcement are more tenuous, less definite.

In regarding mental events as private episodes, stimuli occurring "inside the skin," Skinner wishes to reject the notion that mental events are "way stations," the function of which is to bridge gaps between the occurrence of an external stimulus and a creature's response. So far as the psychologist is concerned, there are just stimuli and behavior. Some stimuli exist outside the skin. Responses to these public goings-on may be reinforced and fine-tuned by the community. Other stimuli, in contrast, arise inside the skin. A creature's response to these private episodes is less easily regulated.

Such a view is consistent with both dualism and materialism. Skinner's own remarks suggest elements of each. Thus mental states are said to be inside the skin, suggesting that they are physiological in character. But they are said, as well, to be private, at least in the sense that they stand in a special relation to the creature possessing them. Such talk lends itself to a dualistic interpretation.

Skinner's apparent ambivalence here is significant, but it need not be taken to be a difficulty for his view. There is no particular reason why, as a psychologist, he ought to take a stand on the matter. Indeed, if the theory entailed, for example, that dualism was false, one might well be suspicious of the character of its commitments.

If we apply the doctrine sketched here to the case of perception, we obtain something like the following view:

Perceiving is a "form of acting." To perceive something is to respond differentially to a particular stimulus. When such responses are suitably reinforced, the perceiving creature may be said to possess what might ordinarily be called *knowledge* of the stimulus. The idea, very roughly, is that when a creature acquires the knack of responding "discriminatively" to a given sort of stimulus, the creature has acquired (again, in ordinary "mentalistic" language) knowledge of the stimulus. The knack of so responding *is* its knowledge, and this knowledge is manifested whenever the creature responds appropriately.

The mechanisms underlying the capacity for differential responses are no doubt complicated. They might include undreamed-of physiological components. What they cannot include, according to Skinner, is a *mental* component. Or rather, if such components exist, they are strictly inessential to the operation of the mechanism. This is because mental episodes are taken to be interior *stimuli*. If these are perceived – inwardly – this means only that they are responded to differentially. If perceiving were taken to include, essentially, a mental episode, we should, or so it seems, be committed to a regress of episodes. If, in order to perceive an external stimulus, I must perceive an internal stimulus, then my perceiving the latter seems to require that I perceive a further, second- – or is it third-? – order stimulus, *and so on*.

This, I think, is one reason Skinner thinks it wise to reject accounts of perception that postulate "mental way stations."

There are many reasons one might object to such a view. I shall mention two. Consider, first, difficulties bound to crop up in attempts to describe stimuli and behavior in a way that does not implicitly require reference to certain of a perceiver's mental states – or at any rate reference to the perceiver's beliefs about the world (see, e.g., Heil 1982). In perceiving, we "respond differentially" not to stimuli *simpliciter*, but to *features* of stimuli. And this seems to require something on the order of a conceptual endowment. It is easy to lose sight of this fact because it is often possible to describe perceptual objects extensionally. I see Clarence, and Clarence happens to be a Cartesian, so I see a Cartesian. Although the latter may be true, it is scarcely helpful to psychologists bent on explaining my behavior unless I, in some sense or other, *appreciate* the fact that Clarence is a Cartesian. It is, of course, open to Skinner to treat appreciation of this sort as a further capacity for differential response – I have the knack of responding differentially to Clarence as a member of the class of persons, say, but I lack the corresponding capacity for responding to him as a member of the class of Cartesians. In spelling all this out, however, the theory risks losing whatever simplicity it might initially have possessed.

A second difficulty is related to the first. Skinner characterizes mental episodes as interior stimuli. In this he seems partly right. Thus, what we ordinarily call sensations seem more or less exclusively describable in this way, and Skinner is surely right in denying that such things are essential for perception. Other sorts of mental states, however, seem to differ from sensations at least in the fact that their existence or operation appears not to depend on their serving as stimuli. I am thinking here of so-called *intentional* states – beliefs, desires, and the like. Such things seem crucially to possess various logical or representational properties. Their effects on behavior depend not on their being *apprehended*, only on their being *had*. It is my *belief* (acquired perceptually) that the cat is on the mat that leads me to respond as I do, not my *awareness* of this belief.

Does this mean that we must have irreducibly mental "way stations" in theories of behavior? The matter is complicated, but the answer, perhaps, is that we must so long as we wish to speak of behavior in the idiom of psychology. We can avoid mental way stations, but only by doing what Davidson describes as "changing the subject" and talking only about retinal stimulation, nerve firings, and muscle contractions (see, e.g., Davidson 1970; also Heil 1983). If this is so – and it would, of course, require a lengthy discussion to show that it is – then the science of psychology as envisaged by Skinner is, strictly, impossible.

BFS: I did not mean to include supposed copies of sensations among mental way-stations. By way-stations I meant precisely the mental events that Heil feels cannot be dealt with as copies, "so-called *intentional* states – beliefs, desires, and the like." These are way-stations in the sense that they are said to intervene between a person's history and the resulting behavior. Thus, I may consult a map and discover what I believe to be the correct route to a city I want to reach, and that belief then leads me to take that route. As a behaviorist I would simply say that one takes the route that one has found leading to the city one is to reach. Taking the route "expresses one's belief" that it is the right route. If asked, one might well say, "Yes, I believe this is the right route." So far as behavior is concerned, consultation with a map has changed the individual in such a way that a given route is taken. One uses the word "belief" in reporting the probability of taking the route. To respond to a cat on a mat does not require an *awareness* of the belief that the cat is on the mat; it does not even require the belief. It requires only that a present setting is sufficiently like earlier settings in which responses to cats on mats have been effective.

Must we say when I am hungry I desire food and that because I desire food I eat? Or that when I am hungry I eat and that I describe the prevailing condition as a desire for food? There is no questioning the strong evidence for states of one's own body to which words like belief and desire have been applied for thousands of years. If we are not too curious about the origin of our behavior, it is perhaps enough to suppose that it begins with these observed states. A more complete account will ask about the origin of the states, will question the accuracy or even the value of introspective observation, and will proceed to formulate the behavior as a direct function of the earlier history.

It is true that talk of a public and a private world "lends itself to a dualistic interpretation," but the dualism is simply that between public and private, not between physical and mental, and the distinction of public and private is one of boundaries, not of nature.

B. F. Skinner's confused philosophy of science

Laurence Hitterdale
Santa Ana, California

Why is B. F. Skinner's behaviorism so famous and influential? In my view, the answer does not lie in the soundness and originality of the position, but in a specious advantage conferred on behaviorism by the fact that it is a confused amalgam of two distinct doctrines. One of these doctrines is a thesis about the relation of the physical to the mental. The other is a thesis about the relation of one sort of physical event – namely, outward, grossly observable bodily behavior – to another sort of physical event – namely, activity in the brain.

The thesis about the physical and mental relation is either materialism or epiphenomenalist dualism. There seems to be a secondary confusion between these two, but the confusion need not be resolved, since my critique of behaviorism holds if Skinner accepts either view. The thesis about the outward behavior – brain activity relation is also unclear. This thesis might be that a science of outward behavior can be developed independently of a science of brain states and even in the face of scientific ignorance about brain states. On the other hand, the thesis might be that the concepts and laws of behavioristic psychology are adequate not only for the science of outward behavior but even for a unified science covering both outward behavior and brain states. Again, the confusion between these two distinct and rather antithetic opinions need not be resolved; as in the previous case, the critique of behaviorism holds if Skinner accepts either view.

The specious advantage accruing to behaviorism from the conflation of a doctrine about the physical–mental relation with a doctrine about the outward behavior–brain activity relation is fairly easy to state. The merit of either doctrine – that is, materialism or epiphenomenalist dualism – about the physical–mental relation is that it deserves to be taken seriously. The defect of such a doctrine (from the standpoint of an assessment of Skinner's behaviorism) is that it is neither original with Skinner nor well presented in his writings. Many other people both before Skinner and contemporaneously with him have formulated these theories more clearly and argued for them more cogently and in more detail. The merit of either doctrine about the relation of outward behavior to brain activity is that the doctrine is original, provocative, and intriguing. Its defect is that it is untrue, even somewhat preposterous.

Both Skinner himself and many of his readers have not noticed that his behaviorism is a conflation of two distinct doctrines on two different topics. Consequently, both Skinner and many of his readers have the impression that the confused amalgam (i.e., Skinner's behaviorism) has the merits of both doctrines but the defects of neither. Actually, behaviorism has the merits of neither, the defects of both, and the additional defect of internal confusion.

So, there are three criticisms of behaviorism:

1. Behaviorism confusedly assimilates a doctrine about the physical and mental relation to a quite different doctrine about the relation of outward behavior to events in the brain.
2. Behaviorism's doctrine about the relation of the physical to the mental is neither original nor well presented.
3. Behaviorism's doctrine about the relation of outward behavior to brain activity is untrue.

I now turn to an analysis of "Behaviorism-50" for a substantiation of these criticisms.

It is evident that Skinner is interested in the metaphysical problem of the relation of body to mind. He explicitly formulates the issue: "Mentalistic psychologists insist that there are other kinds of events uniquely accessible to the owner of the skin within which they occur which lack the physical dimensions of proprioceptive or interoceptive stimuli. They are as different from physical events as colors are from wavelengths of light." Furthermore, Skinner presents his own opinion on the subject. He opposes mentalism, either from a materialist standpoint – "Private and public events have the same kinds of physical dimensions" – or from the standpoint of epiphenomenalism – "The objection is not that these things are mental but that they offer no real explanation."

It is equally evident that Skinner is interested in the scientific problem of the relation between outward behavior and brain activity. He writes, "An adequate science of behavior must consider events taking place within the skin of the organism, not as physiological mediators of behavior but as part of behavior itself. . . . The skin is not that important as a boundary."

There is nothing objectionable in the fact that Skinner deals with both the metaphysical and the scientific questions. He is right to think that both deserve serious attention. Apparently, however, he conflates the two issues, and that is objectionable. These are two very different questions. The dispute between mentalists and their opponents is *not* about the relation between the world outside the skin and the world "within the skin." For mentalists, the entire physical world – that is, *both* outside the skin *and* "within the skin" – is one pole of a contrast; the other pole is an irreducibly mental world of things lacking "physical dimensions." These mental things are, in Skinner's words, alleged to be "as different from physical events as colors are from wavelengths of light." (The term "physical dimensions" refers to physical properties generally; it does not mean simply "spatial dimensions.")

Only a confusion of the two issues can explain the otherwise very puzzling things Skinner says about the brain. For instance, he asserts, "It took us a long time to understand that when we dreamed of a wolf, no wolf was actually there. It has taken us much longer to understand that not even a representation of a wolf is there." I believe that the word "there" in this passage means "in the physical world" rather than "in the mental world"; hence, in the second sentence this word is equivalent to "in the brain." If this interpretation is correct, then the second sentence is false. During a dream of a wolf, the dreamer has a representation of a wolf in his brain. Admittedly, the nature of this representation is unknown, and there can be debate as to the appropriateness of the word "representation." Nevertheless, *something* in the dreamer's brain has *something* to do with a wolf.

Why does Skinner appear to deny this? The explanation, it seems to me, is that he confuses the body–mind problem with the outward behavior–brain activity problem. Skinner knows that he wishes to deny the existence of a representation in the dreamer's *mind*. The denial of mental representation need not necessarily lead to a denial of neural representation, but Skinner slides from one denial to the other.

Or consider this:

> It adds nothing to an explanation of how an organism reacts to a stimulus to trace the pattern of the stimulus into the body. It is most convenient for both organism and psychophysiologist if the external world is never copied – if the world we know is simply the world around us. The same may be said of theories according to which the brain interprets signals sent to it and in some sense reconstructs external stimuli.

Skinner's philosophy of science is wrong, because it does add *something* to an explanation of how an organism reacts to trace the pattern of the stimulus into the body. And Skinner's neurobiology is wrong: The pattern of the stimulus does go into the body; however inconvenient for organism or psychophysiologist, the external world is copied; the brain does interpret signals sent to it to reconstruct external stimuli.

Again one might ask why Skinner would deny this. The answer again is that he has confused a scientific problem with a metaphysical one. He knows that a solution to the scientific problem will not solve the metaphysical problem but might even make it more perplexing. "We must then start all over again and explain how the organism sees the reconstruction." Skinner's solution to the metaphysical problem is to deny the validity of the scientific problem.

Since this commentary has been largely critical, it is only fair to close by saying that the commentary deals exclusively with certain philosophical aspects of behaviorism. Skinner's experimental findings have not been touched, nor can one criticize his insistence on making psychology work effectively for a safer society and happier ives. But if "behaviorism, with an accent on the last syllable, is...a philosophy of science," then behaviorism cannot be accepted.

BFS: I cannot believe that Hitterdale is commenting on my paper. I have nothing to say about "the relation of the physical to the mental" or about the relation of grossly observable bodily behavior to activity in the brain. Hence, I cannot see how my behaviorism can be an amalgam of those "two distinct doctrines."

J. B. Watson's imagery and other mentalistic problems

Francis W. Irwin

Department of Psychology, University of Pennsylvania

Writing about Watson's denial of the existence of images, Skinner sets the tone for "Behaviorism-50" by saying, "He may well have been acting in good faith, for it has been said that he himself did not have visual imagery." Thus, Skinner not only accepts the existence of images, he allows them to have explanatory power over behavior; but they, and other private events "within the skin," are to be drawn within the purview of his behavioristic system, an ambition quite surprising to those familiar with his extraordinarily influential *The Behavior of Organisms* (1938). After reading the target article, I have grave doubts that it can be done.

On seeing without seeing anything. According to Skinner,

> The heart of the behavioristic position on conscious experience may be summed up in this way: Seeing does not imply something seen. We acquire the behavior of seeing under stimulation from actual objects, but it may occur in the absence of these objects under the control of other variables....We also acquire the behavior of seeing-that-we-are-seeing when we are seeing actual objects, but it may also occur in their absence.

Since nothing resembling a definition of such seeing is offered, this appears to be theorizing by fiat. I confess that I utterly fail to comprehend the later discussion of this matter in Skinner (1969, pp. 251–53). The target article goes on to tell us, mysteriously: "To question the reality or the nature of the things seen in conscious experience is not to question the value of introspective psychology or its methods." In addition, it is said that "we have reason to believe" that children "will not see two colors as different – until [they have been] exposed to [appropriate] contingencies" of reinforcement by the verbal community. How these contingencies can be applied prior to the behavior of seeing is not explained, nor is any reference cited. We may wonder how nonhuman animals manage to see at all in the absence of a verbal community to assist them.

On neurophysiology. Skinner vigorously attacks the notion that copies or representations of objects in the real world are transmitted from the sense organs to the brain. "The organism does not create duplicates," he says in the abstract; and, later, "If the real world is, indeed, scrambled in transmission but later reconstructed in the brain, we must then start all over again and explain how the organism sees the reconstruction"; and, finally, "The sooner the pattern of the external world disappears after impinging on the organism, the sooner the organism may get on with these other functions" (of being differentially reinforced for the actions of seeing, hearing, and smelling).

In the 20 years since "Behaviorism-50" was originally published, remarkable advances have been made in sensory neurophysiology. It has been found that far from "scrambling" the real world in transmission and then reconstituting it, which would seem like retrieving eggs, milk, and a pat of butter from a cooked omelet, the primary visual cortex is related to the retina in a highly orderly and organized manner. One might even call it beautiful. The same can be said for the primary auditory cortex and its relation to the basilar membrane (see, e.g., Carlson 1981). The cortical representations are not duplicates or exact copies of the sensory surfaces, but the relations may somewhat loosely be called "point to point." Although it is not yet known how these representations are used in order for the world to be seen or imagined, the answers to these questions will undoubtedly be furthered by both the suggestions about them and the constraints upon them that are rapidly coming to light in neurophysiology.

An alternative behavioral approach. Although I have found fault with some important positions taken by Skinner, there is much that I sympathize with, having often faced similar problems. One statement of his that I heartily agree with is this: "The problem of privacy may be approached in a fresh direction by starting with behavior rather than with immediate experience," although I would prefer to substitute "psychology" for "privacy." SAO theory (Irwin 1971) begins with three primitive terms, situation, act, and outcome, which are undefined in the theory but are left to be characterized by working psychologists in their research. Pairs of situations and outcomes of acts are used as independent variables in binary-choice diagnosis procedures, and three elementary behavioral dispositions are introduced, namely, discrimination; preference and its subtypes, desire and aversion; and act–outcome expectancy. If the subject, human or animal, or, for that matter, a chess-playing microcomputer, gives a significant specified pattern of choices in a diagnostic experiment, it is said to have exhibited a discrimination between the two situations, or a preference for one of the two outcomes, or an act–outcome expectancy that one of the alternative acts is more likely than the other to be followed by a particular one of the two possible outcomes, according to which of the three diagnostic experiments was employed. The experiments contain internal controls against the results being "merely" differential responses rather than true discriminations or merely response biases rather than true preferences. Present chess-playing machines will fail to meet the criteria in any of the three diagnostic experiments, if for no other reason than that they are incapable of the instrumental learning that each experiment requires and thus must be regarded (within the theory) as incapable of discrimination or preference or act–outcome expectancy; but human beings and animals at least as far down the scale as cockroaches have been found capable of each of these processes, given proper choice of the situations, acts, and outcomes used for tests with the organism under study. Note that no reference to consciousness has been found necessary in this development, although still further development would undoubtedly require the introduction of this, or a similar, concept. See Irwin (1971, pp. 107–09) for further remarks on this question. The learning required of the subjects in these experiments is treated as reflecting changes in the relative strengths of act–outcome expectancies, and not as a Skinnerian change of response strength due to reinforcement. "Reinforcement" seems to me to confound the informative and hedonic properties of outcomes.

It is possible from the present state of the SAO theory to define an intentional act as one the occurrence of which depends upon a preference for a particular outcome over another, an expectancy that the act in question is more likely than its alternative to be followed by the preferred outcome, and a complementary expectancy that the alternative act is the more likely to be followed by the nonpreferred outcome. Thus, within the theory, the outcome of an intentional act is both the preferred and the more expected outcome of the act. As Skinner would demand, much is already known about the conditions that control the presence or absence of these dispositions. The theory already covers a broad domain of subjects and circumstances, in spite of its far from complete range over the enormous field of psychology in general. I have called it "behavioral" rather than "behavioristic" argely because the proponents of Skinner's system have effectively appropriated the atter term.

BFS: Irwin claims that in saying that Watson presumably did not have visual imagery, I am accepting "the existence of images," but I am not doing so. I am simply saying that Watson apparently did not do what other people do when they report that they are seeing images – namely, respond as they once responded to stimuli of which the images are said to be copies. When I said that children "will not see two colors as different – until [they have been] exposed to [appropriate] contingencies" of reinforcement by the verbal community, I did not mean that they would not see colored *objects* as different but that they would not name or otherwise respond abstractly to the color alone without verbal reinforcement. I agree that much has been done to relate the visual cortex to the retina "in a highly orderly and organized manner," but I would emphasize that it can only be very "loosely" called point-to-point. In any case, as Irwin says, "it is not yet known how these representations are used in order for the world to be seen or imagined,"

Irwin's SAO theory sounds very much like the operant formulation, and I am fairly sure that it could be reformulated without reference to preference, desire, aversion, or outcome expectancy, all of which sounds very much like E. C. Tolman. I am happy to learn that "no reference to consciousness has been found necessary in [its] development."

What's on the minds of children?

Carl N. Johnson

Program in Child Development and Child Care, University of Pittsburgh

Reading Skinner's "Behaviorism-50" reminded me of the good old days when theoretical controversies shook the very foundations of psychology. I recall that my first contact with Skinner's paper was as an undergraduate, assigned a book of readings entitled *Behaviorism and Phenomenology: Contrasting Bases for Modern Psychology* (Wann 1964). Here, mentalism and behaviorism met head on. On one side were the "humanists," emphasizing the wealth of lived experience; on the other side were the "animalists," claiming that human behavior could be reduced to principles governing rats and pigeons.

In retrospect, it is notable that cognitive psychology was not central to this debate. The case for behaviorism was built in opposition to mentalism, not cognitivism. In fact, the emergence of the cognitive tradition seems to have effectively undermined the debate by providing exacting descriptions of cognitive acts which could neither be located in private conscious experience nor reduced to overt behavioral description. In turn, the study of cognitive development has helped to bridge the seeming chasm between mindless actions and active minds.

Skinner's attack on mentalism rarely challenges cognitivism. In fact, cognitive psychologists are largely in agreement with Skinner's critique. Certainly there is no place in cognitive psychology for "primitive" explanations that refer to "homunculi," "internal copies," or ill-defined mental way stations. Introspective verbal reports do not have a uniquely privileged status in cognitive psychology (e.g., research on infant cognition); ordinary mentalistic concepts are recognized to be inferred from public information (e.g., symbolic interactionism); and the skin is not regarded as a critical boundary (e.g., artificial intelligence).

If cognition was nothing more than mentalism in Skinner's sense, we would all be behaviorists. The problem is that Skinner's mentalism conflates ordinary and scientific explanations in a primitive conception that does justice to neither. He argues that all mentalistic explanations represent a similar mistake, stemming from a primitive animism. Curiously, Skinner neither offers nor appeals to evidence on this point. He rests his case on mere speculation that mentalism is based on dysfunctional attempts to explain extraordinary human events, in other words, dreams, hallucinations, and capricious behavior.

There is, of course, an alternative account. Mentalistic explanations may be primarily derived from functional attempts to explain ordinary behavior. Such a position is supported by a sizable and growing body of literature on children's developing "theory of mind" (see Bretherton, McNew & Beeghly-Smith 1981; Gelman & Spelke 1981; Johnson 1982; Wellman 1985; Wimmer & Perner 1983; Wolf 1982). The point is that at remarkably early ages children are developing the ability to represent the mental status of others in the natural process of trying to communicate, interact, and understand the behavior of others. Moreover, this development emerges in a gradual series of steps from overt behavioral interactions toward increasingly more elaborate inferences about mental status. Instances of primitive animism are clearly the exception rather than the rule. This research, in combination with comparative studies of chimpanzees (Premack & Woodruff 1978; Woodruff & Premack 1978), provides a sound empirical basis for arguing that mentalism is a natural outgrowth of the behavior of organisms, not some primitive aberration. Hence, the study of cognitive development effectively defuses the debate between psychology as the science of mental life and psychology as the science of behavior. Mind is an emergent property of behavior.

This developmental account does not imply that ordinary mentalistic notions are wholly accurate, universal, or the sole object of psychology. Cultures vary in the manner in and degree to which they develop theories of mind (see Heelas & Lock 1981), and cognitive psychologists, like behaviorists, are often rightly critical of indigenous conceptions (see Ross 1981). The point is that human beings are symbolic organisms who must be understood with respect to their indigenous theories of mind within a broader theory of the development of cognitive action.

BFS: Although I did speculate that dreams may first have suggested the notion of a mind separate from the physical body, I did not say, as Johnson argues, that current dualism was *based* on such evidence. It is not so much the nonphysical nature of the world of the mind that causes trouble as its supposed causal effectiveness. Cognitive science is still looking for inner causes. That the causes "develop," presumably for genetic reasons, does not change their role.

I do not, of course, claim that human behavior can be "reduced" to principles governing rats and pigeons. There are principles of behavior common to many different species. They are the same principles. I have discussed a presumably distinguishing feature of human behavior in considerable detail in *Verbal Behavior* (1957).

I do not believe that the cognitive tradition has provided "exacting descriptions of cognitive acts which could neither be located in private conscious experience nor reduced to overt behavioral description," or that comparative studies of chimpanzees have proved that mentalism is a natural outgrowth of the behavior of organisms. Mind is not an emergent property of behavior (*pace* Teilhard de Chardin).

Artificially intelligent mental models

Michael Lebowitz

Department of Computer Science, Columbia University

Skinner's position against the need for mentalistic descriptions in theories of cognition has been debated by psychologists, philosophers, and linguists for many years. From all indications (Skinner 1983a, for example) his basic position remains today much the same as when the target article was written 20 years ago. Artifical intelligence (AI) is a discipline based firmly on the idea of computational mental models. What can the experience of AI researchers with such models add to the debate on the use of mentalistic descriptions in the study of the mind? I argue here that AI can further the case for mental models from two angles – one that supports a pragmatic position already taken by many psychologists and philosophers and another based on AI's unique ability to consider cognitive processes independent of any animate organism.

A strong reason for making use of mentalistic descriptions is summarized by Dennett (1983, p. 344): "The basic strategy of which [using mentalistic descriptions] is a special case is familiar: changing levels of explanation and description in order to gain access to greater predictive power or generality." In pursuit of models with great predictive power, AI research methodology provides strong motivation for selecting the level of abstraction of mental models by providing a valuable tool for testing such theories. In AI, we can not only develop mentalistic theories, but actually implement the algorithms they include with computer programs. This allows us to simulate the models and analyze the behavior they predict. This gives us an experimental tool much like psychology experiments, but able to deal with more complex models. If an AI program behaves differently than a person would with the same input, there must be a problem with the model (although the problem might be at the level of implementing the theory as a computer program). This will lead to refinement of the model. Although the proper behavior of the program does not guarantee a correspondence with the equivalent mechanism in humans, it does suggest that the processes are similar *at some level of abstraction* and that the theory has strong predictive value (which is what we are after).

As an illustration of the use of AI in theory refinement, I would like to describe briefly an example from my research into the process of concept formation through generalization from examples. This research included the development of a computer program, IPP (Lebowitz 1983), that read, remembered, and generalized concepts from newspaper stories (about international terrorism, as it happens). At one point in its development, IPP was tested on a sequence of several stories involving shootings where two people were killed in each. The program made the generalization from these data that shooting victims usually come in pairs, a conclusion unlike that of a human reader. This led us to add to the model (and the program) a method to evaluate confidence in generalizations, either in terms of prior knowledge or future input, giving us a much more complete and robust model. Such refinement can easily be done with algorithmic mental models, but appears much less practical with behaviorist models of any substantial complexity.

The methodological addition to the usefulness of the mentalistic approach is not all that artificial intelligence has to offer in opposition to behaviorism. AI helps separate issues of human abilities from those fundamental to cognition, as the field provides definitive evidence that intelligence need not reside in a human brain. Computer programs are currently able to perform medical diagnosis in certain areas, understand stories, analyze visual scenes, play games, learn new concepts, and perform many other tasks we classify as exhibiting intelligence. (Barr, Cohen, and Feigenbaum 1982 provide many more examples.) Although individual programs cannot, at the moment, perform tasks in as wide a range as people, they nonetheless exhibit intelligence, as will the even more powerful programs under development.

The intelligent behavior of computer programs requires explanation that must be integrated into our overall model of intelligence. Although we could, perhaps, explain the behavior of intelligent programs in behaviorist terms, putting stress on the inputs and outputs of the programs, such analysis seems quite contrived, and, in particular, leaves no role for the computer code to play. Since, unlike human mental models and algorithms, computer programs and their associated data representation can be examined in detail, it seems much more reasonable to include these structures in our analyses. In fact, the programs and data representations are exactly analogous to the internal mental models that Skinner views as unnecessary when discussing human cognition. As long as the mental models used in explaining the intelligent behavior of programs also have predictive value with regard to human cognition, this level of abstraction is clearly worthwhile. Such validity is evident in the manner in which AI has been a fruitful source of theories for researchers in related disciplines.

In summary, we see that artificial intelligence is squarely behind the mentalistic approach to the understanding of cognition. It provides impetus in this direction in two ways. AI simulations of mentalistic models provide a useful research tool and show the predictive nature of such models. Beyond that, AI provides a means for separating issues of human behavior from those of intelligence and cognition, and when the separation is made, mental models remain an important tool for explaining intelligent behavior. In the long run, an added context within which to examine issues of thought that previously only involved biological organisms may prove to be AI's most important contribution to science.

BFS: I agree that AI is "squarely behind the mentalistic approach to the understanding of cognition." It has reached that position in a number of historical stages:

1. The behavior of Homo sapiens prior to the development of verbal behavior, like the behavior of organisms in general, was shaped by contingencies of selection during the evolution of the species and by contingencies of reinforcement in the lifetime of the individual (see "Consequences" and "Phylogeny").

2. With the advent of a highly developed verbal repertoire, contingencies of reinforcement were talked about. One person began to give another advice, warnings, and instruction. Rules and laws were formulated which referred to behavior and it consequences (see "Problem Solving"). In thus

profiting from the experience of others individuals acquired vast repertoires of behavior which far transcended anything that would have been possible during a single lifetime under contingencies of reinforcement alone.

3. The mentalistic hypothesis was proposed that people always responded to contingencies of reinforcement as in (1) by first engaging in behavior of the sort specified in (2). Thus organisms did not respond merely to the world about them; they responded to representations inside them. Their behavior could be affected by contingencies of reinforcement only if they discovered the rules embedded in the contingencies. Mentalism became, as Piaget called it, subjective behaviorism. Private stimuli, private responses, and private consequences became the world of cognitive psychology.

4. AI analyzed contingencies of reinforcement in far greater detail, not by studying the contingencies that prevailed as in (1) (that would be an experimental science), but by constructing models of subjective behavers as they responded to verbal descriptions of contingencies. If representations were accurate copies of the world and if the rules were accurate statements of contingencies of reinforcement, artificial intelligence would support behaviorism. But verbal descriptions of reality are never as detailed as reality itself, and rule-guided or -governed behavior is never as subtle as behavior shaped directly by the contingencies described by the rules. We must also account for the fact that people formulate and follow rules, and to do so we must turn to additional contingencies of reinforcement. They will inject the "motivational and emotional" features which AI models tend to lack.

Skinner and the mind–body problem

William G. Lycan

Department of Philosophy, University of North Carolina at Chapel Hill

Readers have combed Professor Skinner's works for a single, consistent philosophical theory of the mind, and have been disappointed. This is unsurprising – first, because Skinner is not a metaphysician and has no serious prescientific ontological views, but more importantly because his methodological behaviorism prevents the traditional mind–body problem from arising for him. If one's sole theoretical project is the explanation and prediction of behavior, then insofar as one mentions putative mental entities at all, one already knows in outline how those entities are related to the body that is doing the behaving.

Philosophers have nevertheless persisted in thinking that Skinner is addressing their concerns, and that they have useful things to say to or about Skinner. Nowadays the things they do say are predominantly critical. In this commentary on "Behaviorism at Fifty" at 20, I want first to emphasize the extent of my agreement with the views Skinner expresses in that work, and then just to enumerate the remaining points of dispute. I do not flatter myself that Skinner will be much moved by the criticisms of a minor late-20th-century functionalist (still less that he will now finally be able to sleep at night, having won the concurrence of William G. Lycan on the earlier points); rather, I am offering my own views as representative of the general theory of mind that I take to have dominated philosophical thinking for the past two decades. In this way I hope to be able to exhibit some of the relations that do obtain between Skinnerian behaviorism and current philosophy of mind.

First, the points of agreement: (i) The business of psychology is the explanation and prediction of behavior. Moreover, if there is a philosophical case to be made for mental entities it is based on our need for the commonsense explanation and prediction of behavior. (ii) Undischarged homunculi are bad, for just the reasons Skinner says. Homunculi per se have regained some face in recent years thanks to the now well known strategy due to Attneave (1960), Fodor (1968a), and Dennett (1975), of successively breaking down initial homunculi into smaller and smaller and less versatile homunculi which cooperate with each other; I believe that this strategy does allow genuine explanation of capacities complex enough to be counted as intelligent, but I do not think it helps at all in explaining how the intentional can supervene on the nonintentional or how the teleological can supervene on the nonteleological – unless one manages to devise notions of intentionality and teleologicality that come in degrees (cf. Lycan 1981a). (iii) There are no "other kinds" of inner events that are "as different from physical events as colors are from wavelengths of light." We functionalists share Skinner's hostility to spookstuff in any form. (iv) The Movie Theater Model of the Mind is a bad model and is responsible for much philosophical confusion and misguided theorizing. Also, Descartes was wrong in maintaining that we know our own minds better than we know our bodies or our immediate surroundings; "in describing a private way station, one is to a considerable extent making use of public information." (v) The "copy theory" of representation is radically unsatisfactory. Nor do we have representations of wolves in our heads, if by "representation" is meant a little picture or other item whose representational character is entirely determined by the contents of our heads. (Insofar as we do have wolf representors located in our heads, they represent only in virtue of the extrinsic causal and other connections that they and we bear to wolves; see Putnam 1975, Fodor 1980, Lycan 1981b.) Nor does seeing imply something seen.

Now, the disagreements: The copy theory and other "miraculous" accounts of complex capacities are not the only alternatives to behaviorism, either in philosophy or in psychology. As Skinner concedes, mental states (construed by me as functionally rather than neuroanatomically characterized brain states) serve to bridge the gap between stimulus and response, particularly when the gap is temporally very large. Moreover, the positing of underlying mechanisms in the form of mental–functional states affords a *deeper explanation* of behavior than does the mere subsuming of the behavior under a nakedly empirical S–R generalization. (This is just an instance of a general criticism often made by scientific realists against positivistic instrumentalism. Of course, Skinner has always emphasized prediction and control as the goals of science, and shallow instrumentalistic "explanation" yields just as many true predictions as does the same empirical generalization supplemented by a story about an underlying mechanism. But understanding the fine structure of causes is a legitimate aim of science also; and the description of a mechanism will normally spin off further conditional predictions.) Functional states also seem to be required in light of a powerful objection standardly put to Skinner at least by philosophers and linguists (Chomsky 1959; Dennett 1978b; Fodor 1975): that for the most part, S–R correlations in humans are established or presumable only with the aid of tacit but massive assumptions about the subjects' internal organization (utilities, modes of representation, background beliefs, and the like). This point is most vividly illustrated by cases of novel stimuli and novel behavior, particularly verbal utterances. A novel stimulus has not previously been reinforced; yet we predict a subject's response to it with fair reliability if we know enough about the subject's beliefs and desires. (It does not help to suggest that "similar" stimuli have previously been reinforced, unless a respect of similarity is specified, and the only obvious respects of similarity will normally be expressed in intentional terms.) A novel bit of behavior *might* have a distinctive controlling stimulus irrespective of the subject's internal organization, but probably it will not; virtually no complex verbal utterance has its own special stimulus-condition that one might read off the utterer's reinforcement history – unless, again, one introduces a similarity relation and a respect of similarity specified in overtly or covertly intentional terms. The effect of an utterance on a istener depends on the listener's current functional states; the environmental cause of the utterance, to which the utterance is a "response," could be anything at all, depending on the utterer's intervening functional states. Classes of environmental stimuli do not by themselves determine any remotely useful taxonomy of verbal behavior.

Skinner offers three "methodological objections" to the functionalist turn. (a) He says that appeal to "unfinished causal sequences" is nonexplanatory. I do not see why; we can explain an automobile's breakdown in terms of gas-filter clogging without knowing what external events caused the filter to clog, even though a more *complete* explanation would go further back along the causal chain. (b) "A preoccupation with mental way stations burdens a science of behavior with all the problems raised by the limitations and inaccuracies of self-descriptive repertoires." I do not see this either. Theorists need not presume subjects' self-descriptions to be infallible or even generally accurate; they merely count them as further data. (c) "Responses which seem to be describing intervening states alone may embrace behavioral effects." Of course they may. This is another case in which subjects' self-descriptions may be inaccurate; nothing follows about the usefulness in general of positing intervening states to explain behavior patterns as a whole, verbal and nonverbal behavior included.

Finally, if Skinner is to convince us that functionalist posits are methodologically unsound, he will have to produce an argument general enough to apply to biology and to automotive mechanics as well as to the science of behavior. [Cf. the commentary by Stich – *Ed.*]

BFS: I agree that at any given moment a person's behavior is due to the state of his body at that moment and that to some extent a person may observe that state and speak of feelings and states of mind, such as intentions, expectations, desires, and preferences. Traditionally, feelings and states of mind are offered as explanations of behavior: "I took the cake rather than the ice cream because I preferred it." "I shall tell him what I think of him when I see him; that is what I intend to do." "I shall go to the meeting because I expect it will be interesting."

For casual purposes (among which I do not include philosophical purposes), it would be churlish to object to such practices. We all find it useful to ask people what they intend to do, how they feel about things, and so on. Therapists inquire into such matters at length. As a scientist, however (and I hope as a philosopher), I must recognize certain limitations. Reports of feelings and states of mind are notoriously inexact, for reasons I have examined elsewhere (see "Terms"). Nor can I simply look inside the person. That is not yet possible. I have spotted a clogged gas filter and that explains the trouble with my car, but if I want to avoid similar trouble in the future I must know how it came to be clogged.

The available alternative, then, is to discover the processes through which individuals acquire the behaviors and, of course, the bodily states appropriate to them which are observed as feelings and states of mind. It would be absurd to do this for casual purposes or possibly even for professional clinical purposes in therapy, but it seems to me at the moment the only way to go. Rather than attribute behavior to what is felt, let us attribute it to demonstrable external causes and accept the feelings as by-products. That we cannot always do this does not mean that it is not a valid scientific practice. That for casual purposes we seem to move much more quickly in speaking of feelings and states of mind does not mean that we are making greater progress in understanding human behavior.

It is true that "we predict a subject's response to [a novel stimulus] with fair reliability if we know enough about the subject's belief and desires," but it will not do to infer the beliefs and desires from the subject's response. Presumably he must tell us about them, but we shall never get beyond a "fair reliability" when that is the case.

Behaviorism and "the problem of privacy"

William Lyons

Department of Moral Philosophy, University of Glasgow, Scotland

1. It is a distinct pleasure to reread "Behaviorism-50," a classic exposition of the behaviorist position, and to rediscover how well, for the most part, Skinner writes. (Though one must wonder how he could stomach "ongoing ingestive behavior.") Would that his disciples and successors could write as lucidly and cogently.

I am inclined to think that, by now, Skinner's and others' arguments against mentalism or Cartesianism, and copy theories of internal representation, are accepted by those working in the relevant experimental and theoretical disciplines. The move away from Cartesian introspectionist and associationist psychologies to behaviorism was of immense benefit to psychology and related disciplines, but psychology has now moved on from behaviorism, and again, I believe, the move has been beneficial.

Skinner himself, with percipience, realised and acknowledged that the greatest difficulty for behaviorism was in coping with inner cognitive events or, in general, with "the problem of privacy," and I suggest that it was behaviorism's failure to cope with it at certain crucial points that has led to current centralist (brain-centred) psychologies and philosophies. In recent years, centre stage (at least in theoretical matters) has been hogged by latter-day cognitivist psychologies (computational cum artificial intelligence accounts of what goes on *between* environmental input and nonreflex behavioral output in the human organism), and, in philosophy, by, first, eliminative materialism (the elimination or reduction of the mental to brain states and processes), and now, functional materialism (the interpretation of the mental in terms of the abstract, functional, or "program" properties of the brain). Few would want to reinstate Cartesian or mentalist "way stations" but many (most?) feel the need to posit internal cognitive events of some sort.

What I am going to concentrate on, then, is not what behaviorism replaced but its own explanatory accounts, particularly in the area where its explanations have seemed so unconvincing to adherents of succeeding methodologies and schools of psychology and philosophy, namely, in connection with "the problem of privacy." Now one of the crucial points where, I believe, Skinner's behaviorism is found wanting in regard to the problem of privacy is in its treatment of introspection and, in general, our knowledge of such events in ourselves as thinking to oneself, doing mental arithmetic, composing a tune in one's head.

Skinner's most detailed account of how a behaviorist should treat so-called inner mental events is in *Science and Human Behavior* (Skinner 1953, sec. 3). He first points out that "inner" implies nothing more than limited accessibility. So far so good. He then goes on to suggest that, depending on the case in question, inner so-called mental events are to be given one of three possible explanations by a behaviorist.

2. The first explanation is in line with earlier behaviorist accounts of subvocal thoughts. Some inner events, for example doing mental arithmetic or composing a tune in one's head, might turn out to be, Skinner suggests, "covert" or "reduced" or "unemitted" forms of overt behavior, that is, "the private event is incipient or inchoate behavior" (Skinner 1953, p. 263) which, in turn, is to be explained as the internal muscular movements that usually precede overt behavior but which now occur in truncated and impotent form. Thus, presumably, doing mental arithmetic is a stopped-short version of doing arithmetic out loud, and composing a poem in one's head is a truncated unemitted version of composition on paper or in speech. Further, these covert and reduced internal behavioral movements generate the proprioceptive stimulation, that is, the feelings, that accompany some internal bodily movements. It is by means of these, it is suggested, that we become aware of these inner events and so come to refer to them in our talk. The ground-level account of what is going on – truncated, unemitted, reduced, impotent behavioral acts – is similar to the classical accounts of Watson (1921), Tolman (1922), and Lashley (1923). What was new was the suggestion that in some cases introspection amounted merely to the quite unmysterious, nonmental process of registering these truncated behavioral acts as proprioceptive stimulation.

Now the first and major difficulty is that there seems to be little or no evidence to support the view that inner events, such as doing mental arithmetic or composing a poem in one's head are always or even most often accompanied in adults by any inner truncated behavioral acts, such as movements of the tongue or laryngeal muscles. The second difficulty, related to it, is that even if there were a constant correlation between, say, thinking in one's head and such inner truncated behavior, and even if in the future we were to discover this by subtle instrumentation, there seems little or no evidence to suggest that our proprioceptive apparatus would be sufficiently sensitive to register it accurately or, in some cases, at all. (See Woodworth & Schlosberg 1955, chap. 26.)

Skinner's reply to this sort of suggestion used to be that you cannot argue from ignorance, that although there may be little or no evidence *now* as to the existence of such alleged inner truncated speech acts, and as to our ability to register them proprioceptively, quite likely the future will bring the necessary evidence (Skinner 1953, p. 282).

Third, there is still another difficulty with this account of introspection, namely, why it is that we do *not* and cannot make introspective reports in terms appropriate to proprioceptive feelings? As we do not, must a behaviorist postulate a special, internal, compulsory-stop, translation centre for translating proprioceptive data from internal truncated behavior into ordinary cognitive talk?

3. Skinner's second explanation, for other cases of our knowledge of internal so-called mental events, is less easy to pin down. The sort of case he has in mind is that of someone's claimed knowledge of his own intentions, plans, or decisions, Skinner says that when someone is on the point of going home or intending to go home then what is occurring in regard to that person is captured by "describing a history of variables which would enable an independent observer to describe the behavior in the same way if a knowledge of the variables were available to him" (1953, p. 263). I

take this to mean that for a person to say he is on the point of going home is not to report on some inner event at all; it is to make a prediction that he will go home soon, based on his knowledge of his own behavior in similar circumstances in the past. An explanation in terms of "covert" or "unemitted" or "reduced" behavior is inappropriate here. There are no such acts. The person who correctly says "I am on the point of going home" is inferring his future behavior from present environmental factors, for those factors become clues when correlated with his own past behavior in just such circumstances. As an account it has affinities with Ryle's so-called logical behaviorist account of introspection as the retrospection of ordinary behavior (Ryle 1949, esp. chap. 6).

Now there are a number of difficulties with this account as well which makes it look implausible. For a start, it implies that we could not have knowledge of and so assert an intention to go home if we were intending to do so in novel circumstances. Second, it would imply that others could very often (most often if we were introverted persons) know our intentions before we did. Finally, the account implies not merely that we could but also that we continually do gather, retain, then correctly tabulate and correlate information about what sorts of environmental things prompt one (cause one) to go home, such that we predict from environmental conditions what we are about to do. Now, since we are not aware of doing this, Skinner must postulate that we do it subliminally. But if that is so, the words "I'm about to go home" or "I intend to go on holiday this month" must appear out of our mouths, at least if we know nothing of behaviorist psychology, as if by magic. We must just find ourselves saying it.

4. Skinner's third account is aimed at explaining or explaining away any alleged reference to inner mental events when, for example, someone says, "I heard so and so" or "I see a red patch." He argues that the basis for the correct use of such perceptual talk lies in people's ordinary inspection or observation of their own overt discriminative behavior and not in any introspection of internal sense data. Just as we grant that others have heard or seen something if they can perform suitably convincing discriminative tasks (for example, most probably they *have* heard the oboe's part in the symphony if they can hum it afterwards), so we realise that we ourselves have heard or seen something if we catch ourselves performing discriminative tasks that demonstrate we have. "He observes himself as he executes some identifying response" (Skinner 1953, p. 265).

A difficulty with this is that although there may be little support for any sense datum theory of perception, there may be equally little for an account that suggests we make perceptual claims after sitting some sort of examination test for the senses that we have also set ourselves. As children make perceptual statements without any notion of how to check their discriminative behavior, the behaviorist must again resort to the position that the checking is not averted to by the checker, but such a suggestion needs supporting evidence if it is not to appear as a last stand in a forever hidden ditch. Further, the behaviorist will be forced to shore up this sort of explanation with his first sort (the proprioceptive registering of inner unemitted reduced behavior) because when there is no overt discriminative behavior accompanying veridical claims to perceive, the behaviorist will have to say that the discriminative behavior was inner, unemitted, and reduced. In the face of these difficult cases, this third type of account seems to collapse into being a gloss on the first sort of explanation of alleged cases of introspection.

5. So the questions for Skinner are, "At three score years and ten, should behaviorism adhere to these explanations of our knowledge of such things as our inner thoughts, intentions, and awareness of perceptual information, or should it offer a new solution to 'the problem of privacy'?," and "Has your confidence that 'the problem of privacy' would be solved by 'technical advances' been justified?"

Let my last word, however, be that I consider it an honor to be invited to contribute to this festchrift for one who has done so much for psychology and related disciplines.

BFS: I shall do my best (and I know it is not enough) to remedy the defects in my analysis which Lyons has so excellently set forth in his constructive commentary. I agree that the kind of thinking which seems to be merely covert behavior ("truncated, unemitted, reduced, impotent behavioral acts") may be so reduced that there is no muscular involvement to be sensed proprioceptively. Must we appeal to some minute behavior which never reaches a muscle? If so, it is a problem for the physiologist. There is a possibility that the effect is sensory. We may see ourselves behaving rather than actually behave. I believe that my analysis of seeing makes this a possible alternative. And again there is also the possibility that we are reporting some of the external circumstances to which the behavior is appropriate.

The extent to which we can apply the same criteria to knowing the intentions of another person seems to be determined by the extent to which we have shared personal histories. We may have little trouble in assessing the intentions of a friend whom we know particularly well, given the same knowledge of a current situation.

What we report when we say "I see the color of that rose" or "I hear the oboe in that recording of a symphony" is certainly not clear. It means more than "I can mix that color with my paints" or "I can locate it in a color solid" or "I can hum along with the oboe" or (If I am an oboe player) "I can play it covertly along with the oboist." Something less particular seems to be involved. When a teacher says to a child, "Do you see this box?," the child has learned that if he says yes, he will be asked questions which must be answered. He need not review his current repertoire with respect to the box in saying yes. All he needs is some evidence that the box is very much like other boxes to which he has responded in many different ways successfully. It could almost be the case that he sees that he sees the box simply by seeing it a second time. I agree with Lyons that this is far from adequate, but I'm sure that improvements will be made by looking at the circumstances under which people report seeing and hearing rather than by speculating about mental processes.

Philosophy and the future of behaviorism

M. Jackson Marr

School of Psychology, Georgia Institute of Technology

Wittgenstein (1958) has asserted that "there is a kind of general disease of thinking which always looks for (and finds) what would be called a mental state from which all our acts spring as from a reservoir" (p. 143). Skinner attempted to inoculate psychology against this disease by essentially equating public and private (covert) behaviors in relevant dimensions, thereby removing private events as fundamental causes of public behaviors. But this treatment has achieved very limited success – some would say none at all. Modern cognitive psychology largely views the behavior of organisms as *symptomatic* of internal "information processing" – activities comfortably expressed in computer metaphor. Such processing serves as a kind of "mental aether" conducting the *encoded* environment and the *stored* organism's history down to the final common pathway. In the rush to cast creatures into the software of the computing machine, no distinction is being made between essentially arbitrary artificial intelligence programs and adaptive biological mechanisms.

Despite putative advances in cognitive psychology, a Skinner article entitled "Behaviorism at Seventy" would probably not take a significantly different position, as attested by his more recent writings. Cognitive psychology has certainly put radical behaviorism on the defensive, though it is a battle that cognitive psychology itself is hardly aware of in any direct sense. That field, however, is slowly becoming aware of certain of its own conceptual difficulties, as indicated by recent publications of some of its advocates (e.g., Bransford, McCarrel, Franks & Nitsch 1977; Roediger 1980; Tulving 1979). Also, issues raised over the years by philosophers like Wittgenstein, Malcolm, Quine, Austin, and Ryle are receiving belated attention from theorists of psychology. Although very significant differences between (and among) these philosophers and Skinner on the status of "mental way stations" could be pointed out (e.g., Gier 1981), there are enough correspondences to say that Skinner, as a psychologist talking to psychologists, was at the forefront of epistemological theory important for the coherent development of psychology as a science. Although Skinner acknowledges a debt to Mach, Poincaré, Russell, and Bridgman in the early development of his behaviorism, it is not clear from his writings the extent to which, for example, his analysis of privacy, the role of the verbal community in the shaping of consciousness, and his disdain for mental way stations were directly influenced by men like Wittgenstein and Ryle or whether they were derived from other sources. His work makes almost no reference to the modern philosophical literature, and one is tempted to conclude that a more extensive participation in the philosophical community might have better protected him from critics like Dennett (1978a). Dennett's discussion of Skinner's treatment of mentalism is in several ways misguided and misinformed, but it does raise some important issues, particularly regarding the problems and implications of translating statements about mental events into statements about behavior.

Placing radical behaviorism in the context of mainstream philosophy has been left to others (e.g., Day 1969a; 1969b; Harzem & Miles 1978). Putting the radical behaviorist position into coherent philosophical order is an essential task if it is to survive as a vital force in psychological theory. Many would say it is already dead, but there remain significant numbers of advocates, and this issue evokes a continuing interest. The struggle between radical behaviorism and cognitive psychology will not be fought on the battlegrounds of experimental design, or techniques of data analysis, or demonstrations of this or that effect, or of the forms of functional relations, but on the field of philosophical analysis (J. Marr 1983). There are, I think, difficulties for radical behaviorism here in making itself understood and achieving a certain credibility. Its focus is, of course, on the behavior of organisms; this includes the *verba behavior* of the human – including that of the cognitive psychologist, the radical behaviorist, and the philosopher. Cognitive psychologists may claim that their verba behavior provides for more effective delineation and control of variables relevant to complex behavior. This language does not have to "refer" to anything in particular, but encourages a systematic organization of functional relationships – in a word it is heuristic. The adoption of computer metaphors is in part responsible for psychology breaking away in the 1960s from sterile association theories of remembering with their dreary nonsense-syllable methodologies.

The radical behaviorist has to face more effectively the issues raised by translation of statements about mental events into statements about behavior. Are such translations the principal task of behaviorism, as Harzem and Miles (1978) suggest? Is translation impossible, as Quine (1960) asserts? Are reasons and justifications evoking intentions and the like simply provisionary or incomplete explanations for behavior, or are they somehow misguided as, for example, a thermodynamic argument evoking the notion of a caloric fluid?

Finally, rational, philosophical arguments, whether for or against behaviorism, could conceivably be analyzed as elaborate contingency-shaped and rule-governed verbal behavior in a nexus of individual, cultural, and phylogenetic history. There is no way to step out of the system. The development of an "empirical epistemology" is difficult because notions of what is observable and what implications can be drawn thereby are embedded in the contingencies and the rules. As Einstein remarked, it is the theory that tells us what is observable.

BFS: Marr raises a question of my philosophical sources. In the early thirties I read Wittgenstein's *Tractatus*, but although I was at the time writing a "Sketch for an Epistemology" (only one chapter of which was ever published; see Skinner 1979), I doubt very much that Wittgenstein had any important effect on me. Russell was an early and important influence. Ryle and Ayer came later and, so far as I know, did not work any change in me.

I like Marr's statement that "modern cognitive psychology largely views the behavior of organisms as *symptomatic* of internal 'information processing' – activities comfortably expressed in computer metaphor." The important word is "comfortably." The computer is a model of one kind of human *behavior*, anticipated thousands of years earlier with clay tiles, in which "information" is "stored" and "retrieved" for computational purposes. But it is not a useful model of the organism that engages in that behavior, and the comfort will, I am sure, be short-lived.

Mechanism at two thousand

John C. Marshall

Neuropsychology Unit, Neuroscience Group, The Radcliffe Infirmary, Oxford, England

Radical behaviorism is informed by an acute distaste for little men in the role of explanatory variables. The aversion is justified, but quite irrelevant to the mainstream history of information-processing psychology. Despite a passing reference to La Mettrie, nowhere in "Behaviorism-50" does Skinner consider the status of information-processing mechanisms as explanatory constructs in psychological theory; his failure to distinguish between a homunculus and a robot is the most striking example of this oversight.

In a lecture at the University of Basel, Paracelsus (1493–1541) gave an alchemic recipe whereby a miniature human, a homunculus, could be grown from semen in a cucurbit. If theoretical psychology consisted simply in postulating a sequence of homunculi within the skin who were responsible for controlling the behavior of the larger man, Skinner's sceptical attitude towards mentalistic explanation would be amply vindicated. Any modern mentalist from Hero of Alexandria (Marshall 1977) to Kenneth Craik of Cambridge (1943) would agree that little men "offer no real explanation and stand in the way of a more effective analysis." Indeed, the iatrochemists had so little effect upon the development of scientific psychology that Skinner can only cite the arresting graphics of a television program, "Gateways to the Mind," in defence of his claim that mentalistic explanation is committed to little men.

Likewise, any mentalist from Leibniz to Wiener (1948) would agree with Skinner (1947) that to leap *directly* from behavior to neurophysiology is an ill-advised move. Mere correlations between overt behavior and the activity of cells and synapses do not suffice to explain the performance of the organism. Mentalists are neither vitalists nor physiologists, but rather engineers concerned with discovering the type of machine that is man or mouse. The central problem of cognitive psychology is thus to specify the nature of the algorithms and mechanisms that realize the computational capacities (and ultimately the behavioral repertoires) of the organism (D. Marr 1982). Once these mechanisms are specified, one can then inquire into how the functions they carry out are actually implemented by particular neuronal assemblies. But no mentalist would suppose that a knowledge of the properties of cells and synapses (or silicon chips) would in itself be sufficient to explain the activity of the organism (or machine) composed of these elements. As Leibniz writes in *The Monadology* (1714, pp. 227–28):

> Supposing there were a machine so constructed as to think, feel, and have perception, it might be conceived as increased in size, while keeping the same proportions, so that one might go into it as into a mill. That being so, we should, on examining its interior, find only parts which work one upon another, and never anything by which to explain a perception.

If we frame psychological theory within a computational theory of mind (Fodor 1980), it matters little whether any interesting aspect of human performance falls within the domain of the laws and terms of radical behaviorism. Imagine, just for fun, that the action of picking up and drinking a cup of coffee was a "response." That is, the frequency with which the action is performed is determined by the actor's "current motivational state, his current stimulus circumstances, his past reinforcements, and his genetic constitution" (MacCorquodale 1970, p. 83). If human behavior was so controlled, we would have a highly satisfying answer to the philosophical question: *Why* did so-and-so pick up and drink a cup of coffee? Laplace's equations could rejoice, but we would be none the wiser about the nature of the organism that was capable of this feat. The success of the behaviorist enterprise would leave quite untouched the scientific problem of accounting for *how* we are capable of picking up cups (Teuber 1974), perceiving and producing utterances in our native language (Berwick & Weinberg 1983), or deriving form from motion (Ullman 1979). Only an account of the machinery within the skin can explain behavior, quite irrespective of whether or not the principles of operant conditioning suffice to predict behavior.

BFS: I agree that "only an account of the machinery within the skin can explain behavior." When available it will do so, as DNA has explained the laws of genetics. But there were laws of genetics to be explained before the role of DNA was discovered, and there are laws of behavior to be discovered before we can know that an account of the machinery is indeed an explanation.

I have dealt with the supposed success of cognitive psychology in "specify-[ing] the nature of the algorithms and mechanisms that realize the computational capacities. . .of the organism" in reply to other commentaries.

A cognitivist reply to behaviorism

Robert C. Moore

Artificial Intelligence Center, SRI International, Menlo Park, California 94025 and Center for the Study of Language and Information, Stanford University

There are two major themes running through Skinner's various objections to mentalistic psychology. He argues, first, that mentalistic notions have no explanatory value ("The objection is not that these things are mental but that they offer no real explanation"), and second, that since the correct explanation of behavior is in terms of stimuli and responses, mentalistic accounts of behavior must be either false or translatable into behavioristic terms ("behavior which seemed to be the product of mental activity could be explained in other ways"). What I hope to show is that a "cognitivist" perspective offers a way of constructing mentalistic psychological theories that circumvent both kinds of objection.

The first theme appears twice in infinite-regress arguments. Skinner ridicules psychological theories that seem to appeal to homunculi, on the grounds that explaining the behavior of one homunculus would require a second homunculus, and so on. Later he employs the same rationale to criticize theories of perception based on internal representation: If seeing consists of constructing an internal representation of the thing seen, the internal representation would then apparently require an inner eye to look at it, and so on. Skinner's concern for explanatory value is also evident in his view of mental states as mere "way stations" in unfinished causal accounts of behavior. If an act is said to have been caused by a certain mental state, without any account as to how that state itself was caused, there seems to be little to constrain what states we invoke to explain behavior. The limiting case would be to "explain" every action an agent performs by simply postulating a primitive desire to perform that action.

Skinner's concerns about explanatory value should not be taken lightly, and they seem to me to pose serious problems for older-style mentalistic psychological theories. Often these theories appear to allow no direct evidence for the existence of many kinds of mental states and events. According to such theories, "poking around the brain" will not help, because mental entities are not physical; moreover, asking the subject for introspective reports may not help either, because mental entities can be unconscious. But a second consequence of the view that mental entities are nonphysical is that we have no a priori idea as to what the constraints on their causal powers might be. We are thus left in a situation in which we could, at least in principle, postulate any mental states and events we like, adjusting our assumptions regarding their effects on behavior to fit any possible evidence.

How does cognitivism avoid Skinner's charges in this area? I take it that what distinguishes cognitivism from other mentalistic approaches to psychology is the premise that mental states can be identified with *computational* states. This has two consequences for the problem at hand. First, computational states must in some way be embodied in physical states. This means that if behavioral evidence alone were not sufficient to determine what mental state an organism was in, neurological evidence could be brought to bear to decide the question. Second, and of much more immediate practical consequence, is the fact that there is a very well developed mathematical theory of the abilities and limits of computational systems. Hence, once we identify mental states with computational states, we are not free to endow them with arbitrary causal powers.

When a computational account of mental states and events is given, Skinner's infinite-regress arguments lose their force. Although it *is* a characteristic of computational theories of mind to explain the behavior of the whole organism in terms of interactions among systems that may appear to be "homunculi," a computational account, as Dennett (1978a, pp. 123–24) has pointed out, requires each of these homunculi to be less intelligent than the whole they comprise. Thus, although there is indeed a regress, it is not an infinite one, because eventually we get down to a level of homunculi so stupid that they can be clearly seen to be "mere machines." Similar comments apply to Skinner's worries about explaining perception in terms of mental representation. Although he is quite right in maintaining the pointlessness of supposing that the brain contains an isomorphic copy of the image on the retina, computational theories of vision simply do not work that way. Although they make use of internal representations, these express an *interpretation* of the image, not a copy. Although a retinal image might be thought of as a two-dimensional array of light intensities, the postulated representations take as primitives such notions as "convex edge," "concave edge," and "occluding edge." These representations are then manipulated computationally in ways that make sense given their interpretations. Waltz (1975) gives a very clear (albeit already outdated) exposition of this approach.

Skinner's notion of an unfinished causal account is not necessarily answered simply by adopting a computational perspective, but conscientious cognitive theorists do address the problems raised by the tendency to attribute precisely those structures that are needed to account for observed behavior. Some deal with it as Skinner suggests, by investigating the causation of mental states (e.g., studying language acquisition), but the more frequent strategy is to show how a single computational mechanism (or the interaction of a few mechanisms) accounts for a broad range of behavior. If, for example, we can show that a relatively small set of linguistic rules can account for a much larger (perhaps infinite) set of natural-language sentence patterns, then it is certainly not vacuous, or without explanatory value, to claim that those linguistic rules in some sense characterize the mental state of a competent language user.

Whether or not Skinner would acknowledge that the cognitivist framework has the potential to produce mentalistic theories with genuine explanatory value, I suspect he would argue that, because of the other major theme of his paper, any such conclusion is really beside the point. In his view, mentalistic terminology is at best a rather complicated and misleading way of talking about behavior and behavioral dispositions. Skinner's picture seems to be that mental states, rather than being real entities that mediate between stimulus and response, are merely *summaries* of stimulus–response relationships. Thus, hunger, rather than being what causes us to eat when presented with food, would be regarded as the disposition to eat when presented with food. (This interpretation of mental states obviously reinforces Skinner's opinion that mental explanations of behavior are vacuous; attributing eating to a disposition to eat explains nothing.)

The response to this point of view is that, even if we could get a complete description of an organism's "mental state" in terms of behavioral dispositions, that fact would not vitiate attempts to give a causal account of these dispositions in a way that might make reference to mental states more realistically construed. A computer analogy is helpful here. Complex computer systems often have "users' manuals" that are intended, in effect, to be complete accounts of the systems' behavioral dispositions. That is, they undertake to describe for any input (stimulus) what the output (response) of the system would be. But no one would suppose that to know the content of the users' manual is to know everything about a system; we might not know anything at all about how the system achieves the behavior described in the manual. Skinner's response might be that, if we want to know how the behaviora dispositions of an organism are produced, we have to look to neurobiology – but this would miss the point of one of the most important substantive claims of cognitivism Just as in a complex computer system there are levels of abstraction above the leve of electronic components (the analogue, one supposes, of neurons) that comprise coherent domains of the discourse in which causal explanations of behavior can be couched ("The system computes square roots by Newton's method"), so too n human psychology there seem to be similar levels of abstraction – including evels that involve structures corresponding roughly to such pretheoretical mentalistic concepts as belief, desire, and intention.

Finally, it may very well be *impossible* to describe the behavioral dispositions of organisms as complex as human beings without reference to internal states. Skinner seems to assume uncritically that, if the sole objective of psychology is to describe the stimulus–response behavior of organisms, one can always do so without reference to internal states. But this is mathematically impossible for many of the formal models one might want to use to describe human behavior. In particular, given some of the behavioral repertoires that human beings are capable of acquiring (e.g., proving theorems in mathematics, understanding the well-formed expressions of a natural language), it seems likely that no formal model significantly less powerful than a general-purpose computer (Turing machine) could account for the richness of human behavior. In a very strong sense, however, it is generally impossible to characterize the behavior of a Turing machine without referring to its internal states. Now, the behaviorists may be fortunate, and it may turn out that the behavioral dispositions of humans are indeed describable without reference to internal states, but Skinner appears not even to realize that this is a problem.

To summarize:

1. Skinner's arguments against the explanatory value of mentalistic psychology do not apply to properly constructed cognitivist theories.
2. The existence of a complete behavioristic psychology would neither supplant nor render superfluous a causal cognitivist account of psychology.
3. The regularities of human behavior that Skinner's approach to psychology attempts to describe may not even be expressible without reference to internal states.

BFS: I do not formulate behavior in terms of stimuli and responses. It is the cognitivists' computer model that does that, with its input and output. Computers can be designed so that they will be changed by the consequences of their output, but cognitivist models seldom go that far and hence fall that far short of being adequate models of a behaving organism. Computation is something which is done by people in specified ways for specified reasons. If mental states can be identified with computational states, then mental states are human behavior, and that is what I have been saying. The fact that computational systems can be very elaborate adds prestige to computational theory, but it does not advance the identification with mental states.

Whether internal representations are copies or interpretations of images, something called "seeing them" is still required. Notions such as "convex edge," "concave edge," and "occluding edge" are a step in the right direction. They are the beginnings of an *analysis* of an image rather than a replication. But much more is needed before the so-called image is seen. So far as I am concerned, children learn a language when their behavior is modified by the contingencies of verbal reinforcement maintained by a community. (That does not mean, as Chomsky and others seem to suppose, that the community must engage in explicit instruction.) I do not believe that children are discovering the rules of grammar as they learn to speak. They are discovering verbal behavior that is effective in a given community. The contingencies can be analyzed and rules extracted which are helpful to a person learning a language, but to suppose that the rules are *in* the contingencies is a fundamental mistake made by mentalists. Rules are verbal behavior descriptive of contingencies.

Moore's analysis of hunger is incomplete. We observe that an organism sometimes eats and sometimes does not. In general, an organism that has not eaten for some time tends to eat. Deprivation is a controlling variable, and we can induce organisms to eat by depriving them of food. A probability of eating can be evaluated in several ways. It is reasonable to say that deprivation produces a state of the organism in which eating is highly probable, and that state is properly called "hunger," but is it what one feels as hunger, and does what one feels lead one to eat? Stomach pangs are badly correlated with such a state; one may discover that "one was hungrier than one thought" if one eats a surprising amount; and so on. What one feels as hunger is an unreliable clue to the state, and in any case it is the state, not the way it feels, that is responsible for eating. The state is what is felt.

Introspection as the key to mental life

Chris Mortensen

Department of Philosophy, University of Adelaide, Australia

Direct knowledge of the states inside our skins is an important problem of any theory of mental life. Much philosophy of mind has wrestled with accommodating mental *concepts* in a materialist world view, but why bother: Just discard them. Mental states would be no problem for materialism, were it not that what we seem to *know* about them is not easy for a materialist-physicalist to accommodate. That has been the real cause of the fuss. For example, J. J. C. Smart's (1959) topic – neutral "analysis" – was really a theory of what information introspection gives. I argue a weaker thesis here: that we should not hastily discard the deliverances of introspection concerning internal representations or copies of the world.

Skinner remarks "we cannot escape from a toothache as easily as from a deafening noise." This oversimplifies in two ways. First, external events can be quite inescapable: the locomotive bearing down on me. Second, inner states can be escapable. Shut your eyes, open them at t_1, shut at t_2. Now, something distinctive is going on during (t_1, t_2). Such events, moreover, are crucially connected with seeing, hallucinations, and other states inside. And the (t_1, t_2) event is escapable: Just shut your eyes. Indeed, since it is escapable it is inside, because the outside exists after t_2.

Ordinarily we do not inspect our visual experiences. We just have them. Skinner rightly notes that this is no problem for behaviourism (well, materialism anyway). But we also seem to know about the features of inner states. We distinguish visual states from one another along several dimensions, such as colour or shape. The state of having a square patch in your visual field is different from the state of having a triangular, or elliptical, patch in your visual field. There seem to be as many distinguishable part similarities and differences as in some rough spatial topology. Visual states are also among the more directly accessible of our inside states. Freud introduced the idea that we can be quite wrong about out internal states, and more prone to error about certain *kinds*. Humans are more visual than many other species. They are capable of fine discriminations between the visible features of the external world, and fine discriminations between the features of their visual states.

We are being pushed to the view that we know that our inside states have features describable by predicates like "has as part of it a square patch." But would it be so surprising if we, or our evolutionary ancestors, stored *some* information nonverbally, say iconographically? Think of the difference between knowing from a police description that the suspect had brown hair, oval face, . . . ; and knowing by direct acquaintance that he looks like that. Why should Skinner as a materialist deny this? It does not a priori threaten materialism. To be sure, one can imagine such an argument: we know that part of our visual state is a relation to a square patch existing from t_1 to t_2; materialism is the doctrine that whatever exists is physical; no material square patch existing from t_1 to t_2 is identical with the patch in my visual field; therefore materialism is false. Many physicialists have felt it necessary to deny the first premise, but the last might also be denied.

Skinner denies that we store information in "representations" or "copies": "The need for something beyond, and quite different from, copying is not widely understood." But of course the *relationship* between people and their square patch, particularly its causal hookups, could conceivably supply the extra. The relation of *representing* undoubtedly has a causal dimension. I think that Skinner is suspicious of internal knowledge because he fears that its apparent deliverances – that inside we partly copy the universe – might *as a matter of fact* be hard to reconcile with materialism: "The search for copies. . .still goes on, but with discouraging results," and "It is most convenient for both organism and psychophysiologist if the external world is never copied – if the world we know is simply the world around us." But the latter misapplies the principle of parsimony, before evidence the other way has been discounted rather than after. Nor is the opposing view a particularly inconvenient one for a scientist to cope with. It is a nonsequitur to think, as many have, that since a perceiving robot could be built without inner representations, then humans *must* not have them. "If the real world is, indeed, scrambled in transmission but later reconstructed in the brain, we must then start all over again and explain how the organism sees the reconstruction." But a regress threatens here only if we are incautious about the powers of the homunculi inside us. Granted that a mere copy cannot be the *whole* story, since mechanisms for information storage *via* copies are conceivable the regress cannot show that copies are not *part* of the story. Skinner makes the regress easier to swallow, by speaking of "seeing" the reconstruction, though he also says "*seeing-that*-we-are seeing" (italics added). But then: "the heart of the behaviorist position. . . : Seeing does not imply something seen." It is careless to speak about "seeing" our seeing, instead of "knowing"; but even so Skinner's own "seeing *that* we are seeing" blocks the regress. It also weakens his point that seeing does not imply anything seen: Seeing *that p* implies *p*. Nor can I think that there is much to Skinner's view that an inner mechanism adds nothing to an explanation. There might be, if "inner" meant "spooky." But here it just means "inside," and we do not think this about broken-down bodies, cars, or computers.

Eliminative materialism is a powerful strategy: If mental states of a certain kind might be onotologically threatening, deny their existence. Against our capacity for systematic mistakes about our interiors, we need to balance the confidence that we are thereby able to get information. I wish I had a clearer picture of the epistemological weights to assign here. Although it is solipsism to have information about our insides always outweighing information about the outside, the opposite extreme (whenever introspection conflicts with scientific behaviourism, deny the former) is equally misplaced.

BFS: Mortensen apparently attributes to me the position that "Whenever introspection conflicts with scientific behaviorism, deny the former." That is the position of methodological behaviorism which I explicitly rule out. "Behaviorism-50," together with "Terms" [elsewhere in this volume], is concerned with the limits of introspection, not with its rejection.

I said that "we cannot escape from a toothache as easily as from a deafening noise" merely to illustrate that private stimuli are "very much with us." I do not see why it is necessary to prove that we can sometimes not escape from public stimuli.

I doubt very much whether "the *relationship* between people and their square patch, particularly its causal hookups, could conceivably supply" what is needed beyond representations or copies. For Mortensen, a "part of our visual state" is a relation to a square patch existing from t_1 to t_2 in our visual field. If that means that whatever is going on in us is caused by the visual patch, I could scarcely disagree, but the issue is whether there is a copy of the patch inside and if so what part it could play in seeing the patch. I question the reality of representations or copies not because I am "afraid" they would be hard to reconcile with "materialism" but because we have no evidence for them and because they would contribute nothing to the process of seeing if they existed.

Belief-level way stations

Donald Perlis

Computer Science Department, University of Maryland, College Park

"Behaviorism-50" reminds us that Skinner is not a shallow denier of the complex issues surrounding our experiences, as he is sometimes portrayed. He in fact in many respects here (20 years ago) raises the banner of what now seems to be the general attitude of cognitive science: that behavior includes inner events, and that these are to be explained in the same context as the rest of behavior, with physical structures and causes as their basis, and with cognition as nothing more than an aspect of this. That is, homunculi are out of the picture, but inner states that we know as "self" and so on are to be explained as actual physical phenomena of some sort.

Skinner does seem to miss one crucial point in the current cognitive arsenal. In stating repeatedly that there are no internal pictures or representations of externa sources of stimuli, he seems to have in mind only fairly direct "homuncular" copies of these sources, such as two-dimensional projections (visual images) and so on. However, there is a much more profound sense of representation that is available, and that is the touchstone of much current work in artificial intelligence, namely, the representation of beliefs, that is, data that can be reasoned with.

We needn't store a physical picture of an apple in order to store a "belief" that an apple is available in the room. Yet this belief-level "way station" is what allows reasoning (planning, problem solving) to occur. It may lead to action such as eating the apple (easily explained in more S–R fashion, to be sure), or an hour later telling a friend who complains of hunger that the apple is available (slightly less easily explained in S–R fashion), or a day later telling oneself that the apple looked awfully good but actually probably had worms (the action here being only internal), or never telling anyone anything about it and slowly losing the accessibility of the belief (not an action at all, but merely a potential for action).

Skinner is right in pointing to action as the key to perception and cognition, but over strict in denying that any kind of representation occurs. In fact, it may be, as Minsky (1968), Harnad (1982), and others point out, that it is at this level that conscious states have meaning: simply as sentences the organism "tells" itself.

Thus, way stations that contain beliefs can interact via an internal (physical) process ("reason," e.g., modus ponens) to produce further way stations (other beliefs) that can later lead to further external behavior. None of this is outside the paradigm that Skinner defends, but it is important to recognize the distinct character of certain of the inner processes that occur, namely as storing linguistic (logical, amenable to reason) representations of the outside world, and that as such, representations are indeed present and important.

BFS: Cognitive scientists insist upon two kinds of internal copies of the world. Chomsky (1980b) has immortalized them in the title "Rules and Representations." The person, either as Homo sapiens or homunculus sapiens, takes in the environment, observes it, and stores it as a representation of reality, which he can retrieve, observe again, describe, and so on. Perlis seems to agree that this may be wrong and that having been exposed to contingencies of reinforcement involving parts of the world, we are changed in such a way that we can respond in the absence of those parts as if they were present. What we have acquired are not representations of the world but ways of looking at the world.

Beliefs, intentions, knowledge (cognition!) could be said to be copies of contingencies of reinforcement. Having turned on my television set by pushing the button on the right, I henceforth *believe* that that is the way to turn on the set. I now *know* how to turn on the set. If I possess no verbal behavior (if, for example, I have never seen television sets and no one has ever told me about them) the only evidence of my belief or knowledge is the increase in the probability that I will push that button in case the appearance of a picture on a screen has been a reinforcing consequence. Such a "representation of beliefs" is not a datum that can be reasoned with. It is only when one becomes a member of a verbal community which talks about television sets and how to operate them and how they resemble other things that one can know how to turn the set on for merely verbal reasons.

Artificial intelligence and the great computational revolution in cognitive science is concerned not with behavior but with ways in which people talk about behavior. Contingencies of reinforcement can be converted into rules specifying behavior and consequences, including the laws of religions, governments, and science (see "Problem Solving"). Rules can be manipulated to generate new rules applying to novel circumstances. But those who do this have not escaped from the contingencies themselves. One must discover why people formulate rules and follow them.

Ontology and ideology of behaviorism and mentalism

Georges Rey

Department of Philosophy, University of Colorado

Chomsky (1959), Fodor (1968b), and Dennett (1978b; 1978c), to say nothing of many of the actual behaviorist experiments from the twenties through the sixties, are hard acts to follow if one is objecting to behaviorism and defending mentalism. Rather than attempt to improve significantly upon these past efforts, I'll simply try to present them in a summary form that may seem clearer and less question-begging than they may have seemed to Professor Skinner in the past.

A distinction that is crucial to the controversy surrounding mentalism and behaviorism is one drawn by Skinner's colleague Quine. This is the distinction between what Quine (1951) calls the "ontology" and the "ideology" of a theory, or the *objects* that the theory posits and describes, and the particular *terms* in which it describes them. By and large it's a good idea to become clear about a theory's ideology before attempting to determine its ontology: What actually needs to be posited by a theory can depend a lot upon the precise character of the theory's assertions. This is particularly important in view of the "dualistic" and related "private" ontological claims to which Skinner seems to presume mentalism is committed. So, putting aside for a moment questions of ontology, let's compare merely the ideologies of mentalism and behaviorism.

Our ordinary mentalistic explanations of the lives of humans and many other animals involves chiefly two sorts of idioms: the "(propositional) attitude" terms (e.g., "belief," "preference") and "qualitative state" descriptions (e.g., "pain," "itch," "love"). The mentalism that is being most vigorously defended in recent cognitive psychology, and the only sort that I want to defend here, involves only the attitudes. (The qualitative states seem to be a problem for everyone; see, e.g., Block 1980b and Rey 1983.) Very roughly, the view is that the best explanation of the impressive adaptivity of an organism to its environment is in terms of its beliefs and preferences: For example, it wants certain food, and, as a result of its innate endowment, capacities to reason, and past history of stimulation, it acquires some approximately true beliefs about where and how to secure some.

Skinner, of course, will have none of this. Beliefs and preferences are needless "way stations" that distract us from the single important determinant of behavior, the environment. In particular, human and animal behavior can better be understood in terms of ordered triples of physically describable stimuli (S), responses (R), and reinforcements (F) that obey some or other form of the law of effect: The probability of R given S in the future is increased if pairs of S and R have themselves been paired with Fs in certain patterns (e.g., intermittently) in the past. It's an extremely bold theory, purporting to explain an extraordinary complexity of animal behavior by means of virtually a single law.

Although such a theory may well explain *some* behavior (e.g., the turns of the pigeon, phobias, gambling), it seems not to come even close to explaining it all. There are, notoriously, the difficulties in explaining linguistic phenomena raised by Chomsky (1959) in his review of Skinner's *Verbal Behavior* (to which Skinner has yet to make a reply). And then there are all the phenomena that emerged from the behaviorist experiments themselves. Contrary to popular belief, it's not only human behavior that resists behavioristic explanation; the theory doesn't seem to work even for the rats. It runs into serious difficulties in attempting to explain short-cut behavior (Shepard 1933; Tolman & Honzik 1930), passive learning (Gleitman 1963), laten learning (Blodgett 1929), (in the case of monkeys and chimps) learning to learn

(Harlow 1949; 1959), and insightful improvisations (Köhler 1926). What these phenomena in general show is that the probability of a response can be increased in ways other than by the Law of Effect: Mere stimulation even without any specific responses or reinforcements can be enough. Moreover, even in those cases that appear to be covered by the law of effect, the descriptions of the S's R's, and F's exceed mere physical terms (e.g., adequate characterizations of the R's that the rat learns seem to involve descriptions like "to go where it *thinks* the food is"; of the F's, "satisfaction of curiosity"; and of the S's, in the case of humans, not only "is grammatical," or "is a sentential constituent," but, really, most *any* of the arbitrarily complex classifications of stimuli we can conceive). The ideology of the theory and the laws in which it figures simply seem to be inadequate by any standard scientific criteria. The behaviorists' efforts to meet these difficulties have seemed over the years no better than the efforts of Ptolemaics to account for the motion of heavenly bodies, that is, no better, ironically enough, than the very sorts of ad hoc efforts to which Skinner claims mentalism resorts (in this regard see esp. Dennett 1978b, pp. 66–70).

It's not obvious (in fact, it's probably false) that mentalistic explanations are ultimately adequate either. But they seem to many recent theorists to present greater promise. Unlike the case of behaviorism, however, the relevant evidence for them hasn't been quite so thoroughly researched. So why does Skinner reject them a priori? Well, he has what he takes to be some knock-down arguments. In fairness to him, "Behaviorism-50" was written before much of a plausible computational theory of mental processes (e.g., Fodor 1975) had been developed. In the light of particularly that theory, however, all of Skinner's complaints about *cognitive* explanations at least can be answered. Specifically:

1. The no explanation (homunculus) objection. A computational theory of mind explains cognitive processes by appeal to specific computations upon representations that are entokened in the brain. We *know* that we can explain the intelligent behavior of some computers in this way; why shouldn't organisms turn out to be computers of that sort? If such explanations involve appealing to "homunculi," we need only require that in the long run the homunculi become so stupid they can be "replaced by a machine" (Dennett 1978c, pp. 80–81). It's that potential replacement (of *at that point* a mental by a physical explanation) that tells against any "predilection for unfinished causal sequences."

2. "At some point the organism must do more than create duplicates." Quite right: it also had better perform computations upon them. And why shouldn't those "duplicates" include representations of a wolf? If they did, it might then be possible for them to "die in our stead" (Dennett 1978c, p. 77, quoting Popper). (Such a possibility wouldn't entail, by the way, that we "see" the representations. A mentalist can entirely agree with Skinner that "seeing doesn't entail something seen"; see Rey 1980; Smart 1959; but it may still involve a computation on a representation.)

3. Dualism and logical privacy require a special methodology. Given the analogy it exploits between the mind and computer (and particularly its agnosticism with regard to qualitative states), it should be obvious that cognitivism is not committed to dualism. Moreover, given some of the results of its own research on the fallibility of introspection (e.g., Nisbett & Wilson 1977), it should be clear that it's not committed to dualism's associated claims of privacy or anything more than the very sort of *contingently* privileged access that Skinner himself endorses. There is no reason in the world to think that present cognitive research involves any "special methodology" other than the careful framing and public testing of hypotheses that we find in any other science.

4. *"In practice all these [mentalistically describable] ways of changing a man's mind reduce to manipulating his environment, verbal or otherwise."* This is the strong claim of "analytical behaviorism," whose plausibility seems to be based primarily upon a fallacy of confusing the ontology with the ideology of a theory. It may be true that every particular *mental* act that anybody ever performs is a piece of physical behavior; but, as Quine (1951) has shown with an elegant example from number theory, it doesn't follow that the mental terms in which we *describe* that behavior are *translatable* into the physical terms in which it can also be described. Despite the *ontological reducibility* of cognitivism to physics, the two systems of description may so cross-classify that no such "ideological reduction" is possible. A number of famous arguments in the literature (Chisholm 1957, chap. 11; Quine 1960, chap. 2) as well as simply the notorious failure of all efforts at such translation, strongly suggest that this is precisely the case. Mentalistic description seems to be an ideologically irreducible system of description and explanation of the nevertheless ontologically entirely physical states and behaviors of organisms.

The only objection now to such a theory can be that it doesn't explain what it purports to explain. But to establish that we need to look at the diverse empirical evidence cognitive science is presently adducing.

BFS: It is a little late in the day to be defending the experimental analysis of behavior against Köhler (1926), Blodgett (1929), and Tolman and Honzik (1930), as Rey seems to suggest I should be doing. To say that the recent history of the experimental analysis of behavior resembles the efforts of Ptolemy to improve his account by adding epicycles to cycles is to show an extraordinary unfamiliarity with the science. Chomsky will, I am sure, answer himself if I give him enough time. He has already moved slightly in the right direction.

Rey misses the distinction between contingency-governed and rule-governed behavior (see "Problem Solving"). No one denies that those who have the necessary verbal behavior can describe the contingencies to which they are exposed and perhaps specify behavior that will meet them effectively. In doing so they may formulate rules of conduct, and it is possible that new rules may be deduced from old which apply to unexperienced or unpredicted contingencies. By confining oneself to rule-governed behavior, one appears to avoid all the problems of mentalism, but the problems have merely been dropped by the way. We must still explain how and why people compute rules, why they behave in ways guided by rules, and so on. Their behavior is still governed by contingencies of reinforcement which need to be analyzed.

If I must resort to the standard homily: The hungry rat presses a lever and receives food. We observe simply that the rate of pressing the lever increases. Does the rat now believe that pressing a lever produces food? Does it know that pressing a lever produces food? Does it press with the intention of getting food? Does it expect food to appear when it presses? I see no reason to go beyond the facts in any of these ways. But what about a human subject? He pulls the plunger of a vending machine and receives a candy bar. Does he now know that pulling the plunger will produce a candy bar?

Does he believe that the machine is operative? Was it his intention to get a candy bar? Did he expect that a candy bar would appear? In casual discourse we should answer yes to all of these questions, and the man would do so too. But he would do so only if he had been exposed to a verbal community which had taught him "what these words mean," and to do so the community must have observed events very much like those in the case of the rat.

So far as we know both man and rat have private evidence. They feel their bodies at the moment of action. The man, however, has been taught to use words like belief, knowledge, intention, and expectation to describe what he feels. Does he pull the plunger because of the condition he feels or because of his feeling it? That is the question. It is certainly much easier to ask him how he feels about the dispensing machine than to ask about his history with similar machines, and for most practical purposes it would be foolish to do anything else. But if we are interested in explaining his behavior, we must look at the history (at least until we can look at the physiology). Cognitive psychology has tried to improve both observation and inference concerning the state of the body that is felt as belief, knowledge, intention, or expectation. I think it has faced insuperable difficulties, and in the long run it will have done nothing more than improve a vocabulary useful for nonscientific purposes.

Behaviorism at seventy

Daniel N. Robinson

Department of Psychology, Georgetown University

"Behaviorism-50" will remain one of Professor Skinner's most important essays because of its ripeness, its clarity, and its moderation. If he says less in defense of behaviorism than against competing perspectives, his criticisms of the latter are sharp, instructive, insightful, and, I dare say, portentous. They raise the gravest questions about fundamental notions that now animate much of the research and theory in both the neural and the cognitive sciences. The long-range mission of the "brain sciences" is unambiguously specified when Skinner insists that "it adds nothing to an explanation of how an organism reacts to a stimulus to trace the pattern of the stimulus into the body." The long-range mission is to explain the relationship not between the nervous system and the world but between the organism and the world; between events arising from lifeless things and events arising from living ones.

It is another strength of "Behaviorism-50" that it designates behaviorism ("with an accent on the last syllable") as a contribution to *philosophy of science* and not merely a way of doing research or of addressing practical problems. Stripped of its philosophical implications, behaviorism is little more than a refinement of techniques well known to the ancient circus masters. But as a philosophy of science, behaviorism (with accents on *both* the first three and the last syllables) presents a formidable conception of psychology as a science and of the human world as a knowable and manageable realm.

Two decades have now passed since this valuable work appeared, and we are in a position to discover whether behaviorism at 70 has grown or changed in any significant way. Has it been affected by advances in the neurocognitive disciplines? Has its famous position on language been modified to meet the sound rebukes it once invited? Is it really prepared to accept the full weight of Skinner's maxim that "no entity or process which has any useful explanatory force is to be rejected on the ground that it is subjective or mental"? Does it accept at 70 the burden it took on 20 years ago; namely, supplying a scientific psychology not tied to "pure description" but still liberated from appeals to "mentalistic theories"? At the heart of these questions is a concern that behaviorism's immunity to the forces of change is a fatal flaw.

The ontological problem. It simply will not do to declare, without further argument, that "the basic issue is not the nature of the stuff of which the world is made, or whether it is made of one stuff or two." Since behaviorism is presented as an alternative to 'mentalism," one would think that the basic issue is *precisely* whether the world – whether the human person – "is made of one stuff or two." What is moderate in "Behaviorism-50" is the willingness to accept the mental, even to retain it if it proved to have "any useful explanatory force." But its explanatory force, "useful" or otherwise, cannot be assessed until we have decided the issue of its ontological status. *Are there mental events?*

In his artful attempt to say yes and no in reply to this question, Skinner appeals to something he chooses to call the "verbal community." If I understand his thesis, he seems to be claiming that persons, when very young, learn to assign certain terms to interoceptive stimuli. Thus does the lexicon of mentalism arise. He grants that these stimuli "may have a certain intimacy"; that they are "especially familiar"; indeed, that "they may well be of a special kind." Nonetheless, the "awareness" of them is a "social product" forged by a verbal community that supplies the percipient, through differential reinforcement, with self-referential labels.

This is a most disconnected account, to say the least. Philosophers might be tempted to regard it as a clever application of a Wittgensteinian solution to the "private language" problem, but this is a temptation to be avoided. What the account provides is *at most* a theory of how persons come to describe, for example, visceral sensations and come to learn how to make public the difference between these and the sensations arising from exteroceptive stimuli. It is not an account of the *mental* at all. It surely cannot be Skinner's theory that one's experience of pain commences only after one has learned how to refer to it verbally. To refer to it at all, there must be the experience; to teach one *how* (verbally) to refer to it, there must be a percipient who knows that the sensation or experience is *his own*. And there is more to this than is captured by the phrase "a certain intimacy."

It is true, of course, that others – the "verbal community" – will be interested, as Skinner says, "in what a person is doing, has done, or is planning to do." I set aside the question of what it means to be "interested in" and proceed to the exchange Skinner stages to illustrate his theory: "It [the "verbal community"] challenges his verbal behavior by asking, 'How do you know?' and the speaker answers, if at all, by describing some of the variables of which his verbal behavior was a function. The 'awareness' resulting from all this is a social product."

Let us take as an instance an extremely painful toothache. I visit my dentist and declare, "I have an excruciating toothache!" Is it Skinner's proposition that, in the circumstance, the question, "How do you know?" is anything but droll? Or is it his thesis that, if faced with such a question, my "awareness" takes place only after I have successfully met the challenge of my interrogator? What is philosophically interesting about my toothache is not that it is *mine*; this is psychologically interesting. What is *philosophically* interesting is that, with respect to it, I enjoy tota epistemic authority. It is one of those few factual claims I can ever make that canno be overruled by external evidence. I may be utterly wrong in assuming that it is my tooth that is causing the ache, but not in the claim that I have the sensation. I may be wrong, that is, in the theories I hold to account for the sensation, but never *provably* wrong about the sensation itself. Note that Freudian notions of the unconscious and of repression are entirely tangential here and remain, of course, merely theoretical terms.

This property of "incorrigibility" that attaches to first-person accounts of perceptions is usually introduced as evidence against "identity" theories of mind–brain relations (cf. Robinson 1981). I insert it here, however, to underscore the unavoidability of an "aware self" once one attempts to apply Skinner's notions. Quite simply, his "verbal community" (whose very origins raise any number of questions) must get to work on something, and that something must finally be a "mental" thing capable of tagging its private experiences with conventional descriptions. Far from demonstrating that "awareness" is a "social product," Skinner has merely reaffirmed the truism that all of the social functions of language require adherence to social conventions or "rules" regarding the use of language. But minimally a participant here must be able to recognize such conventions or "rules." He must be able to "play the language game." I should think that Noam Chomsky's (1959) critique of the behavioristic explanation of this is sufficient to show that Skinner has yet to tell us even this part of the story. The story of *awareness* is a different one, however, and has not even been begun in "Behaviorism-50".

The problem of explanation. It is only after we accept that the basic issue has to do with just this question regarding the ontological status of the mental that we can test Skinner's proposals regarding explanation. With the accent on the last syllable, behaviorism is a philosophy of science, but more particularly it is a philosophy of explanation. Elsewhere and often Skinner has defended the proposition that the best or the most scientific or the most useful explanation is a "functional" one; one that states the functional relationship between environmental and behavioral variables. His well known defenses of this claim all arise from his conviction that such explanations are the stock and trade of the developed sciences. In more innocent times, we were content to describe such models of explanation as *causal*, but the metaphysicians since the time of Hume have had a chastening effect on the language of science. Yet, the demon of synonymy is a clever one. Since "functional" relationships turn out to be indistinguishable from the older "causal" ones, all of the metaphysical liabilities of "causal" accounts of human actions now infect the "functional" ones.

The chief liability of causal accounts of genuinely psychological events is that the latter do not behave the way "effects" do. It is, no doubt, a source of frustration and disappointment to behaviorists (the accent can be placed anywhere) that much of human history – including the part we are now contributing to – is understood in terms of our *reasons* rather than in terms of external (or even internal) *causes*. Note that one's reason for doing something remains a reason even if we have some behavioristic account of how that particular reason came to be dispositive. With concessions to psychoanalytic theory, we might say that Smith often acts on the basis of considerations to which he is oblivious, but we cannot coherently claim that his reason for acting was not his reason for acting. As with his toothache, Smith may be wrong in the theory he asserts to account for the sensation, but not provably wrong about the sensation itself. Nevertheless, persons can have reasons for acting and not act, whereas there cannot be "causes" without "effects." Reasons and causes have different logics, and thus causal accounts of significant human actions have historically been incomplete and unconvincing.

Let us suppose that every time Smith is to visit his Aunt Mary he misplaces his car keys. His therapist may learn, long before Smith does, that this selective forgetting is grounded in a long-standing hostility toward Aunt Mary of which Smith is unaware.

But it is just to the extent that Smith is unaware of this that his "repressed hostility" cannot be the *reason* he misplaces his keys. What we learn from this is the unsurprising fact that some behavior is quite literally *irrational*, but this fact comes into being in virtue of the more general fact that our actions typically proceed from reasons that enjoy more than "a certain intimacy."

Whether or not a "functional" explanation is better or more useful than some other kind of explanation is itself a metaphysical question that cannot be settled by fiat. Functional explanations may be more "useful" to the experimental psychologist because they are the only variety of explanation yielded by the methods available in a laboratory. Once the decision is made to examine (that is, to count) operants, what else is there but a "functional" explanation? If, however, we choose to examine the details of the battle of Waterloo, or the relationship between slave labor and unemployment in ancient Athens, or the range of effects of the Council of Trent, we may discover that "functional" relationships are entirely beside the point. To know, for example, that Luther had a problematic relationship with his father, may help us explain his reaction, years later, to the authorities in Rome. It will scarcely help us to explain the Reformation! The point here is that *historical* events call for an explanatory model different from the one that is so serviceable in accounting for the motion of balls rolling down the inclined plane. What historical events contain is the element of *agency*. In their recourse to this element, historians, we must agree, have provided useful explanations that are not to be rejected for being "subjective or mental."

It is important to recognize that the failure of causal ("functional") approaches to explanation in history – including the history of a person – is not attributable to the multiplicity of uncontrollable "variables." The failure is not, that is, a "technical" problem but a perspectival one; at base, a metaphysical one that turns on the question of whether the world contains only one or at least two kinds of "stuff." The assumption of the latter is finally incompatible with behaviorism. It is just one of the terms of "mentalism" that human agency is an essential aspect of all significant social and historical occurrences; further, that human agency is not totally determined or "shaped" from without and is not exercised except by a knowing and an aware entity with purposes.

The critique of mentalism. Skinner has reminded us often of the defects of the "homunculus" theory and has put on notice those traditional "humanistic" programs that would construct a scientific psychology by placing little persons within the frame of the visible one. I have applauded this critique elsewhere and have brought it to bear on several trendy "third force" schools (Robinson 1979). But as Skinner would not want to associate himself with everything said under the banner of behaviorism, so too there are "mentalists" who would not accept the burden of defending everything said in behalf of mentalism. I would put forth as the core principles of a defensible mentalism these:

1. Adult persons organize their actions around a set of irreducibly *psychological* considerations that are most aptly and usefully described by such terms as plans, desires, objectives, wishes, duties, and responsibilities. The actions that proceed from these considerations are best *explained* by just such terms in addition to various logical and psychological connectives.

2. The *origins* of these considerations present a separate problem of inquiry although, to a first approximation, behavioristic accounts enjoy the benefit of conformity to common sense. Still, and particularly in the matter of the *mora* dimensions of human psychology, there would seem to be a sturdy barrier blocking environmentalistic explanations of *all* such psychological states and considerations.

3. To the antique empiricist claim that "nothing is in the intellect that was not first

in the senses," the mentalist (and rationalist), drawing on the patrimony from Leibniz, replies, "Nisi intellectus ipse"; nothing but the intellect itself. Mentalism finds it *necessary*, if human actions are to be understood and explained, to grant far more by way of innate faculties and dispositions than behaviorists have been wont to allow. We can all agree that Shakespeare is not "explained" by being called a "genius" or supplied with a "muse." But we retain the right to be impatient with behavioristic attempts to account for his achievements. Such attempts are a species of "psychohistory" in which the theorist has matters too much his own way.

4. Mentalism in a defensible form must also finally take a stand on the issue of *determinism* (both "soft" and "hard") and come down on the side of freedom. (The question of "dignity" arises only after we see how this freedom is used.) The freedom presupposed by mentalism is not *anarchy*. It is a kind of Kantian freedom; in other words the freedom available to a moral being who is (paradoxically) bound by the "laws of freedom." One is not "free" to contravene the law of contradiction. Moral freedom is available only to beings that are *rational* as such. Every suspension of rationality is, therefore, a forfeiture of the freedom itself.

5. In accepting this element of freedom into its psychology, mentalism also rejects the claim that all motives, plans, duties, and the like are externally supplied. Rather, it takes these states or conditions as *authentic*. If Smith's commitment to rationality has been, as it were, installed by others, then although we can say the commitment is "his," we cannot say that it is "his own." Mentalism regards it as *his own*. Interestingly, only Smith's introspections can finally be used to settle this question. Thus, our only means of verifying the authenticity of a psychological disposition is to grant authenticity to the introspective reports of the person whose disposition is under scrutiny.

6. Mentalism is not adopted by its advocates as a lazy habit that has survived during centuries of ignorance about the actual "causes" of behavior. The caveman probably civilized his litter with a stick. Indeed, Skinner is far too dismissive when he refers to "an occasional phrase in classic Greek authors." Plato's *Dialogues*, and especially his *Republic*, provide careful, systematic treatments of environmentalistic and hereditarian attempts to comprehend social and political life. These works are not to be depreciated. As a "social psychology" Plato's *Republic* is nearly radically behavioristic and is, if I may say, rather more sensitive to the limitations of behaviorism than are any number of contemporary writers. But to put the case briefly, I note only that mentalism is adopted when the *facts* of human conduct are most plausibly explained in mentalistic as opposed to behavioristic or physiological terms.

Behaviorism at 70. Skinner would have behaviorism prosper as something richer than mere descriptivism or "Baconian" science. But he has not said what this promised behaviorism will look like or how it will differ from just that "Baconian" body that was propped up 20 years ago. It is my judgment that the triumph of behaviorism in the 1940s and 1950s was due less to its intrinsic merits than to the wearisome and habitual failures of psychoanalytic formulations and primitive "psychobiologies." Watson's early success was built on the defects of structuralism; Skinner's on those of Freudianism. After decades of irrationalism and instinctivism – and after a world war in which both seemed to be at the core of things – the Western psychological community was ready for a Machian housecleaning. Professor Skinner and his able disciples did what was needed then. But it is not at all clear that their program contains within it the potential for anything more than repetition, rediscovery, self-congratulation. If behaviorism is not descriptivism exhaustively applied to reduced and rather mechanical settings, then it is a somewhat overstated and even gaudy utopianism, unalarming because incredible. What is lacking is the intermediary step; the step that elevates us from the handbook-filling tedium of the "rat lab" to a coherent and unavoidably *theoretical* psychology that does more than take jaded Darwinism for granted. Frankly, I can expect only more of the same, for there would seem to be nothing in this *ism* except a method for rediscovering itself.

BFS: Robinson's section "The Ontological Problem" misses my point about awareness. I do not question that animals see, hear, taste, feel, and so on. I was asking whether they are *aware* that they are doing so. I believe that the human animal not only sees but observes that he is seeing, provided that a verbal community has supplied the necessary contingencies, as in asking for further details with questions like, "What are you doing?," "What did you do?," "What are you planning to do?," "Why are you doing it?," and so on. Of course the behavior must be there before it is described. The child must see a bird in the bush before answering yes to the question, "Do you see a bird in the bush?." Neither the question by the verbal community nor the answer is needed in order to see the bird and, unfortunately, one has a toothache whether or not one has been taught to be aware that one has. A perceptive philosopher would not "be tempted to regard [this] as a clever application of a Wittgensteinian solution to the 'private language' problem." Instead, I believe it solves a problem that Wittgenstein failed to solve.

It is far from "a source of frustration and disappointment to behaviorists" that much of human history has been understood in terms of reasons rather than causes. Cognitive scientists are returning to reasons in the mistaken belief that they are dealing with causes. A science of behavior begins with causal relations and in turning to verbal behavior eventually gives a *reasonable* account of reasoning in causal terms. That this is not yet complete should occasion no surprise.

To Robinson's question, "Once the decision is made to examine (that is, to count) operants, what else is there but a 'functional' explanation?" the answer is I think clear enough. It is to go far beyond "a refinement of techniques well known to the ancient circus masters" to a more and more complex and subtle account of a behaving individual, to apply the principles extricated from such an analysis to the management of human affairs (certainly not much can be said for the thousands of years of reason to which Robinson points), and where neither prediction and control nor practica applications are possible to interpret phenomena with principles the validity of which has been established elsewhere (as, for example, astronomy now interprets the universe with the principles of experimental physics).

I shall briefly discuss Robinson's "Critique of Mentalism" point by point.

1. Try a translation with respect to biology, say 150 years ago.
2. The sturdy barrier is all too obvious and regrettable.
3. I leave it to Robinson to explain Shakespeare as he pleases.
4. Many mentalists have been determinists.
5. For the authenticity of introspective reports, see "Terms."

6. I think the historian would find it hard to prove that mentalism has been adopted in an effort to explain the *facts* of human conduct.

Robinson's concluding section again testifies to his limited knowledge of the experimental analysis of behavior.

The behaviorist concept of mind

David M. Rosenthal

Program in Philosophy, Graduate Center, City University of New York

The "central argument" of Skinner's behaviorist position is "that behavior which seemed to be the product of mental activity could be explained in other ways." To the degree to which this argument holds good, mental states are idle when it comes to explaining behavior.

To evaluate this claim, we must understand just what Skinner means by "mental activity" – what it is, according to his conception of the mental, for a state to be a mental state. On the basis of views of the mental that derive from 17th-century rationalist discussions, for example, being mental might definitionally preclude susceptibility to scientific treatment. Relative to such conceptions, it would not only be obvious and uncontroversial that mental states play no role in explaining behavior, it would also be uninteresting. But presumably there are conceptions of the mental that are less loaded, and according to which Skinner's claim would be an empirical hypothesis. We would then have to see whether we could actually dispense with reference to mental states, so conceived, and still explain behavior. Perhaps there are even conceptions of the mental according to which it would seem obvious, in advance of investigation, that mental states would play an active role in explaining behavior.

Some theoretical opposition to Skinner's views seems to reflect the tacit adoption of the third sort of conception of the mental. Following such conceptions, we can dismiss behaviorism on nonempirical grounds. What those critics mean by "mental" makes it clear that mental states will almost certainly be important to explanations of behavior. By contrast, Skinner's own discussions sometimes seem to oscillate between the first two conceptions – between conceiving of mental states neutrally, in a way that leaves open for empirical determination the question of whether those states figure fruitfully in explaining behavior, and conceiving of mental states in a way that precludes that possibility.

Thus Skinner expresses apparent neutrality about this issue when he writes that "no entity or process which has any useful explanatory force is to be rejected on the ground that it is subjective or mental." This seeming receptivity of the mental is in part a product of Skinner's rejection of operationism. "Science often talks about things it cannot see or measure." Accordingly, behaviorism correctly construed does not "exclud[e] so-called sensations, images, thought processes, and so on," at least not "because they are out of reach of [behaviorist] methods." But, operationism aside, "the fact of privacy cannot...be questioned." So, when behaviorists exclude private states for methodological reasons, "the charge is justified that they have neglected the facts of consciousness." Thus, although the study of vision, for example, should focus on discriminative visual behavior, "possible private accompaniments must not be overlooked."

But set against this seeming liberalism about the mental is Skinner's persistent tendency to use "mental" and its cognates as epithets of disapprobation. Mentalism is variously the "theory of an invisible detachable self," the belief in inner events that lack "physical dimensions," and the positing of mental "way stations," which contribute nothing to, and even obstruct genuine explanation. Sometimes Skinner seems almost to use "mentalistic" as short for "antibehaviorist," and his remarks sometimes come close to caricature. Thus, having grouped mentalistic and psychic explanations together, he speculates that both "originated in primitive animism," and that they invariably involve some appeal to a homunculus. These statements strongly suggest a conception of the mental which, by itself, would imply that mental states could not figure in scientific explanations. Skinner's behaviorism would be correct, according to this conception, but at the cost of being made into a truism.

Skinner might seek to defend the empirical status of behaviorism by urging that these two sets of remarks are not actually in conflict. In keeping with the first set of remarks, nothing in the behaviorist position settles in advance whether reference to mental states will be useful in psychological explanation. Perhaps some mental states do have "explanatory force"; perhaps none do. We must examine each kind, case by case, to find out. As Skinner assures us, the objection to "wishes, cognitions, motives, and so on...is not that these things are mental but that they offer no real explanation and stand in the way of a more effective analysis."

But, he might continue, empirical investigation does show that such reference is often, perhaps always, idle. Hence the second set of remarks: Skinner is there simply trying to explain the prescientific, intuitive attraction we have for explanations cast in terms of these scientifically idle states. Mentalistic psychologists are simply those who permit their preconceptions to blind them to the empirical finding that mental states contribute little or nothing to psychological explanations.

It is difficult to know whether to accept this claim about the empirical status of the behaviorist's "central argument." On this account, the objection to mental states is not that they are mental, but that they are idle scientifically. But Skinner tells us too little about his conception of the mental for us to know whether that conception, by itself, precludes the states Skinner calls "mental" from figuring in scientific explanations. Perhaps Skinner conceives of mental states as those about which we can make introspective reports. This answer will not help much without an independent account of what makes some reports introspective reports. Do reports of, say, throbbing veins and churning stomachs count as introspective? Perhaps he conceives of mental events as simply private events, and private events as those that "tak[e] place within the skin of the organism." This account faces the same difficulties as the answer based on introspection. Without some reasonably precise explanation of how Skinner conceives of the mental, we cannot tell whether his conception of the mental does actually allow for the possibility that mental states have "explanatory force."

Even if we accept that behaviorism is an empirical hypothesis, the question about Skinner's conception of the mental arises all over again. For without knowing what states Skinner counts as mental, we cannot test his hypothesis "that behavior which seemed to be the product of mental activity could be explained in other ways." Moreover, we must know what states he counts as mental independent of his particular discussions of experimental situations. For we must take care, in testing his hypothesis, to avoid the danger that the data in such situations may be redescribed or reinterpreted so that the hypothesis automatically comes out true. Having a well-defined, independent account of what it is for a state to be a mental state is an indispensible prolegomenon to a successful formulation and defense of behaviorism.

BFS: I am sure "Behaviorism-50" does not cover all versions of mentalism but I should have supposed that the examples I give, while not offered as a definition of mentalism, would make clear the kinds of alternative accounts of the data to be found in a science of behavior. I spend a good deal of time on conscious content and mental images, on the "intentional" way-stations of feelings and states of mind – in short, on rules and representations – and these are, I believe, the current issues in psychology and cognitive science which are traditionally called mental.

"Behaviorism at fifty" at twenty

Roger Schnaitter

Department of Psychology, Illinois Wesleyan University

Skinner is often taken to be the arch antimentalist of the contemporary scene, and "Behaviorism-50" is as good a source by which to evaluate that interpretation of his position as any. But I think a careful reading shows that Skinner is hardly the antimentalist he is often taken to be. Indeed, he appears to acknowledge or endorse the place of the mental in any comprehensive account ("the fact of privacy cannot, of course, be questioned").

Skinner's primary objection to the mental is not its existence (I will clarify this awkward reification in a moment), but its role in explanation. We might say of Skinner, then, that he is a descriptive mentalist, in that he desires to include in his account *all* psychological events, including those occurring inside the skin (traditionally, the domain of the mental). He is an explanatory antimentalist, however, in that he finds mental events to have no significant explanatory value (but see Zuriff 1979, for certain qualifications). Mental phenomena simply are not the kind of grist from which nourishing explanations of behavior can be milled: Rather, they are phenomena themselves requiring explanation.

Although it is not as clear in "Behaviorism-50" as elsewhere (e.g., Skinner 1974), Skinner distinguishes between mental categories corresponding to private events (e.g., feelings, thoughts) and mental categories that cannot be identified with occurrences in some directly confrontable way (e.g., "memory," as distinct from instances of remembering and recalling). The former are descriptively relevant, the latter not. Indeed, about the former Skinner sounds downright Titchenerian at points ("radical behaviorism. . .restores introspection"; Skinner 1974, p. 16). But he will have no truck with the latter kind of abstract entity.

Skinner's explanatory practices are widely misunderstood by most of his critics. His approach to explanation, indirectly treated in "Behaviorism-50," is essentially the Machian one of providing the most economical account of the interrelationships among variables. Skinner does not hesitate to identify functional relationships between variables where a "cause" occurs at a temporal distance from an "effect" – for example, a punishment occurring in childhood whose effect is seen in adulthood. Interpretatively, at least, some of these temporal gaps span millennia (Skinner 1975a). It is the mentalists who attempt to fill these gaps with conceptual mechanisms to whom Skinner objects most strongly, as such theoretical models are necessarily the product of inference and conjecture rather than the kind of reasonably direct description of observed relationships that Skinner endorses.

The closing section of "Behaviorism-50" on methodological objections to mentalistic explanation is interesting because it suggests the underlying pragmatic foundations of radical behaviorist explanatory practice. The point about a causal order is to identify those nodes between which interesting relationships exist, and where effective action can be taken regarding them. To the mentalists' everlasting dismay, no means are known through which "minds" can be changed directly, nor will they ever be, though much is known about environmental operations effective in changing behavior. That is where Skinner keeps pointing.

For me the most remarkable claim of "Behaviorism-50" is the statement that a range of mental phenomena must be "forms of action rather than of reproduction." Skinner's analysis of action is accomplished, of course, via the functional concept of the operant. This would seem to imply that a wide range of (legitimate) mental phenomena are best understood as events individuated functionally along the lines developed in the operant analysis of overt behavior. Seen in this way, Skinner's position on the mental seems to be one version of central state functionalism, a position of growing appeal to a number of contemporary philosophers of mind (a useful survey is found in Block 1980a). Skinner, it appears, has been occupying that territory for at least two decades.

BFS: Schnaitter has carefully explained what he means when he says that I am in a sense a mentalist. But I myself am content to distinguish merely between the public and private. When cognitive scientists ask their subjects to think out loud so that their behavior can be more effectively studied, I prefer to say that when they are thinking silently they are also behaving rather than engaging in some kind of mental action. As a behaviorist I can, I think, interpret behavior attributed in part to rules and representations by moving outside to settings and contingencies, and I should not like to call these rules and representations mental simulacra of the settings and contingencies, because that implies too much "ontology."

Apparently Schnaitter feels that Zuriff (1979) has effectively qualified my statement that private events have no significant explanatory value. Zuriff has identified in my writing references to private "causes," but they are not initiating causes, and that is the real issue.

Cognitive science at seven: A wolf at the door for behaviorism?

Miriam W. Schustack and Jaime G. Carbonell

Department of Psychology and Social Relations, Harvard University (MWS) and Department of Computer Science, Carnegie–Mellon University (JGC)

1. Introduction. Behaviorism, like any other research paradigm in psychology, strives to understand the behavior of organisms, where *understanding* is defined operationally as successful prediction of behavior in novel but well-specified situations. In evaluating behaviorism, two essential issues must be addressed and resolved. First, does a behavioristic approach help us achieve, to a significant degree, this goal of "understanding"? Second, is it the only approach that is likely to do so, or are other research methodologies likely to prove more successful in certain aspects of psychological inquiry? In this commentary, we address only the latter issue, assuming the former to be true and well documented in the behaviorist literature. We focus on Skinner's insistence on avoiding the postulation of interna representations, and the extent to which this prohibition both restricts productive avenues of research and prevents psychological theories from capturing an essentia feature of human cognition.

2. *Internal representations in scientific discovery.* Consider, as an example, a task simpler than attempting to understand a complex biological organism: A 19th-century scientist has before him a pair of single-band two-way radios. Assume, moreover, that the transistorized internal workings are either unavailable for inspection or beyond comprehension. First, as a true behaviorist, the scientist runs experiments, analyzing the data into the following general observations:

1. Sound emitted into one radio is replicated in the other, but cannot be heard in other locations.
2. Volume and clarity attenuate with distance between transmitter and receiver.
3. It takes longer for a loud sound to be heard far away than it does to transmit that sound the same distance through the radios.

At this point, the scientist departs from approved behaviorist methodology, hypothesizing that the radio converts sound to an unobservable form that travels sotropically at great speed, and the receiving radio converts that form back into sound. This hypothesis in turn raises questions that lead to additional experimentation. For instance, can transmission of the converted form be impeded by anything? Is it unscientific or "mentalistic" to hypothesize radio waves, merely because we cannot observe them directly? Such a hypothesis, akin to the "internal representation" of the sound being transmitted, may indeed provide a greater explanatory and predictive capacity than merely cataloging and analyzing the direct input–output behavior of the radio. Careful experimental analysis is of course necessary, but the question is whether it is sufficient. From the perspective of cognitive science, the kind of research prescribed by behaviorism is an important step, but only a part of the iterative process of hypothesizing internal structures from empirical observations and testing those hypotheses with additional focused, theoretically motivated experimentation.

If we restrict the domain of scientific discourse to observables, do we gain in rigor and control what we lose in power, or do we eliminate the potential for making meaningful discoveries, which can in turn be validated with full experimental rigor? A parallel drawn from the history of modern physics suggests the latter. Many subatomic particles, such as the μ- and π-mesons, were first predicted on theoretical grounds, motivating the experiments that confirmed their existence. Presently, quark theory predicts the existence and nature of a smaller number of more elementary particles not yet empirically confirmed. The subatomic particles and the rules by which they interact to predict the behavior of physical systems are the internal representation of physics. (Note that in this case, there is no serious question as to the existence of an internal representation; the question is *which* variant representation is most appropriate.) Thus, the most powerful and parsimonious atomic theory postulates unobservable entities whose existence can only be confirmed indirectly.

3. *Internal representations in psychology.* An alternative to looking at whether the science can prosper without internal representations is to look at whether the human organism can function as we observe it to function without internal representations. Skinner totally rejects the existence and utility of internal representations, ridiculing those who claim otherwise by equating an internal representation with a direct analogue of the object or concept represented. Thus, the internal representation of a wolf or a person would be as complex as the external entity itself, a position akin to postulating a homunculus for each concept represented. This simplistic extreme, however, bears little resemblance to modern theorizing about internal representations.

3.1. *Representations and recognition.* An internal representation in the mind can be viewed as the total knowledge directly associated with a concept, plus relevant information derivable from other internal knowledge. It follows from this definition that representations can be subject to individual variation, depending on the individual's knowledge and experience. An internal representation of a wolf, for instance, contains perceptual information sufficient to recognize a wolf, partial knowledge of a wolf's typical behavior (e.g., carnivorous pack hunter), associations to some actual events or fictional narratives involving wolves (e.g., Little Red Riding Hood), taxonomic knowledge from which other information may be derived (e.g., a wolf is a mammal, therefore is warm blooded and bears its young alive), linguistic knowledge (e.g., "wolf" is a noun, in other languages called "lobo" and "lupus"), and many other sources of information. The representation of the concept "wolf," groups this knowledge together and makes the rest available when any part of it unique to "wolf" is recognized. The word "wolf," or the baying of a wolf in moonlight, or the description "it's like a wild dog, but bigger and meaner and hunts in packs" matches part of the wolf representation and serves to recall the rest of the information associated with the concept.

A pure stimulus–response paradigm strains to account for the recognition of "wolf" from the description above if the latter had never been presented verbatim. Under a theory that allows the postulation of internal representations, the concept "wolf" is recognized by a partial match to multiple facets of the representation that were learned over time as the person acquired more knowledge about wolves. An internal representation is much more than a collection of features – it includes relations among features, higher-order structures, and associations of these structures with other concepts in memory. It is precisely the presence of such an internal representation that provides generative power, enabling a person to recognize or describe a wolf by any reasonable recombination of existing terms or by the introduction of new terms (perhaps analogically) that convey sufficient meaning to discriminate "wolf" from other concepts in memory.

3.2. The necessity for representations in cognition. The necessity for internal representations becomes even more pronounced when one considers reasoning processes more complex than just recognition or generation of descriptions. Suppose we are given the problem of trapping a wild wolf for a zoo. Knowledge not directly related to wolves must be brought to bear, such as zoos wanting unhurt animals, but let us focus on the necessity of querying our internal representation of wolves in order to attempt a solution to this problem.

What kind of trap should we build? Clearly, a mousetrap will not hold a wolf. How do we infer that without an internal representation of a wolf? Why not build a trap that drops a huge boulder atop an unsuspecting wolf? How do we infer that such a process will hurt or perhaps kill the wolf? We absolutely need to access internal knowledge of wolves to infer expected outcomes from contemplated actions.

How should we bait the trap? Probably not with a $10 bill, although that may prove adequate bait for other quarry. Again, knowledge specific to wolves is necessary, and that knowledge must be used in novel ways not associated with specific past responses.

And why build a trap in the first place? Why not simply walk into the wolf pack and drop a burlap sack over the huskiest wolf around?

We need not have experienced the stimulus of having walked into a wolf pack, or attempted to bait a wolf trap with a monetary inducement, or dropped glacial boulders on wolves, to project the expected responses, and then calculate more reasonable plans. In fact, we need not have ever trapped anything to reason about possible means of trapping animals. Our internal representation of wolves, together with our problem-solving cognitive apparatus, provides us with the necessary reasoning capabilities to foresee the consequences of actions that have never taken place, and thus to plan (however imperfectly) our future actions. Since internal representations play a crucial role in human reasoning, they should clearly be an object of study, in conjunction with the cognitive processes that build them and apply them.

Whereas internal representations may contain significant amounts of information, they in no way replicate the physical objects they represent. The representation of a wolf does not contain detailed physiological information, knowledge of what a wolf is thinking or feeling at a given instant, nor does it replicate the complex instincts and knowledge in the wolf's mind. Hence, there is no "wolf homunculus" in one's head – there is only a structured collection of knowledge about a wolf, which may be labeled collectively the internal representation of a wolf. This representation is open for inspection, recognition, reasoning, and other cognitive processes.

4. *Concluding remarks.* Although situations such as those discussed in the previous sections are potentially describable in behaviorist terms, the behaviorist approach does not adequately meet two basic evaluative criteria: *power* and *parsimony*. Are labored, situation-specific behaviorist descriptions of cognitive processes preferable to more uniform and broadly predictive accounts relying on internal representations? Why shouldn't psychological theory appeal to the canons of simplicity and generative power so prevalent in the natural sciences? A theory that predicts *how* an observable phenomenon may arise motivates further experimentation to confirm, refute, or further elaborate our understanding of the underlying cognitive process.

In psychology, unobservable internal representations include the postulation of a short-term memory capable of holding a small fixed number of "chunks" of information, a well-accepted if nonbehavioristic theoretical concept subject to empirical validation. In artificial intelligence, practical and theoretical results in replicating human problem-solving abilities have been achieved by formalizing the representation of knowledge in a uniform encoding such as first-order predicate logic, semantic networks, frames and schemas, or procedural encodings. Many of these ideas have been used and augmented in cognitive modeling by psychologists, combining theoretical analysis with empirical observation. Behaviorism is not a philosophy whose time has come and gone. Rather, it is a rigorous method of observational analysis that needs to be augmented with modern cognitive modeling to foster continued progress in the field.

BFS: Schustack & Carbonell have taken the word "representation" in some very different senses, though I do not believe I was ridiculing those who used it in those ways. Where I was talking about the supposed internal copy of the stimulus, they include the following:

1. Hypotheses about such directly unobservables as radio waves.

2. "An internal representation in the mind [that] can be viewed as the total knowledge directly associated with a concept, plus relevant information derivable from other internal knowledge." A more traditional expression would perhaps be the "meaning" of the concept. I doubt whether there is ever any single representation of that kind of total knowledge. Bits and pieces are acquired separately and remain to some extent under separate control. Is it possible to identify the "structured collection of knowledge about a wolf, which may be labeled collectively the internal representation

of a wolf"? Although a complete inventory of what the word "wolf" means to a person is probably out of reach, plausible verbal and nonverbal sources can be suggested.

3. The supposed use of a concept of wolf in solving the problem of designing a proper trap to catch one for a zoo – equally out of reach, I am sure, of any kind of rigorous analysis. It is unwise to assume that "our internal representation of wolves, together with our problem-solving apparatus, provides us with the necessary reasoning capabilities to foresee the consequences of action that have never taken place and thus to plan (however imperfectly) our future actions." We certainly have no information at the present time of the internal representations that are said to function this way or of a problem-solving cognitive apparatus. The sentence is only another example of the promise of cognitive science, a promise which has not yet been fulfilled.

Explaining behavior Skinner's way

Michael A. Simon

Department of Philosophy, State University of New York at Stony Brook

What does understanding what goes on under the skin have to do with understanding human behavior? The answer that B. F. Skinner would have us believe is, hardly anything. The arguments he has presented and the successes his research program has generated present a powerful challenge to anyone who would offer any other answer.

The question of how much we can understand of behavior by considering the contingencies of reinforcement depends, of course, on what we mean by understanding. Behaviorism, Skinner notes, is not the science of human behavior; it is the philosophy of that science (1974). That is, it embodies a set of assumptions that define what a science is to be. Specifically, it is for him a philosophy of explanation, one that guarantees that no explanations of behavior will be given in terms of mental states. As Scriven (1956) has pointed out, nothing will count as an explanation for Skinner if it does not rest on observables.

Skinner nevertheless does try to show why behavior is not adequately explained as the product of mental activity. It is neither necessary nor plausible, he argues, to posit "mental way stations" as bridges between environmental and behavioral variables. The view he criticizes – the idea that there are "copies of the real world within the body" – is not the only alternative to behaviorism, however. Remembering and imagining are no less mentalistic for not requiring an internal screen on which a visual image is projected. Showing that it is implausible to claim that mediation of behavior involves replication of external objects is not the same as showing that no form of representation exists whatever. One need not accept a copy theory to believe that memory, for example, involves representation, at least in the sense that a tape recording contains a representation of a voice or performance. That such representation need not be conscious is an important assumption of materialism, but it hardly supports behaviorism.

There are several ways in which Skinner tries to escape the criticism that behaviorism is inadequate because it fails to recognize the need for intervening variables. One of these amounts to broadening the definition of behavior to include everything that is going on within the body when the creature has the disposition to perform that behavior. Thus he speaks of "the behavior of seeing," as though behavior were all that seeing involves. Similarly, when he says that hunger is behavior, he does not deny its physiological basis, but he allows the concept of behavior to embrace the whole state of the organism rather than just its overt manifestations. By thus treating hunger as a unitary phenomenon, he no longer needs to explain hunger behavior itself in terms of either physiological variables or feelings of hunger. In that way Skinner guarantees that hunger will be explained by antecedent occurrences of a behavioral kind rather than by concomitant non-behavioral events.

A second way that Skinner manages to avoid appealing to inner states to explain behavior is simply by disdaining descriptions of behavior that explain as well as describe. Thus he would replace a description of the behavior of a hungry pigeon as "walk[ing] around, hoping...[to] bring the food back again" with a report that indicates merely that "the organism was reinforced when its behavior was of a given kind." So far as reinforcement is a behavioral concept, it does no more than indicate that something – the reinforcer – caused the frequency of the behavior to increase; it gives no explanation of the increase. Since Skinner believes that unobserved internal states cannot be used to explain observed behavior, he does not think that anything is lost by eliminating all mention of attitudes, intentions, and emotional states when rendering an account of a creature's behavior. He would not allow us the explanatory benefit that comes from describing the purposive behavior of animals in intentionalistic terms.

A third way that Skinner makes it appear that the best explanations of behavior are those that mention only contingencies of reinforcement is to interpret or transform each request for an explanation into one that that kind of explanation is best suited to answer. Confronted with the question of why students employ intentional vocabulary to describe the behavior of pigeons, for example, or why a president of the United States decides not to run for reelection, Skinner wants to explain how these people acquired the tendencies to behave as they did under those circumstances, rather than tell what the behavior means either to them or to observers. Skinner is not interested in discovering how creatures make the discriminations they do, or in finding out what expectations and anxieties people have that make them act as they do. His concern is rather with showing how their behavior can be exhibited as effects of the contingencies of past reinforcements.

Aside from his distaste for explanations in terms of theoretical entities or other unobservables, Skinner has a powerful reason, which he freely acknowledges, for preferring explanations that terminate in environmental variables: They yield a technology for changing behavior through the manipulation of mental states. But it would be wrong to suppose that knowing how to produce behavior always implies being able to explain it. Skinner's successes in learning how behavior can be controlled provide no assurance that his explanations will always be the most powerful. And if we acknowledge, as I think we must, that human behavior calls for many different kinds of explanation, then Skinner's philosophy of science – his behaviorism – must be seen as a one-sided approach to the task of understanding why humans behave as they do.

BFS: Simon says that if I were asked what understanding of what goes on under the skin has to do with understanding human behavior, I would reply, "Hardly anything." On the contrary, I would reply, "Everything." The question is, What *does* go on under the skin, and how do we know about it?

My answer is so badly paraphrased by Simon that I can reply only by protesting:

1. I do not say that nothing will count as an explanation if it does not rest on observables.
2. A representation similar to that on a tape recorder is precisely the kind of representation I reject.
3. A disposition to perform behavior is not an intervening variable; it is a probability of behaving.
4. I am not interested in depriving anyone of "the explanatory benefit that comes from describing the purposive behavior of animals in intentionalistic terms"; I question the validity and the expedience.
5. I have long been "interested in discovering how creatures make the discriminations they do."
6. Human behavior may "call for" many different kinds of explanations and if so any one explanation could be called one-sided, but the issue is the validity of whatever explanations are offered.

Skinner's behaviorism implies a subcutaneous homunculus

J. E. R. Staddon

Department of Psychology, Duke University

On rereading "Behaviorism-50" I am struck by the validity of Skinner's attack on the "copy" theory of perception and the acuteness of his discussion of the problems of communicating about private events. But I am also impressed by how his unwillingness to admit of explanatory terms other than actions or environmental events leads him into the homunculus fallacy he presumes to oppose.

If stimuli and responses (albeit broadly defined) are all there is, then private events must also involve stimuli and responses. Private events are, by definition, "events within the skin." Hence the stimuli and responses that go to make them up must also be internal. What, then, receives these stimuli and makes these responses? It cannot be the whole organism, for once we go inside, something is necessarily left out. So what can this actor be but a *homunculus*, the very entity Skinner intends to abolish?

Consider the following statements, with which Skinner parodies the homunculus idea: When a man's finger is pricked, electrical impulses illuminate a television screen in the brain. Then a "little man wakes up, sees the flashing screen [internal stimulus], reaches out, and pulls a lever [internal response]. More flashes of lightning go down the nerve to the muscles, which then contract." The terms in square brackets are mine. Compare this with Skinner's statement later on: "Each of us is in special contact with a small part of the universe enclosed within our own skin. . . . each is uniquely subject to certain kinds of proprioceptive and interoceptive stimulation."

I can see no essential difference between the TV homunculus and Skinner's view of internal events. The notion of internal stimuli and responses makes no sense unless there is some entity to receive those stimuli and make those responses. That entity is then unexplained. Unless one is comfortable with a sort of Chinese-box psychology in which entities contain other entities, world without end, the terms stimuli and response must be reserved for variables we can see and measure. All else are *state* variables. Skinner's reluctance to accept state variables has led him to a self-contradictory position that implies the existence of homunculi while it does not accept them.

BFS: I do not see the parallel between person and homunculus. In the TV portrayal of how a person responds to a painful stimulus, the finger that is pricked is not a finger on the hand that pulls the lever in the brain. I see nothing like that in my statement that "each of us is in special contact with a small part of the universe enclosed within our own skin. . . .each is uniquely subject to certain kinds of proprioceptive and interoceptive stimulation." The essential difference is between the TV homunculus and the "each of us" in that quotation. I could equally well have said, "Each of us is in special contact with a small part of the universe around us. . . .each of us is uniquely subject to certain kinds of exteroceptive stimulation." The main point, as Staddon says, is that private events involve stimuli and responses. They are the only events with respect to which we have developed an interoceptive and proprioceptive nervous system. Unfortunately, the homunculus of cognitive psychology claims to be in contact with many other kinds of things.

Is behaviorism vacuous?

Stephen P. Stich

Center for Advanced Study in the Behavioral Sciences, Stanford, California

In "Behaviorism-50" Skinner writes that behaviorism, with the accent on the last syllable, is a philosophy of science rather than a scientific theory about behavior. But throughout the article, and in many other places, Skinner has made what appear to be strong and substantive claims about the mechanisms and processes that do and do not underlie behavior. It is on these claims that I focus in this commentary. The ones that concern me give every appearance of being empirical. However, it sometimes seems that when Skinner and his followers discuss them they do not treat them as being empirical. Rather, they write in a way that suggests that the claims are compatible with any possible empirical evidence. But if there is no imaginable data that advocates would accept as disconfirming or falsifying a claim, then the claim itself is empirically vacuous. It is my hope that in his response to this commentary Skinner will say whether or not he takes his claims about the processes underlying behavior to be empirical, and thus potentially falsifiable. If he *does* take them to be empirical, then another problem will loom large. For it would appear that if the claims are falsifiable at all, then there is already quite a lot of data indicating that they are in fact false.

Let me begin with some prima facie empirical claims that Skinner makes about the mechanisms and processes underlying behavior. I draw my quoted examples from *About Behaviorism* (Skinner, 1974) in the 1976 Vintage Books edition, though Skinner makes many of the same claims in "Behaviorism-50" and many other publications. According to Skinner, the behavior of organisms can be explained by postulating a number of innate capacities including reflexes, the capacity to undergo respondent conditioning and, most important, the capacity to undergo operant conditioning. In addition to these three innate capacities, Skinner must attribute to organisms a certain number of innately reinforcing stimuli which may vary substantially from species to species. The duckling, for example, "inherits the capacity to be reinforced by maintaining or reducing the distance between itself and a moving object" (p. 46). But since cats and humans do not exhibit so-called imprinting behavior, presumably they are not innately reinforced by this sort of stimulus. Now what is fascinating and powerful about Skinner's theory is not the claim that these innate capacities exist, but rather his contention that these capacities, in conjunction with an organism's history of conditioning, suffice to explain what is most interesting about the behavior of animals and humans. In particular, it would appear that Skinner is committed to holding that these innate capacities, along with my conditioning history, suffice to explain my verbal behavior. They even suffice to explain my behavior as I write this commentary. Moreover, if this is right, it follows that certain other sorts of theoretical posits made by other theorists are mistaken. There is no need to posit innate rules of grammar to account for language learning (p. 14), or internal "problem solving strategies" to account for the way in which people solve problems, or an "inner record-keeping process" to account for memory (p. 122). "There are no 'iconic representations' in [a person's] mind; there are no 'data structures stored in his memory'; he has no 'cognitive map' of the world in which he has lived (p. 93). "There are no images in the sense of private copies" (p. 95). All the phenomena that images, data structures, problem-solving strategies, and the rest were initially posited to explain are in fact explainable in terms of a person's history of conditioning and the various innate capacities mentioned above. These are exciting claims, and they certainly appear to be empirical. The nonexistence of images, data structures, innate grammatical rules, and the like could hardly be a matter of a priori logic or a consequent of methodological strictures.

Perhaps this is the place to begin turning my monologue into a dialogue. My first question to Skinner is whether I have so far represented his views correctly. Does he still wish to claim that there are no internal data structures, innate grammatical rules, internally represented problem-solving heuristics, and the like? And, if he does, does he take these to be factual claims which are true, if they are, because of the way the world happens to be? If, as I would hope, the answer to these questions is affirmative, then we can press on to ask what the world might be like if Skinner were mistaken and these claims were false. (If he does not take these claims to be factual, and thus potentially falsifiable, then, it is to be hoped, he will explain just what their status is.)

There may, of course, be many imaginable worlds in which Skinner's fascinating claims might be false. Let me conjure just one of them. Suppose, to begin, that we were to set out to build a radically non-Skinnerian robot. This robot, whose behavior is controlled by a computer, has all of the things that Skinner claims humans do not have. It has a rich internally represented specification of allowable grammatical structures which it uses in acquiring language. It has complex internal data structures, rich problem-solving heuristics, and detailed cognitive maps of its environment which it uses to get from place to place. There was a time when it was possible to doubt that it made any coherent sense to ascribe such things as internal heuristic rules and data structures to a physical mechanism. And Skinner (along with certain Wittgensteinian philosophers) sometimes writes as though he thought the existence of such things in a physical system was somehow logically impossible or conceptually incoherent. But I would have thought that developments in computer science and technology during the last two decades have laid this particular concern to rest. It is not only possible for a physical mechanism to have internal data structures and heuristic rules that exploit them; such mechanisms actually exist. But here, once again, Skinner should be given the floor to speak for himself. Is he willing to grant that a robot like the one I have described could (in principle) be built? Or does he think that the very description of such a robot is conceptually incoherent? [Cf. Lebowitz commentary – *Ed.*]

In imagining the existence of non-Skinnerian robots, we have not yet succeeded in conjuring a possible world in which Skinner's exciting empirical claims would be false. For his claims are about *organisms*, not robots. So, to imagine a world in which Skinner's empirical claims are false, we will have to suppose that the robots we have been imagining were produced not by some Silicon Valley firm, but by natural selection and evolution. We will have to imagine that they are made of protoplasm rather than electrical hardware, and that they reproduce naturally, rather than being manufactured. So let us suppose that there are such organisms – lots of them. Indeed, let us suppose that most of the higher organisms on the planet are of this sort. Then, it would seem, we have described a world in which the most exciting claims of Skinnerian behaviorism are false. Here, once again, it is crucial to have Skinner's contribution to the dialogue. Is he prepared to grant that if the world were as I have imagined, then his claims about the processes and mechanisms underlying behavior would in fact be false? This is perhaps the crucial question in this commentary. For if Skinner says no, then I confess to being quite at a loss to know what it would take to show that his theory is mistaken. If he does not grant that in the world I have imagined his theory would be wrong, then he owes us an account of what sort of world would falsify his theory. Without such an account we should have to conclude that what appear to be exciting empirical claims are in fact empirically vacuous.

But now suppose Skinner says yes. Suppose he grants that if the world were populated by organisms of the sort I have imagined, his empirical claims would indeed be false. He has then escaped the charge of empirical vacuity. He has granted that his theory is falsifiable, and has indicated one sort of world that would falsify it.

But if Skinner does grant that his claims would be false in our imagined world, then I fear he may have jumped out of the frying pan and into the fire. For how do we know that the imagined world in which Skinner's claims would be false is not *our* world? In the imagined world, as in ours, it would not be possible simply to examne organisms to see if they had internal cognitive maps, problem-solving heuristics, and the rest. Nor would opening the organisms up do much good. (The computer on which I am writing this commentary has an internally stored dictionary of some 20,000–30,000 English words. But you would be hard put to find this out by opening it up and looking inside.) To find out if organisms (real or imagined) have the internal structures and processes whose existence Skinner denies, it would be necessary to elaborate more detailed hypotheses about exactly how these structures and processes work, and then to do experiments to see if the predictions generated by the hypotheses were borne out. But, of course, this is just what has been going on in experimental cognitive psychology. During the past 15 years or so hundreds of researchers have been testing models that postulate internal images, cognitive maps, data structures stored in memory, problem-solving heuristics, and many other internal cognitive mechanisms and processes. Some of these models have been falsified and rejected. Others have done remarkably well, though no one would deny that things are still pretty primitive, and that there is plenty of room for improvement. We now have an enormous collection of experimental data which, it would seem, simply cannot be made sense of unless we postulate something like the mechanisms and processes that were in the heads of organisms in our imaginary world. If this is right, then it would seem we must conclude that if Skinner's claims are falsifiable at all, they have in fact been falsified.

Here I must invite Skinner to have the final word in the dialogue. Can he give us any reason to believe that the data from thousands – perhaps tens of thousands – of experiments that have been taken to support various models involving cognitive maps, problem-solving heuristics, data structures, images, and the rest can be accounted for in some other way? Are there alternative models, more to Skinner's liking, that will account for these data anywhere nearly as well? If not, should he not agree that his claims about the mechanisms and processes underlying behavior are either unfalsifiable or already falsified?

BFS: Do I really contend "that these capacities [behavioral processes, susceptibility to reinforcement, etc.]...suffice to explain what is most interesting about the behavior of animals and humans?" For example, do they explain Stich's behavior in writing his commentary? The answer is no. I think they do suffice to explain the behavior of selected organisms under controlled conditions in laboratory research, and claims made about the data there are falsifiable. That research leads to concepts and principles which are useful in *interpreting* behavior elsewhere. My book *Verbal Behavior* (1957) was an interpretation, not an explanation, and is merely useful, not true or false. I should not want to try to *prove* that there are no innate rules of grammar or internal problem-solving strategies or inner record-keeping processes. I am simply saying that an account of the facts does not require entities of that sort, that we do not directly observe them introspectively, and that an alternative analysis is more likely to be successful in the long run. It is also interesting to interpret the historical ubiquity of explanations of behavior in terms of feelings and states of mind and the (possibly falsifiable) evidence which has encouraged the practice.

To take my place in the "dialogue," I cannot literally claim that there are no internal data structures; I merely undertake to interpret the behavior attributed to them in other ways and to explain why the attribution has been made. Among the (falsifiable) facts of a scientific analysis are the practices through which children are taught to refer to their intentions, beliefs, knowledge, and so on.

Stich imagines a world in which organisms have evolved with internally represented grammatical structures, with problem-solving heuristics, cognitive maps, and so on. Something very much like them could now be simulated on the computer, so the suggestion is plausible. He then asks "the crucial question in this commentary: Am I "prepared to grant...that [my] claims about the processes and mechanisms underlying behavior would in fact be false?" Of course I must say yes, but have I then jumped out of the frying pan into the fire?

I am assuming that organisms from both worlds will behave in precisely the same way, both in the laboratory and in daily life. Stich's hypothetical organism would answer questions about itself in standard ways, and so on. As a mere mortal I should proceed as I have proceeded with existing organisms in analyzing its behavior. Stich has put himself in the position of creator and knows more about the world than can be determined by inspection ("Nor would opening the organisms up do much good"). Stich has created a situation in which he could say "False!," but could anyone else?

Stich's conclusion is that "we now have an enormous collection of experimental data which, it would seem, simply cannot be made sense of unless we postulate something like the mechanisms and processes that were 'n the heads of organisms in our imaginary world." If he means the mechanisms and processes of cognitive science, I should underline the world "seem." If he means neurology, the end of the story lies far in the future.

"Mental way stations" in contemporary theories of animal learning

William S. Terry

Department of Psychology, University of North Carolina at Charlotte

Any current observer of human cognitive psychology would not be surprised to learn that Professor Skinner's arguments against the use of "mental way stations" have been little heeded. What is surprising is the proliferation of such cognitive constructs in theories of animal behavior – this, even though the principles of behavioral psychology were developed in the animal laboratories, and given the belief that at least animal behavior could be described via the mechanisms of reflex, conditioning, and reinforcement. The shift toward cognitive theories began more than a decade ago, and is well illustrated by the titles of some influential monographs from these years: *Animal Memory* (Honig & James 1971); "Rehearsal in animal conditioning" (Wagner, Rudy, & Whitlow 1973); *The Question of Animal Awareness* (Griffin 1976); and *Cognitive Processes in Animal Behavior* (Hulse, Fowler, & Honig 1978). Increasingly, the terminology is also taking on the appearance of mentalism; for example, short-term memory and rehearsal; expectations and surprise; instructed forgetting.

However, the arguments of the radical behaviorists, from the time of Watson on, have not been ignored. The introduction (or in some cases, reintroduction) of mental-sounding constructs has been accompanied by a careful specification of the environmental and behavioral concomitants of the theoretical constructs. This work still bears a strong resemblance to the Hull-Tolman variety of theorizing that was rejected by Skinner (1950). However, it seems that cognitive psychologists are as unlikely to change their behavior as Skinner is to change his. Still, Skinner's analysis of mental constructs in "Behaviorism-50" is vitally instructive in suggesting ways for doing better science. Some illustrations of the behavioral emphasis, and suggestions for further improvement in cognitive theories that derive from Skinner's position, are presented below.

Many of the theoretical terms of Tolman's era are being revived, but with a new emphasis on what these terms objectively imply. This is clearly a reaction to the behaviorists' argument that mental variables were being introduced into an objective science. One of these terms is "expectancy"; for example, an animal is said to acquire an expectancy for the occurrence of food. The Rescorla–Wagner model (1972) of classical conditioning has attempted to operationalize expectancies. This model suggests that the acquisition of conditioning is determined by the degree to which the US (unconditioned stimulus) is expected or surprising. This notion is expressed by a mathematical formula which says that the expectation of the US is a function of the discrepancy between the amount of conditioning possible and the amount that has already occurred. Thus, expectation reduces to empirical statements concerning the amount and kind of prior training. It has also been suggested that expectancy can be further reduced to the discrepancy between amplitudes of the unconditioned and conditioned responses (Donahoe & Wessells 1980).

Similarly, current discussion of cognitive mapping (Menzel 1978; Olton 1978) is concerned with the details of the environment to which the subject is sensitive, and with the subject's ability to perform adaptively in these environments. The term "cognitive map" becomes a descriptive term, which summarizes our knowledge of environment–behavior relationships.

An important influence of behavioral analysis has been determining a more rigorous program for assessing environmental contingencies before resorting to cognitive explanations. Thus, in tasks requiring a time gap to be bridged between stimulus and response, possible external cues such as scent markings (Olton 1978) or mediating behaviors (Blough 1959) are ruled out before invoking a concept such as short-term memory. Unfortunately, there is a tendency to assume that such external events are not factors in any study once they have been excluded from a single study.

An extension of the above idea concerns the necessity of assessing internal stimuli (the private events discussed by Skinner) as potential mediators. Given the present zeitgeist, we are sometimes too ready to assume cognitive processes as explanations. Behavioral views are rejected because knowledge of the external contingencies is insufficient to predict or describe behavior. The possibility of internal, but observable, stimuli is not even considered. Thus, the "concept of an internal representation is useful because it allows us to explain the occurrence of responses that are not entirely governed by external stimuli" (Domjan & Burkhard 1982, p. 304). However, we are clearly aware of sources of internal stimulus control (e.g., interoceptive conditioning, biofeedback). As cognitive theorists, we may want to do more to attempt to separate such internal stimuli (as mediators) from the hypothesized cognitive processes.

Skinner criticized the use of mental way stations when incomplete chains of action are involved. Thus, experience may be said to affect some cognitive state, but no resulting behavior is described. Or, the cognitive state causes behavior, with no statement of what initially determined the mental state. The impact of such criticism today is that theoretical treatments with such incomplete chains are rare, even though the predominant interest of a given theorist may be at one end or the other (stimulus or response) of the chain. No one would suggest that an expectancy or cognitive map appears without environmental experience. Similarly, the goal of much research is to obtain behavioral evidence for the cognitive states. Thus, the chains are complete.

Skinner's argument concerning incomplete chains is more telling in those situations in which the cognitive theorist fails to specify what response will occur. The hallmark of behavioral learning theory is the specification of what response is learned. One of the greatest challenges remaining for cognitive theory is to describe why a particular response occurs. Our theories may make good post hoc sense in explaining why a specific behavior is adaptive, but there is little a priori predictiveness. The response we expect to occur (or change) is determined from our previous research with a given preparation.

Finally, the use of mental-sounding terms does not imply reification of the mental phenomena. Most animal-learning researchers are careful to point out that such terms are theoretical, conceptual, analogical, or metaphorical. The terms are used to describe complex relationships between stimuli and responses (Honig 1978). The impact of Skinner's arguments has been such that researchers now provide detailed specifications of manipulations and recorded behaviors. Although we have not discarded mental way stations from our theories, we have been more objective in their use. Given our current disposition to continue in this cognitive trend, we can continue to use Skinner's advice to do even better.

BFS: There is perhaps a core of cognitive psychologists who are careful to indicate the precursors of mental way-stations and to carry through to their expressions in behavior, but the popularity of cognitive psychology during the past two decades is largely due to a relaxation of critical thinking on the part of those who are concerned with human behavior for largely nonexperimental reasons. Why must we assume expectancy in Pavlov's dog or in a rat in a box? We do so because we have observed the state of our own bodies when we hear the dinner bell or sit down to table. The introspective evidence is unreliable, but it is real, and it comes at just the right time to seem to explain the salivation or the "means–end readiness" with which we pick up our fork. I do not question the fact that there are relevant states of the body at such times or that we have some information about them or that they appear at just the right time to serve as causes, but it is what is felt, not the feeling, that is functional. We do not salivate or pick up the fork because of a felt expectation of food; we do so because of conditions of our body resulting from past experience which we may feel and have learned to call expectancy, though we do not need to do so. To take our observations of the state for the state is a fundamental mistake and particularly so when they are used to eke out incomplete accounts. To say that "'the concept of an internal representation is useful because it allows us to explain the occurrence of responses that are not entirely governed by external stimuli'" is to use the representation in lieu of other variables which should be explored. Some cognitive psychologists have, as Terry says, mended their ways to some extent, but the current fashion in cognitive psychology shows, alas, no acquaintance with the behavioristic objections.

Are radical and cognitive behaviorism incompatible?

Roger K. Thomas

Department of Psychology, University of Georgia

In his synopsis of *250 years* of behaviorism, Ratliff (1962) concluded correctly that behaviorism "amounts to nothing more than the acceptance of the inevitable." "Behaviorism-50" gave Skinner's view of behaviorism, most of which should be acceptable to most behavioral scientists (to be distinguished from nonscientific psychologists). After all, Skinner concluded, "No entity or process which has useful explanatory force is to be rejected on the ground that it is subjective or mental. The data...must, however, be studied and formulated in effective ways." These appear to be reasonable and realizable conditions for behavioral investigations of most traditional subjects in psychology. Why, then, has there been such opposition to Skinner's (radical) behaviorism?

The answer is that Skinner does *not* believe that mental entities or processes have "useful explanatory force." Contrary to the apparent latitude expressed above, included among Skinner's remarks on "Behaviorism-50" (Wann 1964) was, "I find no place in the formulation for anything which is mental." Thus, many behavioral scientists feel that their scholarly interests are rejected by the radical behaviorists, and they oppose behaviorism or, worse, ignore it. This is unfortunate because there is misunderstanding in both camps. Skinner misunderstands (or ignores) alternative views of "mental processes" and what constitutes "useful explanatory force."

Cognitive behavioral scientists believe Skinner to be narrower and less tolerant than he is.

There should be no quarrel with Skinner's criticism of "mental way stations" when mentalistic concepts are substituted for explanations or when mental entities are reified. But the use of mentalistic concepts that are defined only in terms of "behavior and manipulable or controllable variables" (see below) or that are used to characterize, presumably existing, isomorphic neurophysiological processes should be acceptable. Skinner appears to be inconsistent about the acceptability of some concepts, and the ones that he rejects are the ones whose rejection repels the nonradical behaviorist. Consider the following examples.

In "Behaviorism-50" Skinner objected to the students saying that the pigeon came to *associate* its action with the click of the food dispenser. He preferred to say that the bird's action was *temporally related* to the click. More recently (in "Why I Am Not a Cognitive Psychologist," 1977b) he used a similar example. "The standard mentalistic explanation is that the dog 'associates' the bell with the food. But it was Pavlov who associated them!" In a similar vein, he criticized the notion of a child or pigeon "developing a concept."

On the other hand, in "Behaviorism-50" Skinner said, "the child will not *discriminate* among colors...until exposed to...contingencies [of verbal reinforcement]" (italics added). Aside from the error of the assertion about the conditions for color discrimination in children (Bornstein 1975) and the significance that that has for the argument of which it was a part, there is no fundamental difference between Skinner's use of the term discriminate and the use of terms such as associate and conceptualize. All can be defined in relation to behavior and manipulable or controllable variables. In principle all can, but need not, refer to isomorphic neurophysiological processes. Discrimination is a standard term in the radical behaviorists nomenclature. Why can't association and conceptualization be?

To be fair, Skinner usually uses the form "to respond discriminatively," but it appears that "to respond associatively or conceptually" would not be acceptable. Would a definition such as "conceptual behavior refers to reinforced responses which do not depend upon prior experience with the specific stimuli being presented" make "conceptual behavior" or "conceptualization" acceptable? If so, the nonradical behaviorist need not feel rejected by the radical behaviorists and could study conceptualization essentially as it is studied anyway.

Presumably, if pressed, a cognitive behavioral scientist, whether physiologically oriented or not, would say that the use of "associate" or "conceptualize" was only an abbreviated way of characterizing the longer description that a behavioral analysis would yield or, perhaps, that it referred to an assumed, isomorphic neurophysiological process. It may surprise some to know that Skinner pointed to the possibility of the latter at least 20 years ago.

Again, in his remarks on "Behaviorism-50" Skinner indicated what "useful explanatory force" meant to him.

> An explanation is the demonstration of a functional relationship between behavior and manipulable or controllable variables.
>
> A different kind of explanation will arise when a physiology of behavior becomes available. "It will fill in the gaps between terminal events...." It must be arrived a "by independent observation and not by inference, or not by mentalistic construc tions." (Wann 1964, p. 102)

Skinner is unnecessarily restrictive in the last sentence. Mentalistic constructions developed by inference are reasonable and useful provided they are not inappro priately reified or do not become nominal explanations. In the final analysis, the bes explanation is a complete description. In principle, however, there will never be *complete* description in terms of behavioral analysis or otherwise. It is artificially constraining to ignore the probability of eventual neurophysiological correlates for mental–behavioral concepts and to avoid terms such as "associate" and "conceptualize" which function heuristically.

Skinner's place in the history of behavioral science is assured. I hope that in his next 20 years he will work toward a rapprochement with cognitive behavioral science, so that his place in history won't be tainted by dogmatic opposition to such rapprochement.

BFS: I agree that "'The pigeon discriminates' is as objectionable as 'The dog associates.'" Both expressions are dangerous in suggesting an initiating control on the part of the organism. I apologize for my careless usage. It is the behaviorist's dilemma. The English language and so far as I know most other languages put the behaving individual in the position of a controlling agent. We say that a person sees, hears, learns, fears, loves, thirsts, and so on. To rephrase every instance in accordance with good scientific methods would make for very difficult reading, but an analysis of a given instance must assign the initiating control correctly. For many purposes the lay vocabulary is convenient, but convenience is not to be mistaken for heuristics. The current popularity of cognitive psychology "as a revolt against behaviorism" is largely due to the freedom to use a lay vocabulary, not the discovery of an alternative science of comparable rigor.

Models, yes; homunculus, no

Frederick M. Toates

Biology Department, The Open University, Milton Keynes, England

I shall criticize just one aspect of Professor Skinner's excellent argument, that of models in the brain. In so doing, I fully acknowledge the intellectual mine fields and culs-de-sac around which one must try to negotiate. However, I believe that, for parsimony of explanation alone, one can justify postulation of inner representations. Furthermore. much is to be learned by basing explanations upon models and analogies borrowed from engineering.

Skinner quite rightly objects to the idea that once a visual image has been converted into nerve impulses in the optic nerve, it is then reconstructed to be observed by an inner viewer. Indeed, one imagines that there is nothing obviously wolflike about the electrical activity of my visual system when I view a wolf. However, that is not necessarily an argument against internal models, any more than the lack of physical resemblance between "thank you" and "merci" contradicts the notion that they might convey similar information.

Take the simple but revealing case of the rat's circadian rhythm. The rat's nocturnal activity correlates and entrains with, but is not directly dependent upon, darkness (Oatley 1973). Thus, a burrow may be permanently dark, but still the rat emerges at dusk. In continuous illumination, it still exhibits an approximately 24-hr rhythm. Surely it is reasonable to say that the rat runs an internal model of the earth's rotation. It is a model in the way that the movement of a watch *is* a model of the earth's rotation, whereas a sundial *is not* (cf. Oatley 1973). Indeed, it is hard to see how the rat might work without this aspect. Note that, with this description, one is claiming neither (1) that something intrinsic within the rat's head oscillates in light intensity, nor (2) that an inner rat inspects the oscillating signal in order to tell the time. At first, all one need say is that the oscillation influences the neural circuits underlying motivation. If we can establish that, in principle, postulation of models is not ridiculous, then we can build on this. For example, Deutsch (1960) constructed a machinelike representation that exhibited the flexibility of a rat negotiating a maze. Today, the model's internal structure would doubtless be seen as providing a primitive version of a cognitive map (Gallistel 1980). Deutsch did not leave the rat buried in thought, inspecting its own cognitive map. Rather, some simple rules of translation between the map and the appropriate motor command were proposed.

For a similar argument, take sensory preconditioning (Dickinson 1980), which presents difficulty for a traditional behaviourist account. A rat is first exposed to pairing of a tone and light. Later the light is paired with shock. Subsequently, the tone (never having been paired with shock) is seen to have acquired a fear-evoking power. I would suppose that presentation of the light evokes a memory (that is, an internal model) of shock. In turn, the tone can evoke revival of the memory of the light, and thereby that of the shock. The mistake is to assume that belief in this also involves belief that an inner rat inspects such memories. Rather, the rat simply jumps, runs, or freezes, and may thereby avoid the actual shock; this is the response to revival of a memory that is in some respects like a shock. Translation from a model of shock into avoidance behaviour need pose little or no greater conceptual challenge to the scientist than an explanation of how shock induces escape behaviour.

By comparison with Skinner's demonstration of the behaviour of a hungry pigeon to his student audience, it need not be unscientific to say that the rat *expects* shock. The reason is that one can postulate a physically realizable model that generates behaviour of a kind that can economically be described in these terms (whether or not the rat or pigeon has mental states accompanying such an expectation is indeed pure speculation and therefore relatively uninteresting). In using "expects," one is reminded of autoshaping in which the pigeon makes a peck characteristic of whether water or food is the "reinforcer" (Moore 1973).

I think it is a reasonable assumption that Penfield's (1969) patients did indeed have internal models of, say, wolves in their head. This is entirely compatible with Skinner's ideas about reinforcement by the verbal community. One can recognize a wolf as a wolf in so many different ways. Indeed, it is highly likely that one never sees exactly the same wolf twice. Bits of wolves, cartoons of wolves, are all sufficient for the same perception. If you try hard enough you can even "see" wolves where none exist, as Skinner's argument acknowledges. The nervous system often appears to be imposing a wolf "top-down" upon fragmentary and incomplete data. This is as parsimonious an explanation as saying that one invariably *behaves* differently if perceiving, say, a wolf or a fox. Again the intellectual dead end lies in postulating an inner screen onto which the wolf is projected. The challenge comes in looking for rules of translation between the model and the behaviour of, say, crying "wolf" and running.

Finally, let me add that, as two levels of explanation, I see absolutely no contradiction between "cognitive behaviourism," as an explanation of information storage and use, and radical behaviourism, to which I equally strongly subscribe as a technology of behavioural change and philosophy of social change (a similar argument emerged in some commentaries on Bindra 1978). As Skinner notes, it is scientifically reasonable to assume for consistency that the earth moves when he tosses a coin, even though we can't measure it. In a similar vein, I would argue that, on *one* level, consistency demands knowledge acquisition in a form not tied directly to behaviour. Learning that "bar press causes food" is not incompatible with the Skinnerian technology of how to shape such behaviour. The predictions that follow are identical. The competition, insofar as there is any, is for one's time. Have any of us enough time to spare to worry about inner states when the demands for implementation of a technology of behavioural change are so great? I'm not sure.

BFS: A "lack of physical resemblance" such as that "between 'thank you' and 'merci'" does not argue against the usefulness of an internal model. They may, indeed, "convey similar information." The objection is that in substituting one for the other (as in letting an internal representation stand n place of a physical presentation) one makes no progress toward the "use of information" – in this case, perhaps, the traditional reply "Not at all." Toates agrees that it is an intellectual dead end to postulate an inner screen onto which a representation is projected. "The challenge comes," he says, "in looking for rules of translation between the model and the behaviour of" responding to it.

I believe it is possible to account for Toates's examples simply by referring to behavior and a genetic or environmental history. If a model does nothing more than that, I have no objection, but in the process of modeling one tends to add properties which make the relation easier to think about but which actually falsify the account to some extent. There are processes which bring behavior under the control of daily and annual rhythms. They are mainly of phylogenic origin, but it is not difficult to create other behavior that changes in an orderly way with the passage of time. Physical clocks provide external support for behavior of that kind, but is there any reason to suppose that there are internal clocks which are not simply the processes themselves? Machines can be constructed to learn mazes and to respond to other, more clearly defined contingencies of reinforcement, but it does not follow that anything like such machines is to be found as cognitive maps or knowledge of contingencies inside the individual. Though I think sensory preconditioning can be explained in other ways, the explanation Toates gives can be restated as follows: A rat that has been exposed to the pairing of a tone and light is a changed rat. The presentation of the light does not evoke a memory nor does a response indicate "the revival of [a] memory."

I agree that predictions about a model-endowed and a model-free organism could be identical and that the "competition, insofar as there is any, is for one's time." I also agree that "the demands for implementation of a technology of behavioural change" are great. That is why I do not think we can spare the time to worry about internal states as models.

The development of concepts of the mental world

Henry M. Wellman

Department of Psychology, University of Michigan

Skinner's argument is that (1) mental constructs are unnecessary to explain behavior, yet (2) they persist in explanations of human behavior because we feel we have distinctive knowledge of mental states and processes. Upon proper analysis, however, (3) any distinctiveness of knowledge of the mental world disappears. Thus (4) mental constructs have no special claim on our theorizing, and (5) they are actually harmful, because (a) they are imprecise, and (b), as way stations, they lead to unfinished causal explanations. There is much for a cognitive scientist to disagree with here, including the assumed nature of explanation, and the premises of most steps along the way. I have special interest in step 3 and will focus on the analysis presented there. That analysis is central to a number of the other claims and is empirically examinable in ways other sources of disagreement are not.

How do humans come to "know" the mental world, Skinner asks? All knowledge is based on obvious stimuli, in this case internal, private stimuli. Concepts are formed, from this base, by a developmental process of language conditioning. They are taught via reinforcement of appropriate use of terms by the language community. Concepts of the mental world are therefore no different in kind from any other concepts. However, they are, on the average, different in precision. Imprecision results from the difficulty the language community faces in assessing the presence of private stimuli, and hence reinforcing the appropriate use of mental terms.

This analysis is at odds with results from research on the development of such concepts in three ways. First, the array of distinctions contrasting the mental and the physical worlds is collapsed onto the private versus public distinction alone. Second, all concepts are seen as social fabrications: "We have reason to believe that the child will not discriminate among colors – that he will not see two colors as different – until exposed to such [social, language] contingencies." Third, concepts of the mental world are analyzed as specially imprecise, in contrast to concepts of the physical world, which are based on obvious, public stimuli.

Mental phenomena (e.g., thinking, dreaming, knowing) and physical-behavioral phenomena (objective acts and physical objects embedded in space–time) differ in more than privacy. For example, the content of one is symbolic and abstract, the other is spatiotemporally concrete; in one case things can be true or false, in the other they simply are so; in one, logical reversibility obtains, in the other, causal sequences proceed directionally. Consider, as an example, the notion of factuality. A mental proposition can correspond to reality – to the facts – or not, or be distinctly counterfactual. The mind can conceive of things that are not so or indeed not possibly so. Even Skinner admits this, or else people who hold beliefs different from his own could not be wrong. Preschoolers also understand distinctions of this sort between the mental and the physical worlds (Johnson & Wellman 1980). By focusing only on the public versus private distinction Skinner is able to ignore these other essential distinctions which cause people to feel that the mental and the physical are different. It is not necessary to posit different forms of knowing for these two sorts of concepts; their referents are sufficiently different to support claims that the two are distinctive.

Skinner's analysis of the process of concept acquisition is also ill-conceived. Contrary to Skinner's claim, even preverbal infants discriminate different colors (Bornstein 1978) and form rudimentary concepts such as concepts of number (Strauss & Curtiss 1981). Concept development is not solely, or initially, a process of socia tutoring. Skinner resorts to such an analysis, I believe, because he thinks that few natural contingencies dictate the formation of concepts of mental processes (and because he would prefer such concepts to be mostly fabrications). However, as argued above, mental phenomena are different from physical events, and this distinction constantly confronts the child. There are, for example, the commonly experienced differences between one's wishes or expectations and the corresponding events, between one's plans and resulting performances, between one's point of view or understanding and another's. Such things as lies and pretense are frequently confronted – knowing something is so but saying or acting otherwise. Also, the same experience can produce different effects on the mind and the body: times when the mind is clear but the body fatigued, the body at rest but the mind active, and so on. In short, it is no surprise that people consider the mental world distinctive; that world is independent, in the above sense, of the world of behavior and physical events. Given all this evidence, it is not surprising that even $2\frac{1}{2}$ year olds understand many of the essential distinctions between mental and physical phenomena (Shatz, Wellman, & Silber 1983; Wellman, 1985). That is, children consider the mental world distinctive at the *beginning*, not at the end, of a process of acquiring the appropriate use of mental terms.

Finally, the array of evidence cited above means that concepts of the mental world are not necessarily imprecise; they are anchored in a rich context of evidence. At the same time, it is now clear that concepts of the physical world, of colors, or of objects, are themselves imprecise and fuzzy (Rosch, Mervis, Gay, Boyes-Braem, & Johnson 1976). The utility of concepts in one domain versus the other cannot be faulted, or praised, on the basis of precision.

In short, Skinner seems right in his assertion that knowledge of the mental world is acquired developmentally by a process of concept acquisition no different in principle from that which accounts for concepts of the physical world. However, having got the specifics of that process wrong, the hoped-for implications in steps 4 and 5 of his argument break down. In fact, the same reasons that dictate that $2\frac{1}{2}$ year olds conceptually distinguish the mental world underline the scientific utility of doing so. Thoughts are not just terminological way stations to acts. One can act without thinking, think without acting, and indeed think of things that are impossible to do. The dependence and independence of thoughts and acts cannot be dismissed so easily. And the data on the development of the use of mental terms and acquisition of mental concepts contradict, rather than support, such a dismissal.

BFS: Wellman quotes me out of context: "We have reason to believe that the child will not discriminate among colors – that he will not see two colors as different, until exposed to such [social, language] contingencies." I was talking about *naming* a color – that is, responding to colors apart from colored objects. The point was relevant to my argument because the contingencies which lead us to respond to many private events are necessarily "social, language." (Of course, infants discriminate between different colored objects and respond to three objects as different from two objects, but the concepts of color and number as abstract properties are different and I shall be surprised if Wellman can show that there are contingencies generating them which are not social.)

If I were to reply to Wellman's fourth paragraph (beginning "Mental phenomena"), I should have to give my own definitions, and ask him for his, of the following terms: "thinking," "dreaming," "knowing," "symbol," "abstract," "concrete," "true," "false," "logical," "proposition," "mind," and "belief." I have given behavioristic "translations" of all of these elsewhere, but to bring them together here is simply not feasible. Similarly, before I can give a behavioral account of the "experienced differences between one's wishes or expectations and the corresponding events, between one's plans and resulting performances, between one's point of view or understanding and another's," I should have to give my own interpretation of what it means to "wish," to "expect," to "plan," to "have a point of view," and to "understand." I have also dealt with these elsewhere, but a detailed analysis would take far more space than is available here.

Operant conditioning and behavioral neuroscience

Michael L. Woodruff

Department of Anatomy, Quillen–Dishner College of Medicine, East Tennessee State University

The designation "behavioral neurosciences" is intended to subsume any scientific endeavor designed to elucidate the function of the nervous system in the production of behavior. This activity includes manipulation and measurement of biological variables using techniques from the disciplines of, among others, anatomy, biochemistry, and physiology, as well as manipulation and measurement of behavioral variables. Professor Skinner's contribution would presumably be in the area of behavioral analysis. It is therefore necessary to understand Skinner's concept of a science of behavior. For this purpose "Behaviorism-50" seems inadequate. The science in Skinner's contribution to the scientific study of behavior lies behind, not within, this article. However, it is clear from "Behaviorism-50" that Skinner believes that a "science of behavior," equivalent in its rigor to a "science of anatomy" (for example), is possible, and, moreover, that his methodological approach is the best, if not the sole, representative of that science.

The experiments of Skinner and his colleagues and students have emphasized the importance of behavioral impact on the environment for the prediction and control of future behavior. The relationship between stimulus and response is not determined "reflexively," as in Pavlovian conditioning, but is due to the contingencies that exist between the organism's behavior and the environment. Although environmental events are certainly important within the context of an operant approach to behavioral analysis, the response as it operates upon the environment is the center of interest. The particular response is likely to be chosen arbitrarily. The response pattern of a single animal is studied for long periods and inferential statistics are seldom employed. The goal is to eliminate variability in the pattern of response emission over time in the presence of known environmental conditions by managing response–reinforcement contingencies. In other words, the operant psychologist establishes a stable baseline of response emission. Changes in experimental conditions (e.g., presentation of novel exteroceptive stimuli, drug injections, or brain lesions) are introduced after such a stable baseline has been maintained for some period. Finally, the rate of response emission by individual organisms is the chief datum of interest to the operant psychologist (Skinner 1966b).

The usefulness of operant approaches to behavioral analysis and the convenience of using automated testing devices for the maintenance of stable behavioral baselines against which physiological variables may be tested have been recognized by behavioral neuroscientists for some time. For example, operant techniques have been used to study endocrine and autonomic correlates of emotional behavior (Brady 1975); behavioral changes representative of motivational states (Teitelbaum 1966); and learning and memory (Pribram 1971). This list is an abbreviated representation, but an examination of these articles would serve to indicate the general trend, which is that the impact of Skinner's brand of behavioral science upon neuroscience has been in the domain of technique rather than theory. That is, although behavioral neuroscientists have used the techniques of operant analysis, they have not adopted the philosophical constructs of behaviorism. This is not because behavioral neuroscientists are ignorant of the requirements of a science of behavior; rather, the constructs and terms used by those working in behavioral neurosciences tend to remain associated more closely with cognitive rather than behavioristic interpretations, as the problems on which those working in this discipline tend to concentrate are influenced more by clinical neurology and clinical neuropsychology than by operant psychology. Moreover, the heuristic impact of clinical problems such as presenile dementia on research would not be enhanced by replacing terms such as learning, memory, and amnesia with the jargon of operant behaviorism.

In relation to some problems in behavioral neuroscience, operant behaviorism has proven barren not only as a framework within which to conceptualize the problem, but also in the provision of the relevant procedures. For example, the tenets of operant behaviorism have not contributed markedly to the elucidation of the role of the hippocampus in memory. Although it has been accepted for many years that bilateral hippocampal damage in humans causes severe anterograde amnesia, application of operant procedures failed to reveal any such parallel lesion-induced deficit in animals (see Isaacson 1982 for a review). In fact, rats with bilateral hippocampal damage are actually more successful than intact controls when placed on a free operant shock-avoidance schedule (Duncan & Duncan 1971). Determination of whether the hippocampus has a function in memory processing in animals as well as humans is important for several reasons, not the least of which is the desirability of using the animal hippocampus as a model for study of the physical changes in neural structure which may correlate both with the process of memory formation and with pathological states, such as Alzheimer's dementia, in which amnesia is a component and the hippocampus is one of the structures that degenerates.

The procedures of operant analysis, as Skinner (1966b) presents them, rely on nonspatial tasks in which responses are studied continuously. Discrete-trials analyses are not undertaken. Just such an analysis is required when a rat is run in a maze; and although many studies using discrete-trials analysis failed to reveal any obvious memory deficits subsequent to hippocampal removal, recent work, especially by O'Keefe and Nadel (1978) and Olton and his co-workers (Olton, Becker, & Handelmann 1979), using radial arm mazes has revealed a substantial mnemonic mpairment in rats after hippocampal damage. I hasten to add that it is probably possible to construct tasks using operant chambers and manipulanda that could reveal hippocampal lesion-induced memory deficits in rats. However, the radial maze has provided a convenient, species-relevant tool to assess memory function in rats reliably and repeatedly. The behavioral analyses are often done on an individual animal basis, and the results from these experiments are replicable in different aboratories. Although this paradigm would not seem to satisfy behaviorists, it does seem to meet the criteria that specify behavioral science, and the results from these experiments have contributed greatly to understanding the function of the animal hippocampus in memory. Moreover, they do so within a cognitive context that allows ntegration into the literature on human memory deficits subsequent to damage to, or disease of, the brain. Behaviorism has yet to accomplish either of these tasks when dealing with this problem.

BFS: I agree with Woodruff that "the science in [my] contribution to the scientific study of behavior lies behind, not within, this article." That is why I made clear that "Behaviorism-50" was about the philosophy of a science rather than the science itself. Woodruff's criticisms, too, are all about applications of an operant analysis and hence not about my paper. He finds that in relation to some problems within behavioral neuroscience operant behaviorism has proved barren. For example, operant procedures have not contributed markedly to the elucidation of the role of the hippocampus in memory. They were, of course, not designed to do so. But Woodruff's example of barrenness seems to me curious. He says that "it has been accepted for many years that bilateral hippocampal damage in humans causes severe anterograde amnesia," but that application of operant procedures failed to reveal any such lesion-induced deficit in animals. "In fact, rats with bilateral hippocampal damage are actually more successful than intact controls when placed on a free operant shock-avoidance schedule." But is that not a fact about hippocampal damage? It may not agree with Woodruff's conclusions from clinical observation, but it is nevertheless something to be taken into account. If he prefers the radial maze as providing "a convenient, species-relevant tool to assess memory function in rats reliably and repeatedly," is it because the results agree with his expectations? The arbitrary nature of maze scores and the difficulty in relating the behavior to the contingencies of reinforcement established by the maze have long been understood.

Is "Behaviorism at fifty" twenty years older?

Everett J. Wyers

Department of Psychology, State University of New York at Stony Brook

Much of "Behaviorism-50" remains cogent, relevant, or plausible in 1983. I have only one real quarrel with the target article. It has several guises: Can behaviorism avoid all of the excesses of "mentalistic" concepts? Does it need to? Does not its implicit "neorealism" unduly restrict its use?

Skinner tells us that "each of us is uniquely subject to certain kinds of stimulation from a small part of the universe within our skins" and that a science of behavior must be made to deal with the "events within the skin in their relation to behavior, without assuming they have a special nature or must be known in a special way." Paradigmatically, he adds that "seeing-that-we-are-seeing" – being aware of our seeing – is a part of the behavior of seeing – a part occurring "within our skins," even when no seen object is present, and subject to the same rules of discriminative stimulus control as any other behavior. Any "respondent" elements of "seeing" that exist are as subject to "conditioning" as any other respondent.

In one form, Skinner's idea that mental events are in behavior is suggestive of the early Tolman (1932): Intentions and expectations are immanent in behavior. In another form, it is suggestive of the early Hull (1943): Fractional components of response exist internally and follow the rules governing any other response. Unlike both Hull and Tolman, Skinner denies to both forms a causative role in behavior; that is, central mediation of intention and of expectancy (Tolman) is explicitly denied, and the evident respondent element of habit strength (Hull) is at least played down.

I have no objection to viewing mind as behavior, but what of the expanded version of selection by consequences (Skinner 1966c; 1974; 1981 [all commented on in this volume])? Here, natural selection (contingencies of survival and reproductive success) enters as basic, and contingencies of reinforcement are added (superimposed?) as a later derivative. Many animals can "see" colors. Can such a "mind" be explained by behavior? If an animal can discriminate similar colors in only one test trial, the tracing of past contingencies contributing to such discriminative stimulus control is scarcely to be considered (cf. Jarvik 1956; Menzel & Juno 1982).

Either reference to remote contingencies of survival must be made, or reliance must be placed on generalization of specific past experience. The discriminative distinction must be shown to be of value, in terms either of selective contingencies affecting the evolution of the species, or of the development of the individual, or both. In each case a plausible reconstruction is difficult, if not impossible, to derive. Modern population genetics and evolutionary theory do not demand such apt analyses (Gould 1980; Lewontin 1979). An alternative is to assume the existence of representational processes within the skin permitting the degree of behavioral specificity observed and examine the nature of limits of functional utilization those representational processes permit (see Roitblat 1982).

"Science aims at constructing a world which shall be symbolic of the world of commonplace experience. It is not at all necessary that every individual symbol that is used should represent something in common experience or even something explicable in terms of common experience" (Eddington 1958, p. xv).

Science is maplike (Tolman 1935). Its symbols are arranged so as to help us find our way through the phenomena of common experience. They need have no more relation to reality than those of a map. In extending behaviorism into the private realm of human "mental" experience Skinner's effort is to "map" words used to designate private experience onto analytic descriptions of behavior. The obscurity and complexity of the contingencies Skinner refers to as applied by the verbal community in shaping even our simplest, most direct experiences, make such 'mapping" at best a difficult and unreliable procedure.

Today behaviorism accepts the existence of mental events. Instead of mapping behavior onto them, the opposite strategy is adopted; one maps the mental events onto behavior. The mental event is behavior itself. It is a component element (response) of the behavioral action in process. Thus, the question is raised, How can one response cause another response? How can something that is only a portion of the reaction to the current stimulus situation also be a stimulus to that reaction? What is there inside the skin? Skinner asserts that "we" exist within the skin and observe our own behavior in both its internal and external aspects.

This being the case, why not use words denoting mental events as the symbolic content of science? Lack of precision (surplus meaning) is the answer. But the designation of reinforcing contingencies is certainly not without "surplus meaning." A reinforcer can be, and often is, almost anything. Behavior itself can be, and often is, almost anything (Jenkins 1979).

It is reasonable to assume that no response can exist, no instant of behavior occurs, without simultaneous afferent input to the central nervous system. In short, all distinguishable responses have exactly the same status as stimuli insofar as what is inside the skin is concerned. Can we not, by some symbolic system, describe behavior as a continuous sequence of "events" blending into each other?

Some events initiate, others terminate, and still others facilitate or hinder the smooth flow of behavior – the blending of sequential events into each other. The occurrence of events is seldom, if ever, completely predictable – the changeable elements of environment do intrude. Perhaps, like Brunswik (1955), we should seek a symbolic system describing the probabilistic texture of the course of events in time, what we now call stimulus and response being used merely as indicators of achievements relevant to the functioning of representational processes existing within the skin – this, instead of viewing stimulus, response, and reinforcing contingency as the substance of reality.

Such a course could avoid the inherent dualism and neorealism in Skinner's proposals. A system of abstract symbols representing internal causative processes encompassing the provenance of behavior (cf. Tolman 1948) could avoid both the "we" that observes our own behavior and the view that what is observed is "reality." Attention then reverts to what aspects of "reality" constitute the "umwelt" of the individual and how the individual deals with those aspects.

I am not advocating a return to the past. Something new in "intervening variables" is needed. Skinner advances behaviorism by espousing the acceptance of the reality of mentalistic events, but he remains locked in a box created by past and future contingencies of reinforcement, survival, and reproductive success. To enter the box the present state of the individual is the essential key.

How can we characterize for the individual the differences among the situations it enters or finds itself in? Is there a difference between a Skinner box, a maze, and foraging in natural situations? I think there is; a difference first assessable by mentalistic concepts (recognizing their metaphorical nature) in the construction of a system "symbolic of the world of commonplace experience" which does not require "that every individual symbol. . .represent something in common experience." That mentalistic concepts are transposable to something else, where efficiency of description requires, is (or should be) evident to all. This is exactly what Skinner aims at, and what is required in an "experimental analysis of behavior."

When the word "stimuli" (discriminative stimuli) is used to refer to a situation an organism finds itself in, or is presented with, the "stimulus" becomes for the organism, and its observer, something to be dealt with. The situation is interpreted as such. So also with response and reinforcer. In all three cases an interpretative account by and for the organism is needed.

One must refer to mentalistic concepts to divine the nature of a situation for the individual in terms of the three concepts. They do not refer only to physical measures and descriptions and cannot, within the framework of the system, if application of the experimental analysis of behavior is to be feasible. In all cases historical reference is necessary.

To speak of contingencies of reinforcement, discriminative stimuli, and operant response requires a cognitive analysis in terms of "mentalistic" concepts. A sort of three-stage process is involved. First, the behavior is observed, then the meaning of the situation for the organism is inferred, and finally, and only then, is it decided what is discriminative stimulus, what is the operant, and how it is reinforced.

The inferential phase stems from the observer's own private "mentalistic" evaluation of what he has observed and derived from his own past experience. Thus, to "objectify" his key concepts the behaviorist attributes to intervening mentalistic entities (meanings) a causative influence in the initiation and shaping of behavior. In 1983, 20 years after attaining "maturity," the behaviorist has still to find a way to transpose "meanings," as inferred from current observation, into symbolic systems implying future reference without ad hoc "historical" analysis.

Behaviorism at 70 has found the door, but it still lacks the key to what is beyond. "We" do not just sit within the skin and observe. "We" also infer and interpret what we observe. And if "we" are naught but representational processes, then "we" know we exist because those processes "think" ("Cogito, ergo sum").

BFS: I am quite willing to attribute some of the discriminative responses of organisms to phylogenic histories, and I am surprised that Wyers should think I am not. I also suppose that one response "causes" another by creating an eliciting or discriminative stimulus and that a mere "portion" of a response should suffice.

I do not agree that a radical behaviorism, in refusing to dismiss private events as somehow beyond the reach of science because observable by only one person, is restoring mentalism. Perhaps it would do so if it assigned to those private events the initiating direction that Wyers assigns to them. One can "speak of contingencies of reinforcement, discriminative stimuli, and operant response" without inferring the meaning of the situation for the organism. And I should like to ask those who do infer that meaning to explain how they do it without pointing to environmental variables.

In support of cognitive theories

Thomas R. Zentall

Department of Psychology, University of Kentucky

Skinner clearly identifies the quagmire so easily stumbled into by the mentalists. Yet he also acknowledges that a large class of events, those that occur inside the organism and cannot be seen by others, has been denied or ignored by most behaviorists. Skinner's solution is to admit that these events exist, but to claim that they are subject to the same laws as external (observable) events. Thus, according to Skinner, there is no active processing of information, nor is there any inherent central organization. All apparent cognitive processing is mistakenly assumed from overt behavior (e.g., the verbal report that such cognitions exist). But such behavior exists only because it has been shaped by external contingencies.

Skinner justifiably criticizes those who *explain* internal organization in terms of decision-making homunculi and copies of the real world within the body. These concepts give the false impression that the organism's behavior has been explained, and thus further investigation may be deemed unnecessary. Unfortunately, the explanations provided by behaviorists contain the same weakness. To say that all behavior, whether controlled by internal or external stimuli, is determined by external contingencies is highly speculative and may be testable only in principle. The methodological criticism of mental process theories – to the effect that they have "discouraged the completion of the causal sequence" (i.e., they provide the illusion of explanation) – is also applicable to Skinner's behaviorism. To extrapolate from simple conditioning paradigms to all the complex forms of mental behavior gives one a sense of complete understanding in the absence of empirical evidence. Thus, any theory, including behaviorism, can be interpreted erroneously as an end rather than a means, but this fact should not outweigh the great heuristic value of theory. Theories are not ends in themselves; rather, they should provide a framework of prediction that directs research. Theories of mental behavior have resulted in a diversity of experimental procedures that would undoubtedly not have been developed in their absence.

Ultimately, however, one would like the justification for the development of mental theories of behavior to be more than philosophical (i.e., heuristic). Is there any empirical basis for the belief that organisms have the ability to organize incoming stimulation in the absence of external contingencies to do so? Skinner says no, not even humans have this ability. In fact there is considerable evidence for the internal organization of a great variety of stimulus input. Furthermore, this evidence precludes explanation based on reinforcement for the verbal (or nonverbal) expression that such organization exists. Let us consider Skinner's own example of the organization of spectral colors. Skinner proposes that a "child will not discriminate among colors – that he will not see two colors as different – until exposed to [community provided] contingencies." Thus, according to Skinner, there is no internal organization of stimulus values prior to differential reinforcement for responding to those values. It is well established that if an organism is trained to respond to one stimulus value, it will also respond to other stimulus values to an extent predictable from their physical similarity to the training stimulus (i.e., the organism will show a decremental stimulus generalization gradient). Skinner would say that such differences in responding to test stimuli were the result of previous experience in (i.e., differential reinforcement for) making different responses to the different stimulus values. But there is clear evidence that animals can show regular decremental color gradients in the absence of differential reinforcement for responding to color values (Mountjoy & Malott 1968; Riley & Leuin 1971; Tracy 1970). Riley and Leuin (1971) housed chickens in monochromatic light after they had been incubated and hatched in the dark. They then trained the birds to peck the same wavelength of monochromatic light for food reinforcement. When these birds were then exposed to different wavelengths of light (in extinction) they showed a regular generalization gradient. Thus, in the absence of prior experience with different colors the birds clearly discriminated among the colors presented. These data indicate that there exists an internal organization of hues prior to any history of reinforcement for responding to those hues.

Such research is difficult to do with humans, for obvious reasons, but there is suggestive evidence for a genetically based organization of spectral hues in humans. Four-month-old infants habituate faster to (i.e., they spend less time looking at) hues that correspond to adult color prototypes (i.e., "good" examples of red, green, yellow, and blue) than to mixtures of those hues (Bornstein 1981). Furthermore, these infants show generalized habituation within a range of hues that adults categorize as one color (e.g., red) but show renewed interest in hues that fall outside that color category (Bornstein, Kessen, & Weiskopf 1976). Further indirect evidence for genetically based color categories in humans comes from findings that there is almost perfect correspondence in the mapping of color categories across human cultures (Berlin & Kay 1969; Heider 1972; Rosch 1973). Furthermore, color categorization is not limited to humans. There is also evidence for color categorization in pigeons. Under conditions that demonstrate excellent discriminability among colors (viz. red, green, yellow, and blue), pigeons will categorically code red–yellow and blue–green (Zentall, Edwards, Moore, & Hogan 1981) or yellow–green (Zentall & Edwards, 1984). See also Wright and Cumming (1971).

Evidence for the central organization of colors is but one example of the need for theories of central processing. Such theories may appear to Skinner to be unparsimonious. However, I think we have reached the point where a "parsimonious" theory of behavior based *solely* on contingencies of reinforcement is stretched so thin that over large portions of its explanatory domain (e.g., the area of cognition) it has lost its predictive power.

BFS: It is certainly only a hypothesis, "testable only in principle," to say that "all behavior, whether controlled by internal or external stimuli, is determined by external contingencies." A comparable statement would be that it is only a hypothesis, testable only in principle, that the physical processes occurring in outer space are similar to those occurring in the laboratory. One begins wherever possible and proceeds as soon as possible to a more and more adequate account – which, of course, will never be complete.

It is true that theories of mental life have had heuristic value in prompting research, but the question is whether the research would have been done without them. Take, for example, the physiological psychology of Wundt and Titchener. The search for the mental elements that obeyed mental laws in the world of the mind is now the physiology of sensory end organs. Progress has been determined almost entirely by technical advances in instrumentation. Can anything important be said for the heuristic value of the mental theory?

As I have said in response to Wellman, I do not doubt that children will discriminate among colored objects, but they will come to name colors or to respond to color alone in any other way only with the help of a social environment. I am also willing to accept the role of natural selection in the development of color vision. In fact, the experiment to which Zentall refers n which chickens were incubated and hatched in the dark and raised in monochromatic light was first done with ducklings in my laboratory by Neil Peterson (1962). The stimulus generalization gradients investigated by Norman Guttman (e.g., 1956) and his students also apparently reflect a 'genetically based organization of spectral hues" in pigeons. (I question the "almost perfect correspondence in the mapping of color categories across human cultures," however. That may be true of modern cultures, but it is well known that the Greeks had few color words and that their "primaries" were apparently not quite our own.) I do not think that the data offered by Zentall really support cognitive theories. His own account seems to be almost exclusively behavioral.

6 The phylogeny and ontogeny of behavior

Abstract: Responses are strengthened by consequences having to do with the survival of individuals and species. With respect to the provenance of behavior, we know more about ontogenic than phylogenic contingencies. The contingencies responsible for unlearned behavior acted long ago. This remoteness affects our scientific methods, both experimental and conceptual. Until we have identified the variables responsible for an event, we tend to invent causes. Explanatory entities such as "instincts," "drives," and "traits" still survive. Unable to show how organisms can behave effectively under complex circumstances, we endow them with special abilities permitting them to do so.

Behavior exhibited by most members of a species is often accepted as inherited if all members were not likely to have been exposed to relevant ontogenic contingencies. When contingencies are not obvious, it is perhaps unwise to call any behavior either inherited or acquired, as the examples of churring in honey guides and following in imprinted ducklings show. Nor can the relative importance of phylogenic and ontogenic contingencies be argued from instances in which unlearned or learned behavior intrudes or dominates. Intrusions occur in both directions.

Behavior influenced by its consequences seems directed toward the future, but only past effects are relevant. The mere fact that behavior is adaptive does not indicate whether phylogenic or ontogenic processes have been responsible for it. Examples include the several possible provenances of imitation, aggression, and communication. The generality of such concepts limits their usefulness. A more specific analysis is needed if we are to deal effectively with the two kinds of contingencies and their products.

Parts of the behavior of an organism concerned with the internal economy, as in respiration or digestion, have always been accepted as "inherited," and there is no reason why some responses to the external environment should not also come ready-made in the same sense. It is widely believed that many students of behavior disagree. The classical reference is to John B. Watson (1924):

> I should like to go one step further now and say, "Give me a dozen healthy infants, well-formed, and my own specified world to bring them up in and I'll guarantee to take any one at random and train him to become any type of specialist I might select – doctor, lawyer, artist, merchant-chief and, yes, even beggarman and thief, regardless of his talents, penchants, tendencies, abilities, vocations, and race of his ancestors." I am going beyond my facts and I admit it, but so have the advocates of the contrary and they have been doing it for many thousands of years.

Watson was not denying that a substantial part of behavior is inherited. His challenge appears in the first of four chapters describing "how man is equipped to behave at birth." As an enthusiastic specialist in the psychology of learning he went beyond his facts to emphasize what could be done in spite of genetic limitations. He was actually, as P. H. Gray (1963) has pointed out, "one of the earliest and one of the most careful workers in the area of animal ethology." Yet he is probably responsible for the persistent myth of what has been called "behaviorism's counterfactual dogma" (Hirsch 1963). And it is a myth. No reputable student of animal behavior has ever taken the position "that the animal comes to the laboratory as a virtual *tabula rasa*, that species' differences are insignificant, and that all responses are about equally conditionable to all stimuli" (Breland & Breland 1961).

But what does it mean to say that behavior is inherited? Lorenz (1965) has noted that ethologists are not agreed on "the concept of 'what we formerly called innate.'" Insofar as the behavior of an organism is simply the physiology of an anatomy, the inheritance of behavior is the inheritance of certain bodily features, and there should be no problem concerning the meaning of "innate" that is not raised by any genetic trait. Perhaps we must qualify the statement that an organism inherits a visual reflex, but we must also qualify the statement that it inherits its eye color.

If the anatomical features underlying behavior were as conspicuous as the wings of *Drosophila*, we should describe them directly and deal with their inheritance in the same way, but at the moment we must be content with so-called behavioral manifestations. We describe the behaving organism in terms of its gross anatomy, and we shall no doubt eventually describe the behavior of its finer structures in much the same way, but until then we analyze behavior without referring to fine structures and are constrained to do so even when we wish to make inferences about them.

What features of behavior will eventually yield a satisfactory genetic account? Some kind of inheritance is implied by such concepts as "racial memory" or "death instinct," but a sharper specification is obviously needed. The behavior observed in mazes and similar apparatuses may be "objective," but it is not described in dimensions which yield a meaningful genetic picture. Tropisms and taxes are somewhat more readily quantified, but not all behavior can be thus formulated, and organisms selected for breeding according to tropistic or taxic performances may still differ in other ways (Erlenmeyer-Kimling, Hirsch, & Weiss 1962).

The experimental analysis of behavior has emphasized another property. The probability that an organism will behave in a given way is a more valuable datum than the mere fact that it does so behave. Probability may be inferred from frequency of emission. It is a basic datum, in a theoretical sense, because it is related to the question, Why does an organism behave in a given way at a given time? It is basic in a practical sense because frequency has been found to vary in an orderly way with many independent variables. Probability of response is important in examining the inheritance not only of specific forms of behavior but of behavioral processes and characteristics often described as traits. Very little has been done in studying the genetics of behavior in this sense. Modes of inheritance are not, however, the only issue. Recent advances in the formulation of learned behavior throw considerable light on other genetic and evolutionary problems.

The provenance of behavior

Upon a given occasion we observe that an animal displays a certain kind of behavior – learned or unlearned. We describe its topography and evaluate its probability. We discover variables, genetic or environmental, of which the probability is a function. We then undertake to predict or control the behavior. All this concerns a current state of the organism. We have still to ask where the behavior (or the structures which thus behave) came from.

The provenance of learned behavior has been thoroughly analyzed. Certain kinds of events function as "reinforcers," and when such an event follows a response, similar responses are more likely to occur. This is operant conditioning. By manipulating the ways in which reinforcing consequences are contingent upon behavior, we generate complex forms of response and bring them under the control of subtle features of the environment. What we may call the ontogeny of behavior is thus traced to contingencies of reinforcement.

In a famous passage Pascal (1670) suggested that ontogeny and phylogeny have something in common. "Habit," he said, "is a second nature which destroys the first. But what is this nature? Why is habit not natural? I am very much afraid that nature is itself only first habit as habit is second nature." The provenance of "first habit" has an important place in theories of the evolution of behavior. A given response is in a sense strengthened by consequences which have to do with the survival of the individual and species. A given form of behavior leads not to reinforcement but to procreation. (Sheer reproductive activity does not, of course, always contribute to the survival of a species, as the problems of overpopulation remind us. A few well fed breeders presumably enjoy an advantage over a larger but impoverished population. The advantage may also be selective. It has been suggested [Wynne-Edwards 1965] that some forms of behavior such as the defense of a territory have an important effect in restricting breeding.) Several practical problems raised by what may be called contingencies of selection are remarkably similar to problems which have already been approached experimentally with respect to contingencies of reinforcement.

An identifiable unit. A behavioral process, as a change in frequency of response, can be followed only if it is possible to count responses. The topography of an operant need not be completely fixed, but some defining property must be available to identify instances. An emphasis upon the occurrence of a repeatable unit distinguishes an experimental analysis of behavior from historical or anecdotal accounts. A similar requirement is recognized in ethology. As Julian Huxley has said, "this concept...of unit releasers which act as specific key stimuli unlocking genetically determined unit behavior patterns...is probably the most important single contribution of Lorenzian ethology to the science of behavior" (Huxley 1964).

The action of stimuli. Operant reinforcement not only strengthens a given response, it brings the response under the control of a stimulus. But the stimulus does not elicit the response as in a reflex; it merely sets the occasion upon which the response is more likely to occur. The ethologists' "releaser" also simply sets an occasion. Like the discriminative stimulus, it increases the probability of occurrence of a unit of behavior but does not force it. The principal difference between a reflex and an instinct is not in the complexity of the response but in, respectively, the eliciting and releasing actions of the stimulus.

Origins of variations. Ontogenic contingencies remain ineffective until a response has occurred. In a familiar experimental arrangement, the rat must press the lever at least once "for other reasons" before it presses it "for food." There is a similar limitation in phylogenic contingencies. An animal must emit a cry at least once for other reasons before the cry can be selected as a warning because of the advantage to the species. It follows that the entire repertoire of an individual or species must exist prior to ontogenic or phylogenic selection but only in the form of minimal units. Both phylogenic and ontogenic contingencies "shape" complex forms of behavior from relatively undifferentiated material. Both processes are favored if the organism shows an extensive, undifferentiated repertoire.

Programmed contingencies. It is usually not practical to condition a complex operant by waiting for an instance to occur and then reinforcing it. A terminal performance must be reached through intermediate contingencies (perhaps best exemplified by programmed instruction). In a demonstration experiment a rat pulled a chain to obtain a marble from a rack, picked up the marble with its forepaws, carried it to a tube projecting two inches above the floor of its cage, lifted it to the top of the tube, and dropped it inside. "Every step in the process had to be worked out through a series of approximations since the component responses were not in the original repertoire of the rat" (Skinner 1938). The "program" was as follows. The rat was reinforced for any movement which caused a marble to roll over any edge of the floor of its cage, then only over the edge on one side of the cage, then over only a small section of the edge, then over only that section slightly raised, and so on. The raised edge became a tube of gradually diminishing diameter and increasing height. The earlier member of the chain, release of the marble from the rack, was added later. Other kinds of programming have been used to establish subtle stimulus control (Terrace 1963a), to sustain behavior in spite of infrequent reinforcement (Ferster & Skinner 1957), and so on.

A similar programming of complex phylogenic contingencies is familiar in evolutionary theory. The environment may change, demanding that behavior which contributes to survival for a given reason become more complex. Quite different advantages may be responsible for different stages. To take a familiar example the electric organ of the eel could have become useful in stunning prey only after developing something like its present power. Must we attribute the completed organ to a single complex mutation, or were intermediate stages developed because of other advantages? Much weaker currents, for example, may have permitted the eel to detect the nature of objects with which it was in contact. The same question may be asked about behavior. Pascal's "first habit" must often have been the product of "programmed instruction." Many of the complex phylogenic contingencies which now seem to sustain behavior must have been reached through intermediate stages in which less complex forms had lesser but still effective consequences.

The need for programming is a special case of a more general principle. We do not explain any system of behavior simply by demonstrating that it works to the advantage of, or has "net utility" for, the individual or species. It is necessary to show that a given advantage is contingent upon behavior in such a way as to alter its probability.

Adventitious contingencies. It is not true, as Lorenz (1965) has asserted, that "adaptiveness is always the irrefutable proof that this process [of adaptation] has taken place." Behavior may have advantages which played no role in its selection. The converse is also true. Events which follow behavior but are not necessarily produced by it may have a selective effect. A hungry pigeon placed in an apparatus in which a food dispenser operates every 20 seconds regardless of what the pigeon is doing acquires a stereotyped response which is shaped and sustained by wholly coincidental reinforcement (Skinner 1948a). The behavior is often "ritualistic"; we call it superstitious. There is presumably a phylogenic parallel. All current characteristics of an organism do not necessarily contribute to its survival and procreation, yet they are all nevertheless "selected." Useless structures with associated useless functions are as inevitable as superstitious behavior. Both become more likely as organisms become more sensitive to contingencies. It should occasion no surprise that behavior has not perfectly adjusted to either ontogenic or phylogenic contingencies.

Unstable and intermittent contingencies. Both phylogenic and ontogenic contingencies are effective even though intermittent. Different schedules of reinforcement generate different patterns of changing probabilities. If there is a phylogenic parallel, it is obscure. A form of behavior generated by intermittent selective contingencies is presumably likely to survive a protracted period in which the contingencies are not in force, because it has already proved powerful enough to survive briefer periods, but this is only roughly parallel with the explanation of the greater resistance to extinction of intermittently reinforced operants.

Contingencies also change, and the behavior for which they are responsible then changes too. When ontogenic contingencies specifying topography of response are relaxed, the topography usually deteriorates, and when reinforcers are no longer forthcoming the operant undergoes extinction. Darwin (1872) discussed phylogenic parallels in *The Expression of the Emotions in Man and Animals*. His "serviceable associated habits" were apparently both learned and unlearned, and he seems to have assumed that ontogenic contingencies contribute to the inheritance of behavior, at least in generating responses which may then have phylogenic consequences. The behavior of the domestic dog in turning around before lying down on a smooth surface may have been selected by contingencies under which the behavior made a useful bed in grass or brush. If dogs now show this behavior less frequently, it is presumably because a sort of phylogenic extinction has set in. The domestic cat shows a complex response of covering feces which must once have had survival value with respect to predation or disease. The dog has been more responsive to the relaxed contingencies arising from domestication or some other change in predation or disease and shows the behavior in vestigial form.

Multiple contingencies. An operant may be affected by more than one kind of reinforcement, and a given form of behavior may be traced to more than one advantage to the individual or the species. Two phylogenic or ontogenic consequences may work together or oppose each other in the development of a given response and presumably show "algebraic summation" when opposed.

Social contingencies. The contingencies responsible for social behavior raise special problems in both phylogeny and ontogeny. In the development of a language the behavior of a speaker can become more elaborate only as listeners become more sensitive to elaborated speech. A similarly coordinated development must be assumed in the phylogeny of social behavior. The dance of the bee returning from a successful foray can have advantageous effects for the species only when other bees behave appropriately with respect to it, but they cannot develop the behavior until the dance appears. The terminal system must have required a kind of subtle programming in which the behavior of both "speaker" and "listener" passed through increasingly complex stages. A bee returning from a successful foray may behave in a special way because it is excited or fatigued, and it may show phototropic responses related to recent visual stimulation. If the strength of the behavior varies with the quantity or quality of food the bee has discovered and with the distance and direction it has flown, then the behavior may serve as an important stimulus to other bees, even though its characteristics have not yet been affected by such consequences. If different bees behave in different ways, the more effective versions should be selected. If the behavior of a successful bee evokes behavior on the part of "listeners" which is reinforcing to the "speaker," then the "speaker's" behavior should be ontogenically intensified. The phylogenic development of responsive behavior in the "listener" should contribute to the final system by providing for immediate reinforcement of conspicuous forms of the dance.

The speaker's behavior may become less elaborate if the listener continues to respond to less elaborate forms. We stop someone who is approaching us by pressing our palm against his chest, but he eventually learns to stop upon seeing our outstretched palm. The practical response becomes a gesture. A similar shift in phylogenic contingencies may account for the "intentional movements" of the ethologists.

Behavior may be intensified or elaborated under differential reinforcement involving the stimulation either of the behaving organism or of others. The more conspicuous a superstitious response, for example, the more effective the adventitious contingencies. Behavior is especially likely to become more conspicuous when reinforcement is contingent on the response of another organism. Some ontogenic instances, called "ritualization," are easily demonstrated. Many elaborate rituals of primarily phylogenic origin have been described by ethologists.

Some problems raised by phylogenic contingencies

Lorenz has argued that "our absolute ignorance of the physiological mechanisms underlying learning makes our knowledge of the causation of phyletic adaptation seem quite considerable by comparison" (1965). But genetic and behavioral processes are studied and formulated in a rigorous way without reference to the underlying biochemistry. With respect to the provenance of behavior we know much more about ontogenic contingencies than phylogenic. Moreover, phylogenic contingencies raise some very difficult problems which have no ontogenic parallels.

The contingencies responsible for unlearned behavior acted a very long time ago. The natural selection of a given form of behavior, no matter how plausibly argued, remains an inference. We can set up phylogenic contingencies under which a given property of behavior arbitrarily selects individuals for breeding, and thus demonstrate modes of behavioral inheritance, but the experimenter who makes the selection is performing a function of the natural environment which also needs to be studied. Just as reinforcement arranged in an experimental analysis must be shown to have parallels in "real life" if the results of the analysis are to be significant or useful, so the contingencies which select a given behavioral trait in a genetic experiment must be shown to play a plausible role in natural selection.

Although ontogenic contingencies are easily subjected to an experimenta analysis, phylogenic contingencies are not. When the experimenter has shaped a complex response, such as dropping a marble into a tube, the provenance of the behavior raises no problem. The performance may puzzle anyone seeing it for the first time, but it is easily traced to recent, possibly recorded, events. No comparable history can be invoked when a spider is observed to spin a web. We have not seen the phylogenic contingencies at work. All we know is that spiders of a given kind build more or less the same kind of web. Our ignorance often adds a touch of mystery. We are likely to view inherited behavior with a kind of awe not inspired by acquired behavior of similar complexity.

The remoteness of phylogenic contingencies affects our scientific methods, both experimental and conceptual. Until we have identified the variables of which an event is a function, we tend to invent causes. Learned behavior was once commonly attributed to "habit," but an analysis of contingencies of reinforcement has made the term unnecessary. "Instinct," as a hypothetcal cause of phylogenic behavior, has had a longer life. We no longer say that our rat possesses a marble-dropping habit, but we are still likely to say that our spider has a web-spinning instinct. The concept of instinct has been severely criticized and is now used with caution or altogether avoided, but explanatory entities serving a similar function still survive in the writings of many ethologists.

A "mental apparatus," for example, no longer finds a useful place in the experimental analysis of behavior, but it survives in discussions of phylogenic contingencies. Here are a few sentences from the writings of prominent ethologists which refer to consciousness or awareness: "The young gosling ...gets imprinted upon its mind the image of the first moving object it sees" (Thorpe 1951); "the infant expresses the inner state of contentment by smiling" (Huxley 1964); "[herring gulls show a] lack of insight into the ends served by their activities" (Tinbergen 1953); "[chimpanzees were unable] to communicate to others the unseen things in their minds" (Kortlandt 1965).

In some mental activities awareness may not be critical, but other cognitive activities are invoked. Thorpe (1951) speaks of a disposition "which leads the animal to pay particular attention to objects of a certain kind." What we observe is simply that objects of a certain kind are especially effective stimuli. We know how ontogenic contingencies work to produce such an effect. The ontogenic contingencies which generate the behavior called "paying attention" also presumably have phylogenic parallels. Other mental activities frequently mentioned by ethologists include "organizing experience" and "discovering relations." Expressions of all these sorts show that we have not yet accounted for behavior in terms of contingencies, phylogenic or ontogenic. Unable to show how the organism can behave effectively under complex circumstances, we endow it with a special cognitive ability which permits it to do so. Once the contingencies are understood, we no longer need to appeal to mentalistic explanations.

Other concepts replaced by a more effective analysis include "need" or "drive" and "emotion." In ontogenic behavior we no longer say that a given set of environmental conditions first gives rise to an inner state which the organism then expresses or resolves by behaving in a given way. We no longer represent relations among emotional and motivational variables as relations among such states, as in saying that hunger overcomes fear. We no longer use dynamic analogies or metaphors, as in explaining sudden action as the overflow or bursting out of dammed-up needs or drives. If these are common practices in ethology, it is evidently because the functional relations they attempt to formulate are not clearly understood.

Another kind of innate endowment, particularly likely to appear in explanations of human behavior, takes the form of "traits" or "abilities." Though often measured quantitatively, their dimensions are meaningful only in placing the individual in a population. The behavior measured is almost always obviously learned. To say that intelligence is inherited is not to say that specific forms of behavior are inherited. Phylogenic contingencies conceivably responsible for "the selection of intelligence" do not specify responses. What has been selected appears to be a susceptibility to ontogenic contingencies, leading particularly to greater speed of conditioning and the capacity to maintain a larger repertoire wtihout confusion.

It is often said that an analysis of behavior in terms of ontogenic contingencies "leaves something out of account," and this is true. It leaves out of account habits, ideas, cognitive processes, needs, drives, traits, and so on. But it does not neglect the facts upon which these concepts are based. It seeks a more effective formulation of the very contingencies to which those who use such concepts must eventually turn to explain their explanations. The strategy has been highly successful at the ontogenic level, where the contingencies are relatively clear. As the nature and mode of operation of phylogenic contingencies come to be better understood, a similar strategy should yield comparable advantages.

Identifying phylogenic and ontogenic variables

The significance of ontogenic variables may be assessed by holding genetic conditions as constant as possible – for example, by studying "pure" strains or identical twins. The technique has a long history. According to Plutarch (*De Puerorum Educatione*) Licurgus, a Spartan, demonstrated the importance of environment by raising two puppies from the same litter so that one became a good hunter while the other preferred food from a plate. On the other hand, genetic variables may be assessed either by studying organisms upon which the environment has had little opportunity to act (because they are newborn or have been reared in a controlled environment) or by comparing groups subject to extensive, but on the average probably similar, environmental histories. The technique also has a long history. In his journal for 24 January 1805, Stendahl refers to an experiment in which two birds taken from the nest after hatching and raised by hand exhibited their genetic endowment by eventually mating and building a nest two weeks before the female laid eggs. Behavior exhibited by most of the members of a species is often accepted as inherited if it is unlikely that all the members could have been exposed to relevant ontogenic contingencies.

When contingencies are not obvious, it is perhaps unwise to call any behavior either inherited or acquired. Field observations, in particular, will often not permit a distinction. Friedmann (1956) has described the behavior of the African honey guide as follows:

> When the bird is ready to begin guiding, it either comes to a person and starts a repetitive series of churring notes or it stays where it is and begins calling....
>
> As the person comes to within 15 or 20 feet,...the bird flies off with an initial conspicuous downward dip, and then goes off to another tree, not necessarily in sight of the follower, in fact more often out of sight than not. Then it waits there, churring loudly until the follower again nears it, when the action is repeated. This goes on until the vicinity of the bees' nest is reached. Here the bird suddenly ceases calling and perches quietly in a tree nearby. It waits there for the follower to open the hive, and it usually remains there until the person has departed with his loot of honey-comb, when it comes down to the plundered bees' nest and begins to feed on the bits of comb left strewn about.

The author is quoted as saying that the behavior is "purely instinctive," but it is possible to explain almost all of it in other ways. If we assume that honey guides eat broken bees' nests and cannot eat unbroken nests, that people (not to mention baboons and ratels) break bees' nests, and that birds more easily discover unbroken nests than people, then only one other assumption is needed to explain the behavior in ontogenic terms. We must assume that the response which produces the churring notes is elicited either (i) by any stimulus which frequently precedes the receipt of food (comparable behavior is shown by a hungry dog jumping about when food is being prepared for it) or (ii) when food, ordinarily available, is missing (the dog jumps about when food is not being prepared for it on schedule). An unconditioned honey guide occasionally sees people breaking nests. It waits until they have gone, and then eats the remaining scraps. Later it sees people near but not breaking nests, either because they have not yet found the nests or have not yet reached them. The sight of a person near a nest, or the sight of people when the buzzing of bees around a nest can be heard, begins to function in either of the ways just noted to elicit the churring response. The first step in the construction of the final pattern is thus taken by the honey guide. The second step is taken by the person (or baboon or ratel, as the case may be). The churring sound becomes a conditioned stimulus in the presence of which a search for bees' nests is frequently successful. The buzzing of bees would have the same effect if the person could hear it.

The next change occurs in the honey guide. When a person approaches and breaks up a nest, the behavior begins to function as a conditioned reinforcer which, together with the fragments which are left behind, reinforces churring, which then becomes more probable under the circumstances and emerges primarily as an operant rather than as an emotional response. When this has happened, the geographical arrangements work themselves out naturally. People learn to move toward the churring sound, and they break nests more often after walking toward nests than after walking in other directions. The honey guide is therefore differentially reinforced when it takes a position which induces people to walk toward a nest. The contingencies may be subtle, and the final topography is often far from perfect.

As we have seen, contingencies which involve two or more organisms raise special problems. The churring of the honey guide is useless until people respond to it, but people will not respond in an appropriate way until the churring is related to the location of bees' nests. The conditions just described compose a sort of program which could lead to the terminal performance. It may be that the conditions will not often arise, but another characteristic of social contingencies quickly takes over. When one honey guide and one person have entered into this symbiotic arrangement, conditions prevail under which other honey guides and other people will be much more rapidly conditioned. A second person will more quickly learn to go in the direction of the churring sound because the sound is already spatially related to bees' nests. A second honey guide will more readily learn to churr in the right places because people respond in a way which reinforces that behavior. When a large number of birds have learned to guide and a large number of people have learned to be guided, conditions are highly favorable for maintaining the system. (It is said that, where people no longer bother to break bees' nests, they no longer comprise an occasion for churring, and the honey guide turns to the ratel or baboon. The change in contingencies has occurred too rapidly to work through natural selection. Possibly an instinctive response has been unlearned, but the effect is more plausibly interpreted as the extinction of an operant.)

Imprinting is another phenomenon which shows how hard it is to detect the nature and effect of phylogenic contingencies. In Thomas More's *Utopia*, eggs were incubated. The chicks "are no sooner out of the shell, and able to stir about, but they seem to consider those that feed them as other chickens do the hen that hatched them." Later accounts of imprinting have been reviewed by Gray (1963). Various facts suggest phylogenic origins: The response of following an imprinted object appears at a certain age; if it cannot appear then, it may not appear at all; and so on. Some experiments by Peterson (1960), however, suggest that what is inherited is not necessarily the behavior of following but a susceptibility to reinforcement by proximity to the mother or mother surrogate. A distress call reduces the distance between mother and chick when the mother responds appropriately, and walking toward the mother has the same effect. Both may therefore be reinforced (Hoffman, Schiff, Adams, & Serle 1966), but they appear before these ontogenic contingencies come into play and are, therefore, in part at least phylogenic. In the laboratory, however, other behavior can be made effective which phylogenic contingencies are unlikely to have strengthened. A chick can be conditioned to peck a key, for example, by moving an imprinted object toward it when it pecks or to walk away from the object if, through a mechanical arrangement, this behavior actually brings the object closer. To the extent that chicks follow an imprinted object simply because they thus bring the object closer or prevent it from becoming more distant, the behavior could be said to be "species specific" in the unusual sense that it is the product of *ontogenic* contingencies which prevail for most members of the species.

Ontogenic and phylogenic behavior are not distinguished by any essence or character. The form of response seldom if ever yields useful classifications. The verbal response *Fire*! may be a command to a firing squad, a call for help, or an answer to the question, *What do you see*? The topography tells us little, but the controlling variables permit us to distinguish three very different verbal operants (Skinner 1957). The sheer forms of instinctive and learned behavior also tell us little. Animals court, mate, fight, hunt, and rear their young, and they use the same effectors in much the same way in all sorts of learned behavior. Behavior is behavior whether learned or unlearned; it is only the controlling variables which make the difference. The difference is not always important. We might show that a honey guide is controlled by the buzzing of bees rather than by the sight of a nest, for example, without prejudice to the question of whether the behavior is innate or acquired.

Nevertheless the distinction is important if we are to undertake to predict or control the behavior. Implications for human affairs have often affected the design of research and the conclusions drawn from it. A classical example concerns the practice of exogamy. Popper (1957) writes:

> Mill and his psychologistic school of sociology...would try to explain [rules of exogamy] by an appeal to "human nature," for instance to some sort of instinctive aversion against incest (developed perhaps through natural selection...); and something like this would also be the naive or popular explanation. [From Marx's] point of view...however, one could ask whether it is not the other way round, that is to say, whether the apparent instinct is not rather a product of education, the effect rather than the cause of the social rules and traditions demanding exogamy and forbidding incest. It is clear that these two approaches correspond exactly to the very ancient problem whether social laws are "natural" or "conventions."

Much earlier in his *Supplement to the Voyage of Bougainville*, Diderot (1796) considered the question of whether there is a natural basis for sexual modesty or shame (*pudeur*). Though he was writing nearly a hundred years before Darwin, he pointed to a possible basis for natural selection. "The pleasures of love are followed by a weakness which puts one at the mercy of his enemies. That is the only natural thing about modesty; the rest is convention." Those who are preoccupied with sex are exposed to attack (indeed, may be stimulating attack); hence, those who engage in sexual behavior under cover are more likely to breed successfully. Here are phylogenic contingencies which either make sexual behavior under cover stronger than sexual behavior in the open or reinforce the taking of cover when sexual behavior is strong. Ontogenic contingencies through which organisms seek cover to avoid disturbances during sexual activity are also plausible.

The issue has little to do with the character of incestuous or sexual behavior, or with the way people "feel" about it. The basic distinction is between provenances. And provenance is important because it tells us something about how behavior can be supported or changed. Most of the controversy concerning heredity and environment has arisen in connection with the practical control of behavior through the manipulation of relevant variables.

Interrelations among phylogenic and ontogenic variables

The ways in which animals behave compose a sort of taxonomy of behavior comparable to other taxonomic parts of biology. Only a very small percentage of existing species has as yet been investigated. (A taxonomy of behavior may indeed be losing ground as new species are discovered.) Moreover, only a small part of the repertoire of any species is ever studied. Nothing approaching a fair sampling of species-specific behavior is therefore ever likely to be made.

Specialists in phylogenic contingencies often complain that those who study learned behavior neglect the genetic limitations of their subjects, as the comparative anatomist might object to conclusions drawn from the intensive study of a single species. Beach, for example, has written (1950):

> Many...appear to believe that in studying the rat they are studying all or nearly all that is important in behavior...How else are we to interpret ... [a] 457-page opus which is based exclusively upon the performance of rats in bar-pressing situations but is entitled simply *The Behavior of Organisms?*

There are many precedents for concentrating on one species (or at most a very few species) in biological investigations. Mendel discovered the basic laws of genetics – in the garden pea. Morgan worked out the theory of the gene – for the fruitfly. Sherrington investigated the integrative action of the nervous system – in the dog and cat. Pavlov studied the physiological activity of the cerebral cortex – in the dog.

In the experimental analysis of behavior many species differences are minimized. Stimuli are chosen to which the species under investigation can respond and which do not elicit or release disrupting responses: Visual stimuli are not used if the organism is blind, nor very bright lights if they evoke evasive action. A response is chosen which may be emitted at a high rate without fatigue and which will operate recording and controlling equipment; we do not reinforce a monkey when it pecks a disk with its nose or a pigeon when it trips a toggle switch – though we might do so if we wished. Reinforcers are chosen which are indeed reinforcing, either positively or negatively. In this way species differences in sensory equipment, in effector systems, in susceptibility to reinforcement, and in possible disruptive repertoires are minimized. The data then show an extraordinary uniformity over a wide range of species. For example, the processes of extinction, discrimination and generalization, and the performances generated by various schedules of reinforcement are reassuringly similar. (Those who are interested in fine structure may interpret these practices as minimizing the importance of sensory and motor areas in the cortex and emotional and motivational areas in the brain stem leaving for study the processes associated with nerve tissue as such, rather than with gross anatomy.) Although species differences exist and should be studied, an exhaustive analysis of the behavior of a single species is as easily justified as the study of the chemistry or microanatomy of nerve tissue in one species.

A rather similar objection has been lodged against the extensive use of domesticated animals in laboratory research (Kavanau 1964). Domesticated animals offer many advantages. They are more easily handled, they thrive and breed in captivity, they are resistant to the infections encountered in association with people, and so on. Moreover, we are primarily interested in the most domesticated of all animals – man. Wild animals are, of course, different – possibly as different from domesticated varieties as some species are from others, but both kinds of differences may be treated in the same way in the study of basic processes.

The behavioral taxonomist may also argue that the contrived environment of the laboratory is defective since it does not evoke characteristic phylogenic behavior. A pigeon in a small enclosed space pecking a disk which operates a mechanical food dispenser is behaving very differently from pigeons at large. But in what sense is this behavior not "natural"? If there is a natural phylogenic environment, it must be the environment in which a given kind of behavior evolved. But the phylogenic contingencies responsible for current behavior lie in the distant past. Within a few thousand years – a period much too short for genetic changes of any great magnitude – all current species have been subjected to drastic changes in climate, predation, food supply, shelter, and so on. Certainly few land mammals are now living in the environment which selected their principal genetic features, behavioral or otherwise. Current environments are almost as "unnatural" as a laboratory. In any case, behavior in a natural habitat would have no special claim to genuineness. What an organism does is a fact about that organism regardless of the conditions under which it does it. A behavioral process is none the less real for being exhibited in an arbitrary setting.

The relative importance of phylogenic and ontogenic contingencies cannot be argued from instances in which unlearned or learned behavior intrudes or dominates. Breland and Breland (1961) have used operant conditioning and programming to train performing animals. They conditioned a pig to deposit large wooden coins in a "piggy bank."

> The coins were placed several feet from the bank and the pig required to carry them to the bank and deposit them. . . . At first the pig would eagerly

> pick up one dollar, carry it to the bank, run back, get another, carry it rapidly and neatly, and so on....Thereafter, over a period of weeks the behavior would become slower and slower. He might run over eagerly for each dollar, but on the way back, instead of carrying the dollar and depositing it simply and cleanly, he would repeatedly drop it, root it, drop it again, root it along the way, pick it up, toss it up in the air, drop it, root it some more, and so on.

They also conditioned a chicken to deliver plastic capsules containing small toys by moving them toward the purchaser with one or two sharp straight pecks. The chickens began to grab at the capsules and "pound them up and down on the floor of the cage," perhaps as if they were breaking seedpods or pieces of food too large to be swallowed. Since other reinforcers were not used, we cannot be sure that these phylogenic forms of food-getting behavior appeared because the objects were manipulated under food reinforcement. The conclusion is plausible, however, and not disturbing. A shift in controlling variables is often observed. Under reinforcement on a so-called fixed-interval schedule, competing behavior emerges at predictable points (Skinner & Morse 1957). The intruding behavior may be learned or unlearned. It may disrupt a performance or, as Kelleher (1962) has shown, it may not. The facts do not show an inherently greater power of phylogenic contingencies in general. Indeed, the intrusions may occur in the other direction. A hungry pigeon which was being trained to guide missiles (Skinner 1960) was reinforced with food on a schedule which generated a high rate of pecking at a target projected on a plastic disk. It began to peck at the food as rapidly as at the target. The rate was too high to permit it to take grains into its mouth, and it began to starve. A product of ontogenic contingencies had suppressed one of the most powerful phylogenic activities. The behavior of civilized people shows the extent to which environmental variables may mask an inherited endowment.

Misleading similarities

Since phylogenic and ontogenic contingencies act at different times and shape and maintain behavior in different ways, it is dangerous to try to arrange their products on a single continuum or to describe them with a single set of terms.

An apparent resemblance concerns intention or purpose. Behavior which is influenced by its consequences seems to be directed toward the future. We say that spiders spin webs in order to catch flies and that fishermen set nets in order to catch fish. The "order" is temporal. No account of either form of behavior would be complete if it did not make some reference to its effects. But flies or fish which have not yet been caught cannot affect behavior. Only past effects are relevant. Spiders which have built effective webs have been more likely to leave offspring, and a way of setting a net that has effectively caught fish has been reinforced. Both forms of behavior are therefore more likely to occur again, but for very different reasons.

The concept of purpose has had, of course, an important place in evolutionary theory. It is still sometimes said to be needed to explain the variations upon which natural selection operates. In human behavior a "felt intention" or "sense of purpose" which precedes action is sometimes proposed as a current surrogate for future events. Fishermen who set nets "know why they are doing so," and something of the same sort may have produced the spider's web-spinning behavior which then became subject to natural selection. But people behave because of operant reinforcement even though they cannot "state their purpose"; and, when they can, they may simply be describing their behavior and the contingencies responsible for its strength. Self-knowledge is at best a by-product of contingencies; it is not a cause of the behavior generated by them. Even if we could discover a spider's felt intention or sense of purpose, we could not offer it as a cause of the behavior.

Both phylogenic and ontogenic contingencies may seem to "build purpose into" an organism. It has been said that one of the achievements of cybernetics has been to demonstrate that machines may show purpose. But we must look to the construction of the machine, as we look to the phylogeny and ontogeny of behavior, to account for the fact that an ongoing system acts as if it has a purpose.

Another apparent characteristic in common is "adaptation." Both kinds of contingencies change the organism so that it adjusts to its environment in the sense of behaving in it more effectively. With respect to phylogenic contingencies, this is what is meant by natural selection. With respect to ontogeny, it is what is meant by operant conditioning. Successful responses are selected in both cases, and the result is adaptation. But the processes of selection are very different, and we cannot tell from the mere fact that behavior is adaptive which kind of process has been responsible for it.

More specific characteristics of behavior seem to be common products of phylogenic and ontogenic contingencies. Imitation is an example. If we define imitation as behaving in a way which resembles the observed behavior of another organism, the term will describe both phylogenic and ontogenic behavior. But important distinctions need to be made. Phylogenic contingencies are presumably responsible for well-defined responses released by similar behavior (or its products) on the part of others. A warning cry is taken up and passed along by others; one bird in a flock flies off, and the others fly off; one member of a herd starts to run, and the others start to run. A stimulus acting upon only one member of a group thus quickly affects other members, with plausible phylogenic advantages.

The parrot displays a different kind of imitative behavior. Its vocal repertoire is not composed of inherited responses each of which, like a warning cry, is released by the sound of a similar response in others. It acquires its imitative behavior ontogenically, but only through an apparently inherited capacity to be reinforced by hearing itself produce familiar sounds. Its responses need not be released by immediately preceding stimuli (the parrot speaks when not spoken to); but an echoic stimulus is often effective, and the response is then a sort of imitation.

A third type of imitative contingency does not presuppose an inherited tendency to be reinforced by behaving as others behave. When other organisms are behaving in a given way, similar behavior is likely to be reinforced, since they would not be behaving in that way if it were not. Quite apart from any instinct of imitation, we learn to do what others are doing because we are then likely to receive the reinforcers they are receiving. We must not overlook distinctions of this sort if we are to use or cope with imitation in a technology of behavior.

Aggression is another term which conceals differences in provenance. Inherited repertoires of aggressive responses are elicited or released by specific stimuli. Azrin, for example, has studied the stereotyped, mutually aggressive behavior evoked when two organisms receive brief electric shocks. But he and his associates have also demonstrated that the opportunity to engage in such behavior functions as a reinforcer and, as such, may be used to shape an indefinite number of "aggressive" operants of arbitrary topographers (Azrin, Hutchinson, & Laughlin 1965). Evidence of damage to others may be reinforcing for phylogenic reasons because it is associated with competitive survival. Competition in the current environment may make it reinforcing for ontogenic reasons. To deal successfully with any specific aggressive act we must respect its provenance. (Emotional responses, the bodily changes we feel when we are aggressive, like sexual modesty or aversion to incest, may conceivably be the same whether of phylogenic or ontogenic origin; the importance of the distinction is not thereby reduced.) Konrad Lorenz's *On Aggression* (1963) could be seriously misleading if it diverts our attention from relevant manipulable variables in the current environment to phylogenic contingencies which, in their sheer remoteness, encourage a nothing-can-be-done-about-it attitude.

The concept of territoriality also often conceals basic differences. Relatively stereotyped behavior displayed in defending a territory, as a special case of phylogenic aggression, has presumably been generated by contingencies involving food supplies, breeding, population density, and so on. But cleared territory, associated with these and other advantages, becomes a conditioned reinforcer and as such generates behavior much more specifically adapted to clearing a given territory. Territorial behavior may also be primarily ontogenic. Whether the territory defended is as small as a spot on a crowded beach or as large as a sphere of influence in international politics, we shall not get far in analyzing the behavior if we recognize nothing more than "a primary passion for a place of one's own" (Ardrey 1961) or insist that "animal behavior provides prototypes of the lust for political power" (Dubos 1965).

Several other concepts involving social structure also neglect important distinctions. A hierarchical "pecking order" is inevitable if the members of a group differ with respect to aggressive behavior in any of the forms just mentioned. There are therefore several kinds of pecking orders, differing in their provenances. Some dominant and submissive behaviors are presumably phylogenic stereotypes; the underdog turns on its back to escape further attack, but it does not follow that the vassal prostrating himself before king or priest is behaving for the same reasons. The ontogenic contingencies which shape the organization of a large company or governmental administration show little in common with the phylogenic contingencies responsible for the hierarchy in the poultry yard. Some forms of human society may resemble the anthill or beehive, but not because they exemplify the same behavioral processes (Allee 1938).

Basic differences between phylogenic and ontogenic contingencies are particularly neglected in theories of communication. In the inherited signal systems of animals the behavior of a "speaker" furthers the survival of the species when it affects a "listener." The distress call of a chick evokes appropriate behavior in the hen; mating calls and displays evoke appropriate responses in the opposite sex; and so on. De Laguna (1927) suggested that animal calls could be classified as declarations, commands, predictions, and so on, and Sebeok (1965) has attempted a similar synthesis in modern linguistic terms, arguing for the importance of a science of zoosemiotics.

The phylogenic and ontogenic contingencies leading respectively to instinctive signal systems and to verbal behavior are quite different. One is not an early version of the other. Cries, displays, and other forms of communication arising from phylogenic contingencies are particularly insensitive to operant reinforcement. Like phylogenic repertoires in general, they are restricted to situations which elicit or release them and hence lack the variety and flexibility which favor operant conditioning. Vocal responses which at least closely resemble instinctive cries have been conditioned, but much less easily than responses using other parts of the skeletal nervous system. The vocal responses in the human child which are so easily shaped by operant reinforcement are not controlled by specific releasers. It was the development of an undifferentiated vocal repertoire which brought a new and important system of behavior within range of operant reinforcement through the mediation of other organisms (Skinner 1957).

Many efforts have been made to represent the products of both sets of contingencies in a single formulation. An utterance, gesture, or display, whether phylogenic or ontogenic, is said to have a referent which is its meaning, the referent or meaning being inferred by a listener. Information theory offers a more elaborate version: The communicating organism selects a message from the environment, reads out relevant information from storage, encodes the message, and emits it; the receiving organism decodes the message, relates it to other stored information, and acts upon it effectively. All these activities, together with the storage of material, may be either phylogenic or ontogenic. The principal terms in such analyses (input, output, sign, referent, and so on) are objective enough, but they do not adequately describe the actual behavior of the speaker or the behavior of the listener responding to the speaker. The important differences between phylogenic and ontogenic contingencies must be taken into account in an adequate analysis. It is not true, as Sebeok (1965) contends, that "any viable hypothesis about the origin and nature of language will have to incorporate the findings of zoosemiotics." Just as we can analyze and teach imitative behavior without analyzing the phylogenic contingencies responsible for animal mimicry, or study and construct human social systems without analyzing the phylogenic contingencies which lead to the social life of insects, so we can analyze human verbal behavior without taking into account the signal systems of other species.

Purpose, adaptation, imitation, aggression, territoriality, social structure, and communication – concepts of this sort have, at first sight, an engaging generality. They appear to be useful in describing both ontogenic and phylogenic behavior and in identifying important common properties. Their very generality limits their usefulness, however. A more specific analysis is needed if we are to deal effectively with the two kinds of contingencies and their products.

POSTSCRIPT

This paper was given at a conference on genetics at the University of Kentucky in November 1965. I took the opportunity to present what seemed to me to be a reasonable view of the relevance of genetics to the experimental analysis of behavior. It seemed appropriate to make clear that psychology as a science of behavior did not reject genetic contributions, and I began accordingly with that classic quotation from John B. Watson which, in spite of the fact that Watson himself immediately challenged it, furthered the misunderstanding that behaviorists ignored or denied the role of natural selection in the determination of behavior. I then surveyed a number of problems common to ethology and the analysis of behavior. In a given organism, phylogenic and ontogenic sources of behavior are intricately interwoven, and I considered some of the problems which arise in trying to untangle them. The paper did not pretend to be a survey of the current status of genetics or of behavioral sciences.

My interest in the genetics of behavior was actually long-standing. Most of the experiments reported in *The Behavior of Organisms* (1938) were done with rats from the Bussey Institute strains used by William Castle in studying mammalian genetics. I used them because I hoped to find behavioral differences which could then be treated genetically. It was a different strategy from that of R. C. Tryon, who was creating strain differences by the selective breeding of rats which scored well or poorly in maze performance.

My paper was an ecumenical gesture. Konrad D. Lorenz had given the Dunham Lectures at the Harvard Medical School a few years earlier, and I had had a brief exchange with him. Daniel Lehrman had also visited our laboratory, and a young colleague, William Verplanck, had spent a year with Lorenz and Tinbergen and was full of the ethological revolution. Operants resembled in many ways the released behaviors of Lorenz and the other ethologists, contingencies of reinforcement resembled contingencies of selection, and many problems were common to the two fields. But there were differences, and I thought they were worth discussing.

COMMENTARIES AND RESPONSES

Skinner's circus

Stuart A. Altmann

Department of Biology, University of Chicago

Skinner's article on the phylogeny and ontogeny of behavior resembles a good circus: The sideshows are at least as interesting as the main event, if for no other reason than that they satisfy our morbid curiosity. Skinner satisfies that curiosity by giving us his viewpoint on a wide variety of topics.

The main event, an exposition of similarities and differences between ontogenetic and phylogenetic processes affecting behavior, suffers from a narrow perspective. Just as the ontogeny of behavior involves far more than learning, and learning more than operant conditioning, so evolution requires more than natural selection.

Of the many parallels and relationships between the ontogeny and phylogeny of behavior that remain unexplored in Skinner's article, one aspect of learning is especially important from our anthropocentric viewpoint. All social animals with overlapping generations have the potential for transmission of learned information from one generation to the next, resulting in two parallel systems of inheritance, one genetic, the other ontogenetic. In humans, the second system is extraordinarily developed and forms the basis for social and cultural phylogenetic evolution. The analogy with organic evolution leads to a variety of questions about this learning process. How extensive are errors in the transmission of cultural behavior from one generation to the next? Is such behavior preferentially transmitted within lineages or other trait groups and is it restricted or even prohibited among others? Are there components of transmitted behavior that are primarily adaptations to the internal organization of the behavior system rather than to external exigencies? The rich parallels between biological and cultural evolution have been the focus of several recent studies by Boyd and Richerson, Cavalli-Svorza and Feldman, Lumsden and Wilson, Pulliam, and others.

Another overlooked relationship is this: The ontogenetic process itself has evolved. For learned behavior this suggests the possibility that animals of each species most readily learn those types of behavior that are most important to them in their natural habitat and that these species differences are to some extent heritable and thus subject to natural selection. Of course, the limitations of sensory and effector systems place limits on what animals can perceive and how they can respond. Rats cannot be conditioned to pantothenic acid in their food, apparently because it has no distinctive taste to them, and a dog, with limited ability to rotate its shoulder, cannot be trained to brachiate like a gibbon. But within such sensory and motor limits is there evidence for adaptive specialization in learning abilities, or is all learning a broad-band capacity?

Skinner's "phylogeny" has essentially nothing to say about such issues. He is aware of species differences in behavior and he pays lip service to their study, but it is apparent that to him they are essentially a nuisance. He attends to them primarily to guarantee that a response is chosen that can be emitted at a high rate without fatigue. "In this way species differences...are minimized."

Now to some of Skinner's sideshows: At various places in "Phylogeny" he makes claims and arguments that seem dubious. He identifies behavioral processes with changes in the frequency of response, requiring for their analysis repeatable and thus countable units. However, most behavior modifications, both ontogenetic and phylogenetic, have probably been graded changes in the behavior patterns themselves. Such qualitative changes are not detected in the usual operant experiment, in which a microswitch is either tripped or not. Although counting is often easier than measuring, we should not let logistical considerations obscure for us the importance to animals of graded changes in the form of behavior.

Skinner claims that "both phylogenic and ontogenic contingencies 'shape' complex forms of behavior from relatively undifferentiated material." That claim is one side of an old dispute in behavioral embryology, to which Skinner does not refer. The contrary claim is not so easily dismissed.

Skinner, like several other behavioral scientists, believes that genetic effects can be assessed by studying neonates or animals raised under controlled environmental conditions. Evidence obtained entirely from within one generation, with no data from or about relatives, can tell us nothing whatsoever about the genetics of any trait, behavioral or otherwise. This is so essentially because inheritance is a process that takes place between, not within, generations.

Skinner refers to humans as "the most domesticated of all animals," and uses this as one justification for research on domestic animals. But we are not domesticated. A domestic animal is one whose activities, particularly breeding activities, are manipulated by another species. In the case of the domestic laboratory rat, the consequences have been extensive alterations in behavior.

Having compared and contrasted the processes of operant conditioning and natural selection, Skinner tries in "Phylogeny" to divide the behavior patterns of individuals into corresponding categories, which he refers to variously as learned versus unlearned behavior, ontogenetic versus phylogenetic behavior, acquired versus inherited behavior, and so forth. I hope that today Skinner no longer tries to maintain this false dichotomy. Nor will it do to argue that each behavior pattern of an organism falls somewhere along a continuum between the two extremes. Although one can partition the variance of a trait (behavioral or otherwise) into heritable and nonheritable components, such an analysis of what R. A. Fisher (1918) called *heritability* is a statement about differences between individuals. It is not a measure of the relative role of either genetic or ontogenetic processes in the development of an individual.

The most astonishing part of Skinner's article is his deprecation of naturalistic behavior, or rather, his defense of essentially ignoring it. He believes that evolutionary processes no longer operate. This is incorrect. Furthermore, even in the mid-1960s, when "Phylogeny" was published, there was a considerable literature, based on both experiments and observations, on adaptive aspects of behavior that are responsible for its selection, past and present. Skinner argues, however, that "within a few thousand years...all current species have been subjected to drastic changes in climate, predation, food supply, shelter, and so on." This is simply false. The vast majority of animals on earth live today under conditions that have changed so little as to have a negligible effect on attempts to study evolutionary aspects of behavior. Beyond that, the exceptions can be illuminating, as exemplified by Kettlewell's (1961) studies of industrial melanism in moths.

Finally, Skinner argues that "in any case, behavior in a natural habitat would have no special claim to genuineness. What an organism does is a fact about that organism regardless of the conditions under which it does it." He continues: "A behavioral process is none the less real for being exhibited in an arbitrary setting." Wha is one to make of this? Is this an ontological argument, a claim that behavior in arbitrary settings does indeed exist? Or does Skinner really believe that all behaviors, human induced or otherwise, are equally worthy of study?

It is evident that Skinner has no professional interest in the vast panorama of life on earth or of the role of behavior in it. His focus is entirely on similarities, not differences, and in particular, on one small component, the common denominators of learned aspects of behavior. Put the other way around, any aspect of an animal's learned behavior that is not also an aspect of every other animal's learned behavior is considered to be a nuisance.

Skinner is entitled to this narrow perspective in his research, but he must pay the penalty. Such research is woefully inadequate to explain the role of behavior in the life histories of animals, its ontogenetic development, or its phylogenetic history.

Ironically, the most valuable contribution made by "Phylogeny" is Skinner's repeated warning against dismissing the possibility of learning for every behavior that occurs in the natural environment and that is demonstrably adaptive. There is now growing interest among experimental psychologists in applying their methods of analysis to naturalistic behavior. In the process, behavioral biology is being considerably enriched.

BFS: Altmann has read "Phylogeny" as one attends a circus and has suffered a common complaint. Too many things are going on, and he has missed the main feature. He reports that the ontogenic inheritance of behavior remains "unexplored" in my article. It was being explored in a different ring (see "Consequences"). Altmann missed "Methods" in another ring (although he glanced in that direction when I was paying "lip service to their study"). He apparently did not see me distinguishing between the study of behavior and the physiology of the organism.

He also misses the point of some of my "sideshows." Though I identify "behavioral processes with changes in the frequency of response," I have paid attention to (one could almost say I have specialized in) the shaping of behavior, which Altmann speaks of as "graded changes in the form of behavior." I have specifically rejected a parallel with embryology, leaving that to those who speak of the "development" of behavior.

I do not say that "genetic *effects* can be assessed by studying neonates or animals raised under controlled. . .conditions" (italics added). Behavior due to natural selection is most easily detected when the possibility of environmental effects is held to a minimum.

When I said that humans are "the most domesticated of all animals," I was referring to the extent to which their behavior is due to human culture.

I do not try to "divide the behavior patterns of individuals into corresponding categories" referred to as learned versus unlearned, and so on. I do make the distinction between natural selection and operant conditioning, but whether these bring about the same kind of changes in the organism is a question I do not try to answer.

I certainly do not believe "that evolutionary processes no longer operate," but they operate slowly – too slowly to make current "naturalistic behavior" merely natural. The appropriateness of "naturalistic behavior" (Altmann's substitute for unlearned behavior) should not be estimated on the assumption that the current environment selected the behavior.

Since he has missed so much of my "circus," it is not surprising that Altmann should say that I have "no professional interest in the vast panorama of life on earth or of the role of behavior in it." He should buy another ticket and come again.

Ontogenetic or phylogenetic – another afterpain of the fallacious Cartesian dichotomy

Gerard P. Baerends

Department of Zoology, University of Groningen, The Netherlands

Skinner originally presented "Phylogeny" on 11 November 1965 in Lexington on the occasion of the centennial of the founding of the University of Kentucky, thus shortly after the publication in 1965 of Lorenz's *Evolution and Modification of Behavior.* It seems to be a reaction to this book (actually the English version of a paper published in 1961 in German), and it can be seen as an attempt to bridge the gap between behaviorism and ethology. Although both disciplines claimed to study behavior with objective scientific methods, the strong emphasis laid in behaviorism on learning processes as determinants of behavior and its neglect of possibly underlying genetic factors had made zoologists interested in the variation of behavior between species search for an approach more suitable to their purposes.

In contrast to the behaviorists, the early ethologists emphasized the study of stereotyped behavior patterns typical for a species or larger taxonomical group, instead of for individuals. They considered such behavior to be controlled by genes and for this reason called it innate. Consequently, behaviorists and ethologists found themselves on opposite sides of the barrier put up by Descartes when he sharply distinguished between behavior that resulted from reasoning and behavior that resulted from instinct and so gave rise to the dichotomy of learned versus innate or nature versus nurture, which has persistently survived until now. In 1953 Lehrman made an attempt to surmount this barrier. Attacking Lorenz's use of the term innate, but without depreciating the role of genetic factors, Lehrman urged the ethologists to pay more attention to the exact way in which genes underlying the form of behavior patterns actually exert their effects, thus to the processes through which genes and factors external to them, including experience, interact during ontogeny. Lorenz's abovementioned papers, in which he now attempted to define the concepts "innate" as well as "learned" without excluding the other, were a reaction to this critique. He argued that the essential difference between principles lies in the provenance of the information incorporated. "Innate" information is obtained in the course of several generations in a population of genetically related individuals as the result of differences in survival rate of mutation and recombinations of genes in the process of natural selection. In contrast, "learned" information is obtained by the individual as a direct result of its experiences in interacting with the environment. Although Lorenz points to the analogy between mutation and natural selection on the one hand and learning through trial and error or success on the other, he particularly stresses the differences in the way both types of information become stored (genes versus memory) and consequently in the way they are transferred to other individuals.

In "Phylogeny" Skinner pushes the analogy a step further, arguing that both phylogeny and ontogeny are based on the reinforcing effect of consequences contingent upon the behavior performed changing its probability to occur again in the future. A merit of this analogy is that it stresses that selection through evolutionary processes as well as through learning only takes place on the basis of some contingency, and does not result from the selection process, which has already had its effect. I agree with Skinner that it is consequently incorrect to state that any adaptiveness is always the outcome of selection. Although in biology this is recognized by the existence of the misleading and awkward term "preadaptation," in practice this notion often seems to have been overlooked in evolutionary considerations. I am ready to accept that in other respects too, thinking in terms of the reinforcement of contingencies can be helpful in studies of the evolutionary development of behavior. However, Skinner's claim that contingency can successfully replace many concepts commonly used in the causal analysis of behavior (Skinner mentions for instance "drive" and "motivational state" but has actually selected a sample of terms never commonly favored for serious use in ethology) seems to disregard the fact that such terms, including contingencies, reinforcement, and learning are not meant to be real explanatory entities but transitory stages in the path toward a proper description of the underying physiological mechanisms.

Skinner's analogy made him distinguish between ontogenetic and phylogenetic *contingencies*. To me this terminology does not seem quite correct: The difference is not in the contingency but in the kind of questions asked when considering it. The distinction has further led Skinner to speak of ontogenetic and phylogenetic *variables*, which I would not support because it is unclear whether the role of genes in ontogeny is recognized. However, I wish to object even more strongly to the distinction between ontogenetic and phylogenetic *behavior* than to Lorenz's casual use of the terms innate and learned *behavior*. Whereas the latter terminology may lead to neglect of the study of the ontogeny of "innate behavior." Skinner's distinction even suggests that phylogenetic behavior has no ontogeny at all! Our present knowledge of the ontogeny of taxon-specific behavior, for instance of the development of bird song, shows how closely influences passed through the genes and developmental processes are intertwined in giving form to a behavior pattern. The learning processes discovered by Skinner and his many followers are likely to be of great importance here – if not in shaping species-specific activities, certainly in promoting their proper use. Control of the developmental program by the genes functions to protect an individual from developing behavior patterns that would seriously reduce the implementation of its need to cooperate for various purposes with other similar individuals; in other words, for what we have for a long time called the maintenance of the species.

I am afraid that Skinner pushes the analogy too far when he speaks of a "sort of phylogenic extinction." The use of the same term, particularly when it might be interpreted as having some explanatory value, for phenomena that only show some superficial resemblances but are most likely to result from entirely different processes, tends to impede further research. The cases mentioned would need documentation. Do wild species of dogs really cover their feces by scraping with the forepaw like cats?

BFS: I find Baerends's disagreement puzzling. Environmental contingencies select variations in genes which contribute to the "innate" behavior of a species, and different environmental contingencies contribute to the selection of variations which compose "learned" behavior. That a given instance of behavior is clearly due to both (as, apparently, is bird song) should not be surprising. I used the inadequate covering of feces in the dog as a possible example of phylogenic "extinction" not in comparing wild and domesticated dogs but rather on the assumptions that in the remote past a more adequate covering may have had survival value which has since been lost and that when those contingencies of survival no longer prevailed the behavior deteriorated. (See also my reply to Timberlake in "Consequences.")

Contingencies of selection, reinforcement, and survival

David P. Barash

Departments of Psychology and Zoology, University of Washington

To reread B. F. Skinner's "The Phylogeny and Ontogeny of Behavior" is to be impressed with his grasp not only of psychology (to say that Skinner has a "grasp" of psychology is like saying that Einstein had a "grasp" of physics!) but of evolutionary biology as well. Notably, his emphasis upon the parallels between reinforcement and natural selection shows how creative and undogmatic his thought actually is, and how unfair it is to caricature the "Skinnerian" approach as one that denies a role to biological evolution. Indeed, I must personally plead guilty to having done the same myself, and willingly do penance in this brief commentary. All too often, the work of a giant is deformed in the retelling, especially by us Jacks who would do better to stop styling ourselves as giant killers and instead find room for ourselves at the giant's table. Skinner's ideas offer a sumptuous repast, especially for those interested in reconciling seemingly contradictory views as to the origin of behavior; indeed, rarely have the distinctions – and mutual interdependence – of proximate and ultimate causation been more clearly enunciated, and this nearly a decade before "sociobiology" was even a gleam in the eyes of its current practitioners!

Skinner also shows much greater sensitivity to species differences than I had previously appreciated, and in fact, more than he had shown in earlier writings, when he (like sociobiology during the past decade or so) was eager to establish a new intellectual tradition and in the process was understandably inclined to overstate the virtues of an emerging paradigm. In the competitive world of scientific ideas, it seems that success leads to moderation of views. More to the point, perhaps immoderate views are simply unlikely to withstand the acid test of empirical findings. In any event, Skinner's views, as expressed in this *Science* article of 1966, have stood the test of time and seem likely to continue doing so. (Here I discount such minor aberrations as the anachronistic reference to "the good of the species," a locution I am sure Skinner would no longer use.)

Another great psychologist, the social psychologist and semanticist Charles Osgood, coined a phrase that has also stood the test of time and seems due for a renewal, appropriate not only to the political climate of the early 1980s, but also to a retrospective on the ideas of Skinner. Thus, in his *An Alternative to War or Surrender*, more than 20 years ago, Osgood (1962) briefly described the "Neanderthal mentality," referring not to anthropological fact, but rather to the regrettable persistence of primitive, widespread patterns of thought and behavior among modern-day *Homo sapiens*. Thus, Einstein earlier recognized that "the splitting of the atom has changed everything but our way of thinking, and hence we drift toward unparalleled catastrophe" (Einstein 1960, p. 376). That way of thinking, which has not changed, is probably attributable to the contingencies of selection which operated for the 99.99% of our evolutionary history that preceded the invention of nuclear weapons. Now, modern-day Neanderthals confront the means of their own annihilation with a mentality that has quite suddenly become inappropriate (see Barash & Lipton, 1985).

Admittedly, these assertions are not amenable to the clearcut experimental testing that has made operant psychology such a powerful intellectual tool, but I shall nonetheless assert that the Neanderthal mentality is alive and well, and that it threatens us all. Among other things, it induces us to feel that "more is better," that we enhance our own security by threatening our opponent, that the techniques of violent conflict resolution – so successful in the past – will continue to serve us today, and that our opponents aren't quite human (or certainly, less human than we). These mental predispositions have served us well during our long evolutionary history: The evolutionist might say they have been adaptive; the Skinnerian would recognize that such attitudes have been positively reinforced.

There are other important components to the Neanderthal mentality, such as the (adaptive, and also often reinforced) disinclination to suffer pain – emotional as well as physical – which inhibits most of us from confronting the issue of nuclear war in the first place, as well as the tendency to feel safe when the threatening weapons cannot readily be perceived; that is, since nuclear weapons lack psychological reality, most of us go about our daily lives, seeking the immediate positive reinforcers available to us. Moreover, just as it was doubtless maladaptive for Neanderthalers to wrestle with oversized adversaries (sabertooths yes, volcanoes no), they were – and still are – reinforced for dealing with manageable problems – not oversized ones like nuclear war. So, once again, the contingencies of selection and of reinforcement reinforce each other, paradoxically turning adaptive strategies into dangerous ones, and making our own long-term survival *less* likely than ever before.

But even though the Neanderthal mentality is well entrenched and widely reflected in the behavior of human beings, it is not immutable. Thus, in discussing the origin of human aggression, Skinner himself warns us against excessive reliance on instinctivist interpretations, since they could divert "our attention from relevant manipulable variables in the current environment to phylogenetic contingencies which, in their sheer remoteness, encourage a nothing-can-be-done-about-it attitude." Perhaps Skinner's own work, seeking to train pigeons to guide missiles, suggests the alternative possibility: Can we train ourselves *not* to guide missiles? Can we overcome our Neanderthal mentality, perhaps by appropriate manipulation of the contingencies of reinforcement operating in the world of the 1980s? (Certainly, we cannot wait for the contingencies of selection to reveal the Neanderthal's maladaptiveness.)

It seems likely that either we shall overcome, or we shall be, and indeed, the enormous flexibility of human behavior makes the former prospect feasible if not likely. After all, modifications in the contingencies of reinforcement regularly induce Homo sapiens, a stubbornly messy arboreal primate, to become toilet trained; perhaps someday soon people who cannot control their Neanderthal mentality will seem as inappropriate as those who cannot control their bowels. If so, the contingencies for our own survival will have been established.

BFS: While I agree with Barash that Neanderthal man may survive in us and cause trouble, the problem today is not so much our animal instincts as the failure to solve our problems by methods which most people would regard as the use of reason. For "reasons" read "reinforcing consequences." We are still too much controlled by the more immediate consequences of our behavior to act effectively with respect to remote consequences. I have developed that point in detail elsewhere (e.g., Skinner 1982).

Of false dichotomies and larger frames

Jerome H. Barkow

Department of Sociology and Social Anthropology, Dalhousie University, Canada

Skinner is making at least two assumptions with which I must disagree. The less important is that selection operates primarily at the level of the group. The more serious is that the unlearned versus learned or innate–acquired dichotomy is meaningful.

From the instant of conception, nothing in the organism is either innate or acquired: Everything is generated through complex feedbacks and interactions between organism and environment. Genes interact with other genes, for example, as well with their biochemical environment. Both subsequent behavior and morphology are generated through these complex processes. There are no blueprints, only processes that involve large numbers of endogenous and "environmental" variables.

The illusion of some behaviors being "innate" and some "acquired" stems from inadequate attention to this processual nature of behavioral and morphological development. Environmental inputs are essential for the development of all behavior. But some behaviors (and structures) are so vital in terms of biological fitness that natural selection has resulted in their canalization. That is, these behaviors will occur in the presence of a wide range of environmental inputs rather than being dependent on a small number of phylogenetically unreliable "stimuli."

Skinner's "unlearned" behaviors are those so canalized by selection that even varying environments (a wide range of inputs) all result in their generation. The "learned" behaviors are those under such weak selection pressure for their specific occurrence that they require highly particular inputs from the environment. The distinction between "learned" and "unlearned" is that between ends of a continuum and is not of overwhelming importance, Skinner (see the beginning of the final section) notwithstanding. Wherever a particular behavior happens to fall on the continuum, after all, our research goal remains that of understanding the processes that generate it.

(It is also important to note that the requirements of natural selection are quite satisfied – that is, that the behavior in question will have a high probability of being generated – even if it is on the "learned" side of Skinner's dichotomy, provided that the crucial environmental inputs are constant aspects of the organism's ecological setting.)

Because biological evolution is a rather slow process, many species have been selected for various kinds of general learning abilities. A wide range of outputs can therefore result from a wide variety of inputs. Skinner's chief contribution has been to further our understanding of the ontogenetic processes involved in general learning. Note that these "general learning" capacities are quite as much products of natural selection as are any "instincts." Note, too, that except in cases of convergent and parallel evolution we would expect different species to have different kinds of "general learning" abilities – an expectation that Skinner has hardly emphasized.

I must respectfully consider Skinner's lack of emphasis on biological evolution a disservice to our understanding of behavior. Skinnerian psychology is a branch of evolutionary biology and ethology, not something apart from it. If we are to understand a species it behooves us to understand its ecological niche, its ethology and sociobiology. We may then explore, via Skinner's methods, the nature of the general learning abilities for which the species has been selected. The latter are part of the species's ethogram, rather than something apart from it.

Placing Skinnerian psychology into its proper position in biology is not merely a matter of neatness. It is a matter of whether he and his followers are to be considered scientists or behavioral alchemists. Science is not just a methodology, it is a consistency: The laws of any one field are perfectly consistent with the laws of all others. For example, evolutionary theory is entirely consistent with modern chemistry and physics. And Skinnerian theory, if it is to be part of modern science and not an isolated island, must be consistent with evolutionary biology – which it is, of course. Skinner, judging from "Phylogeny," now seems to understand and accept this. Perhaps, eventually all of those who have followed him in the past will follow him in this direction too.

Skinner does retain his prejudice against "mentalistic" constructs. In this he is hardly alone, even today. And it is true that our models of "mental apparatus" are probably as crude as was Bohr's first model of the hydrogen atom. Particle physics has gone a long way since that early model, of course. But had Skinner been an influential physicist rather than psychologist, one wonders whether physics today would largely consist of mechanics, where direct measurement is possible and long chains of inference regarding the unseen are unnecessary. Models of cognitive abilities and, yes, even of self-awareness, are both necessary and, I hope, respectable (see Barkow 1976; 1983).

BFS: Barkow's commentary raises many interesting issues. I must first, however, correct his impression that I believe that selection operates primarily at the level of the group. Quite the contrary. Nor do I believe that I am guilty of a lack of emphasis on biological evolution. The point of "Phylogeny" was to establish a relative equality between ontogeny and phylogeny. I also believe that all behavioral processes are the products of evolution and that the organism as a whole is nothing else.

The really interesting question concerns the meaningfulness of the dichotomy of learned versus unlearned or innate versus acquired. I agree that this is meaningless if we are talking about stored products such as instincts and habits. Selection changes the individual and, if transmission occurs, the group; the result is a changed species, not the storage of any representation of the contingencies of selection. Contingencies of reinforcement change the individual; as a result the individual now behaves in a different way. My quarrel with cognitive psychology is primarily on the grounds of the metaphor of storage. The organism does not take in the world as representations (see "Behaviorism-50") or contingencies of reinforcement as rules of conduct (see "Problem Solving"). It is changed by its encounter with the world and behaves in changed ways. As Barkow puts it, there are no blueprints, only processes.

While I agree with Barkow as to the achievements of theoretical physicists, I would nevertheless insist on the importance of particle physics as an experimental science, and I would certainly not equate it with mechanics. How far would the theoretical physicists have gone without the experimental work?

A new experimental analysis of behavior – one for all behavior

D. Caroline Blanchard, Robert J. Blanchard, and Kevin J. Flannelly

John A. Burns School of Medicine (DCB, RJB) and Department of Psychology (all), University of Hawaii

In the period between about 1930 and the time "Phylogeny" was written the study of behavior in America featured a number of divergent approaches. Most of these approaches involved highly structured theories with elaborate systems of intervening variables, complex analogies with concepts from the physical sciences, mathematical models, and the like. Skinner's radical empiricism, created against this background, offered a stark and elegant alternative.

By the decade of the sixties, much of the tension had gone out of this theoretical argument. Many of the more cumbersome theoretical models were on their last legs, because of their own excess weight and predictive inadequacies. But a new challenge had arisen in the form of ethological models, as well as in the accumulated evidence from both physiological and comparative psychology, that biological or phylogenetic variables must be considered in a science of behavior.

As suggested in the subheading of the original paper ("Contingencies of Reinforcement Throw Light on Contingencies of Survival in the Evolution of Behavior"), Skinner here draws parallels between the evolutionary processes acting on behavior, and reinforcement contingencies at the ontogenetic level. This at first appears to be a thoughtful and conciliatory recognition of possible analogies between ethological approaches and his own experimental analysis of behavior.

Alas, the conciliatory position was short-lived. Instead, Skinner reaffirmed basic tenets of his own system, among them a refusal to study response topography, avoidance of terms or concepts dealing with organismic variables, and a belief that standard laboratory conditions are entirely adequate for the study of behavior. Moreover, he proposed that this approach may be just as satisfactory for the study of phylogenetic effects as it is for the investigation of learning.

Since just these points, attention to response topography, analysis of organismic variables, and an emphasis on natural environments, are core features of more biological approaches to behavior, Skinner's rationales for rejecting them are worth examining critically.

Stimulus variables. Skinner states that, because "few land animals are now living in the environment which selected their principal genetic features...current environments are almost as 'unnatural' as a laboratory." Now the first statement may be true, though perhaps misleading; but the conclusion is such cheerful nonsense that one would be tempted to ignore it, were it not for the fact that quite a number of psychologists, apparently taking such statements as gospel, continue to deny that there is a real world out there that is very different from the laboratory environments they create.

In fact, having attempted little by little over about a decade to identify essential features of the natural environment of rats and to incorporate these into a model for studying aggressive and defensive behaviors, we feel qualified to assert that most laboratory tests and environments are so unlike the real world that they do not support the development of many important behavior patterns. Certainly it is possible, once one has identified such essential features, to bring them into a laboratory setting. However, a belief that the laboratory is already equivalent to the natural environment makes such an attempt superfluous. The resulting problem is not only that these behaviors are missing in the laboratory; on occasion, behaviors that are easier to obtain and manipulate in laboratory settings have simply been misidentified as the missing patterns.

Response variables. Skinner provides very little actual explanation of his rejection of analysis of response topography in favor of response frequency or probability measures. He simply asserts that "the form of response seldom if ever yields useful classifications. The verbal response *Fire!* may be a command to a firing squad, a call for help, or an answer to the question, *What do you see?* The topography tells us little."

This example is deeply interesting, as it provides so tantalizing a glimpse of some of the consequences of long-term adherence to standard operant conditioning methodologies. The behavioral topography of a word is not its spelling, recorded on a sheet of paper. It is how that word is spoken. We submit that, even in this best-case scenario, an astute observer watching the subject alone could not only discriminate between the three examples given, but could also provide a consistent and predictive rationale for doing so. Moreover, acoustical measures could probably do the same. This is true even though human language is purely learned, and perhaps does contain less of topographic interest than most other human and animal behavior patterns.

We are not, incidentally, suggesting that the analysis proposed above constitutes a satisfactory scientific methodology. It is not a matter of looking at *either* response topography *or* antecedent contingencies and current stimulus situations. To use either approach alone is the analytic equivalent of fighting with one hand tied to one foot.

Organismic variables. The abhorrence of organismic concepts perhaps constitutes the most characteristic and salient feature of Skinner's approach to behavior, and one that was taken up with relief by many psychologists reared in the great theory-building era. This position has a number of aspects, some of which are rather reasonable (rejection of poorly anchored mentalistic concepts) whereas others are more dubious. In this latter category is the extreme focus on only such processes (extinction, discrimination, generalization, and performance under different reward schedules are the examples given) as are resistant to species differences and other types of nonlearned variation. Skinner asserts that these are "the processes associated with nerve tissue as such" and consigns sensory, motor, motivational, and emotional processes to a kind of neurological limbo – the product of gross anatomy rather than nerve tissue "per se."

In similar fashion Skinner dismisses the objections (at that time made by ethologists, now more generally expressed) to the use of only domesticated animals in research. He claims that, at worst, they are simply different species, and thus presumably as good to use as any other.

The problem, of course, is that domesticated animals are systematically, not randomly, different from their wild congeners, being among other things much less fearful of man, and of novel stimuli in general, and much more willing to breed under abnormal conditions (Blanchard & Blanchard 1980). This difference is linked to robust and systematic changes in specific behavior patterns. The point again is that Skinner's position is insensitive to an accumulated body of information from an important biological discipline, and unlikely to lure persons from this discipline into cooperative research efforts. In fact, Skinner's extreme distaste for organismic variables and analyses – although perhaps partly justified in terms of the history of psychology – nevertheless discourages participation not only by neuroscientists and behavioral biologists, but also by those behaviorists who are explicitly interested in emotional or motivational states. It may be possible, as he claims, that experimental analysis "does not neglect the facts upon which these concepts are based," but it is unlikely ever to encounter many of the relevant "facts" of behavior unless it becomes more open to different biological disciplines and the methodologies they customarily employ.

Historical perspectives. In the period of nearly two decades since "Phylogeny" was published, profound changes have occurred in the study of behavior. The highly structured "grand theories" against which Skinner fought are clearly dead, while neuroscience and behavioral biology have gobbled up much of what used to be called physiological and comparative psychology. Where there was once a clear mainstream – learning theory – there are now also a number of smaller topic-oriented groups, focused on sexual and social behavior, aggression, stress, and the like. Though limited in focus, these groups tend to be much more electic in methodology and interdisciplinary in spirit, working with hormonal and brain-function variables as well as demonstrating a specific interest in evolutionary processes. A wider range of species is being used, and there is probably more willingness to create new paradigms, measures, and concepts than at any time in the past 50 years.

It is obvious, then, that researchers continue to be interested in the biological basis of behavior, but that they have largely failed to take up Skinner's invitation to use his approach to investigate phenomena of joint phyletic and ontogenetic provenance. The reason, we think, is well illustrated in "Phylogeny" and in some of our reactions to it, expressed herein. In the long run a science of behavior will not consist of a study of phylogenetic instead of ontogenetic variables; it will not be studied in a laboratory setting instead of the real world, be analyzed as response topography rather than response frequency, or involve behaviors that reflect properties of nervous tissue per se, rather than neuroanatony. Skinner's own rallying cry, "The Experimental Analysis of Behavior," does indeed encompass what we see behaviorists doing in the immediate future; but we hope this analysis will start with adequate attention to the complexity, diversity, and multiplicity of determining factors that characterize the behavior of higher animals.

BFS: I would point out that in my thesis, published in 1931, I hazarded a guess that there were three kinds of variables of which behavior would prove to be a function. I referred to them with the terms conditioning, drive, and emotion. Blanchard et al. would call the last two organismic. Over the years I have spent a good deal of time on them, but simply as different sets of variables of which the probability of response is a function. "Phylogeny" deals only with operant conditioning because I wanted to draw the parallel with natural selection. (Incidentally, I have studied the differentiation of response topography in many ways.)

I have certainly never said that "standard laboratory conditions are entirely adequate for the study of behavior" and certainly not "for the study of phylogenetic effects." Blanchard et al. agree that "few land animals are now living in the environment which selected their principal genetic features," but they feel that my conclusion that "current environments are almost as 'unnatural' as a laboratory" is "cheerful nonsense." There is no point in quibbling over the word "natural." I certainly did not mean to say that there is not "a real world out there that is very different from the laboratory environments" of the experimental analysis of behavior. All I said was that what a rat does in an experimental apparatus is the behavior of a rat, though not by any means all the behavior the rat would display under other circumstances – or even in different apparatuses. As to response variables, I agree that a careful study of the topography of the response "Fire!" would permit inferences about the controlling variables, but a good actor could duplicate them for quite different reasons which a study of topography would not discover. The important point is that the lexicographer's word tells us very little about verbal behavior. We need to know something about the instance in which the "word is used."

As I have already said, I do not relegate motivational and emotional processes to a kind of neurological limbo, but they raise problems very different from those which are attacked by a study of such processes as extinction, discrimination, generalization, and so on. It may be that one difference between domesticated and wild animals is that the latter are more fearful of man and of novel stimuli. I am not insensitive to such facts; they are simply not part of what I am studying. I quite agree that "in the long run, a science of behavior will not consist of the study of phylogenetic versus ontogenetic variables; it will not be studied in the laboratory setting instead of the real world, be analyzed as response topography rather than response frequency," and so on. It is researchers like Blanchard et al. who insist upon emphasizing the distinctions rather than the processes encountered in both cases.

Cost–benefit models and the evolution of behavior

Jerram L. Brown

Department of Biological Sciences, State University of New York at Albany

When "Phylogeny" first appeared, my Skinnerian friends were proud. As an evolutionary biologist, however, I was disappointed. Personally, I could find nothing in the paper that was not already fully appreciated by most of my colleagues in the mid-sixties. There was no evidence in the paper that Skinner was familiar with the relevant literature on evolution. True, there was the usual psychologist's preoccupation with Lorenz, instinct, and its abuses, but the references to evolutionary biology were few, derisive, and superficial. The paper had no impact on evolutionary biology. It missed the main event of the sixties.

"Phylogeny" expresses a misunderstanding that is widespread in psychology even today, namely, that since evolution occurred in the past, it cannot be studied in the present. Remember, however, that natural selection is the mechanism of evolutionary adaptation and that it can very well be studied in the present. Indeed, the 1960s saw a new ferment brought to evolutionary biology and ethology by the introduction of stimulating models with which to study the action of natural selection on behavior. Hamilton's (1964) rule, the polygyny threshold, optimal foraging theory, and economic defendability have suggested how the evolution of behavior can be studied in the present, namely by detailed studies of cost and benefit, not to the species but to the individual and to the gene.

"The contingencies responsible for unlearned behavior" act today.

BFS: I am willing to concede that Brown knew everything that I had to say in "Phylogeny" before I said it, and I quite agree that he knows more about the "stimulating models" with which "the action of natural selection on behavior" is studied. I also agree that "'the contingencies responsible for unlearned behavior' act today." But to what extent can the effect of that action be followed? How many new species have been produced experimentally?

Ethology and operant psychology

Gordon M. Burghardt

Department of Psychology, University of Tennessee

B. F. Skinner's "Phylogeny" appeared during my last year in graduate school. My course work had included considerable study of animal learning with particular emphasis upon operant conditioning. But ethology was far more attractive to me because it was explicitly concerned with the analysis, evolution, and diversity of behavior patterns animals actually performed in their normal day-to-day life. Yet with regard to human psychology, I always felt Skinner's criticisms were relevant, incisive, and largely ignored.

I thought then that Skinner's comparisons and contrasts between natural selection and contingencies of reinforcement in "Phylogeny" were most useful for nonpsychologically trained students of animal behavior and for operant conditioners themselves, most of whom had studiously avoided evolution and regarded ethology skeptically if they paid any attention to it at all. But I viewed the paper primarily as a belated attempt to defend a system of thought against the growing evidence from ethology that something was awry in his elegant psychological world view that could no longer be ignored. The appearance of the apostate paper by Breland and Breland (1961) in a prestigious journal and the widely acclaimed popularizations of ethology by Lorenz, Ardrey, and Morris that drew implications for human behavior now made a response for Skinner's educated lay followers necessary; their attitudes have always seemed more important to Skinner than the views of his scientific critics. Ethology seemed to attack his system from a direction he never expected. My rereading of this paper has changed my attitude little, and thus I will not repeat earlier specific comments (Burghardt 1973). But is there any truth to these speculations? Perhaps Skinner can enlighten us.

To attribute political motives to a paper does not aid in its analysis as science. And much of the paper *is* provocative and should surely have stimulated the thinking of those unaware of the nature of behavioristic operant analysis. My commentary, in the spirit of this volume, is based on a brief look at some points on which I would like a response. The paper touches on many important controversial topics where I largely agree with Skinner. These, along with other areas where I dissent, cannot be addressed here. The insightful notes added when the paper was reprinted (Skinner 1969) will not be discussed.

Skinner begins by trying to lay to rest the oft-quoted statement by J. B. Watson about the malleability of human behavior. But he protests too much. Kuo (1921; 1924) and others actually did try to rule out genetics in their haste to rid psychology of instinct. Skinner certainly hasn't forgotten Watson's (1924) wonderful boomerang metaphor wherein he dismissed endogenous forces in behavior. Beach (1955) documented this "anti-instinct revolt," and Lashley (1938), who was the coauthor with Watson of some of the early work Skinner indirectly uses to establish Watson's credibility as an ethologist, saw clearly that genetics and evolution were made scapegoats in a misdirected attack upon "the hypostatization of psychic energies" (p. 329). No, the rise of ethology was not due to behaviorism as *conceptually formulated and practiced* being ignored or misunderstood by zoologists.

Learning is equated with operant conditioning throughout "Phylogeny." In his earlier writings Skinner also discussed classical conditioning, a process that also has a role in the natural behavior of animals, as does habituation. Even more problematic is his reduction of the entire area of behavioral ontogeny to the study of contingencies of reinforcement. Skinner here seems as guilty of overgeneralizing a concept as those he criticizes in his last paragraph for using aggression, communication, and other "concepts."

Developmental psychobiology is a growing field involving, of necessity, studies in embryology, genetics, endocrinology, sensory abilities, and effector mechanisms. The learned–unlearned dichotomy at the heart of Skinner's analysis is ultimately both too broad and too restrictive when answering specific questions about ontogeny (Burghardt 1977). Ironically, this lack of interest in mechanisms is as pronounced in Skinner as it was in the early sociobiologists who were only interested in behavior insofar as it was heritable and affected reproductive success. Certainly an operant interpretation of African honey-guide behavior is a valuable heuristic example, but if not followed up by research it is as much a "just so" story as the plausible adaptive explanations that sociobiologists subsequently popularized. Both have had value, but plausibility proves nothing.

Skinner's most important contribution was the development and working out of a technology useful in answering specific questions. What Skinner omitted was a naturalistic context in which to employ his technology with nonhuman animals. Was there any contact over the years with the Museum of Comparative Zoology and the many behaviorally oriented zoologists there during Skinner's many years at Harvard? E. O. Wilson's (1975) sociobiological synthesis arose at Harvard, and although Wilson cites "Phylogeny," the thrust of his approach is in many ways antithetical to Skinner's; he relies upon the hypothetico-deductive strategy Skinner so effectively countered in learning theory [see "Methods," this volume].

After developing a powerful method and exploring its ramifications in standard apparatus, Skinner appeared *with animals* content to teach rats carnival tricks, pigeons to play Ping-Pong, or in a more deadly vein, to guide missiles to their targets. This apparent lack of appreciation for nature, living diversity, and the processes of evolution is perhaps what most disturbed behavioral biologists and made many reluctant to consider how operant methods could help answer intractable questions and even aid in improving the welfare of diverse captive animals. "Phylogeny" went some distance to address these concerns.

Skinner's defense here of the reliance on lever-pressing rats in *The Behavior of Organisms* (1938) is based upon analogies with genetics and physiology. But the analogy may be suspect because in the other areas those applying the postulated principles to various species were genuinely interested in differences; indeed, when they weren't, questionable generalizations also invaded their literature. Similar forced arguments are advanced to defend the reliance upon arbitrary responses, unnatural environments, and domesticated species. The arguments ultimately rest upon an uncompromisingly narrow conception of *human* behavior and a lack of interest in understanding nonhuman animals as diversified organisms that may operate in differentiated ways. Evolutionary thought seems to originate in a concern for differences; experimental psychology's in similarities, both within and across species. Although Skinner elegantly challenged the pooled-data mentality of his peers, the profound implications of his innovative single-subject designs for looking beyond environmental contingencies in the external world of the individual seem to have had no interest for him.

In recent years we have seen a resurgence in theories of animal learning of the type Skinner attacked in his writings of the late forties and fifties. There has also been a return to more mentalistic cognitive theories in both animal learning and ethology. There are problems with this cognitivism that certainly merit behavioristic critiques of the type leveled here. But being aware of traps along a road does not justify traveling a different route if you have good reasons for heading a particular way. Skinner *has* often been proved right in his criticisms of the dangers in reifying terms. But the main philosophical issue appears to be where we should be headed as well as how to get there.

But what of the impact of "Phylogeny"? I checked 21 introductory textbooks designed for courses in comparative psychology, ethology, and evolution of behavior to see which ones cited Skinner at all and which ones cited this particular paper. The dates of these books were 1972–1983; I set a criterion of at least five years after publication of "Phylogeny" for a text to be included. While two-thirds (14) cited at least one of his writings, only five cited "Phylogeny," not all of them favorably. (The five were Denny 1980; Eibl-Eibesfeldt 1975; Mortenson 1975; Nevin & Reynolds 1973; and Wilson 1975.) The most frequent point made is that there is a parallel between individual behavior change and the evolution of behavior. This comparison is not at all new, having been made, perhaps most presciently, by E. L. Thorndike (1900a; 1900b), the founder of American animal learning psychology, in his astute 1899 lectures on instinct and learning at Woods Hole that followed a previous series of lectures by C. O. Whitman (1899), whom Lorenz and other ethologists hold to be the founder of comparative ethology (Burghardt 1973).

Ethologists have frequently argued that the field of animal learning has left out comparative, ecological, and evolutionary considerations in its rush to formulate general principles. A push for this impatience certainly arose from a primary interest in human learning and the desire to use controlled "scientific" studies with animals to legitimize applications to people. Certainly the power and successes of behavior modification principles in diverse areas of human behavior are a lasting tribute to Skinner. Yet even these successes have been most marked when a relatively eclectic approach is taken with respect to the behaviors recorded and the contexts employed. This is in marked contrast to the animal operant conditioning work which, with few exceptions, has continued to focus not only on rat lever pressing and pigeon pecking but has become insular, extremely esoteric, and removed from most of the concerns and issues of other students of animal behavior.

Indeed today, as behavioral ecology formulates models that cry out for the operant methodology, people other than traditional Skinnerians have had to examine the parallels and applications (e.g., Crawford 1983). I personally find extremely stimulating work such as Timberlake's (1983), which tries to apply a knowledge of the principles of animal learning and the evolved behavioral repertoires of their subjects in a way that makes me think a true integration of ontogeny and phylogeny, ethology and experimental psychology, just might be possible. Skinner's contribution to the study of animal behavior will endure; context and style have slowed, but not prevented, their incorporation into ethology.

BFS: Burghardt contributes some interesting historical background to the issues raised (not for the first time) by "Phylogeny." Nevertheless, he misunderstands several points. It is not true that "learning is equated with operant conditioning throughout 'Phylogeny.'" My paper is about the kind of learning that shows a marked parallel with natural selection. The existence of other kinds is not questioned.

Burghardt says that my "arguments ultimately rest upon an uncompromisingly narrow conception of *human* behavior. . . the profound implications of his innovative single-subject designs for looking beyond environmental contingencies in the external world of the individual seem to have had no interest for him." But only 10 years after publishing *The Behavior of Organisms* (1938) I published *Walden Two* (1948b) all about human behavior, and five years later *Science and Human Behavior* (1953), very largely about human behavior. I then embarked upon an extensive program in education and programmed instruction, and in 1971 published *Beyond Freedom and Dignity* – all based upon the implications of my research.

Of course I was not the first to point to the parallel between natural selection and what I called operant conditioning, but the study of animal learning has come a long way beyond Thorndike and Whitman, and I believe my comparison goes into many new details.

Operant conditioning and natural selection

Andrew M. Colman

Department of Psychology, University of Leicester, England

Who says Skinner has no sense of humor? In "Phylogeny" he tells us that fishermen do not set nets because of any internal intention, purpose, or desire to catch fish. They do so merely because their net-setting behavior has been reinforced in the past and has therefore become more frequent, just as spiders do not spin webs because of any intention, purpose, or desire to catch flies, but merely because their web-spinning behavior has been naturally selected in the past and has therefore become more frequent. "Even if we could discover a spider's felt intention or sense of purpose," says Skinner, "we could not offer it as a cause of the behavior"; presumably the fisherman's felt intention, which we *can* easily discover, is equally irrelevant to the explanation of his behavior, or can supply only a "fictional explanation" (Skinner 1953, p. 278).

Variations on this familiar theme can be found throughout Skinner's writings over the past half-century. Is he willing to confirm, after all these years, with the tide of cognitive psychology running high, that he never intended these statements to be taken literally? If not, then will he certify the following behavioral analyses, which suggest (as Blanshard 1967 and others have pointed out) that novelists, dramatists, historians, philosophers, and ordinary people the world over have been governed by a unanimous illusion?

(a) Romeo's feeling of love for Juliet, and his mistaken belief that she was dead, were in no sense causes of his suicide; his suicide can be explained only as the result of external influences which somehow increased the frequency of his suicidal response from zero to one.

(b) Hitler's feeling of hatred toward the Jews is irrelevant in explaining his genocidal policies; the Final Solution must be attributed to contingencies of reinforcement which increased the frequency of his genocidal behavior.

(c) Skinner does not propound this doctrine because he believes it to be true; he propounds it (frequently) merely because he has been reinforced in the past for doing so.

This last example suggests, by the way, that Skinner's behaviorism is a self-defeating doctrine, since whenever he propounds it he implicitly denies that he believes it, or at least that it has any valid claim to truth (see Branden 1963; Locke 1966).

In "Phylogeny" Skinner draws an analogy between operant conditioning and natural selection in the provenance of behavior. A certain response is more likely to recur if it is associated with ontogenic contingencies that are reinforcing, just as a different response may be more likely to recur if it is associated with phylogenic contingencies that favor it through natural selection. I have always felt suspicious of this analogy, and I now think I have put my finger on one cardinal deficiency of operant conditioning theory in comparison with the theory of natural selection. *Operant conditioning theory offers no mechanism to explain changes in response frequency*. In the (modern) theory of natural selection, responses become more frequent because, when exposed to certain phylogenic contingencies, organisms that possess genes for these responses produce more offspring, on average, than do other organisms that lack such genes, and these offspring tend to resemble their parents because they inherit their parents' genes. In the theory of operant conditioning, on the other hand, responses become more frequent when organisms are exposed to certain ontogenic contingencies of reinforcement, but no mechanism is offered to account for this. In fact, the events that function as reinforcers are defined simply as those that increase the frequency of the responses they follow: "the only defining characteristic of a reinforcing stimulus is that it reinforces" (Skinner 1953, p. 72); the theory does not presume to explain how or why response frequency increases. Operant theory, in sharp contrast to natural selection theory, purports to be merely descriptive rather than explanatory (see, e.g., Skinner 1938, p. 44; 1950), and therein lies one of its crucial weaknesses.

But in spite of its purportedly atheoretical character, operant theory does entail claims that can, at least in principle, be empirically falsified. For example, in "Phylogeny" Skinner asserts that "what we may call the ontogeny of behavior [can be] traced to contingencies of reinforcement." Mills (1978a; 1978b) has raised several objections to this assertion, but I shall confine my remarks to just one, which arises from experiments on autoshaping. Brown and Jenkins (1968) demonstrated that the key-peck response in pigeons develops when the key in a Skinner box is illuminated, even when the pecking does not speed up the delivery of food reinforcements. Williams and Williams (1969) showed that the ontogeny of this kind of behavior cannot be traced to any accidental or adventitious reinforcement. More recently, Stiers and Silberberg (1974) found that, although rats will not learn to press a bar if there is a random relationship between the presentation of the (retractable) bar and food reinforcement, they will do so if there is a predictable relationship, even when bar pressing *delays* the delivery of food reinforcement.

Skinner has recently gone on record as saying: "I do not often read my critics" (Skinner 1983c, p. 28). Since he will undoubtedly read this commentary, and the others in this volume, I only hope that I shall be able to understand his response.

BFS: Colman devotes his commentary to three issues, only one of which is relevant to "Phylogeny." I do not say that feelings are irrelevant to action. To put it roughly, they are by-products of the causes of action. As I said in my debate with Blanshard (1967), Hitler's treatment of the Jews can be traced to many well documented events in his life. Those events and his action with respect to Jews were also responsible for conditions of his body which he could feel as hatred of the Jews. To say that he first experienced these events and hence felt hatred and that his hatred then led him to act gives the feelings an apparent causal status which "novelists, dramatists, historians, philosophers, and ordinary people the world over" have also assigned to them. There is an apparent priority in feelings; when we act we have better evidence of how we feel than of the long history of events which have led to what is felt and the related action.

Colman has indeed put his finger on a "cardinal deficiency of operant conditioning theory in comparison with the theory of natural selection." No one has yet analyzed the central nervous system in the same detail as chromosomes and genes. I assume that Colman would have been equally "suspicious" of both fields when, not so long ago, genetics and evolutionary theory rested on the same kind of evidence as operant conditioning. Genetics was a respectable science prior to the discovery of the "mechanism" to which Colman refers.

I have discussed the problem of autoshaping in several places (e.g., Skinner 1983b). I myself was interested in the basic phenomenon long before

Brown and Jenkins (1968) reported it, but did not think it important enough to publish. W. H. Morse and I used it with pigeons precisely for the purpose of evoking a particular type of response to the key. It involves classical conditioning rather than operant conditioning and so far as I know raises no real problem.

Consequence contingencies and provenance partitions

Juan D. Delius

Experimentelle Tierpsychologie, Psychologisches Institut, Ruhr-Universität, Federal Republic of Germany

When, about 15 years ago, I had to prepare a lecture intended to inform a conference of neuroscientists about the views of ethologists on the development of behavior, I thought it would be a good idea to contrast these views with those of behaviorists. One of the themes I thought of featuring was the behaviorists' Olympian disregard of biological evolution. The title of the lecture was going to be "The Phylogeny of Behavior Ontogeny." My dismay was great when idly leafing through a pile of *Science* ssues left by my office predecessor I stumbled upon B. F. Skinner's "Phylogeny." There was the preeminent theoretician of behaviorism holding forth on the very topic I supposed he and his brethren chose to ignore. I quickly modified both the tack and the title of my presentation (Delius 1970).

However, as laudable as I found Skinner's late interest in evolution, I was disappointed by "Phylogeny." It was neither a source of theoretical inspiration nor a reflection of the state of the art. On the contrary, it seemed intent on reversing hard-won progress. It reified in the guise of "ontogenic behavior" and "phylogenic behavior" the strict dichotomy between innate and learned behavior, a division that even ethological diehards had by then been forced to give up. All the arguments and the evidence against such a black-or-white distinction that had been marshaled by then (see Hinde 1966; Marler & Hamilton 1966) seemed to have bypassed Skinner. A rigid commitment leads him to equate behavioral ontogeny exclusively with the changes of response probabilities due to reinforcement contingencies, that is, with operant conditioning. Not even classical conditioning is expressly acknowledged to play a role in the development of behavior. Imprinting is, summarily and wrongly, dismissed as just another instance of operant conditioning. Nonlearning influences of environmental variables on the ontogeny of behavior are ignored. The provenance of "ontogenic behavior" is simply and purely operant conditioning and nothing else.

In contrast, Skinner ascribes the provenance of "phylogenic behavior" to the contingencies of natural selection acting upon a collection of fixed action patterns and does not allow it any ontogeny. This is logically consistent within his conceptual framework but ignores the fact that it conflicts with the evidence then already extant. That phylogeny exerts control over behavior via ontogeny and through genes is conveniently ignored. Behavior genetics is all but dismissed on the technical ground that its results do not square with Skinner's expectation that genes should express themselves in "units" of behavior.

Conversely, "ontogenic behavior" apparently does not have a phylogeny except that Skinner admits obliquely that baseline responding and certain reinforcers may have an evolutionary provenance. Considering that Skinner equates ontogeny with operant conditioning, that might be a fair reflection of contemporary behaviorist opinion. But there were already signs that it would not endure (Garcia & Koelling

1966). Following earlier ethological suggestions (Lorenz 1965; Tinbergen 1951) it soon became apparent that the phylogeny of learning is a more complex and incisive issue (Seligman 1970).

Instead, attention is drawn to the analogy that exists between the processes underlying phylogeny and ontogeny (sensu Skinner). Contingencies of selection in one case and contingencies of reinforcement in the other are identified as the moving agents. This parallel still has some reality, but it would have been fair to point out that other authors, more recent than Descartes, had dealt with it in some detail (e.g., Pringle 1951). The comparison of the outcomes of schedules of reinforcement with the effect of schedules of selection that might have been illuminating remains superficial; Skinner, perhaps sensing that it would have shown up the limitations of the analogy, chose not to find out what evolutionary biologists had to say about the matter. The exciting possibility of an "experimental analysis of phylogenic behavior" is surprisingly negated by alluding to natural selection's action in the unrecoverable past. Artificial selection is unnatural and thus deemed not really relevant. Ad hoc pleading is then necessary to immunize from a similar criticism artificial reinforcement, the basis of what should now correctly be the "experimental analysis of ontogenic behavior." Arguably, the failure to provide objective, as opposed to hypothetical, accounts of the natural ontogeny of behaviors as a product of natural reinforcement contingencies was already in 1966 corroding the attractiveness of radical behaviorism.

Why has the paper had so little impact, even among Skinner's own following? It is simply that the attempt to contain the explosion of knowledge that had in the meantime occurred within the very lean ontological framework conceived some 30 years earlier (Skinner 1938) yielded an inadequately narrow account. It could not compete against the up and coming eclectic, much richer, multidisciplinary account of behavior (Delius 1985), which, to be sure, incorporates a great deal of what Skinner and his disciples have discovered and described with truly admirable acumen. The sad fact is that simplicity, contrary to widespread opinion, is not a principle that organisms often care to respect.

BFS: Like many other commentators, Delius is concerned more with what I do not say than with what I say. He contends that the fact "that phylogeny exerts control over behavior via ontogeny and through genes is conveniently ignored." But was it really necessary for me to state my belief that the organism as a whole is nothing more than a member of an evolved species and that all its processes, including operant conditioning, operate "through genes"? I do not "dismiss" imprinting as just another instance of operant conditioning; I merely note that an imprinted stimulus can be used as an operant reinforcer.

I do not believe in a strict dichotomy between "ontogenic behavior" and "phylogenic behavior," if by behavior one means a stored habit or an instinct, but I think it is quite easy to distinguish between ontogenic and phylogenic *contingencies of selection*, and that was one of the points of "Phylogeny." (See also "Consequences.")

My reference to units of behavior was inspired by Julian Huxley's (1964) accolade of Lorenz. The released behavior of the ethologists is strikingly similar to operant behavior in its stimulus control. Neither is elicited, as in a reflex, conditioned or unconditioned.

As I have pointed out elsewhere, my "late" interest in evolution began with the first five pieces of research I ever undertook, and most of the work reported in *The Behavior of Organisms* (1938) was conducted on well-established strains of rats in the hope that differences would appear which could be subjected to genetic experiments.

Difficulties with phylogenetic and ontogenetic concepts

Irenäus Eibl-Eibesfeldt

Forschungstelle für Humanethologie, Max-Planck-Institut für Verhaltensphysiologie, Seewiesen, Federal Republic of Germany

Skinner complains that explanatory entities such as "instincts," "drives," and "traits" still survive. But evidently he fails to realize that these concepts have been redefined and in most cases replaced. "Phylogenetically adapted," for example, is preferred to "instinctive" nowadays. The term refers to the source of information controlling the process of differentiation during embryogenesis and ontogeny. If, for example, motor patterns develop without corresponding patterned input from the environment then it is reasonable to assume that the wiring of the neuronal networks underlying these skills developed in a process of self-differentiation according to the developmental recipes encoded in the genome of the individual in question. To argue that some unidentified environmental factors might have contributed to the patterning comes close to referring to some mystical force. Those poor mice whose forelimbs were amputated by Fentress (1973) at birth and which nonetheless developed the complete coordinated pattern of preening the head with the (nonexisting) forelimbs – as could be deduced from the movement of the stumps, the contraction of the remaining muscles, and the head and eye movements coordinated to the movement patterns of the "arms" – could not possibly have learned by any of the traditional ways of learning. All the details of how a nervous system can get wired for its function by genome-controlled growth processes are not known, but the investigations by Sperry (1971) and his group have provided valuable insight. The fact that we still lack information about many details of these processes should not discourage us from investigating the phenomenon. Skinner, after all, is not discouraged from studying the processes of conditioning, even though he does not know how an engram is coded.

In answering Lehrman's (1953) critique that innate was only defined as what was not learned, Lorenz (1965) provided the positive definition and explained in detail that phylogenetic adaptations determine behavior in well-defined ways, on the motor side as well as on the receptor side (innate releasing mechanisms), in the form of motivating mechanisms, templates, central feedback systems, and the like. Since I have already reviewed the concepts elsewhere (Eibl-Eibesfeldt 1979) I do not intend to go into the details. The concept of drive refers to factors of inner motivation. It is a functional term used to describe one set of variables. Ethologists have often emphasized that the term does not refer to one particular causal mechanism.

Skinner's contribution is certainly of great historical interest. He is certainly right that one can study imitative behavior the same way as any other behavior without analyzing the phylogenetic contingencies. A believing creationist can indeed be a brilliant physiologist and professional medical doctor without further inquiring into ultimate causes.

The contingencies of reinforcement certainly play an important role, and Skinner's contribution to their investigation is not to be belittled. But there are other questions to be answered. As to the statement that no reputable student of animal behavior has ever taken the position that an animal is born as a tabula rasa, what about Kuo? As late as 1967 he wrote that if he were able to exchange the brain of a man with that of a chimpanzee and vice versa, both would still behave the same way as before, since it is the organs of the body that determine behavioral capacity. Perhaps Kuo is not reputable in Skinner's eyes, but he is certainly often quoted by those who adopt an extreme environmentalist stand. It is fashionable nowadays to pay lip service to genetics by saying that the environment and the genes interact, but only to emphasize shortly afterward in a defeatist way that the two contributions cannot be separated. And this simply is not true. If we take a specific adaptation into consideration we can indeed explore and find an answer. At the time Skinner wrote "Phylogeny" Lorenz's (1965) book *Evolution and Modification of Behavior*, in which he provided the theoretical background for any such analyses, was already available. Skinner in fact cites it, but from his paper I gather that he failed at that time to understand fully the value of Lorenz's contribution. And some seem to have difficulties even today, as can be seen from Segall's (1979) theoretical discussion of Lorenz's work in his otherwise stimulating book.

BFS: The thrust of "Phylogeny" was to compare contingencies of selection, both phylogenic, insofar as they affect behavior, and ontogenic. The latter can readily be observed and more easily arranged for experimental purposes. Eibl-Eibesfeldt raises a question about the product. Both kinds of contingencies change the organism – "the wiring of the neuronal networks." Phylogenic contingencies do so in a way involving the genome, ontogenic contingencies in a different way, in the individual organism. It is an interesting question as to whether the changes are of the same kind. Certainly the two systems, whether they exist in the same form or not, interact in the life of the individual and the interaction will be understood only when both have been analyzed.

I do not think that much progress is made toward understanding either change by speaking of "motivating mechanisms, templates, central feedback systems, and the like." Eibl-Eibesfeldt sees behavior as a product of traits and abilities. These aspects or properties of the human organism have two practical shortcomings:

1. They have not yet been directly measured. (Tests, inventories, and questionnaires are of arbitrary length and complexity, and scores are arbitrary. Meaningful quantities refer only to the position of an individual in a sample of the population at large. Particularly in the case of intelligence, the problem of sampling has been acute.)
2. They cannot be directly manipulated. Teachers cannot readjust the intelligence of their students; therapists cannot readjust the introversion–extraversion ratio of their clients. Practices which seem to have these effects involve environmental operations and are subject to a different interpretation.

I am not denying that many interesting correlations have been established between abilities and traits so measured and between traits or abilities and physiological or genetic factors. Although the experimental analysis of behavior and most of its applications deal with individual organisms, it is obviously helpful to know as much about an organism as possible before beginning to study it. With a lower species one may seek genetic uniformity, a uniform environmental history, and so on. That is usually impossible with human subjects, but the help that can be reasonably obtained from measures of abilities and traits is less than an adequate substitute. To say this, as Eysenck suggests in the next commentary, is not to disregard "completely . . .the accomplishments of other psychologists."

The needs of Eibl-Eibesfeldt and the needs, drives, and emotions of Eysenck are other internal states which Eibl-Eibesfeldt regards as essential. More than 50 years ago in two papers on drive and reflex strength, I pointed to external functional variables which could take the place of the inferred psychological state, leaving open the possibility of a physiological analysis. I developed the same theme with respect to emotion in *Science and Human Behavior* (1953). Does Eibl-Eibesfeldt believe with Eysenck that the practices of Pavlovian therapy, the importance of which I do not question, involve the extinction of a state of anxiety, or of the so-called symptoms? Reinforcement is another concept which depends upon a state of the organism which, unfortunately, we must leave to the physiologist, who has or will have the appropriate techniques and methods.

Skinner's blind eye

H. J. Eysenck

Department of Psychology, Institute of Psychiatry, University of London, England

There are several similarities between B. F. Skinner and Lord Nelson. Both favour a very aggressive tendency; both have shown considerable leadership potential; and both have a tendency to put the telescope to their blind eye – Nelson at the Battle of Copenhagen, to avoid seeing the signal for retreat, Skinner to avoid seeing the wide extent of behaviour not susceptible to simplification in terms of his law of operant conditioning. In all these respects, Skinner also resembles Freud, and it is no wonder that both men have formed a tightly knit group of supporters, founded their own journals, and have, in their attempt to inaugurate a new psychology, separated themselves from the broad basis of general psychology.

Both Skinner and Freud make their work easier by disregarding completely both the accomplishments of other psychologists and the problems that arise in the applications of their own theories. Both succeed in spinning a web of words around a cocoon of an idea, but these words do not come to grips with reality. Consider Skinner's assertion that

> although ontogenic contingencies are easily subjected to an experimental analysis, phylogenic contingencies are not. When the experimenter has shaped a complex response, such as dropping a marble into a tube, the provenance of the behavior raises no problem. The performance may puzzle anyone seeing it for the first time, but it is easily traced to recent, possibly recorded, events. No comparable history can

> be invoked when a spider is observed to spin a web. We have not seen the phylogenic contingencies at work.

This, surely, is a wrong comparison. Skinner contrasts an experimental study with everyday life behaviour. To be acceptable, the comparison should be between likes, not unlikes – an experimental psychological study should be compared with an experimental genetic study, such as breeding rats for emotionality, or the comparison should be between everyday life behaviour and phylogenic features dating back over the millennia. Skinner really has nothing to say about ontogenic contingencies of everyday life behaviour, other than to make unwarranted assumptions about possible reinforcements; no one has observed these reinforcements, there is no history of them, and indeed the behaviour may have been shaped along quite different lines. The law of reinforcement is not a demonstrated reality but an assumption; the assumption is hidden behind Skinner's prose, but is nonetheless no more than an assumption.

Or consider Skinner's assertion that "other concepts replaced by a more effective analysis include 'need' or 'drive' and 'emotion.' In ontogenic behaviour, we no longer say that a given set of environmental conditions first gives rise to an inner state which the organism then expresses or resolves by behaving in a given way." Do we not? Who in fact is this "we" other than a small group of followers of Skinner? It certainly is not the great mass of experimental or theoretical psychologists, who still speak about needs, drives, and emotions. It is very difficult to speak about the complex behaviour of neurotics without postulating such an "inner state" as anxiety, and the reduction of anxiety by various methods such as desensitization, flooding, or modelling. Skinner and his followers have made no real contribution to the treatment of neurotic disorders, where Pavlovian conditioning seems to be the major cause of the disorder and Pavlovian extinction a major means of treatment (Eysenck 1982). Theoretical contributions to psychology should not, like Skinner's, simply provide assertions; they should argue the case, taking care to deal with the most successful alternative hypotheses, and demonstrating that these, in fact, are inferior to the new theory proposed. Skinner never deals in detail with alternative theories. Often he does not even mention them. He simply asserts that "we" do not have need of these concepts any longer, but without demonstrations that these assertions have any rational meaning, any empirical content, or any predictive value. This is not the way of scientific argument, and it only leads to the polarisation of psychology, and its division into hostile camps, such as the Skinnerian, the Freudian, and so on.

As the third and last example of this unfortunate method of argument, consider another of Skinner's assertions. He mentions that an analysis of behaviour in terms of ontogenic contingencies leaves something out of account, and goes on to say:

> This is true. It leaves out of account habits, ideas, cognitive processes, needs, drives, traits, and so on. But it does not neglect the facts upon which these concepts are based. It seeks a more effective formulation of the very contingencies to which those who use such concepts must eventually turn to explain their explanations. The strategy has been highly successful at the ontogenic level, where the contingencies are relatively clear.

This is not my reading of the literature. It is precisely by neglecting traits, such as extroversion–introversion, that Skinner and his followers have made it difficult and almost impossible to attach very much meaning to ontogenic analysis in terms of histories of reinforcement. Thus, what is a positive reinforcement to an extrovert may be a negative reinforcement to an introvert (Eysenck 1967). This makes difficult the precise definition of a reinforcer other than in terms of a circular argument: The stimulus leads to behaviour repetition; therefore it is a reinforcement. This makes prediction impossible and is about as useful as a postulation of instincts was 100 years ago. Unless you can specify a reinforcer *independently* of the actual observation that it leads to consequences that we associate with reinforcers, the argument s simply circular, trivial, and of no scientific interest. Nor is it clear how Skinnerian analysis can do away with concepts such as general intelligence. Again we have a simple assertion that this is so, and not even a shadow of an attempt at evidence. Science cannot disregard facts, and it would be interesting to know how Skinner would explain, in terms of his own method of analysis, the existence of a "positive manifold" in the intelligence field, or the tendency in intercorrelations between IQ tests to form a matrix of unit rank (Eysenck 1979). Skinner arbitrarily disregards such facts, but it is difficult to follow him in doing so; they demand an explanation, and no explanation is possible without postulation of abilities of various kinds.

Of course Skinner is right in stating that the rewarding or punishing consequences of an act influence future behaviour; psychologists and philosophers from Plato to Thorndike have subscribed to this view, and the man in the street would hardly have disagreed at any time. Thus a certain amount of behaviour can be explained in these terms. Skinner attempts to extend this basis to all behaviour, again very much like Freud's attempt to extend a very modest sexual basis to all behaviour. But this is impossible, as will be clear to anyone who is not a member of the magic circle. Attempts to extend reinforcement principles to all behaviour have had adverse effects on the community of psychology; they have misled many people into embracing a belief that is religious rather than scientific and to deny the importance of phenomena the reality of which can hardly be doubted. Not along these lines are we ever likely to arrive at a truly scientific psychology, which will take its place with the hard sciences. Skinner, like Freud, has made a modest but genuine contribution to psychology; again like Freud, he has also made it more difficult for the science of psychology to come of age and to leave behind the time when schools and individuals are more important than scientific laws and principles.

BFS: The telescope through which Eysenck looks at behavior is pointed at "phylogenic features dating back over the millennia" which I am said to completely disregard. They include emotionality, needs, drives, and traits like introversion, extraversion, a "'positive manifold' in the intelligence field, or the tendency in intercorrelations between IQ tests to form a matrix of unit rank." These have to do with states of the organism of phylogenic or ontogenic origin. They are products. They have a bearing on behavior but are not themselves forms of behavior. I do not believe I have seriously neglected their so-called behavioral manifestations. I have certainly not ignored them. But traits like introversion or intelligence are quantified not in the individual but in the position of the individual in a population. The function of an "inner state" of anxiety in mediating the causal relation between behavior and some feature of the history of the individual I have discussed in several places (e.g., Skinner 1953; "Behaviorism-50"). Pavlovian conditioning is not more appropriate to therapy because it deals with states like anxieties, phobias, and so on. It is different from operant therapy because it deals with a different kind of contingency, and the contingencies are easier to arrange in a clinic.

I prefer to leave it to the reader of these papers to decide whether I "really [have] nothing to say about ontogenic contingencies of everyday life behaviour, other than to make unwarranted assumptions," or "simply provide assertions" in place of theoretical contributions, or "have misled many people into embracing a belief that is religious rather than scientific."

It is not true that "unless you can specify a reinforcer *independently* of the actual observation that it leads to consequences that we associate with reinforcers, the argument is simply circular, trivial, and of no scientific interest." As I point out in my reply to Gallup (see "Behaviorism-50," this volume) we discover the events that reinforce an individual's behavior and use them subsequently for that purpose. Why they are reinforcing is another question.

I know of no way in which a reinforcer can be identified in advance. If certain kinds of food are usually reinforcing to a hungry organism, the reasons must be found in the phylogeny of the species, but I should not use food as a reinforcer until I had demonstrated its power to reinforce. It evidently does not reinforce the eating of those who suffer from anorexia nervosa. Why salt and sugar should be reinforcing even to the nonhungry I have discussed elsewhere (e.g., reply to Wyrwicka, "Consequences").

B. F. Skinner versus Dr. Pangloss

Michael T. Ghiselin

Department of Invertebrates, California Academy of Sciences

Two publications that appeared in 1966 have had a major influence on my work. One was George C. William's book *Adaptation and Natural Selection*. Another was the target article, B. F. Skinner's "Phylogeny and Ontogeny of Behavior." William's book was seminal in getting biologists to abandon the notion that anything exists "for the good of the species." It encouraged a return to the Darwinian principle that whatever evolves has to be explained in terms of advantages to individuals, including higher-level individuals such as families (see Ghiselin 1981). In 1969 I published a book and a paper of my own: the one explaining the Darwinian methodology, the other replacing species-level explanations for hermaphroditism with individualistic ones, such as the "size-advantage model" (Ghiselin 1969a, 1969b). Later I criticized at length the teleological approach to biology in general, and its application to aspects of sociobiology and reproduction in particular (Ghiselin 1974). Skinner's paper now has an old-fashioned flavor to it because he refers to utility for species, but a shift to individualism is precisely the sort of improvement in approach that he has championed so often and so well.

The similarities between Williams's book and Skinner's paper would not have been apparent had it not been for an article in which Dennett (1983) attempted to defend a watered-down Panglossianism and its analogue in cognitive ethology. This provides a fine opportunity to continue this discussion, in which Skinner plays a major role. Those who study living beings deal with at least three kinds of change. In the first place, we have phylogeny, which is the transformation of species and lineages through time. Second, we have ontogeny, which is the transformation of organisms in their life cycles. Third, we have learning, which is a transformation of what an organism does behaviorally. All these changes are changes of individuals; they must be, for only individuals can change. All these changes are subject to laws of nature and one goal of science is to discover such laws. But much change is historically contingent, so that we need to know about the past to explain many of the particulars.

There would seem to be high-level generalizations that we can make about change in different kinds of objects. Hence the so-called analogies among the three processes are very likely manifestations of laws of nature that govern all of them. From a methodological or epistemological point of view there are additional parallels. Right thinking about change is characteristic of more than one kind of object.

For one thing, we do not wish to posit with Dr. Pangloss that this is the best of all possible worlds. (Or to accept the view of Pope, who might better have said that whatever is, is trite.) It may be true, as Dennett (1983) claims, that a lot of scientists blunder along through tenure to retirement presupposing optimality. But I repeat that we have no need for that fatuous question, What is good? All we need ask is, What has happened? Dennett is absolutely right when he compares this position with that taken by Skinner. He seems unaware, however, of how respectable it is among knowledgeable biologists, and for what good reasons.

How, pray tell, ought we to explain the appearances of embryology? Surely not, as Dr. Pangloss did, by invoking the homunculus, putatively observed by Hartsoeker in the human spermatozoon (Leibniz 1695). Nor do we need a *vis essentialis*, a *nisus formativus*, or an entelechy. What we do need is a clearly formulated hypothesis about the underlying morphogenetic processes, with experiments and observations that will back it up. We also need to understand such historical accidents as are responsible for the presence of gill slits in mammalian embryos. So too with evolutionary biology: We do not need a lot of empty talk about "tendencies to perfection." Rather, we need to ask questions about how organisms compete reproductively and to find a way to answer those questions by means of observations on real organisms in the real world. In cognitive psychology these days we have far too many homunculi and their little friends. Mental representations are a fine example. These have an embryological analogue in the notion that the germ somehow contains a "blueprint" of the soma. Of course one can readily invoke some other metaphor, drawing upon computer jargon. Part of the trouble is that there are various ways in which organized beings can be organized. In embryology, again, we have the precedent of mosaic and regulatory eggs. Skinner recognizes such a wealth of possibilities, and rightly insists that we face up to it. The trouble with Panglossians is not that their hypotheses are illegitimate, but that they are not treated as hypotheses that have to be tested. They are posits, so that where formerly we had providence, now we have programs.

Perhaps it would be a good idea to sidestep certain issues and deal with what look like soluble problems. This is part of Skinner's strategy, and it has a good biological precedent. The best book ever written on the relationship between ontogeny and phylogeny is *The Variation of Animals and Plants under Domestication* (Darwin 1868; cf. the analyses by Ghiselin 1969b and Gould 1977). Darwin was unable to discover the laws of inheritance, as we can see from his theory of pangenesis. On the other hand, he did show how the mechanisms of development constrain the course of evolution. Thus he sidestepped genetics and succeeded with embryology. Now that we have a good understanding of genetics we can accomplish more than Darwin could. Let us hope that psychology can do the same.

The examples Skinner gives of maladaptation (e.g., superstition) clearly show him to be no Panglossian. Probably most everybody begins as a rather naive adaptationist, until perhaps having to deal with a problem in which it does not suffice. We may have been selected for thinking that way, but the ease with which it is unlearned suggests that it gets socially reinforced. The difficulties should not militate against our studying adaptation, but, as Skinner points out, we have to do more than just note "the mere fact that behavior is adaptive." There is of course a danger that something will be left out for spurious methodological reasons. Skinner answers his critics on that point, but it seems to me that more needs to be said, for example, with respect to the study of behavioral diversity. He gives the impression of believing that there are behavioral laws, true of all organisms. However, taxa, such as species, are individuals, and there are no laws for individuals (see Ghiselin 1981). Much of what is true about a taxon is the result of history, and one has to survey a wide range of organisms to differentiate between that which is accidental and that which is necessary. *Drosophila* is diploid, but some insects happen to be haplodiploid, and this is thought to affect their social behavior profoundly. Furthermore, the best way to get an understanding of the phylogenetic aspects of behavior is by means of comparison.

The quotation from Watson at the beginning of "Phylogeny" is symptomatic of the hyperbole we find in the literature on behaviorism. Of course Watson didn't really believe what he asserted. Then why did he say it? I am struck by the parallel with the exchange between Dennett (1983) and Lewontin (1983). In both cases we have what is on the face of it a discussion of scientific methodology and fact. But those who know what is really going on can detect the underlying political motivation. Gould and Lewontin (1979) had written an ideological diatribe, not a serious effort to deal with a scientific problem. Small wonder that Dennett was puzzled by the inconsistencies, and small wonder that Skinner had to explain away the behavior of Watson. There are all sorts of Panglossians. For some, like Dennett, perhaps, this is the best of all possible worlds, but everything in it is a necessary evil. For others, like Lewontin, perhaps, the necessary evil becomes the class struggle and all will be fine in the end. It is Panglossianism on the installment plan.

Are the organisms no more than ink blots to the hopes and dreams of metaphysicians? One stock example of useless features, the bands on snails, turns out to be something for which the adaptive significance is particularly well documented (as A. J. Cain, who did much of the work, has urged upon me). For us scientists, adaptation, be it anatomical or behavioral, is a datum of experience to be studied in the laboratory and in the field. Given a lot of hard work and clear thinking, we can answer those questions about it that are both interesting and answerable. Let us not wander too far into the wasteland of metaphysics. *Il faut cultiver notre jardin.*

BFS: I have complained of the extent to which many of those who have commented upon these papers have simply misunderstood what I have said and the extent to which I am forced to offer correction. If all the other contributors understood my position as well as Ghiselin, I should have found myself with little or nothing of that sort to say. His commentary might well have appeared first as a general introduction to my paper. It would have made my position clearer than I myself have been able to make it, and a more productive discussion might then have followed.

Lingering Haeckelian influences and certain other inadequacies of the operant viewpoint for phylogeny and ontogeny

Gilbert Gottlieb

Department of Psychology, University of North Carolina at Greensboro

In proposing a dichotomy of two sources or "provenances" of behavior, one ontogenetic and the other evolutionary or phylogenetic, Skinner follows a long line of intellectual descent that includes such unlikely cohorts as Thorndike (1911) and Lorenz (1965) and their respective offspring – general behavior theory and classica ethological theory (cf. Johnston 1982). These otherwise rather disparate viewpoints share the assumption that if a behavior is ontogenetically fixed (unmodifiable) its form was established during the course of the evolution of the species (phylogenesis), whereas if a behavior is modifiable or experientially dependent it is a consequence of ontogenetic events. Although the view is not uncontroversial, it is conventionally accepted that some behaviors that arise during ontogenesis are innate (in the sense of not being directly dependent upon specific prior experiential events) and some are experientially dependent. However, the acceptance of that dichotomy does not attest to the validity of the conclusion that innate behavior stems from phylogenesis and experientially dependent behavior stems from ontogenesis. This conclusion, no matter how appealing and how seemingly tight its logic, is incorrect or misleading for at least three reasons.

1. It represents a long-outmoded Haeckelian (1891) way of thinking about the influence of phylogeny on ontogeny, to the singular effect that "ontogeny recapitulates phylogeny."
2. It relies on the erroneous assumption that genes control innate behavior and experience controls acquired behavior, whereas genes coming down from ancestors are in fact involved in the ontogenetic development of all behavior (Gottlieb 1971; 1976a; Lehrman 1970).
3. The phylogeny–ontogeny dichotomy, shared by many current authors, is based on a lack of appreciation of the relationship between phylogeny and ontogeny, namely, that evolution (phylogeny) is a consequence of an altered ontogeny.

I would like to elaborate briefly on these three related points concerning the influence of phylogeny on ontogeny and then close by commenting on the inadequacy of the operant viewpoint for an understanding of the various roles that experience plays in the ontogenetic development of behavior.

Haeckel's view (1891) that ontogeny recapitulates phylogeny placed the mechanical cause of ontogeny in the remote evolutionary history of the species ("Die Phylogenie ist die mechanische Ursache der Ontogenese," p. 7) and thus long thwarted the establishment of a truly experimental embryology, which aimed to place the causes of animal form in the immediate and observable mechanical events of ontogenesis (Oppenheimer 1967). Skinner writes as if innate or instinctive behavior was formed in phylogenesis, à la Haeckel. This view came under the most trenchant empirical and conceptual attack in the writings of Garstang (1922) and de Beer (1940). It was the latter's thinking, in particular, that put the current view of the relation between ontogeny and phylogeny in such clear relief. De Beer's insights into the influence of various alterations in developmental timing (heterochrony) for the more or less enduring evolutionary changes in animal form show us once and for all that phylogeny is intimately dependent on changes in ontogeny, rather than the other way around (reviewed and extended by Gould 1977).

A final weakness in the operant view vis-à-vis the analysis of the ontogeny of behavior is the requirement that "the entire repertoire of an individual or species must exist prior to ontogenic or phylogenic selection." Although experience certainly can function to *maintain* behavior that has already developed, experience also functions during ontogeny to *facilitate* and *induce* behavior that has not yet occurred or developed at the time of the experience (Gottlieb 1976a; 1976b). In fact, one of the features distinguishing the developmental study of behavior from the study of mature or adult behavior is the necessity of understanding how experience functions to bring about or otherwise influence behavior *prior* to its expression. Thus, although recognizing the contribution of operant psychology to developmental analysis (especially its methodological contributions), the operant view shares with other traditional learning theories an inability to describe adequately the various ways in which experience functions in the ontogeny of species-typical behavior. As a result, it has become necessary to fashion a new vocabulary that better fits the various experiential contingencies of typical behavioral development. To date the new framework has been applied to such diverse topics as the development of speech perception in human infants (Aslin 1981; Aslin & Pisoni 1980), olfactory experience and huddling preferences in rat pups (Brunjes & Alberts 1979), maintenance of emotionality in gerbils (Clark & Galef 1979), flying ability (Krischke 1983), and auditory perception in young birds (Kerr, Ostapoff, & Rubel 1979), to cite but a few examples.

Since it would be unfair as well as inappropriate to criticize the operant framework for failing to do what it does not try to do, in the latter part of this critique I am merely calling attention to a significant ontogenetic problem that is not addressed by the operant viewpoint. It is widely recognized that operant methods or procedures are often used to good advantage in developmental studies that are motivated by other conceptual or theoretical concerns. Operant conditioning often works powerfully and effectively in maintaining or shaping behavior (or components of behavior) that is already in an organism's repertoire – it does not deal with problems of the induction and facilitation of behavior yet to be expressed, which are prominent experiential occurrences in ontogenetic development. That is, the operant framework focuses on the maintenance (or extinction) of already existing behavior, not on the experiences responsible for the initial establishment or expression of the behavior in ontogenetic development. Operant psychology usually comes into play after the behavioral phenotype is already developed and expressed, whereas a major task of developmental psychobiology is to describe and analyze the experiences that interact with maturation to bring about the original expression of species-typical behavior. To state the difference most succinctly, operant analysis is concerned with behavior that is controlled by its consequences, whereas the developmental approach is concerned with behavior that is controlled by its antecedents.

Skinner recognizes that experiential contingencies in the development of species-typical behavior are often not obvious, and recent evidence supports that view with the experimental discovery of nonobvious cases of maintenance as well as facilitation and induction (Gottlieb 1981).

BFS: I find Gottlieb's paper merely puzzling. What could lead him to think that I believe the following?

1. "Ontogeny recapitulates phylogeny." Natural selection and operant conditioning work through the selection of variations, but the variations and the contingencies of selection are quite different.
2. "Genes control innate behavior and experience controls acquired behavior." All behavior is due to genes, some more or less directly, the rest through the role of genes in producing the structures which are modified during the lifetime of the individual.
3. "Evolution is [not] a consequence of an altered ontogeny." A trait must occur as a variation before being selected to become a trait of the species, but it does not follow that "the entire repertoire of an individual or species must exist prior to ontogenic or phylogenic selection." How complex behavior is shaped bit by bit through operant reinforcement as very small variations are differentially reinforced is a staple of operant behaviorism.

Ethology ignored Skinner to its detriment

Jack P. Hailman

Department of Zoology, University of Wisconsin–Madison

It is difficult to comment usefully on an essay that is more than 15 years old and today shows its senility. One must put the work among its contemporaries in the flow of science, and then with the prowess of hindsight attempt to evaluate its place.

In one form or another, the "nature–nurture" question has enticed man's inquiring mind since antiquity. Charles Darwin (1859), however, sharpened attempts to deal with the problem in the form of the evolution of "instincts." His alter ego, George Jean Romanes (1884; 1889), took up the mantle in supporting the notion that consciously learned behavior became so habitual through practice that it was established in the individual as unconscious reflex, and then passed to offspring by some sort of Lamarckian inheritance. William James (1890) knew better, and by the 20th century empirical workers were focusing on separate aspects of the "phylogeny and ontogeny" of behavior. As I have attempted to document elsewhere (Hailman 1984), early studies of learning revealed keen interest in observing "instincts," while early observational studies frequently dealt with behavioral changes due to learning. Nevertheless, Thorndike (1898) established a psychological tradition focusing upon learning and Heinroth (1911) a zoological tradition focusing upon "instincts," the separate paths of inquiry having little direct interaction until Tinbergen's (1951) classic *Study of Instinct* and Lehrman's (1953) seminal criticism of the ethological tradition. The ferment of the ensuing decade yielded Lorenz's (1965) book, *Evolution and Modification of Behavior*, and Skinner's (1966) article, "Phylogeny." It is no accident that Lorenz was the most visible practitioner of Heinroth's comparative method and Skinner the most visible practitioner of Thorndike's conditioning paradigm.

What we can now see in the nearly simultaneous publication of the works by Lorenz (1965) and Skinner (1966) is basic acknowledgement of each other's tradition. But how different the two works! Lorenz was argumentative and contorted, continually altering the implied definitions of "behavior we formerly called innate," castigating "English-speaking ethologists" who deserted the old dogma, and trying to establish learning phenomena as mere frosting on the behavioral cake. Skinner was considerably more clever, disarming critics by citing Beach's (1950) quote about the presumptuous title *Behavior of Organisms*, breaking down differences into discrete issues, and all the while showing subtly how much we know about operantly conditioned behavior and how little about "instincts."

Skinner's "Phylogeny," however, had almost no influence on zoologists, whereas Lorenz's (1965) book is still frequently cited today. I cannot profess to account fully for the difference in influence, but I can point to aspects of Skinner's essay that make it easy for an ethologist to dismiss it as naive and unimportant. First, it does not directly address a question of great importance to zoologists: How and why do species differ in behavior? Indeed, the essay emphasizes the idea that by simplifying the animal's environment in the laboratory, one can find great similarities among species' operant responding, a fact that ethologists then found uninteresting. Second, the essay does not deal directly with the heart of the ethological tradition of Heinroth (1911): the comparative method used to parse similarities and differences in behavior according to factors of common descent and presumed selective pressures. Third, the essay repeatedly contains phrases such as "survival of species" and "advantage to species," revealing the author's endorsement of group selection, which at that time was roundly discredited in biological circles, as evidenced by fierce attacks on the viewpoint of Wynne-Edwards (1965, and later publications). It is easy to draw the conclusion that Skinner just did not understand evolutionary theory at the time of writing "Phylogeny." Fourth, the essay clearly equates analysis of the ontogeny of behavior with analysis of operant responding, a viewpoint that was too simple for students of wild animals to accept seriously. Fifth, Skinner was already well known for his viewpoint, reflected in this essay, that the understanding of behavior required not only accurate prediction but also "experimental control" over the process studied. Such a viewpoint defines historical studies out of existence, thus depriving ethologists of the core of their evolutionary interests. And finally, the essay considers behavior to be composed of "responses" (as evidenced by the very first word of the abstract). All ethologists then "knew" that behavior was often spontaneous, exhibited in the absence of any identifiable stimuli in the environment: No work that dealt solely with responses and ignored "sponses" could be taken seriously.

That Lorenz, in a sense, won the struggle for recognition is clear from the award of the 1973 Nobel Prize for Physiology or Medicine to him jointly with Niko Tinbergen and Karl von Frisch. At the time there was much talk in the halls of academe concerning the difficulty the committee must have experienced in excluding B. F. Skinner, Julian Huxley, and perhaps Harry Harlow (of whom only Skinner today still lives). If this recognition sealed the fate of Skinner's attempt to influence the ethological tradition and bring about some cross-talk with operant conditioning, it is indeed a shame. For what comes through in "Phylogeny," standing tall above the aforementioned differences that separated the camps, is Skinner's most important point: Science should deal with operationally measured variables. The essay tries to say how ethology might become more operational by patterning itself after the operant conditioning paradigm. Unfortunately, the do as I do and you shall succeed format may have resulted in throwing the baby out with the bath. More than a decade and a half later, ethology is today creeping only slowly toward becoming an operational science (Hailman 1982; 1982b). It might have progressed much more rapidly had the central message of "Phylogeny" been taken lovingly to heart.

BFS: I shall take Hailman's use of the word "senility" to refer to the seniority of my paper rather than any sign of the feebleness and decay of the standard stereotype. I accept some of the reasons Hailman advances for the lack of attention paid by ethologists to my paper, though I do not like all of them.

1. By simplifying an environment (removing most of the normal releasers) one can show great similarities in the operant responding of different species as, after allowing for gross differences in anatomy, one can show similarities in the structure of their nervous systems.
2. I did not deal directly with "factors of common descent and presumed selective pressures" (as ethologists have not dealt directly with the "selective pressures" of operant reinforcement).
3. I used phrases such as "survival of species" and "advantage to the species," carelessly, perhaps, but scarcely "revealing [my] endorsement of group selection."
4. Students of "wild animals" could not seriously accept the equation of "the analysis of the ontogeny of behavior with [the] analysis of operant responding." (Alas!)
5. By insisting upon prediction and control I "define[d] historical studies out of existence." But that is the difference between the laboratory and the field in many sciences.

6. In using the word "response," I seemed to be on the side of stimulus–response psychologists, but the whole point of the term "operant" was to emphasize the apparent spontaneity and lack of specific stimulus control.

With these modifications, I am happy to accept Hailman's explanation of why ethologists have paid so little attention to the operant field.

The structure versus the provenance of behavior

Jerry A. Hogan

Department of Psychology, University of Toronto, Canada

What we find interesting and important depends on the questions we are asking. This point was made by Lehrman (1970) when discussing his views on the nature–nurture problem, and the same point is applicable to Skinner's discussion of the same issue. Skinner's basic question is, What is the provenance of behavior? He seeks an answer in terms of ontogenetic contingencies (an organism's history of reinforcement) and phylogenetic contingencies (a species' history of selection pressures in the course of evolution).

Skinner's framework allows him to make a number of sensible, insightful, and thought-provoking comparisons between ontogenetic and phylogenetic contingencies. For example, whether or not his analysis of the development of the behavior of the African honey guide is correct, the point is well taken that it is necessary to make such an analysis of any complex behavior before drawing conclusions about its provenance. Likewise, he emphasizes the fact that phylogenetic and ontogenetic contingencies bring about their results in different ways, and similarities in outcome do not imply similarities in provenance.

Even within Skinner's own framework, though, there are a few points with which one can disagree. For example, he refers to "survival of the species" whereas evolutionary biologists currently believe that selection operates at the level of individual survival (Williams 1966). And many authors would not agree that the consequences of adventitious contingencies are as pervasive as Skinner suggests, either phylogenetically (Holliday & Maynard Smith 1979) or ontogenetically (Staddon 1977). But these and similar examples do not really affect his main arguments.

If one asks questions somewhat differently, however, several points in Skinner's account of behavior seem incomplete or unduly emphasized. Suppose we accept the premise that our main interest is to determine the probability that an organism will behave it a given way. One set of variables that affects the probability is indeed the one related to ontogenetic and phylogenetic contingencies as Skinner discusses. But to know the entire history of reinforcement of the rat that possesses a marble-dropping habit or the entire course of the evolution of the web spinning of a spider would be useless if our task is to demonstrate either of these behaviors to a class of undergraduate students. For such a task, other variables are much more important.

Of importance for demonstrating the behavior of the rat would be variables such as the state of hunger and the strength of competing states such as fear (caused by the presence of students) that could interfere with the expression of marble dropping. For the spider, variables such as temperature, light conditions, and hunger state might be relevant, as well as an appropriate situation for the spider to build in. All these variables belong to a class that is often called motivational, and it is simply not true that such variables are used "because the functional relations [ethologists] attempt to formulate are not clearly understood." Contingencies are important when answering developmental questions (such as questions about learning), and motivational variables are important when answering questions about immediate causation.

We can ask yet other questions about behavior. For example, many species of spiders have a web-spinning instinct. But the webs they spin are often radically different. These differences do not reflect differences in ontogenetic contingencies or in motivational factors. They do reflect differences in behavioral structure. If one wishes to ask questions about the evolution of these structures, one would look for answers in terms of phylogenetic contingencies. But if one is interested in functional questions (e.g., what are the different types of web good for?), the structure of the web itself is the important variable. In such a case we are more interested in the particular way a spider will behave than in the probability that it will behave that way.

Another question concerned with the structure of behavior is, What events are reinforcing for a particular species (or individual)? There is a wide variety of events that have been shown to be reinforcing, but some of them are effective only for a particular species or even for a particular individual (Hogan & Roper 1978). Whether or not an event is reinforcing depends on the structure of the organism.

I agree that concepts such as habit, instinct, drive, and the like have often been misused. That may be reason for using them with caution, but I do not find it reason enough for dispensing with them. Habits and instincts are facts of behavioral structure and are necessary concepts when asking structural questions. Structural concepts cannot explain the development of behavior nor do they give us insight into the immediate causation of behavior. Contingencies and motivational concepts are necessary for that. Which concepts we use depend on the questions we are asking.

BFS: In general, I accept the modifications in my paper that Hogan suggests. As I have already admitted, it was careless of me to refer to the survival of the species without making it clear that the first selection (cf. "Consequences") is due to the survival of the individual. Of course one must take other variables into account and hold some of them constant in order to study the effects of others. I do not believe I have neglected "motivational" variables, though the word "motivation" is, I think, commonly misused.

Of course differences in structure are important, but they are themselves the results of contingencies of selection. Structures are what is selected. Organisms have evolved in such a way that when they are hungry, food strongly reinforces their behavior. Other reinforcers are merely conditioned. But both reinforce because of the structure of the organism. The structure is not an initiating cause of anything, however.

Behavior in the light of identified neurons

Graham Hoyle

Institute of Neuroscience, University of Oregon

Since Skinner's 1966 article "Phylogeny," we have enjoyed a quarter-century of research on the neural mechanisms underlying behavior, which has used the ability to identify individual neurons and address them repeatedly in preparations showing a variety of behaviors. The scene has changed dramatically since the 1965 remark by Lorenz, quoted by Skinner, that we have an "absolute ignorance of the physiologica mechanisms underlying learning." The November 1983 issue of *Discover*, "America's eading science magazine," is dedicated to memory – how it works. The article quotes Eric Kandel as saying "we found that everyday molecular machinery is used for *mental* activity, but in novel ways. It helps de-mystify learning." Daniel Alkon is reported as having achieved "a tour de force of memory research." I must admit to gulping out loud when I read each of these statements: Can Kandel really be attributing to two neurons of his beloved molluscan gut ganglion the highest of all nervous system activities? His purpose was surely loftier than that of drawing attention to the imitations of semantics! Memory is derived from the Latin memoria, which is indeed translatable as "mindful." Memory has also come to mean any readdressable store of neural information. Kandel and his associates have shown how the information acquired during an aversive conditioning is established cellularly. It is a modified synaptic transmission between two identified neurons. This type of plasticity in neurons does not meet the criteria of some of the more careful definitions of memory, but it cannot be denied that it meets some. Nor need other forms of neuronal plasticity use the same molecular mechanisms. But the point is that every kind of mental activity must be associated with molecular events whose nature it is now, in principle, within our power to ascertain experimentally.

Behavior is animal movement, especially controlled motion, and it is of two distinct types. One kind is generated within the organism independently of input information; the other is a response to input. Almost every conceivable combination of the two occurs. Skinner grew up in an era in which animals were exclusively regarded as input–output mechanisms. The sole function of a nervous system was thought to be to relate input to output. Enlightenment came only in mid-century, after ethologists had demonstrated that many behavioral acts, even some of the most complex, are generated without any input at all. For organisms without a nervous system, such as house-building amoebas likę *Difflugia*, the intrinsic generation of behavior is being related to subtle patterns of timed ion-channel openings and closings. For neural organisms emergent properties, arising out of neuronal connectivity and synaptic interactions, occur in addition, but the fundamental activity remains based upon the opening and closing of specific ion channels of neuronal membrane, as well as those at synapses. Time, voltage, inorganic-, and organic-substance dependencies, themselves linked to metabolism and other aspects of intracellular chemistry, provide a constant, complex dynamism.

The biggest surprise arising as the outcome of recent detailed studies of neural networks has been the extent to which the dominant synaptic event is inhibition, not excitation as had been expected. Many neurons are powerfully active intrinsically (phylogenic mainly, but with some ontogeny) with periodicities ranging from circannual to 1 kHz, several of which may be generated in a single neuron. The evolution of nervous systems evidently proceeded by the emergence of inhibitory synapses suppressing overly eager neurons in such a way that subtle patterns of neural action are produced among them. These patterns are in turn used to generate behaviors on which natural selection operates.

Skinner's first word in the abstract (which occurs repeatedly in his text) is *responses*. How distressing! I have thought (naively?) that the whole point of Skinnerian operant conditioning (of which I have long been a disciple) is that it is the reinforcement of endogenously generated movements. The reinforcement of a *response*, by contrast, is surely classical or Pavlovian? Especially distressing is the statement "it is usually not practical to condition a complex operant by waiting for an instance to occur and then reinforcing it." Shame! I honestly thought Skinner succeeded by being a patient man. Did he then prod, cajole, provide a source for imitation, and so on? No matter. In my laboratory we have had our successes with insect operant conditioning by using a computer (fortunately they have almost infinite patience) to wait for and detect the operant.

Finally, Skinner wrote that "the contingencies responsible for unlearned behavior acted long ago," as though evolution of the mechanisms for generating endogenous behavior is somehow over, generally set for ever, so that only ontogenic variants are now relevant. I submit that in every organism, including man, there are constant gene mutations affecting neurons, circuits, modulators, transmitters, and ion channels which result in genetically determined behavioral variation. Natural selection is acting on the resulting variants in behavior right now. The genetic changes may do no more than alter the time dependencies of a single ion channel, but they could change the world.

BFS: It is no doubt regrettable that I continue to speak of operant "responses," but "actions" or acts would be confusing in other ways. As Hoyle points out, I have spent a great deal of time making clear that the etymology of "response" is irrelevant (for that matter, the etymologies of "chemistry" and "physics" are irrelevant too). In my reply to Konorski and Miller (Skinner 1937) I particularly made the point that the nature of operant reinforcement was obscured by using eliciting stimuli.

When I said that "the contingencies responsible for unlearned behavior acted long ago," I did not mean to imply that comparable contingencies were not now acting. I was speaking of the contingencies responsible for current repertoires of behavior.

With these exceptions (and the usual behavioristic caveat against speaking of "mental activity" where "behavior" would do as well) I have no quarrel with Hoyle's commentary.

The use of evolutionary analogies and the rejection of state variables by B. F. Skinner

Alejandro Kacelnik and Alasdair Houston

Edward Grey Institute of Field Ornithology, Department of Zoology, University of Oxford, England

In "Phylogeny" Skinner argues against the use of state variables such as "hunger" or "fear" as explanatory entities or causes of behaviour. His arguments are supported by making analogies between ontogenic and phylogenic formation of behavioural patterns. The ontogeny–phylogeny analogy has appeared in highly disparate contexts, from Haeckel's biogenetic law of recapitulation to Freud's (1939) attempt to reconstruct human evolutionary history from observations of emotional development of individuals or, in a rather more sophisticated way, Piaget and Garcia's (1982) study of the convergence between psychogenesis and the history of science. As Gould (1977) points out, although it is not objectionable to compare two independent processes to formulate generalizations about how complexity can be built, it is wrong to assume that a detailed correspondence is to be expected, or that the identification of an element or relation at one level must imply a counterpart at the other. We believe that Skinner has fallen into this trap.

To give an example, in his discussion of adventitious contingencies, Skinner states: "Behavior may have advantages which played no role in its selection. The converse is also true. Events which follow behavior but are not necessarily produced by it may have a selective effect." The point is illustrated by the acquisition of so-called superstitious behaviour in pigeons. It is beyond our aim here to discuss Skinner's accoun of superstitious behaviour (but see Staddon & Simmelhag 1971). Instead, we look at the evolutionary conclusion derived from this example. Basing his argument on the explicit assumption that there must be a phylogenetic parallel, Skinner suggests that there must be genetic traits that are not adaptive but are nevertheless selected. This claim is misleading. Although it is reasonable to expect that environmental transitions may cause selection to generate behaviour ill adapted to new conditions, natural selection will not produce this in globally stable environments. Notice that Skinner's argument is not about frequency variations of neutral traits, but about features that become fixated by selection because of random contingencies. If "contingency" is taken to mean differential fitness, natural selection will not favour traits that imply lower fitness. Although the analogy between evolution and learning can be dangerous, it can also be amusing. Controversies in evolution about gradual versus sudden changes (Eldredge & Gould 1972) resemble the arguments in psychology concerning gradual versus all-or-none learning (Mackintosh 1974). Also, opponents of the so-called adaptationist programme argue that developmental constraints and lack of genetic variation prevent any arbitrary phenotype being achieved (Gould & Lewontin 1979), whereas opponents of what might be called omnipotent conditioning argue that constraints on learning and lack of behaviour variation prevent any arbitrary association between reinforcement and response frequency (Hinde & Stevenson-Hinde 1973).

We agree with Skinner that it is always past events that shape behaviour as we see it, but this does not imply that notions of state are not justified. Perhaps part of Skinner's dislike of the concept of internal states comes from his linking them with "mentalistic explanations." He says that if dynamic analogies are still used in ethology, this is because of a fundamental lack of understanding of the situation. We would dispute such a view. Attempts to develop a rigorous approach to ethology regard the concept of state as fundamental. Using the framework of control theory, behaviour is seen as changing the animal's state, while the animal's state determines its behaviour (e.g., McFarland & Houston 1981).

Skinner's reference to hunger and fear serves to introduce a relevant example. Milinski and Heller (1978) and Heller and Milinski (1979) studied the foraging behaviour of sticklebacks (*Gasterosteus aculeatus*) simultaneously facing several containers with water fleas at various densities. Before the test, some fish were exposed to the silhouette of a predator (a kingfisher), and others were not. The fish that had seen a predator preferred lower densities of water fleas, a choice that presumably results in a greater chance of detecting an attacking predator, but a lower capture rate. Milinski and Heller showed that this choice is to be expected from an optimality analysis based on the combination of hunger and predation risk. Clearly the predation risk that is controlling behaviour cannot be the risk while behavior is taking place, since even from a mentalistic point of view this cannot be known to the fish, but some function of the fish's individual and phylogenetic history that correlates well with current risk. If this presumption of good correlation is followed, the ethologist can estimate the value of this function from an independent assessment of risk and can formulate accurate predictions without knowledge of past contingencies. It could be argued that complete knowledge of past contingencies would make this exercise unnecessary, but this would imply a loss of generality, since the same state might result from different histories.

In a similar example, Kacelnik, Houston, and Krebs (1981) found that the previous observation of a territorial intruder altered the foraging behaviour of great tits (*Parus major*) in a way that would make detection of new intrusions more effective. As in the previous example, it is economical and of convenient generality to model the problem by postulating a state variable that is assumed to correlate with risk of territorial intrusion instead of limiting all predictions to specifying the outcome of a particular history.

Yet another area in which the notion of state is crucial is the analysis of risk sensitivity in foraging, where risk refers to danger of starvation. Caraco (1980) argues that a foraging animal should be sensitive to the mean and variance of food rewards. Subsequent theoretical work (Houston & McNamara 1982; McNamara & Houston 1982; Stephens 1981) has shown that the behaviour that minimizes the risk of starvation depends on the animal's energy reserves. Various experiments have shown that small birds behave in the way that the theory requires, preferring variability when reserves are low with respect to what is needed to avoid starvation (e.g., Caraco 1983; Caraco, Martindale, & Whittam, 1980). These examples show both the use of state in modern ethology and the way in which optimality considerations are used. Skinner may well argue that state can be replaced by a detailed description of the history of the organism up to the time of the experiment. We would not argue with such a claim, in that a state is actually defined as a set of equivalent histories (McFarland & Houston 1981; Metz 1977). To the extent that an organism's history influences the contingencies that operate, the concept of state is logically justified and is here to stay.

BFS: Kacelnik and Houston consider the concept of state important, but whether or not it is here to stay is a question. If by state one simply means the organism as it has been affected by a given variable, I agree. I made that point nearly 50 years ago in a two-part paper called "Drive and Reflex Strength" (Skinner 1932a; 1932b). An organism that has not eaten for some time is more likely to eat. To say that the deprivation has made it hungry and that the hunger prompts it to eat adds nothing to that statement. And when additional padperties are assigned to the state, trouble arises. Do people eat because they *feel* hungry? How does hunger *prompt one* to look for food? Do starving people who eat nonnutritious materials to stop hunger pangs treat their hunger? Perhaps some single state of the organism will eventually be identified that is correlated with all the so-called manifestations of hunger, but until then it seems wise to deal with each one of them as it is observed and to deal with it as a function of an environmental variable.

As to adventitious contingencies, I have no doubt of the validity of my observations. Could there have been something wrong in the Staddon and Simmelhag (1971) experiment? In "Phylogeny" I say merely that "there is *presumably* a phylogenic parallel" (italics added). My doubt was not about the process but about the selective contingencies, which were not likely to be purely adventitious. But a variation which involved an adaptive trait adventitiously linked to a nonadaptive one could lead to the evolution of a nonadaptive trait "for adventitious reasons."

Molar concepts and mentalistic theories: A moral perspective

Stephen Kaplan

Departments of Psychology and Computer and Communication Sciences, University of Michigan

Skinner would have us discard such molar concepts as purpose, adaptation, and imitation. Although he implies that they only appear to be useful, in many contexts such concepts have proved to be not merely useful, but powerful and effective. There are many issues here; certainly misunderstandings concerning reductionism, "mentalism," and evolution deserve to be clarified. Given limited space, however, I shall leave these issues to my colleagues and focus on yet another issue, that of the moral implications of opting for theory that is molar, mentalistic, and sensitive to evolutionary factors in behavior.

Skinner is, quite properly, concerned with the moral issues implicit in the nature–nurture controversy. He cautions against a "phylogenic" approach which could "encourage a nothing-can-be-done-about-it attitude." Although Skinner's concern is commendable, his logic is backward. If indeed all human behavior is malleable through appropriate arrangement of contingencies, then we need not worry about how people are treated since we can always adjust them to fit new circumstances. It is only when we begin to understand human nature that we can meaningfully speak of constraints on how people are to be treated. Given such aspects of people that are not readily changed, it may be more appropriate to change the environment to fit people than vice versa. We may, for example, discover that people inherently dislike confusion and disorientation. It might be more humane and effective to modify the environment than to attempt to change people in this respect. The attempt to change people even though it violates their basic nature is not without precedent, even in recent times. Left-handed people still face pressures to function in the "normative" fashion; the deaf still face pressures to communicate via speech (e.g., through lip-reading) rather than by signing.

Fortunately there has been increasing interest in recent years in the appropriateness of environmental patterns to human activities and human goals. Environmental psychology, a newly developing subdiscipline, has made considerable progress in studying the impact of the physical environment; in many instances changes in design can greatly enhance human effectiveness and human satisfaction (Newman 1980). Interestingly enough, such concepts as territory, privacy, and choice figure centrally in this new research area. The very concept of human–environment compatibility (Kaplan 1983) points to the possibility of factors within humans whose identification makes possible a more penetrating analysis of environmental arrangements.

Practitioners of the "experimental analysis of behavior" are often insensitive to those human constraints that would incline one to adjust the environment rather than the organism. Perhaps one reason for this is the centrality of the laboratory in their research strategy. The nature of any organism includes inclinations and preferences hard to get at in the artificial and often coercive setting of the laboratory. Skinner questions the appropriateness of the natural setting as a context for research. On the other hand, the laboratory, a "blank room," may provide little clue as to the normal functioning of the organism. As George Schaller (1964) pointed out, people believed gorillas to be fierce and aggressive animals until field studies showed them to be gentle and docile. Their behavior in cages was apparently not indicative of their characteristics in an environment that fit them. Perhaps the radical behaviorist's inclination to believe in a "blank slate," came from too much observation of behavior in a "blank room."

Given Skinner's moral concern, his fear that we might fall into "nothing-can-be-done-about-it" patterns, he should favor molar concepts rather than criticize them. There is, as George Miller (1969) has so effectively pointed out, a danger that psychological knowledge, rather than becoming a constructive force, will fall into the hands of a few powerful and manipulative individuals. His solution to this problem is "to give psychology away," to make it as widely available as possible so that it belongs to everyone rather than a manipulative few. If this is to happen it must be in terms people can understand and use. It must, in other words, be expressed in terms of territory and communication and aggression and the other molar terms that Skinner criticizes.

There are, in fact, many well intentioned individuals shaping the human environment at this very moment. These people are administrators, policy makers, managers, designers. Unfortunately the good intentions of these individuals tend not to be backed by knowledge about people. Further facts about people are unlikely to correct the problem. To make use of such facts they need nothing less than an internal model of human behavior.

From a Skinnerian perspective such a statement undoubtedly qualifies as the ultimate in mentalism. Nonetheless, it is supported by recent developments in cognitive psychology, as well as by practical experience.

For many years the power of an internal model of the environment has been evident (Craik 1943; Gregory 1969), but until recently the concept has not been extensively used in research. Something of a breakthrough, however, has been made through application of the internal-model concept to the learning of mathematics and science on the part of grade-school children. In a stimulating and inspiring discussion of this work, Resnick (1983) pointed out that the conception of the schoolchild as a passive recipient of information is not supported by the research evidence. These children already have a model if the world, although it is admittedly intuitive and incomplete. Whatever its flaws, however, it plays a central role in meeting their need to understand what is going on around them. Their classroom efforts are best understood as a struggle to relate the new information that is presented to them to that preexisting model. The resulting accommodation is often a compromise, and a tenuous one at that. When the new perspective fails, they promptly revert to their old model. Siegler's (1983) review shows that this sort of "mentalistic" approach has made possible impressive strides in understanding the process whereby children learn arithmetic. Given the sorts of concepts that have proved fruitful here, it seems unlikely that an approach restricted to the analysis of environmental contingencies would be able to come to grips with these data.

Like grade-school children, planners, managers, and other experts also function on the basis of internal models (Kaplan 1977). Unlike grade-school children, however, one does not have control of their intellectual activities for hours each day for many years. If experts are to incorporate information about human requirements and constraints in their decision making, it must be in a form that is readily learned and easy to use. They are often eager for such information, but are unlikely to use it unless it is in a form that is sufficiently compact and intuitive that they can carry it around in their heads. Such a "portable model" (Kaplan & Kaplan 1982) not surprisingly consists of concepts at a molar level.

Thus the interest of scientific understanding and the interest of practical application will benefit from an approach to human behavior that is sensitive to evolutionary constraints, open to "mentalistic" (or, as we would now speak of them, "cognitive") perspectives, and free of even a trace of prejudice against molar concepts.

BFS: I am sorry to contradict Kaplan, but I do not ask behavioral scientists to discard "molar concepts" such as adaptation or imitation, or theories sensitive to evolutionary factors in behavior. I do not advise violating the basic nature of people. I am quite willing to speak of preferences and inclinations if those terms are defined (as they may quite easily be) in behaviora terms. I have dealt at length with the question of who is to control behavior and to what effect (see "Consequences" and my book *Beyond Freedom and Dignity*, 1971).

I am not sure what Kaplan means when he says that "practitioners of the experimental analysis of behavior' are often insensitive to those human constraints that would incline one to adjust the environment rather than the organism." Is he recommending adjusting the environment or the organism? If he means the latter and the molar concepts he speaks of in his commentary, I should be interested to see how he proposes to adjust them without changing the environment.

In arguing that cognitive psychology offers terms that can be used to give psychology away, Kaplan may be right. These are the terms which have been used by "administrators, policy makers, managers, [and] designers" for thousands of years. But to offer them cognitive psychology is to give psychology away in another sense – to reveal the secret that cognitive psychology has nothing of any value beyond laymanship. The practical applications of the experimental analysis of behavior are to date far more impressive. That is particularly true in education. While "impressive strides in understanding the process whereby children learn arithmetic" have been made to the satisfaction of cognitive psychologists, children have been *taught* arithmetic in highly efficient ways through programmed instruction.

B. F. Skinner and the flaws of sociobiology

Anthony J. Perzigian

Departments of Anthropology and Anatomy, University of Cincinnati

Nearly two decades have passed since Skinner's "Phylogeny" originally appeared. This work remains a timely and timeless reminder of the intractabilities of behavioral studies. It is timely because his insights into phylogeny have clear implications for modern sociobiology; it is timeless since a full and satisfying decipherment of the ontogenic and phylogenic contingencies responsible for behavior continues to be scientifically elusive. Skinner effectively portrayed this elusiveness; nevertheless, those scholars who have hastily penned their sociobiological pronouncements either do not appreciate or choose to ignore his message. With a disregard for the immense uncertainties of disentangling ontogenic and phylogenic contingencies, sociobiologists have unflinchingly gravitated toward phylogenic explanations for various behaviors. A good example of reckless "phylogeneticizing" is Wilson's (1978) *On Human Nature*. It would thus appear that Skinner's cogent plea for more rigorous analysis of ontogenic and phylogenic contingencies went largely unheeded in some circles.

In addressing the difficult problems raised by phylogenic contingencies, Skinner, in 1966, certainly articulated and perhaps even anticipated the fundamental criticisms directed at modern sociobiology. For example, he noted that "natural selection of a given form of behavior, no matter how plausibly argued, remains an inference." Nevertheless, contemporary sociobiologists typically offer such seductively simple and evolutionarily plausible explanations for behavior that we can easily forget Skinner's reminder that those "explanations" are essentially only inferences. Wilson's (1978) sociobiological explanation for human religious behavior is an illustration. Given the ubiquity of human religious behavior. Wilson argues for its phylogenetic underpinnings. He notes that "predisposition to religious belief...is... an ineradicable part of human nature" (p. 169) and that "the highest forms of religious practice...can be seen to confer biological advantage" (p. 188). In short,

Wilson and others idly speculate on the inaccessible and remote past and then conjure up adaptive, genetic explanations for human behavior. Again, Skinner pointed out in 1966 that the phylogenic provenance of behavior is not only deeply concealed by time but also obscured or even suppressed by ontogenic contingencies. Whereas Wilson can make a claim for the adaptive and selective value of an adherence to religious beliefs, Skinner, in contradistinction, notes that "we cannot tell from the mere fact that behavior is adaptive which kind of process [i.e., phylogenic or ontogenic] has been responsible for it."

As Skinner implies, the phylogenic infrastructure of behavior is incontestable. He notes, also, that specific characteristics of behavior, for example imitation, aggression, and territoriality, seem to be common products of phylogenic and ontogenic contingencies. However, tracing that tortuous pathway from base pairs to behavior is like untying the Gordian knot. If, as he suggests, phylogenic contingencies were selectively favored if the organism showed an extensive, undifferentiated repertoire, then the resultant ontogenic malleability will forever shroud phylogenic provenance. Will our understanding of behavior ever expand beyond such conclusions as that *Homo sapiens* has an inherited capacity for aggression, or, as Skinner states, that a parrot's imitative calls stem from an "inherited capacity to be reinforced by hearing itself produce familiar sounds?" Let me suggest that behavioral scientists and sociobiologists, who together rarely deal with specific genes, need to apply and embrace more effectively Waddington's (1957) concept of "epigenetic landscape." Here, at least, we have a potentially useful model for dealing with phylogenic–ontogenic contingencies. Fishbein (1976), for example, implemented the Waddington model in a study of children's learning and development.

Finally, as Skinner points out, the very remoteness of phylogenic contingencies provides ineluctible difficulty in determining the provenance of behavior. This difficulty is potentially magnified by the implications of Gould and Vrba's (1982) concept of "exaptation." They define exaptations as those features that now enhance a species' fitness but were not built directly by natural selection for their current role. The older term, adaptation, is thus reserved for any feature built directly by selection for its current role. To illustrate exaptation, they use the evolution of birds. The current function of feathers for flight may not have been the original purpose. Paleontologic data suggest that the initial development of feathers was probably for insulation and thermoregulation. Exaptations thus begin as adaptations for other functions in ancestors and are later coopted for their current use. Gould and Vrba primarily address anatomical features; nevertheless, their notion of exaptation would seem to have implications for the study of phylogenic behavior. That virtual inextractability of phylogenic provenance is further emphasized if phylogenic behaviors like morphologic structures can also be exaptations. This is all the more reason to heed Skinner's appeal for more specific analysis of those contingencies that underlie behavior.

BFS: Perzigian brings "Phylogeny" up to date with respect to sociobiology. The ubiquity of religions (like the ubiquity of the universals of grammar to which Chomsky appeals) is a product of cultural evolution. All languages and all religions serve similar functions, but at the level of the operant behavior of the individual and the survival of the group. A god, usually patterned after a king or father, is someone to ask for help and to thank for favors when no one else is available. He (not she!) is the punisher to whom the group turns to keep the individual in line. Among the advantages of a culture (and hence of the species) is peaceful behavior and mutual aid. Among the disadvantages is religious warfare.

The exaptations of Gould and Vrba (1982) to which Perzigian refers should not be confused with the effects of adventitious contingencies as exemplified n "superstitious" operant behavior and less clearly (or possibly not at all) in natural selection when a nonadaptive trait is carried by an adaptive one.

I welcome Perzigian's call for a more vigorous joint exploration of these ssues.

Hereditary ≠ innate

Robert Plomin and Denise Daniels

Institute for Behavioral Genetics, University of Colorado

In drawing an analogy between natural selection and operant conditioning, Skinner frequently uses the word *heredity* as if it were synonymous with *innate*, *phylogenetic*, and *unlearned*. *Ontogenetic* is equated with *learned*. The point of this commentary is to emphasize that Skinner addresses average differences between species, not differences among individuals within a species. *Heredity* usually refers to the latter. Genetic contributions to behavioral variability among individuals are the focus of an entire field of research, behavioral genetics, which Skinner does not mention even though he asks the question, "Why does an organism behave in a given way at a given time?" and answers it by saying that "very little has been done in studying the genetics of behavior in this sense." We disagree with this answer.

Why *Homo sapiens* talks and walks bipedally are interesting questions, but they refer only to universal or average features of our species. Another set of questions with considerable social importance concerns differences among individuals within a species – why some people are more fluent verbally than others, why some children are reading disabled, why some individuals are gifted athletically, and why some are particularly aggressive. These views – intergroup universals and intragroup individual differences – are perspectives and, as such, are not right or wrong: They are more or less useful in understanding specific problems. Most important is the need to be clear about which question one is addressing, and Skinner's "Phylogeny" clouds the distinction by using the word *heredity* in the context of genetic *constants* produced at the phylogenetic level by natural selection, rather than using heredity in its usual sense: genetic transmission of *deviations* such as deviations in height, eye color, and psychopathology from one generation to the next. The distinction is important because causal factors explaining average differences between species are not necessarily related to the causes of individual differences within a species. For example, genetics, part of our phylogenetic conditioning, might be responsible for the fact that *Homo sapiens* is a natural user of language as compared to other primate species. However, differences among people in verbal fluency, reading ability, and disability, and the ability to learn additional languages could be independent of genetic differences among individuals.

It is interesting that, early in his career, Skinner evidenced an interest in genetic differences among individuals within a species. For example, he described his experiences with inbred strains of rats:

> As soon as I brought them into my new laboratory, I began to see...many genetic differences....One strain was so wild that it had to be handled with forceps, but another could be held loosely in the hand. One strain would immediately leap out of a shallow box in which another would remain indefinitely. (Skinner 1979, p. 36)

One of Skinner's few unsuccessful experiments involved an attempt to violate genetic principles: "I tried a Lamarckian experiment. I thought it worthwhile to see whether they [pigeons] had inherited any tendency to strike a target to which their parents had responded vigorously for many months. . . . But neither bird pecked the plate at all" (1979, p. 280).

Although some of the issues raised by Skinner in the context of ethology and average differences among species could also be raised in relation to behavioral variability within a species, it is clear that Skinner's arguments are aimed at the level of average differences among species: why the African honey guide leads people to bees' nests or why chicks follow an imprinted object. We agree with Skinner who indicates "how hard it is to detect the nature and effect of phylogenic contingencies" which is why, for example, the controversy about the provenances of human language has persisted. In contrast, the study of individual differences within a species has at its disposal methodologies to untangle the roles of nature and nurture – heredity and environment – in the etiology of differences among individuals in a species (Plomin, DeFries, & McClearn 1980).

Studies employing these behavioral genetic methods have demonstrated that genetic variance accounts for a significant portion of variance observed for diverse behavioral characters in fruitflies (for example, activity, geotaxis, phototaxis, mating speed), in mice (performance in learning tasks, alcohol responses, reactivity, social behavior), and in human beings (cognitive abilities such as verbal and spatial ability, temperament such as shyness and emotionality, and psychopathology including schizophrenia and manic-depressive psychosis). Behavioral genetics does not study universals, either genetic constants that are shared by all members of a species or environmental constants such as oxygen, sunlight, or the law of effect which is the essence of operant conditioning. As a first step in understanding the provenances of individual differences within a species, behavioral genetics asks the extent to which observed behavioral differences among individuals can be ascribed to genetic sources of variance and then ascribes the rest of the variance to environmental – more specifically, nongenetic – factors. Behavioral genetics thus describes the functional relationship between genes and behavior without specifying the processes by which genetic variability surfaces in the form of behavioral differences among individuals; this is much like the attempt of operant conditioning to describe the functional relationship between environmental contingencies of reinforcement and behavior without specifying the physiological events that mediate the relationship. In some cases, the links between genes and behavior might be hard wired, relatively impervious to environmental perturbations. In most cases, however, behavioral genetics data demonstrate that environmental variation plays a significant role in producing the behavioral variability we observe. Operant conditioners rarely study the sources of differences among individuals, assuming that such differences are brought about by differing reinforcement histories and being content to change behavior regardless of its provenance. Because cures are not necessarily related to causes, this puts operant conditioning in the position of focusing on intervention rather than prevention (Plomin 1985). Regarding the causes of change within individuals, it should be noted that genetic influence can also be responsible for change. Evidence is now emerging (Plomin 1983) that indicates that genes turn on and off during development, and thus genes can explain change as well as continuity during development.

Although the distinction between the perspectives of intergroup universals and intragroup variability is critical in discussions of phylogeny and ontogeny, we do not mean to imply that behavioral genetics and operant conditioning are in opposition. In October 1983, a conference was sponsored by the National Institute of Child Health and Human Development to bring together researchers interested in the relationship between behavioral genetics and operant conditioning. Although i would be difficult to pick two fields in the behavioral sciences farther apart concep tually and methodologically than behavioral genetics and operant conditioning, interaction between the two fields is most likely to take place at the interface of individual differences in learning. Operant conditioning provides sensitive measures of learning processes; behavioral genetics offers tools for untangling genetic and environmental differences as they affect interindividual differences in learning.

In summary, Skinner distinguishes phylogenic and ontogenic provenances. Phylogeny usually refers to species universals even though natural selection also plays a role in maintaining variability within a species. Ontogeny refers to development and is used both in the sense of universals and in the sense of individual differences. The distinction between universals and individual differences must be crossed with Skinner's distinction between phylogenic and ontogenic provenances if we are to be clear in our discussions of the effects of environmental contingencies and genetic factors on behavioral development.

BFS: It is true that I was addressing "average differences between species, not differences [of phylogenic origin] among individuals within a species." There are no doubt purposes for which it is worthwhile to do the latter. Variations may reach only part of the population of a species. But they presumably do so only because of genetic transmissions, and the results are therefore properly called phylogenic.

I would not quarrel with reserving *heredity* for features common to individuals or small groups, but I am not sure that verbal behavior is a good example. Homo sapiens is distinguished from all other species by the speed with which its vocal behavior can be modified through operant conditioning. A very important genetic change must have occurred to make that possible, and if we compare the species with its nearest relatives it would appear that the change came relatively late. Can we be sure that the variations have yet reached all members of the species? Or is some small part of the subtle anatomical and physiological requirements still missing upon occasion?

I cannot agree that operant conditioning focuses on "intervention rather than prevention." In solving a behavior problem that appears to be due to a history of reinforcement, the operant conditioner may intervene by arranging conditions in which the behavior is extinguished or in which incompatible behavior is strengthened. That is intervention. But the main thrust of applied behavior analysis is preparation for an effective future, part of which could be called prevention.

Nature and nurture revisited

H. C. Plotkin

Department of Psychology, University College London, England

The controversy over heredity and environment, represented in the target article by phylogeny and ontogeny, is not primarily a matter concerning the practical control of behaviour, which is what Skinner asserts. It is a theoretical issue of deep importance to behavioral science. Nor, contrary to innumerable claims over the last few decades, has the problem been solved or the issue resolved by interactionist accounts.

Interactionism implies two or more separate factors that interact to result in some outcome. This is an incorrect conception of the nature–nurture problem. To draw a none too adequate analogy from computer science, ontogeny and phylogeny bear to one another the relationship of routine and subroutine, with the one nested under the other. A case can be made for either being the main routine, although traditionalists would vote phylogeny into that role. Some epigeneticists (Ho & Saunders 1979; 1982; Johnston & Gottlieb 1981; Piaget 1979) would disagree. But I stress that the analogy is weak. The real relationship between ontogeny and phylogeny involves each being simultaneously main routine and subroutine. Phylogeny is partly caused by a succession of ontogenies, and ontogeny is partly caused by phylogeny. Biology does not yet have an adequate language for describing this complex causal nexus, and biologists are certainly not conceptually at ease with it. But Waddington exhorted us "to think in terms of circular and not merely unidirectional causal sequences" (Waddington 1960, p. 401), and indeed we must do so. Causes are consequences and consequences are causes. Ontogeny is both caused and causal. When it is viewed as caused, then one of those causes is its nested relationship to phylogeny (Plotkin & Odling-Smee 1979; 1981). For this reason there is no behaviour, including learned behaviour, that is solely ontogenetic in origin. All behaviour is both ontogenetically and phylogenetically caused. Thus there can be no valid either–or arguments for the provenance of behaviour. Skinner's analysis, it seems to me, is invalid precisely because it is based on a sometimes explicit, always implicit, either–or argument.

As regards the way in which a form of explanation (in this case evolutionary events buried in the past of a species) relates to some kind of empirical programme, evolutionary events do have an accessible, laboratory-based, experimental, getatable programme. It is called genetics. There is nothing dubious or mysterious about behaviour genetics. Skinner knows, surely, that when one refers to the web-spinning instinct of a spider, what that means is that the cause of that behaviour is partly to be found in the genetic constitution of that spider; and spiders who do not spin webs will have a different genetic constitution from those that do. There is no need to speculate on the history of natural selection acting on a range of web-spinning spider phenotypes, though it may be of theoretical interest to do so. Insofar as phylogeny is causal, and it always is to some degree, those causes are to be understood in genetic terms. It is simply incorrect to say that phylogenetic contingencies are empirically less accessible (if not wholly inaccessible) than ontogenetic contingencies. They are merely different and require different methodologies.

Throughout "Phylogeny" there runs a constant thread. This is the notion of learning by operant reinforcement. Skinner seems to believe that it is the most important, if not the sole, form of learning – presumably in all species that do learn. Early in the article he claims that "what we may call the ontogeny of behavior is thus traced to contingencies of reinforcement." Circular definitions linking behavioural ontogeny and operant learning aside, does Skinner really mean what he seems to be saying? Does he believe that behavioural development is explicable entirely, or even in large part, only in terms of operant learning? What exactly is one to make of the effects of, say, low-level lead (Pb) exposure, or exposure to any other toxin, on the development of behaviour in children? How does one account for the findings of the effects of specific visual environments on the subsequent visually guided behaviour of kittens (Hirsh & Jacobson 1975)? Or of maternal deprivation on subsequent social behaviour in macaque monkeys (Mineka & Suomi 1978)? How does one account for the effects of malnutrition on a wide range of behaviours in a wide range of species? Or for the development of song in songbirds? The developmental and general experimental journals are full of such findings, and so the list can be made very long. None appears to involve operant reinforcement. In some instances, as in the effects of temperature on the way *Drosophila* develop the behaviour of flight, the attempt to account for the consequences to behavioural development of some condition in terms of operant reinforcement becomes downright absurd.

Finally, it is difficult not to respond with personal comment when the essay is pervaded by the royal "we," as in "In ontogenic behavior we no longer say." But the 'we" refers to a very small section of the scientific community interested in and working on behaviour. And the whole stance of "Phylogeny," that curious mix of Puritan inductivism and intellectual imperialism that marked the "experimental analysis of behaviour" in the 1960s, is strangely out of place now. Cognitivism is rampant, even if not triumphant. The "experimental analysis of behaviour" has not generated a flood of new journals and books in the way that cognitive science has. The "experimental analysis of behaviour" does not have the ear of the artificial intelligence people in the way that the cognitivists have. The "experimental analysis of behaviour" has not contributed to the language and thinking of behavioural biology in the way that cognitivism has. By these measures, Skinner and his followers have failed. They did not convince a significant number of behavioural scientists that theirs was the way. The fault may, of course, lie with the majority. But it may also be due to the narrowness of vision and conceptual inadequacies of the "experimental analysis of behaviour." What does Skinner himself think?

BFS: In challenging my belief that behavioral development is explicable entirely, or even in large part, in terms of operant learning, Plotkin cites three kinds of studies:

1. The effects of low-level lead and other toxins and of malnutrition on the development of behavior. (But certainly it is no threat to the validity of a process to show that it can be physiologically damaged.)
2. The effects of early visual experiences of kittens and early maternal deprivation in monkeys. (But terms like exposure and deprivation lack specificity. What did the kittens and monkeys do or not do?)
3. Bird song and the flight of *Drosophila*. (These may be modified by operant conditioning, but they are primarily phylogenic.)

Nothing in that list shakes my faith in operant conditioning. (As for Pavlovian conditioning and other processes, see my other replies, especially to Eysenck.)

Plotkin objects to my use of the royal "we," or as we should say in America, the editorial "we." As an example he gives "In ontogenic behavior we no longer say." The experimental analysis of behavior is, he thinks, a "curious mix of Puritan inductivism and intellectual imperialism" and holds that it is now strangely out of place. "Cognitivism is rampant, even if not triumphant." In favor of cognitive psychology is a flood of new journals and the attention of artificial intelligence people and behavioral biologists. I shall not go into my own reasons for the popularity of cognitive psychology. It has nothing to do with scientific advances but rather with the release of the floodgates of mentalistic terms fed by the tributaries of philosophy, theology, history, letters, media, and worst of all, the English language.

Is evolution of behavior operant conditioning writ large?

Anatol Rapoport

Institute for Advanced Studies, Vienna, Austria

Demystification is an important component of the enlightenment imparted by science. This is not to say that the scientific mode of cognition is incompatible with the sort of "mystical feelings" attested to by some outstanding scientists when confronted with the immensities of the cosmos – feelings that stem from an aesthetic sense. What the insights imparted by science dispel are perplexities and superstitious fears (or awe, if you will) traceable directly to ignorance. Foremost among the conceptions of our world that science tirelessly demolishes is animism.

Along with wills and goals attributed to forces of nature and inanimate objects, teleology, a more abstract form of animism, has been under steady attack by proponents of the analytic view in the philosophy of science. Whether causation can beckon from ahead instead of pushing from behind is a question posed in the language of metaphysics, hence unanswerable in the scientific mode. It is a matter of record, however, that alleged examples of teleological causation have been reduced to ordinary causation that can be described in analytic terms, that is, as a set of conditions at some specified time that imply an expected set of conditions at a later time. The confirmation of the expectations lends credence to the scientific explanation of the events.

This approach pervades the natural selection theory of biological evolution and has been extended to a behavioristic theory of learning, from which "mentalistic" concepts are deliberately excluded. Perhaps the greatest intellectual dividend of this approach has been a synthesis of theories of phylogenic and ontogenic development of behavior. In the light of this synthesis, the phylogeny of learning can be seen as an analogue of ontogeny stretched over millions of generations. Indeed, the shaping of behavior, as in operant conditioning, can be regarded as a "natural selection" of facilitated neural pathways, reinforcement as an analogue of a favorable procreation ratio, inhibition as an analogue of extinction.

Both the theory of natural selection and the reinforcement theory of behavior are based on an analogous pair of assumptions. Behavioral units selected for in phylogeny must have been present, at least minimally, in the genetic pool of the evolving species. The behavioral unit learned in progressive conditioning must already have been present, at least minimally, in the behavioral repertoire of the learning organism. This latter assumption is convincingly supported by demonstrations of operant conditioning, as most complex forms of behavior are synthesized from simple ones before our eyes, as it were. Here is demystification in its most dramatic manifestation.

I sometimes indulge in a fantasy, I imagine seeing my direct ancestors assembled. Assuming 25 years to be the average length of a human generation, I would see a Jew in 17th-century garb already among the first dozen ancestors. Among 100, I would perhaps see some speaking Akkadian. In a crowd that can easily fit into a medium-sized auditorium, perhaps half might be cave dwellers. In a stadium full of ancestors, most would not be human. And so on to fishes, trilobites, and protozoa, all observable in a crowd that could be spanned by sight.

Suppose now all of these ancestors passed in front of me, at first rapidly (the protozoa could move at a million per second), then more and more slowly at a rate inversely related to the rate of evolutionary modification. Viewing the process, which would take no more than a few months, would be analogous to viewing an experiment in operant conditioning of comparable duration. If I were to witness it (I would give a lot to be able to do so), I could see how "I" with all my behavior patterns, predilections, "ideas", and so on (may Professor Skinner forgive the use of a mentalistic term) was "put together" from those primitive beginnings. It is just such a process that the demystifiers of "instincts" (Skinner foremost among them) wish us to magine.

If, as I assume, demystification should be welcomed, the fantasy is an attractive one. There remains, however, the nagging question of whether there has been enough time for the imagined events to occur. The greatest difficulty is to account for the incompletely synthesized phases of an unlearned fully adaptive behavior. As pointed out above, the components of behavior patterns selected for must have already been in the genetic pool of the species. We must therefore justify on adaptive grounds a bird's flying about for a million years or so with a twig in its beak before it "gets the idea" of using it in building its nest. We must suppose that the behavioral repertoire of the working bee at some time contained not only a tendency to orient its dance so as to indicate the direction of the food but also to orient it in every other conceivable way. If we suppose, as Skinner suggests, that different bees may have at first behaved in different ways and that more effective ways were selected for, we face the task of explaining genetic selection of a worker bee's behavior, since the worker bee has no progeny – the crushing argument against the doctrine of transmission of acquired characteristics. Of course we could argue that the germ plasm of the bee was progressively modified, so that more and more bees came to respond properly to phototropic stimuli, and (at the same time, be it noted) more and more came to respond properly to the dance of the foragers. The trouble is that ingenious arguments of this sort tend to make explanations of unlearned behavior in terms of natural selection unfalsifiable. In the case of operant conditioning, the synthesis of complex forms of behavior has actually been demonstrated, for which Skinner justly deserves his reputation as one of the greatest experimental psychologists of our age. In the context of phylogeny, we can only exercise our imagination, and we cannot evade the question of whether there has been enough time. The question will not go away. After all, if there were enough time, the method of random permutations would with certainty eventually produce all the works of Shakespeare and of everyone else, for that matter, both written and unwritten. This is not to repeat the naive arguments of creationists about the a priori improbability of complex structures or patterns. The *conditional* probabilities of successive modifications surely reduce the required time scale by many orders of magnitude. But do they reduce it enough to make all the marvelous results of evolution fit into even the most liberal estimate of the time since the creation of the universe?

Some estimation of orders of magnitude of time required for a credible explanation of "instincts" in terms of natural selection should be assigned a high priority as a problem of theoretical biology.

BFS: "Has there been enough time?," asks Rapoport. Anyone who has thought much about evolution must have struggled with that nagging question. It is the kind of question one would rather forget than answer, but Rapoport's commentary brings it starkly to our attention. He is certainly right that it should be assigned a high priority. Perhaps the behavioral geneticists who are bringing about evolutionary changes will be able to help. Unfortunately, it is not so much a matter of the selection which follows when contingencies are arranged as the provenance of the contingencies.

I am not quite sure I understand Rapoport's paragraph about teleology, but a discussion of that point would be more appropriate in connection with "Consequences."

Skinner's practical metaphysic may be impractical

S. N. Salthe

Department of Biology, Brooklyn College, City University of New York

According to Skinner (using his 1981 "Consequences," [this volume] to interpret his 1966 "Phylogeny"), the form of a system is a selective expression of environmental contingencies, selected by well-understood mechanisms from a system-generated, variable, "relatively undifferentiated" repertoire. The environmental contingencies are more informative of the result than is the intrinsic repertoire. The intrinsic repertoire itself has in any case a form that reflects past environmental contingencies, which are now lost to inspection and manipulation – mere "plausible inferences." Reifying this intrinsic repertoire with concepts like "structure" or "stored information" ("insight," "instinct," "disposition") brings us no closer to the mechanisms by which it was generated and tends to focus our attention on these relatively trivial entities (operant units) rather than upon the process of generating them, which is more important because we can harness it in our own interests.

Ironically, this view is largely isomorphic with that now called the panselectionist view of evolutionary biology, which tends to ignore intrinsic "developmental constraints" in generating its adaptive scenarios (e.g., Bonner 1982). Yet it was in argument against essentially this same selectionist viewpoint that the 1966 paper was launched. But Skinner has no quarrel with the process of natural selection, other than the impossibility of observing or interfering with its erstwhile production of the biological repertoires now in place.

There are four points in Skinner's thought on these matters that I would like to mark:

1. He plays down the importance of intrinsic constraints in favor of environmental ones. This is essentially a systems-theoretic move, leading us to examine the behavior of black boxes in some environment. From this perspective experimental environments are just as interesting as "natural" ones, having all the same formal properties with the added boon of being at least in part under our own control (he is no naturalist). Skinner does not go on to consider the forms of experimental environments as themselves the results of selective contingencies, but behaviorist preoccupation with experimental design is no doubt a circuitous way of struggling with this concept.

2. In this connection, Skinner's zeal to eschew intrinsic factors leads him to make the extraordinary suggestion that the current environments of the organisms in a given species are more or less standardized, and so there is no need to consider intrinsic constraints inherited in common to explain behaviors that are species specific and evinced by all of its parts. Hence, these contingencies are not really contingent, being regularities. This attitude is directly in conflict with the neo-Darwinian interpretation of synthetic evolutionary theory, which insists upon *chance* contingencies at all levels. This attitude also has implications for the reality of higher-level forms. If they exist, were they also the results of some process of selection by contingencies? I wonder how far Skinner would be willing to push this notion – or was it really only a contingent move in the flow of argument?

3. Skinner's identification of intrinsic constraints as mere outcomes of earlier selective events brings us squarely to the issue of levels of organization, faced more directly by him in "Consequences." He views relevant processes at different levels as being structurally isomorphic and argues that we can better focus upon that structure if we confine our observations to those operating at a scale closer to our own immediate observational processes. In his view "phylogenic contingencies" defeat or enhance different products of ontogenetic contingencies (expressions of the "rela

tively undifferentiated" repertoire), whereas "ontogenetic contingencies" regulate the products (intrinsic stored information) of the action of phylogenetic contingencies. We must eventually deal with the fact that defeating or enhancing (selecting) and regulating (conditioning, etc.) here take place at different organizational levels, even though they are formally similar. Skinner's suggestion appears to be that we forget the higher-level process and focus only on those more readily accessible to us.

4. Skinner's preference for the language of process over the language of entities appears to be an attempt, rather in conflict with the systems flavor of most of his convictions, to reduce phenomena to simpler components, seeking "basic processes." Thus, "instinct" can be reduced to "operants," "conditioning," and so forth. Presumably the ultimate goal of such a replacement of metaphors in the present context might be to converge upon some sort of machine language. I think, however, that Skinner would not want to push that far down since the style of discourse he favors is eminently conducive to practical control and appears to him already to be at hand with "operants" and the like. In other words, his reductionism here was probably more a rhetorical device made in a time susceptible to it than a metaphysical commitment.

I believe that what best characterizes Skinner's viewpoint is that the urgent purpose of science is practical manipulation, and once that appears to be a possibility no further theoretical work is required in an area (in this and other more proximate views, including 1 above, he has interesting points of convergence with many Marxists). The often-pointed-out problem with this view emerges primarily in contemplating practical applications. What portion of the Gross National Product would it take to make sunbirds or weaver finches lead anyone to honey? Even if it is some noncontingent aspect of the honey guides' environment that conditions them to perform this work, the cost of trying to find the right environment to induce this in the other kinds of birds would probably be prohibitive. Leaving aside the power of intrinsic (genetic and developmental) constraints, this is because environments and their organisms are not readily separable (Lewontin 1982; Patten 1982).

BFS: I agree with Salthe that experimental environments are themselves the result of selective contingencies, but I do not agree that my "behaviorist preoccupation with experimental design is no doubt a circuitous way of struggling with this concept." As I have often said, the behavior of scientists is shaped by their subject matters. My rats and pigeons have changed my behavior as much as I have changed theirs. What my experimental animals have done is responsible for the design of further research and the analysis of the data. I do not suggest that "we forget the higher-level process and focus only on those more readily accessible to us."

If a comparison between natural selection and operant conditioning is at all relevant, it would not follow that in a standardized environment "there is no need to consider intrinsic constraints inherited in common to explain behaviors that are species specific and evinced by all of its parts. Hence, these contingencies are not really contingent, being regularities." But contingencies work to maintain as well as to produce.

I see nothing reductionistic about my analysis. I do not say "that 'instinct' can be reduced to 'operants,' 'conditioning,' and so forth." Instinct is a presumed entity resulting from natural selection, not the process itself or the selective contingencies responsible for it. It is analogous to habit, which

Salthe might better have used but which also represents a supposed product or entity rather than process.

(I am puzzled by Salthe's treatment of "Phylogeny" as a kind of verbal dance. Something I say may be due to "a contingent move in the flow of argument," "a style of discourse [I favor]," or "more a rhetorical device... than a metaphysical commitment.")

Reinforcement is the problem, not the solution: Variation and selection of behavior

J. E. R. Staddon

Department of Psychology, Duke University

The major contribution of "Phylogeny" is to emphasize the similarities between phylogeny and ontogeny. In both, adaptiveness comes about because of what Skinner terms "contingencies" – predictive relations between some aspect of behavior and a consequence: "survival" (differential reproduction) for "phylogenic contingencies," and "reinforcement" for "ontogenic" ones.

This resemblance between Darwinian selection and learning through reward and punishment has been noted before by Spencer and others after him (see Campbell 1960). To these earlier accounts. Skinner adds theoretical analyses of some examples – imprinting, the bee dance, the behavior of the honey guide – and his own view of the process of operant conditioning and the special terminology – of operants, of discriminative versus eliciting stimuli, of frequency and probability of response, and the like – that appertains thereto.

The essence of Darwin's theory is of course not selection alone, but the interplay between selection and (heritable) variation. The major flaw in Skinner's approach is that he unnecessarily plays down the role of (behavioral) variation. A positive message that can be drawn from his analyses of particular examples is that species-specific behavior, often equated with "instinct," may nevertheless involve learning. Skinner's insistance on a behavioristic vocabulary, whose terms are often obscure, and his attacks on apparently mentalistic terms (which can often be given perfectly objective interpretations), seem unnecessarily restrictive today. His analysis of so-called superstitious behavior no longer commands universal assent. I take up each of these points in turn.

Certain words, such as "dimension" and "probability," play key roles, yet are never adequately defined. For example, Skinner writes "the behavior observed in mazes and similar apparatuses may be 'objective,' but it is not described in dimensions which yield a meaningful genetic picture." What is the meaning of *dimensions* here? The biologist might interpret the term as an oblique reference to the mechanisms, developmental and physiological, that permit some particular behavior to occur under specified circumstances: Genes guide development, both directly and by determining the effects of environment. Presumably a "meaningful genetic picture" must include some notion of how genes affect development in such a way as to permit the occurrence of the target behavior. But Skinner's conclusion is very different. He sees *probability of response* as the dimension that "yield[s] a meaningful genetic picture." I cannot imagine what this statement would mean to a developmental biologist. I cannot see what possible link Skinner himself sees between probability of response, however assessed, and genetics. The concept of response probability recurs frequently, is never defined, and seems to have a special significance. "A behavioral process, as a change in frequency of response, can be followed only if it is possible to count responses" – so much for bird-song learning, orientation, and the learning of bees. The words "probability" and "dimension" seem to have acquired for Skinner an almost talismanic property that makes further inquiry into their meaning unnecessary, if not improper – and rules out any other way of looking at behavioral processes.

Skinner is unduly harsh on anything that smacks of mentalism. For example, he criticizes Tinbergen (1953) for asserting that herring gulls "lack...insight into the ends served by their activities." Yet Tinbergen's remark is susceptible of a perfectly objective interpretation: He asserts merely that the act will continue even if its usual consequence does not follow, and will not be modified if the usual relation between act and consequence is interfered with in other ways. In Skinner's terms, Tinbergen is merely saying that the herring gull's behavior is controlled by the situation and not by its consequences.

Skinner goes on to discuss the fascinating relations between nature and nurture, between habit – the product of learning – and instinct, the product of phylogeny. He sees, with Pascal, a resemblance between the two, a more sophisticated and correct view than the old dichotomy between learning and instinct. But he goes no further than to assimilate habit and instinct by pointing to the similar "contingencies" responsible for each. The notion that habits and instincts may be related because one is built from ingredients provided by the other – as the sheepdog trainer builds on a repertoire delivered to him by nature in the form of "herding," "circling," and other elements shown by the young sheepdog without special training – finds no place in Skinner's analysis. On the contrary, in discussing the "origins of [behavioral] variations" Skinner explicitly discounts the possibility that nature provides anything in the way of structure: "Both phylogenic and ontogenic contingencies 'shape' complex forms of behavior from relatively undifferentiated material. Both processes are favored if the organism shows an extensive, undifferentiated repertoire." This view is true neither of ontogeny nor of phylogeny: "Punctuated equilibrium" is now a respected view, and whatever the details, it seems clear that sharp and constrained changes play an important if not dominant role in macroevolution (see Raff & Kaufman 1983). Similarly, species and even individual differences in learning abilities rule out Skinner's view that behavioral repertoires exist before operant conditioning only in the form of "minimal units." Much work on animal learning in recent years has focused on innate repertoires and their differential susceptibility to different kinds of operant and classical conditioning (see Garcia, Clarke, & Hankins 1973; Holland 1977; Shettleworth 1975; Staddon 1983).

Moreover, exclusive reliance on "undifferentiated material" makes no adaptive sense. An animal's phylogeny can tell it much about which class of activities is most likely to be useful in securing particular kinds of "reinforcers." It would be strange indeed if animals reacted identically to signals for food and sex, for example. When Skinner is "shaping" one of his pigeons, the first food delivery defines the situation for the animal as one in which food-related activities are much more likely than agonistic or sexual ones. Skinner must build up the target behavior out of these far from arbitrary ingredients, not from "undifferentiated material."

A key role in Skinner's scheme is played by what he terms *adventitious contingencies*. He draws an interesting parallel between the "superstitious" behavior shown by hungry pigeons given periodic free food, and the "useless structures" that are "selected" by accidental contingencies during phylogeny. This comparison is instructive because it shows up an inconsistency in Skinner's view of contingency. On the one hand, he writes "We do not explain any system of behavior simply by demonstrating that it works to the advantage of...the individual or species. It is necessary to show that a given advantage is contingent upon behavior in such a way as to alter its probability." It is hard to be certain what this last sentence means, but given the usual meaning of contingency, it implies that we must demonstrate a real causal connection between the behavior and its beneficial consequence, Darwinian fitness or reinforcement, if the consequence is to be used as an explanation for the behavior. Yet in the next paragraph Skinner is explaining superstitious behavior by reference to "adventitious" contingencies, that is, accidental response-reinforcer conjunctions without causal significance.

Once again, evolutionary theory provides a better account. Darwin's "useless structures," the vermiform appendix and the like, are explained, not by selection, but by *variation*, that is, by constraints on developmental mechanisms. Constraints act either to force development of one structure when selection favors another (epistasis; see Mayr 1963), or to maintain a structure after selection for it has ceased. Selection (current selection, at least), by definition, plays no role. Similarly, superstitious behavior is best explained not by (ontogenetic) selection, for there is none when reinforcement is response independent, but by variation – the processes that provide the raw material on which operant contingencies can then act. Important among these is learning about *stimulus*-reinforcer contingencies (see Holland 1977; Hollis 1982; Moore 1973; Staddon & Simmelhag 1971; Trapold & Overmier 1972) and the behavioral "candidates" to which this learning gives rise. If a situation signals food, then food-related activities are likely to occur even if they have no consequence; or a negative one. Much "superstitious" behavior is of this adaptively sensible sort.

In his accounts of the evolution of bee dances and the behavior of the honey guide Skinner shows us that evolutionary biologists have no monopoly on "just so" stories. But he also makes the excellent point that when the story refers to ontogeny, to the selection of behavior by immediate consequences, rather than to phylogeny (natural selection), we can at least observe the action rather than being forced to infer it. Moreover, his account of honey-guide behavior makes a plausible case for the involvement of learning mechanisms in a pattern often interpreted without them. Recent work on the border between behavioral ecology and experimental psychology attempts to analyze how learning mechanisms work in natural environments, a research program implicit in Skinner's analysis.

But my major quarrel with Skinner is that he seems not to acknowledge that *selection* and *variation* are complementary concepts, whether used to explain ontogeny or phylogeny. Neither is adequate by itself. Because he relegates variation to the production of "undifferentiated material" or "minimal units" he seems to feel it necessary to give all explanatory weight to selection. For example, he writes: "Unable to show how the organism can behave effectively under complex circumstances, we endow it with a special cognitive ability which permits it to do so. Once the contingencies are understood, we no longer need to appeal to mentalistic explanations." By implication, contingencies (phylogenetic or ontogentic) explain everything. This assertion of the total hegemony of contingencies is either trivial – or strains belief. It is trivial if by "contingencies" Skinner just means "environment" – its own history or the environments of an organism's ancestors. Creationism aside, obviously every feature of every organism is ultimately traceable to environmental effects. But if Skinner means just reinforcement contingencies, then the assertion is incredible. If we choose "approach" as our response, then light is a "reinforcer" for a phototactic bug, yet we cannot train it to discriminate Bach from Beethoven, no matter how subtle the contingencies. Skinner explains *imitation* by saying "we learn to do what others are doing because we are then likely to receive the reinforcers they are receiving." Yet many animals fail to imitate, even when doing so would yield reinforcement; and others imitate even when imitation has no effect. A given set of contingencies will be effective with one creature and not another, and to understand the difference we need to know more about the creatures, not the contingencies.

In addition to ignoring variation, Skinner assumes that we know much more about the process of (ontogenetic) *selection* than we do. Since the work on contingency by

Rescorla (1967) and others (Catania & Keller 1981), none can assume that contiguity (between response or stimulus and reinforcer) is a sufficient selection rule. But what other processes are needed? In general we do not know.

By assuming that variation can be neglected and selection is a process that is perfectly understood, Skinner is able to treat operant conditioning as a unitary mechanism that is sufficient explanation for anything where ontogenetic consequences have an effect. But *reinforcement*, the process by which a rewarded behavior comes to predominate, remains a major problem for current research. Anomalies like superstitious behavior and instinctive drift are not to be explained by reinforcement but rather provide clues to how it works. Much the same can be said about forms of learning. In "Phylogeny" and subsequent papers (e.g., Skinner 1983b), Skinner ignores problems with reinforcement as an explanation and often seems intent on explaining away research done during the past 15 years that has attempted to solve them. This is an unfortunate response from the man whose brilliant early work created the field in which so many now labor. It does not detract from Skinner's contribution to say that he did not discover everything of interest about the operation of reward and punishment. It is unfortunate that he evidently still espouses a theoretical view within which questions of mechanism and cognitive structure can barely be asked, let alone answered.

BFS: I am sorry that so many of my replies must consist of a series of corrections, but nothing else seems to serve; that is especially true in reply to Staddon. To wit:

I do not play down variation. The shaping of behavior by taking advantage of slight variations in topography is a key principle in the analysis of operant behavior.

I do not define "dimensions," but I think my use of the term is clear when I characterize the measures of behavior in mazes and discrimination boxes (time required, number of errors made, preference for response *A* against response *B*, and so on) as dimensions peculiar to a particular apparatus and procedure. Rate of responding is not without its problems as a measure of probability, but it has a much greater generality from one experimental setting to another. To say that "a behavioral process, as a change in frequency of response, can be followed only if it is possible to count responses" does not dismiss the subject of bird song, orientation, or the behavior of bees – these are behavior, not behavioral processes. Although it may be difficult to trace the learning of bird song or how bees learn to return to a target, changes in frequency are certainly observed in both cases.

I do not think I am "unduly harsh on anything that smacks of mentalism." Staddon's translation of the expression of Tinbergen's to which I object is a good behavioral paraphrase.

It is not true that "the notion that habits and instincts may be related because one is built from ingredients provided by the other. . . finds no place in [my] analysis." Operant behavior is, however, much more easily shaped from "an extensive, undifferentiated repertoire" of behavior, and the evolution of such a repertoire is, I believe, an important stage in the evolution of behavior in general.

There is nothing inconsistent in insisting that a consequence must be temporally contingent on behavior in speaking of adventitious contingencies. In a standard apparatus, the delivery of food is contingent upon pressing a lever. That is the way the apparatus is built. There is nothing adventitious about it. But food can appear simply by accident immediately after a response is made and will be equally effective in reinforcing the response. (I have argued that only the immediacy rather than the causal mediation could have operated in the natural selection of the process of operant conditioning. I have been puzzled by the effects reported by Staddon and Simmelhag (1971). I have repeated my experiment on superstitious behavior many times and have never got the uniformity they observed. Could they have got hold of pigeons in which pecking had already been reinforced?)

I have certainly said that neither variation nor selection could be adequate by itself. I do not think that "superstitious behavior and instinctive drift are not to be explained by reinforcement but rather provide clues to how it works." I believe superstitious behavior is explained by reinforcement and instinctive drift is quite clearly phylogenic.

Each behavior is a product of heredity and experience

Douglas Wahlsten

Department of Psychology, University of Waterloo, Canada

In "Phylogeny" Skinner makes two points quite effectively. First, he argues that it is not possible to know either the phylogenetic or the ontogenetic origin of a behavior from knowledge of its apparent purposiveness or adaptiveness. Second, he maintains that ontogenetic contingencies can be well investigated and understood without analyzing the phylogenetic contingencies that may have contributed to the evolution of the behavioral processes. By this he does not mean that species or strain differences should be ignored or that exhaustive knowledge of one mammalian species can substitute for in-depth study of other mammals. Although his earlier writings did imply these erroneous views, this 1966 article does not.

When Skinner ventures an opinion on the relation between heredity, experience, and behavior, however, he seems to concur with the views of the "classical" ethologists. Lorenz (1981) and Eibl-Eibesfeldt (1979), for example, stubbornly maintain that a behavior that is resistant to modification by experience is therefore innate and genetically encoded. This view is false. There is no necessary relation between the modifiability of a behavior during ontogeny and its degree of heritability in a population. In some instances the symptoms of a genetic disease may be altered dramatically by changing the diet, as in certain forms of diabetes (Lee & Bressler 1981), whereas a morphological characteristic that is established by environmental conditions during a critical period of development may later be almost impossible to change, such as the determination of the sex of certain reptiles by nest temperature during incubation (Bull & Vogt 1979; Ferguson & Joanen 1982). For this reason, as well as others discussed previously (Wahlsten 1979), the only way to demonstrate a genetic influence on behavior or morphology is to do a genetic experiment whereby the genetic material is modified.

Skinner states that "genetic variables may be assessed . . . by studying organisms upon which the environment has had little opportunity to act (because they are newborn or have been reared in a controlled environment)." He is wrong for the same reasons the ethologists are wrong. He should also note that the organism's environment begins to act when the organism begins to exist, at conception. A vast number of environmental influences on the development of vertebrate animals prior to birth or hatching have been documented.

There are several statements in "Phylogeny" that indicate that Skinner agrees with the view that there are two mutually exclusive and exhaustive categories of behavior, inherited and acquired. This view is also false. First of all, no behavior is inherited. Skinner recognizes this problem and qualifies his statements about "inherited behavior" by suggesting that "bodily features" are actually inherited or genetically specified. In fact, no characteristic of the adult organism is inherited as such. Substances comprising the egg and, in most cases, the sperm are inherited, and these develop epigenetically through interaction with the environment. The notion that specific phenotypes are inherited is a vestige of the preformationist view of development. Today it is valid only for single-celled organisms wherein body parts such as cilia are replicated and transmitted directly to "offspring" and persist in essentially the same form during the life of the animal (Nanney 1977). In vertebrates, the chromosomal genes are part of a complex chemical and physiological system which is inherited and develops. Mutation of a specific gene may modify the course of development and consequently modify later behavior, but this does not mean that the normal form of the gene codes specifically for that behavior or for a brain structure that organizes the behavior (Stent 1981; Webster & Goodwin 1981).

Furthermore, a specific behavior is often found to be influenced by both heredity and experience. A behavior that appears to be instinctive, in that it is performed relatively competently on the first attempt, may be modified by experience. The work of Hailman (1969) on the pecking behavior of newly hatched gull chicks is a good example of this. The species-typical song of the cowbird occurs despite rearing by another species of songbird, but controlled experiments reveal that the song pattern can be changed by auditory experience (West, King, & Eastzer 1981). The literature in behavioral genetics provides abundant evidence of behaviors modified by both heredity and learning (Wahlsten 1978).

Physical structures or "bodily features" are also modified by both heredity and experience. The living organism is not analogous to an electronic computer wherein there is a clear distinction between prewired "hardware" and acquired "software." Heredity does not code for brain structure in the sense that a wiring diagram or blueprint specifies how to arrange wires and transistors to make a computer. Memories in the adult brain can be stored without the growth of new axons or synapses, but experience can also change the organizational structure or wiring of the brain, especially during the formative period when the nervous system is becoming organized. Even the structure of bones can be altered dramatically by the early experience of the organism's own movement (Drachman & Sokoloff 1966). Two bones do not fit together and articulate well purely because genes code precisely for the shape of each one separately; rather, they are custom fit to each other during ontogeny through mutual contact and motion. Genes undoubtedly play an important role in the development of structures, but they are certainly not the sole source of information directing construction of a brain or a bone.

It seems to me that Skinner gave too much weight to the dogmatic opinions of Lorenz and adopted certain of them as his own without first exploring the extensive literature of behavioral genetics or developmental biology. Eighteen years ago the paper was thought provoking and timely, but its discussion of the problem of heredity, evolution, and behavior was not sufficiently precise or authoritative to make it a real classic in this area of study. It may be relevant that in the commentaries on the BBS article by Eibl-Eibesfeldt (1979) on human ethology, no one referred to Skinner's 1966 paper or any other work by him. Perhaps it is a little unfair to judge something written long ago in the light of extensive evidence and detailed discussions published subsequent to it. Perhaps it would be better to inquire whether Skinner still adheres to everything he wrote in the 1966 paper. The real measure of a scientist is the extent to which he responds adaptively to ontogenetic contingencies occasioned by new evidence and argumentation.

BFS: I agree with most of the points Wahlsten makes except his implications that I do not agree with them. I do not believe my earlier writings imply such a disagreement. Thus, I agree that "there is no necessary relation between the modifiability of a behavior during ontogeny and its degree of heritability in a population." I agree that an organism's environment begins to act as soon as the organism begins to exist. I agree that there are not two mutually exclusive and exhaustive categories of behavior, inherited and acquired. I agree that behavior that appears to be instinctive may be modified by experience. I disagree with Lorenz on almost every count. I still believe, though Wahlsten disagrees, that "genetic variables may be assessed . . . by studying organisms upon which the environment has had little opportunity to act (because they are newborn or have been reared in a controlled environment)." That is to say, I believe in holding one variable as nearly constant as possible when studying the effects of another.

Neuropsychology vis-à-vis Skinner's behaviouristic psychology

Gerhard D. Wassermann

Reader in the Theory and Philosophy of Biology, University of Newcastle upon Tyne, England

Skinner's approach to the differences and similarities of (learning-acquired) ontogeny and (predominantly genetically controlled) phylogeny of behaviour follows the holist tradition of stimulus–response (SR) behaviourist theorizing, which is also adopted by ethologists. This theorizing assumes that the organism can be treated like a black box, whose stimulus inputs can be related to its response outputs. Inside the black box reinforcement and partly genetically controlled processes occur, as appropriate. Yet SR theory makes no attempt to explain either ontogenic or phylogenic aspects of behaviour in terms of the machinery of the black box. At most there are oblique hints, as when Skinner states "But we must look to the construction of the machine, as we look to the phylogeny and ontogeny of behaviour, to account for the fact that an ongoing system acts as if it has a purpose."

The philosophy of SR theory, whether dealing with the ontogeny or the phylogeny of behaviour, is based on the belief that a few "molar variables" can suffice to formulate complex behaviour. This outlook is closely analogous to the belief of some bygone generations of physicists who thought that simple physical relationships such as Ohm's law, or van der Waals's equation of state for gases, were paradigmatic for all physics. Indeed, statistical mechanics, by averaging over the energy states of an ensemble of gas molecules, was able to derive equations of state of reasonably simple kinds. Yet it must be stressed that a gas, or for that matter simple solids (such as a piece of metal), are compositionally relatively uniform compared to a central nervous system (say of a mammal) which, at the molecular level, is probably intercellularly extremely heterogenous (Clowes & Wassermann 1984; Wassermann 1978). It is for this reason that one cannot apply statistical mechanics (as distinct from thermodynamics) to a complex multineuronal system. Instead, many people have come to recognize that cognitive processes of man depend on a host of parameters, whose effects cannot be expressed in terms of simple laws with the help of statistical mechanics (and thermodynamics) or otherwise.

To invoke "reinforcement" in the ontogeny of behaviour, as frequently as Skinner prefers, seems to me not unlike the wholesale invocation of "natural selection" to explain almost any facet of evolutionary adaptation, as practiced by panselectionists (cf. Dennett 1983), or like attributing all this to divine creation as is done by creationists. Realizing this, one group of scientists has abandoned realism, for the time being, and has resorted to (usually) computer-simulated formulations of cognitive processes (the simulating system being the computer program, i.e., its software, and not the computer hardware) in terms of artificial intelligence (AI) systems. Other theorists (including myself) have tried to relate the functions of nervous systems and behaviour more directly in terms of neuropsychological theories (cf. Hebb 1949; Sommerhoff 1974; Wassermann 1978, particularly chap. 6, for discussions of various types of neuropsychological theories, including my own). In contrast to various theoretical neuropsychologists and AI theorists, Skinner's SR theorizing, as he admits, "leaves out of account habits, ideas, cognitive processes, needs, drives, traits, and so on. But it does not neglect the facts upon which these concepts are based." To some extent this applies also to those neuropsychologists, who, like Skinner, try to rid themselves of "mentalistic ghosts" without ignoring the facts related to these ghosts, and, who, like myself, are hard-faced materialists (cf. Wassermann 1979; 1982a; 1983a; 1983b). It is therefore worthwhile to compare Skinner's approach with that of the latter group of neuropsychological theorists.

Although Skinner does not assume that the nervous system (NS) is a tabula rasa at birth, he leaves aside the high degree of developmental organization of the NS, which seems to be largely gene dominated (even if environmental factors determine ultimate details). Jacobson (1969, p. 543) remarked pertinently that in *normal* embryonic development

> developing neurons sprout slender processes, their axons and dendrites, which in some cases grow to relatively great lengths to form connections with other neurons. The direction of growth of these processes and the targets on which they terminate appear to be constant in all individuals of the same species. Anatomical and physiological methods have shown the remarkable invariance of neuronal circuits and have given no evidence of random connectivity. A distinguished neuroanatomist (Palay 1967) has recently written, "The nervous system is not a random net. Its units are not redundant. Its organization is highly specific, not merely in terms of the connections between particular neurons, but also in terms of number, style, and location of terminals upon different parts of the same cell and the precise distribution of terminals arising from each cell."

Elsewhere I have written (Wassermann 1978, p. 33), "Perkel (1970) also noted that 'increasing evidence for the homology of neurons identifiable from individual to individual (Bullock 1970) bespeaks a more basic role for "wired-in" neural connections than has been attributed to them.'" Such observations led me to conclude that neural nets are highly species-specifically wired-in under predominant genetic guidance (at least in *normal*, i.e., nonexperimental, development). This suggests that learned behaviour (LB) as well as phylogenetically derived ("innate") behaviour (PB) can be interpreted as due, in part, to modifications of essentially genetically wired-in nervous systems. Modifications of NSs related to either LB or PB could be similar in kind, except that the modifications related to PB could become developmentally established under genetic control. If one deals with similar *types* of modifications of NSs in PBs and LBs, then it is not surprising to discover the numerous parallels between LBs and PBs which Skinner has elegantly presented (explicitly or implictly).

Although a holistic analysis of Skinner's type is valuable in its own right, it has its limits in that it only elucidates what (quasi–black box) organisms do in SR situations. It does not tell us anything, however, about the mechanisms that are involved in PBs and LBs. Behavioural science, if it is to be ranked as a science, must also be committed to the discovery of mechanisms, notably nervous system mechanisms at the physiological and molecular biological levels. The latter levels ultimately link with genes (Wassermann 1978) and, hence, with evolution (Wassermann 1981b; 1982b; 1982c). Granted that "reinforcers" play a role in LB, we must understand their neural equivalents. Moreover, we can be sure that LBs and PBs of all kinds, whether occurring in simple SR chains or in complex cognitive behaviour, are hierarchically organized into units. I suggested elsewhere that cognitive hierarchies could inter alia comprise hierarchies of concept-representing units (Wassermann 1978). If so, what is wired into NSs are possibly genetically provided macromolecular concept-representing units (CRUs) rather than specific concepts (with a few possible exceptions). Learning processes could then determine, on the basis of contingencies, to which genetically established CRU a particular (learned) concept becomes allocated. This is where Skinner's environmental contingencies become relevant. CRUs could form a hierarchy of associated systems (Wassermann 1978). It seems to me that although reinforcement processes are likely to play an important role in strengthening genetically established connections between CRUs, ultimately extensive neuropsychological research will be required in this area. (It is not good enough to state like Skinner, at the end of his section "Interrelations among Phylogenic and Ontogenic Variables" that "the behavior of civilized people shows the extent to which environmental variables may mask an inherited endowment." *How much* behaviour is inherited and how much learned seems to me to be a practically insoluble problem; cf. Wassermann 1983a.)

Long ago Hebb (1949) clearly recognized, like others before him, that cognitive structures such as "sets," although learnable (Allport 1955), are represented within NSs, and SR talk cannot explain this away. Moreover, many "sets" are goal directed, and how goal direction is neurally (or intraneurally?) represented remains an unresolved problem (pace Sommerhoff 1974). Indeed, notwithstanding detailed analyses of teleology (MacKay 1951; 1952; Sommerhoff 1950; Wassermann 1981a; Woodfield 1976) there exists no agreement on how to define "goals." It seems to me that Skinner's discussion of "sense of purpose" (in his final section) or "intention" disregards the fact that goal-directed behaviour of people or animals is probably more than an expression of "operant reinforcements." At least this assertion remains tenable until the nature of goal directedness and of "operant reinforcement" has been resolved in terms of experimental and theoretical neuropsychology. I conclude that Skinner's type of comparative analysis, although molar, is an important step in the right direction. His type of analysis must ultimately be extended to the level of neural mechanisms, where the relationship between the ontogenesis and the phylogeny of behaviour can become more fully elucidated. I am not advocating reductionism for its own sake, but recommend it in the belief that it may afford a deeper level of understanding of various aspects of behaviour than unsupplemented holistic analyses.

BFS: It is hard to reply to anyone who, like Wassermann, regards me as a stimulus–response psychologist. I have not been one for more than 50 years. The essence of operant conditioning and, for that matter, of "Phylogeny," is that behavior is not triggered by the environment but selected by it. The distinction cannot be made by speaking of goal directedness, even when that has been "resolved in terms of experimental and theoretical neurospsychology." We are always speaking of the behavior of an organism, most of it mediated by the nervous system. Neurology will eventually give behavioral science what DNA has given genetics, but it has not done so yet, nor will the "reduction" of behavioral facts to neurological facts be helpful until the behavioral facts are correct. The phylogeny and ontogeny of behavior are subjects in their own right, as was genetics prior to the discovery of the structure of DNA, and they need to be studied both as basic science and for the sake of their practical applications.

Summing up

7 What are the scope and limits of radical behaviorist theory?

Stevan Harnad

The following is an attempt to make explicit some of the questions to which commentators appear to have furnished default answers of their own, answers that have perhaps given rise to certain misunderstandings. It is hoped that in this explicit form the questions will allow Professor Skinner's position to be equally explicitly formulated (Please note that there is some overlap with Professor Catania's questions 3, 4, 5, 7, 8, and 10.)

A. What is the current status of theory in radical behaviorism? It is generally held by scientists and philosophers of science that data do not speak for themselves. Hence even so-called descriptive theories involve at least rudimentary interpretation and explanation. But even so, the history of science seems to suggest that descriptions of the phenomena and regularities observed are superseded by explanatory theory as a science matures and its depth and breadth of understanding increase. To what extent do these considerations apply to radical behaviorism?

B. What are the theoretical concepts of radical behaviorism? In general, a scientific theory will attempt to account for a class of observed phenomena (data) in terms of concepts that predict and explain them. The concepts will include terms referring to observations as well as to inferred entities, events, and processes underlying the observations and hypothesized to give rise to them. What (if any) are these theoretical concepts in radical behaviorism? And to what extent do these general considerations apply to radical behaviorism?

C. What is behavior? To a first approximation, behavior seems to be something an organism *does*, but this raises questions because what one does can be described at so many levels, from the sequential movement of the fingers to writing behavior to signing a check to committing a fraud to betraying one's country. Moreover, there are questions about what *parts* of an organism do: A hand moves, a muscle twitches, a neuron fires. All these are, in a sense, things the organism *does*, but which of them are or are not "behavior," and why? The difficult special cases seem to be the very high order ones (betraying one's country) and the very low order ones (firing one's neurons).

D. What is the status of neuroscientific theory in radical behaviorism? Related to the foregoing, the question of brain theory concerns radical behaviorism's stance on the relation between accounts of what an organism does and what its nervous system does. Both are based on observable data, and sometimes the boundary between the two domains seems fuzzy or arbitrary (as when correct responses are preceded by a scalp macropotential). Perhaps this is related to the question of the relation of operant to respondent theory (see E, below).

E. What is the scope of radical behaviorism? What kinds of phenomena usually regarded as related to psychology *can* radical behaviorism account for in its own theoretical terms, and what kinds of phenomena can it *not* account for? In particular, please consider the cases of operant versus respondent behavior, neural activity, and unlearned behaviors. (The special cases of language and of perception are taken up separately below.)

F. How does radical behaviorism account for language? Language capacity includes the ability to *produce* and *comprehend* everything said in a natural language. Comprehension can perhaps be equated with the ability to respond appropriately, verbally or nonverbally, to everything said in a natural language. Contemporary linguistics seems to have arrived at the conclusion that the structure underlying language is much more complex than a response "shaping" view can encompass. In particular, if current linguistic theory is correct, then the kinds of rules, principles, and constraints that *any* mechanism must somehow encode internally to be able to exhibit linguistic behavior at all *cannot be shaped by experience*. The basis for this radical claim is in part (i) formal and mathematical (it is provable that no simple inductive mechanism could induce certain kinds of formal rules from finite samples of data) – these are limits on "learnability" – and in part (ii) empirical (the samples of linguistic experiences a child encounters, and the behavior the child produces, are claimed to be too impoverished a basis for shaping the requisite rules). What (short of denying the validity of current formal linguistic theory) is radical behaviorism's reaction to this? The answer would seem to be very important because any theoretical distinction between "contingency-shaped" and "rule-governed" behavior in which the "rules" are verbal appears first to require confronting the problem of the source and nature of the rules underlying language capacity itself.

G. How does radical behaviorism account for discrimination? On the face of it, *discrimination* is a behavioral phenomenon par excellence. It is differential responding to stimuli. But again, as with language, the question of how *any* mechanism can accomplish the complex and elaborate discriminations we are able to make seems to require a theoretical reply in analytic, information-processing terms rather than in terms of response shaping. If a discrimination can be shaped by appropriate consequences, that just shows *that the stimuli concerned were discriminable by the organism and that it* somehow succeeded in *discriminating* them. But some would hold that the real problem of discrimination begins where the radical behaviorist story seems to end: Given that a discrimination was shaped by a certain history of reinforcement, how did the perceptual mechanism *do* it? How could *any* input-processing mechanism do it? The kinds of candidate computational, geometric, and statistical theories that seem capable of providing answers to these questions do not appear to be within the scope of radical behaviorist theory.

H. What is the status of data in radical behaviorism? Related to the questions about theory and about behavior, this question concerns the methodoogical strictures and the motivation for the word "behavior" in "radical behaviorism." As a constraint on methodology it certainly seems appropriate to remind psychologists that their only data will be behavior (possibly including neural behavior). But that still seems to leave the theoretical branch of psychology to *account for* those data in whatever terms parsimony and the evidence will allow. Hence hypothetical processes can be proposed to account for the observable input–output data of language, discrimination, or what have you. Radical behaviorism's theoretical repertoire seems to be concerned largely with factors in the experiential history of the organism that shape its responding. But what about the unobservable factors that allow responding to be shaped in certain ways but not others? And the unobservable way in which the permissible responses are converged on? Language, pattern discrimination, and even complex motor skills seem to require going far beyond the observable input–output history in order to provide a viable explanatory theory.

I. What is the status of internal representation and analysis in radical behaviorism? The way that contemporary cognitive theory confronts the questions of discrimination and language is to hypothesize representations of information within the organism, together with active analytic processes. These internal representations and processes are neither homuncular nor animistic, as demonstrated by the fact that they have been successfully implemented in computer programs (which involve neither homunculi nor nonphysical forces). Moreover, these models *work* (within the admittedly limited domains in which they have so far been attempted) in that, given the right input, they will generate the right output. Is there a reason that such theories are illicit from the viewpoint of radical behaviorism? And if not, what is the relation, in the overall enterprise of psychology, of this kind of cognitive work to radical behaviorism?

J. Where would radical behaviorism's contribution fit into a complete neurocognitive theory of our behavioral performance and competence? Many psychologists and philosophers are profoundly skeptical that the complexities of a complete and adequate explanatory theory of what people *can* and *do* do – a theory along the lines of successful theories in other branches of science, both physical and biological – will be in any way relevantly similar to the shaping of bar pressing in the rat or key pecking in the pigeon by differential reinforcement histories. Whenever radical behaviorism has claimed that the operant story will be the *whole* story, or even the relevant substantive part of the whole story, such skeptics have raised questions of the kind raised above. But perhaps Professor Skinner sees the relation between radical behaviorism and cognitive psychobiology as a more complementary one (he certainly seems to do so in the case of evolutionarily "prepared" behaviors). His explicit position on the questions raised here concerning scope, limits, and theory should help to put the status of radical behaviorism into perspective in modern psychological theory.

SKINNER'S REPLY TO HARNAD

A. What is the current status of theory in radical behaviorism? Radical behaviorism is antitheoretical in the sense that it attacks and rejects traditional explanations of behavior in terms of internal initiating causes. It is anticreationist. It turns instead, as Darwin did, to the selection of presumably random variations by contingencies of survival (ethology) and contingencies of reinforcement (the experimental analysis of behavior). In that analysis, rate of responding is taken as a basic datum and studied as a function of many contingencies of reinforcement. The results are factual, not theoretical. The analysis has "matured" by successfully analyzing more and more complex arrangements of variables. If rate of responding is taken as a measure of probability of response, an element of theory no doubt arises, and theory may be necessary in *interpreting* facts about behavior which are out of reach of precise prediction and control. As in modern astronomy, a laboratory science of behavior will continue, I believe, to give the best possible explanation of facts beyond experimental control – events in the world at large in the case of behavior, the waves and particles reaching the earth from outer space in the case of astronomy. The depth and breadth of both fields depend not upon improvements in theory but upon success in the analysis of presumably similar phenomena where some degree of prediction and control is possible.

Over the centuries we have had many theories of the very large and the very small, both spiritual and materialistic. Have they been theoretical anticipations of the facts, or metaphors suggested by the facts available at the time? An answer to such a question will require a better understanding of human behavior, toward which both the data of an experimental analysis and the theory of radical behaviorism are slowly moving.

B. What are the theoretical concepts of radical behaviorism? If my answer to A is acceptable, there are very few "concepts...referring to...inferred entities, events, and processes underlying the observations and hypothesized to give rise to them" in either a science or a philosophy of behavior. The neurology of behavior is currently rich in such concepts, but only because it is poor in relevant facts. Covert behavior is often merely inferred, but even so not as an explanatory entity but as more of the subject matter to be accounted for. Probability of response is inferred from rate and from other evidence, but as a state of behavior – not something that gives rise to behavior. The history of the experimental analysis of behavior has shown a steady increase in the discovery of observable and manipulable variables of which observed behavior is a function. It is not one of the subject matters (like the very small or the very large) requiring theory.

C. What is behavior? There is no essence of behavior. The very expression "what an organism does" is troublesome because it implies that the organism initiates its behavior. There are many kinds of organisms, and they do many different things. When one analyzes a single instance, boundary problems arise. Is talking to oneself behavior? I would say yes, but I do not think behavior is necessarily muscular action. We observe it either through introspection (of which radical behaviorism can give a much better account than most people suppose) or through physiological measures that "invade privacy." Lacking better data, a science of behavior can merely offer an interpretation.

The word "behavior" means something very different when applied to betraying one's country or even to some detail in doing so, such as telling a secret. A behavior analyst can talk about that kind of behavior only as a geneticist might talk about the population problem in Africa. Another mistake is to take topography of behavior as a datum in itself. Muscle twitches or the products of muscle twitches (saying "hello") are the stuff of structuralism. Ethologists often describe the innate behavior of organisms simply as structure because the contingencies of natural selection are not visible. All the ethologist can do is say that under certain circumstances organisms do certain things. But an analysis of operant behavior can do more. It can go beyond the setting and the topography of response to a full statement of the contingencies. A given instance is not adequately described unless the selective contingencies (the operations performed upon the organism by the environment) are specified.

D. What is the status of neuroscientific theory in radical behaviorism? Sherrington (1906) wrote *The Integrative Action of the Nervous System* after performing only one operation on the nervous system – severing the spinal cord. Pavlov's (1927) book was subtitled *An Investigation into the Physiological Activity of the Cerebral Cortex*, although he got no nearer the cerebral cortex than a salivary fistula. These men were studying the Conceptual Nervous System. Since their time, neurology has come a long way. We now know much more about the chemistry and the architecture of the nervous system, but I believe it is still true, as I said in 1938 in *The Behavior of Organisms*, that no fact about the nervous system has yet told us anything new about behavior. It has, of course, told us much that is new about the relation between the nervous system and behavior and has indicated things to be done to the nervous system to change behavior. We have not yet learned anything about the behavior of an organism in an experimental space from its physiology except when measures are employed which directly alter the physiology. The neurological measures are, of course, very much worth studying.

A science of behavior is not yet indebted to neuroscience, but there is an enormous debt in the other direction. Behavioral science gives neuroscience its assignment, just as the early science of genetics, exploring the numerical relationships among the traits of successive generations, gave the study of genes its assignment.

A behavioral analysis has two necessary but unfortunate gaps – the spatial gap between behavior and the variables of which it is a function and the temporal gap between the actions performed upon an organism and the often deferred changes in its behavior. These gaps can be filled only by neuroscience, and the sooner they are filled, the better.

E. What is the scope of radical behaviorism? An answer would have to cover all the kinds of facts which are "usually regarded as related to psychology," but take, for example, individual differences – in intelligence, personality, ability, and so on. These have no physical dimensions. An intelligence test is of arbitrary length and difficulty. Scores are "meaningful" only when a large number of scores from a population are collected and a single score given a number representing its place in the distribution. A behavioral analysis cannot make much use of those quantities. Instead, it would have to look at the speed with which changes in behavior take place, the subtleties of the control exerted by complex stimuli, the size of repertoire that can be acquired and maintained without confusion, and so on. These are the kinds of facts which are within the range of the science of which radical behaviorism is the philosophy.

As to the operant-respondent distinction, respondent behavior is composed of reflexes, conditioned or unconditioned, presumably due to natural selection and Pavlovian conditioning. For the most part it is concerned with glandular secretion and the responses of smooth muscles. Most of the contingencies responsible for operant conditioning include stimuli which also elicit respondent behavior, but operant conditioning does not require them. Unlearned behavior is the product of natural selection. These are all parts of the subject matter of a comprehensive science. Both operant and respondent behavior have been brought under rather precise control in the laboratory, with results which can be used to interpret behavior in the world at large, where precise prediction and control are not possible. Neural activity is presumably involved in all behavior.

F. How does radical behaviorism account for language? I have, of course written a rather large book about verbal behavior (Skinner 1957). Chomsky's (1959) attack on it seems to have kept it out of the hands of linguists – to their eventual regret, I am sure. In the book I make no use of such concepts as idea, meaning, information, or any other thing said to be communicated by a speaker to a listener. I do not endow the listener with a faculty of comprehension, and I certainly do not distinguish between behavior and competence. In short, I do "[deny] the validity of current formal linguistic theory," insofar as it employs terms of that kind. When a dog learns to catch a ball, I do not think it "encodes" any principle of dynamics, and when a child learns to talk, I do not think he encodes any linguistic principle or rule. A verbal community arranges the contingencies under which people formulate rules in the sense of descriptions of contingencies, and its members can then adjust to the contingencies by following the rules. (The rules are useful both to those who formulate them and to others who have not been exposed to the contingencies.) The mistake is to say that the rule is *in* the contingencies and responsible for their effects. Verbal behavior being the extraordinary field that it is, I am afraid that all current theories must be called impoverished. I do not believe that that fact suggests any constraint on learnability. The only constraints imposed upon my analysis of verbal behavior are, so far as I am concerned, traditional views of language, which have kept my analysis from being widely understood and used. The constraints are really on linguistic theory, not on a behavioral analysis.

G. How does radical behaviorism account for discrimination? As a behavioral problem, discrimination raises no question if one stops talking about input-processing mechanisms. The behavioral facts are well known. They are often astonishing, and a neurological explanation is badly needed. In reporting my original work on discrimination (*The Behavior of Organisms*, 1938) I used the word "discrimination" mainly because of current interest in the subject in psychology. The choice was unfortunate. The issue is not discriminability but how stimuli acquire control of behavior from their role in contingencies of reinforcement. I agree that not all the answers to these questions are "within the scope of radical behaviorist theory" at the present time, but the behavioral facts are reasonably well established. They include my early experiments on establishing a discrimination without errors (Skinner, 1934), the extensive work by Terrace (1963b) and by Sidman and Stoddard (1967) on the transfer of discriminations through fading, Guttman's (1959) exploration of stimulus generalization and the peak shifts produced by a discrimination, Herrnstein, Loveland, and Cable's (1976) work on concept formation, and so on. These well-established facts are seldom if ever mentioned by cognitive psychologists concerned with concept formation, abstraction, or other forms of discrimination.

H. What is the status of data in radical behaviorism? The question seems very much like question E. We are always talking about the behavior of an organism which, as the product of natural selection, possesses a repertoire of unlearned behavior due to natural selection, and which subsequently acquires a vast learned repertoire through conditioning. Species differences are important. It is almost impossible to shape vocal behavior as an operant in any species except man, but this is not a constraint; it is a simple fact about the evolution of species. The human species took an enormous step forward when its vocal musculature came under operant control. Different consequences have different reinforcing effects for genetic reasons or because of individual histories of respondent or operant conditioning. If blushing does not change under operant reinforcement, it is not because of a constraint but because variations contributing to the operant conditioning of blushing have never had very much survival value. The "unobservable factors" mentioned in the question are not *easily* observed because they lie in the natural selection of the species, now largely out of reach. I do not believe that language, pattern discrimination, or complex motor skills require "going far beyond the observable" data unless the "viable explanatory theory" concerns physiological mechanisms, and they are not my province.

I. What is the status of internal representation and analysis in radical behaviorism? My objection to representations and processes (rules) is not that they are homuncular or animistic but that they are unnecessary. I do not believe that the world to which a person is exposed is in any sense "represented" inside that person or that the behavior the person acquires is stored in the form of rules of action. The fact that a computer can be programmed with the equivalent of representations and rules simply means that when so constructed it is not a good model of the human organism. Copy theories of perception are due to a misunderstanding of both direct perception and recall. As I have said in a recent paper (Skinner 1985a), a storage battery would be a better model of the organism. Electricity is put into the battery and the battery puts electricity out, but there is no electricity in the battery. Nor are there copies of stimuli or rules describing contingencies in the organism. Organisms are changed by contingencies of selection, they do not store them.

J. Where would radical behaviorism's contribution fit into a complete neurocognitive theory of our behavioral performance and competence? In my experience, the skepticism of psychologists and philosophers about the adequacy of behaviorism is an inverse function of the extent to which they understand it. I have mentioned many instances in my replies to these commentaries. In a recent paper (Skinner 1985a) I have accused cognitive scientists, in particular, of misusing the metaphor of storage and retrieval, speculating about internal processes about which they have no reliable information, studying behavior in response to descriptions of experimental settings rather than in response to the settings themselves, studying reports of intentions rather than the behavior intended, attributing behavior to feelings and states of mind instead of the contingencies of reinforcement of which they are current surrogates, and inventing explanatory systems which are admired for a profundity that is better called inaccessibility.

In abandoning the position of behaviorism (in asking that behaviorism be declared legally dead), psychology and much of philosophy have escaped from the strain of rigorous thinking but have suffered a serious reversal in their progress toward an effective understanding of human behavior.

8 Problems of selection and phylogeny, terms and methods of behaviorism

A. Charles Catania

We have had a grand tour of operant behaviorism ranging over evolutionary time and the breadth of human cultures. It has included both verbal and nonverbal behavior, and it has visited both their public and their private domains. To test my understanding of some of the issues discussed and to offer what I hope will be constructive contributions to the treatments, I here address to Professor Skinner several questions and comments on some of the topics stopped at along the way (I will treat his responses as my souvenirs of the trip).

1. What is selected? Of the three levels of selection you discussed in "Consequences," the commentators gave particular attention to selection at the cultural level, especially with regard to the issue of group selection. The major question is that of what is selected (e.g., Dawkins ["Consequences"]): Speaking of the survival of a group, and therefore of the individuals within it, is substantially different from speaking of the survival of their practices. If some individuals from a culture were separated from it and did not pass their practices on to their descendants, we would not point to them as examples of the survival of a culture. On the other hand, if they had learned new practices from another group and continued those practices even after the other group was destroyed, theirs might be regarded as an appropriate example of the survival of the culture they had acquired even if no biological relation existed between the two groups. In other words, we should speak of the survival of practices and not of their practitioners: classes of behavior survive as cultural practices, and not the group, the individuals in it, or their descendants. The parallel you drew with the distinction between the selection of organs and other physiological features as opposed to the selection of individuals or populations was instructive (e.g., your replies to Dawkins, Harris, and Maynard Smith ["Consequences"]).

Through phylogenic mechanisms operating over generations, the behavior of a parent can survive in the behavior of its offspring. Through ontogenic mechanisms operating over the lifetime of a single organism, some types of behavior are more likely than others to survive in that organism's behavior. When the offspring can acquire behavior from the parent or from any other organism (e.g., through observation, imitation, verbal behavior), a third arena for selection is created. Such selection is nonphylogenic. The question is whether it is necessary to invoke a third mechanism for this transmission of behavior from one organism to another. When Donahoe ("Consequences") raised this question by asking whether cultural evolution involves a different kind of selection, your answer was affirmative, but you went on to say that it involved no new behavioral process.

The issue is how behavior gets from one organism to another (see also Boulding, Harris ["Consequences"]). It is possible to imagine ways in which imitation or observational learning could be established either phylogenically or ontogenically, but there must be constraints on the imitative class. The unfledged hatchling in a nest on a high limb, for example, imitates its parents' flight at its peril, and generalized imitation must be limited by those instances, such as imitating another organism that has just injured itself, in which imitation has aversive consequences. Still another problem is how the correspondence between the imitator and its model is established. For example, how does an organism learn that a particular felt position of its own limbs corresponds to the seen position of the limbs of another organism? And, finally, verbal behavior is a different way in which behavior can be transmitted from one organism to another, through control by instructions or rules (see "Problem Solving"). Verbal behavior is, par excellence, behavior that is replicated, and its effectiveness depends on that property. Yet the contingencies that maintain the effectiveness of control by instructions have a paradoxical effect: Rule-governed behavior inevitably becomes behavior that is insensitive to contingencies (e.g., Matthews, Shimoff, Catania & Sagvolden 1977).

In a paper on the evolution of behavior (Skinner 1984), you briefly discussed possible sources of imitation and other means by which behavior may be moved from one organism to another. The analysis of these processes is perhaps a field of study in its own right. I offer the remarks above as an occasion for your elaboration on these issues, and in particular for a statement of your current views on the relative contributions of phylogeny and ontogeny to such processes.

2. Phylogenic–ontogenic parallels. Some commentaries questioned the adequacy of the analogy between phylogenic and ontogenic selection (e.g., Timberlake ["Consequences"]). As one example, you have discussed the evolution of homing and migration in terms of shaping (Skinner 1975). To supplement that discussion, here is another example of shaping by phylogenic contingencies.

> The same is true of intraspecific competition, where the optimum size, say, for an individual can be slightly larger than the present population mode, *whatever the present population mode may be*. "...in the population as a whole there is a constant tendency to favor a size slightly above the mean. The slightly larger animals have a very small but in the long run, in large populations, decisive advantage in competition....Thus, populations that

> are regularly evolving in this way are always well adapted as regards size in the sense that the optimum is continuously included in their normal range of variation, but a constant asymmetry in the centripetal selection favors a slow upward shift in the mean." (Dawkins 1982, p. 104, quoting Simpson 1953, p. 151; Dawkins's italics)

As discussed in some commentaries (e.g., Altmann, Kacelnik & Houston ["Phylogeny"], Campbell ["Consequences"]), an issue in evolutionary theory is whether evolution is continuous or saltatory. I see no reason why some features might not be selected in a relatively continuous way while the selection of others is punctuated. A parallel exists in the ontogenic shaping of behavior.

In a demonstration apparatus you once designed for an undergraduate course, a rat's presses on a counter-weighted lever produced food. The topography of its pressing consisted of its resting one or both forepaws on the lever and pushing down. Lever presses began with the counterweight set at a modest level. As successive presses were reinforced, the counterweight was gradually increased until a point at which depression of the lever required a force exceeding the rat's weight. At that point, continued success in shaping depended on the emergence of a new topography of lever pressing. Whereas pushing down on the lever with both hindlegs on the floor had previously worked, an effective press now required that the rat's feet lift to the wall of the chamber, on which a wire mesh allowed it a firm grip. By pulling between forelegs and hindlegs, the rat could then depress the lever even with the counterweight exceeding its own weight (jumping on the lever – more appropriate to the saltatory metaphor – was a third topography that was occasionally successful, but the rat who pressed above its own weight in this way was less likely to move on to the more effective foreleg–hindleg topography). This performance, usually shaped within a single class session, illustrates two kinds of ontogenic selection, one gradual and the other saltatory: the relatively continuous change in the rat's pressing while the counterweight remained less than its own weight, and the relatively discontinuous change when that weight was exceeded. Furthermore, the saltatory part of this shaping makes a point about the source of new topographies: The likelihood of producing the foreleg–hindleg topography depends jointly on the rat's anatomy and on its environment (e.g., whether the chamber wall allows a firm grip for its hind feet and whether the height of the lever makes it likely that it will lift its feet off the floor as the counterweight approaches its own weight).

Although the analogies between phylogenic and ontogenic selection must break down somewhere, I assume and you have suggested that there are other parallels. Delius ("Phylogeny") sees schedules of reinforcement as ontogenic phenomena without phylogenic analogues. Yet just as fixed-interval performance depends on temporal cyclicities, the cyclicities of the seasons undoubtedly make the timing of reproductive behavior crucial to some species. Longer cycles may operate in other circumstances (e.g., 13-

year and 17-year cicadas), but there is also the possibility that depletion of resources favors long fallow periods, in a manner analogous to schedules that differentially reinforce low rates of responding.

The population biologist distinguishes between *K*-selection, in stable environments with heavy competition for limited resources, and *r*-selection, in unstable environments that favor rapid reproduction over other types of adaptation. Do the contingencies of survival under *r*-selection then have some properties in common with variable-ratio schedules?

Variability itself has consequences. Should it not therefore be a property of behavior that can be selected? For example, if certain environments existed only periodically in evolutionary time, might relevant behavior be more likely to remain available in a population (e.g., in recessive form) than if those environments were continuously in existence? The argument is of course relevant to physiology as well as to behavior (cf. arguments for the evolution of sexual reproduction; e.g., Maynard Smith 1958). Just as ontogenic shaping will proceed more slowly with stereotyped than with variable behavior, a population that has become relatively homogeneous in genotype as a result of extended exposure to a stable environment may be less likely to survive environmental disruptions than one that has become relatively heterogeneous in changing environments (cf. Dawkins ["Consequences"] on a possible role of displacement activity).

Behavior analysis and biology may reap reciprocal benefits by exploring these analogies. I welcome your reactions to any of the above remarks, with a special interest in what you may have to say about phylogenic analogues of schedule effects.

3. Explanation, description, and taxonomy. For some commentators, the model for behavioral science seems to be physics rather than biology (e.g., Nicholas ["Methods"]). Perhaps this accounts for the frequent concern not with behavior taxonomy but rather with explanation. For example, Stich ("Behaviorism-50") sees reflexes and operant behavior as postulates requiring explanation (see also Cohen, Dodwell ["Problem Solving"], Rey, Robinson, Rosenthal ["Behaviorism-50"]). Yet in an argument I once heard put to good use by Peter Dews and have lately found effective myself (e.g., Catania 1978; 1983), the point has been made that reinforcement, stimulus control, elicitation, and so on are not explanatory terms but rather are names of phenomena, of a status in our field comparable to that of terms like osmosis or cell or respiration in biology. (If similar issues of explanation had existed in biology, imagine then how the theory of osmosis might have been challenged by the discovery of active transport.)

In experimental analyses, explanation is derivative. Our first task is to identify the classes of phenomena into which behavior can be fractionated. Learning theories were once concerned with "botanizing" reflexes or drives, and those commentators who suggested taxonomies of problems (e.g., Kaufmann, Raaheim ["Problem Solving"]) seemed to have analogous interests.

But a taxonomy of types of behavior is different from a taxonomy of behavioral processes (Rapoport ["Problem Solving"] saw the importance of this point in his discussion of the distinction between rule-governed and contingency-shaped behavior).

The issue is not even one of explanation versus description. Once we have learned to see reinforcement, either in the laboratory or outside of it, it is neither description nor explanation when we identify it in new situations. When we see a response increase in probability because it has produced some change in the environment, we may then speak of reinforcement. We may also effectively use other procedures that reinforcement makes possible (e.g., shaping). This particular constellation of events is thus the discriminative stimulus that sets the occasion on which both verbal behavior and nonverbal behavior have consequences. The three-term contingency, at the heart of so many other aspects of behavior analysis, therefore enters into this most fundamental part of scientific behavior. Yet I see little that is relevant to this point in the contemporary philosophy of science. What then are the processes that make up our taxonomy, and how shall we treat explanation and description in a behavioral account?

4. Copies, representations, and analyses of stimuli. In "Behaviorism-50" you say that the organism "does more than make copies." In your response to Moore ("Behaviorism-50"), you elaborate by noting, about edge receptors in vision, that they are "a step in the right direction. They are the beginnings of an *analysis* of an image rather than a replication." In your response to Farrell ("Behaviorism-50"), you expand this point to include not only stimuli but also contingencies: "That some copy of the contingencies is taken into the organism to be used at a later date is a fundamental 'cognitive' mistake. Organisms do not store the phylogenic or ontogenic contingencies to which they are exposed; they are changed by them."

An argument similar to that about following copies through the sensory system can be made with respect to the purported functions of representations. Terrace ("Terms") says that the organism codes features of stimuli and then represents them to itself. Terrace justifies this argument with the claim that organisms cannot respond directly to some properties of stimuli; he apparently rejects the idea that an organism might respond to relational properties of the environment (e.g., "to the left of," "same"). Terrace uses matching-to-sample in the pigeon as an example. The pigeon, according to Terrace, cannot respond to the sameness of the sample and the matching stimuli. It codes these stimuli in some way, however, and later responds to its coding of "sameness." Yet if this property was not in the stimuli as the pigeon encountered them, how could it ever emerge indirectly in some coding of the stimuli? Is it not the case that an organism responding to the sameness of its own coding responses poses as much of a problem as its responding to the sameness of the stimuli themselves? Here too the distinction between replications and analyses is presumably relevant. Is it not more appropriate to say that the organism analyzes stimuli than to say that it represents them to tself?

5. What is behavior? Behaviorism was once called muscle-twitch psychology. Although that label is no longer appropriate, several commentaries raise questions about the nature of behavior. I assume that when Kochen ("Problem Solving") says, "Are we to stretch the concept of behavior to include reflection?" your answer is affirmative, and that you object when Harré ("Problem Solving"), in discussing reflection, asserts that "the formation of hypotheses prior to their expression is hardly behavior." More often, commentators accept seeing as an act, thinking as an act, and so on (e.g., Belth ["Behaviorism-50"]). But their opinions differ on whether behavior is necessarily movement (e.g., Schagrin ["Methods"]), or is muscular movement in particular, or is something else (e.g., Shimp ["Methods"], who speaks of not knowing what behavior is). In your reply to Gunderson ("Behaviorism-50"), you speak of silent thinking as behavior that may have "little if any muscular involvement," and in your reply to Lyons ("Behaviorism-50") you go further: It may have "no muscular involvement" or may be "some minute behavior which never reaches a muscle." It seems clear that behavior need not involve muscles, but can there then be behavior without movement?

Some commentaries discuss thinking as a way of trying out contingencies privately, as in simulations. I assume that you have no objections when Dawkins ("Consequences") speaks of imagination or simulation or when Gamble ("Consequences") speaks of "vicarious selection systems such as thought trials," provided that they acknowledge that these are instances of behavior. If so, it follows that the problem with Schull's statement ("Consequences") that "intelligent agents 'experiment mentally' with potentially productive courses of action...before...behaving," is simply that it implies that this "experi-mental" activity is something other than behavior.

It is a different question whether these are effective classes of behavior. Dawkins (1976, pp. 62–63) has put it as follows:

> No amount of simulation can predict exactly what will happen in reality, but a good simulation is enormously preferable to blind trial and error. Simulation could be called vicarious trial and error, a term unfortunately preempted by rat psychologists. If simulation is such a good idea, we might expect that survival machines would have discovered it first.... Well, when you yourself have a difficult decision to make involving unknown quantities in the future, you do go in for a form of simulation. You *imagine* what would happen if you did each of the alternatives open to you....[I]t is unlikely that somewhere laid out in your brain is an actual spatial model of the events you are imaging....[T]he details are less important than the fact that it is able to...predict possible events. Survival machines which can simulate the future are one jump ahead of survival machines who can only learn on the basis of overt trial and error.

But simulations cannot be useful unless imagined outcomes correspond reasonably well to actual ones. The task of an analysis of simulations as behavior, then, is to show how (and whether) they can generate outcomes similar in effect to the natural consequences of the corresponding overt behavior. Presumably some of the behavior you have discussed in "Problem Solving" is relevant.

6. The definition of reinforcers. Many commentaries either implicitly or explicitly addressed the purported circularity of the definition of a reinforcer (e.g., Rosenberg ["Consequences"], Cohen, Rein ["Problem Solving"], Gallup ["Behaviorism-50"], Eysenck ["Phylogeny"]). You have discussed the difficulty of identifying a reinforcer in advance (e.g., your reply to Eysenck ["Phylogeny"]). Sometimes evolutionary considerations help (e.g., your replies to Wyrwicka ["Consequences"] and Gallup ["Behaviorism-50"]).

One way the problem has been treated is in terms of the relativity of reinforcers (Premack 1959; 1971). The account first considers reinforcers as stimuli that set the occasion for behavior and then examines the relative probabilities of behavior occasioned by different stimuli. For example, water can set the occasion for a rat's drinking, and the availability of a running wheel can set the occasion for its running. At times when the rat is more likely to drink than to run, the opportunity to drink can be used to reinforce running, but at other times when it is more likely to run than to drink, the opportunity to run can be used to reinforce drinking. This reversibility demonstrates that there are no absolute classes of reinforcers. Instead, reinforcers are defined relative to the responses to be reinforced.

Given that response probabilities can be manipulated by restricting the organism's opportunities to engage in behavior, this account makes easy contact with deprivation as a method for establishing reinforcers (e.g., Eisenberger, Karpman, & Trattner 1967).

The relative probabilities of the different responses have been assessed in various ways (e.g., relative times spent engaging in each, or momentary probabilities when both are available concurrently, or relative frequencies of larger units of responding variously defined), and the account has been complicated by the ways in which changes in the probability of one response can change the probability of another (as when water deprivation changes the likelihood that an organism will eat; e.g., see Bernstein & Ebbesen 1978; Rachlin & Burkhard 1978). Nevertheless, these phenomena have been well documented, and in many situations the relative probabilities of responding have been shown to be good predictors of whether one response will be reinforced by the opportunity to engage in another. It would therefore be of interest to know your views on the relativity of reinforcement and its bearing on the purported circularity of the definition of reinforcers.

7. The problem of structure. Accounts in terms of structure have often substituted for analyses of contingencies. Several commentaries appeal to structure both in phylogeny and in ontogeny (e.g., Hallpike, ["Consequences"]

Scandura ["Problem Solving"], Hogan ["Phylogeny"]). The structures are said to have various properties, such as carrying information (e.g., Maynard Smith ["Consequences"]). Yet structures are themselves simply networks of contingencies. The difference between a sphere and a cube, for example, can be expressed in terms of whether and in what manner one encounters an edge as one explores the surfaces of the two solids. Structure, therefore, cannot have a role in behavior separate from that of contingencies.

Structure is said to be a property of behavior as well as environment. The structure of response chains, in which each response produces a consequence that sets the occasion for the next, is different from that of temporal sequences organized in other ways. The difference can often be found in environmental constraints; for example, it is difficult to walk through a door before it has been opened, whereas the notes of an arpeggio are playable in many orders. As you point out in your reply in Shimp ("Methods"), "Behaviorists ...are accused of saying that the successive responses of a skilled pianist are triggered one by one by the preceding responses, which, of course, is absurd." In your analysis of verbal behavior, chaining was involved in the class you called intraverbal, but that class would have been unnecessary if there were only one kind of sequential verbal behavior (see also Grossberg ["Problem Solving"], and the misunderstanding of this point in Chomsky's 1959 review of *Verbal Behavior*).

The treatment of structure becomes even more complicated when some sets of contingencies are nested within others. Verbal behavior provides the most obvious example; analyses can proceed at the levels of morphemes, phonemes, words, phrases, sentences, paragraphs, or entire compositions. Such relations are often discussed in terms of hierarchical structure or organization, but the same problems can be addressed in terms of the different units of behavior that are shaped by the components of a nested set of contingencies. And, finally, novel behavior, both verbal and nonverbal, has often been discussed in terms of structure, but in your treatments of creativity and of multiple causation in verbal behavior you have dealt with such cases in terms of the combination of response classes. Are there then any circumstances in which reducing the issue of structure to one of contingencies is inappropriate?

8. Language acquisition. Several commentaries were concerned with language (e.g., Solomon ["Consequences"], Rapoport ["Problem Solving"]), and in particular with the role of consequences in establishing verbal discriminations such as the color name "red" (e.g., Gopnik, Thomas, Zentall ["Behaviorism-50"]). It is hard to imagine how children could learn vocabulary with any consistency if what they said was unaffected by its consequences or, in other words, if the verbal community failed to respond to their verbal behavior in any way (the linguist's proof that the environment is inadequate to the child's development of verbal behavior reminds me of the mathematician's proof that bees cannot fly). Perhaps the problem has to do with which consequences are thought to count as reinforcers. I assume that praise or consumable reinforcers such as candy are relatively minor consequences in the acquisition of language, and that the consequences we should look at are more subtle and more variable over time even though more important: hearing oneself saying something similar to what one has heard others say, getting something one has asked for, hearing a remark relevant to something one had just said, and so on. One of the problems faced by those with only a passing acquaintance with behavior analysis, I suspect, is a narrow view of the kinds of consequences that can function as reinforcers; perhaps some regard praise or candies as possible reinforcers but do not consider that other more natural consequences of what we say may also qualify.

Some see cases in which vocabulary is acquired through observation or imitation as an embarrassment to an account in terms of consequences. Yet the significant consequences of echoic speech are the correspondences between sounds one has heard and sounds one has produced oneself. It is not too great a leap to extend such correspondences to include other properties of verbal behavior, especially given the many months over which they can develop. It is presumably important to discover that the relations between words and things in one's own behavior correspond to these relations in the behavior of others. You dealt with some of these issues in "Terms" (and the research by Johnson and Wellman ["Behaviorism-50"] on the acquisition of the language of metacognition might profitably consider how the verbal community establishes such vocabularies). The verbal community provides the discriminative stimuli as well as the consequences that shape the child's verbal behavior and maintain its consistency, but the complexity of these processes must not be underestimated. It would be useful, therefore, if you could provide other examples of subtle consequences that might be overlooked in the acquisition of verbal behavior.

It is also tempting to address here the question of the innateness of language. But if any aspects of language are phylogenically determined, it would seem more likely that they would be functional than structural properties. In particular, control by instructions has features in common with elicited behavior or behavior produced by releasers. It is easy to specify contingencies that maintain the following of rules (disobedience is typically punished). But might not phylogenic contingencies operate to create coordinated behavior in social groups? Might some rule-governed behavior depend more on phylogenic than ontogenic contingencies (cf. Lowe ["Terms"])? Is there anything special about the contingencies that maintain rule-governed behavior?

9. Private events as causal. Here I try a few statements to test my understanding of the causal status of private events, a recurrent issue in the commentaries (e.g., Heil, Schnaitter, and Zuriff ["Terms"]). First, the public–private dimension is different from the physical–mental dimension. The former has to do with accessibility whereas the latter has to do with the kinds of stuff of which the world is made. Thus, saying that mental events are not causes of behavior follows simply from rejecting the physical–mental distinction, but it does not follow that *private* events cannot be causes of behavior. As elaborated in "Problem Solving," one can create discriminative stimuli that affect one's subsequent behavior (e.g., writing the intermediate products in the multiplication of large numbers). Sometimes such stimuli are accessible only to the problem solver (e.g., the intermediate products when the multiplication is mental rather than written). The public origins of such private stimuli are obvious enough. Yet if they are part of the causal chain leading to other behavior (e.g., the solution to the multiplication problem), should they not be regarded as causes of behavior? I assume the resolution involves the distinction between initiating causes and other kinds of causes: To the extent that private events are parts of causal chains they can be *intermediate* causes, but they cannot be *initiating* causes.

10. Active versus passive organisms. Much of the concern with control and who might exert it (e.g., Dahlbom ["Consequences"], Sternberg ("Problem Solving"]) seems to ignore the many varieties of control that exist already in human cultures. If human behavior is in fact influenced in these ways, it is unfortunate that so many are reluctant to consider the implications. It would be inappropriate to review here your arguments in *Science and Human Behavior* and elsewhere (Skinner 1953; 1956). But one detail seems worth further comment. To say that an individual is not an initiating agent or that the behavior of an individual is controlled is different from saying that the individual is passive. Brinker & Jaynes ("Terms"), for example, argue against the passive organism, but the distinction between active and passive is not the same as that between initiating and controlled. The opposite side of control by the environment is that the operant acts on the environment; it is implicit in the concept of the operant that what the organism does makes a difference in the world. Curious and active organisms have evolved from organisms that gained survival advantages by exploring and changing their worlds. Is it then correct to say that the argument that behavior is caused or determined should not be construed as an argument that the organism is passive?

With these ten sections, I have completed my comments. Behavior analysis is often an exercise in parsimony, and I hope I have not introduced too much excess baggage. You may wish to respond not only to my specific items but also to these treatments as a whole. For your guidance on this tour I now simply offer my thanks.

SKINNER'S REPLY TO CATANIA

1. What is selected? Around the turn of the century, Samuel Butler made the point that a hen is only an egg's way of making another egg. He was anticipating the view that the organism is the servant of the gene. But the organism is needed by the gene. Variations occur in genes but must be selected in organisms. If we regard a culture as a social environment that shapes the behavior of new members of a group, then we can say that a culture is simply an individual's way of producing other enculturated individuals. Variations occur in the individual, but it is the culture with its practices that survives. Many practices evolve and survive independently of particular cultures, just as eyes, ears, wings, and legs – the "practices" of species – evolve and survive independently of particular species.

Imitation and modeling are not foolproof behavioral processes, but they were the best natural selection could do. (Compare the point that it would be better if a reinforcer strengthened responses only when produced by them, but the best natural selection could do was to make a reinforcer effective when it followed a response, for whatever reason, with the risk that adventitious consequences would be effective, as in "superstition.")

With the advent of verbal behavior and the possibility of the transmission of behavior by rules rather than by imitation and modeling, the human species moved rapidly toward effective culture, but cultures that continue to rely on rule-governed behavior are less efficient than those in which contingencies of reinforcement derived from the physical environment and from face-to-face interaction in social environments can take over. Cultures of the latter kind do not need to maintain the contingencies under which rules are followed.

2. Phylogenic–ontogenic parallels. Larger animals may have an advantage, but only up to a point, beyond which greater size is a handicap. The strong man has an advantage, but also only up to the point at which his excessive use of strength leads to joint countercontrolling action on the part of weaker persons.

Whether evolution is continuous or saltatory is still moot, and I am not sure the weight-lifting rat is relevant. In that demonstration one topography reached its limit, and a different topography then appeared (as a "mutation"?). That is not, as I understand it, the point of punctuated evolution.

I have never been sure about the place of intermittent contingencies in natural selection or the evolution of cultures. The time scales are very different, of course. Contingencies of selection need not be invariable; in a sense they are merely statistical. An evolved trait survives for a long time when the contingencies are no longer selective, and I dare say an occasiona reinstatement of the contingencies would further postpone "extinction."

3. Explanation, description, and taxonomy. I have never liked models oı postulates. Could anything be more factual than the effect of reinforcement either in a single instance or when scheduled? What is hypothetical about it? What needs to be modeled? The Law of Effect states a fact not a hypothesis. Consequences affect behavior.

4. Copies, representations, and analyses of stimuli. If I said that an organism "does more than make copies," I was speaking carelessly. It does not make copies at all. I must have meant "more than" in the sense of "something other than." And, of course, that holds for internal rules as "copies" of contingencies. People do make copies of things for later use and do formulate rules as statements about contingencies, but they do not do so when their behavior is simply shaped by the contingencies. I don't agree with Terrace that representations are necessary. I see no reason why the red sample in the matching experiment cannot be the occasion upon which pecking a red key is reinforced – or pecking a green one in "choosing the opposite." (Whether a pigeon ever generalizes so that matching occurs with new colors is hard to say because one soon runs out of colors.)

5. What is behavior? It is more than muscle twitches, certainly, because controlling variables need to be specified. But are muscles needed? It is too simple to say that "seeing is behavior." As Pere Julià and I (1985b) have been saying, seeing is only the early part of an instance of behavior. When the same early part is common to many different operants, something close to a generalized seeing emerges. (This is very close to "tacting" in my analysis of verbal behavior; if seeing is what happens in behavior "up to the point of action" – and hence probably to be studied only by neurology – the tact carries the matter one step further by adding an action but only "up to the point of reinforcement.") If action is not reached, no muscle responses are involved. I see no reason why we should not also call the action of efferent nerves behavior if no muscular response is needed for reinforcement. That may occur in the thinking that retreats beyond the point at which muscular action can be detected (As in *Verbal Behavior* [1957], I equate "thinking" with "behaving.")

Thought trials, like Tolman's (1948) "vicarious trial-and-error" (and for that matter the concept of trial itself), need a more careful analysis. A response is made that is less than complete but still enough to produce a consequence that alters its probability of occurrence. (It is not an "error" just because no effective change follows.) I would distinguish in a different way between "survival machines which can simulate the future" and "machines who [*sic*] can only learn on the basis of. . .trial and error." The second are . . .contingency shaped; the first follow rules and report consequences.

6. The definition of reinforcers. I do not see any significant "reversibility" in the fact that an occasion for running can reinforce drinking and an occasion for drinking can reinforce running. An occasion for drinking can reinforce a thousand different behaviors, and so can an occasion for running. (Why would you ever need to use occasion for weak behavior to reinforce behavior that is already strong?) Some 50 years ago, when I was using the term drive, I said that there must be a drive for every reinforcer. The effect of any consequence depends upon a degree either of deprivation (in positive reinforcement) or the strength of aversive stimulation (in negative reinforcement).

There is nothing circular in learning about the power of a reinforcer from observing its effect. (There might be if I were talking about an internal process.) I do not know why food is reinforcing to a hungry organism. I am sure it is not because "it reduces a need." Rather, it is a fact about phylogeny. There must have been great survival value if the probability of eating varied with the degree of food deprivation.

7. The problem of structure. I have already assumed that structure meant form or topography. Structuralists (in the old days, Gestalters) argue that certain principles of structure play causal roles. Developmental psychologists emphasize structure because age is an uncontrollable variable and they seem to feel they need something else, but developmental schedules are really schedules of changing environments. Erikson's (1963) stages are changes in the way in which behavior acts upon and is reinforced by the (primarily social) environment. If there are any significant properties of structure that affect the probability that a response will occur (either as a restraint or a help), they will be related to the prevailing contingencies.

8. Language acquisition. Chomsky and others often imply that I think that verbal behavior must be taught, that explicit contingencies must be arranged. Of course I do not, as *Verbal Behavior* makes clear. Children learn to speak in wholly noninstructional verbal communities. But the contingencies of reinforcement are still there, even though they may be harder to identify. Most intraverbals, for exàmple, are not taught. You don't teach a child to say *home* when you say *house*. But *house* and *home* appear near each other so often that one of them as a stimulus acquires some control over the other as a response.

The organized verbal behavior that is said to "follow rules" of grammar evolved very late, and in only one species. Grammatical behavior could not have had much of an advantage over ungrammatical in natural selection, and I do not think there has been enough time for the evolution of innate properties of verbal behavior such as those said to show a knowledge of the rules of grammar. The functions of verbal behavior, as seen in its effects upon the behavior of a listener, suffice to explain the rules and their supposed universality.

9. Private events as causal. As I indicate in "Terms," private events can be brought under the control of (especially public) behavior. In that case they may be called causes, but not initiating causes. The only possible exceptions I can imagine would arise if, when someone had acquired extensive public behavior, a set of private events (serving as stimulus, response, and consequence) would resemble a public set well enough to come into existence through generalization. We do engage in productive private verbal behavior in which some initiation certainly occurs, if that term means anything, but if my analysis is correct, public versions must have been established first. In that case, the initiation passes to the environment.

10. Active versus passive organisms. Selection by consequences assigns the initiation of behavior to contingencies of selection, but the organism is not therefore passive in the sense of being submissive. We do not call digestion, respiration, gestation, and other physiological processes passive, even though we explain them in terms of natural selection. Our culture may have gained a great deal by emphasizing the possibility that individuals are responsible for their behavior, can take active steps to change it, and are therefore in control. It is also possible that such a philosophy has remoter consequences which will prove to be dangerous. Whatever the ultimate consequences, the origination of behavior is still to be sought in natural selection, operant conditioning, and the evolution of cultural practices.

As to my reaction to the treatments in this volume as a whole: it has been my experience that when I write something in one setting at one time and come back to it in a different setting at a different time I see other implications and relations. I had thought that something of the same sort would happen when other people read these papers. They would add things which occurred to them because of their special interests and special knowledge, and a joint contribution would be possible. Too often, this has not happened. The misunderstandings triggered by my papers apparently did not suggest further implications to many commentators.

Why have I not been more readily understood? Bad exposition on my part? All I can say is that I worked very hard on these papers, and I believe they are consistent one with another. The central position, however, is not traditional, and that may be the problem. To move from an inner determination of behavior to an environmental determination is a difficult step. Many governmental, religious, ethical, political, and economic implications might also have been considered, but most of the contributions do not venture that far afield.

Why is discussion in the behavioral sciences so often personal? I do not believe that Einstein, finding it necessary to challenge some basic assumptions of Newton, alluded to Newton's senility. I do not think that Mendel and the other early geneticists, discovering facts that Darwin so badly needed, then accused him of "totally ignoring" the genetic basis of evolution. I do not think that those who propounded the gas laws for so-called ideal or perfect gases were condemned for their prejudice against the individual gas molecule. Why has it been so tempting to say, as one commentator does, that I am "strangely provincial," that my reluctance to acknowledge something or other is "quixotic," or that something else is "a tragic irony"? Are points of that sort relevant in a scientific discussion?

I have tried to keep the personal tone out of my replies, but the temptation was great, and at a few points I have failed. In any case, I have been unable to avoid spending time and space on the simple correction of misstatements of fact and of my position, where I would have welcomed the opportunity for a more productive exchange. Whatever current usefulness this volume may have, it should at least be of interest to the future historian as a sample of the style of discussion among behavioral scientists near the end of the 20th century.

Appendix: Biographical sketch and bibliography of works by B. F. Skinner

Biographical sketch

B. F. Skinner was born March 20, 1904 in Susquehanna, a small town in northeastern Pennsylvania, the son of a lawyer. He attended 12 years of public school in Susquehanna and went to Hamilton College, Clinton, New York, for his AB degree. His family had moved to Scranton, Pennsylvania, and after college he spent about two years there, first in testing himself as a writer of fiction and then writing a technical book for the coal mining industry. He had read books by John B. Watson, Jacques Loeb, and Pavlov and had become a committed behaviorist by the time he entered Harvard University as a graduate student in psychology in 1928. His doctoral thesis was on "the concept of the reflex," but his research led him quickly to operant behavior. He spent five postdoctoral years (as a National Science Foundation Fellow and as a Junior Fellow in the Harvard Society of Fellows) in the biological laboratories at Harvard. In 1936, he became an instructor at the University of Minnesota and in 1938 published *The Behavior of Organisms*. He married Yvonne Blue. They have two daughters: Julie (Mrs. Ernest Vargas) and Deborah (Mrs. Barry Buzan). In 1945, he became Chairman of Psychology at Indiana University, but before going to Indiana he wrote *Walden II*, a utopian novel. In 1947, he gave the William James Lectures at Harvard and was invited to return there as professor, which he did in 1948. He designed a new introductory course and wrote *Science and Human Behavior* as a text for it. In 1954 he developed a type of teaching machine which he used in that course in the late fifties. A long-term interest in verbal behavior culminated in the publication of his book *Verbal Behavior* in 1957. During the fifties, in collaboration with Charles B. Ferster and, later, with William Morse and Lewis Gollub, he conducted research on schedules of reinforcement.

A career award in 1964 enabled him to close his laboratory and stop teaching. He has since devoted his time to some of the implications of an operant analysis, publishing several books on technical issues. A popular book in 1971 called *Beyond Freedom and Dignity* became a best seller. He has recently been concerned about the future of the world and has published rather widely on the possibility that a behavioral science may help in solving our problems.

Bibliography

1. The progressive increase in the geotropic response of the ant *Aphaenogaster*. *Journal of General Psychology*, 1930, *4*, 102–12 (with T. C. Barnes).
2. On the inheritance of maze behavior. *Journal of General Psychology*, 1930, *4*, 342–46.
3. On the conditions of elicitation of certain eating reflexes. *Proceedings of the National Academy of Sciences*, 1930, *16*, 433–38.
4. The concept of the reflex in the description of behavior. *Journal of General Psychology*, 1931, *5*, 427–58.
5. Drive and reflex strength. *Journal of General Psychology*, 1932, *6*, 22–37.
6. Drive and reflex strength: II. *Journal of General Psychology*, 1932, *6*, 38–48.

7. On the rate of formation of a conditioned reflex. *Journal of General Psychology*, 1932, 7, 274–86.
8. A paradoxical color effect. *Journal of General Psychology*, 1932, 7, 481–82.
9. On the rate of extinction of a conditioned reflex. *Journal of General Psychology*, 1933, *8*, 114–29.
10. The measurement of "spontaneous activity." *Journal of General Psychology*, 1933, *9*, 3–23.
11. The rate of establishment of a discrimination. *Journal of General Psychology*, 1933, *9*, 302–50.
12. "Resistance to extinction" in the process of conditioning. *Journal of General Psychology*, 1933, *9*, 420–29.
13. The abolishment of a discrimination. *Proceedings of the National Academy of Sciences*, 1933, *19*, 420–29.
14. Some conditions affecting intensity and duration thresholds in motor nerve, with reference to chronaxie of subordination. *American Journal of Physiology*, 1933, *106*, 721–37 (with E. F. Lambert and A. Forbes).
15. Has Gertrude Stein a secret? *Atlantic Monthly*, January 1934, *153*, 50–57.
16. The extinction of chained reflexes. *Proceedings of The National Academy of Sciences*, 1934, *20*, 234–37.
17. A discrimination without previous conditioning. *Proceedings of the National Academy of Sciences*, 1934, *20*, 532–36.
18. The generic nature of the concepts of stimulus and response. *Journal of General Psychology*, 1935, *12*, 40–65.
19. Two types of conditioned reflex and a pseudo type. *Journal of General Psychology*, 1935, *12*, 66–77.
20. A discrimination based upon a change in the properties of a stimulus. *Journal of General Psychology*, 1935, *12*, 313–36.
21. A failure to obtain "disinhibition." *Journal of General Psychology*, 1936, *14*, 127–35.
22. The reinforcing effect of a differentiating stimulus. *Journal of General Psychology*, 1936, *14*, 263–78.
23. The effect on the amount of conditioning of an interval of time before reinforcement. *Journal of General Psychology*, 1936, *14*, 279–95.
24. Conditioning and extinction and their relation to drive. *Journal of General Psychology*, 1936, *14*, 296–317.
25. Thirst as an arbitrary drive. *Journal of General Psychology*, 1936, *15*, 205–10.
26. The verbal summator and a method for the study of latent speech. *Journal of Psychology*, 1936, 2, 71–107.
27. Two types of conditioned reflex: A reply to Konorski and Miller. *Journal of General Psychology*, 1937, *16*, 272–79.
28. Changes in hunger during starvation. *Psychological Record*, 1937, *1*, 51–60 (with W. T. Heron).
29. The distribution of associated words. *Psychological Record*, 1937, *1*, 71–76.
30. Effects of caffeine and benzedrine upon conditioning and extinction. *Psychological Record*, 1937, *1*, 340–46 (with W. T. Heron).
31. *The behavior of organisms: An experimental analysis*. New York: Appleton-Century-Crofts, 1938, 1966.
32. An apparatus for the study of animal behavior. *Psychological Record*, 1939, *3*, 166–76 (with W. T. Heron).
33. Some factors influencing the distribution of associated words. *Psychological Record*, 1939, *3*, 178–84 (with S. W. Cook).
34. The alliteration in Shakespeare's sonnets: A study in literary behavior. *Psychologica Record*, 1939, *3*, 186–92.
35. The rate of extinction in maze-bright and maze-dull rats. *Psychological Record*, 1940 *4*, 11–18 (with W. T. Heron).

36. A method of maintaining an arbitrary degree of hunger. *Journal of Comparative Psychology*, 1940, *30*, 139–45.
37. The psychology of design. In *Art education today*. New York: Bureau Publications, Teachers College, Columbia University, 1941, pp. 1–6.
38. A quantitative estimate of certain types of sound-patterning in poetry. *American Journal of Psychology*, 1941, *54*, 64–79.
39. Some quantitative properties of anxiety. *Journal of Experimental Psychology*, 1941, *29*, 390–400 (with W. K. Estes).
40. The processes involved in the repeated guessing of alternatives. *Journal of Experimental Psychology*, 1942, *30*, 495–503.
41. Reply to Dr. Yacorzynski, *Journal of Experimental Psychology*, 1943, *32*, 93–94.
42. The operational analysis of psychological terms. *Psychological Review*, 1945, *52*, 270–77, 291–94.
43. Baby in a box. *Ladies' Home Journal*, October 1945, *62*, 30–31, 135–36, 138.
44. An automatic shocking-grid apparatus for continuous use. *Journal of Comparative and Physiological Psychology*, 1947, *40*, 305–07 (with S. L. Campbell).
45. Experimental psychology. In W. Dennis et al., *Current trends in psychology*. Pittsburgh: University of Pittsburgh Press, 1947, pp. 16–49.
46. 'Superstition' in the pigeon. *Journal of Experimental Psychology*, 1948, *38*, 168–72.
47. Card-guessing experiments. *American Scientist*, 1948, *36*, 456, 458.
48. *Walden Two*. New York: Macmillan, 1948, 1976.
49. Are theories of learning necessary? *Psychological Review*, 1950, *57*, 193–216.
50. How to teach animals. *Scientific American*, December 1951, *185*, 26–29.
51. Some contributions of an experimental analysis of behavior to psychology as a whole. *American Psychologist*, 1953, *8*, 69–78.
52. *Science and human behavior*. New York: Macmillan, 1953.
53. The science of learning and the art of teaching. *Harvard Education Review*, 1954, *24*, 86–97.
54. A critique of psychoanalytic concepts and theories. *Scientific Monthly*, 1954, *79*, 300–05.
55. The control of human behavior. *Transactions of the New York Academy of Sciences*, 1955, *17*, 547–51.
56. Freedom and the control of men. *American Scholar*, Winter 1955–56, *25*, 47–65.
57. A case history in scientific method. *American Psychologist*, 1956, *11*, 221–33.
58. What is psychotic behavior? In *Theory and treatment of the psychoses: Some newer aspects*. St. Louis: Committee on Publications, Washington University, 1956, pp. 77–99.
59. Some issues concerning the control of human behavior: A symposium. *Science*, 1956, *124*, 1057–66 (with C. R. Rogers).
60. The psychological point of view. In H. D. Kruse (Ed.), *Integrating the approaches to mental disease*. New York: Hoeber–Harper, 1957, pp. 130–33.
61. The experimental analysis of behavior. *American Scientist*, 1957, *45*, 343–71.
62. A second type of superstition in the pigeon. *American Journal of Psychology*, 1957, *70*, 308–11 (with W. H. Morse).
63. Concurrent activity under fixed-interval reinforcement. *Journal of Comparative and Physiological Psychology*, 1957, *50*, 279–81 (with W. H. Morse).
64. *Verbal behavior*. New York: Appleton–Century–Crofts, 1957.
65. *Schedules of reinforcement*. New York: Appleton–Century–Crofts, 1957 (with C. B. Ferster).
66. Diagramming schedules of reinforcement. *Journal of the Experimental Analysis of Behavior*, 1958, *1*, 67–68.
67. Some factors involved in the stimulus control of operant behavior. *Journal of the Experimental Analysis of Behavior*, 1958, *1*, 103–07 (with W. H. Morse).
68. Reinforcement today. *American Psychologist*, 1958, *13*, 94–99.

69. Teaching machines. *Science*, 1958, *128*, 969–77.
70. Sustained performance during very long experimental sessions. *Journal of the Experimental Analysis of Behavior*, 1958, *1*, 235–44 (with W. H. Morse).
71. Fixed-interval reinforcement of running in a wheel. *Journal of the Experimental Analysis of Behavior*, 1958, *1*, 371–79 (with W. H. Morse).
72. John Broadus Watson, behaviorist. *Science*, 1959, *129*, 197–98.
73. The programming of verbal knowledge. In E. Galanter (Ed.), *Automatic teaching: The state of the art*. New York: John Wiley, 1959, pp. 63–68.
74. Animal research in the pharmacotherapy of mental disease. In J. Cole and R. Gerard (Eds.), *Psychopharmacology: Problems in evaluation*. Washington, D. C.: National Academy of Sciences–National Research Council, 1959, pp. 224–28.
75. The flight from the laboratory. In B. F. Skinner, *Cumulative record*. New York: Appleton–Century–Crofts, 1959, pp. 242–57.
76. *Cumulative record*. New York: Appleton–Century–Crofts, 1959. Enlarged edition, 1961. Third edition, 1972.
77. Special problems in programming language instruction for teaching machines. In F. J. Oinas (Ed.), *Language teaching today*. Bloomington, Indiana: Indiana University Research Center in Anthropology, Folklore, and Linguistics, 1960, pp. 167–74.
78. Concept formation in philosophy and psychology. In S. Hook (Ed.), *Dimensions of mind: A symposium*. Washington Square: New York University Press, 1960, pp. 226–30.
79. The use of teaching machines in college instruction (Parts II–IV). In A. A. Lumsdaine and R. Glaser (Eds.), *Teaching machines and programmed learning: A source book*. Washingon, D. C.: Department of Audio-Visual Instruction, National Education Association, 1960, pp. 159–72 (with J. G. Holland).
80. Pigeons in a pelican. *American Psychologist*, 1960, *15*, 28–37.
81. The design of cultures. *Daedalus*, 1961, *90*, 534–46.
82. Why we need teaching machines. *Harvard Educational Review*, 1961, *31*, 377–98.
83. Learning theory and future research. In J. Lysaught (Ed.), *Programmed learning: Evolving principles and industrial applications*. Ann Arbor: Foundation for Research on Human Behaviors, 1961, pp. 59–66.
84. Teaching machines. *Scientific American*, November 1961, *205*, 90–102.
85. *The analysis of behavior: A program for self-instruction*. New York: McGraw-Hill, 1961 (with J. G. Holland).
86. Technique for reinforcing either of two organisms with a single food magazine. *Journal of the Experimental Analysis of Behavior*, 1962, *5*, 58 (with G. S. Reynolds).
87. Operandum. *Journal of the Experimental Analysis of Behavior*, 1962, *5*, 224.
88. Squirrel in the yard: Certain sciurine experiences of B. F. Skinner. *Harvard Alumni Bulletin*, 1962, *64*, 642–45.
89. Two "synthetic social relations." *Journal of the Experimental Analysis of Behavior*, 1962, *5*, 531–33.
90. Conditioned and unconditioned aggression in pigeons. *Journal of the Experimental Analysis of Behavior*, 1963, *6*, 73–74 (with G. S. Reynolds and A. C. Catania).
91. Behaviorism at fifty. *Science*, 1963, *140*, 951–58.
92. Operant behavior. *American Psychologist*, 1963, *18*, 503–515.
93. Reply to Thouless. *Australian Journal of Psychology*, 1963, *15*, 92–93.
94. Reflections on a decade of teaching machines. *Teachers College Record*, 1963, *65*, 168–77.
95. L'avenir des machines à enseigner. *Psychologie Française*, 1963, *8*, 170–80.
96. New methods and new aims in teaching. *New Scientist*, 1964, *122*, 483–84.
97. "Man." *Proceedings of the American Philosophical Society*, 1964, *108*, 482–85.
98. The technology of teaching. *Proceedings of the Royal Society*, 1965, *162*, 427–43.
99. Stimulus generalization in an operant: A historical note. In D. I. Mostofsky (Ed.), *Stimulus generalization*. Stanford: Stanford University Press, 1965, pp. 193–209.

100. Why teachers fail. *Saturday Review*, October 16, 1965, *48*, 80–81, 98–102.
101. The phylogeny and ontogeny of behavior. *Science*, 1966, *153*, 1205–13.
102. An operant analysis of problem solving. In B. Kleinmuntz (Ed.), *Problem solving: Research, method, and theory*. New York: John Wiley, 1966, pp. 225–57.
103. Conditioning responses by reward and punishment. *Proceedings of the Royal Institution of Great Britain*, 1966, *41*, 48–51.
104. Contingencies of reinforcement in the design of a culture. *Behavioral Science*, 1966, *11*, 159–66.
105. What is the experimental analysis of behavior? *Journal of the Experimental Analysis of Behavior*, 1966, *9*, 213–18.
106. Some responses to the stimulus "Pavlov." *Conditional Reflex*, 1966, *1*, 74–78.
107. B. F. Skinner (An autobiography). In E. G. Boring and G. Lindzey (Eds.), *A history of psychology in autobiography* (Vol. 5). New York: Appleton–Century–Crofts, 1967, pp. 387–413.
108. Visions of utopia. *The Listener*, January 5, 1967, *77*, 22–23.
109. Utopia through the control of human behavior. *The Listener*, January 12, 1967, *77*, 55–56.
110. The problem of consciousness – a debate. *Philosophy and Phenomenological Research*, 1967, *27*, 317–37 (with B. Blanshard).
111. The science of human behavior. In *Twenty-five years at RCA laboratories 1942–1967*. Princeton, New Jersey: RCA Laboratories, 1968, pp. 92–102.
112. Teaching science in high school – what is wrong? *Science*, 1968, *159*, 704–10.
113. Edwin Garrigues Boring, *Year Book of the American Philosophical Society*, 1968, pp. 111–15.
114. The design of experimental communities. In *International encyclopedia of the social sciences* (Vol. 16). New York: Macmillan, 1968, pp. 271–75.
115. *The technology of teaching*. New York: Appleton–Century–Crofts, 1968.
116. Contingency management in the classroom. *Education*, 1969, *90*, 93–100.
117. The machine that is man. *Psychology Today*, April 1969, *2*, 22–25, 60–63.
118. *Contingencies of reinforcement: A theoretical analysis*. New York: Appleton–Century–Crofts, 1969.
119. Creating the creative artist. In A. J. Toynbee and others. *On the future of art*. New York: Viking Press, 1970, pp. 61–75.
120. Humanistic behaviorism. *The Humanist*, May/June 1971, *31*, 35.
121. Autoshaping. *Science*, 1971, *173*, 752.
122. A behavioral analysis of value judgments. In E. Tobach, L. R. Aronson, and E. Shaw (Eds.), *The biopsychology of development*. New York: Academic Press, 1971, pp. 543–51.
123. B. F. Skinner says what's wrong with the social sciences. *The Listener*, September 30, 1971, *86*, 429–31.
124. *Beyond freedom and dignity*. New York: Alfred A. Knopf, 1971.
125. Some relations between behavior modification and basic research. In B. F. Skinner, *Cumulative record* (3rd ed.). New York: Appleton– Century–Crofts, 1972, pp. 276–82.
126. Compassion and ethics in the care of the retardate. In B. F. Skinner, *Cumulative record* (3rd ed.). New York: Appleton–Century–Crofts, 1972, pp. 283–91.
127. A lecture on "having a poem." In B.F. Skinner, *Cumulative record* (3rd ed.), New York: Appleton–Century–Crofts, 1972, pp. 345–55.
128. Humanism and behaviorism. *The Humanist*, July/August 1972, *32*, 18–20.
129. Freedom and dignity revisited. *New York Times*, August 11, 1972, p. 29.
130. *The freedom to have a future* (The 1972 Sol Feinstone Lecture). Syracuse, New York: Syracuse University, 1973.
131. Reflections on meaning and structure. In R. Brower, H. Bendler, and J. Hollander (Eds.), *I. A. Richards: Essays in his honor*. New York: Oxford University Press, 1973, pp. 199–209.

132. Answers for my critics. In H. Wheeler (Ed.), *Beyond the punitive society*. San Francisco: W. H. Freeman, 1973, pp. 256–66.
133. Some implications of making education more efficient. In C. E. Thoresen (Ed.), *Behavior modification in education*. Chicago: National Society for the Study of Education, 1973, pp. 446–56.
134. Are we free to have a future? *Impact*, 1973, *3*(1), 5–12.
135. *Walden* (One) and *Walden Two*. *The Thoreau Society Bulletin*. Winter 1973, *122*, 1–3.
136. The free and happy student. *New York University Education Quarterly*, Winter 1973, *4*, 2–6.
137. Designing higher education. *Daedalus*, 1974, *103*, 196–202.
138. *About behaviorism*. New York: Alfred A. Knopf, 1974.
139. Comments on Watts's "B. F. Skinner and the Technological Control of Social Behavior. *The American Political Science Review*, 1975, *69*, 228–29.
140. The shaping of phylogenic behavior. *Acta Neurobiologiae Experimentalis*, 1975, *35*, 409–15. Also published in *Journal of the Experimental Analysis of Behavior*, 1975, *24*, 117–20.
141. The steep and thorny way to a science of behaviour. In R. Harré (Ed.), *Problems of scientific revolution: Progress and obstacles to progress in the sciences*. Oxford: Clarendon Press, 1975, pp. 58–71.
142. The ethics of helping people. *Criminal Law Bulletin*, 1975, *11*, 623–36.
143. Farewell, my LOVELY! *Journal of the Experimental Analysis of Behavior*, 1976, *25*, 218.
144. *Particulars of my life*. New York: Alfred A. Knopf, 1976.
145. The force of coincidence. In B. C. Etzel, J. M. LeBlanc, and D. M. Baer (Eds.), *New developments in behavioral psychology: Theory, methods, and application*. Hillsdale, New Jersey: Lawrence Erlbaum Associates, 1977, pp. 3–6.
146. The experimental analysis of operant behavior. In R. W. Rieber and K. Salzinger (Eds.), *The roots of American psychology: Historical influences and implications for the future* (*Annals of the New York Academy of Sciences*, Vol. 291). New York: New York Academy of Sciences, 1977, pp. 374–85.
147. Freedom, at last, from the burden of taxation. *New York Times*, July 26, 1977, p. 29.
148. Why I am not a cognitive psychologist. *Behaviorism*, Fall 1977, *5*, 1–10.
149. Between freedom and despotism. *Psychology Today*, September 1977, *11*, 80–82, 84, 86, 90–91.
150. Herrnstein and the evolution of behaviorism. *American Psychologist*, 1977, *32*, 1006–12.
151. *Reflections on behaviorism and society*. Englewood Cliffs, New Jersey: Prentice-Hall, 1978.
152. Why don't we use the behavioral sciences? *Human Nature*, March 1978, *1*, 86–92.
153. *The shaping of a behaviorist: Part two of an autobiography*. New York: Alfred A. Knopf, 1979.
154. A happening at the annual dinner of the Association for Behavioral Analysis, Chicago, May 15, 1978. *The Behavior Analyst*. Winter 1979, *2*(1), 30–33.
155. My experience with the baby tender. *Psychology Today*, March 1979, *12*(10), 28–31, 34, 37–38, 40.
156. Le renforgateur arrangé. *Revue de modification du comportement*, 1979, *9*, 59–69 (translated into French by Raymond Beausoleil).
157. Symbolic communication between two pigeons (*Columba livia domestica*). *Science* 1980, *207*, 543–45 (with R. Epstein and R. P. Lanza).
158. Resurgence of responding after the cessation of response-independent reinforce ment. *Proceedings of the National Academy of Sciences*, 1980, *77*, 6251–53 (with R Epstein).
159. *Notebooks*. Englewood Cliffs, New Jersey: Prentice-Hall, 1980.
160. The species-specific behavior of ethologists. *The Behavior Analyst*, 1980, *3*, 51.

161. Pavlov's influence on psychology in America. *Journal of the History of the Behavioral Sciences*, 1981, *17*, 242–45.
162. "Self-awareness" in the pigeon. *Science*, 1981, *212*, 695–96 (with R. Epstein and R. P. Lanza).
163. Charles B. Ferster – A personal memoir. *Journal of the Experimental Analysis of Behavior*, 1981, *35*, 259–61.
164. How to discover what you have to say – a talk to students. *The Behavior Analyst*. 1981, *4*, 1–7.
165. Selection by consequences. *Science*, 1981, *213*, 501–04.
166. The spontaneous use of memoranda by pigeons. *Behavior Analysis Letters*, 1981, *1*, 241–46 (with R. Epstein).
167. Contrived reinforcement. *The Behavior Analyst*, 1982, *5*, 3–8.
168. "Lying" in the pigeon. *Journal of the Experimental Analysis of Behavior*, 1982, *38*, 201–03 (with R. P. Lanza and J. Starr).
169. *Skinner for the Classroom*. Champaign, Illinois: Research Press, 1982.
170. Intellectual self-management in old age. *The American Psychologist*, March 1983, *38*(3), 239–44.
171. Can the experimental analysis of behavior rescue psychology? *The Behavior Analyst*, Spring 1983, *6* (1), 9–17.
172. *Enjoy Old Age*. New York: W. W. Norton & Company, 1983 (with M. E. Vaughan).
173. A better way to deal with selection. *The Behavioral and Brain Sciences*, 1983, *3*, 377.
174. *A Matter of Consequences*. New York: Alfred A. Knopf, Inc., 1983.
175. The evolution of behavior. *Journal of the Experimental Analysis of Behavior*, 1984, *41*(2), 217–21.
176. Canonical papers of B. F. Skinner. *The Behavioral and Brain Sciences*, December 1984, *7*(4), 473–724.
177. The shame of American education. *American Psychologist*, September 1984, *39*(9), 947–54.
178. Evolution of verbal behavior. *Journal of the Experimental Analysis of Behavior*, 1986, *45*, 115–22.
179. News from nowhere, 1984. *The Behavior Analyst*, Spring 1985, *8* (1), 5–14.
180. Toward the cause of peace: What can psychology contribute? *Applied Social Psychology Annual*, 1985, 21–25.
181. Cognitive science and behaviorism. *British Journal of Psychology*, 1985, *76*, 291–301.
182. Reply to Place: "Three senses of the word 'tact'." *Behaviorism*, Spring 1985, *13*(1), 75–76.
183. Some thoughts about the future. *Journal of the Experimental Analysis of Behavior*, 1986, *45*(2), 299–35.
184. What is wrong with daily life in the western world? *American Psychologist*, May 1986, *41*(5), 568–74.
185. Sleeping in peace. *Free Inquiry*, Summer 1986, *6*(3), 57.
186. *Upon Further Reflection*. Englewood Cliffs, New Jersey: Prentice-Hall, 1986.
187. Programmed instruction revisited. *Phi Delta Kappan*, October 1986, *68*(2), 103–10.
188. Outlining a science of feeling. *The Times Literary Supplement*, 1987, May 8, 490–96.
189. Whatever happened to psychology as the science of behavior? *American Psychologist*, 1987, *42*(8), 780–86.

Acknowledgments and notes

The editors would like to acknowledge here the invaluable help of Helaine Randerson who, as Assistant Editor of *BBS* during the preparation of the special Skinner issue, skillfully organized and coordinated the complex communications and editorial work entailed by the *BBS* treatments. We also thank Michael Gnat of Cambridge University Press for his expert editorial work on this volume, and Glorieux Dougherty for her careful and thorough indexing.

Preparation of A. C. Catania's introduction and concluding remarks was supported in part by NSF grant BNS82-03385 to the University of Maryland Baltimore County. Some passages from the introduction were excerpted from Catania (1980), with permission of the publisher. The University College of North Wales provided helpful resources during the editorial preparation of the book.

1. Selection by consequences

B. F. Skinner's "Selection by consequences" originally appeared in *Science* 213:501–04, 3 July 1981. Copyright 1981 by the American Association for the Advancement of Science (reprinted with permission).

The commentary by C. B. G. Campbell has been reviewed by the Walter Reed Army Institute of Research, and there is no objection to its presentation or publication. The opinions or assertions contained therein are the private views of the author and are not to be construed as official or as reflecting the views of the Department of the Army or the Department of Defense.

Preparation of the commentary by M. J. Katz was supported by the Whitehall Foundation.

Preparation of the commentary by D. M. Rumbaugh was supported by National Institute of Child Health and Human Development no. 06016 and National Institutes of Health Animal Resources Branch no. RR-00165.

P. R. Solomon is grateful to Andrew Crider for helpful comments on an earlier version of his commentary.

W. Timberlake thanks Don Gawley, Ted Melcer, and especially Gary Lucas for comments. Preparation of the commentary was supported by a grant from the National Science Foundation.

2. Methods and theories in the experimental analysis of behavior

B. F. Skinner's "Methods and theories in the experimental analysis of behavior" is a combination and condensation of "The flight from the laboratory," which appeared in *Current trends in psychological theory* edited by Wayne Dennis et al. and is reprinted by permission of the University of Pittsburgh Press (copyright 1961 by University of Pittsburgh Press), "Are theories of learning necessary?," which appeared in *Psychological Review* 57:193–216, 1950, and the Preface to *Contingencies of reinforcement: A theoretical analysis* (copyright 1969, Prentice-Hall, Inc., Englewood Cliffs, N.J.: reprinted with permission).

A version of the commentary by Hershberger has also appeared in *American Psychologist*, and is published with permission. Copyright 1988 by the American Psychological Association.

Preparation of S. Roberts's commentary was supported by NIMH grant 1 RO 1 MH38358-01. Some of the ideas came from conversations with Steven Maier and N. J. Mackintosh.

3. The operational analysis of psychological terms

B. F. Skinner's "The operational analysis of psychological terms" is slightly revised from the original, which appeared in *Psychological Review* 52:270–77, 291–94, 1945.

D. T. Kenrick and R. C. Keefe wish to thank Peter R. Killeen for very helpful editorial suggestions concerning their commentary.

Preparation of H. S. Terrace's commentary was supported by an NSF grant (BNS-82-02423).

4. An operant analysis of problem solving

B. F. Skinner's "An operant analysis of problem solving" is an edited version of a chapter from *Problem solving: Research, method, and theory*, edited by B. Kleinmuntz, copyright 1966, John Wiley & Sons, Inc. Publishers (reprinted with permission). The article incorporates a portion of the notes that followed an earlier reprinting in *Contingencies of reinforcement: A theoretical analysis* (pp. 159–62, 166–67; copyright 1969, Prentice-Hall, Inc., Englewood Cliffs, N.J.; reprinted with permission).

Preparation of S. Grossberg's commentary was supported in part by the Air Force Office of Scientific Research (AFOSR 82-0148), and the Office of Naval Research (ONR-N00014-83-K0337).

Partial support from the National Science Foundation on grant IST-800-7433 in preparing M. Kochen's commentary is gratefully acknowledged.

J. G. Rein thanks P. Saugstad and L. Stinessen for valuable discussion.

5. Behaviorism at fifty

B. F. Skinner's "Behaviorism at fifty" is an edited version of an article that originally appeared in *Science* 140:951–58, 31 May 1963, Copyright 1963 by the American Association for the Advancement of Science (reprinted with permission).

Preparation of M. Lebowitz's commentary was supported in part by the Defense Advanced Research Projects Agency under contract N00039-82-C-0427.

In the commentary by M. W. Schustack and J. G. Carbonell, the order in which the authors are listed is not significant.

S. P. Stich's commentary was written while he was a fellow at the Center for Advanced Study in the Behavioral Sciences. He is grateful for financial support provided by the Andrew Mellon Foundation and the National Endowment for the Humanities.

6. The phylogeny and ontogeny of behavior

B. F. Skinner's "The phylogeny and ontogeny of behavior" originally appeared in *Science* 153:1205–13, 9 September 1966. Copyright 1966 by the American Association for the Advancement of Science (reprinted with permission).

The preparation of J. D. Delius's commentary was supported in part by the Deutsche Forschungsgemeinschaft through its Sonderforschungsbereich 114.

References

The references are keyed to the section in which they were cited first by section number according to the following list and second by the initials of the citing author.

0. Introduction
1. Selection by consequences ("Consequences")
2. Methods and theories in the experimental analysis of behavior ("Methods")
3. The operational analysis of psychological terms ("Terms")
4. An operant analysis of problem solving ("Problem Solving")
5. Behaviorism at fifty ("Behaviorism-50")
6. The phylogeny and ontogeny of behavior ("Phylogeny")
7. Summing up

For example, [1-RD] indicates a citation by Richard Dawkins in the treatment of "Consequences," and [4-EH] indicates a citation by Earl Hunt in the treatment of "Problem Solving." References to citations in the original articles by B. F. Skinner precede other citations (e.g., [3-BFS] for a citation in "Terms"). Citations in B. F. Skinner's responses to commentators are shown in the format: [7-BFS on SH]; this identifies B. F. Skinner's response to Stevan Harnad in the final section. Thus, [6-BFS, MTG, BFS on JPH] indicates three citations within the treatment of "Phylogeny": in B. F. Skinner's article, in M. T. Ghiselin's commentary, and in B. F. Skinner's reply to Hailman.

Adams, C. D. & Dickinson, A. (1981) Actions and habits: Variations in associative representations during instrumental learning. In: *Information processing in animals: Memory mechanisms*, ed. N. E. Spear & R. R. Miller. Erlbaum. [1-WKH]

Adrian, E. D. (1928) *The basis of sensations: The action of the sense organs*. W. W. Norton. [4-BFS]

Allee, W. C. (1938) *Cooperation among animals*. Abelard-Schuman. [6-BFS]

Allport, F. H. (1955) *Theories of perception and the concept of structure*. Wiley. [6-GDW]

Anderson, J. A. (1973) A theory for the recognition of items from short memorized lists. *Psychological Review* 80:417-38. [2-RDL]

Anderson, J. R. (1978) Arguments concerning representations for mental imagery. *Psychological Review* 85:249-77. [3-LCR]

Anderson, J. R. & Bower, G. H. (1973) *Human associative memory*. Winston. [2-CPS]

Arbib, M. A. & Caplan, D. (1979) Neurolinguistics must be computational. *Behavioral and Brain Sciences* 2:449-84. [4-EPS]

Ardrey R. (1961) *African genesis*. Atheneum. [6-BFS]

Armstrong, D. M. (1971) Meaning and communication. *Philosophical Review* 80:427-47. [3-JB]

Ashby, W. R. (1952) *Design for a brain*. Wiley & Sons. [1-TJG]

(1956) *An introduction to cybernetics*. Chapman and Hall. [1-SCS]

Aslin, R. N. (1981) Experiential influences and sensitive periods in development: A unified model. In: *Development of perception: Psychobiological perspectives*, vol. 2, ed. R. N. Aslin J. R. Alberts & M. R. Petersen. Academic Press. [6-GG]

Aslin, R. N. & Pisoni, D. B. (1980) Some developmental processes in speech perception. In: *Child phonology: Perception and production*, ed. G. H. Yeni-Komshian, J. F. Kavanagh & C. A. Ferguson. Academic Press. [6–GG]

Attneave, F. (1960) In defense of homunculi. In: *Sensory communication*, ed. W. Rosenblith. MIT Press. [5–WGL]

Austin, J. L. (1961) *Philosophical papers*. Clarendon Press. [3–PH]

Azrin, N. H., Hutchinson, R. R. & Laughlin, R. (1965) The opportunity for aggression as an operant reinforcer during aversive stimulation. *Journal of the Experimental Analysis of Behavior* 8:171–80. [6–BFS]

Bacon, F. (1620) *Novum organum*. J. Billius. [4–LJC]

Baer, D. M. (1982) Some recommendations for a modest reduction in the rate of current recommendations for an immodest increase in the rate of exclusive usages of rate as a dependent measure. Paper presented at the meeting of the Association for Behavior Analysis, Milwaukee. [2–SMD]

Baerends, G. P. (1941) Fortpflanzungsverhalten und Orientierung der Grabwespe *Ammophilia campestris* Jur. Tijdschrift Entomologie 84:68–275. [1–GWB]

Baldwin, J. M. (1896). A new factor in evolution. *American Naturalist* 30:441–51. [1–JS]

(1900) *Mental development in the child and race*. Macmillan. [1–TJG]

Barash, D. P. & Lipton, J. E. (1985). *The caveman and the bomb*. McGraw-Hill. [6–DPB]

Barkow, J. (1976) Attention structure and the evolution of human psychological characteristics. In: *The social structure of attention*, ed. M. R. A. Chance & R. R. Larsen. Wiley. [6–JHB]

(1983) Begged questions in behavior and evolution. In: *Animal models of human behavior*, ed. G. Davey. [6–JHB]

Barr, A., Cohen, P. R. & Feigenbaum, E. A., eds. (1982) *The Handbook of Artificial Intelligence*, vols. 1–3. William Kaufmann. [5–ML]

Bates, E. (1976) *Language and context: The acquisition of pragmatics*. Academic Press. [3–RPB]

Bateson, G. (1963). The role of somatic change in evolution. *Evolution* 17:359–69. [1–JS]

Bateson, P. (1980) Optimal outbreeding and the development of sexual preferences in Japanese quail. *Zeitschrift für Tierpsychologie* 53:231–44. [1–GWB]

Beach, F. A. (1950) The snark was a boojum. *American Psychologist* 5:115–24. [6–BFS, JPH]

(1955) The descent of instinct. *Psychological Review* 62:401–10. [6–GMB]

Bealer, G. (1978) An inconsistency in functionalism. *Synthese* 38:332–72. [2–RJN]

de Beer, G. (1940) *Embryos and ancestors*. Oxford University Press. 3d rev. ed. 1958. [6–GG]

Bem, D. J. (1967) Self-perception: An alternative interpretation of cognitive dissonance phenomena. *Psychological Review* 74:183–200. [3–DTK, BFS on DTK, HST]

Bem, D. J. & Allen, A. (1974) On predicting some of the people some of the time: The search for cross-situational consistencies in behavior. *Psychological Review* 81:506–20. [3–DTK]

Bennett, J. (1975) Stimulus, response, meaning. *American Philosophical Quarterly* 9:55–88. [3–JB]

(1976) *Linguistic behavior*. Cambridge University Press. [3–JB]

Bergmann, G. & Spence, K. W. (1941) Operationism and theory in psychology. *Psychological Review* 48:1–14. [3–JM]

Berlin, B. & Kay, P. (1969) *Basic color terms: Their universality and evolution*. University of California Press. [5–TRZ]

Berlyne, D. E. (1966) Discussions of papers by Israel Goldiamond, B. F. Skinner, and Arthur W. Staats. In: *Problem solving: Research, method and theory*, ed. B. Kleinmuntz. Wiley. [4–EH]

(1969) The reward-value of indifferent stimulation. In: *Reinforcement and behavior*, ed. J. T. Tapp. Academic Press. [4–SG]

Bernstein, D. J. & Ebbesen, E. B. (1978) Reinforcement and substitution in humans: A multiple-response analysis. *Journal of the Experimental Analysis of Behavior* 30:243–53. [7–ACC]

Berwick, R. C. & Weinberg, A. (1983) *The grammatical basis of linguistic performance*. MIT Press. [5–JCM]

Bindra, D. (1978) How adaptive behavior is produced: A perceptual-motivational alternative to response-reinforcement. *Behavioral and Brain Sciences* 1:41–91. [5–FMT]

Bitterman, M. E. (1975) The comparative analysis of learning. *Science* 188:699–709. [4–NEW]

Black, M. (1962) *Models and metaphors*. Cornell University Press. [5–MB]

Blanchard, R. J. & Blanchard, D. C. (1980) The organization of aggressive behaviors in rodents. In: *The biology of aggression*, ed. P. F. Brain & D. Benton. Nordhoof. [6–DCB]

Blanshard, B. (1967) The problem of consciousness – a debate. *Philosophy and Phenomenological Research* 27:317–24. [6–AMC, BFS on AMC]

Block, N. (1978) Troubles with functionalism. In: *Perception and cognition: Issues in the foundations of psychology*. Minnesota studies in the philosophy of science, vol. 9, ed. C. W. Savage. University of Minnesota Press. [3–GG]

(1980a) *Readings in the philosophy of psychology*, vol. 1. Harvard University Press. [5–RS]

(1980b) Troubles with functionalism. In: *Readings in the philosophy of psychology*, vol. 1, ed. N. Block. Harvard University Press. [5–GR]

(1980c) What is functionalism? In: *Readings in the philosophy of psychology*, vol. 1, ed. N. Block, Harvard University Press. [5–LHD]

ed. (1981) *Readings in philosophy of psychology*, vol. 2. Methuen. [4–GK]

Blodgett, H. (1929) The effect of the introduction of reward upon the maze performance of rats. In: *University of California publications in psychology*. University of California Press. [5–GR, BFS on GR]

Bloomfield, T. M. (1969) Behavioral contrast and the peak shift. In: *Animal discrimination learning*, ed. R. M. Gilbert & N. S. Sutherland. Academic Press. [4–SG]

Blough, D. S. (1956) Dark adaptation in the pigeon. *Journal of Comparative and Physiological Psychology* 49:425–30. [5–BFS]

(1959) Delayed matching in the pigeon. *Journal of the Experimental Analysis of Behavior* 2:151–60. [5–WST]

(1963) Interresponse time as a function of continuous variables: A new method and some data. *Journal of the Experimental Analysis of Behavior* 6:237–46. [2–SR]

(1972) Recognition by the pigeon of stimuli varying in two dimensions. *Journal of the Experimental Analysis of Behavior* 18:345–67. [2–SR]

(1978) Reaction times of pigeons on a wavelength discrimination task. *Journal of the Experimental Analysis of Behavior* 30:163–67. [2–SR]

(1982) Pigeon perception of letters of the alphabet. *Science* 218:397–98. [2–SR]

Blough, D. S. & Schrier, A. M. (1963) Scotopic spectral sensitivity in the monkey. *Science* 139:493–94. [5–BFS]

Boden, M. (1972) *Purposive explanation in psychology*. Harvard University Press. [3–JDR]

Bohr, N. (1958) *Atomic physics and human knowledge*. [2–BFS, MNR]

Bolter, D. J. (1984) *Turing's man*. University of North Carolina Press. [5–MB]

Bonner, J. T., ed. (1982) *Evolution and development*. Springer Verlag. [6–SNS]

Boring, E. G. (1936) Temporal perception and operationism. *American Journal of Psychology* 48:519–22. [3–JM]

(1945) The use of operational definitions in science. *Psychological Review* 52:243–45. [3–BFS]

Bornstein, M. H. (1975) Qualities of color vision in infancy. *Journal of Experimental Child Psychology* 19:401–19. [5–RTK]

(1978) Chromatic vision in infancy. In: *Advances in child development and behavior*, vol. 12, ed. H. W. Reese & L. H. Lipsitt. Academic Press. [5–HMW]

(1981) Psychological studies of color perception in human infants: Habituation, discrimination and categorization, recognition and conceptualization. In: *Advances in infancy research*, ed. L. P. Lipsitt & C. K. Rovee-Collier. Ablex. [5–TRZ]

Bornstein, M. H., Kessen, W. & Weiskopf, S. (1976) Color vision and hue categorization in young human infants. *Journal of Experimental Psychology: Human Performance and Perception* 2:115–29. [5–TRZ]

Borowsky, R. (1978) Social inhibition of maturation in natural populations of *Xiphophorus viriatus* (Pisces: Poeciliidae). *Science* 201:933–35. [1–GWB]

Bousfield, A. K. & Bousfield, W. A. (1966) Measurement of clustering and of sequential constancies in repeated free recall. *Psychological Reports*. 19:935–42. [3–HST]

Bower, G. H. (1972) A selective review of organizational factors in memory. In: *Organization of memory*, ed. E. Tulving & W. Donaldson. Academic Press. [3–HST]

Boyd, R. & Richerson, P. J. (1980) Sociobiology, culture and economic theory. *Journal of Economic Behavior and Organization* 1:97–121. [1–TJG]

Brady, J. V. (1975) Conditioning and emotion. In: *Emotions: Their parameters and measurement*, ed. L. Levi. Raven Press. [5–MLW]

Branden, N. (1963) The contradiction of determinism. *Objectivist Newsletter* 2:17–20. [6–AMC]

Bransford, J. D., McCarrel, N. W., Franks, J. J. & Nitsch, K. E. (1977) Towards unexplaining memory. In: *Perceiving, acting, and knowing: Toward an ecological psychology*, ed. R. E. Shaw & J. D. Bransford. Erlbaum. [5–MJM]

Breland, K. & Breland, M. (1961) The misbehavior of organisms. *American Psychologist* 16: 661–64. [1–WKH, BFS on WKH; 2–RM; 6–BFS, GMB]

Bretherton, I., McNew, S. & Beeghly-Smith, M. (1981) Early person knowledge as expressed in gestural and verbal communication: When do infants acquire a "Theory of Mind?" In: *Social cognition in infancy*, ed. M. Lamb & L. Sherrod. Erlbaum. [5–CNJ]

Bridgman, P. W. (1928) *The logic of modern physics*. Macmillan. [3–BFS, RPB, JDR]

(1945a) Some general principles of operational analysis. *Psychological Review* 52:246–49. [3–BFS]

(1945b) The prospect for intelligence. *Yale Review* 34:444–61. [2–LW]

(1952) *The nature of some of our physical concepts*. Philosophical Library. [4–BFS]

(1959) *The way things are*. Harvard University Press. [4–BFS; 5–BFS]

Brinker, R. P. (1982) Contextual contours in the development of language. In: *Children thinking through language*, ed. M. Beveridge. Edward Arnold. [3–RPB]

Broadbent, D. E. (1958) *Perception and communication*. Pergamon. [5–BAF, BFS on BAF]

Brown, P. L. & Jenkins, H. M. (1968) Auto-shaping of the pigeon's key-peck. *Journal of the Experimental Analysis of Behavior* 11:1–8. [6–AMC, BFS on AMC]

Bruner, J. S. (1975) The ontogenesis of speech acts. *Journal of Child Language* 2:1–19. [3–RPB]

Brunjes, P. C. & Alberts. J. R. (1979) Olfactory stimulation induces filial preferences for huddling in rat pups. *Journal of Comparative and Physiological Psychology* 93:548–55. [6–GG]

Brunswik, E. (1952) *The conceptual framework of psychology*. University of Chicago Press. [4–RMH]

(1955) Representative design and probabilistic theory in a functional psychology. *Psychological Review* 62:193–217. [5–EJW]

Bull, J. J. & Vogt, R. C. (1979) Temperature-dependent sex determination in turtles. *Science* 206:1186–88. [6–DW]

Bullock, T. H. (1970) *The reliability of neurones*. Jacques Loeb memorial lectures. Woods Hole, Woods Hole Oceanographic Institution and Marine Biological Laboratory Massachusetts. [6–GDW]

Bunge, M. (1968) *Scientific research, vol. 2, The search for truth*. Springer. [4–PCD]

(1980) *The mind-body problem: A psychological approach*. Pergamon Press. [2–MNR]

Burghardt, G. M. (1973) Instinct and innate behavior: Toward an ethological psychology. In: *The study of behavior*, ed. J. A. Nevin & G. S. Reynolds. Scott, Foresman & Co. [6–GMB]

(1977) Ontogeny of communication. In: *How animals communicate*, ed. T. A. Sebeok. Indiana University Press. [6–GMB]

Bush, R. R. (1960) A survey of mathematical learning theory. In: *Developments in mathematical psychology*, ed. R. D. Luce, R. R. Bush & J. C. R. Licklider. Free Press. [2–KMS]

Camerer, C. F. (1981) The validity and utility of expert judgment. Ph.D. dissertation. University of Chicago. [4–RMH]

Campbell, D. T. (1956) Perception as substitute trial and error. *Psychological Review* 63:330–42. [1–RCB, TJG]

(1960) Blind variation and selective retention in creative thought as in other knowledge processes. *Psychological Review* 67:380–400. [1–WKH, BFS on WKH; 6–JERS]

(1974a) Downward causation in hierarchically organized biological systems. In: *Studies in the philosophy of biology*, ed. F. J. Ayala & T. Dobzhansky. Macmillan. [1–HCP]

(1974b) Evolutionary epistemology. In: *The philosophy of Karl Popper*, ed. P. A. Schlipp. Open Court Publishing Co. [1–TJG]

(1975) On the conflicts between biological and social evolution and between psychology and moral tradition. *American Psychologist* 30:1103–26. [1–GWB]

Caraco, T. (1980) On foraging time allocation in a stochastic environment. *Ecology* 61:119–28. [6–AK]

(1983) White-crowned sparrows (*Zonotrichia Peucophrys*): Foraging preferences in a risky environment. *Behavioral Ecology and Sociobiology* 12:63–69. [6–AK]

Caraco, T., Martindale, S. & Whittam, T. S. (1980) An empirical demonstration of risk-sensitive foraging preferences. *Animal Behaviour* 28:820–30. [6–AK]

Carey, S. (1978) The child as word learner. In: *Linguistic theory and psychological reality*, ed. M. Halle, J. Bresnan, & G. Miller. MIT Press. [5–AG]

Carlson, N. R. (1981) *Physiology of behavior*. 2d ed. Allyn and Bacon. [5–FWI]

Carnap, R. (1934) *The unity of science*. K. Paul, Trench, Trubner & Co. [3–BFS]

(1962) *Logical foundations of probability*. 2nd ed. University of Chicago Press. [3–CW]

Caswell, H. (1983) Phenotypic plasticity in life-history traits: Demographic effects and evolutionary consequences. *American Zoologist* 23:35–46. [1–SCS]

Catania, A. C. (1978) The psychology of learning: Some lessons from the Darwinian revolution. *Annals of the New York Academy of Sciences* 309:18–28. [7–ACC]

(1979) *Learning*. Prentice-Hall. [3–RBP]

(1980) Operant theory: Skinner. In: *Theories of learning*, ed. G. M. Gazda & R. Corsini. F. E. Peacock. [0–ACC]

(1983) Behavior analysis and behavior synthesis in the extrapolation from animal to human behavior. In: *Animal models of human behavior*, ed. G. Davey. Wiley. [7–ACC]

Catania, A. C. & Keller, K. (1981) Contingency, contiguity, correlation, and the concept of causation. In: *Advances in the study of behaviour*, vol. 2. *Predictability, correlation and contiguity*. Wiley. [6–JERS]

Cavalli-Sforza, L. & Feldman, M. W. (1973) Models for cultural inheritance. *Theoretical Population Biology* 4:12–55 [1–TJG]

(1981) *Cultural transmission and evolution: A quantitative approach*. Princeton University Press. [1–TJG, SCS]

Changeux, J.-P. (1983) *L'homme neuronal*. Favard. [2–MNR]

Changeux, J.-P. & Danchin, A. (1976) Selective stabilization of developing synapses as a mechanism for the specification of neuronal networks. *Nature* 264:705–12. [2–MNR]

Charnov, E. L. & Bull, J. (1977) When is sex environmentally determined? *Nature* 266:829–30. [1–SCS]

Cheek, J. M. (1982) Aggregation, moderator variables, and the validity of personality tests: A peer-rating study. *Journal of Personality and Social Psychology* 43:1254–69. [3–DTK]

Chi, M. T. H., Glaser, R. & Rees, E. (1982) Expertise in problem solving. In: *Advances in the psychology of human intelligence*, vol. 1, ed. R. J. Sternberg. Erlbaum Associates. [4–EH]

Chisholm, R (1957) *Perceiving: A philosophical study*. Cornell University Press. [5–GR]

Chomsky, N. (1959) A review of Skinner's Verbal Behavior. *Language* 35:26–58. [1–BD, JWD; 2–RM, MNR, CPS, BFS on CPS, ES; 3–RPB, JDR; 4–PJ; 5–WGL, GR, DNR; 7–BFS on SH, ACC]

(1965) *Aspects of the theory of syntax*. MIT Press. [2–RM]

(1966) *Cartesian linguistics*. Harper & Row. [1–JWD]

(1968) *Language and mind*. Harcourt, Brace and Jovanovich. [2–MNR]

(1969) Comments on Harman. In: *Language and philosophy*, ed. S. Hook. New York University Press. [4–EPS]

(1975) *Reflections on language*. William Collins. [3–CFL]

(1980a) Discussion of Putnam's comments. In: *Language and learning: The debate between Jean Piaget and Noam Chomsky*. Harvard University Press. [1–JWD]

(1980b) Rules and representations. *Behavioral and Brain Sciences* 3:1–15. [1–JWD; 4–EPS]

Churchland, P. (1981) Eliminative materialism and propositional attitudes. *Journal of Philosophy* 78:67–90. [3–JB]

Churchland, P. M. & Churchland, P. S. (1981) Functionalism, qualia, and intentionality. *Philosophical Topics* 12:121–45. [3–GG]

Clark, H. H. & Haviland, S. E. (1977) Comprehension and the given-new contract. In: *Discourse production and comprehension*, ed. R. O. Freedle. Ablex. [4–EH]

Clark, J. H. (1963) Adaptive machines in psychiatry. In: *Nerve, brain and memory models*, ed. J. Wiener & J. P. Schade. Amsterdam. [4–BFS]

Clark, M. M. & Galef, B. G., Jr. (1979) A sensitive period for the maintenance of emotionality in Mongolian gerbils. *Journal of Comparative and Physiological Psychology* 93:200–210. [6–GG]

Cloak, F. T. (1975) Is a cultural ethology possible? *Human Ecology* 3:161–82. [1–RD]

Clowes, J. S. & Wassermann, G. D. (1984) Genetic control theory of developmental events. *Bulletin of Mathematical Biology* 46:785–825. [6–GDW]

Cohen, L. J. (1986) Semantics and the computational metaphor. In: *Logic, methodology and philosophy of Science*, vol. 7, ed. R. Barcan Marcus, G. J. W. Dorn & P. Weingartner. North-Holland. [4–LJC]

Colwell, R. K. (1981) Group selection is implicated in the evolution of female-biased sex ratios. *Nature* 290:401–4. [1–SCS]

Commons, M. L., Herrnstein, R. J. & Rachlin, H. eds. (1982) *Quantitative analyses of behavior, vol. 2, Matching and maximizing accounts*. Ballinger. [3–HR]

Craig, W. (1953) On axiomalizability within a system. *Journal of Symbolic Logic* 18:30–32. [2–ES]

(1956) Replacement of auxiliary expressions. *Philosophical Review* 65:38–55. [2–ES]

Craik, K. J. W. (1943). *The nature of explanation*. Cambridge University Press. [5–JCM; 6–SKR]

Crawford, L. (1983) Local contrast and memory windows as proximate foraging mechanisms. *Zeitschrift für Tierpsychologie* 63:283–93. [6–GMB]

Cumming, W. W. & Berryman, R. R. (1965) Stimulus generalization. In: *Stimulus generalization*, ed. D. I. Mostofsky. Stanford University Press. [3–HST]

Danto, A. C. (1983) Science as an intentional system. *Behavioral and Brain Sciences* 6:359–60. [5–MB]

Darwin, C. (1859) *On the origin of species by means of natural selection*. R. West. [6–JPH]

(1868) *The variation of animals and plants under domestication*. John Murray. [6–MTG]

(1872) *The expression of the emotions in man and animals*. R. West. [6–BFS]

Darwin, F., ed. (1888) *The life and letters of Charles Darwin*, vol. 3. Murray. [1–JWD]

Davidson, D. (1970) Mental events. In: *Experience and theory*, ed. L. Foster & J. W. Swenson. University of Massachusetts Press. [5–JH]

Davis, L. H. (1982) Functionalism and absent qualia. *Philosophical Studies* 41:231–49. [5–LHD]

Dawes, R. M. & Corrigan, B. (1974) Linear models in decision making. *Psychological Bulletin* 81:95–106. [4–RMH]

Dawkins, R. (1976) *The selfish gene*. Oxford University Press. [1–BD, SCS, WV; 7–ACC]

(1978) Replicator selection and the extended phenotype. *Zeitschrift für Tierpsychologie* 47:61–76. [1–HCP]

(1982) *The extended phenotype*. W. H. Freeman. [1–RD; 7–ACC]

Dawson, M. E. (1973) Can classical conditioning occur without contingency learning? A review and evaluation of the evidence. *Psychophysiology* 10:82–86. [5–JJF]

Dawson, M. E. & Furedy, J. J. (1976) The role of awareness in human differential autonomic

classical conditioning: The necessary gate hypothesis. *Psychophysiology* 13:50–53. [5–JJF]
Day, W. (1969a) On certain similarities between the philosophical investigations of Ludwig Wittgenstein and the operationism of B. F. Skinner. *Journal of the Experimental Analysis of Behavior* 12:489–506. [5–MJM]
(1969b) Radical behaviorism in reconciliation with phenomenology. *Journal of the Experimental Analysis of Behavior* 12:315–28. [5–MJM]
Deitz, S. M. (1978) Current status of applied behavior analysis: Science versus technology. *American Psychologist* 33:805–14. [2–SMD]
(1982) Defining applied behavior analysis: An historical analogy. *Behavior Analyst* 5:53–64. [2–SMD]
Deitz, S. M. & Arrington, R. L. (1983) Factors confusing language use in the analysis of behavior. 11:117–32. *Behaviorism*. [2–SMD]
De Laguna, G. (1927) *Speech: Its function and development*. Yale University Press. [6–BFS]
Delius, J. D. (1970) The ontogeny of behaviour. In: *The neurosciences second study program*, ed. F. O. Schmitt. Rockefeller University Press. [6–JDD]
(1985) Behaviour, free for all. In: *Behavior analysis and contemporary psychology*, ed. C. F. Lowe, M. Richelle, D. E. Blackman & C. M. Bradshaw. Lawrence Erlbaum Associates. [6–JDD]
Dennett, D. C. (1975) Why the law of effect will not go away. *Journal of the Theory of Social Behaviour* 5:169–87. [5–WGL]
(1978a) *Brainstorms*. Bradford Books. [1–AR; 4–PJ, GK; 5–LHD, MJM, RCM]
(1978b) Skinner skinned. In: *Brainstorms*. Bradford Books. [1–BD; 4–EPS; 5–JEA, WGL, GR]
(1978c) Why the law of effect won't go away. In: *Brainstorms*. Bradford Books. [1–BD, JS; 5–GR]
(1983) Intentional systems in cognitive ethology: The "Panglossian paradigm" defended. *Behavioral and Brain Sciences* 6:343–90. [1–AR; 5–ML; 6–MTG]
Denny, M. R., ed. (1980) *Comparative psychology*. Wiley. [6–GMB]
Deutsch, J. A. (1960) *The structural basis of behavior*. University of Chicago Press. [5–FMT]
Dickinson, A. (1980) *Contemporary animal learning theory*. Cambridge University Press. [5–FMT]
Diderot, D. (1796) *Supplement au Voyage de Bougainville*. [6–BFS]
Dodwell, P. C. (1977) Criteria for a neuropsychological theory of perception. *Cahiers de psychologie* 20:175–82. [4–PCD]
Domjan, M. & Burkhard, B. (1982) *The principles of learning and behavior*. Brooks-Cole. [5–WST]
Donahoe, J. W., Crowley, M. A., Millard, W. J. & Stickney, K. A. (1982) A unified principle of reinforcement. In: *Quantitative analyses of behavior*, vol. 2. *Matching and maximizing accounts*, ed. M. L. Commons, R. J. Herrnstein & H. Rachlin. Ballinger. [1–JWD]
Donahoe, J. W. & Wessells, M. G. (1980) *Learning, language and memory*. Harper & Row. [5–WST]
Drachman, D. B. & Sokoloff, L. (1966) The role of movement in embryonic joint development. *Development Biology* 14:401–20. [6–DW]
Dubos, R. (1965) Humanistic biology. *American Scientist* 53:4–19. [6–BFS]
Duncan, P. M. & Duncan, N. C. (1971) Free-operant and T-maze avoidance performance by septal and hippocampal-damaged rats. *Physiology & Behavior* 7:687–93. [5–MLW]
Eccles, J. C. (1979) *The human mystery*. Springer [2–MNR]
Eddington, A. (1958) *The nature of the physical world*. University of Michigan Press. [5–EJW]
Eibl-Eibesfeldt, I. (1975) *Ethology: The biology of behavior*. 2d ed. Holt, Rinehart & Winston. [6–GMB]
(1979) Human ethology: Concepts and implications for the sciences of man. *Behavioral and Brain Sciences* 2:1–57. [6–IE-E, DW]
Einhorn, H. J. (1980) Overconfidence in judgment. In: *New directions for methodology of socia and behavioral science: Fallible judgment in behavioral research*, vol. 4, ed. R. Shweder Jossey-Bass. [4–RMH]

Einhorn, H. J. & Hogarth, R. M. (1982) Prediction, diagnosis, and causal thinking in forecasting. *Journal of Forecasting* 1:23–36. [4–RMH]

(1983) *Diagnostic inference and causal judgment: A decision making framework*. University of Chicago, Center for Decision Research. [4–RMH]

Einstein, A. (1960) Fund-raising telegram for the Emergency Committee of Atomic Scientists, 23 May 1946. In: *Einstein on peace*, ed. O. Nathan & H. Norden. Simon & Schuster. [6–DPB]

Eisenberger, R., Karpman, M. & Trattner, T. (1967) What is the necessary and sufficient condition for reinforcement in the contingency situation? *Journal of Experimental Psychology* 74:342–50. [7–ACC]

Eldredge, N. & Gould, S. J. (1972) *Punctuated equilibria: An alternative to phyletic gradualism. In: Models in paleobiology*, ed. T. J. M. Schopf. Freeman, Cooper & Co. [1–CBGC; 6–AK]

Ellegård, A. (1958) *Darwin and the general reader*. Göteborgs Universitets Årsskrift. [1–JWD]

Epstein, R., Lanza, R. P. & Skinner, B. F. (1980) Symbolic communication between two pigeons (Columba Livia domestica). *Science* 207:543–45. [2–CPS]

Epstein, W., ed. (1977) *Stability and constancy in visual perception: Mechanisms and processes*. Wiley. [4–SG]

Erickson, E. H. (1963) *Childhood and society*. Rev. ed. W. W. Norton. [7–BFS on Acc]

Erlenmeyer-Kimling, E., Hirsch, J. & Weiss, J. M. (1962) Studies in experimental behavior genetics: III. Selection and hybridization analyses of individual differences in the sign of geotaxis. *Journal of Comparative and Physiological Psychology* 55:722–31. [6–BFS]

Eysenck, H. J. (1967) *The biological basis of personality*. C. C. Thomas. [6–HJE]

(1979) The conditioning model of neurosis. *Behavioral and Brain Sciences* 2:155–99. [6–HJE]

(1982) Neobehavioristic (S–R) theory. In: *Contemporary behavior therapy*, ed. G. T. Wilson & C. M. Franks. Guilford Press. [6–HJE]

Fantino, E., Dunn, R. & Meck, W. (1979) Percentage reinforcement and choice. *Journal of the Experimental Analysis of Behavior* 32:335–40. [4–SG]

Feigl, H. (1945) Operationism and scientific method. *Psychological Review* 52:250–59. [3–BFS, RPB]

Felsenstein, J. (1974) The evolutionary advantage of sexual recombination. *Genetics* 78:737–56. [1–SCS]

Fentress, J. C. (1973) Development of grooming in mice with amputated forelimbs. *Science* 179:794–5. [6–IE–E]

Ferguson, M. W. J. & Joanen, T. (1982) Temperature of egg incubation determines sex in *Alligator mississippiensis*. Nature 296:850–53. [6–DW]

Ferster, C. B. & Skinner, B. F. (1957) *Schedules of reinforcement*. Appleton-Century-Crofts. [0–ACC; 1–BFS on JWD; 6–BFS]

Fishbein, H. D. (1976) *Evolution, development, and children's learning*. Goodyear Publishing Company. [6–AJP]

Fisher, R. A. (1918) The correlation between relatives on the supposition of Mendelian inheritance. *Transactions of the Royal Society* (Edinburgh) 52:399–433. [6–SAA]

Fodor, J. A. (1968a) The appeal to tacit knowledge in psychological explanation. *Journal of Philosophy* 65:627–40. [5–WGL]

(1968b) *Psychological explanation*. Random House. [5–GR]

(1975) *The language of thought*. Crowell. [4–LJC, EPS; 5–WGL, GR]

(1980) Methodological solipsism considered as a research strategy in cognitive psychology. *Behavioral and Brain Sciences* 3:63–73. [3–JB; 4–LJC; 5–WGL, JCM]

(1981a) The mind-body problem. *Scientific American* 244:114–23. [2–SMD]

(1981b) *Representations*. Harvester. [4–LJC]

(1983) *The modularity of mind*. MIT Press. [5–LHD]

Fodor, J. A., Bever, T. G. & Garrett, M. F. (1974) *The psychology of language*. McGraw-Hill. [3–JDR; 4–EPS]

Freeman, W. J. (1979) EEG analysis gives model of neuronal template-matching mechanism for sensory search with olfactory bulb. *Biological Cybernetics* 35:221–34. [4–SG]

Freud, S. (1939) *Moses and monotheism*. Random House. [6–AK]

Friedmann, H. (1956) Quoted in article entitled "African honey-guides." *Science* 123:55. [6–BFS]

Furedy, J. J. (1973) Some limits of the cognitive control of conditioned autonomic behavior. *Psychophysiology* 10:108–11. [5–JJF]

Furedy, J. J. & Riley, D. M. (1982) Classical and operant conditioning in the enhancement of biofeedback: Specifics and speculations. In: *Clinical biofeedback: Efficacy and mechanisms*, ed. L. White & B. Tursky. Guilford Press. [5–JJF]

Furedy, J. J., Riley, D. M. & Fredrickson, M. (1983) Pavlovian extinction, phobias, and the limits of the cognitive paradigm. *Pavlovian Journal of Biological Psychology* 18:126–35. [5–JJF]

Gallistel, C. R. (1980) *The organization of action: A new synthesis*. Erlbaum. [5–FMT]

Gallup, G. G., Jr. (1983) Toward a comparative psychology of mind. In: *Animal cognition and behavior*, ed. R. L. Mellgren. North Holland Publishing Co. [5–GGG]

Galton, F. (1983) *Inquires into human faculty and its development*. J. M. Dent and Company. [5–BFS]

Garcia, J., Clarke, J. & Hankins, W. G. (1973) Natural responses to scheduled rewards. In: *Perspectives in ethology*, ed. P. P. G. Bateson & P. Klopfer, Plenum Press. [6–JERS]

Garcia, J. & Koelling R. A. (1966) The relation of cue to consequence in avoidance learning. *Psychonomic Science* 5:121–22. [6–JDD]

Garcia, J., McGowan, B. K., & Green, K. F. (1972) Biological constraints on conditioning. In: *Classical conditioning*. vol. 2, ed. A. H. Black & W. H. Prokasy. Appleton-Century-Crofts. [1–PRS]

Garstang, W. (1922) The theory of recapitulation: A critical restatement of the biogenetic law. *Journal of the Linnean Society of London* 35:81–101. [6–GG]

Gauld, A. & Shotter, J. (1977) *Human action and its psychological investigation*. Routledge & Kegan Paul. [4–JGR]

Gelman, R. & Spelke, E. (1981) The development of thoughts about animate and inanimate objects: Implications for research on social cognition. In: *Social cognitive development*, ed. J. H. Flavell & L. Ross. Cambridge University Press. [5–CNJ]

Ghiselin, M. T. (1969a) The evolution of hermaphroditism among animals. *Quarterly Review of Biology* 44:189–208. [6–MTG]

(1969b) *The triumph of the Darwinian method*. University of California Press. [6–MTG]

(1973) Darwin and evolutionary psychology. *Science* 179:964–68. [1–TJG]

(1974) *The economy of nature and the evolution of sex*. University of California Press. [6–MTG]

(1980) Natural kinds and literary accomplishments. *Michigan Quarterly Review* 29:73–88. [1–MTG]

(1981) Categories, life, and thinking. *Behavioral and Brain Sciences* 4:269–83. [1–TJG, MTG, AR, JS; 6–MTG]

(1982) On the mechanisms of cultural evolution, and the evolution of language and the common law. *Behavioral and Brain Sciences* 5:11. [1–MTG]

Gibbon, J. (1977) Scalar expectancy theory and Weber's law in animal timing. *Psychologica Review* 84:279–325. [2–CPS]

Gier, N. F. (1981) *Wittgenstein and phenomenology*. State University of New York Press. [5–MJM]

Gleitman, H. (1963) Place-learning. *Scientific American* 209:116–22. [5–GR]

Glymour, C. (1979) *Theory and evidence*. Princeton University Press. [2–JMN]

Goffman, E. (1959) *The presentation of self in everyday life*. Doubleday Anchor. [5–JEA]

Gottlieb, G. (1971) *Development of species identification in birds*. University of Chicago Press. [6–GG]

(1976a) Conceptions of prenatal development: Behavioral embryology. *Psychological Review* 83:215–34. [6–GG]

(1976b) The roles of experience in the development of behavior and the nervous system. In: *Neural and behavioral specificity*, ed. G. Gottlieb. Academic Press. [6–GG]

(1981) Roles of early experience in species-specific perceptual development. In: *Development of perception: Psychological perspectives*, vol. 1, ed. R. N. Aslin, J. R. Alberts & M. R. Petersen. Academic Press. [6–GG]

Gould, S. J. (1977) *Ontogeny and phylogeny*. Harvard University Press. [1–WW; 6–MTG, GG, AK]

(1980) *The panda's thumb: More reflections in natural history*. W. W. Norton & Co. [5–EJW]

Gould, S. J. & Lewontin, R. C. (1979) The spandrels of San Marco and the panglossian paradigm: A critique of the adaptationist programme. *Proceedings of the Royal Society of London* B 205:581–98. [1–BD, AR; 6–MTG, AK]

Gould, S. J. & Vrba, E. S. (1982) Exaptation – a missing term in the science of form. *Paleobiology* 8:4–15. [6–AJP, BFS on AJP]

Grant D. S. (1983) Rehearsal in pigeon short-term memory. In: *Animal cognition*, ed. H. L. Roitblat, T. G. Bever & H. S. Terrace. Lawrence Erlbaum Associates. [3–HST]

Gray, P. H. (1963) The descriptive study of imprinting in birds from 1863 to 1953. *Journal of General Psychology* 68:333–46. [6–BFS]

Green, S. & Marler, P. (1979) The analysis of animal communication. In: *Handbook of behavioral neurobiology*, vol. 3, *Social behavior and communication*, ed. P. Marler & J. G. Vandenbergh. Plenum Press. [1–GWB]

Greenfield, P. M. & Smith, J. H. (1976) *The structure of communication in early language development*. Academic Press. [3–RPB]

Gregory, R. L. (1969) On how so little information controls so much behavior. In: *Towards a theoretical biology, two sketches*, ed. C. H. Waddington. Edinburgh University Press. [6–SK]

Grene, M. (1959) Two evolutionary theories. *British Journal for the Philosophy of Science* 9:110–27, 185–93. [1–BD]

Grice, H. P. (1957) Meaning. *Philosophical Review* 66:377–88. [3–JB]

Griffin, D. R. (1976) *The question of animal awareness*. Rockefeller University Press. [5–WST]

Grossberg, S. (1975) A neural model of attention, reinforcement, and discrimination learning. *International Review of Neurobiology* 18:263–327. [4–SG]

(1978a) Behavioral contrast in short-term memory: Serial binary memory models or parallel continuous memory models? *Journal of Mathematical Psychology* 17:199–219. [4–SG]

(1978b) A theory of human themory: Self-organization and performance of sensory-motor codes, maps, and plans. In: *Progress in theoretical biology*, vol. 5., ed. R. Rosen & F. Snell. Academic Press. [4–SG]

(1980) How does a brain build a cognitive code? *Psychological Review* 87:1–51. [4–SG]

(1982a) Processing of expected and unexpected events during conditioning and attention: A psychophysiological theory. *Psychological Review* 89:529–72. [4–SG]

(1982b) A psychophysiological theory of reinforcement, drive, motivation, and attention. *Journal of Theoretical Neurobiology* 1:286–369. [4–SG]

(1982c) *Studies of mind and brain: Neural principles of learning, perception, development, cognition, and motor control*. Reidel Press. [4–SG]

(1983a) The adaptive self-organization of serial order in behavior: Speech and motor control. In: *Perception of speech and visual form: Theoretical issues, models, and research*, ed. E. C. Schwab & H. Nusbaum. Academic Press. [4–SG]

(1983b) Some psychophysiological and pharmacological correlates of a developmental, cognitive, and motivational theory. In: *Brain and information: Event related potentials*, ed. R. Karrer, J. Cohen & P. Tueting. New York Academy of Sciences. [4–SG]

Gudmondsson, K. (1983) The emergence of B. F. Skinner's theory of operant behaviour. Ph.D. thesis, University of Western Ontario. [2–JMN]

Gunderson, K. (1971) Asymmetries and mind–body perplexities. In: *Minnesota studies in the philosophy of science*, vol. 4, ed. M. Radner & S. Winokur. University of Minnesota Press. [5–KG]

Gustavson, C. R., Garcia, J., Hankins, W. G. & Rusiniak, K. W. (1974) Coyote predation control by aversive conditioning. *Science* 184:581–83. [2–SR]

Guttman, N. (1956) The pigeon and the spectrum and the other perplexities. *Psychological Reports* 2:449–60. [5–BFS on TRZ]

(1959) Generalization gradients around stimuli associated with different reinforcement schedules. *Journal of Experimental Psychology* 58:335–40. [7–BFS on SH]

Haeckel, E. (1891) *Anthropogenie oder entwicklungsgeschichte des Menschen: Keimes- und Stammes-Geschichte*. 4th rev. enl. ed. Engelmann. [6–GG]

Hailman, J. P. (1969) How an instinct is learned. *Scientific American* 221:98–106. [6–DW]

(1982a) Evolution and behavior: An iconoclastic view. In: *Learning, development, and culture*, ed. H. C. Plotkin, Wiley. [6–JPH]

(1982b) Ontogeny: Toward a general theoretical framework for ethology. In: *Perspectives in ethology*, vol. 5, ed. P. P. G. Bateson & P. H. Klopfer. Plenum Press. [6–JPH]

(1984) Historical notes on the biology of learning. In: *Issues in the ecological study of learning*, ed. T. D. Johnston & A. T. Pietrewicz. Lawrence Erlbaum Associates. [6–JPH]

Hamilton, W. (1964) The genetical theory of social behavior. *Journal of Theoretical Biology* 7:1–52. [1–JWD; 6–JLB]

(1967) Extraordinary sex ratios. *Science* 156:477–88. [1–SCS]

(1972) Altruism and related phenomena, mainly in social insects. *Annual Review of Ecology and Systematics* 3:193–232. [1–SCS]

(1980) Sex versus non-sex versus parasite. *Oikos* 35:282–90. [1–SCS]

Hanson, N. R. (1969) *Perception and discovery*. Freeman, Cooper, and Co. [2–CPS]

Hanson, S. J. & Timberlake, W. (1983) Regulation during challenge: A general model of learned performance under schedule constraint. *Psychological Review* 90:261–82. [1–WT]

Harlow, H. F. (1949) The formation of learning sets. *Psychological Review* 56:51–65. [5–GR]

(1959) Learning set and error factor theory. In: *Psychology: A study of science*, vol. 2, ed. S. Koch, McGraw-Hill. [5–GR]

Harnad, S. (1982) Consciousness: An afterthought. *Cognition and Brain Theory* 5:29–47. [5–DP]

Harré, R. & Secord, P. F. (1972) *The explanation of social behaviour*. Blackwell. [3–CFL]

Harris, C. S., ed. (1980) *Visual coding and adaptibility*. Erlbaum Associates. [4–SG]

Harris, M. (1964) *The nature of cultural things*. Random House. [1–MH]

(1979) *Cultural materialism: The struggle for a science of culture*. Random House. [1–MH]

Harzem, P. & Miles, T. R. (1978) *Conceptual issues in operant psychology*. Wiley. [2–SMD; 3–PH; 5–MJM]

Hebb, D. (1949) *The organization of behavior*. Wiley [2–MNR; 6–GDW]

Heelas, P. & Lock, A., eds. (1981) *Indigenous psychologies*. Academic Press. [5–CNJ]

Heider, E. R. (1972) Universals in color naming and memory. *Journal of Experimental Psychology* 93:10–20. [5–TRZ]

Heil, J. (1982) Seeing is believing. *American Philosophical Quarterly* 19:229–39. [5–JH]

(1983) *Perception and cognition*. University of California Press. [5–JH]

Heinroth, O. (1911) Beiträge zur Biologie, namentlich Ethologie und Psychologie der Anatiden, *Verhandlung V. Internationale Ornithologische Kongress*. [6–JPH]

Held, R. (1961) Exposure-history as a factor in maintaining stability of perception and co-ordination. *Journal of Nervous and Mental Diseases* 132:26–32. [4–SG]

Heller, R. & Milinsky, M. (1979) Optimal foraging of sticklebacks on swarming prey. *Animal Behaviour* 27:1127–41. [6–AK]

Helmholtz, H. von (1852) On the theory of compound colors. *Philosophical Magazine* 4:519–34. [1–PRS]

Hempel, C. G. (1965a) The concept of rationality and the logic of explanation by reasons. In: *Aspects of scientific explanations*. Free Press. [3–JDR]

(1965b) Empiricist criteria of cognitive significance: Problems and changes. In: *Aspects of scientific explanation*. Free Press. [3–JDR]

(1965c) A logical appraisal of operationism. In: *Aspects of scientific explanation*. Free Press. [3–JDR]

(1980) The logical analysis of psychology. In: *Readings in philosophy of psychology*, vol. 1, ed. N. Block. Harvard University Press. [2–RM]

Herrnstein, R. J. (1977) The evolution of behaviorism. *American Psychologist* 32:593–603. [3–RPB]

Herrnstein, R. J., Loveland, D. H. & Cable, C. (1976) Natural concepts in pigeons. *Journal of Experimental Psychology: Animal Behavior Processes* 2:285–311. [4–BFS on AR; BFS on SH]

Herrnstein, R. J. & van Sommers, P. (1962) Method for sensory scaling with animals. *Science* 135:40–41. [5–BFS]

Hinde, R. A. (1966) *Animal behaviour: A synthesis of ethology and comparative psychology*. 1st ed. McGraw-Hill. [6–JDD]

Hinde, R. A. & Stevenson-Hinde, J. (1973) *Constraints on learning: Limitations and predispositions*. Academic Press. [6–AK]

Hinsie, L. E. & Campbell, R. J., eds. (1970) *Psychiatric Dictionary*. 4th ed. Oxford University Press. [3–PEM]

Hinson, J. M. & Staddon, J. E. R. (1978) Behavioral competition: A mechanism for schedule interactions. *Science* 202:432–31. [4–SG]

Hirsch, J. (1963) Behavior genetics and individuality understood. *Science* 142:1436–42. [6–BFS]

Hirsh, H. V. B. & Jacobson, M. (1975) The perfectible brain: Principles of neuronal development. In: *Handbook of psychobiology*, ed. M. S. Gazzaniga & C. Blakemore. Academic Press. [6–HCP]

Ho, M. W. & Saunders, P. T. (1979) Beyond neoDarwinism: An epigenetic approach to evolution. *Journal of Theoretical Biology* 78:673–91. [6–HCP]

(1982) The epigenetic approach to the evolution of organisms. In: *Learning, development and culture: Essays in evolutionary epistemology*, ed. H. C. Plotkin, Wiley. [6–HCP]

Hoffman, H. S., Schiff, D., Adams, J. & Serle, J. L. (1966) Enhanced distress vocalization through selective reinforcement. *Science* 151:352–54. [6–BFS]

Hogan, J. A. & Roper, T. J. (1978) A comparison of the properties of different reinforcers. *Advances in the Study of Behavior* 8:155–255. [6–JAH]

Hogben, L. (1957) *Statistical theory*. Allen and Unwin. [5–BFS]

Holland, P. C. (1977) Conditioned stimulus as a determinant of the form of the Pavlovian conditioned response. *Journal of Experimental Psychology: Animal Behavior Processes* 3:77–104. [6–JERS]

Holliday, R. & Maynard Smith, J., ed. (1979) The evolution of adaptation by natural selection. *Proceedings of the Royal Society of London* 205: whole issue. [6–JAH]

Hollis, K. L. (1982) Pavlovian conditioning of signal-centered action patterns and autonomic behavior: A biological analysis of function. *Advances in the Study of Behavior* 12:1–64. [6–JERS]

Honig, W. K. (1978) On the conceptual nature of cognitive terms: An initial essay. In: *Cognitive processes in animal behavior*, ed. S. W. Hulse, H. Fowler & W. K. Honig. Erlbaum. [5–WST]

(1981) Working memory and the temporal map. In: *Information processing in animals: Memory mechanisms*, ed. N. E. Spear & R. R. Miller. Erlbaum. [1–WKH]

Honig, W. K. & James P. H. R. (1971) *Animal memory*. Academic Press. [5–WST]

Hooke, R. (1980) Getting people to use statistics properly. *American Statistician* 34:39–42. [2–LW]

Hospers, J. (1958) What means this freedom? In: *Determinism and freedom*, ed. S. Hook, Collier Books. [5–JEA]

Houston, A. I. & McNamara, J. M. (1982) A sequential approach to risk taking. *Animal Behaviour* 30:1260–61. [6–AK]

Hull, C. L. (1943) *Principles of behavior*. D. Appleton-Century. [2–BFS, LW; 5–EJW]

Hull, D. L. (1972) Darwinism and historiography. In: *The comparative reception of Darwinism* ed. T. F. Glick. University of Texas Press. [1-JWD]

(1980) Individuality and selection. *Annual Review of Ecology and Systematics* 11:311-32. [1-HCP]

Hulse, S. H., Fowler, H. & Honig, W. K. (1978) *Cognitive processes in animal behavior* Erlbaum. [5-WST]

Hulse, S. H. & O'Leary, D. K. (1982) Serial pattern learning: Teaching an alphabet to rats. *Journal of Experimental Psychology: Animal Behavior Processes* 8:260-73. [2-CPS]

Hume, D. (1739) *A treatise of human nature*. J. Noon. [4-LJC]

Hunt, E. (1981) The design of a robot mind: A theoretical approach to some issues in intelli gence. In: *Intelligence and learning*, ed. M. P. Friedman, J. P. Das & N. O'Connor. Plenum Press. [4-EH]

Hunt, E. & Pixton, P. (1982) A general model for simulating information processing experi ments. *Proceedings of the 4th Annual Conference of the Cognitive Science Society*, pp. 164-66 [4-EH]

Hunter, W. S. (1913) The delayed reaction in animals. *Behavior Monographs* 2:6. [3-HST]

Hutchison, V. H. & Maness, J. D. (1979) The role of behavior in temperature acclimation and tolerance in ectotherms. *American Zoologist* 19:367-84. [1-GWB]

Huxley, J. S. (1942) *Evolution: The modern synthesis*. Allen and Unwin. [1-SCS]

(1964) Psychometabolism: General and Lorenzian. *Perspectives in Biology and Medicine* 7:399-432. [6-BFS]

Irwin, F. W. (1971) *Intentional behavior and motivation: A cognitive theory*. J. B. Lippincott Co. [5-FWI]

Isaacson, R. L. (1982) *The limbic system*. Plenum Publishing. [5-MLW]

Jacobs, H. L. & Sharma, K. N. (1969) Taste versus calories: Sensory and metabolic signals in the control of food intake. *Annals of the New York Academy of Sciences 157:1084-1125. [1-WW]*

Jacobson, M. (1969) Development of specific neuronal connections. *Science* 163:543-47. [6-GDW]

James, W. (1890) *The principles of psychology*. Henry Holt & Co. [1-JS; 6-JPH]

Jarvik, M. E. (1956) Simple color discrimination in chimpanzees: Effects of varying contiguity between cue and incentive. *Journal of Comparative and Physiological Psychology* 49: 492-95. [5-EJW]

Jaynes, J. (1976) *The origin of consciousness in the breakdown of the bicameral mind*. Houghton Mifflin. [3-HST]

Jenkins, H. M. (1979) Animal learning and behavior theory. In: *The first century of experimental psychology*, ed. E. Hearst, Erlbaum. [5-EJW]

Jenkins, H. M. & Moore, B. R. (1973) The form of the autoshaped response with food and water reinforcers. *Journal of the Experimental Analysis of Behavior* 20:163-81. [1-WKH, BFS on WKH]

Jennings, H. S. (1906) *Behavior of the lower organisms*. Macmillan. [0-ACC]

Jepsen, G. L., Simpson G. G. & Mayr, E. (1949) *Genetics, paleontology, and evolution*. Princeton University Press. [1-CBGC]

Johnson, C. N. (1982) Acquisition of mental verbs and the concept of mind. In: *Language development*, vol. 1, ed. S. Kuczaj. Erlbaum. [5-CNJ]

Johnson, C. N. & Wellman, H. M. (1980) Children's developing understanding of mental verbs: Remember, know, and guess. *Child Development* 51:1095-1102. [5-HMW]

Johnston, T. D. (1982) Learning and the evolution of developmental systems. In: *Learning, development, and culture: Essays in evolutionary epistemology*, ed. H. C. Plotkin. Wiley. [6-GG]

Johnston, T. D. & Gottlieb, G. (1981) Epigenesis and phylogenesis: Reordering the priorities. *Behavioral and Brain Sciences* 4:243. [6-HCP]

Julià, P. (1983) *Explanatory models in linguistics: A behavioral perspective*. Princeton University Press. [4-PJ]

Kacelnik, A., Houston, A. & Krebs, J. R. (1981) Optimal foraging and territorial defence in the great tit (*Parus major*). *Behavioral Ecology and Sociobiology* 8:35–40. [6–AK]

Kamil, A. C. & Sargent, T. D. (1981) *Foraging behavior: Ecological, ethological, and psychological approaches*. Garland Press. [1–SCS]

Kamin, L. J. (1969) Predictability, surprise, attention, and conditioning. In: *Punishment and aversive behavior*, ed. B. A. Campbell & R. M. Church. Appleton-Century-Crofts. [1–WKH]

Kandel, E. R. (1976) *Cellular basis of behavior*. W. H. Freeman. [1–PRS]

Kandel, E. R. & Schwartz, J. (1982) Molecular biology of learning: Modulation of transmitter release. *Science* 218:433–42. [1–AR]

Kaplan, S. (1977) Participation in the design process: A cognitive approach. In: *Perspectives on environment and behavior*, ed. D. Stokols. Plenum Press. [6–SK]

(1983) A model of person-environment compatibility. *Environment and Behavior* 15:311–32. [6–SK]

Kaplan, S. & Kaplan, R. (1982) *Cognition and environment: Functioning in an uncertain world*. Praeger. [6–SK]

Katz, J. L. & Bever, T. G. (1976) The fall and rise of empiricism. In: *An integrated theory of linguistic ability*, ed. T. G. Bever, J. L. Katz & D. T. Langendoen. Crowell. [1–JWD]

Katz, M. J. (1983) Ontophyletics: Studying evolution beyond the genome. *Perspectives in Biology and Medicine* 26:323–33. [1–MIK]

Katz, M. J. & Grenander, U. (1982) Developmental matching and the numerical matching hypothesis for neuronal cell death. *Journal of Theoretical Biology* 98:501–17. [1–MJK]

Kavanau, J. L. (1964) Behavior: Confinement, adaptation, and compulsory regimes in laboratory studies. *Science* 143:490. [6–BFS]

Kelleher, R. T. (1962) Variables and behavior. *American Psychologist* 17:659–60. [6–BFS]

Keller, F. S. & Schoenfeld, W. N. (1950) *Principles of psychology: A systematic text in the science of behavior*. Irvington. [1–MH]

Kendall, P. C. & Hollon, S. D. (1979) *Cognitive-behavioral interventions: Theory, research and procedures*. Academic Press. [3–CFL]

Kenrick, D. T. & Dantchik, A. (1983) Interactions, idiographics, and the social psychological invasion of personality. *Journal of Personality* 51:286–307. [3–DTK]

Kenrick, D. T. & Stringfield, D. O. (1980) Personality traits and the eye of the beholder: Crossing some traditional philosophical boundaries in the search for consistency in all of the people. *Psychological Review* 87:88–104. [3–DTK]

Kerr, L. M., Ostapoff, E. M. & Rubel, E. W. (1979) Influence of acoustic experience on the ontogeny of frequency generalization gradients on the chicken. *Journal of Experimental Psychology: Animal Behavior Processes* 5:97–115. [6–GG]

Kettlewell, H. B. D. (1961) The phenomenon of industrial mechanism in Lepidoptera. *Annual Review of Entomology* 6:245–62. [1–SCS; 6–SAA]

Killeen, P. (1982) Incentive theory, 2: Models for choice. *Journal of the Experimental Analysis of Behavior* 38:217–32. [4–SG]

Koch, S. (1964) Psychology and emerging conceptions of knowledge as unitary. In: *Behaviorism and phenomenology*, ed. T. W. Wann. University of Chicago Press. [3–JDR]

Koestler, A. (1967) *The ghost in the machine*. Hutchinson. [3–CFL]

Köhler, W. (1926) *The mentality of apes*. Harcourt. Brace and World. [5–GR, BFS on GR]

Kortlandt, A. (1965) On the essential morphological basis for human culture. *Current Anthropology* 6:320–25. [6–BFS]

Krischke, N. (1983) Beitrage zur Ontogenese der Flug- und Manövrierfähigkeit der Haustaube (Columba livia var. domestica). *Behaviour* 84:265–86. [6–GG]

Kuhn, T. S. (1970) *The structure of scientific revolutions*. University of Chicago Press. [3–JDR; 5–MB]

Kuo, Z. Y. (1921) Giving up instincts in psychology. *Journal of Philosophy* 17:645–64. [6–GMB]

(1924) A psychology without heredity. *Psychological Review* 31:427–51. [6–GMB]

(1967) *The dynamics of behavior development*. Random House. [6–IE–E]

Lacey, H. (1974) The scientific study of linguistic behavior: A perspective on the Skinner-Chomsky controversy. *Journal for the Theory of Social Behaviour* 4:17–51. [3–JDR]

Larkin, J. H., McDermott, J., Simon, D. P. & Simon, H. A. (1980) Expert and novice performance in solving physics problems. *Science* 208:1335–42. [4–EH]

Lashley, K. (1923) The behavioristic interpretation of consciousness. *Psychological Review* 30:237–72, 329–53. [5–WL]

(1938) Experimental analysis of instinctive behavior. *Psychological Review* 45:445–71. [6–GMB]

Lebowitz, M. (1983) Generalization from natural language text. *Cognitive Science* 7:1–40. [5–ML]

Ledgwidge, B. (1978) Cognitive-behavior modification: A step in the wrong direction? *Psychological Bulletin* 85:353–75. [3–CFL]

Lee, S. M. & Bressler, R. (1981) Prevention of diabetic nephropathy by diet control in the *db/db* mouse. *Diabetes* 30:106–11. [6–DW]

Lehrman, D. S. (1953) A critique of Konrad Lorenz's theory of instinctive behavior. *Quarterly Review of Biology* 28:337–63. [6–GPB, IE–E, JPH]

(1970) Semantic and conceptual issues in the nature-nurture problem. In: *Development and evolution of behavior*, ed. L. R. Aronson, E. Tobach, D. S. Lehrman & J. S. Rosenblatt. Freeman. [6–GG, JAH]

Leibniz, G. W. (1695) New system of the nature and communication of substances, as well as of the union existing between the soul and the body. Transl. in G. H. R. Parkinson (1973) *Leibniz: Philosophical writings*. J. M. Dent & Sons. [6–MTG]

(1714) *The monadology and other philosophical writings*. Trans. R. Latta. Oxford University Press. [5–KG, JCM]

Lenneberg, E. H. & Lenneberg, E. (1975) *Foundations of language development*, vols. 1 & 2. Academic Press. [1–GWB]

Lewin, K. (1936) *Principles of topological psychology*. McGraw-Hill. [4–BFS, MK]

Lewontin, R. C. (1970) The units of selection. *Annual Review of Ecology and Systematics* 1:1–18. [1–SCS]

(1979) Sociobiology as an adaptationist paradigm. *Behavioral Science* 24:5–14. [5–EJW]

(1982) Organism and environment. In: *Learning, development, and culture*, ed. H. C. Plotkin. Wiley. [1–HCP; 6–SNS]

(1983) Elementary errors about evolution. *Behavioral and Brain Sciences* 6:367–68. [6–MTG]

Locke, E. A. (1966) The contradiction of epiphenomenalism. *British Journal of Psychology* 57:203–4. [6–AMC]

(1979) Behavior modification is not cognitive and other myths: A reply to Ledgwidge. *Cognitive Therapy and Research* 3:119–25. [3–CFL]

Lorenz, K. (1961) Phylogenetische Anpassung und adaptive Modifikation des Verhaltens. *Zeitschrift für Tierpsychologie* 18:139–87. [6–GPB]

(1963) *On aggression*. Harcourt, Brace & World. [6–BFS]

(1965) *Evolution and modification of behavior*. University of Chicago Press. [6–BFS, GPB, JDD, IE–E, GG, JPH]

(1966) *Evolution and modification of behavior*. Methuen. [1–RD]

(1981) *The foundations of ethology*. Simon and Schuster. [6–DW]

Lowe, C. F. (1979) Determinants of human operant behaviour. In:*Advances in analysis of behaviour*. vol. 1, *Reinforcement and the organisation of behaviour*, ed. M. D. Zeiler & P. Harzem, Wiley. [3–CFL]

(1983) Radical behaviorism and human psychology. In: *Animal models of human behavior*, ed. G. C. L. Davey, Wiley [3–CFL, BFS on CFL]

Lowe, C. F., Beasty, A. & Bentall, R. P. (1983) The role of verbal behavior in human learning: Infant performance on fixed-interval schedules. *Journal of the Experimental Analysis of Behavior* 39:157–64. [3–CFL]

Lowe, C. F. & Higson, P. J. (1981) Self-instructional training and cognitive behaviour modification: A behavioral analysis. In: *Applications of conditioning theory*, ed. G. C. L. Davey. Methuen. [3-CFL]

Luria, A. (1961) *The role of speech in the regulation of normal and abnormal behavior*. Liveright. [3-CFL]

Lycan, W. G. (1981a) Form, function, and feel. *Journal of Philosophy* 78:24-50. [3-GG; 5-WGL]

(1981b) Toward a homuncular theory of believing. *Cognition and Brain Theory* 4:139-59. [5-WGL]

MacCorquodale, K. (1970) On Chomsky's review of Skinner's *Verbal Behavior. Journal of the Experimental Analysis of Behavior* 13:83-99. [3-JDR; 5-JCM]

McFarland, D. J. (1966) On the causal and functional significance of displacement activities. *Zeitschrift für Tierpsychologie* 23:217-35. [1-RD]

McFarland, D. J. & Houston, A. I. (1981) *Quantitative ethology: The state space approach*. Pitman. [6-AK]

Mach, E. (1893) *The science of mechanics*. Open Court Publishing Company. [3-BFS]

(1919) *The science of mechanics*. Translated by T. J. McCormack. 4th ed. Open Court Publishing Company. [3-JDR]

MacKay, D. M. (1951) Mindlike behaviour in artifacts. *British Journal for the Philosophy of Science* 2:105-21. [6-GDW]

(1952) Mentality in machines. *Proceedings of the Aristotelian Society Suppl*. 26:61-86. [6-GDW]

Mackintosh, N. J. (1974) *The psychology of animal learning*. Academic Press. [6-AK]

McNamara, J. M. & Houston, A. I. (1982) Short-term behaviour and life-time fitness. In: *Functional ontogeny*, ed. D. J. McFarland. Pitman. [6-AK]

Mahoney, M. J. (1977) Reflections on the cognitive-learning trend in psychotherapy. *American Psychologist* 32:5-13. [3-CFL]

Malcolm, N. (1964) Behaviorism as a philosophy of psychology. In: *Behaviorism and phenomenology: Contrasting bases for modern psychology*, ed. T. W. Wann. University of Chicago Press. [3-GG, BFS on GG]

(1977) *Memory and mind*. Cornell University Press. [2-SMD]

Mandler, G. (1967) Organization and memory. In: *The psychology of learning and motivation*, ed. K. W. Spence & J. T. Spence. Academic Press. [3-HST]

Marler, P. & Hamilton, W. J. (1966) *Mechanisms of animal behavior*. Wiley. [6-JDD]

Marr, D. (1982) *Vision*. W. H. Freeman. [2-RM; 4-EPS; 5-JCM]

Marr, J. (1983) Memory: Models and metaphors. *Psychological Record* 33:12-19. [5-MJM]

Marshall, J. C. (1977) Minds, machines and metaphors. *Social Studies of Science* 7:475-88. [5-JCM]

Maslow, A. (1962) *Toward a psychology of being*. Van Nostrand. [4-BFS]

Matthews, B. A., Shimoff, E., Catania, A. C. & Sagvolden, T. (1977) Uninstructed human responding: Sensitivity to ratio and interval contingencies. *Journal of the Experimental Analysis of Behavior* 27:453-67. [7-ACC]

Maynard Smith, J. (1958) *The theory of evolution*. Penguin Books. [7-ACC]

(1964) Group selection and kin selection: A rejoinder. *Nature* 201:1145-47. [1-SCS]

(1978) *The evolution of sex*. Cambridge University Press. [1-SCS]

Mayr, E. (1961) Cause and effect in biology. *Science* 134:1501-6. [1-HCP]

(1963) *Animal species and evolution*. Harvard University Press. [6-JERS]

(1976a) *Evolution and the diversity of life*. Harvard University Press. [1-WV]

(1976b) Typological versus population thinking. In: *Evolution and the diversity of life*, ed. E. Mayr. Harvard University Press. [1-JWD]

(1982) *The growth of biological thought: Diversity, evolution, and inheritance*. Harvard University Press. [1-BD, JWD, HCP]

Maze, J. R. (1953) On some corruptions of the doctrine of homeostasis. *Psychological Review* 60:405-12. [5-JJF]

Meck, W. H. (1983) Selective adjustment of the speed of internal clock and memory processes. *Journal of Experimental Psychology: Animal Behavior Processes* 9:171–201. [2–SR]
Mehler, J. (1974) Connaitre par desapprentissage. In: *L'unité de l'homme*, ed. E. Morin & Piatelli-Palmarini. Le Seuil. [2–MNR]
Menzel, E. W. (1978) Cognitive mapping in chimpanzees. In: *Cognitive processes in animal behavior*, ed. S. W. Hulse, H. Fowler & W. K. Honig. Erlbaum. [5–WST]
Menzel, E. W., Jr. & Juno, C. (1982) Marmosets (*Saguinus fuscicollis*): Are learning sets learned? *Science* 217:750–52. [5–EJW]
Metz, J. A. J. (1971) State space models for animal behaviour. *Annals of Systems Research* 6:65–109. [6–AK]
Meyer, M. (1921) *The psychology of the other-one*. Missouri Book Co. [3–GEZ]
Michotte, A. (1946) *La perception de la causalité*. Vrin. [4–RMH]
Milinski, M. & Heller, R. (1978) Influence of a predator on the optimal foraging behaviour of sticklebacks (*Gasterosteus aculeatus* L.) *Nature* 275:642–44. [6–AK]
Miller, G. A. (1951) *Language and communication*. McGraw-Hill. [3–JB, BFS on JB]
Miller, G. A. (1969) Psychology as a means of promoting human welfare. *American Psychologist* 24:1063–75. [6–SK]
Mills, J. A. (1978a) A summary and criticism of Skinner's early theory of learning. *Canadian Psychological Review* 19:215–23. [6–AMC]
(1978b) A summary and criticism of Skinner's second theory of learning. *Canadian Psychological Review* 19:328–37. [6–AMC]
Mineka, S. & Suomi, S. J. (1978) Social separation in monkeys. *Psychological Bulletin* 85: 1376–1400. [6–HCP]
Minsky, M. (1968) Matter, mind, and models. In: *Semantic information processing*, ed. M. Minsky, MIT Press. [5–DP]
Monod, J. (1970) *Le hasard et la necessité*. Le Seuil. [2–MNR]
Moore, B. R. (1973) The role of directed Pavlovian reactions in simple instrumental learning in the pigeon. In: *Constraints on learning*, ed. R. A. Hinde & J. Stevenson-Hinde. Academic Press. [5–FMT; 6–JERS]
Morse, W. H. & Skinner, B. F. (1958) Some factors involved in the stimulus control of operant behavior. *Journal of the Experimental Analysis of Behavior* 1:103–7. [2–BFS on WWR]
Mortenson, F. J. (1975) *Animal behavior: Theory and research*. Brooks/Cole. [6–GMB]
Mountjoy, P. P. & Malott, M. K. (1968) Wave-length generalization curves for chickens reared in restricted portions of the spectrum. *Psychological Record* 18:575–83. [5–TRZ]
Mowrer, O. H. & Jones, H. M. (1943) Extinction and behavior variability as functions of effortfulness of task. *Journal of Experimental Psychology* 33:369–86. [2–BFS]
Müller, M. (1872) Max Müller on Darwin's philosophy of language. *Nature* 1:145. [1–JWD]
Näätänen, R., Hukkanen, S. & Järvilechto, T. (1980) Magnitude of stimulus deviance and brain potentials. In: *Progress in brain research*, vol. 54, *Motivation, motor and sensory processes of the brain*, ed. H. H. Kornhuber and L. Deecke. Elsevier-North Holland. [4–SG]
Nagel, T. (1974). What is it like to be a bat? *Philosophical Review* 83:435–50. [4–LJC]
Nanney, D. L. (1977) Molecules and morphologies: The perpetuation of pattern in the ciliated protozoa. *Journal of Protozoology* 24:27–35. [6–DW]
Neisser, U. (1963) The limitation of man by machine. *Science* 138:193–97. [4–BFS]
Nelson, R. J. (1969) Behaviorism is false. *Journal of Philosophy* 66:417–51. [2–RJN]
(1982) *The logic of mind*. Reidel. [2–RJN]
Neurath, O. (1970) Foundations of the social sciences. In: *The foundations of the unity of science*, ed. O. Neurath et al. University of Chicago Press. [5–MB]
Nevin, J. A. & Reynolds, G. S., eds. (1973) *The study of behavior: Learning, motivation, emotion, and instinct*. Scott, Foresman & Co. [6–GMB]
Newell, A. (1981) The knowledge level. *AI Magazine* 2:1–20. [2–RM]
Newell, A. & Simon, H. A. (1972) *Human problem solving*. Prentice-Hall. [4–JMS]
Newman, O. (1980) *Community of interest*. Doubleday. [6–SK]

Neyman, J. & Pearson, E. S. (1967) *Joint statistical papers*. Cambridge University Press. [2–FHCM]
Nisbett, R. E. & Ross, L. (1980) *Human inference: Strategies and shortcomings of social judgment*. Prentice-Hall. [4–RMH, EPS]
Nisbett, R. E. & Wilson, T. D. (1977) On saying more than we can know. *Psychological Review* 84:231–59. [5–GR]
Oatley, K. (1973) Simulation and theory of thirst. *The neuropsychology of thirst: New findings and advances in concepts*, ed. A. N. Epstein, H. R. Kissileff & E. Stellar. V. H. Winston. [5–FMT]
Ogden, C. K. & Richards, I. A. (1938) *The meaning of meaning*. Harcourt, Brace. [3–BFS on DS]
O'Keefe, J. & Nadel, L. (1978) *The hippocampus as a cognitive map*. Oxford University Press. [5–MLW]
Olton, D. S. (1978) Characteristics of spatial memory. In: *Cognitive processes in animal behavior*, ed. S. W. Hulse, H. Fowler & W. K. Honig. Erlbaum. [5–WST]
Olton, D. S., Becker, J. T. & Handelmann, G. E. (1979) Hippocampus, space, and memory. *Behavioral and Brain Sciences* 2:313–65. [5–MLW]
Olton, D. S. & Samuelson, R. J. (1976) Remembrance of places past: Spatial memory in rats. *Journal of Experimental Psychology: Animal Behavior Processes* 2:97–116. [3–HST]
Oppenheimer, J. M. (1967) *Essays in the history of embryology and biology*. MIT Press. [6–GG]
Osgood, C. (1962) *An alternative to war or surrender*. University of Illinois Press. [6–DPB]
Paige, J. M. & Simon, H. A. (1966). Cognitive processes in solving algebra word problems. In: *Problem solving: Research, method, and theory*, ed. B. Kleinmuntz. Wiley. [4–EH]
Paivio, A. (1975) Neomentalism. *Canadian Journal of Psychology* 29:263–91. [5–RMG]
Palay, S. L. (1967) Principles of cellular organization. In: *The neurosciences*, ed. G. C. Quarton, T. Melnechuk & F. O. Schmitt. Rockefeller University Press. [6–GDW]
Paley, W. (1836) *Natural theology* Charles Knight. [1–JS]
Palmer, S. E. (1978) Fundamental aspects of cognitive representation. In: *Cognition and categorization*, ed. E. Rosch & B. Lloyd. Lawrence Erlbaum Associates. [3–LCR]
Pascal, B. (1670) *Pensées*. [6–BFS]
Patten, B. C. (1982) Environs: Relativistic elementary particles for ecology. *American Naturalist* 119:179–219. [6–SNS]
Pavlov, I. P. (1927) *Conditioned reflexes*. Trans. G. V. Anrep. Oxford University Press. [1–PRS; 7–BFS on SH]
Peirce, C. S. (1878) How to make our ideas clear. *Popular Science Monthly*, January. [2–ES]
Pelham, G. F. (1982) The psychological writings of B. F. Skinner. Doctoral dissertation, University of Bradford, England. [4–RH]
Penfield, W. (1969) Consciousness, memory and man's conditioned reflexes. In: *On the biology of learning*, ed. K. H. Pribram. Harcourt, Brace and Jovanovich. [5–FMT]
Perkel, D. H. (1970) Spike trains as carriers of information. In: *The neurosciences second study program*, ed. F. O. Schmitt. Rockefeller University Press [6–GDW]
Peterson, G. B., Wheeler, R. L. & Trapold, M. A. (1980) Enhancement of pigeons' conditional discrimination performance by expectancies of reinforcement and nonreinforcement. *Animal Learning and Behavior* 8:22–30. [1–WKH]
Peterson, N. (1960) Control of behavior by presentation of an imprinted stimulus. *Science* 132:1395–96. [1–BFS; 6–BFS]
(1962) Effect of monochromatic rearing on the control of responding by wavelength. *Science* 136:774–75. [5–BFS on TRZ]
Piaget, J. (1929) *The child's conception of the world*. Harcourt, Brace. [3–HST]
(1979) *Behaviour and evolution*. Routledge and Kegan Paul. [6–HCP]
Piaget, J. & Garcia, R. (1982) *Psicogenesis e historia de la ciencia*. Siglo XXI. [6–AK]
Piaget, J. & Inhelder, B. (1969) The gaps in empiricism. In: *Beyond reductionism*, ed. A. Koestler & J. R. Smythies. Hutchinson. [3–RPB]

Place, U. T. (1981a) Skinner's *Verbal behavior* I – Why we need it. *Behaviorism* 9:1–24. [3–UTP]

(1981b) Skinner's *Verbal Behavior* II – What is wrong with it. *Behaviorism* 9:131–52. [3–UTP]

Plomin, R. (1983) Developmental behavioral genetics. *Child Development* 54:253–59. [6–RP]

(1985) Behavioral genetics, behavioral analysis, and development. In: *Developmental behavioral genetics and learning*, ed. D. B. Gray. Lawrence Erlbaum Associates. [6–RP]

Plomin, R., DeFries, J. C. & McClearn, G. E. (1980) *Behavioral genetics*. Freeman. [6–RP]

Plotkin, H. C. & Odling-Smee, F. J. (1979) Learning, change and evolution. *Advances in the Study of Behaviour* 10:1–41. [1–HCP; 6–HCP]

(1981) A multiple-level model of evolution and its implications for sociobiology. *Behavioral and Brain Sciences* 4:225–68. [1–TJG, HCP; 6–HCP]

Polanyi, M. (1958) *The study of man*. Routledge. [4–BFS]

(1960) *Personal knowledge*. University of Chicago Press. [3–BFS on JM; 4–BFS]

Popper, K. R. (1957) *The open society and its enemies*. Routledge & Kegan Paul. [6–BFS]

(1961) *Logic of scientific discovery*. Science Editions. [2–ES]

(1963) *Conjectures and refutations: The growth of scientific knowledge*. Routledge & Kegan Paul. [4–PCD]

(1969) Science: Conjectures and refutations. In: *Conjectures and refutations*. Basic Books. [2–ES]

Popper, K. R. & Eccles, J.-C. (1977) *The self and its brain*. Springer. [2–MNR]

Pounds, W. (1969) The process of problem finding. *Industrial Management Review* 11(1):1–19. [4–CK]

Powers, W. T. (1973) *Behavior: The control of perception*. Aldine. [2–WH]

(1978) Quantitative analysis of purposive systems: Some spadework at the foundations of scientific psychology. *Psychological Review*, 85:417–35. [2–WH]

Prelec, D. (1982) Matching, maximizing, and the hyperbolic reinforcement feedback function. *Psychological Review* 89:189–230. (2–RDL)

Premack, D. (1959) Toward empirical behavior laws: I. Positive reinforcement. *Psychological Review* 66:219–33. [7–ACC]

(1971) Catching up with common sense or two sides of a generalization: Reinforcement and punishment. In: *The nature of reinforcement:* ed. R. Glaser. Academic Press. [7–ACC]

(1976) *Intelligence in ape and man*. Lawrence Erlbaum Associates. [3–HST]

Premack, D. & Woodruff, G. (1978) Does the chimpanzee have a theory of mind? *Behavioral and Brain Sciences* 4:515–26. [5–GGG, LCNJ]

Pribram, K. H. (1971) *Languages of the brain: Experimental paradoxes and principles in neuropsychology*. Prentice-Hall. [5–MLW]

Price, G. R. (1972) Extension of covariance selection mathematics. *Annals of Human Genetics* 35:485–90. [1–SCS]

Pringle, J. W. S. (1951) On the parallel between learning and evolution. *Behaviour* 3:174–215. [1–GWB; 6–JDD]

Pulliam, H. R. & Dunford, C. (1980) *Programmed to learn*. Columbia University Press. [1–TJG]

Putnam, H. (1975) The meaning of "meaning." In: *Minnesota studies in the philosophy of science*, vol. 7, *Language, mind and knowledge*, ed. K. Gunderson. University of Minnesota Press. [5–WGL]

Pylyshyn, Z. (1980) Computation and cognition: Issues in the foundation of cognitive science. *Behavioral and Brain Sciences* 3:11–169. [4–EPS]

Quine, W. V. O. (1951) Notes on the theory of reference. In: *From a logical point of view and other essays*. Harper & Row. [5–GR]

(1953) Two dogmas of empiricism. In: *From a logical point of view*. Harvard University Press. [5–MB]

(1960) *Word and object*. MIT Press. [3–JDR; 5–MJM, GR]

(1970) Methodological reflections on current linguistic theory. *Synthese* 27:325–29. [3–JDR

Raaheim, K. (1961) Problem solving: A new approach. *Acta Universitatis Bergensis, Series Humaniorum Litterarum*, no. 5 [4–KR]

(1974) *Problem solving and intelligence*. Universitetsforlaget. [4–KR]

Rachlin, H. & Burkhard, B. (1978) The temporal triangle: Response substitution in instrumental conditioning. *Psychological Review* 85:22–47. [7–ACC]

Raff, R. A. & Kaufman, T. C. (1983) *Embryos, genes, and evolution*. Macmillan. [6–JERS]

Ratliff, F. (1962) Some interrelations among physics, physiology, and psychology in the study of vision. In *Psychology: A study of a science*, study 2, vol. 4, ed. S. Koch. McGraw-Hill. [5–RKT]

Rein, J. G. & Svartdal, F. (1979) Limitations of Skinner's concept of an "operant." *Scandinavian Journal of Psychology* 20:65–70. [4–JGR]

Rescorla, R. A. (1967) Pavlovian conditioning and its proper control procedures. *Psychological Review* 74:71–80. [6–JERS]

Rescorla, R. A. & Wagner, A. R. (1972) A theory of Pavlovian conditioning: Variations in the effectiveness of reinforcement and nonreinforcement. In: *Classical conditioning*, vol. 2, *Current research and theory*, ed. A. H. Black & W. F. Prokasy. Appleton-Century-Crofts. [1–JWD; 2–SR; 5–WST]

Resnick, L. B. (1983) Mathematics and science learning: A new conception. *Science* 220:477–78. [6–SK]

Rey, G. (1980) What are mental images? In: *Readings in the philosophy of psychology*, vol. 2, ed. N. Block. Harvard University Press. [5–GR]

(1983) A reason for doubting the existence of consciousness. In: *Consciousness and self-regulation*, vol. 3, ed. R. Davidson, G. Schwartz & D. Shapiro. Plenum. [5–GR]

Rice, W. R. (1983) Parent–offspring pathogen transmission: A selective agent promoting sexual reproduction. *American Naturalist* 121:187–203. [1–SCS]

Richelle, M. (1976) Formal analysis and functional analysis of verbal behavior: Notes on the debate between Chomsky and Skinner (transl. W. S. Foster & J. A. Rondal). *Behaviorism* 4:209–21. [2–MNR]

(1977) *B. F. Skinner ou le péril behavioriste*. Mardaga. [2–MNR]

Riley, D. A. & Leuin, T. G. (1971) Stimulus-generalization gradients in chickens reared in monochromatic light and tested with single wavelength values. *Journal of Comparative and Physiological Psychology* 75:399–402. [5–TRZ]

Ringen, J. (1977) On evaluating data concerning linguistic intuition. In: *Current themes in linguistics*, ed. F. Eckman. Wiley. [3–JDR]

(1980) Quine on introspection in linguistics. In: *A festschrift for a native speaker*, ed. F. Coulmas. Mouton. [3–JDR]

Roberts, S. (1981) Isolation of an internal clock. *Journal of Experimental Psychology: Animal Behavior Processes* 7:242–68. [2–SR]

(1982) Cross-modal use of an internal clock. *Journal of Experimental Psychology: Animal Behavior Processes* 8:2–22. [2–SR]

Roberts, S. & Holder, M. D. (1984) What starts an internal clock? *Journal of Experimental Psychology: Animal Behavior Processes*. 10:273–96. [2–SR]

Roberts, W. A. & Kraemer, P. J. (1982) Some observations of the effects of intertrial interval and delay on delayed matching to sample in pigeons. *Journal of Experimental Psychology: Animal Behavior Processes* 8:342–53. [3–HST]

Robinson, D. N. (1979) *Systems of modern psychology: A critical sketch*. Columbia University Press. [5–DNR]

(1981) *An intellectual history of psychology*. Rev. ed. Macmillan. [5–DNR]

Roediger, H. L. (1980) Memory metaphors in cognitive psychology. *Memory and Cognition* 8:231–46. [5–MJM]

Rogers, C. (1961) *On becoming a person: A therapist's view of psychotherapy*. Houghton Mifflin. [4–BFS]

Roitblat, H. L. (1980) Codes and coding processes in pigeon short-term memory. *Animal Learning and Behavior* 8:341–51. [3–HST]

(1982) The meaning of representation in animal memory. *Behavioral and Brain Sciences* 5:353–406. [5–EJW]

Romanes, G. J. (1884) *Mental evolution in animals*. Kegan, Paul, Trench & Co. [6–JPH]

(1889) *Mental evolution in man*. D. Appleton. [6–JPH]

(1892) *Animal intelligence*. D. Appleton. [2–BFS]

Rorty, R. (1979) *Philosophy and the mirror of nature*. Princeton University Press. [2–CPS]

Rosch, E. H. (1973) Natural categories. *Cognitive Psychology* 4:49–53. [5–TRZ]

Rosch, E., Mervis, C. B., Gay, W. D., Boyes-Braem, P. & Johnson, D. N. (1976) Basic objects in natural categories. *Cognitive Psychology* 8:382–439. [5–HMW]

Rosenberg, A. (1983) Fitness. *Journal of Philosophy* 80:457–73. [1–AR]

Ross, L. (1981) The "intuitive scientist" formulation and its developmental implications. In: *Social cognitive development*, ed. J. H. Flavell & L. Ross. Cambridge University Press. [5–CNJ]

Roughead, W. G. & Scandura, J. M. (1968) "What is learned" in mathematical discovery. *Journal of Educational Psychology* 59:283–89. [4–JMS]

Routtenberg, A. & Lindy, J. (1965) Effects of the availability of rewarding septal and hypothalamic stimulation on bar pressing for food under conditions of deprivation. *Journal of Comparative and Physiological Psychology* 60:158–61. [1–WW]

Rozeboom, W. W. (1958) "What is learned?" – an empirical enigma. *Psychological Review* 65:22–33. [2–WWR]

(1961) Ontological induction and the logical typology of scientific variables. *Philosophy of Science* 28:337–77. [2–WWR]

(1966) Scaling theory and the nature of measurement. *Synthèse* 16:170–233. [2–WWR]

(1967) Conditioned generalization, cognitive set, and the structure of human learning. *Journal of Verbal Learning and Verbal Behavior* 6:491–500. [2–WWR]

(1970) The art of metascience, or, what should a psychological theory be? In: *Toward unification of psychology*, ed. J. R. Royce. Toronto University Press. [2–WWR]

(1972) Scientific inference: The myth and the reality. In: *Science, psychology and communication*, ed. S. R. Brown & D. J. Brenner. Teachers College Press. [2–WWR]

(1973) Dispositions revisited. *Philosophy of Science* 40:59–74. [2–WWR]

(1982) Let's dump hypothetico-deductivism for the right reasons. *Philosophy of Science* 49: 637–47. [2–WWR]

(1984) Dispositions do explain. In: *Annals of theoretical psychology*, vol. 1, ed. J. R. Royce & L. P. Mos. Plenum Press. [2–WWR]

Russell, B. (1940) *An inquiry into meaning and truth*. G. Allen & Unwin. [3–BFS]

Ryle, G. (1949) *The concept of mind*. Hutchinson. [2–SMD; 3–PH, UTP; 5–JJF, WL]

Salaman, R. A. (1957) Tradesmen's tools. In: *A history of technology*, vol. 3. Oxford University Press. [4–BFS]

Scandura, J. M. (1964) An analysis of exposition and discovery modes of problem solving instruction. *Journal of Experimental Education* 33:145–48. [4–JMS]

(1969) New directions for theory and research on rule learning. II. Empirical research. *Acta Psychologica* 29:101–33. [4–JMS]

(1970) The role of rules in behavior: Toward an operational definition of what (rule) is learned. *Psychological Review* 77:516–33. [4–JMS]

(1971) Deterministic theorizing in structural learning: Three levels of empiricism. *Journal of Structural Learning* 3:21–53. [4–JMS]

(1973) *Structural learning*, vol. 1, *Theory and research*. Gordon & Breach Science Publishers. [4–JMS]

(1976) ed. *Structural learning*, vol. 2, *Issues and approaches*. Gordon & Breach Science Publishers. [4–JMS]

(1977) *Problem solving*. Academic Press. [4–JMS]

(1981) Problem solving in schools and beyond: Transitions from the naive to the neophyte to the master. *Educational Psychologist* 16:139–50. [4–JMS]

(1982) Structural (cognitive task) analysis. I. Background and empirical research. *Journal of Structural Learning* 7:101–14. [4–JMS]

Scandura, J. M. & Scandura, A. B. (1980) *Structural learning and concrete operations: An approach to Piagetian conservation*. Praeger. [4–JMS]
Schaller, G. B. (1964) *The year of the gorilla*. University of Chicago Press. [6–SK]
Schick, K. (1974) Operants. *Journal of the Experimental Analysis of Behavior* 15:413–33. [4–JGR]
Schiffer, S. R. (1972) *Meaning*. Oxford University Press. [3–JB]
Schneider, W. & Shiffrin, R. M. (1977) Controlled and automatic human information processing. 1. Detection, search and attention. *Psychological Review* 84:1–66. [4–EH]
Schwartz, B. (1974) On going back to nature: A review of Seligman and Hager's *Biological boundaries of learning*. *Journal of the Experimental Analysis of Behavior* 21:183–98. [2–BM]
Scriven, M. (1956) A study of radical behaviorism. In: *The foundations of science and the concepts of psychology and psychoanalysis*. Minnesota Studies in the Philosophy of Science, vol. 1, ed. H. Feigl & M. Scriven. University of Minnesota Press. [3–JDR; 5–MAS]
Sebeok, T. A. (1965) Animal communication. *Science* 147:1006–14. [6–BFS]
Segal, E. F. (1975) Psycholinguistics discovers the operant: A review of Roger Brown's *A first language: The early states*. *Journal of the Experimental Analysis of Behavior* 23:149–58. [3–RPB]
Segall, M. H. (1979) Cross-cultural psychology. Brooks/Cole. [6–IE–E]
Seligman, M. E. P. (1970) On the generality of the laws of learning. *Psychological Review* 77:406–18. [6–JDD]
Seligman, M. E. P. & Hager, J. L., eds. (1972) *Biological boundaries of learning*. Appleton-Century-Crofts. [2–BM]
Shatz, M., Wellman, H. M. & Silber, S. (1983) The acquisition of mental verbs: A systematic investigation of the first reference to mental state. *Cognition* 14:301–21. [5–HMW]
Shepard, J. (1933) Higher processes in the behavior of rats. *Proceedings of the National Academy of Sciences* 19:149–52. [5–GR]
Shepard, R. N. (1975) Form, formation and transformation of internal representations. In: *Information processing and cognition*, ed. R. L. Solso. Lawrence Erlbaum Associates. [3–HST]
Shepard, R. N. & Metzler, J. (1971) Mental rotation of three-dimensional objects. *Science* 171:701–3. [3–LCR]
Sherman, P. W. (1977) Nepotism and the evolution of alarm calls. *Science* 197:1246–53. [1–SCS]
Sherrington, C. (1906) *The integrative action of the nervous system*. Scribner's. [0–ACC; 1–PRS; 7–BFS on SH]
Shettleworth, S. J. (1975) Reinforcement and the organization of behavior in golden hamsters: Hunger, environment and food reinforcement. *Journal of Experimental Psychology* 104: 56–87. [6–JERS]
Shimp, C. P. (1975) Perspectives on the behavioral unit: Choice behavior in animals. In: *Handbook of learning and cognitive processes*, ed. W. K. Estes, vol. 2. Lawrence Erlbaum Associates. [2–CPS]
(1976a) Organization in memory and behavior. *Journal of the Experimental Analysis of Behavior* 26:113–30. [2–CPS]
(1976b) Short-term memory in the pigeon: Relative recency. *Journal of the Experimental Analysis of Behavior* 25:55–61. [3–HST]
(1984a) Relations between memory and operant behavior, according to an associative learner (AL). *Canadian Journal of Psychology* 38:269–84. [2–CPS]
(1984b) Timing, learning and forgetting. In: *Timing and time perception*, ed. J. Gibbon & L. Allen. New York Academy of Sciences. [2–CPS]
Sidman, M. (1978) Remarks. *Behaviorism* 6:265–68. [2–SMD]
(1979) Remarks. *Behaviorism* 7:123–26. [2–SMD]
Sidman, M. & Stoddard, L. T. (1967) The effectiveness of fading in programming a simultaneous form discrimination for retarded children. *Journal of the Experimental Analysis of Behavior* 10:3–15. [7–BFS on SH]

Siegel, S. (1979) The role of conditioning in drug tolerance and addiction. In: *Psychopathology in animals: Research and treatment implications*, ed. J. D. Keehn. Academic Press. [2–SR]

Siegler, R. S. (1983) Review of *The development of mathematical thinking*. *Science* 221:1042–43. [6–SK]

Simon, H. A. (1966) Thinking by computers. In: *Mind and cosmos*, ed. R. C. Colodny. University of Pittsburgh Press. [1–TJG]

Simpson, G. G. (1953) *The major features of evolution*. Columbia University Press. [7–ACC]

Skinner, B. F. (1931) The concept of the reflex in the description of behavior. *Journal of General Psychology* 5:127–58. [1–RCB; 2–JMN; 3–BFS, PNH, JDR]

(1932a) Drive and reflex strength, I. *Journal of General Psychology* 6:22–37. [2–BFS on RJN; 6–BFS on AK]

(1932b) Drive and reflex strength, II. *Journal of General Psychology* 6:38–48. [6–BFS on AK]

(1932c) On the rate of formation of a conditioned reflex. *Journal of General Psychology* 7:274–86. [1–BFS on TJG]

(1934) A discrimination without previous conditioning. *Proceedings of the National Academy of Sciences* 20:532–36. [7–BFS on SH]

(1935a) The generic nature of the concepts of stimulus and response. *Journal of General Psychology* 12:40–65. [0–ACC; 2–BFS on ES; 3–RPB, PNH]

(1935b) Two types of conditioned reflex and a pseudo-type. *Journal of General Psychology* 12:66–77. [3–PNH]

(1937) Two types of conditioned reflex: A reply to Konorski and Miller. *Journal of General Psychology* 16:272–79. [1–RCB; 3–PNH; 6–BFS on GH]

(1938) *The behavior of organisms*. Appleton-Century-Crofts. [0–ACC; 2–BFS; 3–RPB, CFL, PEM, DS; 4–JGR; 5–FWI; 6–BFS, GMB, AMC, JDD; 7–BFS on SH]

(1945) The operational analysis of psychological terms. *Psychological Review* 42:270–77; 291–94. [0–ACC]

(1947) Current trends in experimental psychology. In: *Current trends in psychology*. University of Pittsburgh Press. [5–JCM]

(1948a) "Superstition" in the pigeon. *Journal of Experimental Psychology* 38:168–72. [6–BFS]

(1948b) *Walden two*. Macmillan. [0–ACC; 6–BFS on GMB]

(1950) Are theories of learning necessary? *Psychological Review* 57:193–216. [0–ACC; 1–RCB; 3–PNH, BFS on PNH, HST; 5–WST; 6–AMC]

(1953) *Science and human behavior*. Macmillan. [0–ACC; 1–BFS on WKH, on PRS; 2–WWR, ES; 3–CFL, HST; 4–JGR, BFS on MK, on WSV; 5–BFS, BAF, KG, WL, BFS on WL; 6–AMC, BFS on IE–E; 7–ACC]

(1956) Freedom and the control of men. *American Scholar* 25:47–65. [7–ACC]

(1957) *Verbal behavior*. Appleton-Century-Crofts. [0–ACC; 1–BFS; 2–BFS on BM, MNR, ES; 3–KRG, GG, CFL, JM, UTP, JDR; 4–BFS, PJ; 5-BFS on MB, on CNJ; 6–BFS; 7–BFS on SH]

(1959a) A case history in scientific method. In: *Psychology: A study of science*, ed. S. Koch. McGraw-Hill. [1–PRS]

(1959b) John Broadus Watson, behaviorist. *Science* 129:197–98. [3–JDR]

(1960) Pigeons in a pelican. *American Psychologist* 15:28–37. [0–ACC; 6–BFS]

(1961) The flight from the laboratory. In: *Current trends in psychological theory*, ed. Wayne Dennis et al. University of Pittsburgh Press. [0–ACC]

(1963a) Behaviorism at fifty. *Science* 140:951–58. [0–ACC; 1–AR; 3–CFL; 4–BFS]

(1963b) Operant behavior. *American Psychologist* 18:503–15. [4–BFS]

(1966a) An operant analysis of problem solving. In: *Problem solving: Research, methods, and theory*, ed. B. Kleinmuntz. John Wiley & Sons. (0–ACC; 3–PNH]

(1966b) Operant behavior. In: *Operant behavior: Areas of research and application*, ed W. K. Honig. Appleton-Century-Crofts. [2–CPS; 5–MLW]

(1966c) The phylogeny and ontogeny of behavior. *Science* 153:1205–13. [0–ACC; 1–JS 5–EJW]

(1966d) Preface to paperback ed. of *The behavior of organisms*. 1st ed. 1938. Appleton-Century-Crofts. [4–BFS]
(1968) *The technology of teaching*. Appleton-Century-Crofts. [4–BFS]
(1969) *Contingencies of reinforcement: A theoretical analysis*. Appleton-Century-Crofts. [0–ACC; 2–SMD, KMS; 3–RPB, UTP, HST, GEZ; 4–JGR; 5–FW; 6–GMB]
(1971) *Beyond freedom and dignity*. Knopf (1973, Penguin). [1–BFS, BD; 2–BM; 4–BFS on EH; 5–BFS on JEA, BAF; 6–BFS on SK]
(1972) *Cumulative record: A selection of papers*. Appleton-Century-Crofts. [2–JMN]
(1974) *About behaviorism*. Knopf (1976, Vintage). [1–CBGG, PRS; 2–BFS on JMEM, WWR; 3–PH, CFL, DS, HST, GEZ; 4–BFS on MK; 5–RS, MAS, SPS, EJW]
(1975a) The shaping of phylogenic behavior. *Journal of the Experimental Analysis of Behavior* 24:117–20. [1–BFS; 5–RS; 7–ACC]
(1975b) The steep and thorny way to a science of behavior. In: *Problems of scientific revolution*, ed. R. Harré. Clarendon Press. [5–BAF]
(1976) *Particulars of my life*. Knopf. [0–ACC]
(1977a) Herrnstein and the evolution of behaviorism. *American Psychologist* 32:1006–12. [3–RPB, PNH]
(1977b) Why I am not a cognitive psychologist. *Behaviorism* 5:1–10. [3–HST; 5–RKT]
(1979) *The shaping of a behaviorist*. Knopf. [0–ACC; 2–JMN; 5–BFS on MJM; 6–RP]
(1981) Selection by consequences. *Science* 213:501–4. [0–ACC; 3–PNH; 5–EJW; 6–SNS]
(1982) Contrived reinforcement. *Behavior Analyst* 5:3–8. [6–BFS on DPB]
(1983a) A better way to deal with selection. *Behavioral and Brain Sciences* 6:377–78. [5–ML]
(1983b) Can the experimental analysis of behavior rescue psychology? *Behavior Analyst* 6:9–17. [1–BFS on WKH, on PRS; 6–BFS on AMC, JERS]
(1983c) Origins of a behaviorist. *Psychology Today* 17(9):22–33. [6–AMC]
(1983d) *A matter of consequences*. Knopf. [0–ACC; 1–BFS on WKH; 4–BFS on PCD]
(1984) The evolution of behavior. *Journal of the Experimental Analysis of Behavior* 41:217–21. [7–ACC]
(1985a) Cognitive science and behaviorism. *British Journal of Psychology* 76:291–301. [7–BFS on SH]
(1985b) Reply to Place: "Three senses of the word 'tact'". *Behaviorism* 13:75–6. [7–BFS on ACC]
Skinner, B. F. & Morse, W. H. (1957) Concurrent activity under fixed-interval reinforcement. *Journal of Comparative and Physiological Psychology* 50:279–81. [6–BFS]
Skinner, B. F. & Vaughan, M. E. (1983) *Enjoy old age*. Norton. [2–MNR]
Slater, E. & Glithero, E. (1965) A follow up of patients diagnosed as suffering from hysteria. *Journal of Psychosomatic Research* 9:9–13. [3–DTK]
Smart, J. (1959) Sensations and brain processes. *Philosophical Review* 68:141–56. [5–CM, GR]
Sokolov, A. N. (1972) *Inner speech and thought*. Plenum [3–CFL]
Sommerhoff, G. (1950) *Analytical biology*. Oxford University Press. [6–GDW]
(1974) *Logic of the living brain*. Wiley. [6–GDW]
Sperry, R. W. (1971) How a developing brain gets itself properly wired for adaptive function. In: *The biopsychology of development*, ed. E. Tobach, L. R. Aronson & E. Shaw. Academic Press. [6–IE–E]
Squires, K., Wickens, C., Squires, N. & Donchin, E. (1976) The effect of stimulus sequence on the waveform of the cortical event-related potential. *Science* 193:1142–46. [4–SG]
Stabler, E. P. (1983) How are grammars represented? *Behavioral and Brain Sciences* 6:391–421. [4–EPS]
Staddon, J. E. R. (1977) Schedule-induced behavior. In: *Handbook of operant behavior*, ed. W. K. Honig, & J. E. R. Staddon. Prentice-Hall. [6–JAH]
(1983) *Adaptive behavior and learning*. Cambridge University Press. [6–JERS]
Staddon, J. E. R. & Simmelhag, V. (1971) The "superstition" experiment: A reexamination of its implications for the principles of adaptive behavior. *Psychological Review* 78:3–43. [6–AK, BFS on AK, JERS, BFS on JERS]

Stearns, S. C. (1983) The evolution of life-history traits in mosquitofish since their introduction to Hawaii in 1905: Rates of evolution, heritabilities, and developmental plasticity. *American Zoologist* 23:65–75. [1–SCS]

Stearns, S. C. & Crandall, R. E. (1983) Plasticity for age and size at sexual maturity: A life-history response to unavoidable stress. In: *Proceedings of the international symposium of the British Fisheries Society*, ed. R. J. Wootton. Academic Press. [1–SCS]

Stent, G. (1981) Strength and weakness of the genetic approach in the development of the nervous system. *Annual Review of Neuroscience* 4:163–94. [6–DW]

Stephens, D. W. (1981) The logic of risk-sensitive foraging preferences. *Animal Behavior* 29:628–29. [6–AK]

Sternberg, R. J., ed. (1982) *Handbook of human intelligence*. Cambridge University Press. [4–KR]

Stevens, S. S. (1935) The operational basis of psychology. *American Journal of Psychology* 47:323–30. [5–BFS]

(1939) Psychology and the science of science. *Psychological Bulletin* 36:221–63. [3–BFS, JM]

(1957) On the psychophysical law. *Psychological Review* 64:153–81. [2–JTT]

Stiers, M. & Silberberg. A. (1974) Lever-contact responses in rats: Automaintenance with and without a negative response-reinforcer dependency. *Journal of the Experimental Analysis of Behavior* 22:497–506. [6–AMC]

Stinessen, L. (1983) Intentionality, problem solving, and rule-governed behavior. Doctoral dissertation. University of Trondheim. [4–JGR]

Straub, R. O., Seidenberg, M. S., Bever, T. G. & Terrace, H. S. (1979) Serial learning in the pigeon. *Journal of the Experimental Analysis of Behavior* 32:137–48. [2–CPS]

Strauss, M. S. & Curtis, L. E. (1981) Infant perception of numerosity. *Child Development* 52:1146–52. [5–HMW]

Strawson, P. F. (1968) Freedom and resentment. In: *Studies in the philosophy of thought and action*, ed P. F. Strawson. Oxford University Press. [5–JEA, BFS on JEA]

Suppes, P. (1975) From behaviorism to neobehaviorism. *Theory and Decision* 6:269–86. [2–RJN]

Swanson, L. W., Teyler, T. J. & Thompson, R. F. (1982) Hippocampal long term potentiation: Mechanisms and implications for memory. *Neurosciences Research Program Bulletin* 5. [1–PRS]

Taube, M. (1961) *Computers and common sense: The myth of thinking machines*. Columbia University Press. [4–BFS]

Taylor, C. (1964) *The explanation of behavior*. Routledge & Kegan Paul. [3–JDR; 4–PJ]

Tecce, J. J. (1972) Contingent negative variation (CNV) and psychological processes in man. *Psychological Review* 77:73–108. [4–SG]

Teitelbaum, P. (1966) The use of operant methods in the assessment and control of motivational states. In: *Operant behavior: Areas of research and application*, ed. W. K. Honig. Appleton-Century-Crofts. [5–MLW]

Terrace, H. S. (1963) Discrimination learning with and without "errors." *Journal of the Experimental Analysis of behavior* 6:1–27. [6–BFS]

(1963) Errorless transfer of a discrimination across two continna. *Journal of the Experimental Analysis of Behavior* 6:223–32. [7–BFS on SH]

(1970) Towards a doctrine of radical behaviorism. *Contemporary Psychology* 15:531–35. [3–HST]

(1982) Can animals think? *New Society* 4:339–42. [3–HST]

(1983a) Animal cognition. In *Animal Cognition*, ed. H. L. Roitblat, T. G. Bever & H. S. Terrace. Lawrence Erlbaum Associates. [3–HST]

(1983b) Simultaneous chaining: The problem it poses for traditional chaining theory. In: *Quantitative studies in operant behavior: Acquisition*, ed. M. L. Commons, A. R. Wagner & R. J. Herrnstein. Ballinger. [3–HST]

Teuber, H. L. (1974) Key problems in the programming of movements. *Brain Research* 71:535–68. [5–JCM]

Thomas, L. (1983) *The youngest science: Notes of a medicine watcher*. Viking Press. [4–RMH]
Thompson, R. F. (1976) The search for the engrain. *American Psychologist* 31:209–27. [1–PRS]
Thorndike, E. L. (1898) Animal intelligence: An experimental study of the associative processes in animals. *Psychological Reviews*, Monographic Supplement 8:1–109. [6–JPH]
(1900a) The associative processes in animals. *Biological Lectures from the Marine Biological Laboratory of Woods Hole, 1899*, 7:69–91. [6–GMB]
(1900b) Instinct. *Biological Lectures from the Marine Biological Laboratory of Woods Hole, 1899*, 7:57–67. [6–GMB]
(1911) *Animal intelligence: Experimental studies*, Macmillan. [1–JS; 6–GG]
Thorpe, W. H. (1951) The learning abilities of birds. Part I. *Ibis* 93:1–52. [6–BFS]
Thurstone, L. L. (1924) *The nature of intelligence*. Harcourt Brace. [1–TJG]
Timberlake, W. (1983) Rats' responses to a moving object related to food or water: A behavior-systems analysis. *Animal Learning and Behavior* 11:309–20. [6–GMB]
Tinbergen, N. (1951) *The study of instinct*. Oxford University Press. [6–JDD, JPH]
(1953) *The herring-gull's world*. Collins. [6–BFS, JERS]
Todd, J. T. & Morris, E. K. (1983) Misconception and miseducation: Presentations of radical behaviorism in psychology textbooks. *Behavior Analyst* 6:153–60. [0–ACC]
Tolman, E. C. (1922) A new formula for behaviorism. *Psychological Review* 29:44–53. [5–WL]
(1926) A behavioristic study of ideas. *Psychological Review* 33:352–69. [1–TJG]
(1932) *Purposive behavior in animals and men*. Century. [5–EJW]
(1935) Psychology versus immediate experience. *Philosophy of Science* 2:356–80. [5–EJW]
(1948) Cognitive maps in rats and men. *Psychological Review* 55:189–208. [5–EJW; 7–BFS on ACC]
Tolman, E. & Honzik, C. (1930), "Insight" in rats. In: *University of California publications in psychology*. University of California Press. [5–GR, BFS on GR]
Townsend, J. T. (1972) Some results concerning the identifiability of parallel and serial processes. *Journal of Mathematical Psychology* 25:168–199. [2–JTT]
Townsend, J. T. & Ashby, F. G. (1983) *The stochastic modeling of elementary psychological processes*. Cambridge University Press. [2–JTT]
Tracy, W. K. (1970) Wavelength generalization and preference in monochromatically reared ducklings. *Journal of the Experimental Analysis of Behavior* 13:163–78. [5–TRZ]
Trapold, M. A. & Overmier, J. B. (1972) The second learning process in instrumental conditioning. In: *Classical conditioning*, vol. 2, *Current research and theory*, ed. A. H. Black & W. F. Prokasy. Appleton-Century-Crofts. [6–JERS]
Trivers, R. (1971) The evolution of reciprocal altruism. *Quarterly Review of Biology* 46:35–57. [1–JWD]
Tukey, J. W. (1980) Teaching of statistics: We need both exploratory and confirmatory. *American Statistician* 34:23–25. [2–LW]
Tulving, E. (1979) Memory research: What kind of progress. In: *Perspectives in memory research*, ed. L. A. Nilsson. Erlbaum. [5–MJM]
Tuomela, R., ed. (1978) *Dispositions*. Reidel. [2–WWR]
Ullman, S. (1979) *The interpretation of visual motion*. MIT Press. [4–EPS; 5–JCM]
Valenstein, E. S. (1967) Selection of nutritive and nonnutritive solutions under different conditions of need. *Journal of Comparative and Physiological Psychology* 63:429–33. [1–WW]
Verplanck, W. S. (1962) Unaware of where's awareness: Some verbal operants – notates, monents, and notants. In: *Behavior and awareness*. Duke University Press. [4–WSV]
Vygotsky, L. (1962) *Thought and language*. Wiley. [3–CFL]
de Waal, F. (1982) *Chimpanzee politics*. Jonathan Cape. [5–GGG]
Waddington, C. H. (1957) *The strategy of genes*. Allen and Unwin. [AJP]
(1960) Evolutionary adaptation. In: *The evolution of life*, ed. S. Tax. University of Chicago Press. [6–HCP]
(1968) The human evolutionary system. In: *Darwinism and the study of society*, ed. M. Banton. Quadrangle Books. [1–TJG]

(1969) Paradigm for an evolutionary process. In: *Towards a theoretical biology*, vol. 2, ed. C. H. Waddington. Edinburgh University Press. [1-HCP]

Wade, M. J. (1978) A critical review of the models of group selection. *Quarterly Review of Biology* 53:101-14. [1-SCS]

Wagner, A. R., Rudy, J. W. & Whitlow, J. W. (1973) Rehearsal in animal conditioning. *Journal of Experimental Psychology* 97:407-26. [5-WST]

Wahlsten, D. (1978) Behavioral genetics and animal learning. In: *Psychopharmacology of aversively motivated behavior*, ed. H. Anisman & G. Bignami. Plenum Press. [6-DW]

(1979) Some logical fallacies in the classical ethological point of view. *Behavioral and Brain Sciences* 2:48-49. [6-DW]

Wallach, H. & Karsh, E. B. (1963) Why the modification of stereoscopic depth-perception is so rapid. *American Journal of Psychology* 76:413-20. [4-SG]

Wallis, W. A. & Roberts, H. V. (1956) *Statistics: A new approach*. Free Press. [2-LW]

Waltz, D. L. (1975) Understanding line drawings of scenes with shadows. In: *The psychology of computer vision*, ed. P. Winston. McGraw-Hill. [5-RCM]

Wann, T. W. (1964) *Behaviorism and phenomenology: Contrasting bases for modern psychology*. University of Chicago Press. [5-CNJ, RKT]

Wanner, E. & Gleitman, L. R. (1982) *Language acquisition: The state of the art*. Cambridge University Press. [4-EPS]

Wassermann, G. D. (1978) *Neurobiological theory of psychological phenomena*. Macmillan and University Park Press. [6-GDW]

(1979) Reply to Popper's attack on epiphenomenalism. *Mind* 88:572-75. [6-GDW]

(1981a) Book review of *Teleology* by Andrew Woodfield. *Philosophia* 10:125-32. [6-GDW]

(1981b) On the nature of the theory of evolution. *Philosophy of Science* 48:609-28. [6-GDW]

(1982a) Materialism and mentality. *Review of Metaphysics* 35:715-29. [6-GDW]

(1982b) TIMA part 1. TIMA as a paradigm for the evolution of molecular complementarities and macromolecules. *Journal of Theoretical Biology* 96:77-86. [6-GDW]

(1982c) TIMA part 2. TIMA-based instructive evolution of macromolecules and organs and structures. *Journal of Theoretical Biology* 99:609-28. [6-GDW]

(1983a) Human behaviour and biology. *Dialectica* 37:169-84. [6-GDW]

(1983b) Quantum mechanics and consciousness. *Nature and System* 5:3-16. [6-GDW]

Watson, J. B. (1913) Psychology as the behaviorist views it. *Psychological Review* 20:158-77. [3-CFL]

(1921) Is thinking merely the action of the language mechanisms? *British Journal of Psychology* 11:87-104. [5-WL]

(1924) *Behaviorism*. W. W. Norton. [6-BFS, GMB]

Webster, G. & Goodwin, B. (1981) History and structure in biology. *Perspectives in Biology and Medicine* 25:39-62. [6-DW]

Weimer, W. B. (1973) Psycholinguistics and Plato's paradoxes of the Meno. *American Psychologist* 28:15-33. [1-JWD]

Weiskrantz, L., Warrington, E. K., Sanders, M. D. & Marshall, J. (1974) Visual capacity in the hemianopic field following a restricted occipital ablation. *Brain* 97:709-28. [5-RMG]

Weismann, A. (1889) *Essays on heredity and kindred biological problems*. Oxford University Press. [1-JMS]

Wellman, H. M. (1985) The origins of metacognition. In: *Metacognition, cognition and human performance*; ed. D. Forrest-Pressley, G. E. MacKinnon & T. G. Waller, Academic Press. [5-CNJ, HMW]

Wells, G. (1981) *Learning through interaction: Study of language development*. Cambridge University Press. [3-RPB]

West, M. J., King, A. P. & Eastzer, D. H. (1981) The cowbird: Reflections on development from an unlikely source. *American Scientist* 69:56-66. [6-DW]

Westby, G. (1966) Psychology today: Problems and directions. *Bulletin of the British Psychological Society* 19(65). [2-BFS]

Whewell, W. (1967) *History of the inductive sciences*. 1st ed. 1837. Cass. [2-MLS]

Whitlock, F. A. (1967) The aetiology of hysteria. *Acta Psychiatrica Scandinavica* 43:144–62. [3–DTK]

Whitman, C. O. (1899) Animal behavior. *Biological Lectures from the Marine Biological Laboratory of Woods Hole, 1898*, 6:285–338. [6–GMB]

Wiener, N. (1948) *Cybernetics, or control and communication in the animal and the machine*. Wiley. [5–JCM]

Williams, D. R. & Williams, H. (1969) Automaintenance in the pigeon: Sustained pecking despite contingent non-reinforcement. *Journal of the Experimental Analysis of Behavior* 12:511–20. [6–AMC]

Williams, G. C. (1966) *Adaptation and natural selection*. Princeton University Press. [1–RD, SCS; 6–MTG, JAH]

Wilson, D. S. (1975) A theory of group selection. *Proceedings of the National Academy of Sciences* 72:143–46. [1–GWB]

(1980) *The natural selection of populations and communities*. Benjamin/Commings. [1–GWB]

Wilson, E. B. (1952) *An introduction to scientific research*. McGraw-Hill. [2–BFS]

Wilson, E. O. (1975) *Sociobiology: The new synthesis*. Harvard University Press. [1–GWB, JWD; 6–GMB]

(1978) *On human nature*. Harvard University Press. [6–AJP]

Wilson, T. (1978) Cognitive behavior therapy: Paradigm shift or passing phase? In: *Cognitive behavior therapy: Research and application*, ed. J. Foreyt & D. Rathjen. Plenum. [3–CFL]

Wimmer, H. & Perner, J. (1983) Beliefs about beliefs: Representation and constraining function of wrong beliefs in young children's understanding of deception. *Cognition* 13:103–28. [5–CNJ]

Winokur, S. (1976) *A primer of verbal behavior: An operant view*. Prentice-Hall. [3–JDR]

Wisdom, J. (1938) Metaphysics and verification. 1. *Mind* 47:452–98. [4–PCD]

(1952) *Other minds*. Basil Blackwell. [5–KG]

Wittgenstein, L. (1953) *Philosophical investigations*. Macmillan. [2–SMD, CPS; 3–KPG, PH]

(1958) *The blue and brown books*. Harper & Row. [5–MJM]

Wolf, D. (1982) Understanding others: A longitudinal case study of the concept of independent agency. In: *Action and thought*, ed. G. E. Forman. Academic Press. [5–CNJ]

Woodfield, A. (1976) *Teleology*. Cambridge University Press. [3–JDR; 6–GBW]

Woodruff, G. & Premack, D. (1979) Intentional communication in the chimpanzee: The development of deception. *Cognition* 7:333–62. [5–CNJ]

Woodworth, R. S. & Schlosberg, H. (1955) *Experimental psychology*. Methuen. [5–WL]

Woolridge, D. (1963) *The machinery of the brain*. McGraw-Hill. [4–EPS]

Wright, A. A. & Cumming, W. W. (1971) Color-naming functions for the pigeon. *Journal of the Experimental Analysis of Behavior* 15:7–17. [5–TRZ]

Wright, L. (1976) *Teleological explanations*. University of California Press. [3–JDR]

Wynne-Edwards, V. C. (1963) Intergroup selection in the evolution of social systems. *Nature* 200:623–26. [1–JWD]

(1965) Self-regulating systems in populations of animals. *Science* 147:1543–48. [6–BFS, JPH]

Wyrwicka, W. (1975) The sensory nature of reward in instrumental behavior. *Pavlovian Journal of Biological Science* 10:23–51. [1–WW]

(1980) Mechanisms of motivation in avoidance behavior. *Acta Neurobiologiae Experimentalis* 40:371–80. [1–WW]

Zentall, T. R. (1983) Cognitive factors in conditional learning by pigeons. In: *Animal cognition*, ed. H. L. Roitblat, T. G. Bever & H. S. Terrace. Lawrence Erlbaum Associates. [3–HST]

Zentall, T. R. & Edwards, C. A. (1984) Categorical color coding by pigeons. *Animal Learning and Behavior* 12:249–55. [5–TRZ]

Zentall, T. R., Edwards, C. A., Moore, B. S. & Hogan, D. E. (1981) Identity: The basis for both matching and oddity learning in pigeons. *Journal of Experimental Psychology: Animal Behavior Processes* 7:70–86. [5–TRZ]

Zettle, R. D. & Hayes, S. C. (1982) Rule-governed behavior: A potential theoretical frame-

work for cognitive behavior therapy. In: *Advances in cognitive-behavioral research and therapy*, vol. 1, ed. P. C. Kendall. Academic Press. [3–CFL]
Ziff, P. (1960) *Semantic analysis*. Cornell University Press. [3–JB]
(1970) A response to stimulus meaning. *Philosophical Review* 79:63–74. [3–JB]
Zuriff, G. E. (1979) Ten inner causes. *Behaviorism* 7:1–8. [5–RS, BFS on RS]

Name index

Subject index

Made in the USA
San Bernardino, CA
03 August 2013